# 500
## BUNGALOWS

DOUGLAS KEISTER

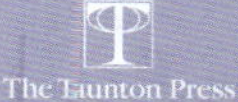

DEDICATED TO THE BUNGALOW HOMEOWNERS
WHO PRESERVE THE PAST TO BETTER THE FUTURE.



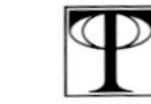

The Taunton Press

The Taunton Press, Inc.
63 South Main Street, PO Box 5506
Newtown, CT 06470-5506
e-mail: tp@taunton.com

Editor: Pam Hoenig

Jacket/Cover design: Chika Azuma
Interior design: Chika Azuma
Layout: Cathy Cassidy
Photographer: Douglas Keister

Library of Congress Cataloging-in-Publication Data

Keister, Douglas.
500 bungalows / Douglas Keister
p. cm.
ISBN-13: 978-1-56158-842-8
ISBN-10: 1-56158-842-3
1. Bungalows--United States--Pictorial works. I. Title: Five hundred bungalows.
II. Title.
NA7571.K39 2006
728'.373--dc22

2006006351

Printed in China
10 9 8 7 6 5 4 3 2 1

# C O N T E N T S

# INTRODUCTION

I am often asked, "Exactly what is a bungalow?" I'm happy to attempt an answer, but the fact is that the word's definition is less than definitive.

Scholars generally agree that the term comes from the word *bangala* (or a variation), referring to a thatched-roof building with a shaded veranda that British colonialists encountered in India. The concept was imported to England, where it became associated not only with small residences but with seaside summer homes, many of which were quite expansive. In the late 1800s the bungalow's relaxed character found good company with England's Arts and Crafts movement, which advocated modest living, handcrafted objects, and an appreciation of nature.

The word—and the house form—jumped the Atlantic and rapidly caught on among the ballooning middle class here in the United States. During the nineteen-teens and twenties, most every newlywed couple of modest means wanted a bungalow. They were romanticized; popular songs were written about them. Bungalows signified independence and respectability, a home that boasted the quality and artistry of the mansions of the wealthy but on a scale that was affordable and could be managed without servants.

But how does one identify a bungalow? The typical specimen built in the Unites States was a cozy, one- or one-and-a-half-story house with a horizontal orientation, a gently pitched roof, overhanging eaves, and a prominent front porch. It gets a little fuzzy beyond that. Then, like today, realtors and developers labeled their product whatever they thought would sell it and, for many years, *bungalow* sold like crazy. They were also happy to vary the concept to satisfy the customer. Did a young bride dream of the romantic locales in motion pictures? A Spanish bungalow fulfilled her fantasies. Was a home buyer captivated by the allure of the East? An oriental-style bungalow domesticated the exotic. Did a couple appreciate Frank Lloyd Wright's progressive designs but lack the funds to hire him? A Prairie-style bungalow was within their means.

So don't worry too much about trying to nail down a precise definition of the bungalow. Just spend some time with the examples in these pages, and you'll surrender to their charm, artistry—and variety.

—Tim Counts, president,
Twin Cities Bungalow Club
Minneapolis–St. Paul, Minnesota

# PRAIRIE-STYLE BUNGALOWS

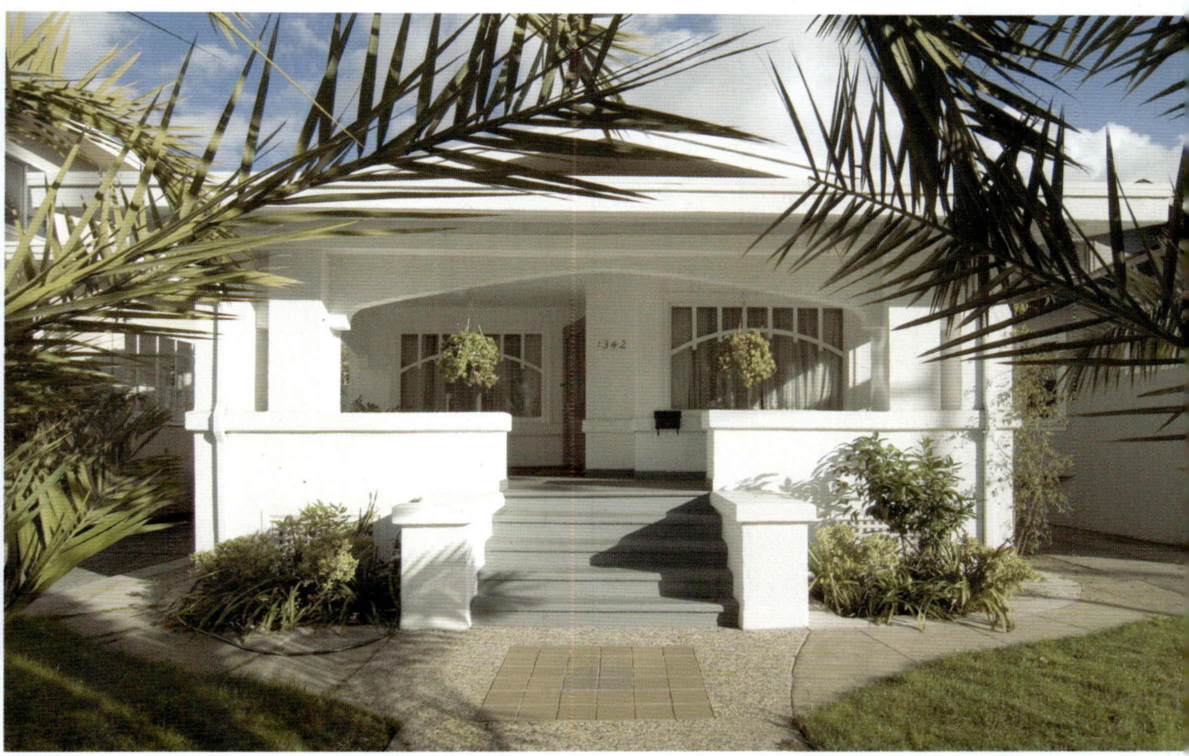


Alameda, California

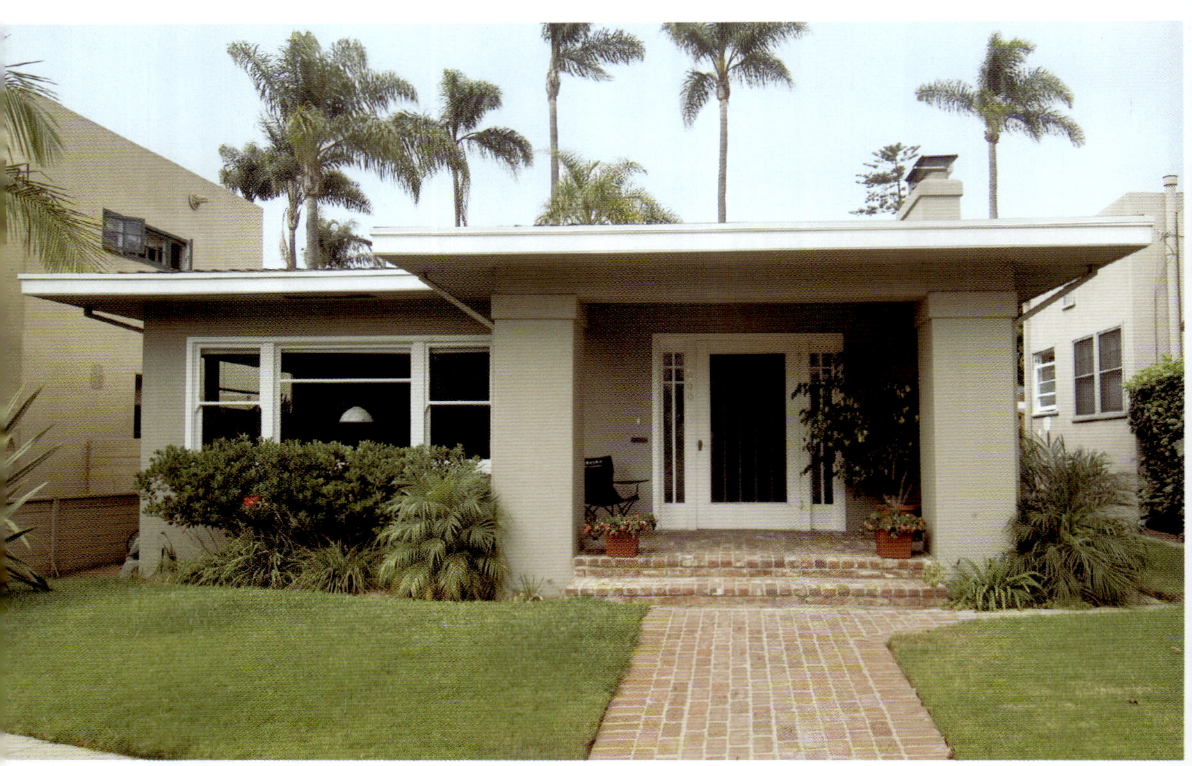

 San Diego, California

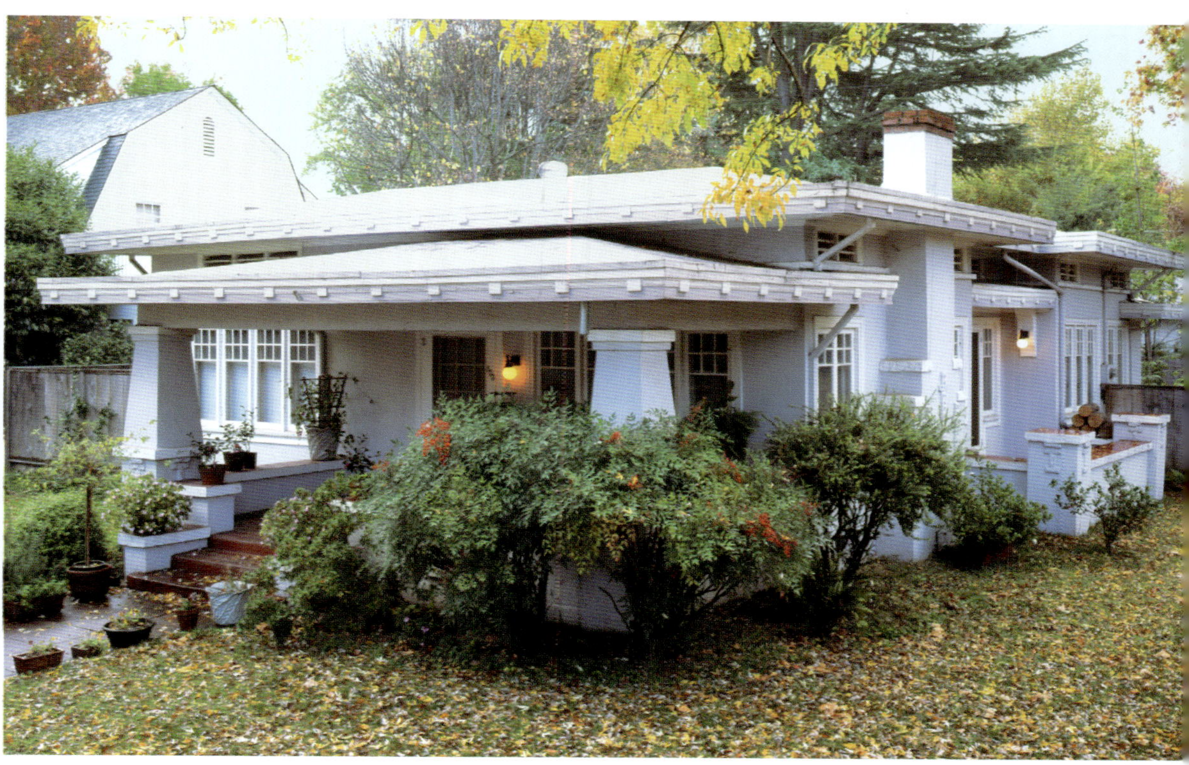

Chico, California

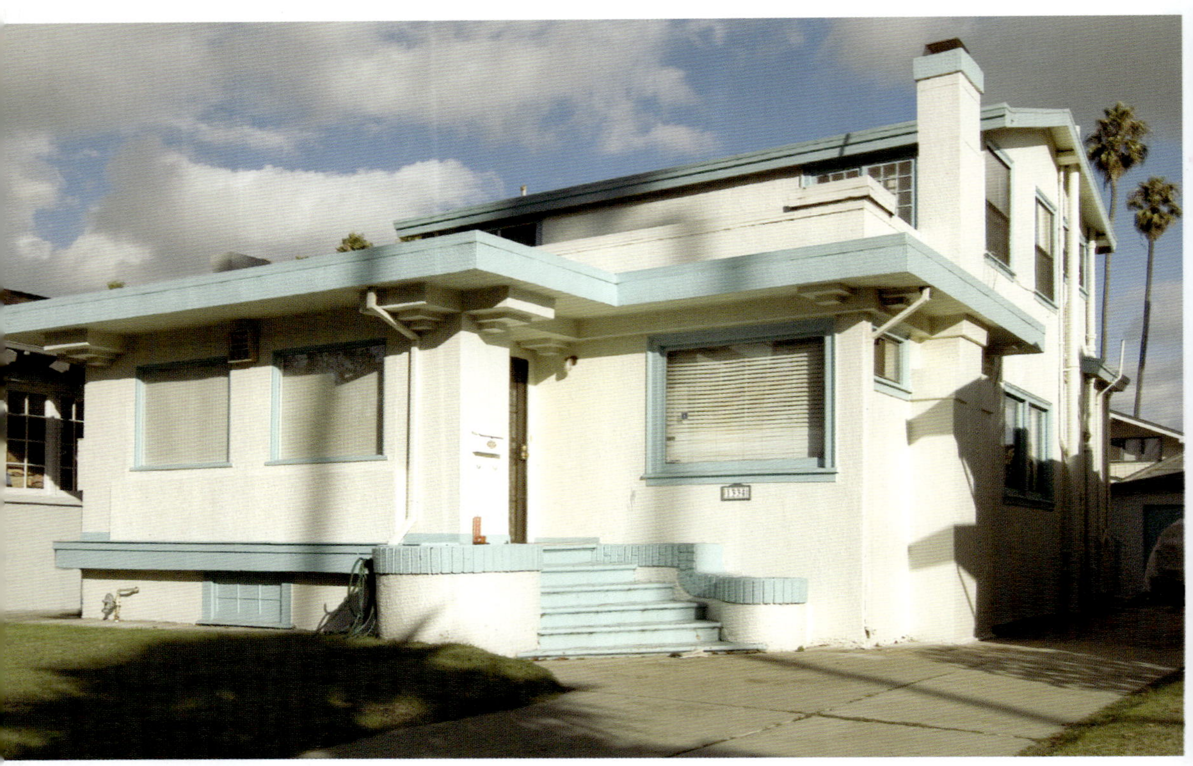

8 Alameda, California

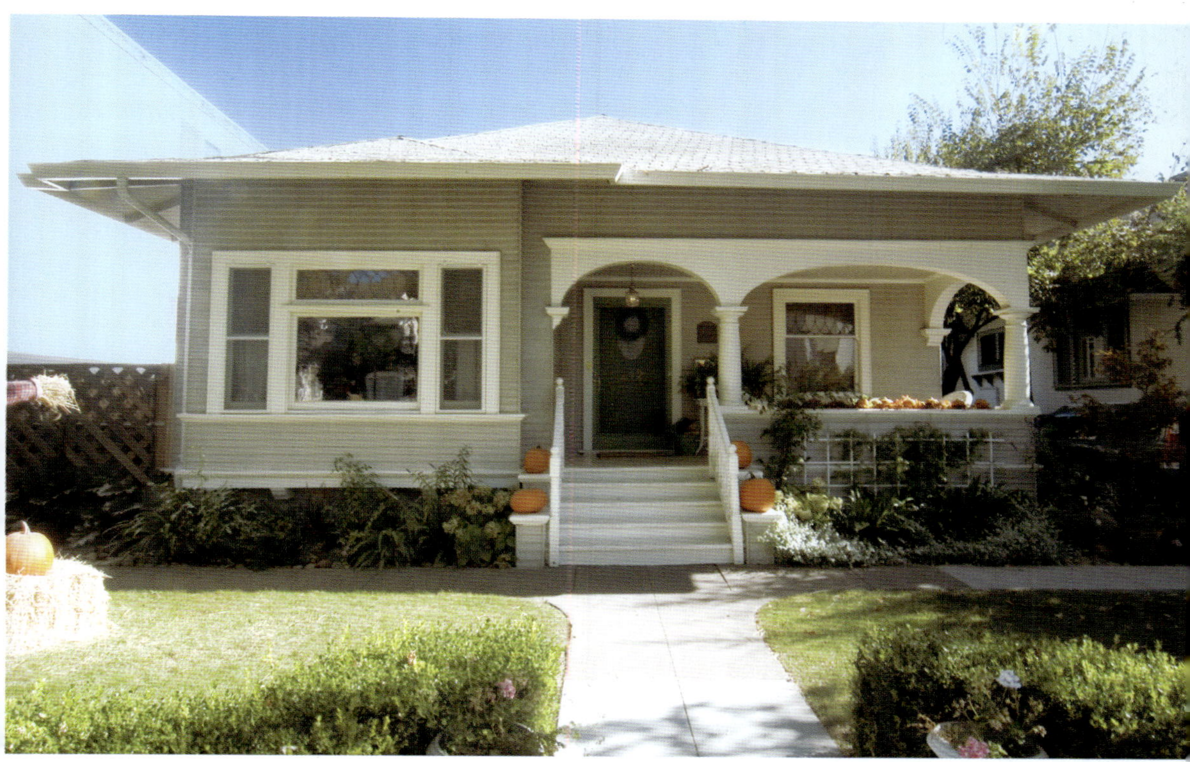

San Jose, California

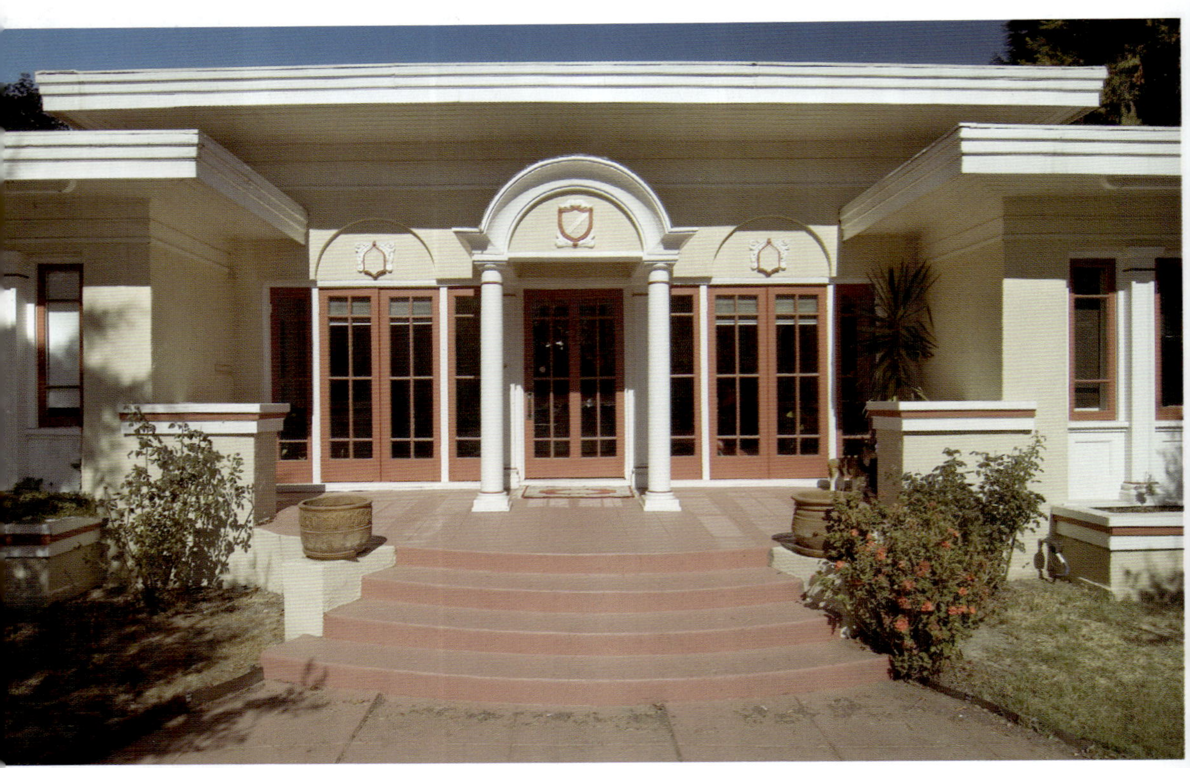

 SAN JOSE, CALIFORNIA

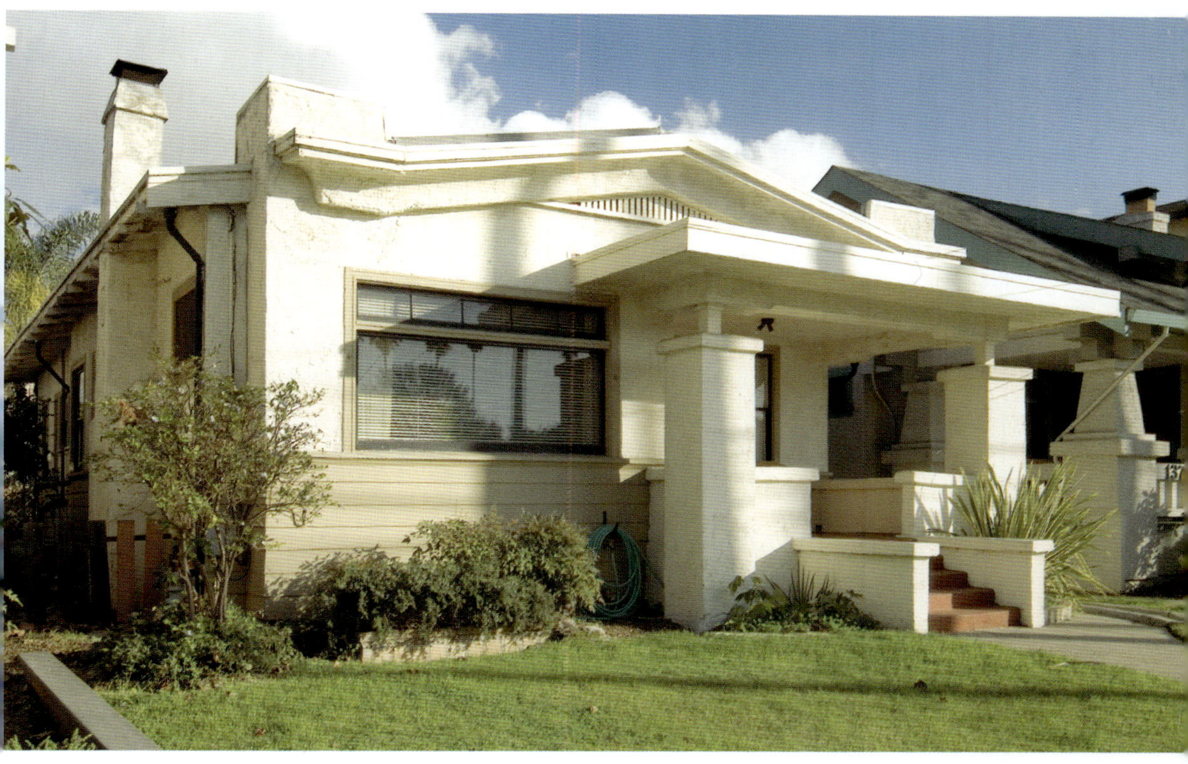

Alameda, California

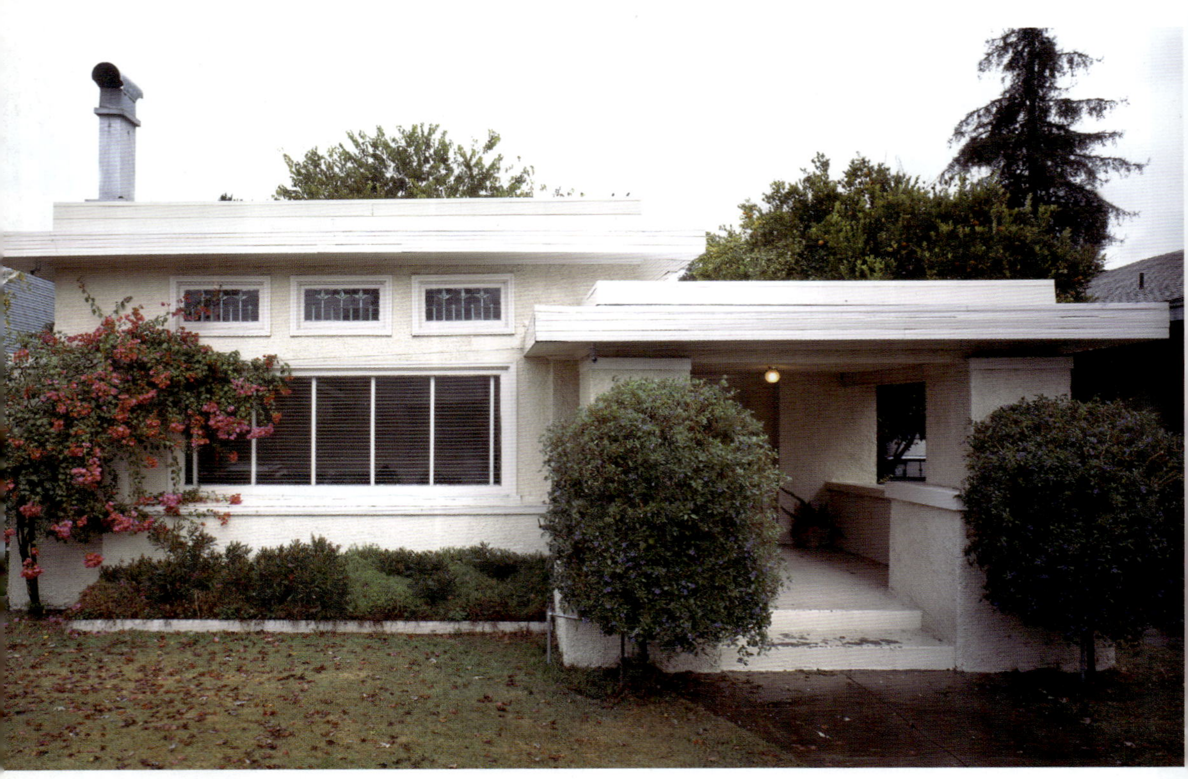

 San Jose, California

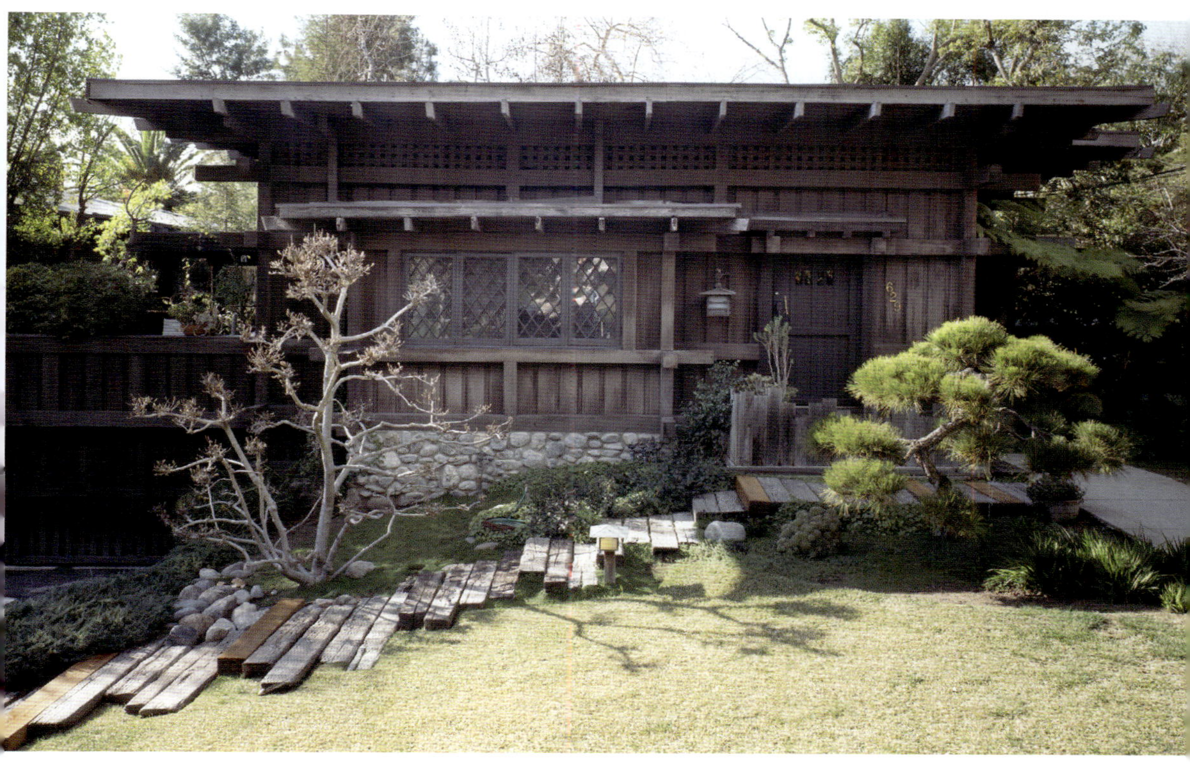
629

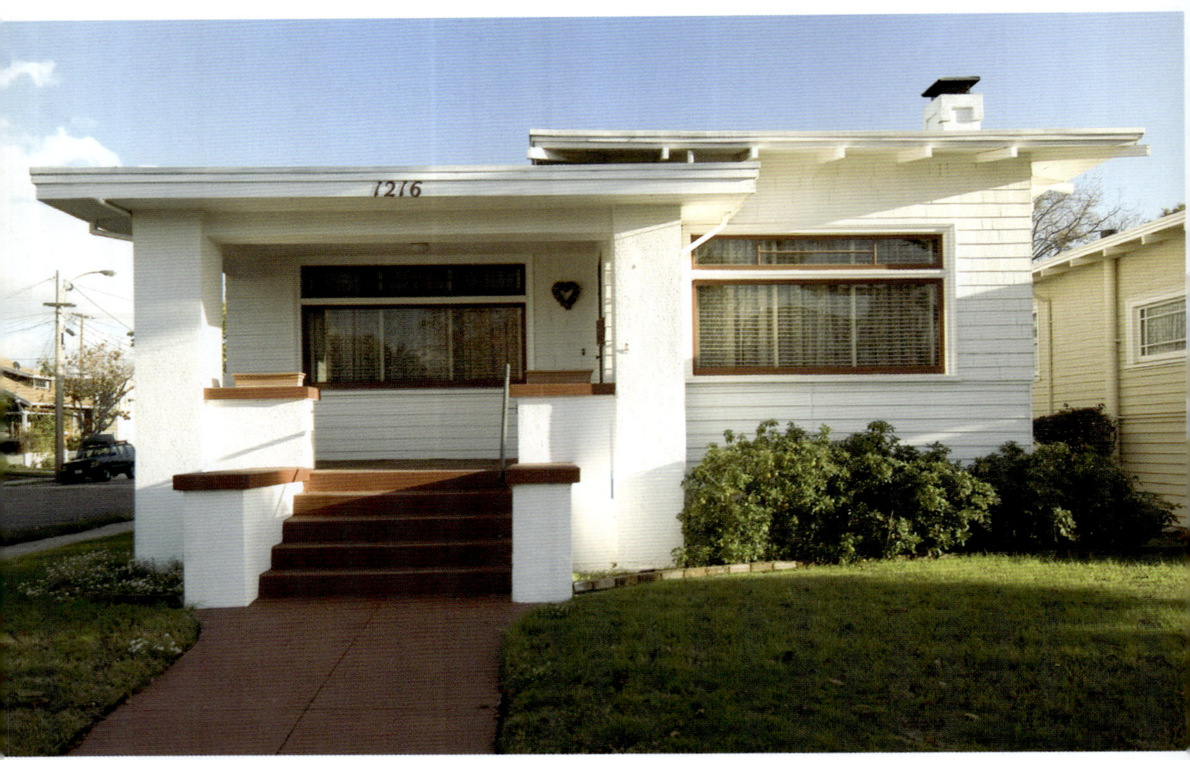


 Alameda, California

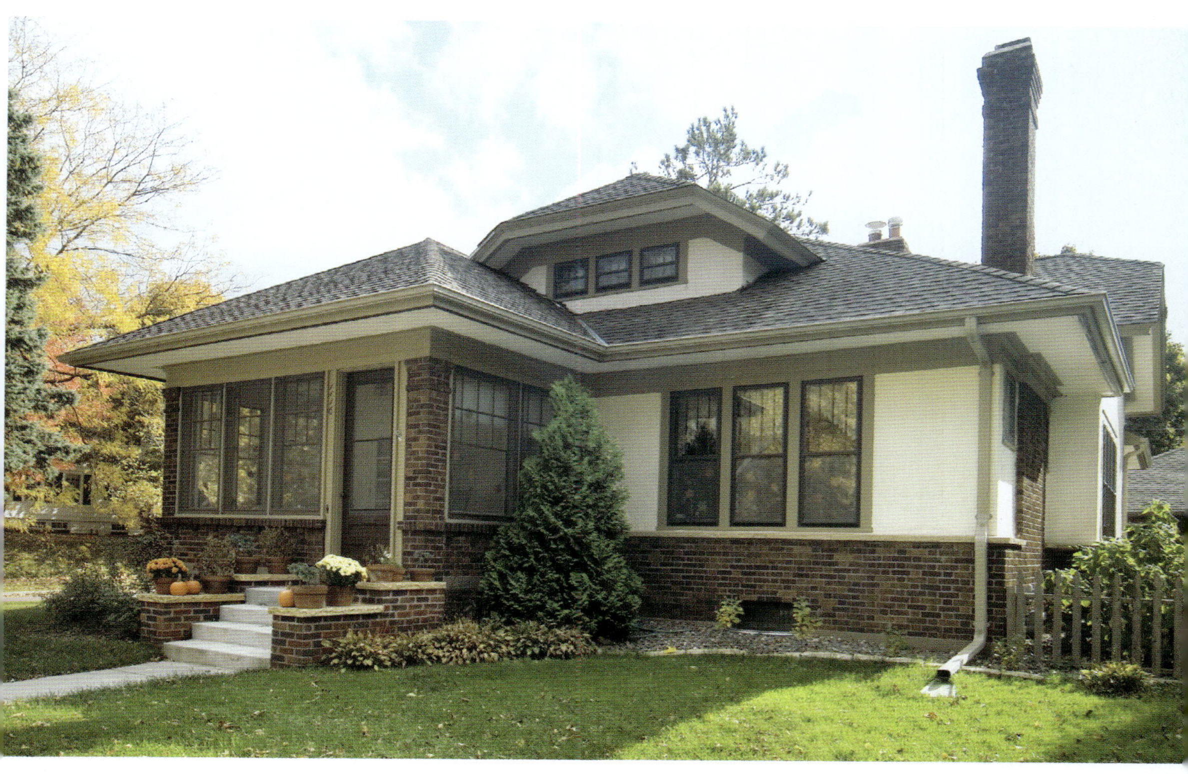

St. Paul, Minnesota

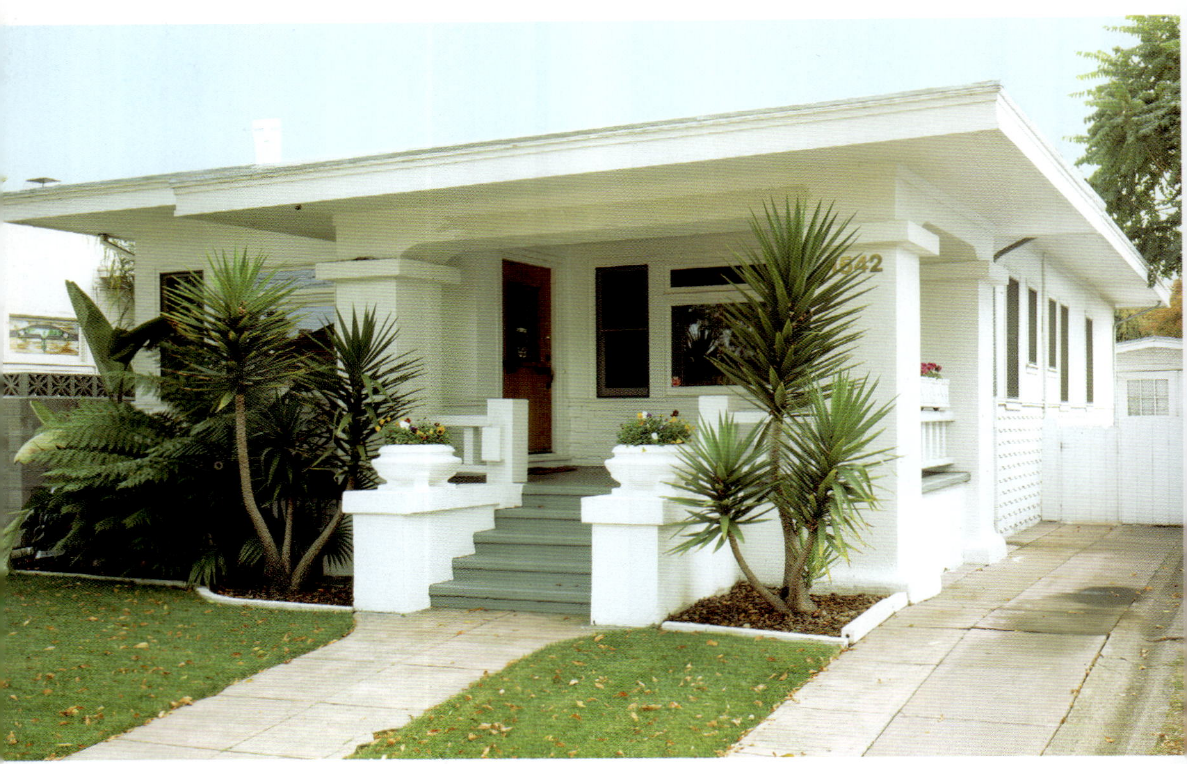

 Alameda, California

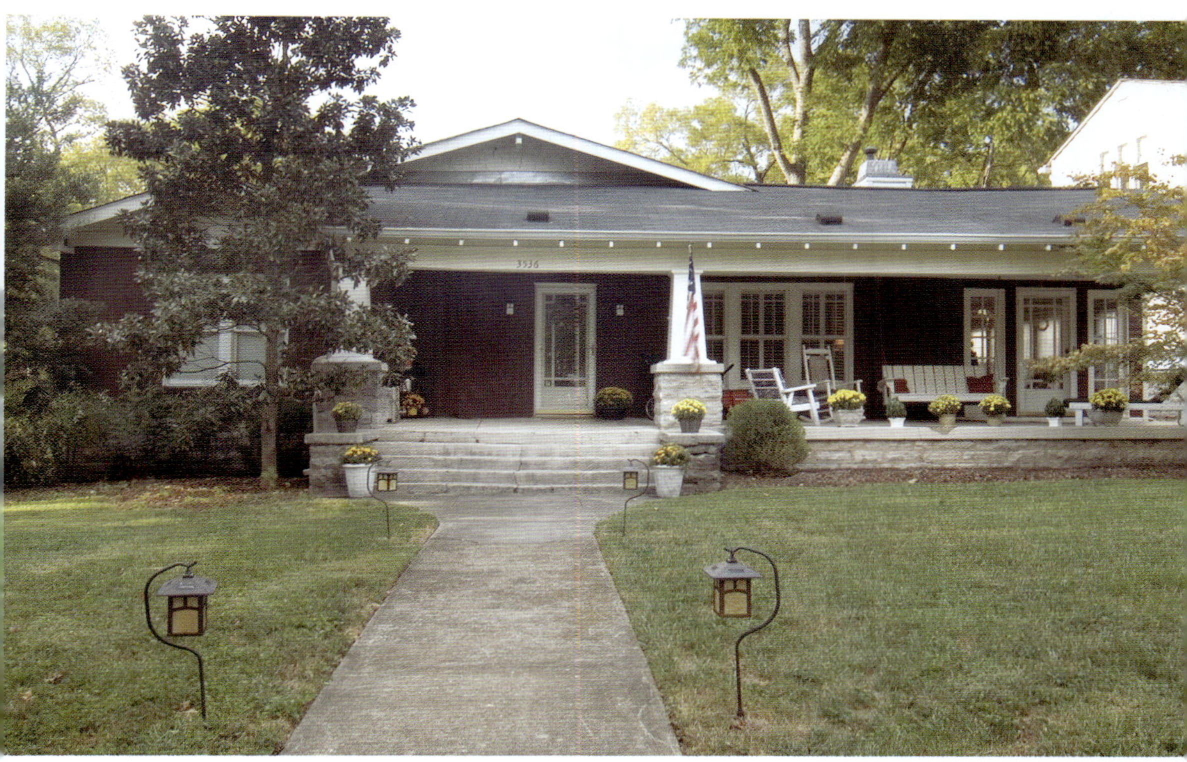

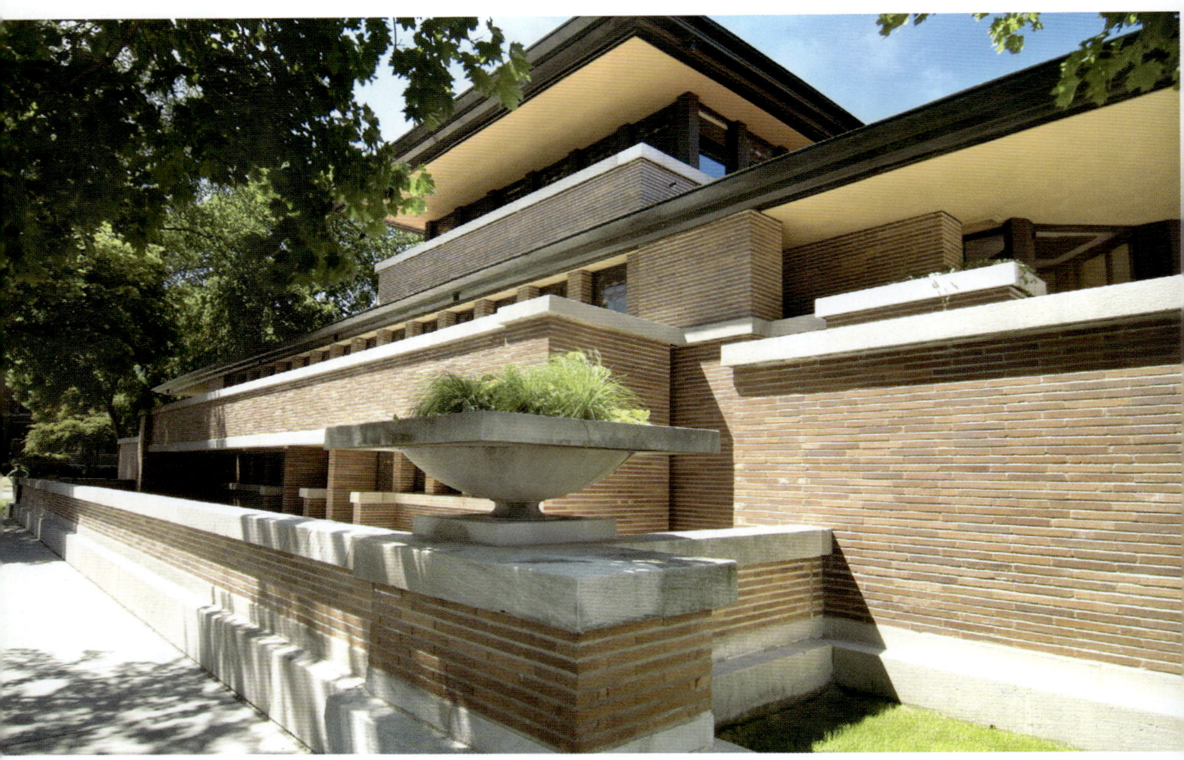

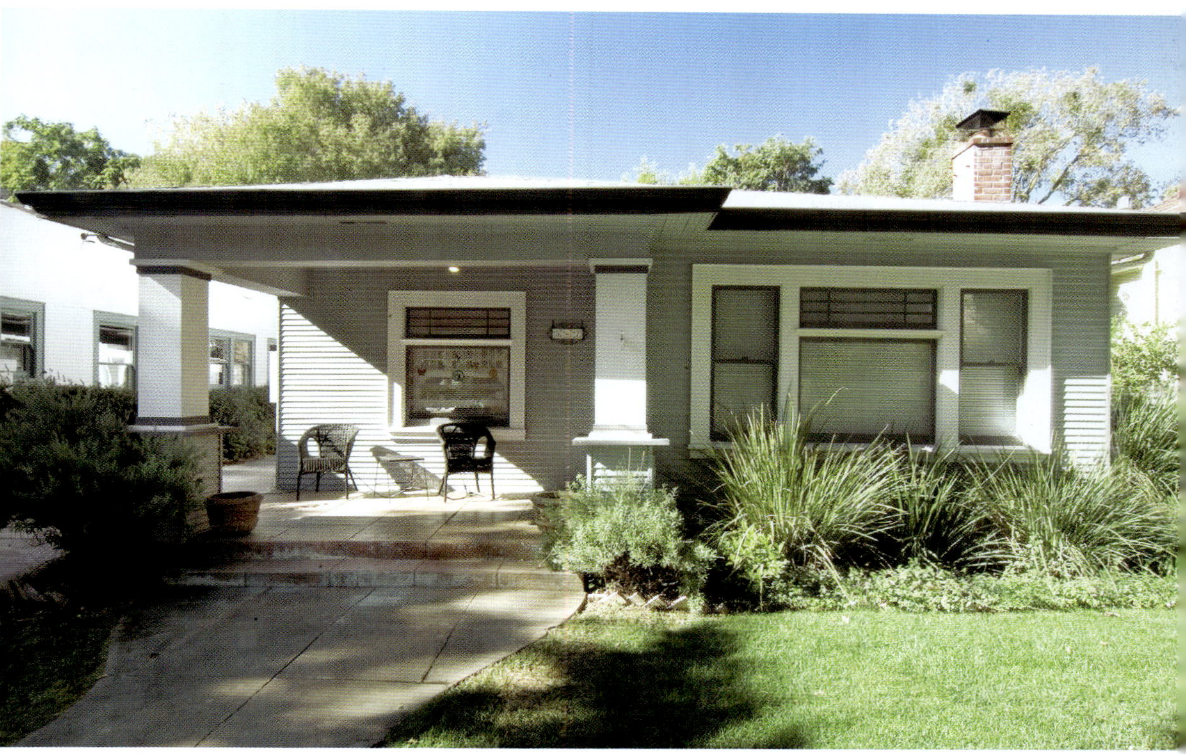

San Jose, California

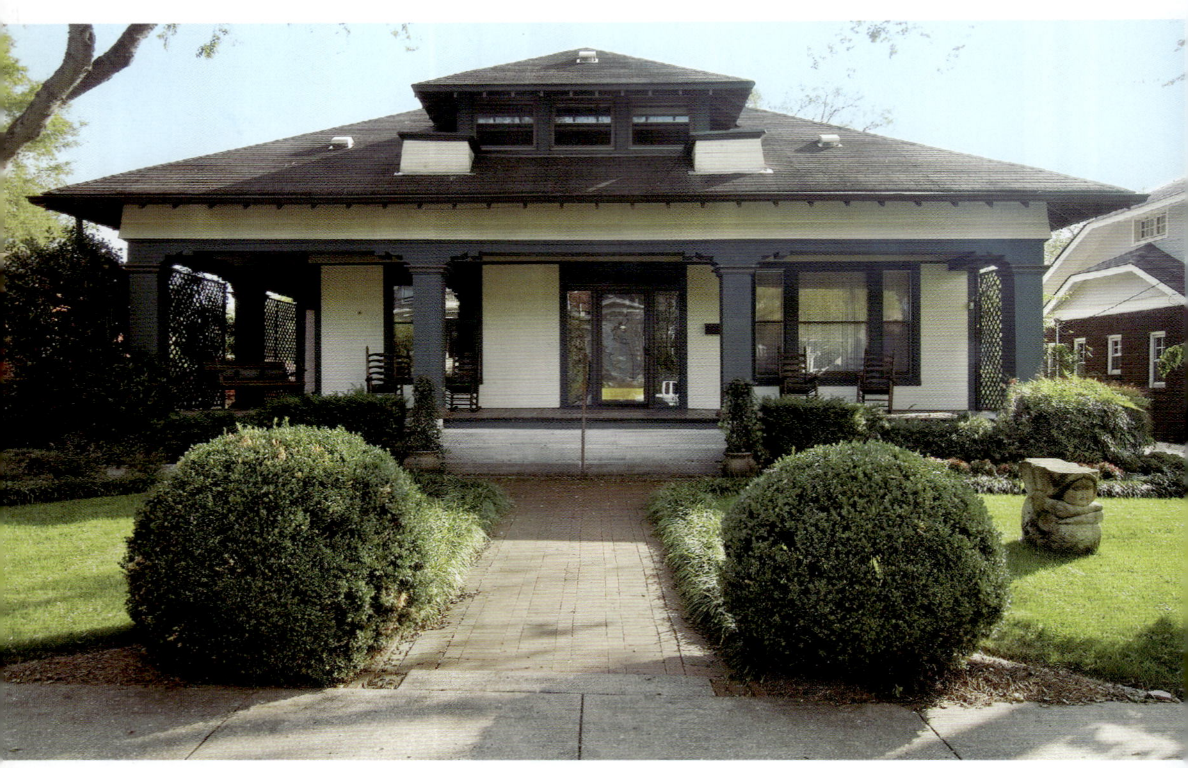

 San Jose, California

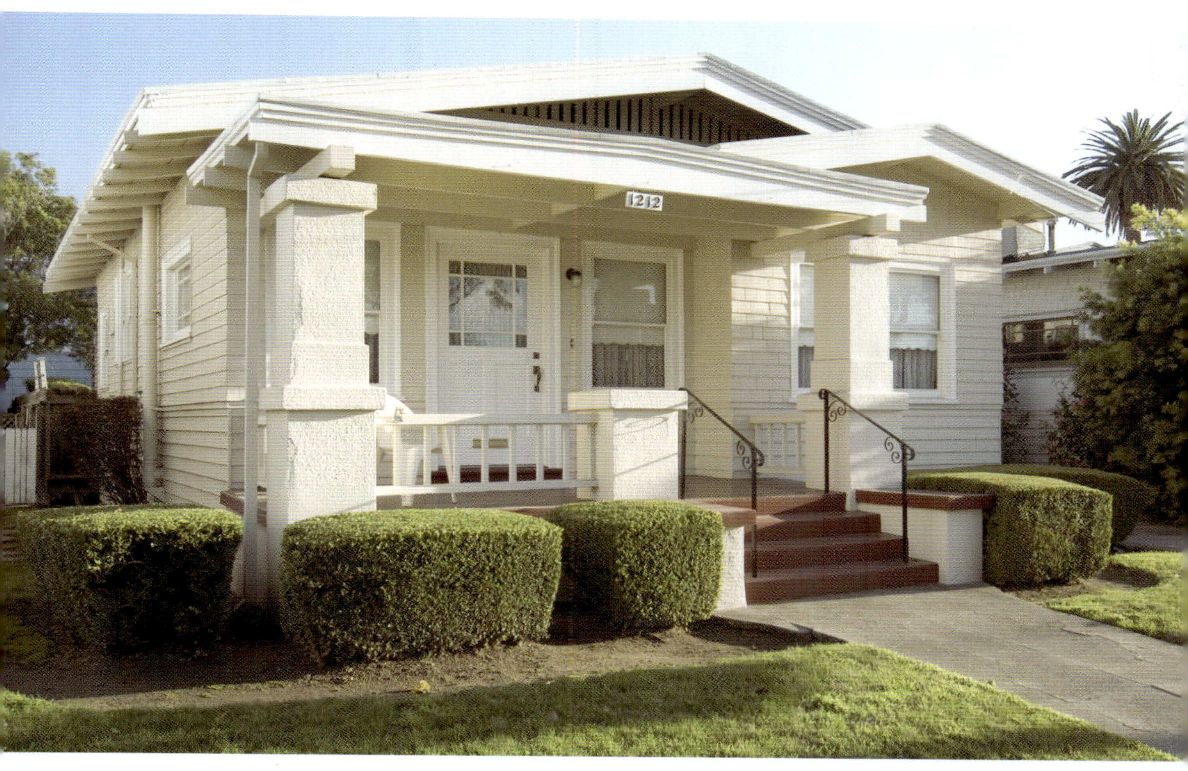


ALAMEDA, CALIFORNIA

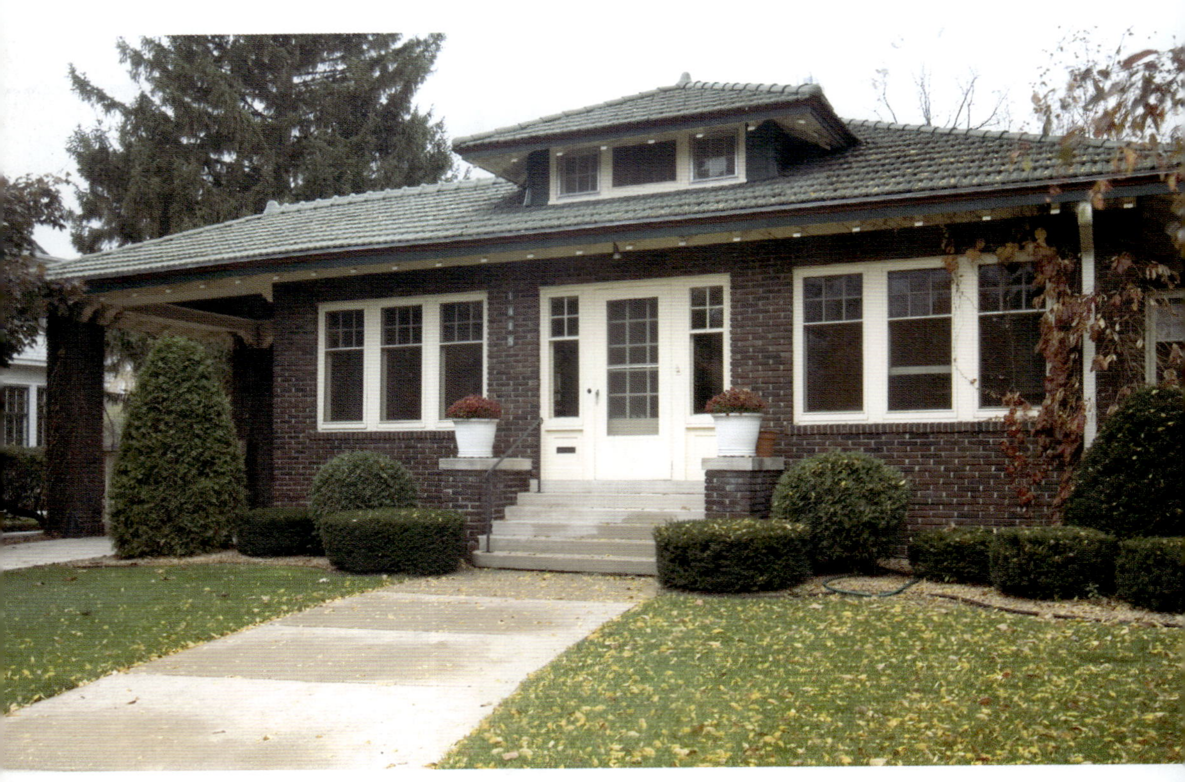

 St. Paul, Minnesota

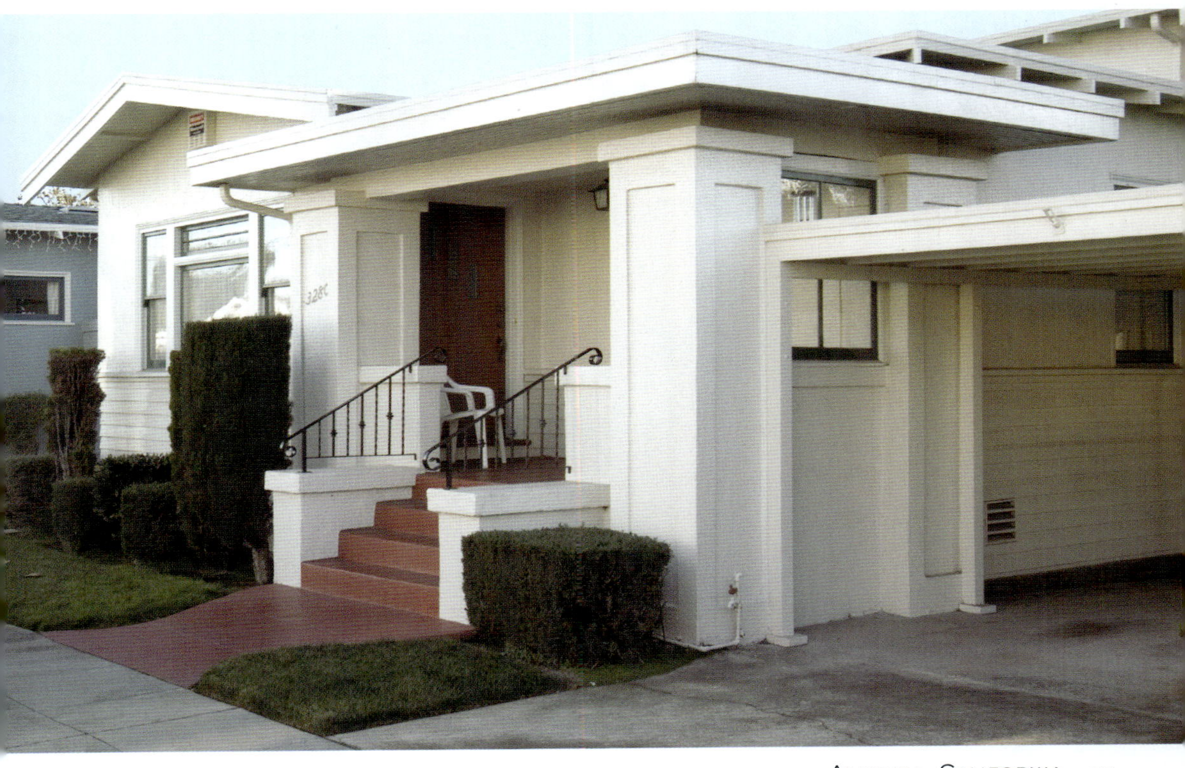

Alameda, California

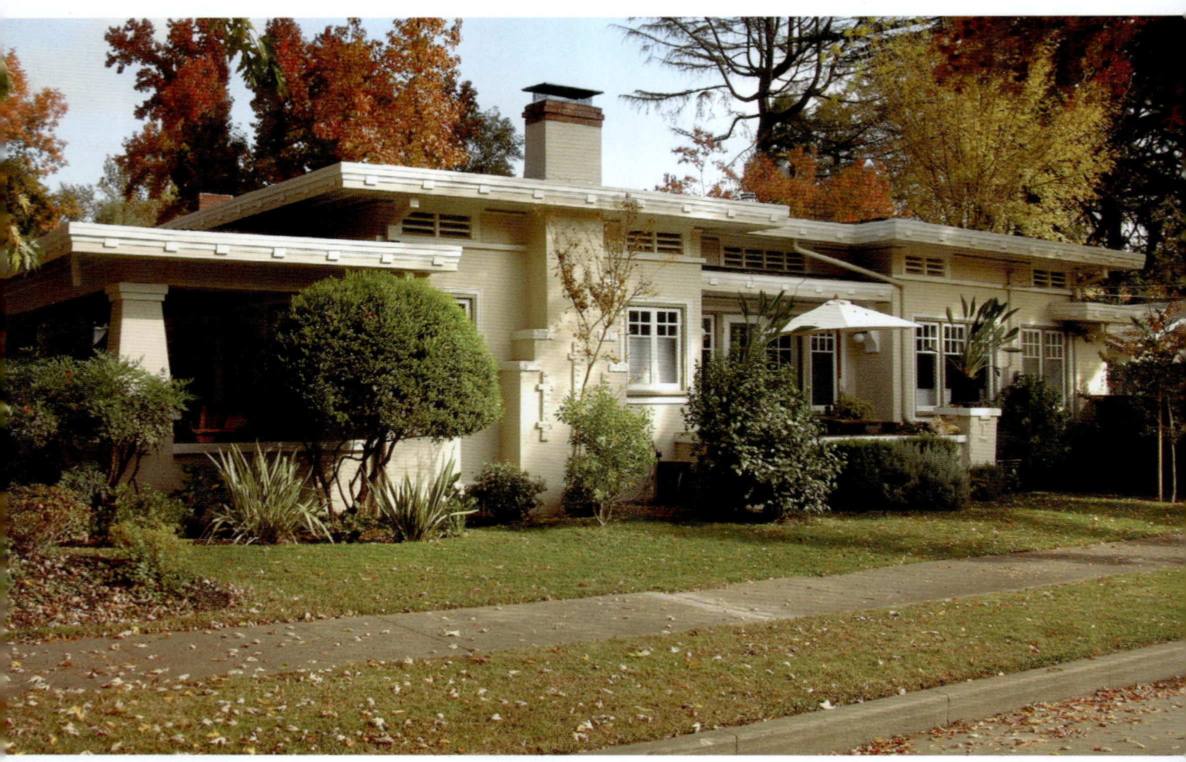

 Chico, California

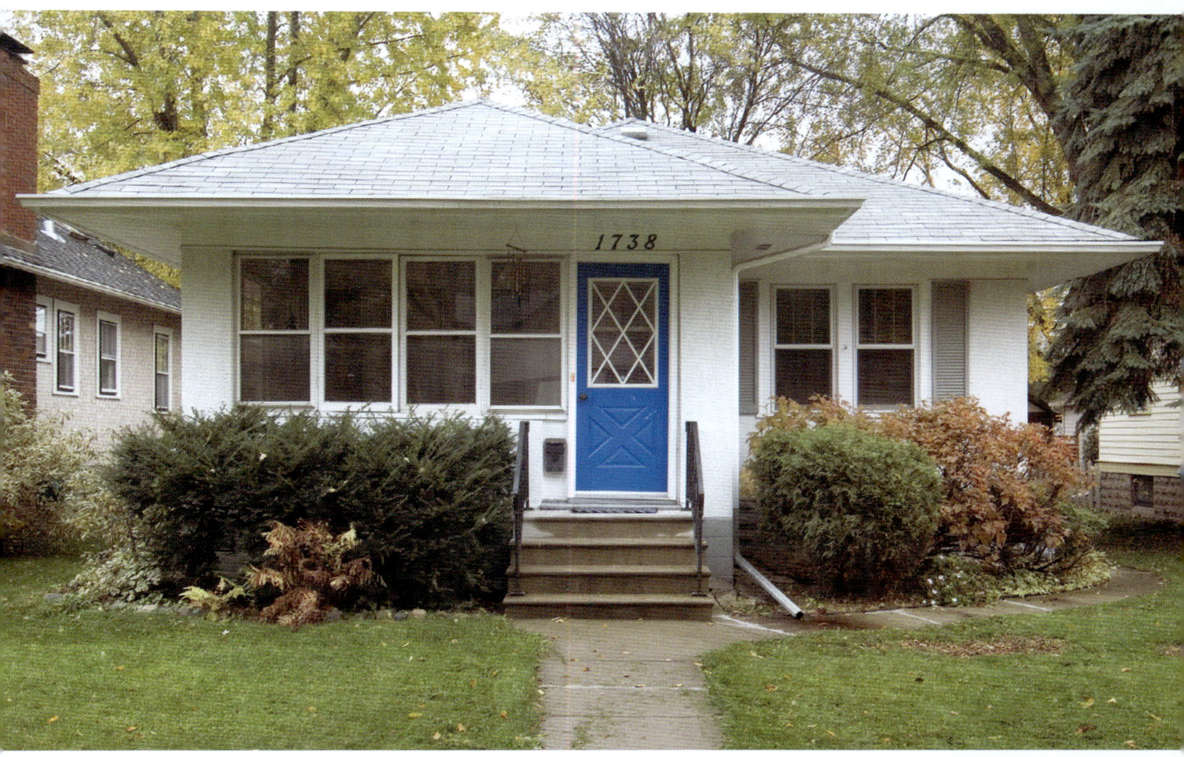
1738

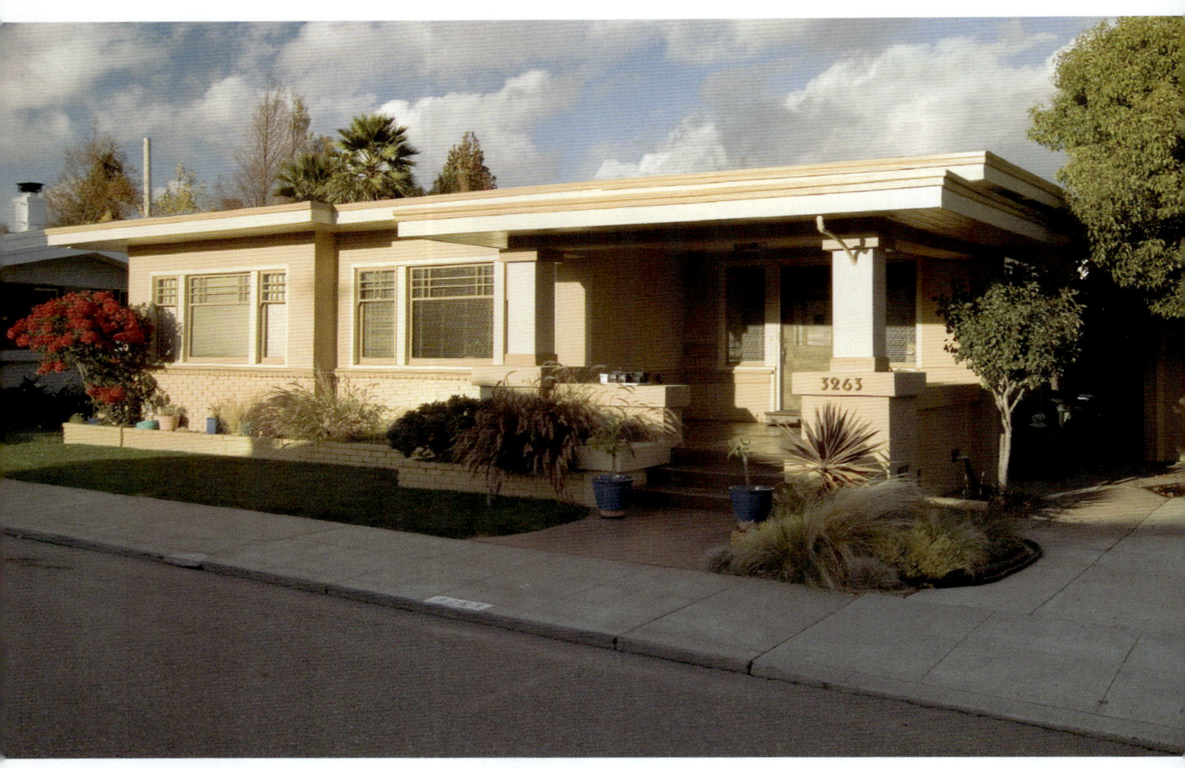


 Alameda, California

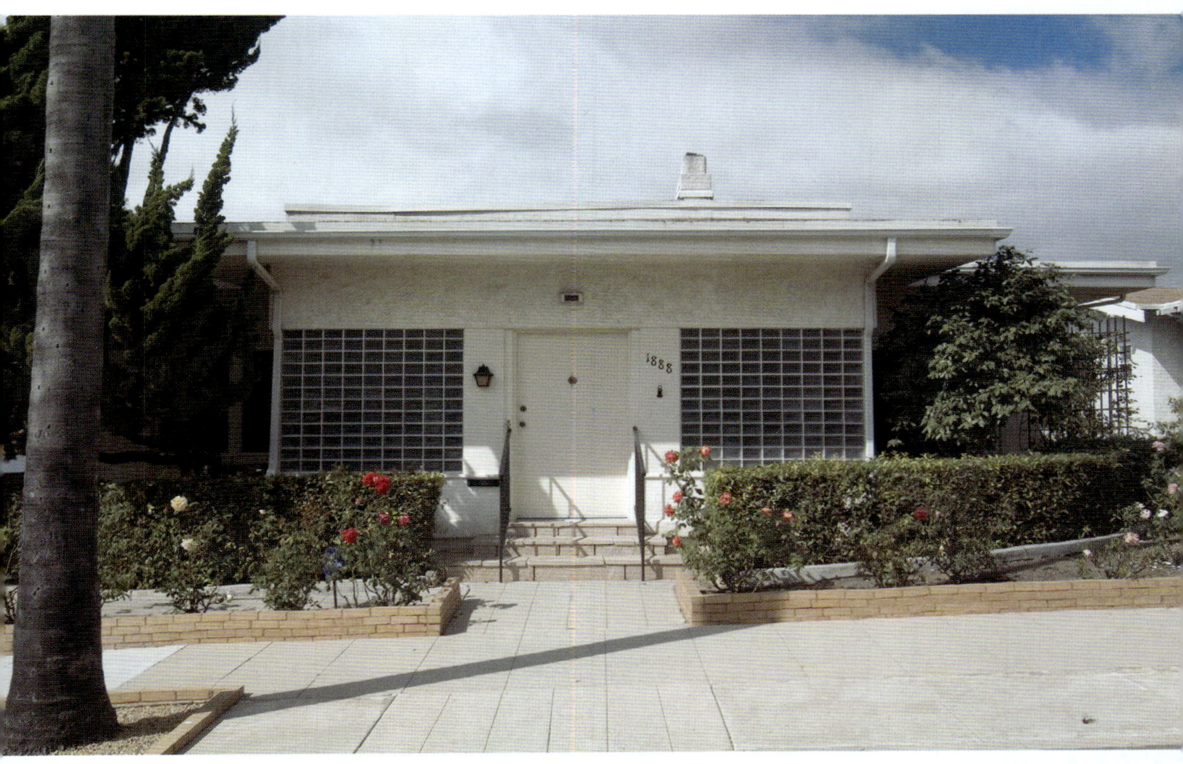


San Diego, California

# SPANISH-STYLE BUNGALOWS

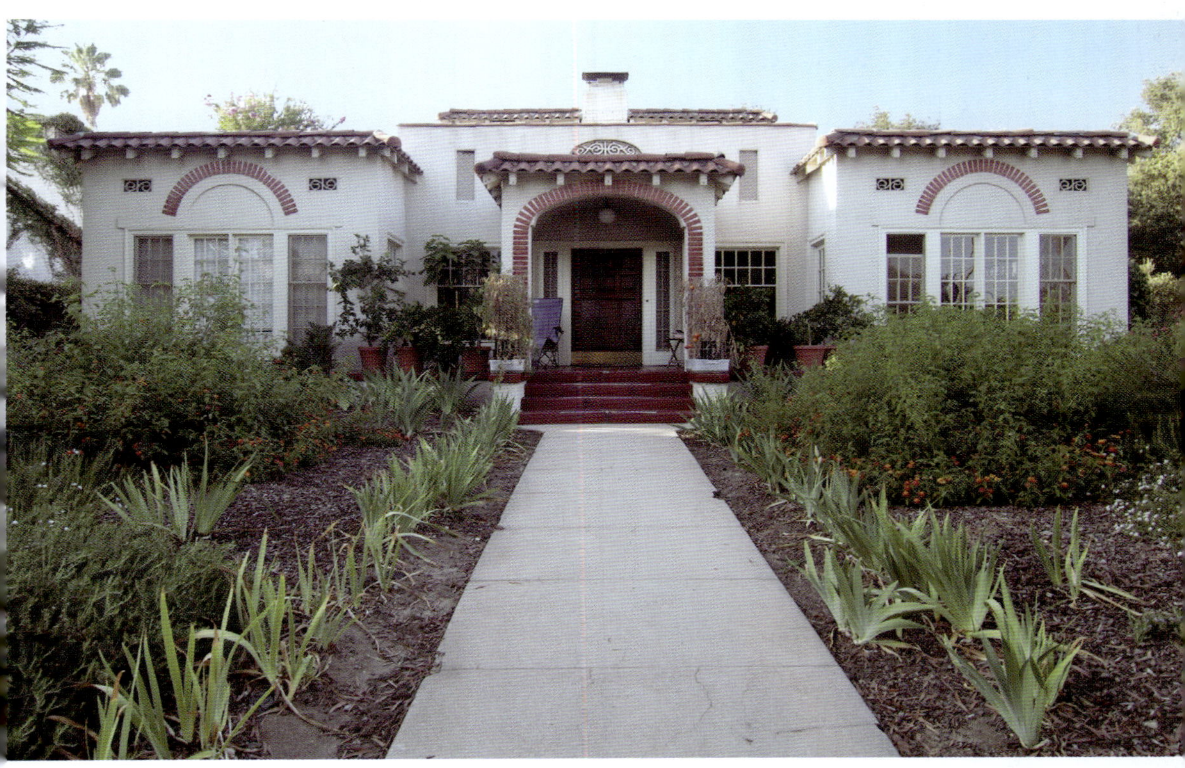

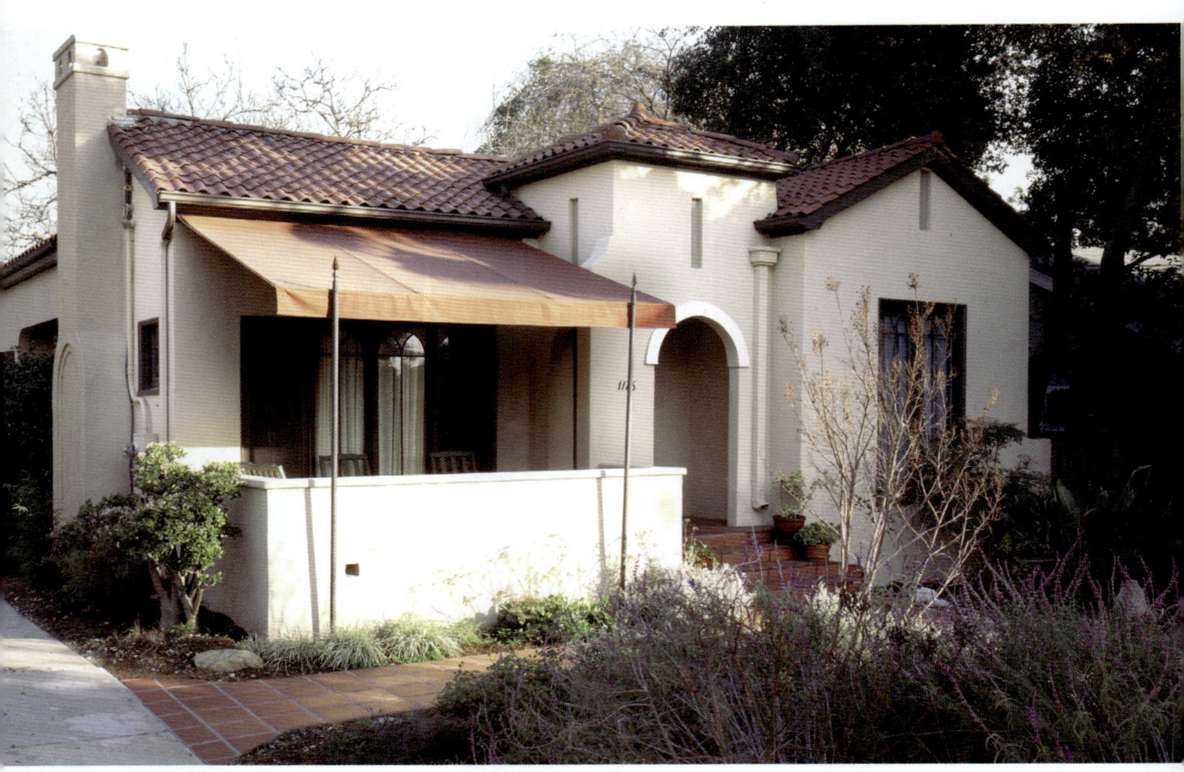

 Pasadena, California

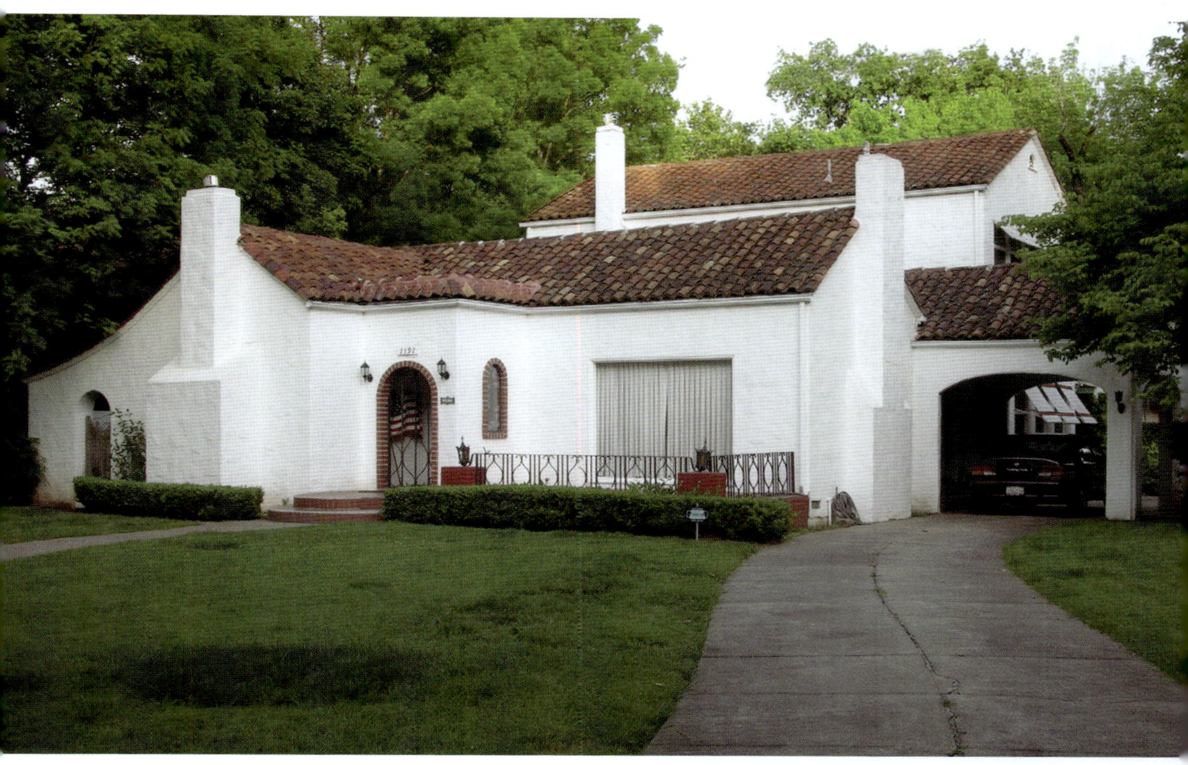

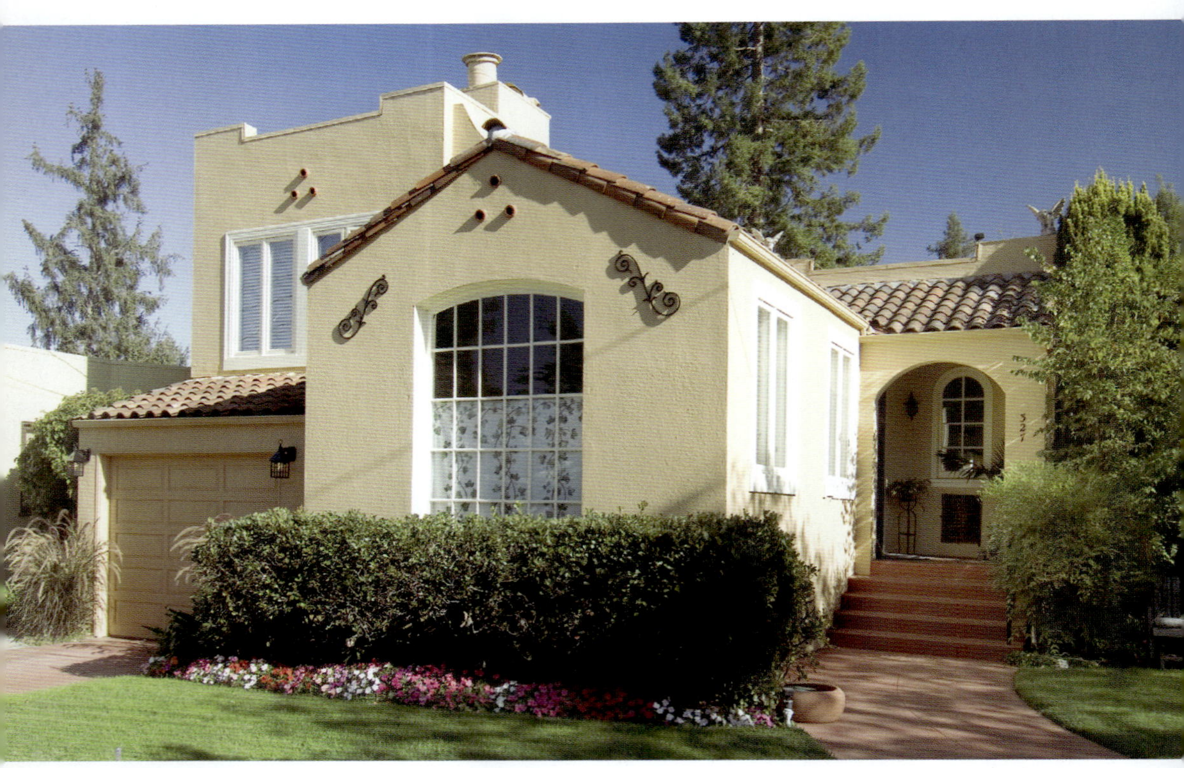

 REDWOOD CITY, CALIFORNIA

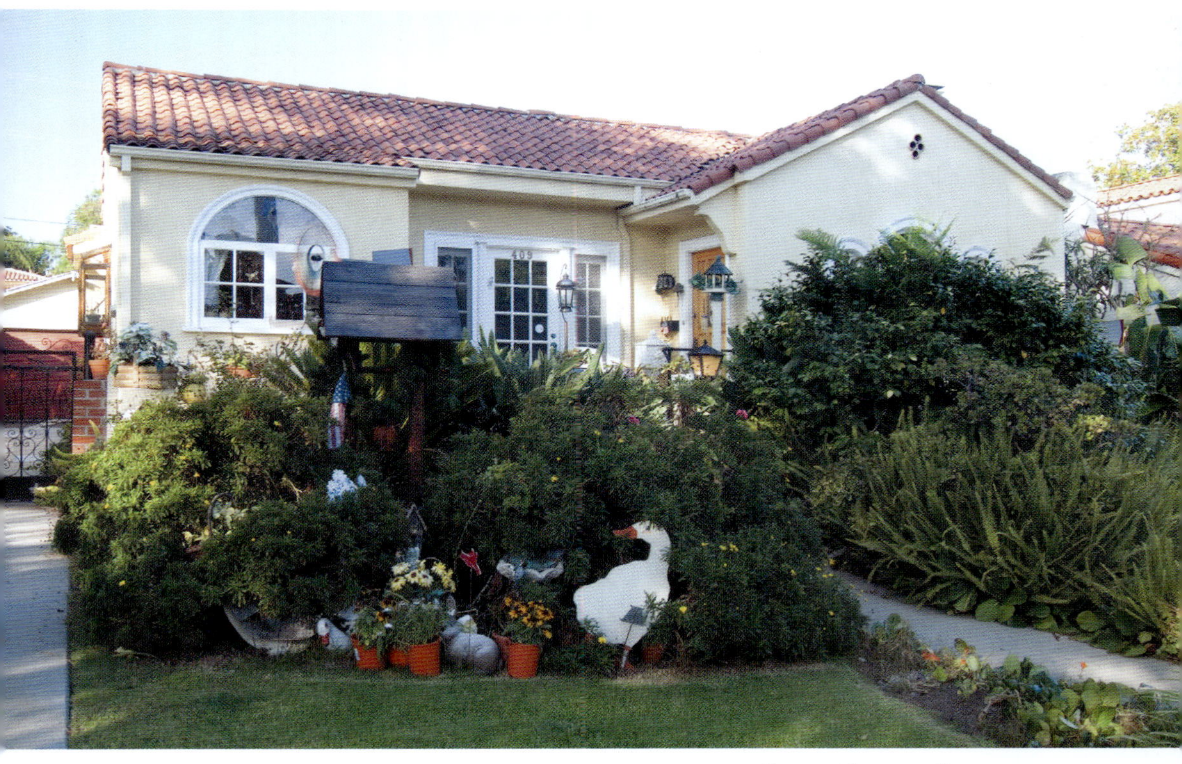


Santa Monica, California

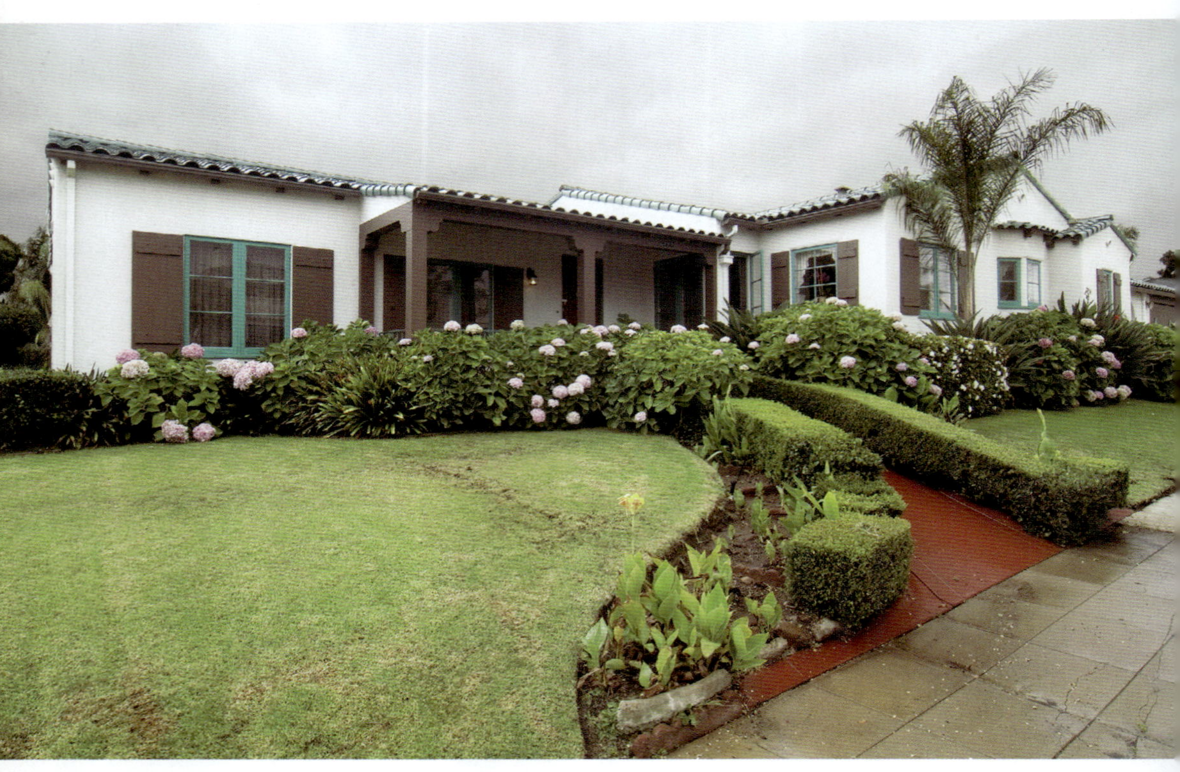

 San Diego, California

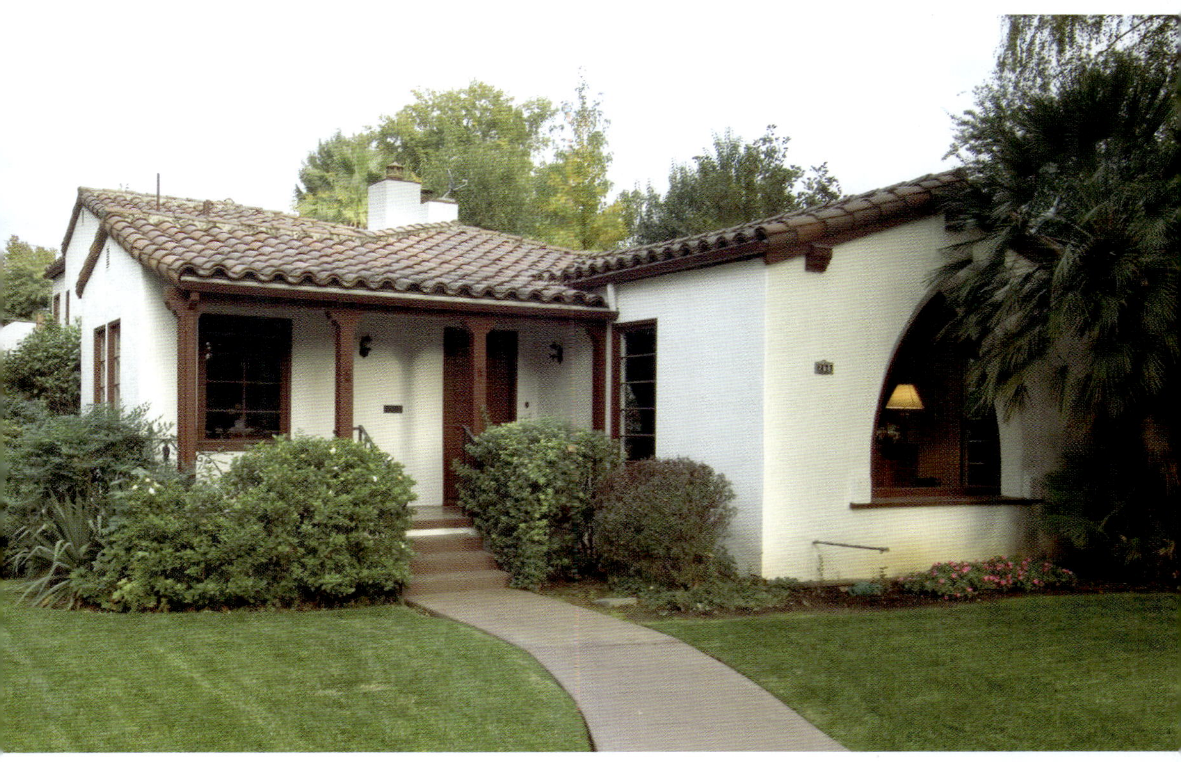

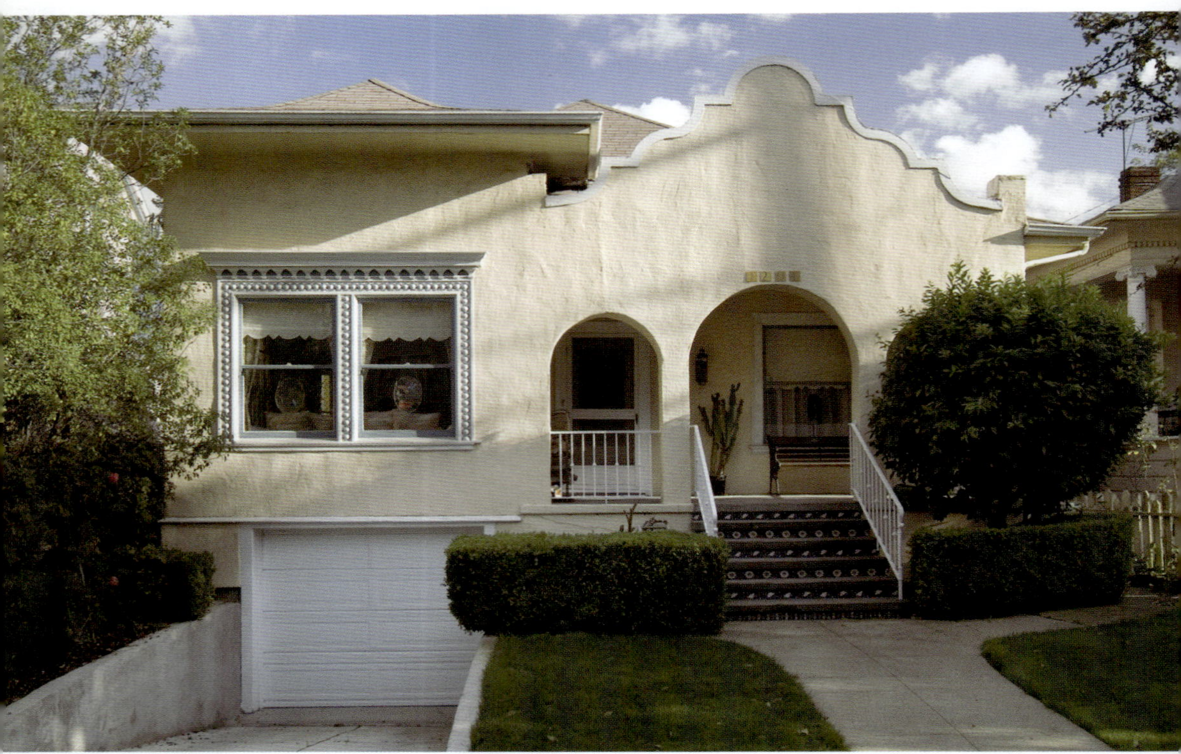

 Alameda, California

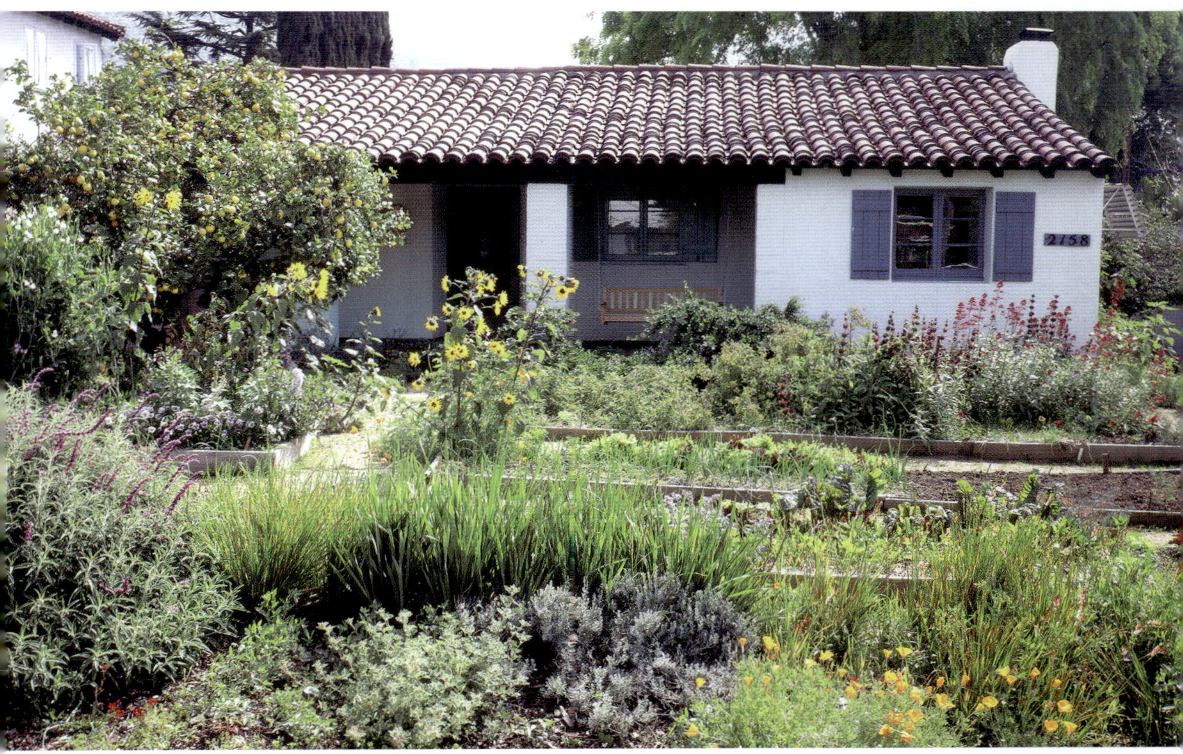
2158

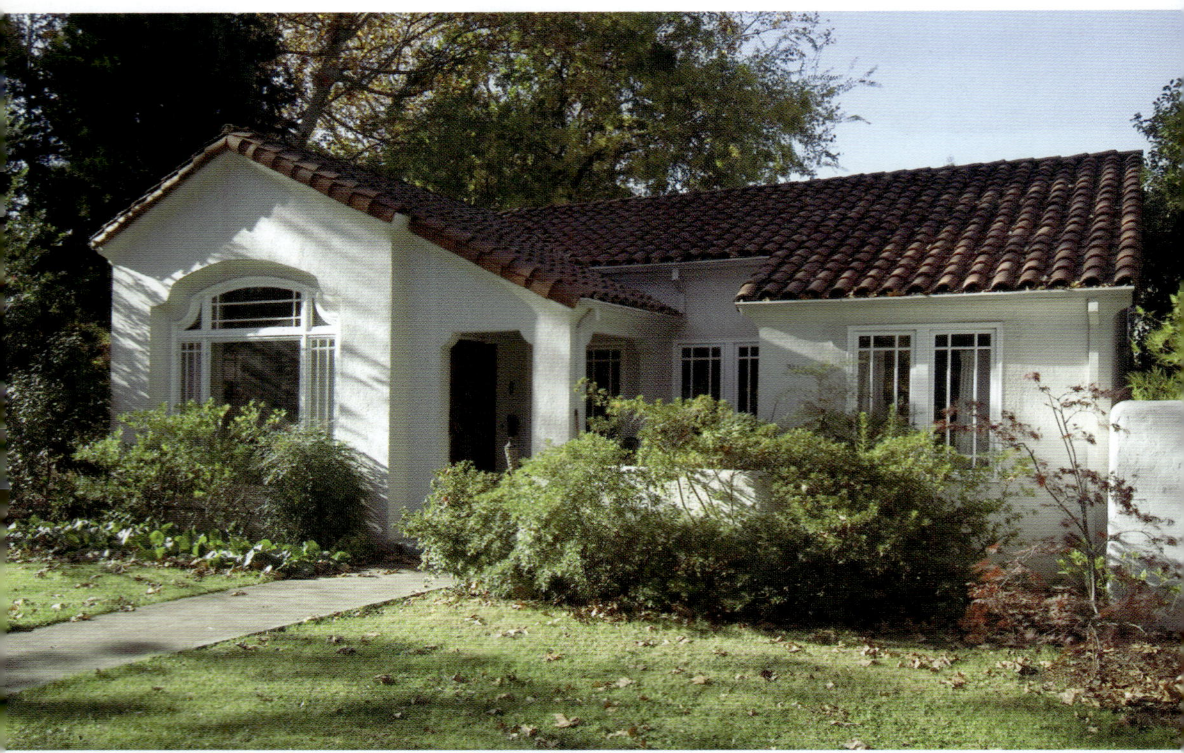

 Chico, California

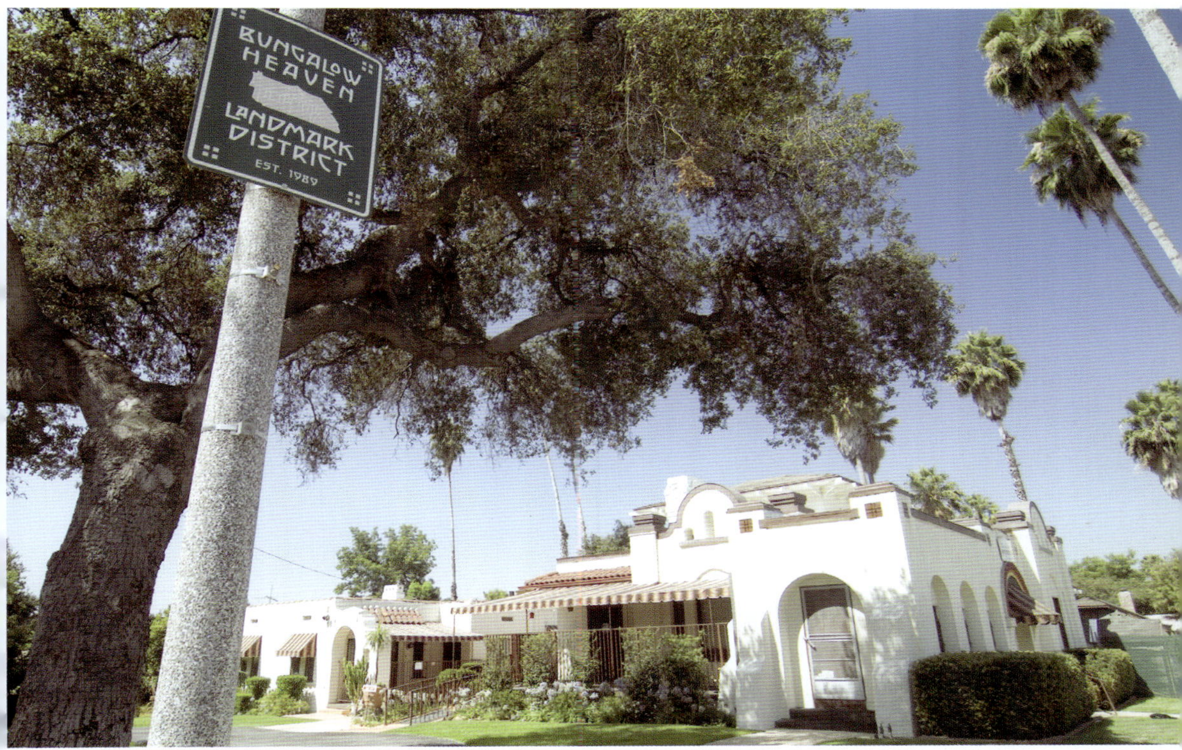
BUNGALOW
HEAVEN
LANDMARK
DISTRICT
EST. 1989

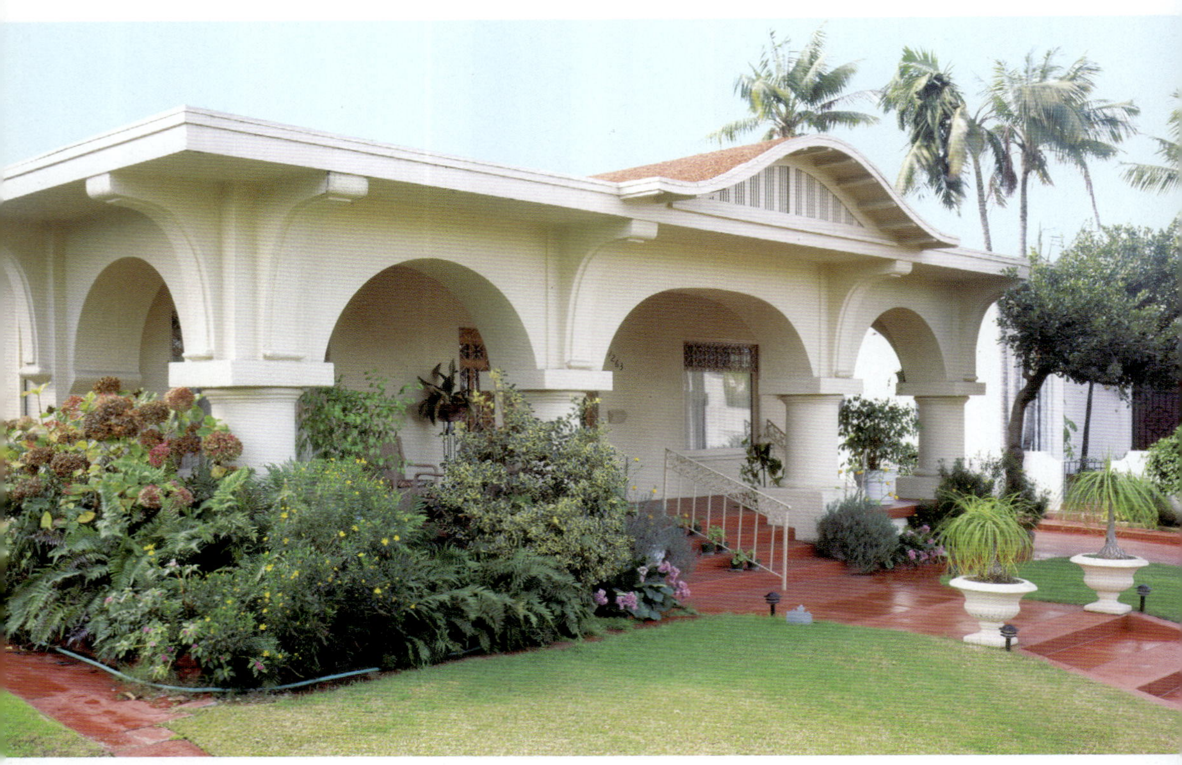

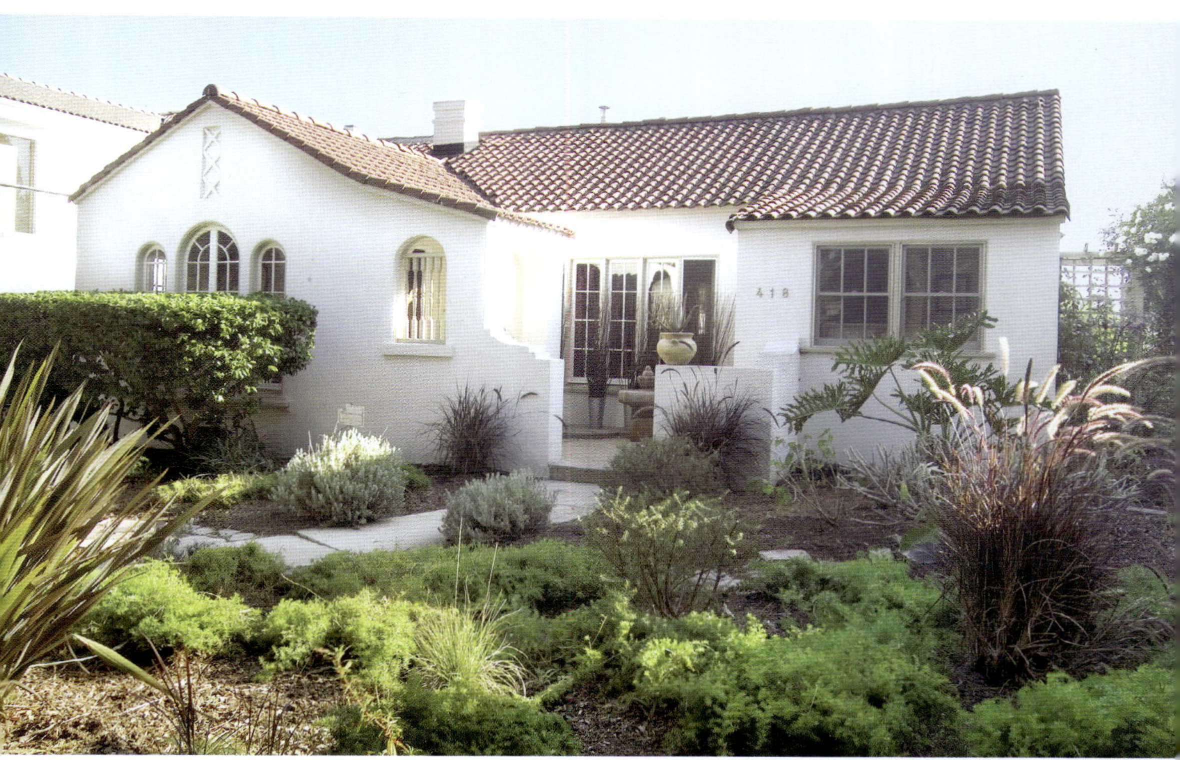


Santa Monica, California

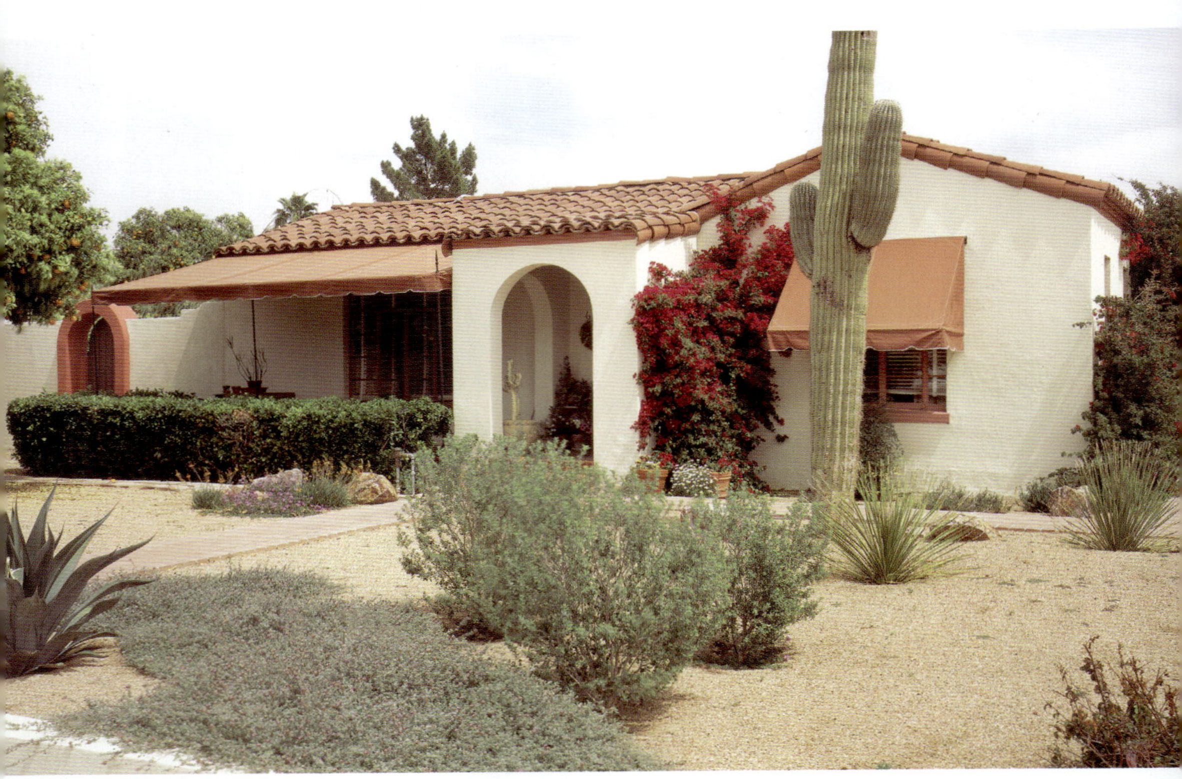

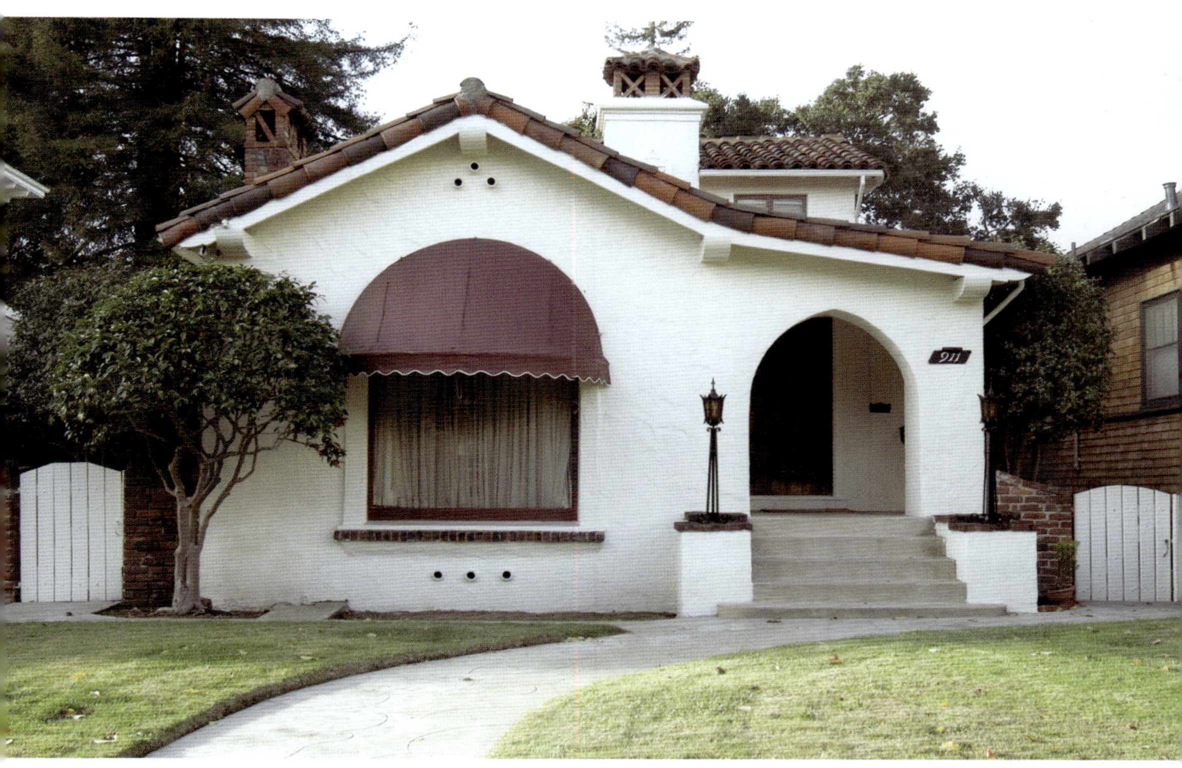


ALAMEDA, CALIFORNIA

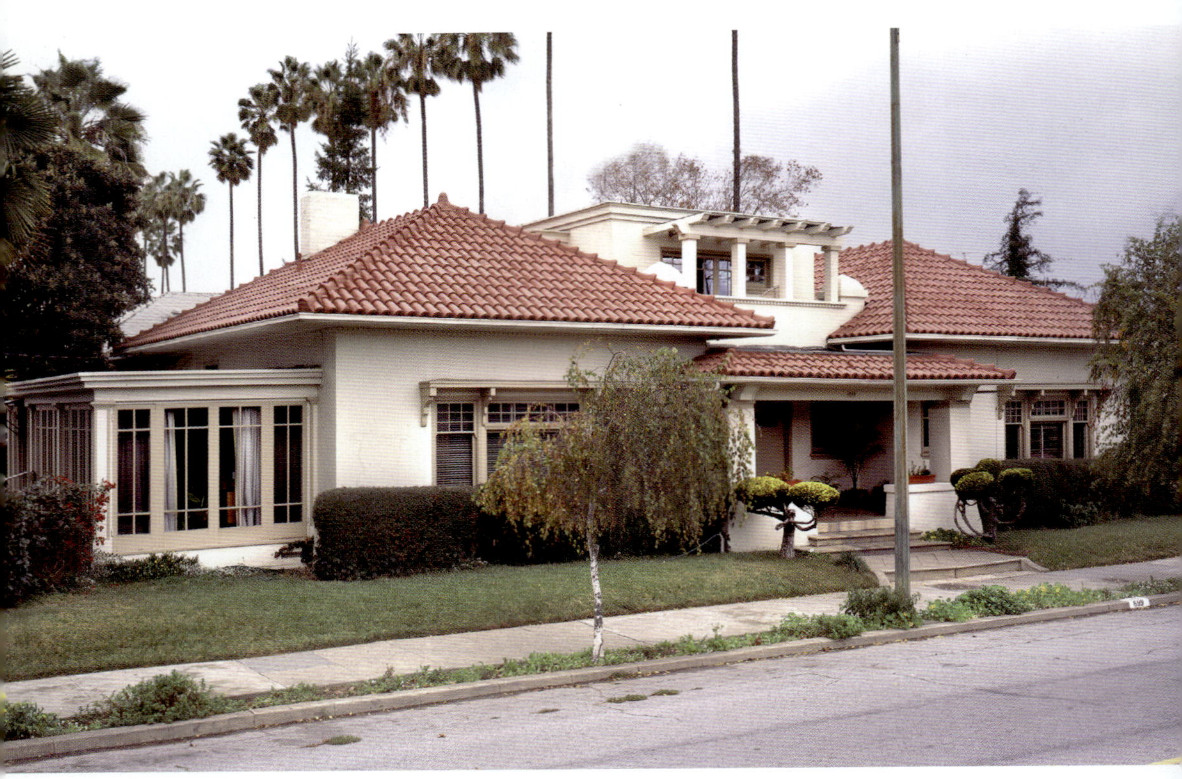

 San Jose, California

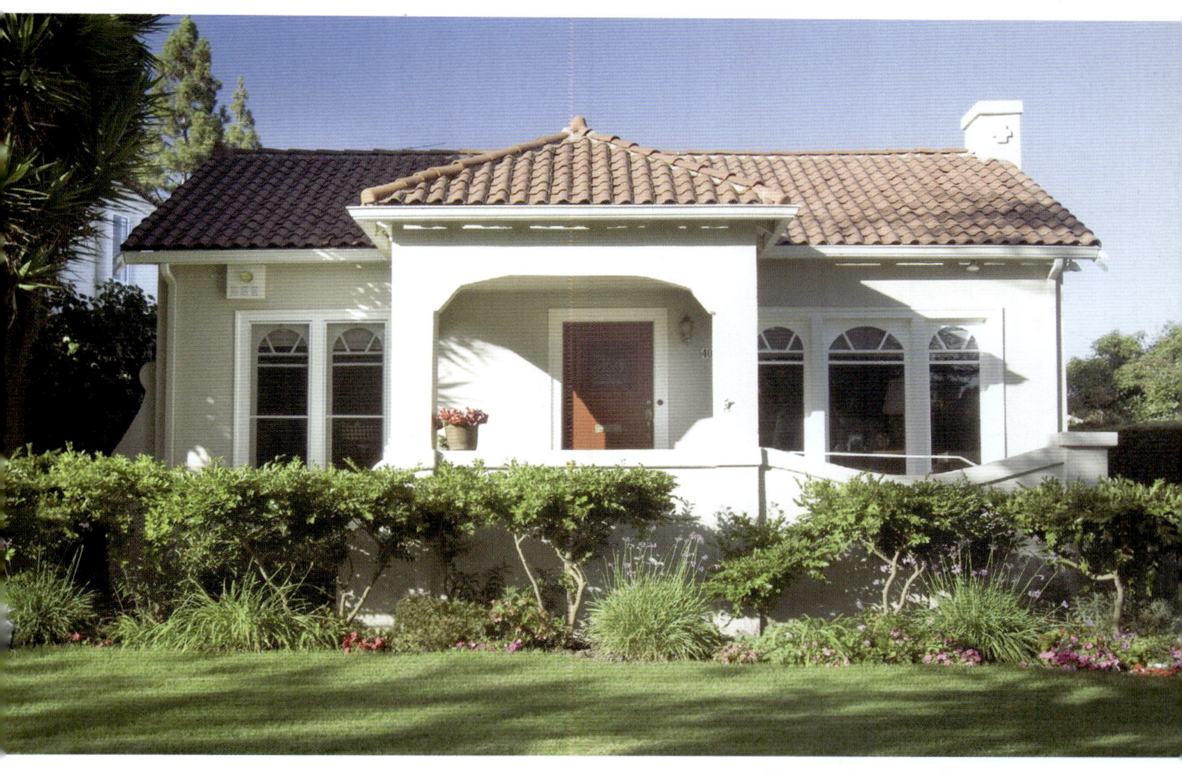

Santa Monica, California

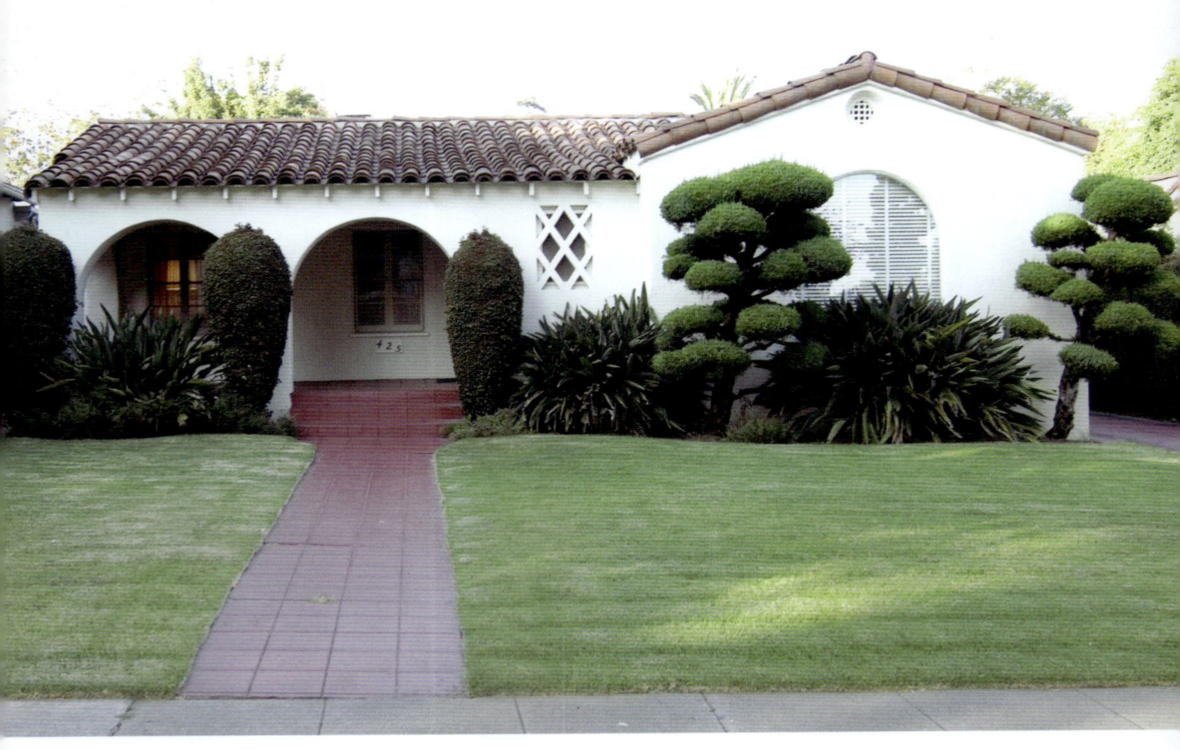


 Santa Monica, California

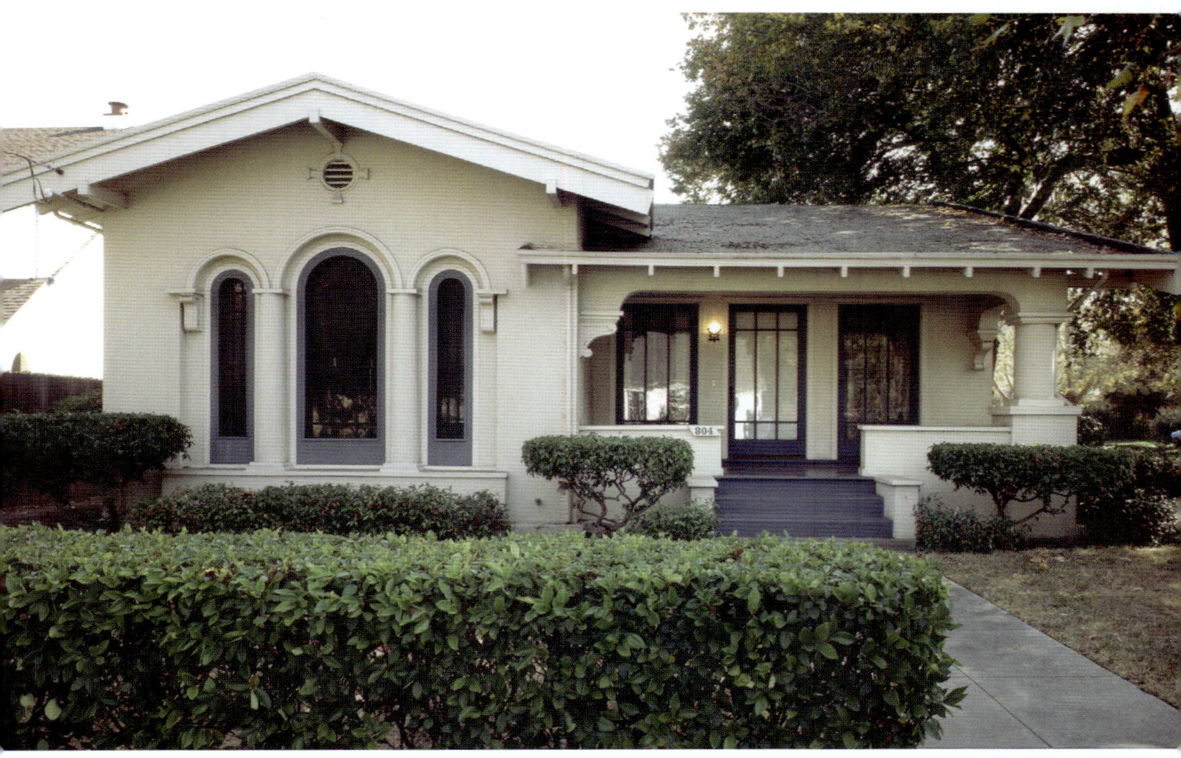
804

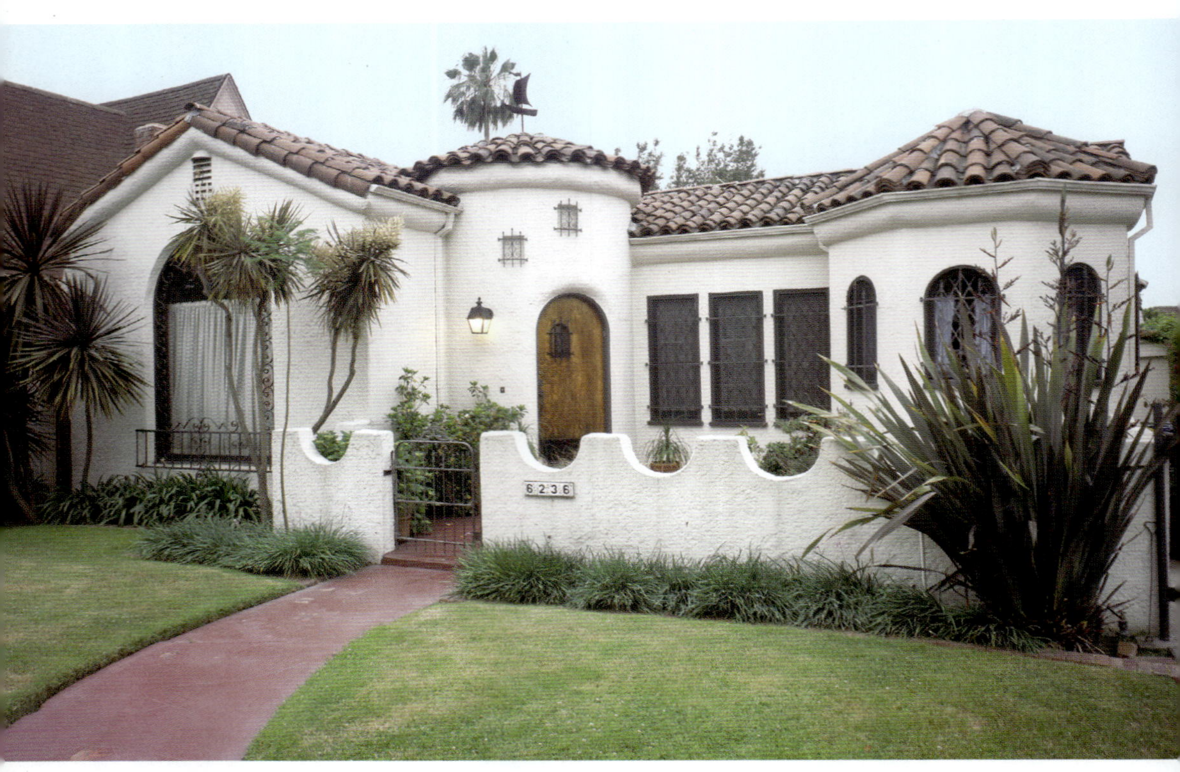


 Los Angeles, California

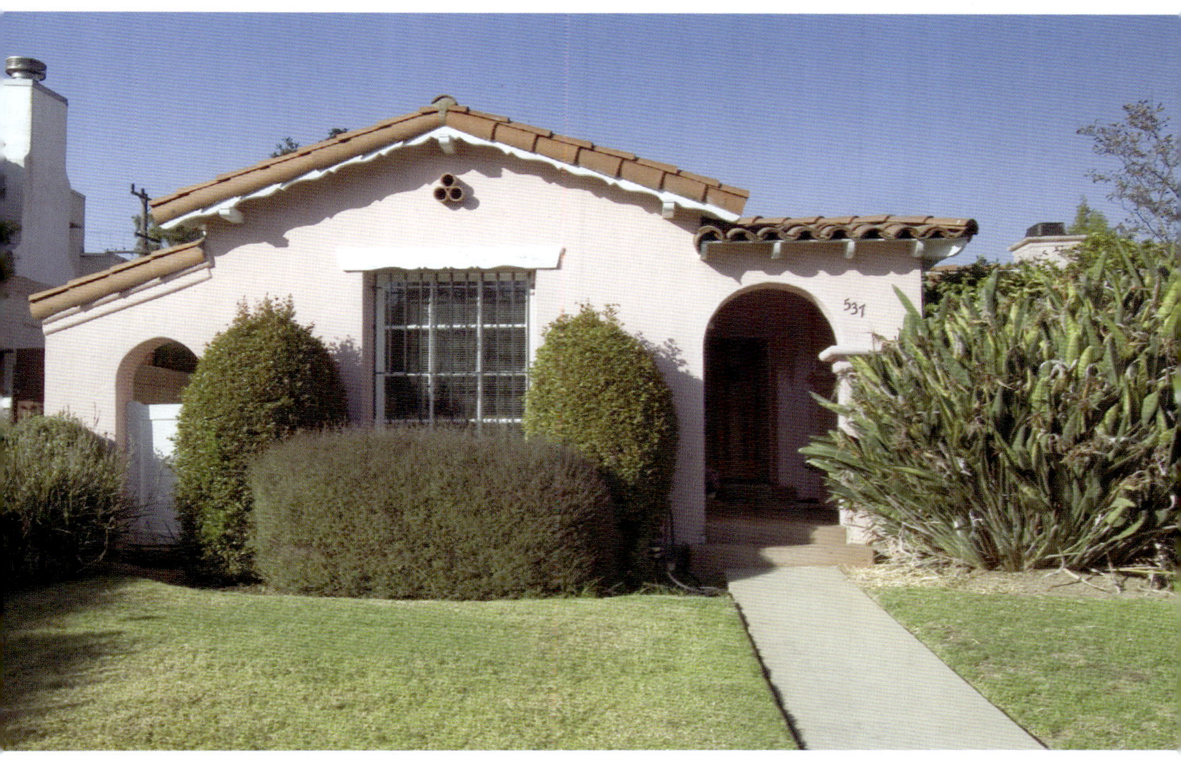

Santa Monica, California

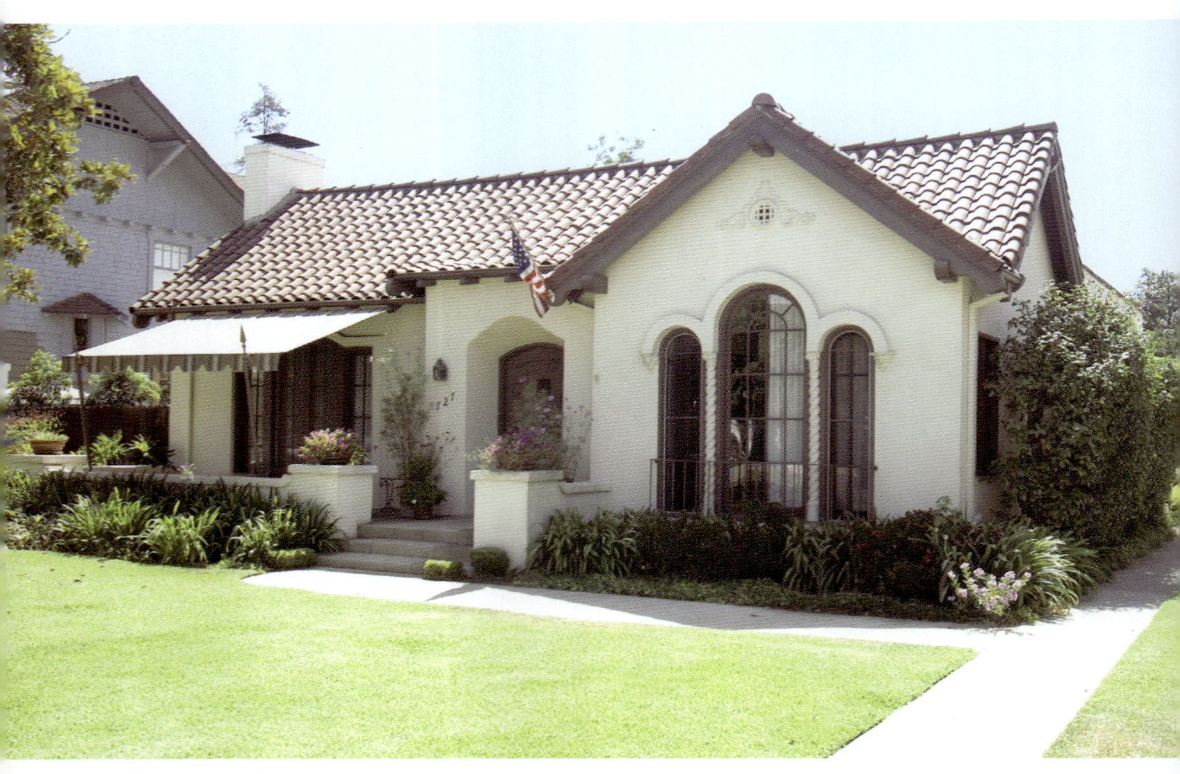

 PASADENA, CALIFORNIA

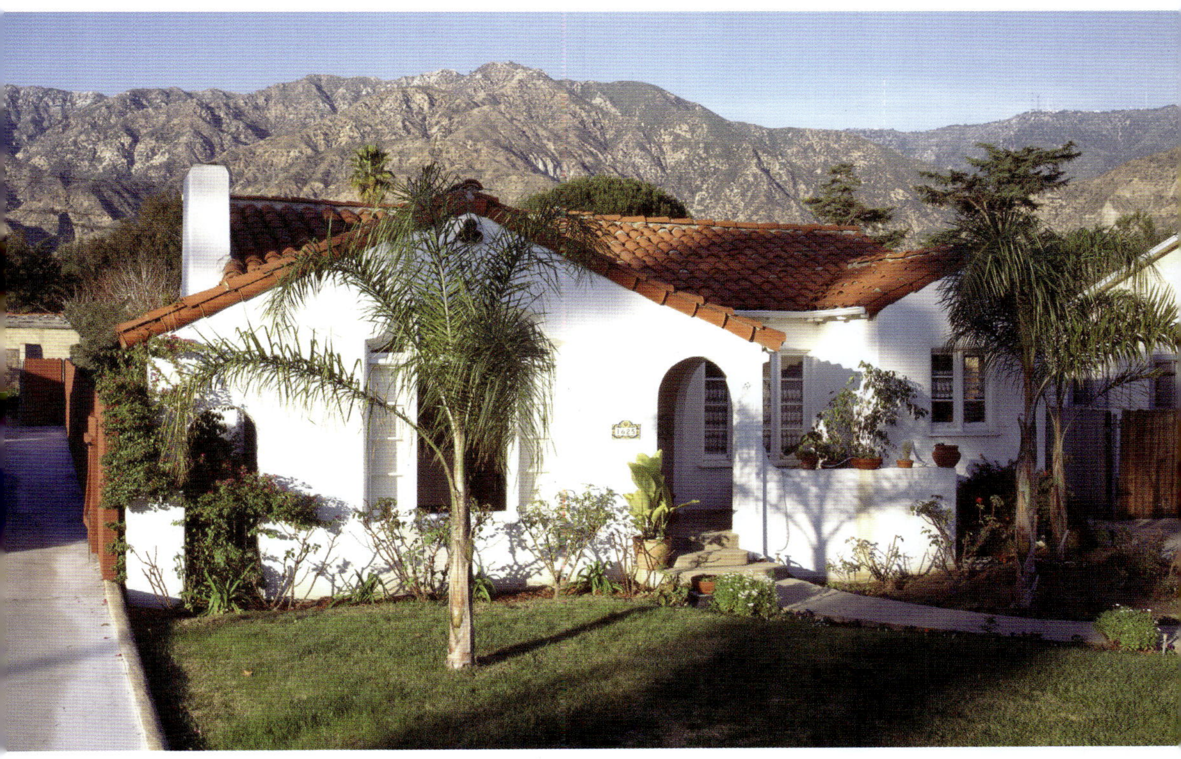

Altadena, California

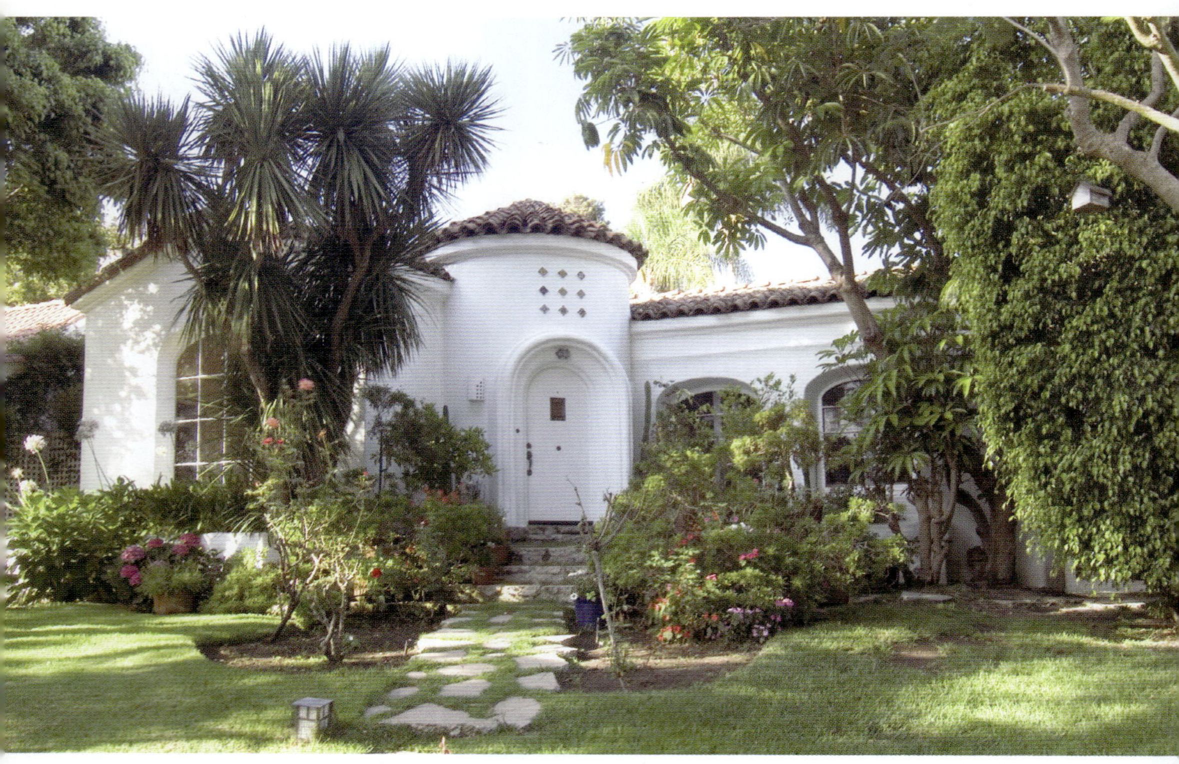

 Santa Monica, California

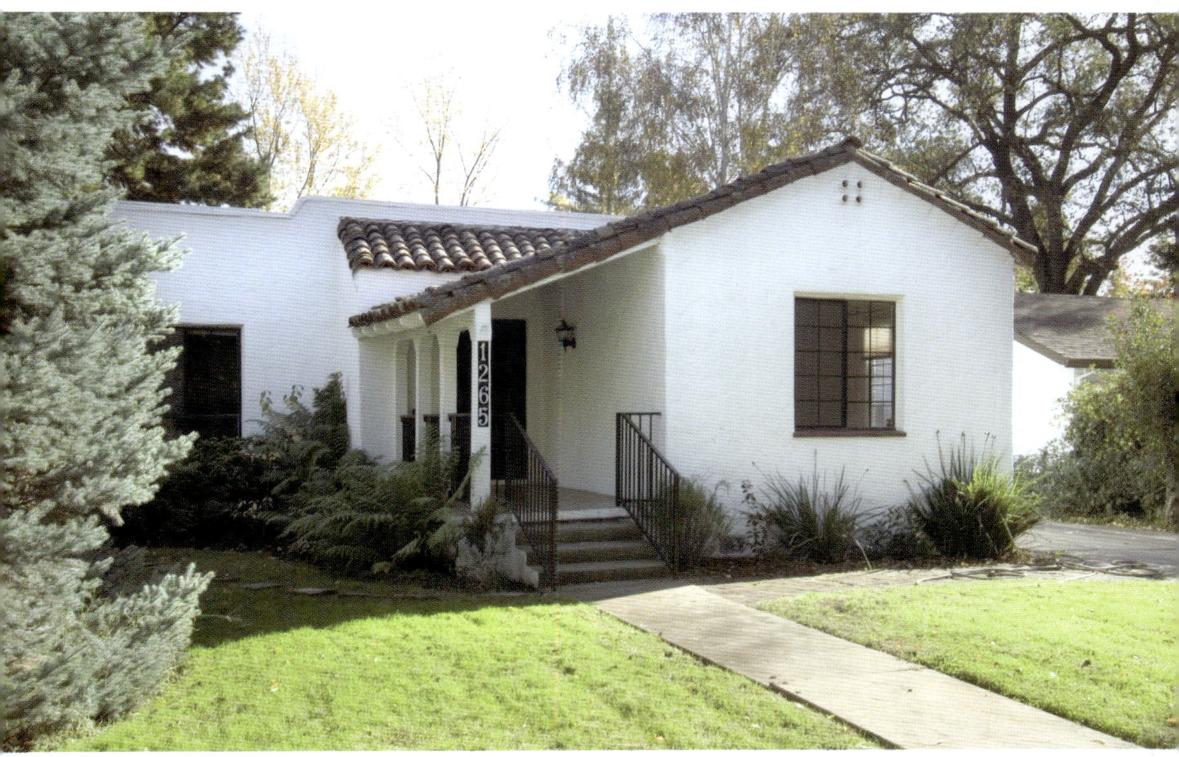


Chico, California

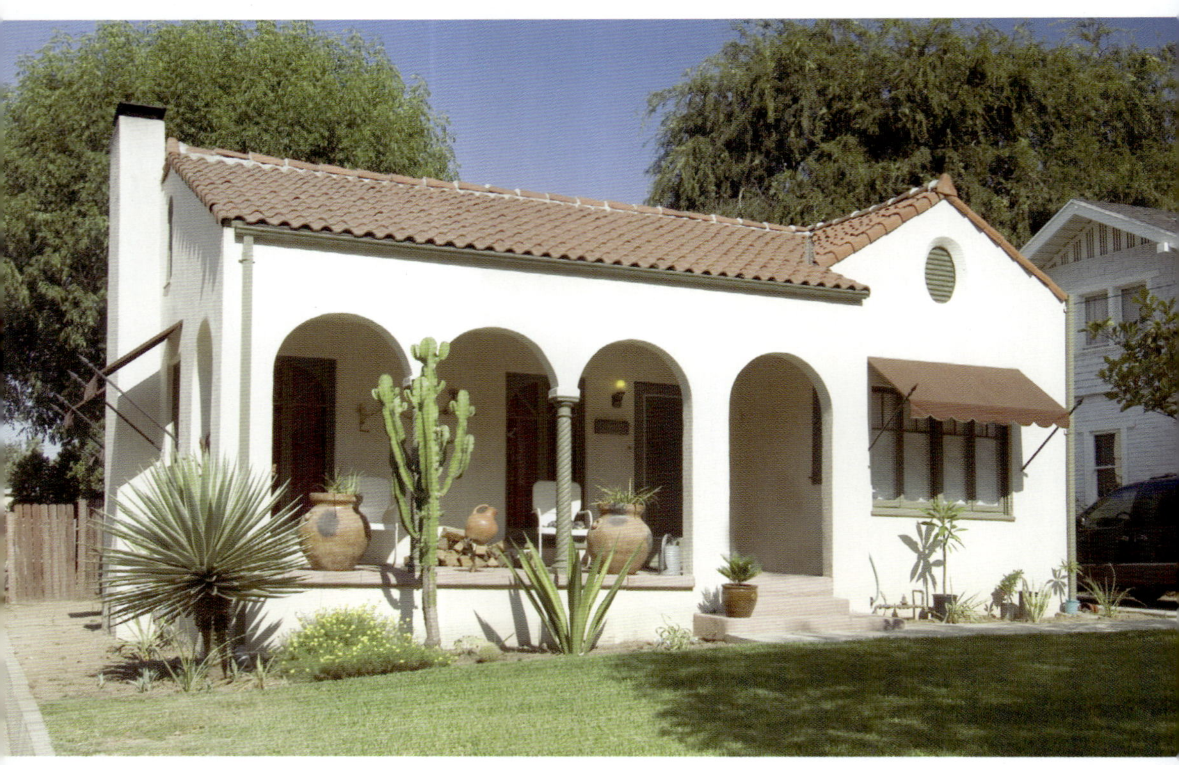

 Pasadena, California

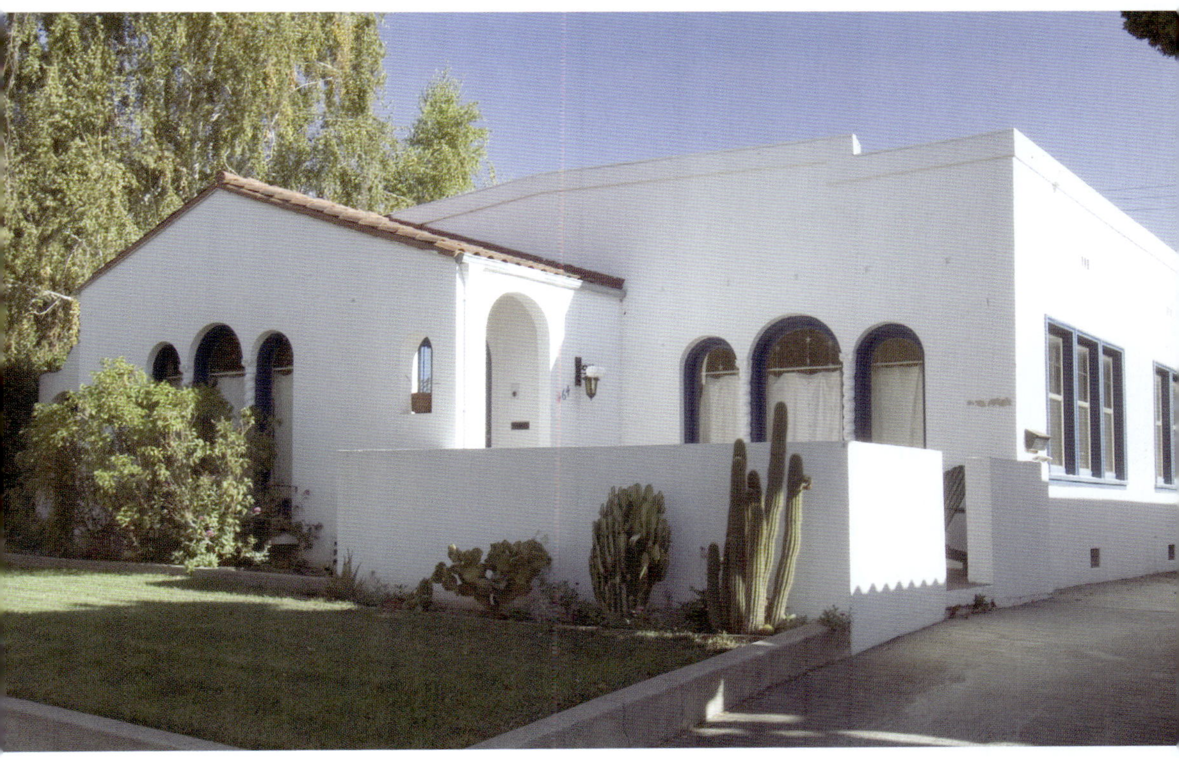

San Jose, California

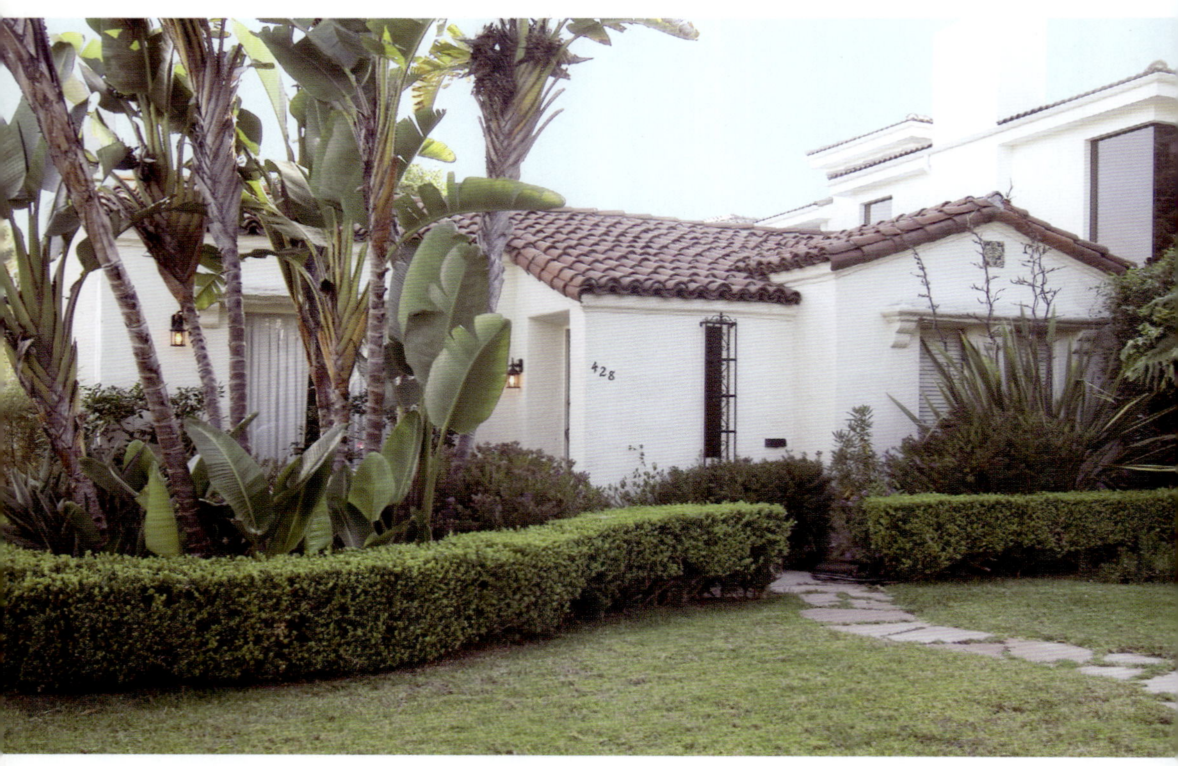




SANTA MONICA, CALIFORNIA

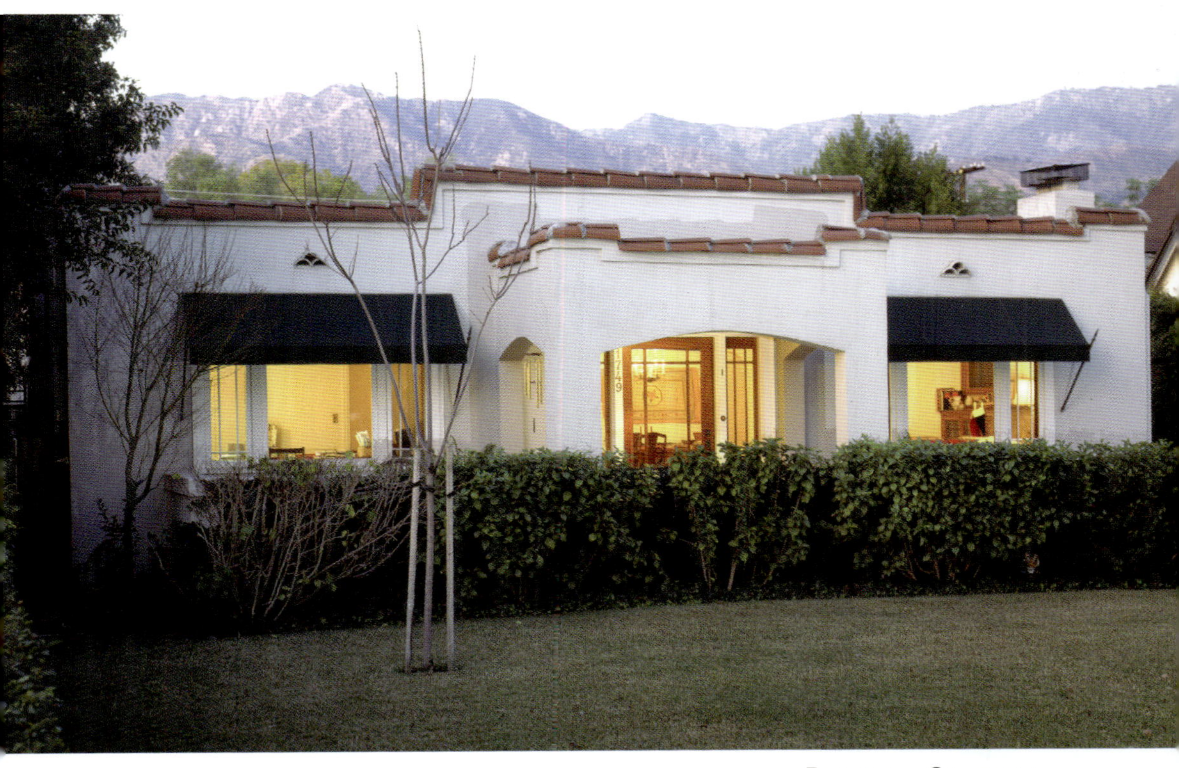

Pasadena, California

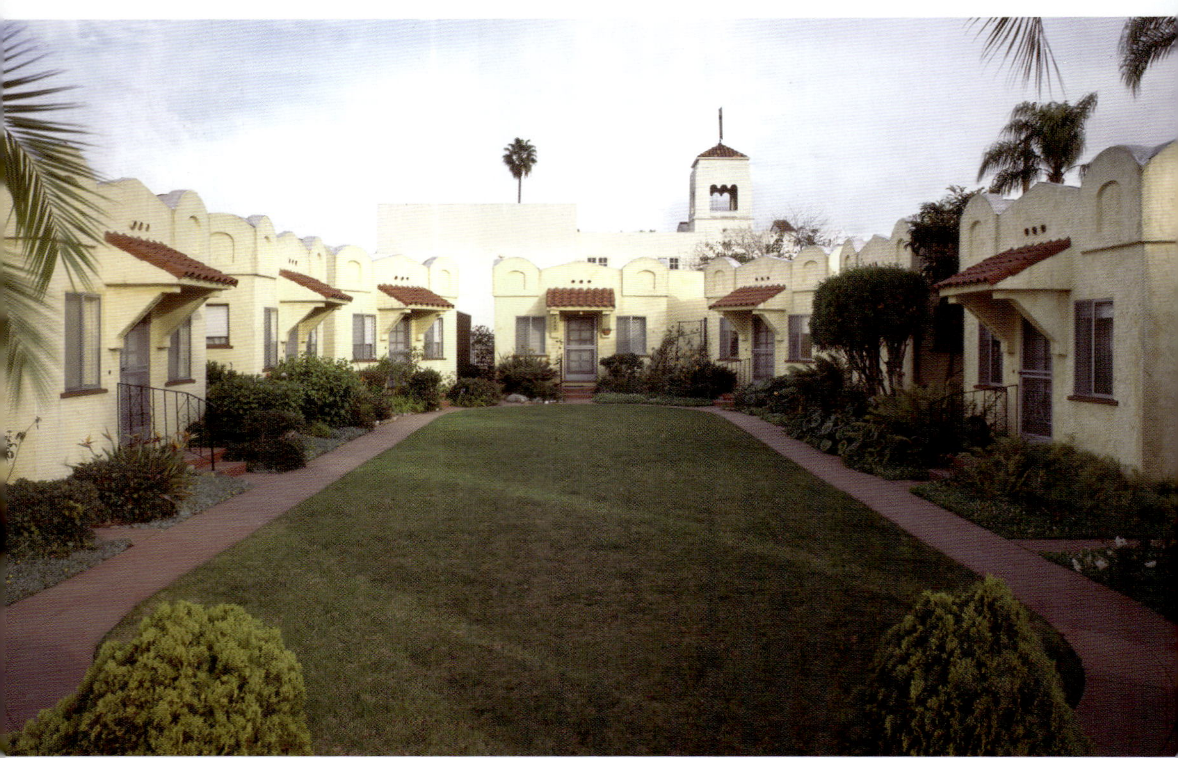

 San Diego, California

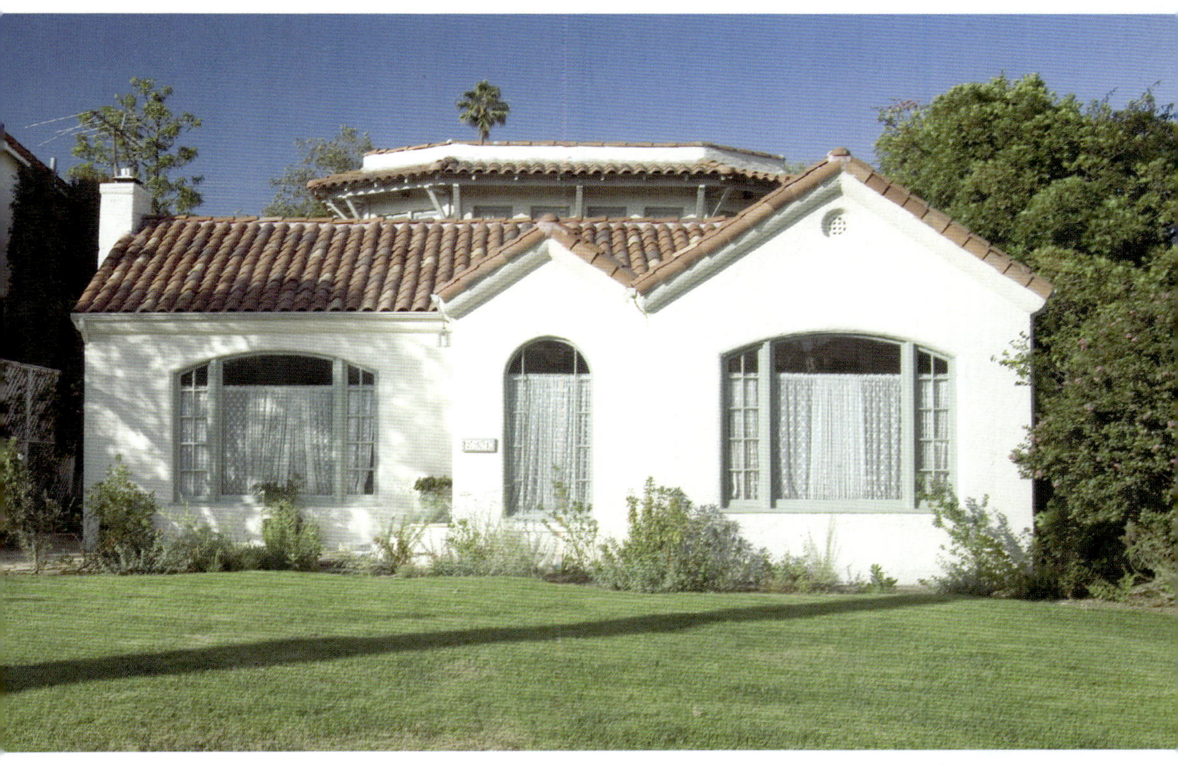

Santa Monica, California

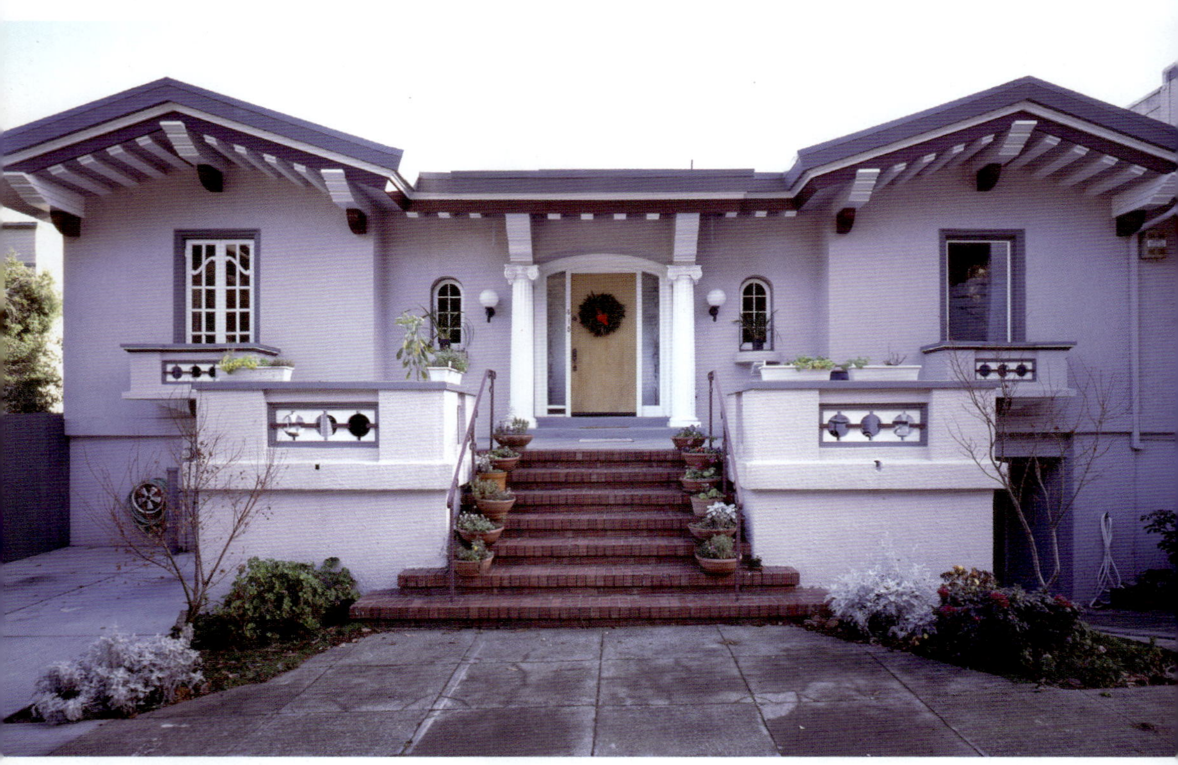


SAN FRANCISCO, CALIFORNIA

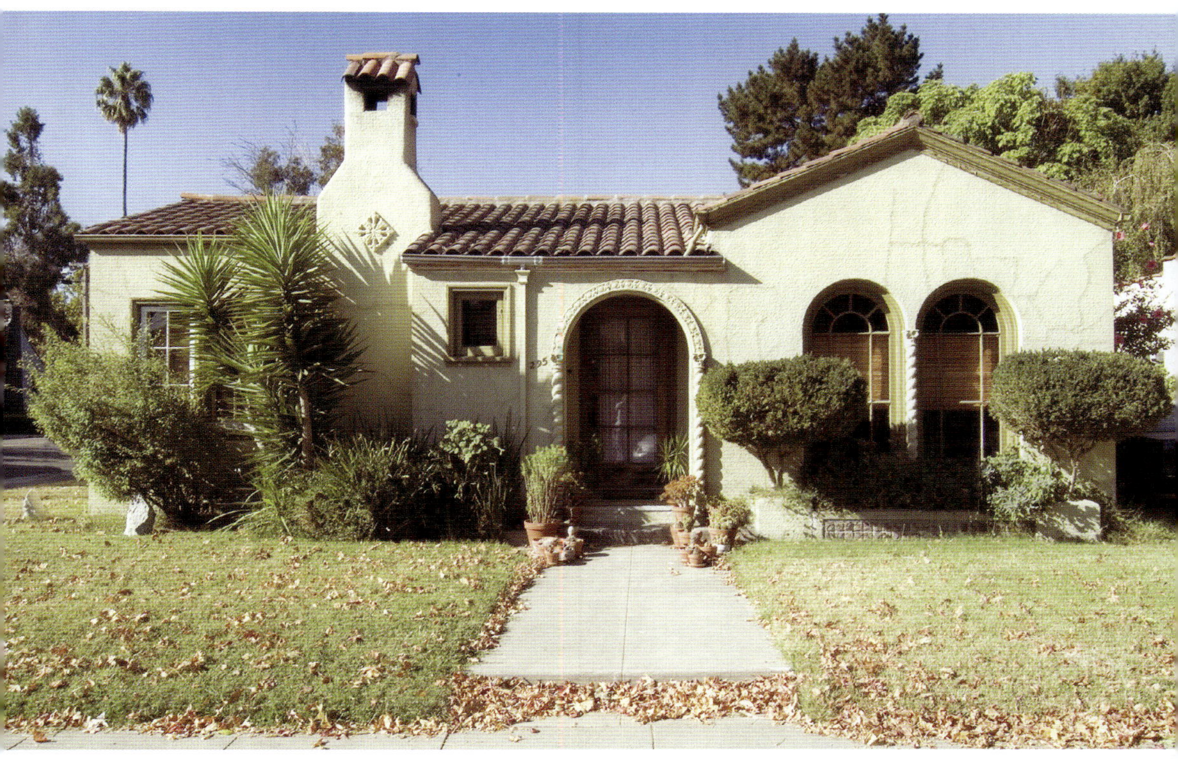

San Jose, California

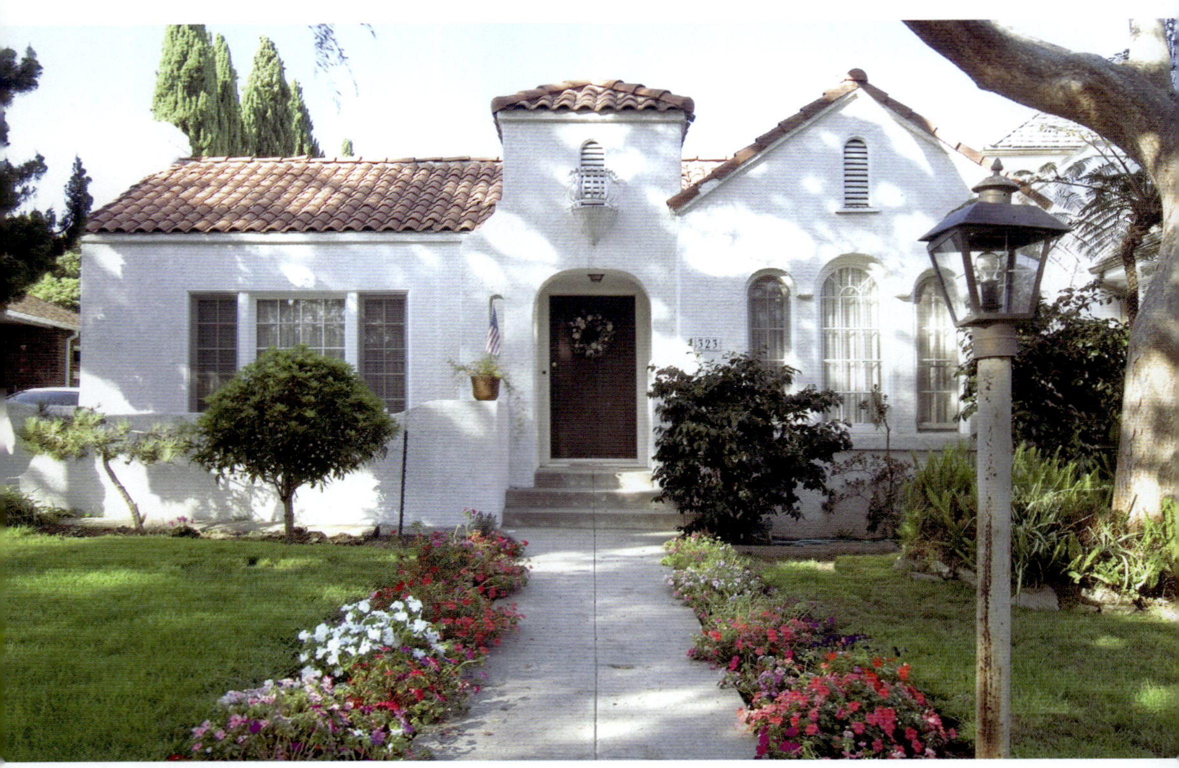


 Santa Monica, California

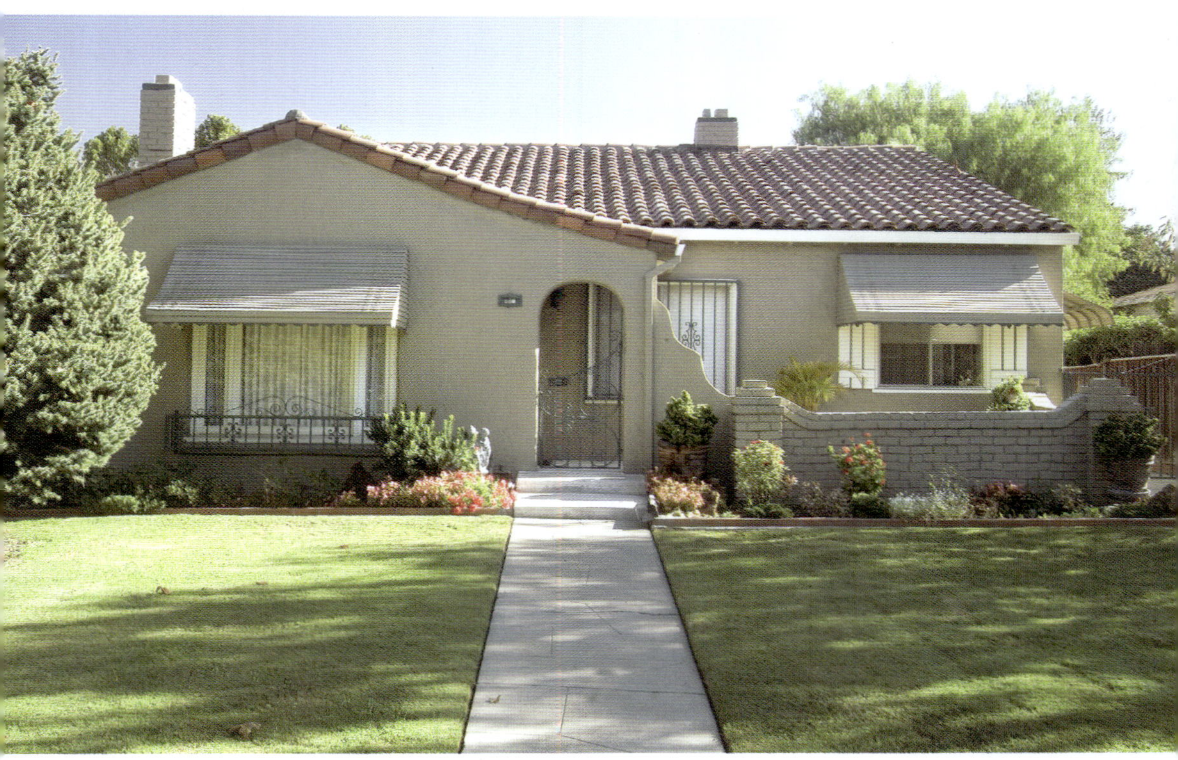

San Jose, California 

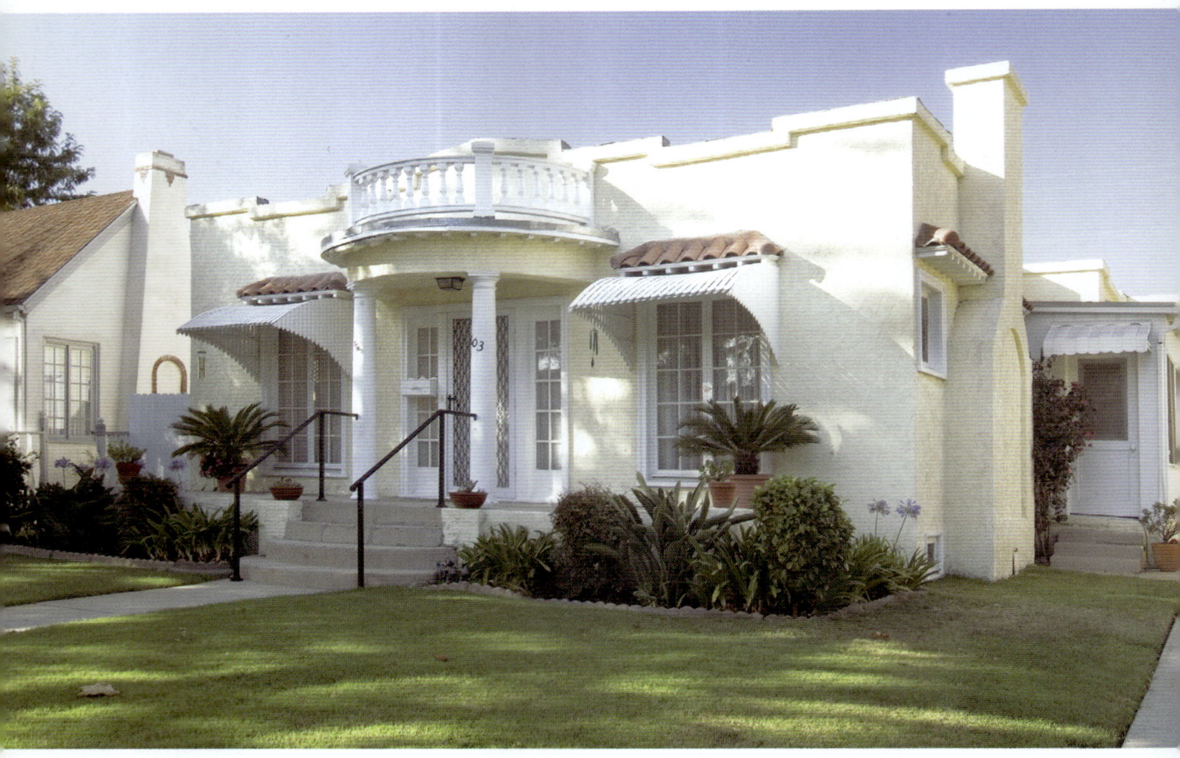

 Santa Monica, California

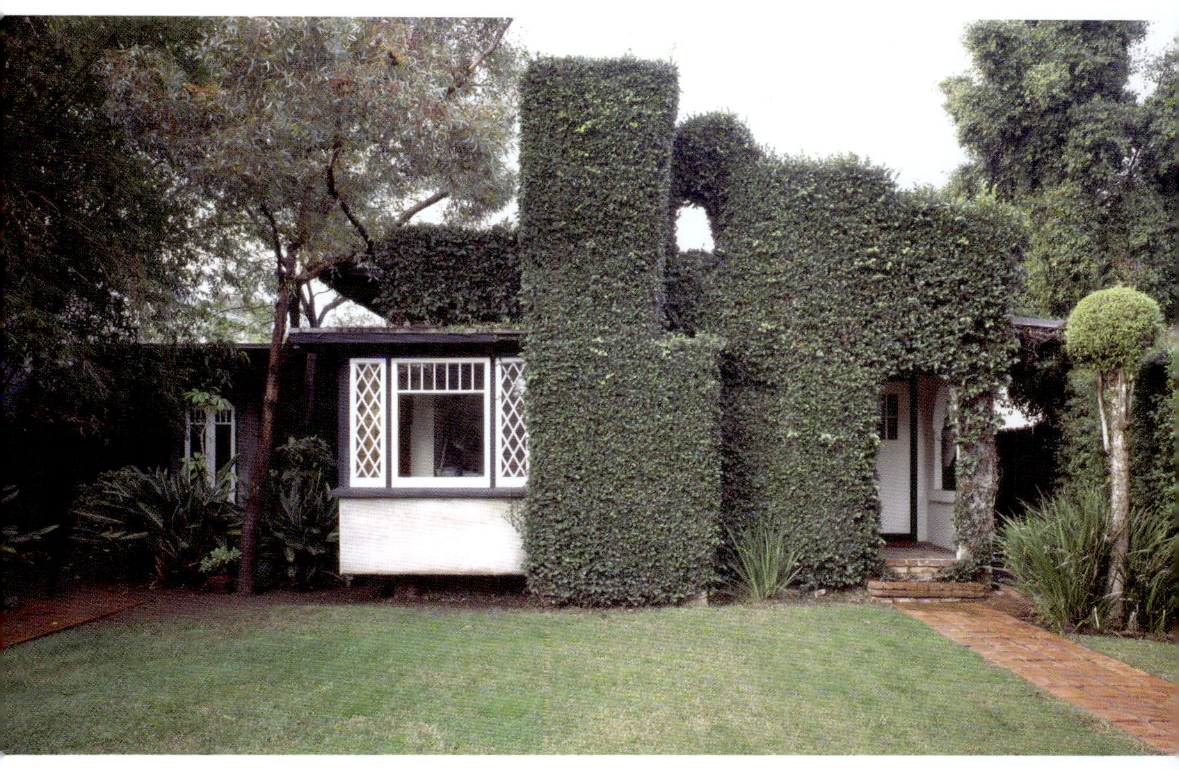

# CRAFTSMAN BUNGALOWS

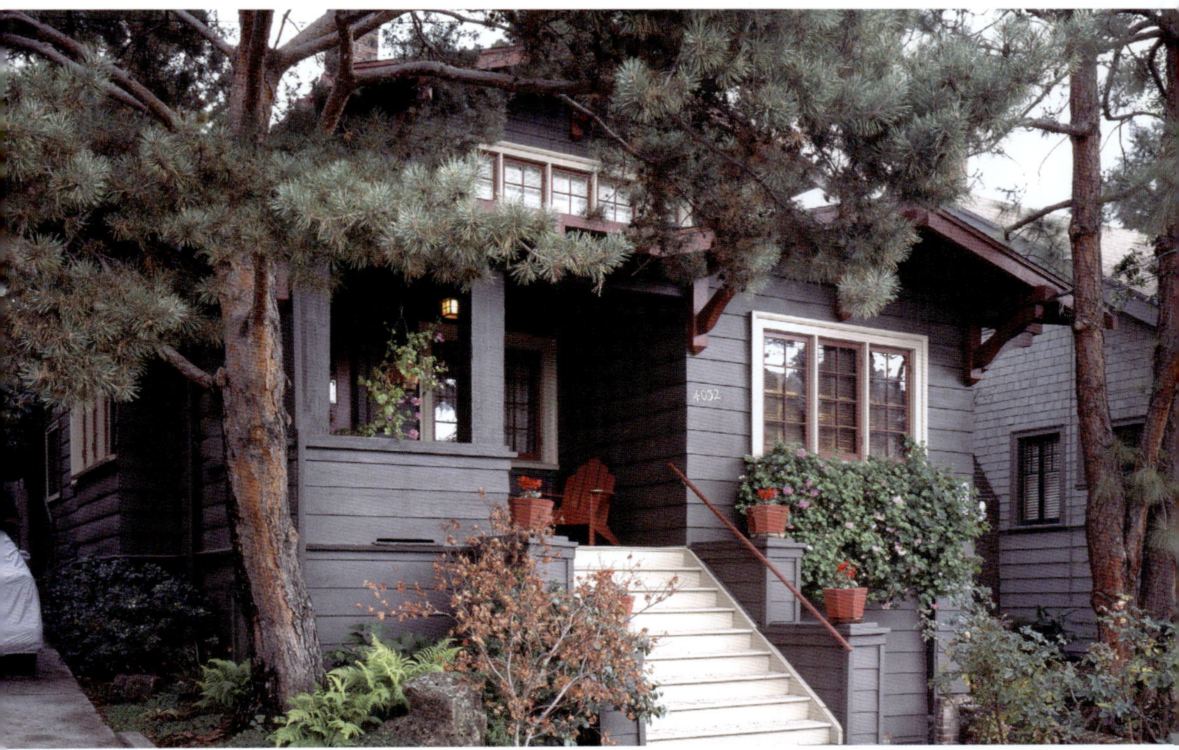


Oakland, California

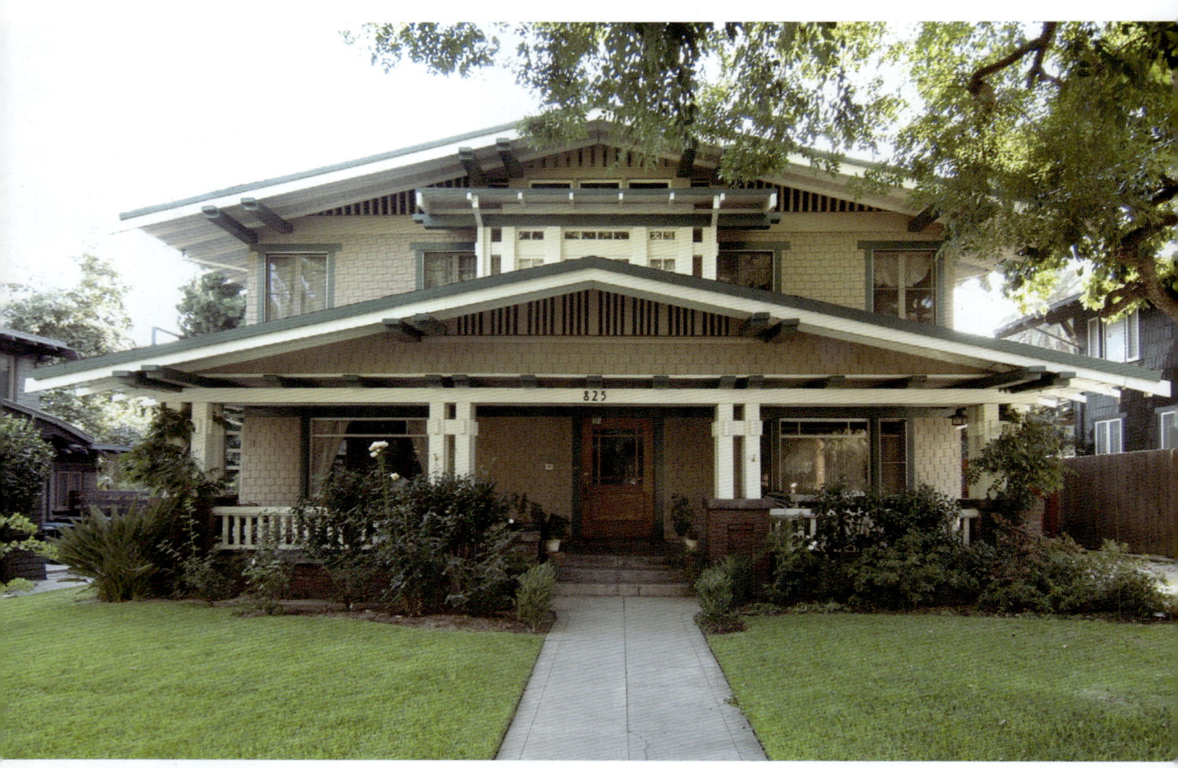




Santa Monica, California

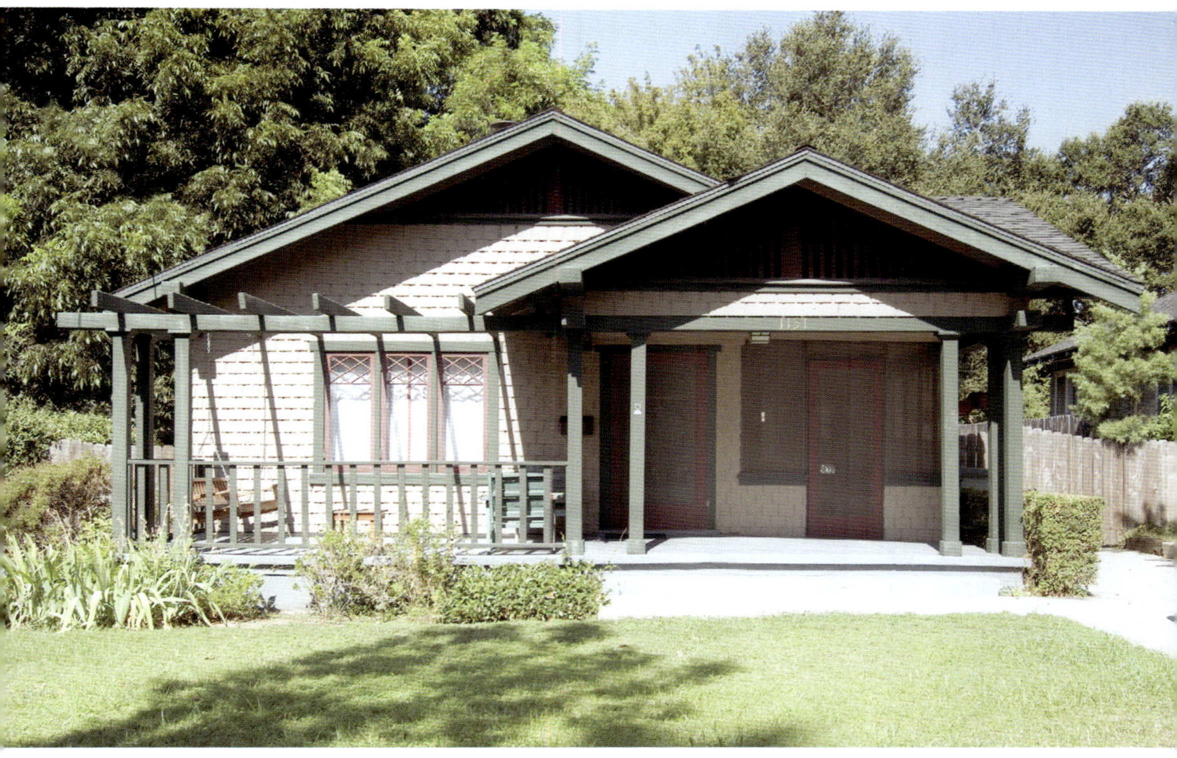

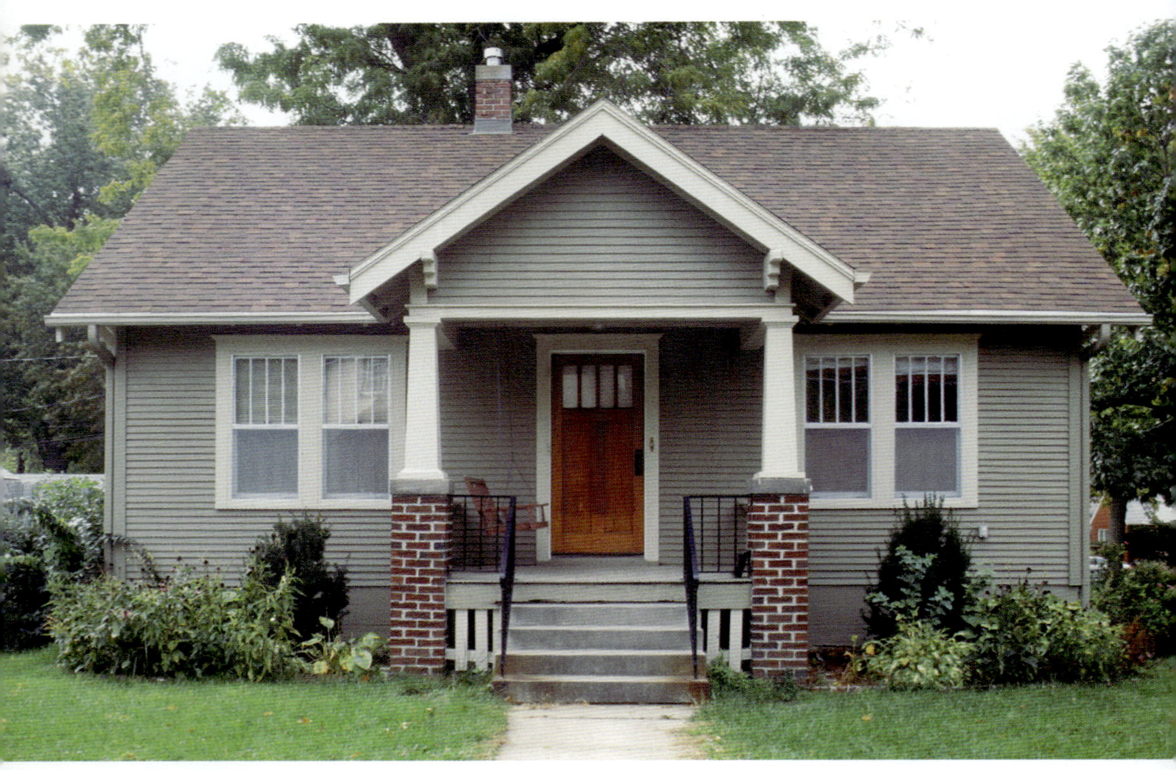

 Lincoln, Nebraska

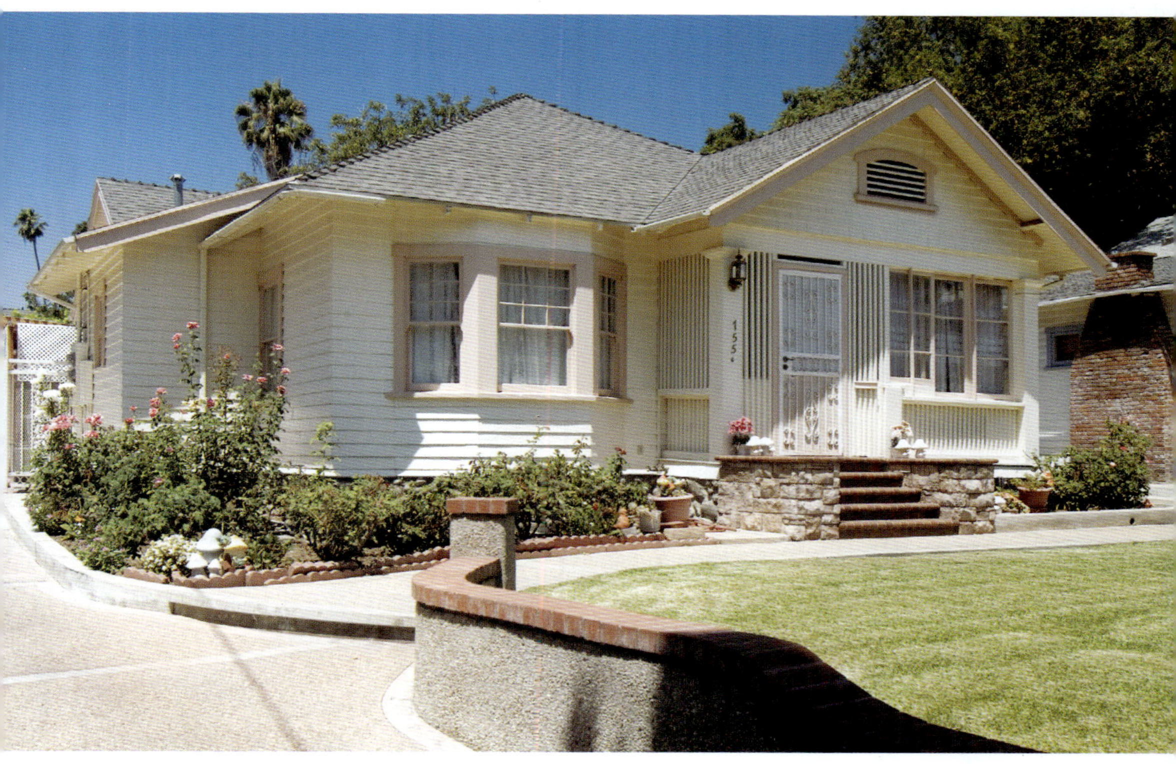


Pasadena, California

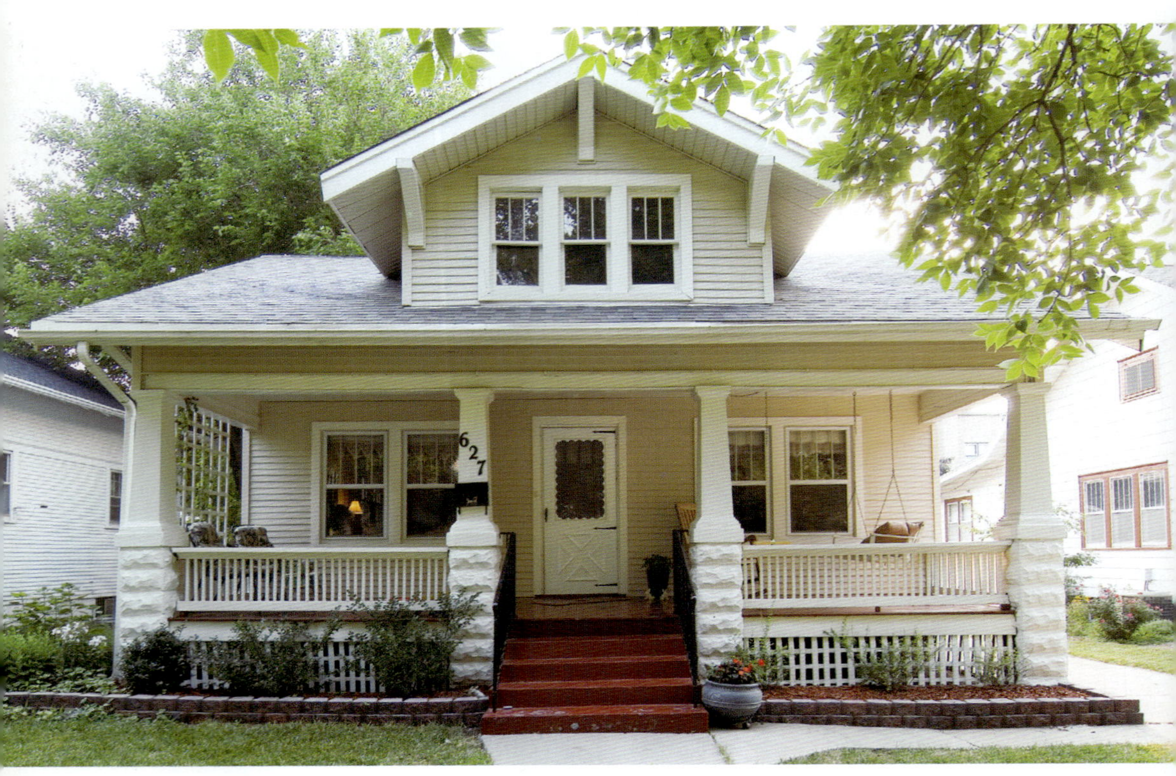


 Lincoln, Nebraska

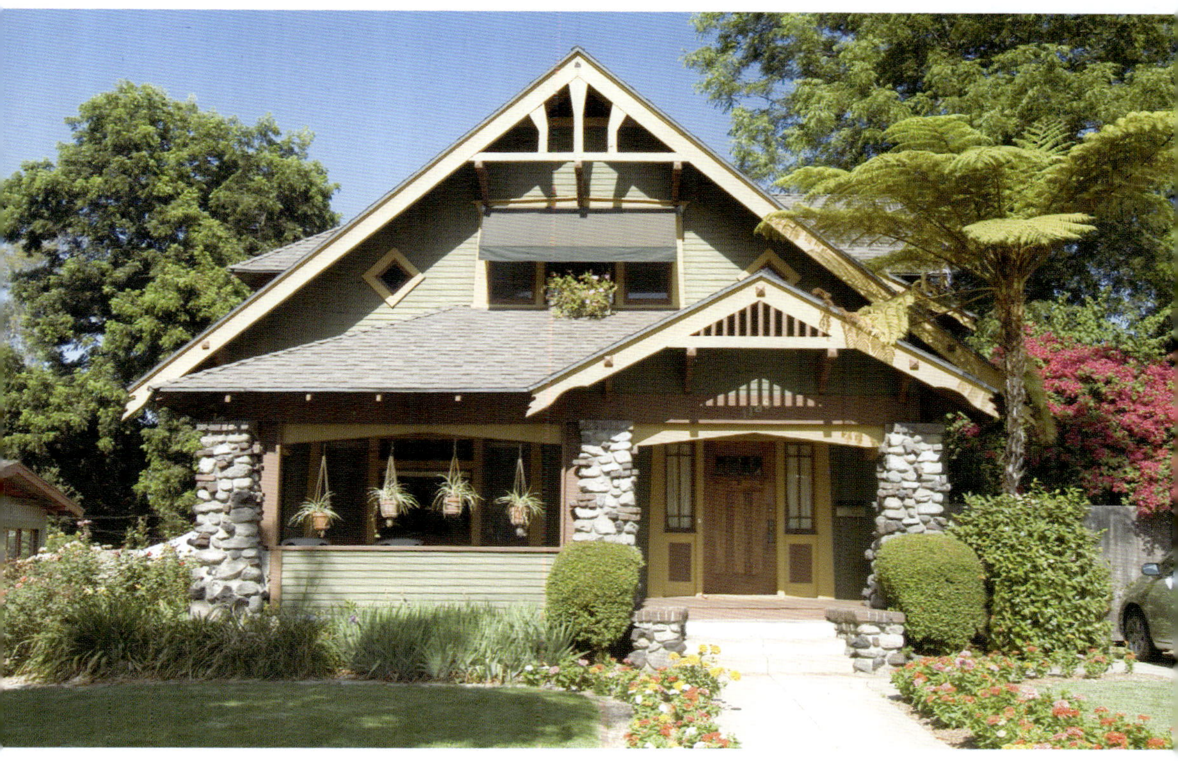

Pasadena, California

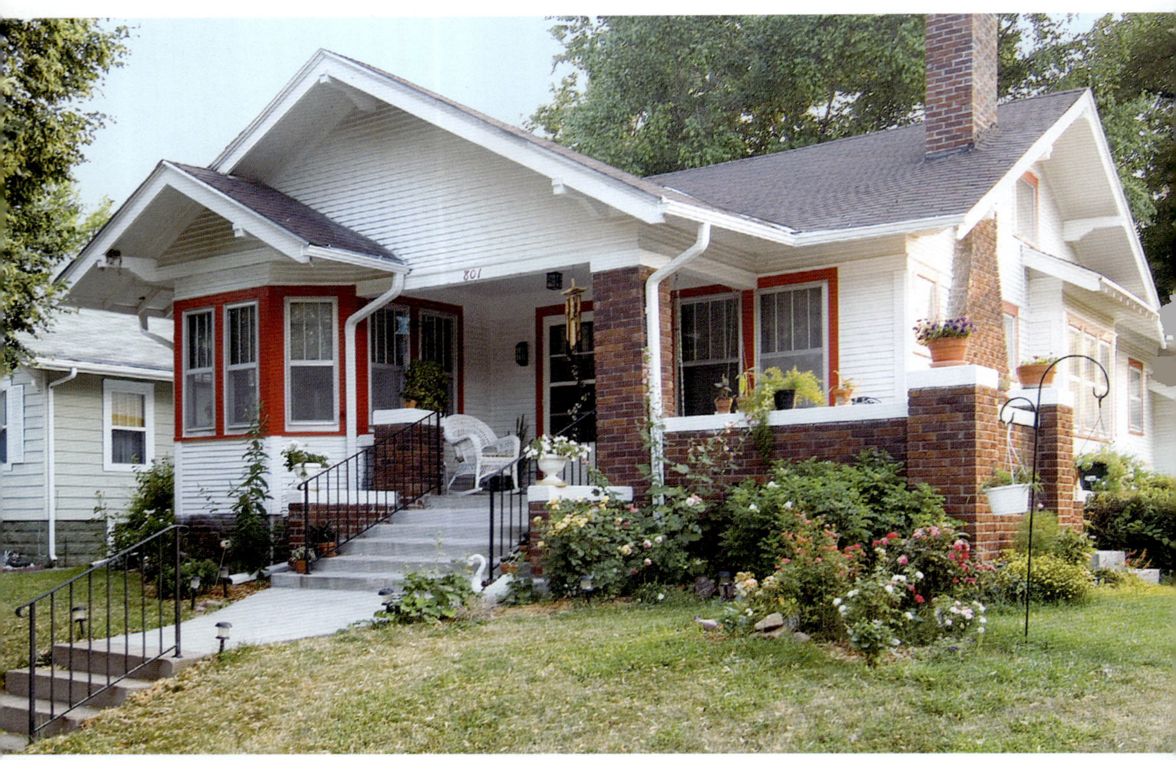
801

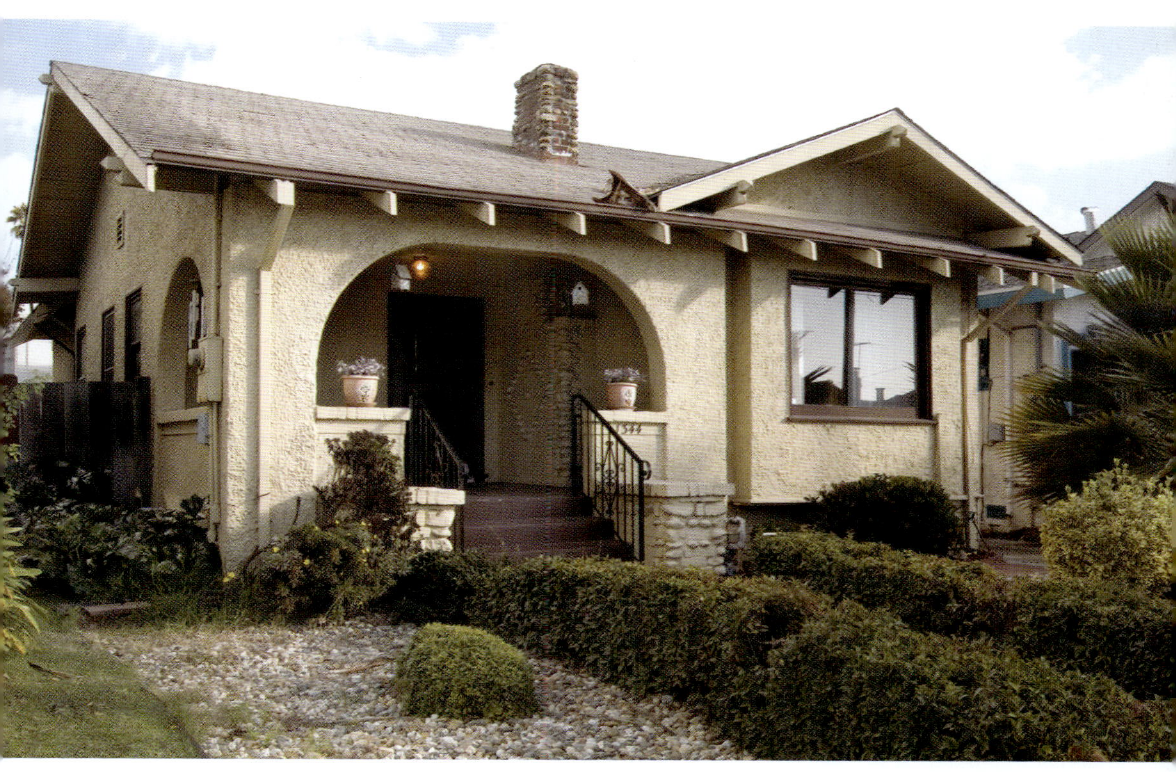

Alameda, California

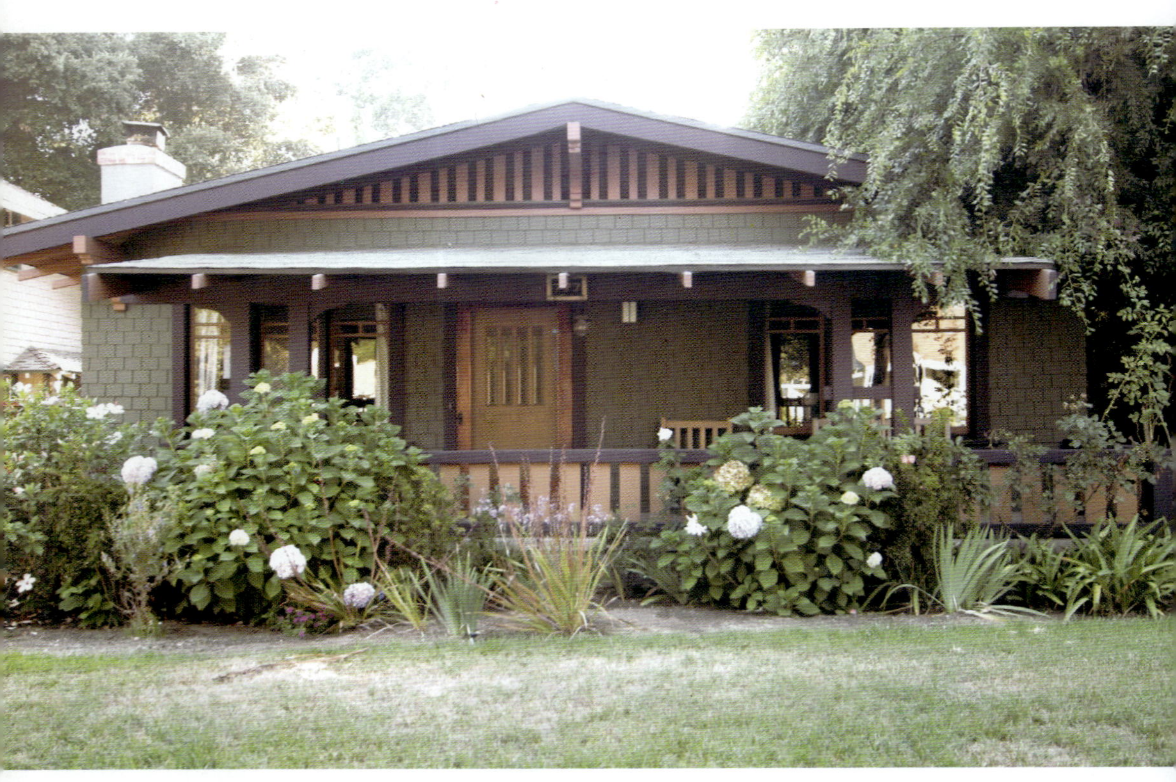

 Pasadena, California

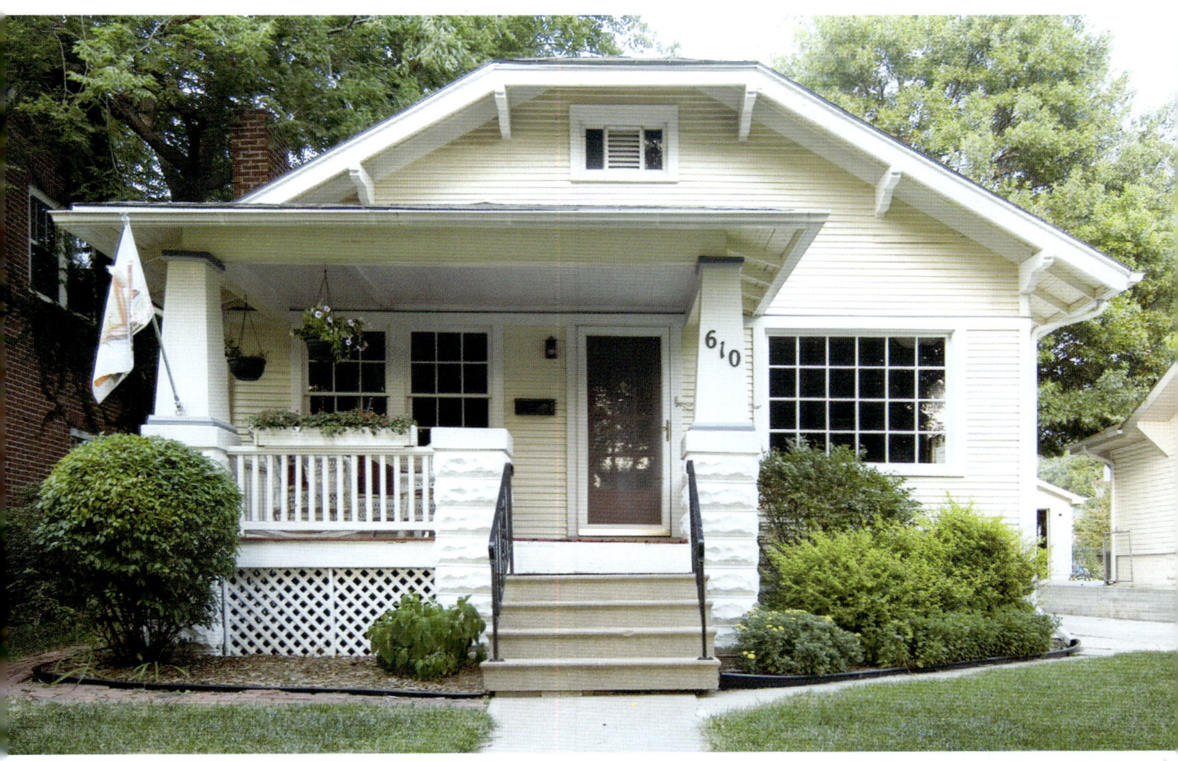
610

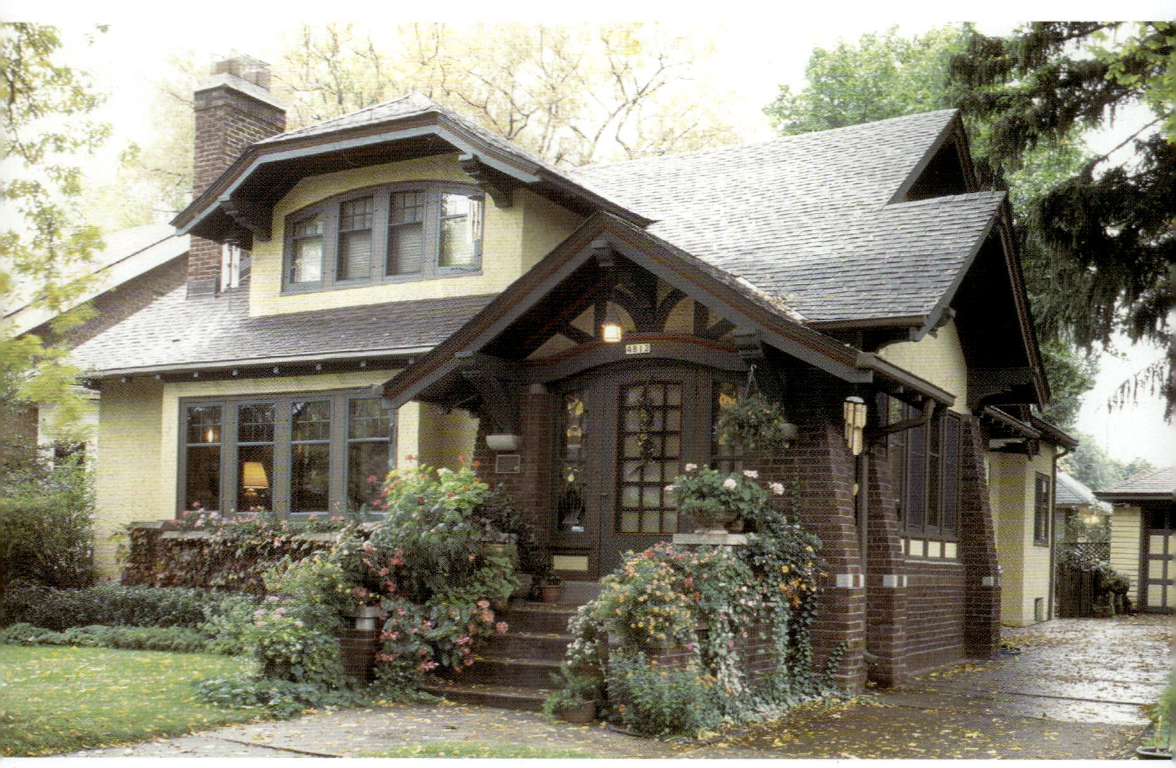




Milwaukee, Wisconsin

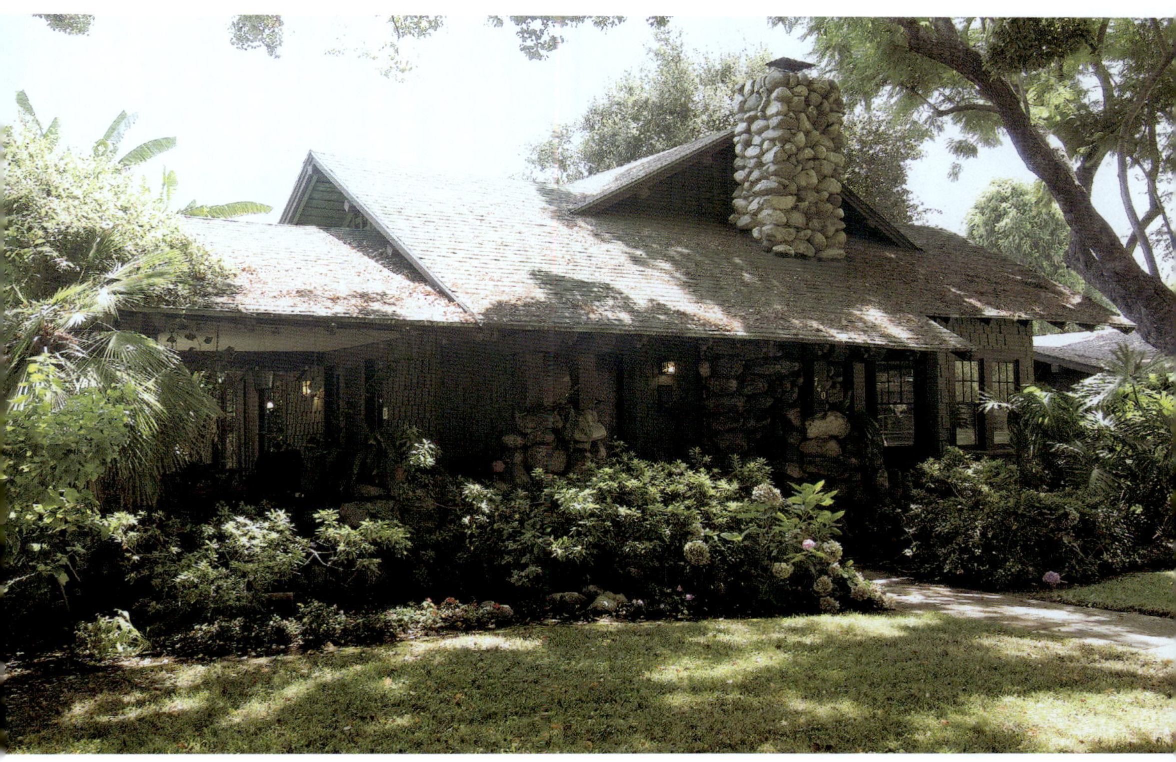

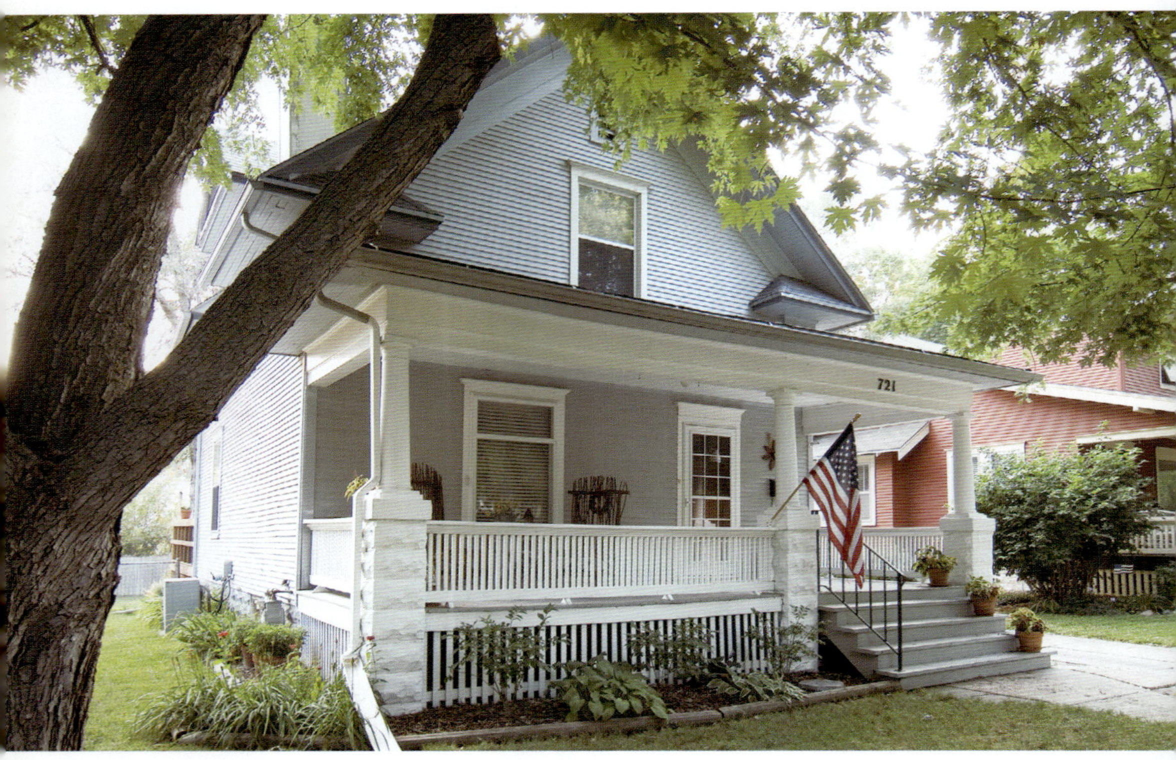
721

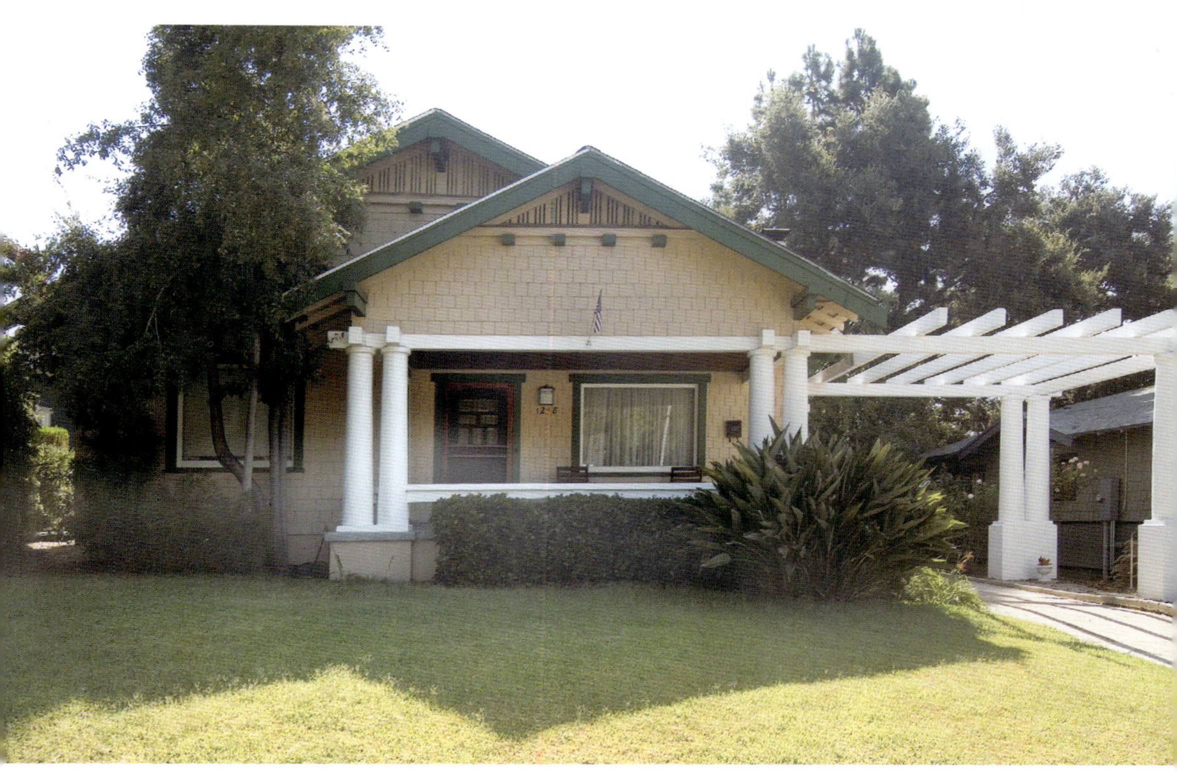

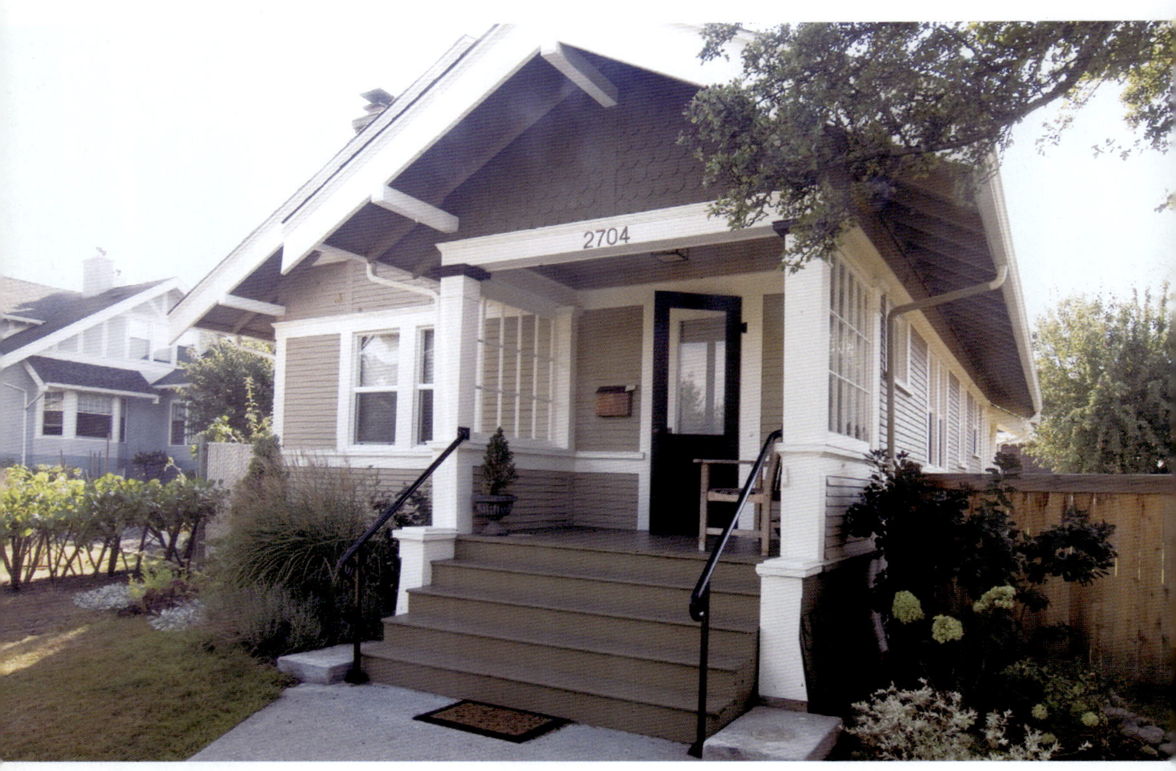
2704

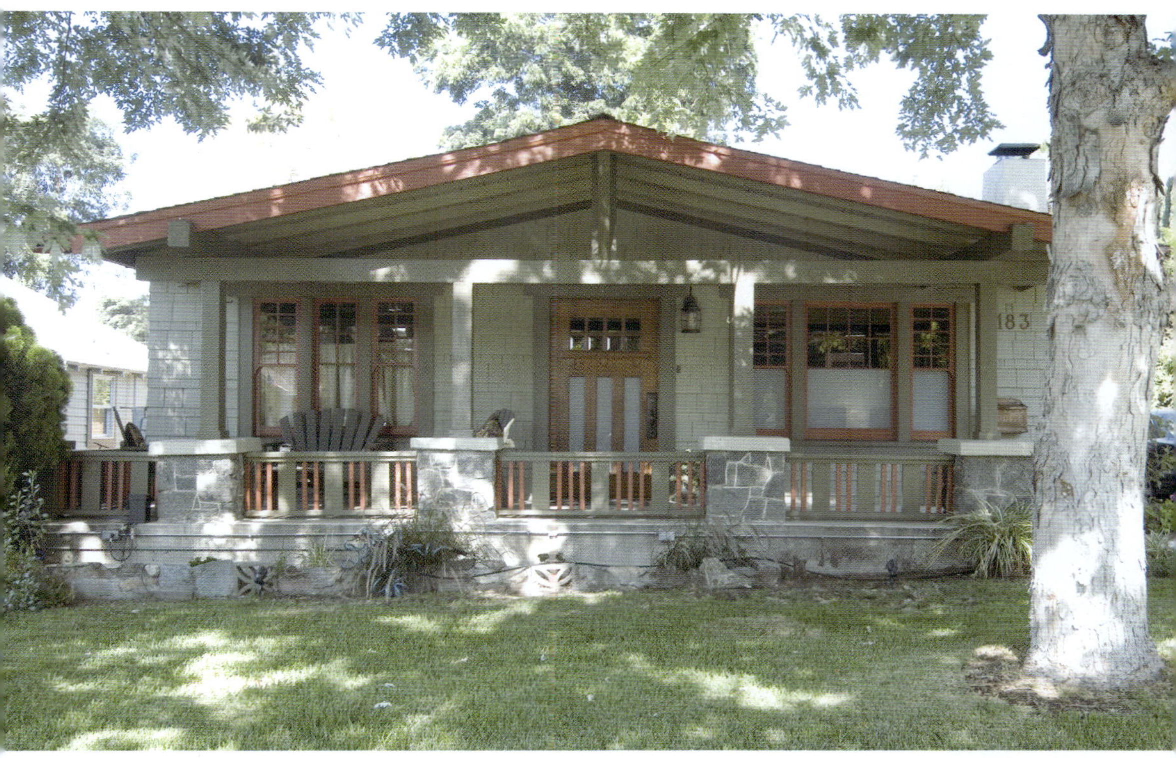


Pasadena, California 

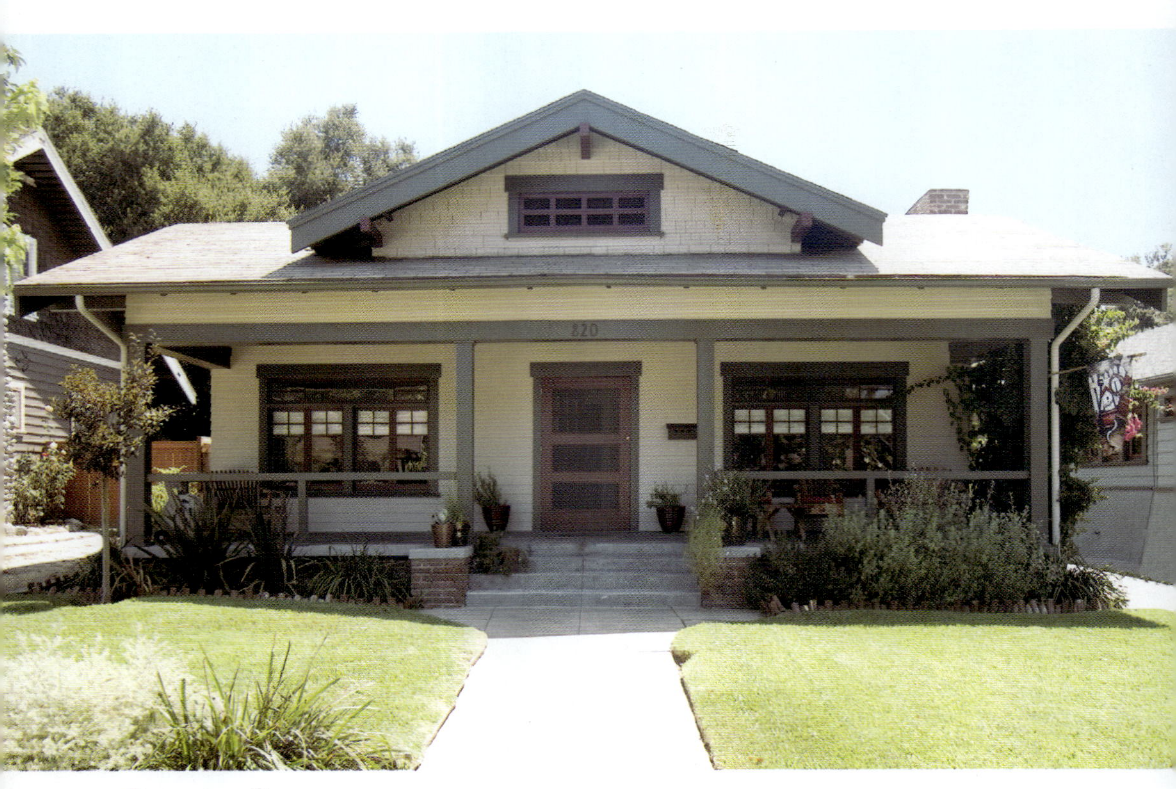


 Pasadena, California

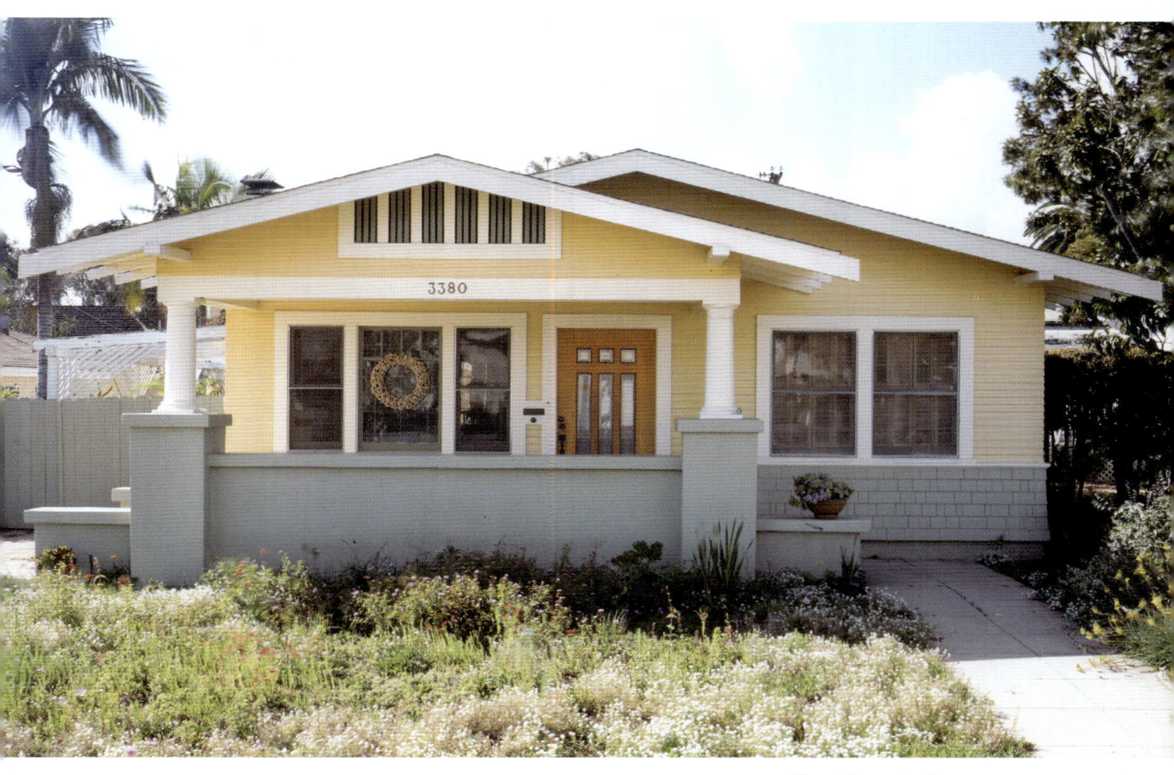


San Diego, California 

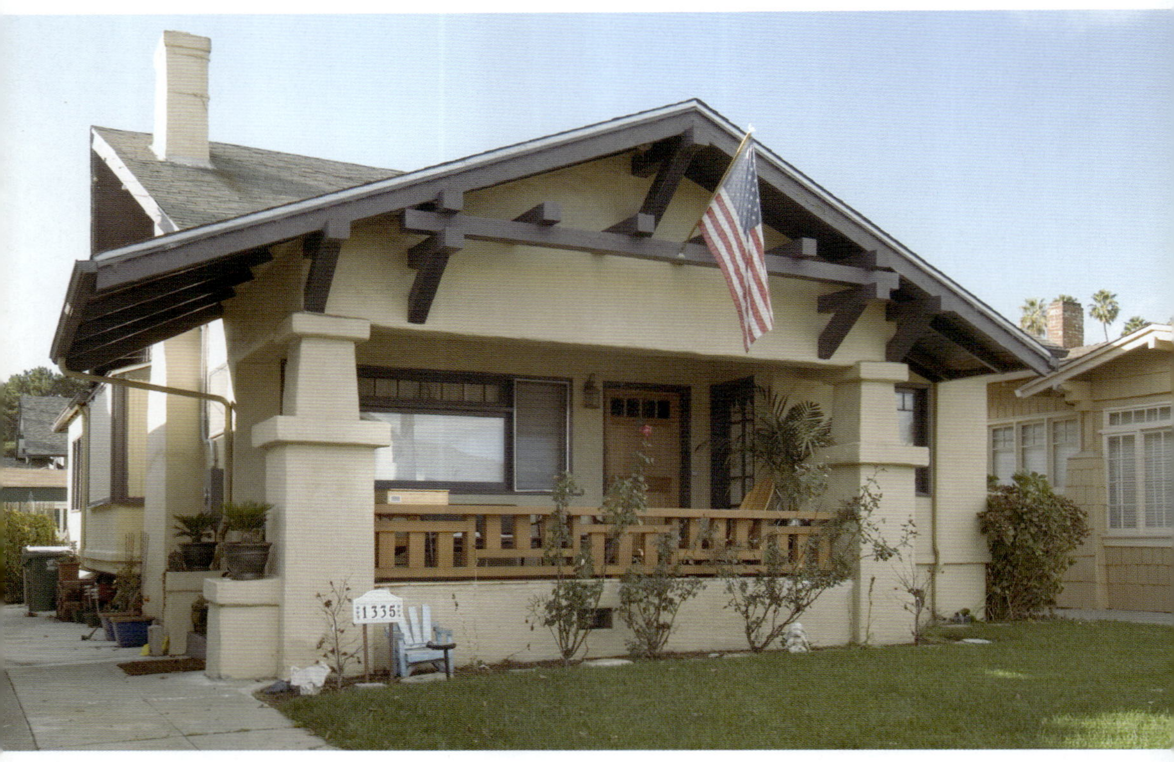


 Alameda, California

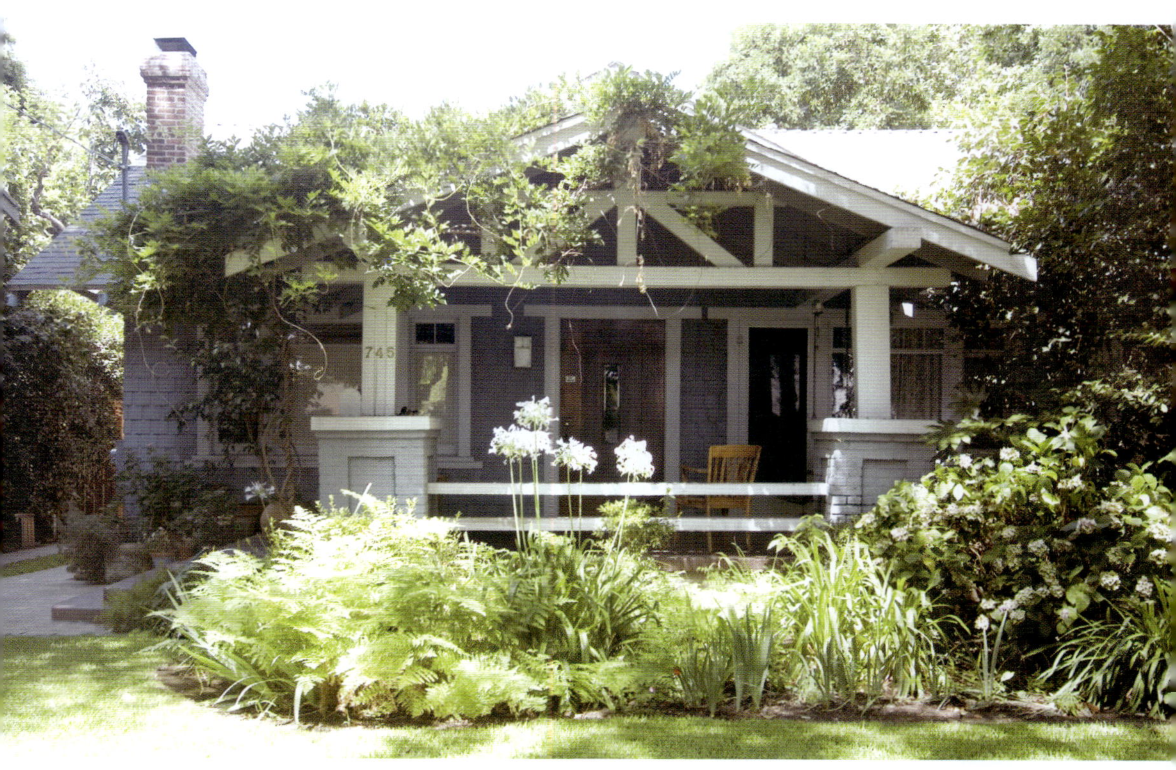


Pasadena, California

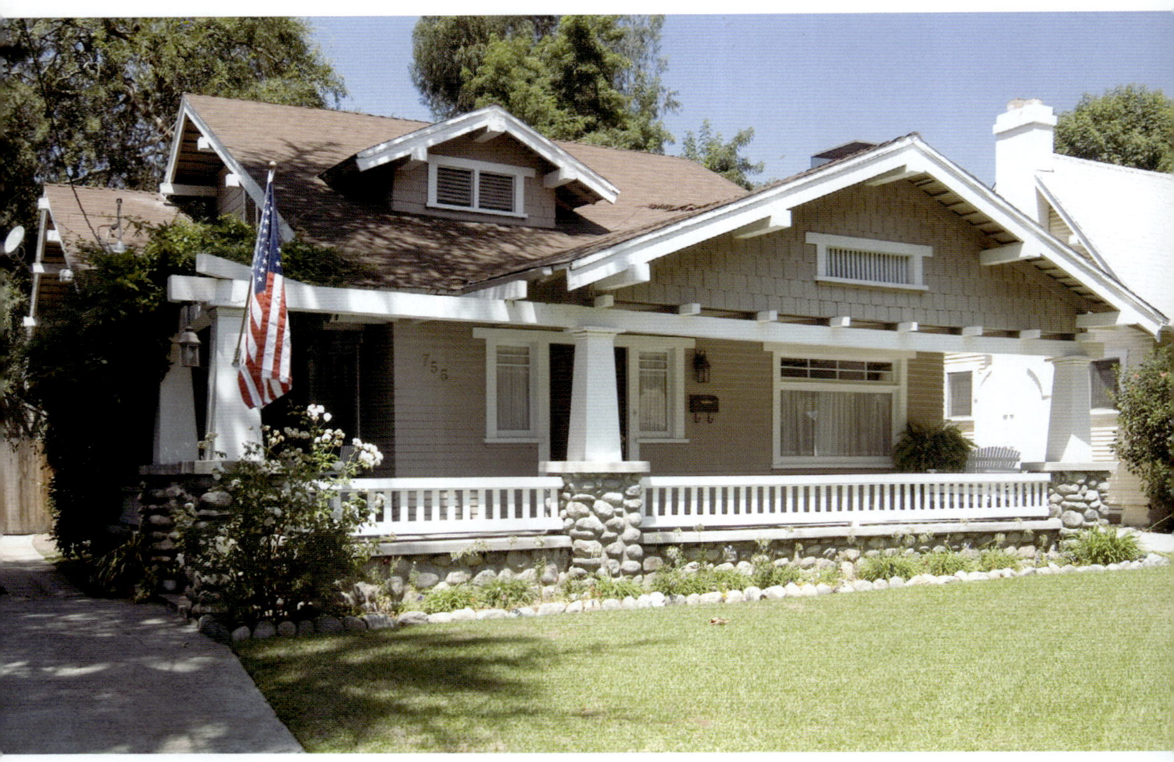

 PASADENA, CALIFORNIA

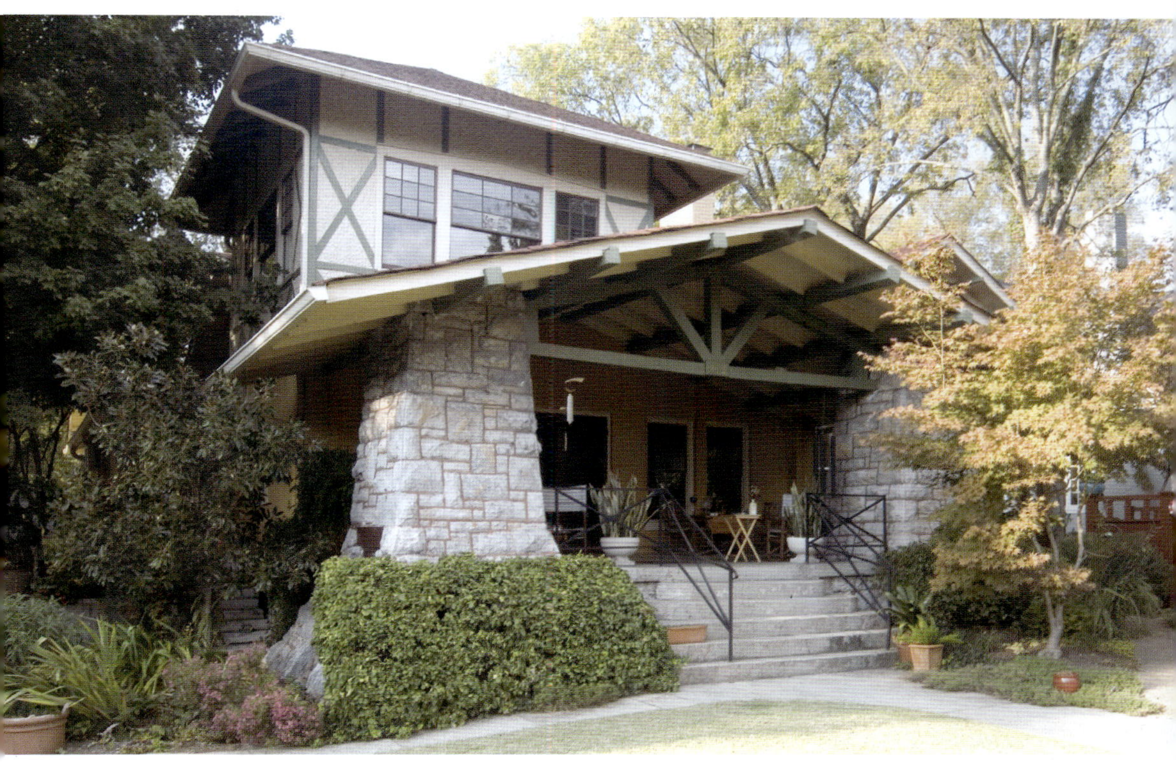

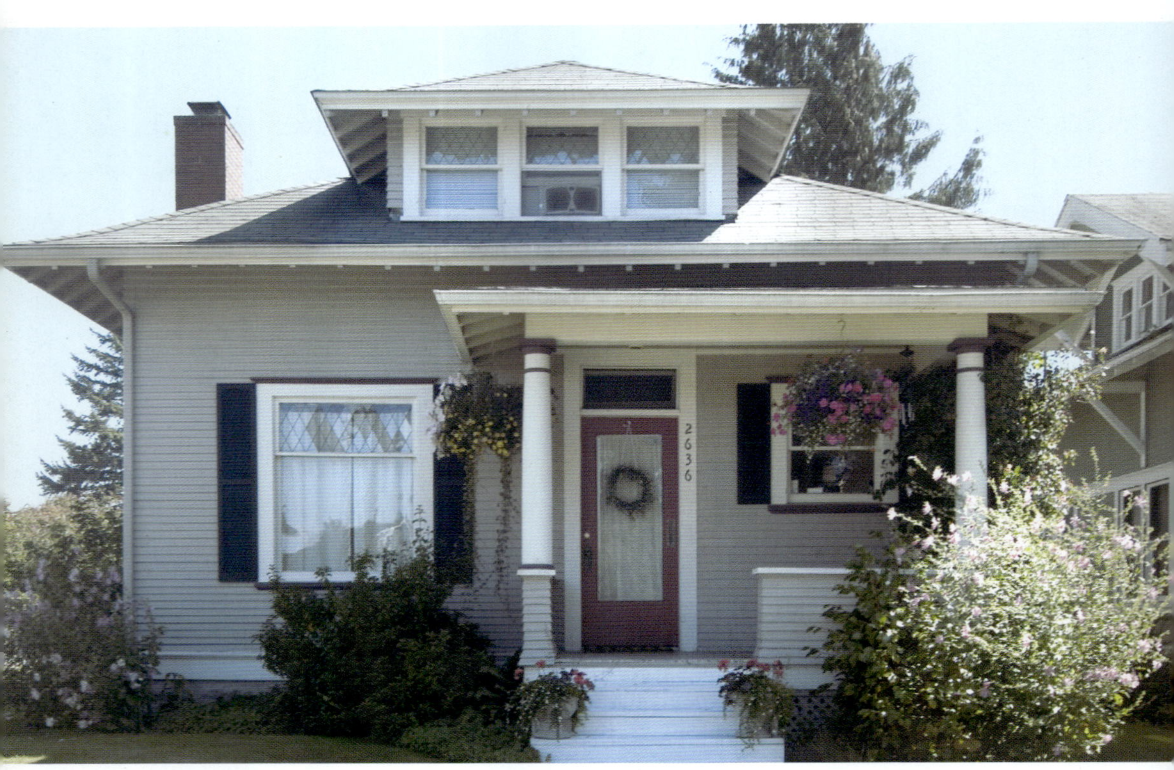


 Bellingham, Washington

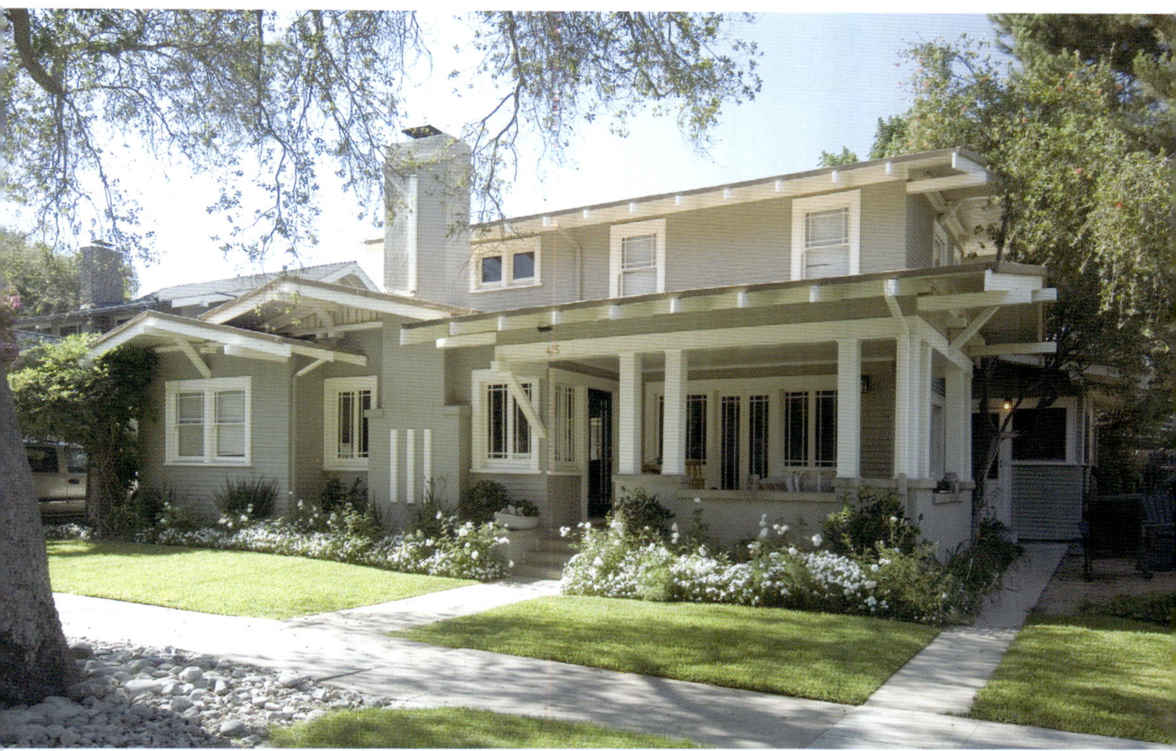

Pasadena, California

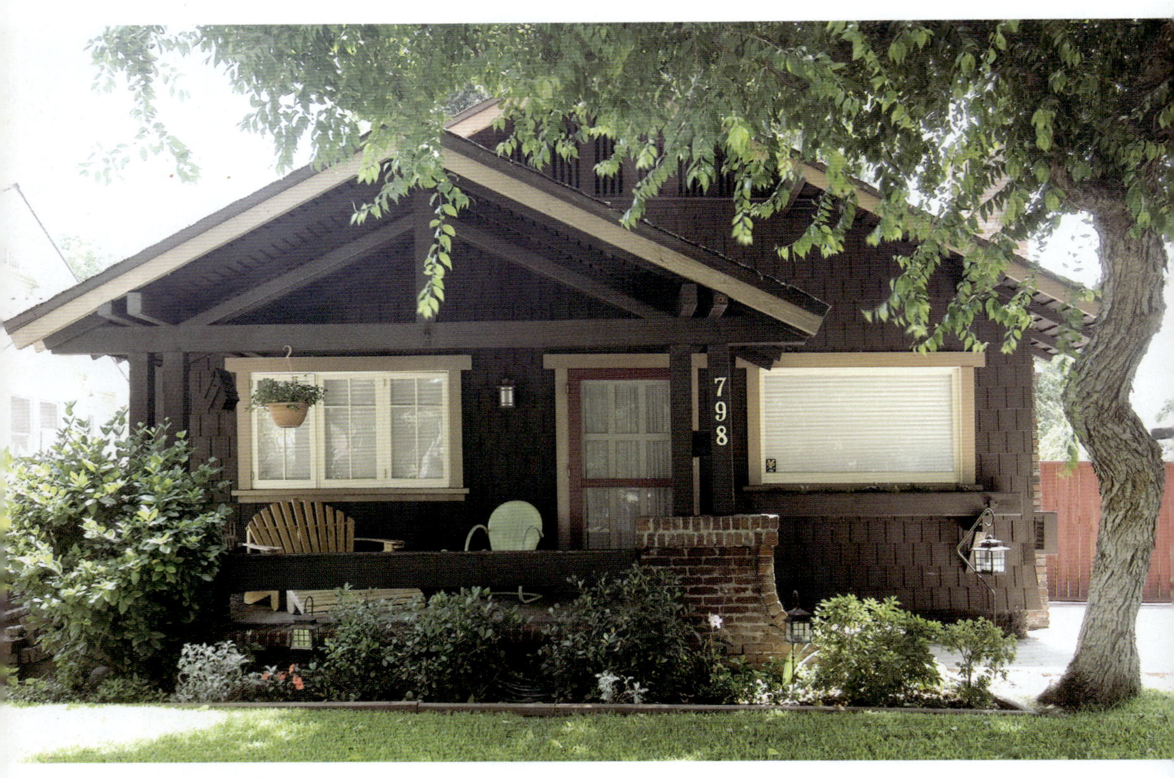




Pasadena, California

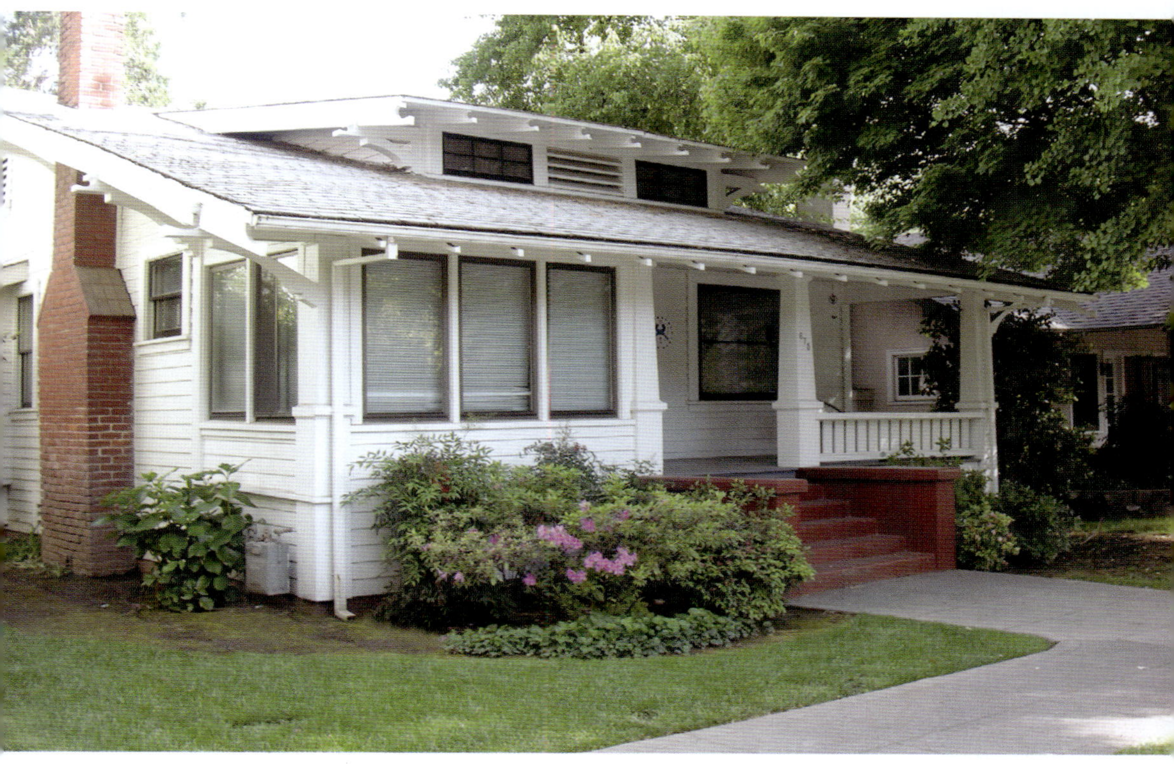

CHICO, CALIFORNIA

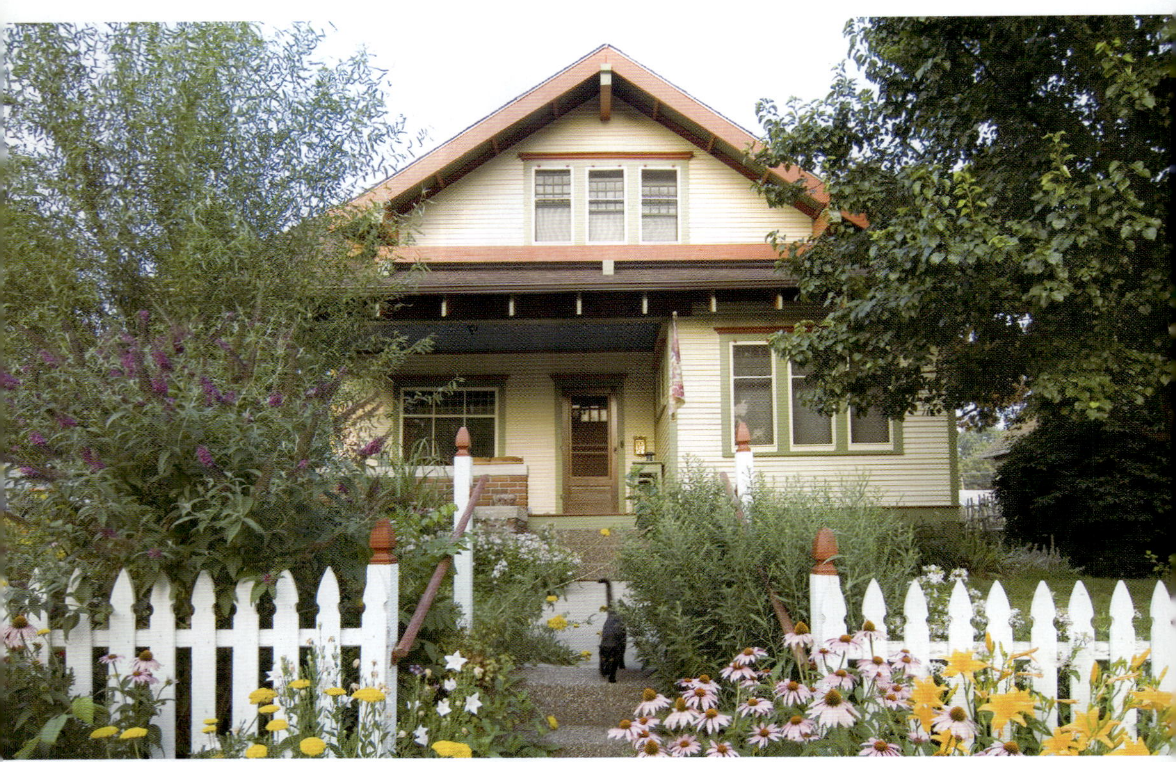

 Lincoln, Nebraska

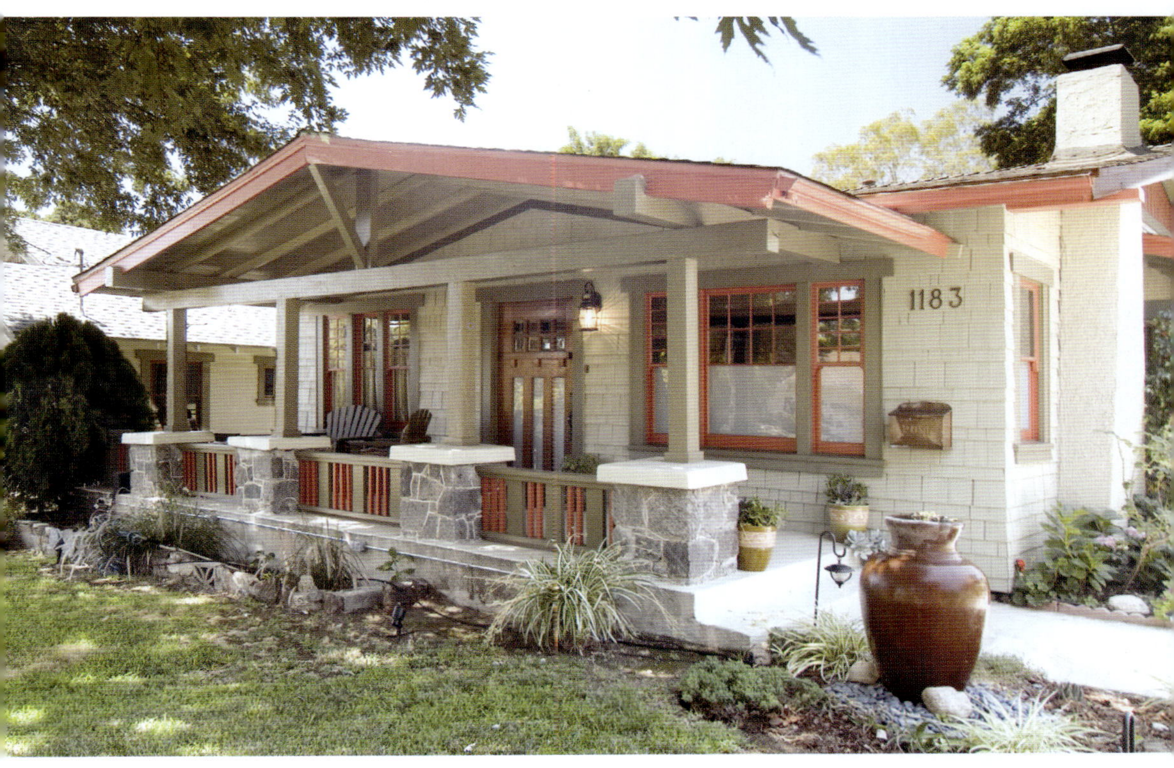


Pasadena, California

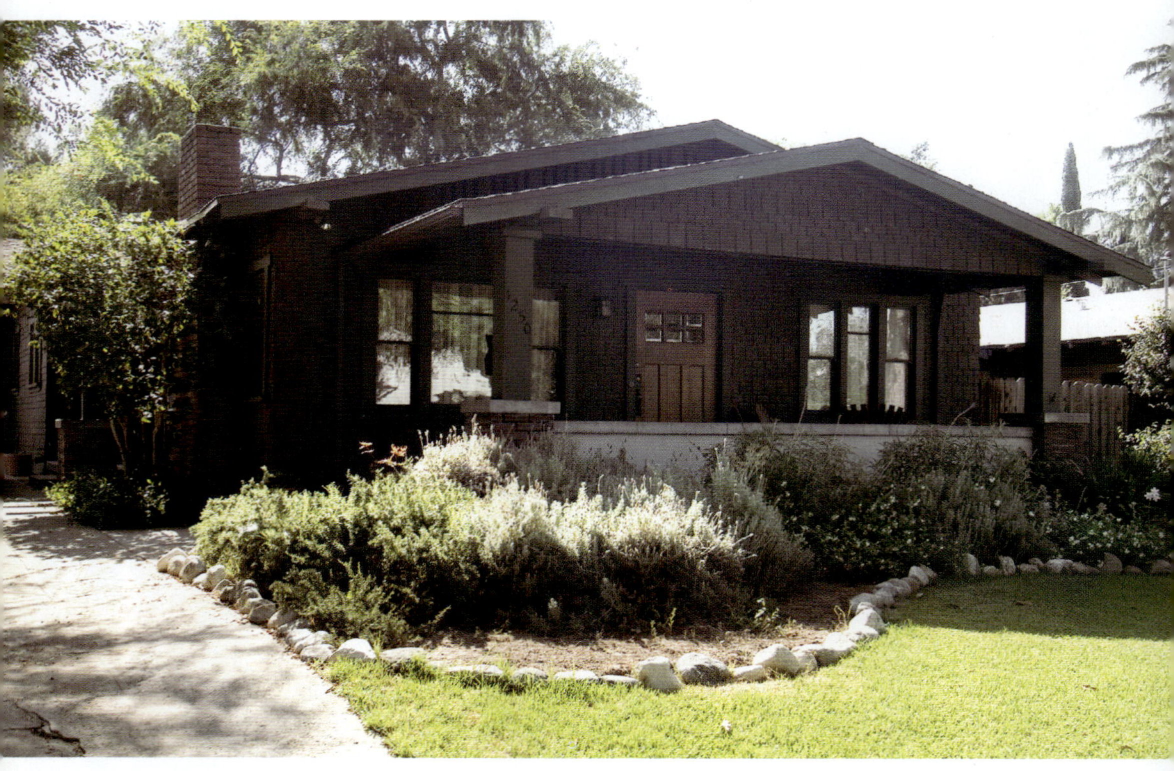

 Pasadena, California

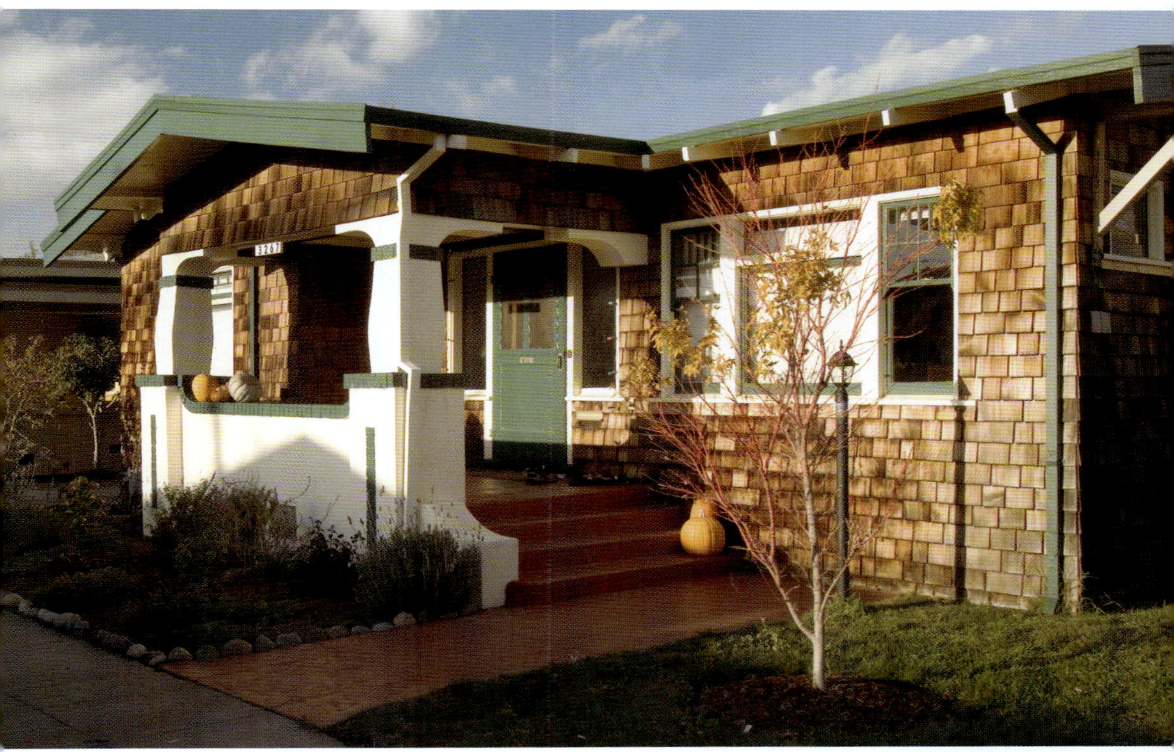


Alameda, California

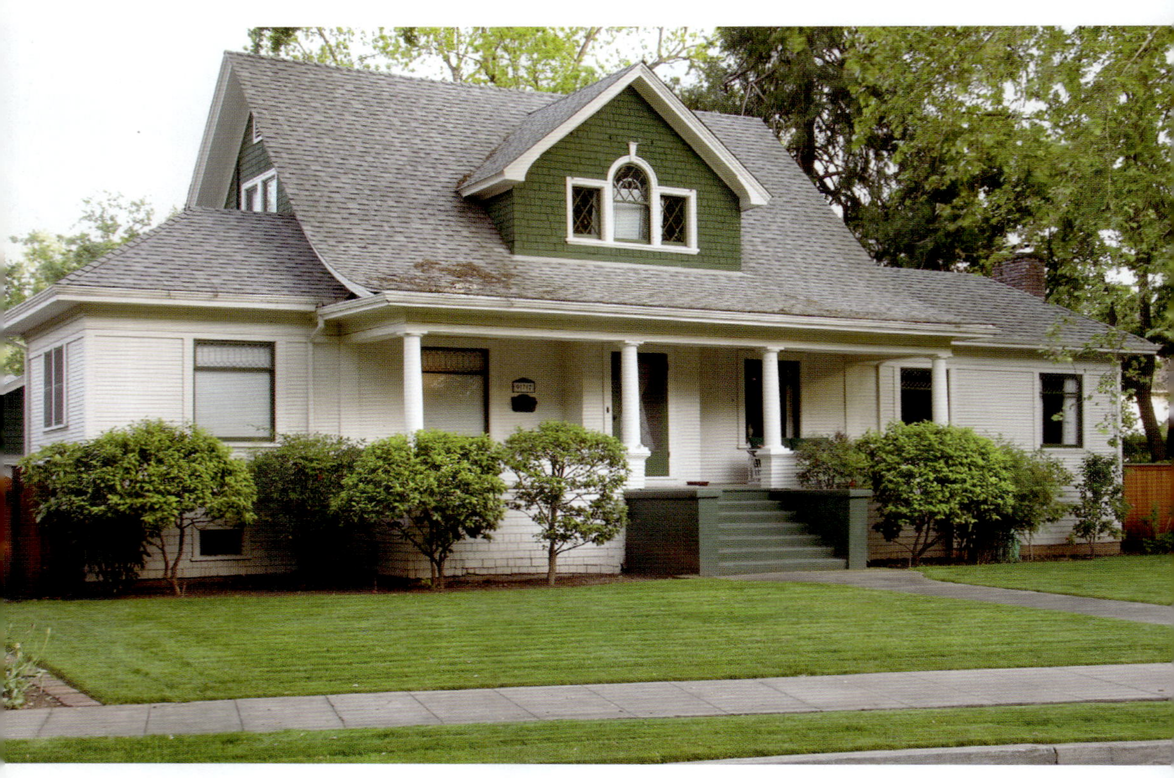

 Chico, California

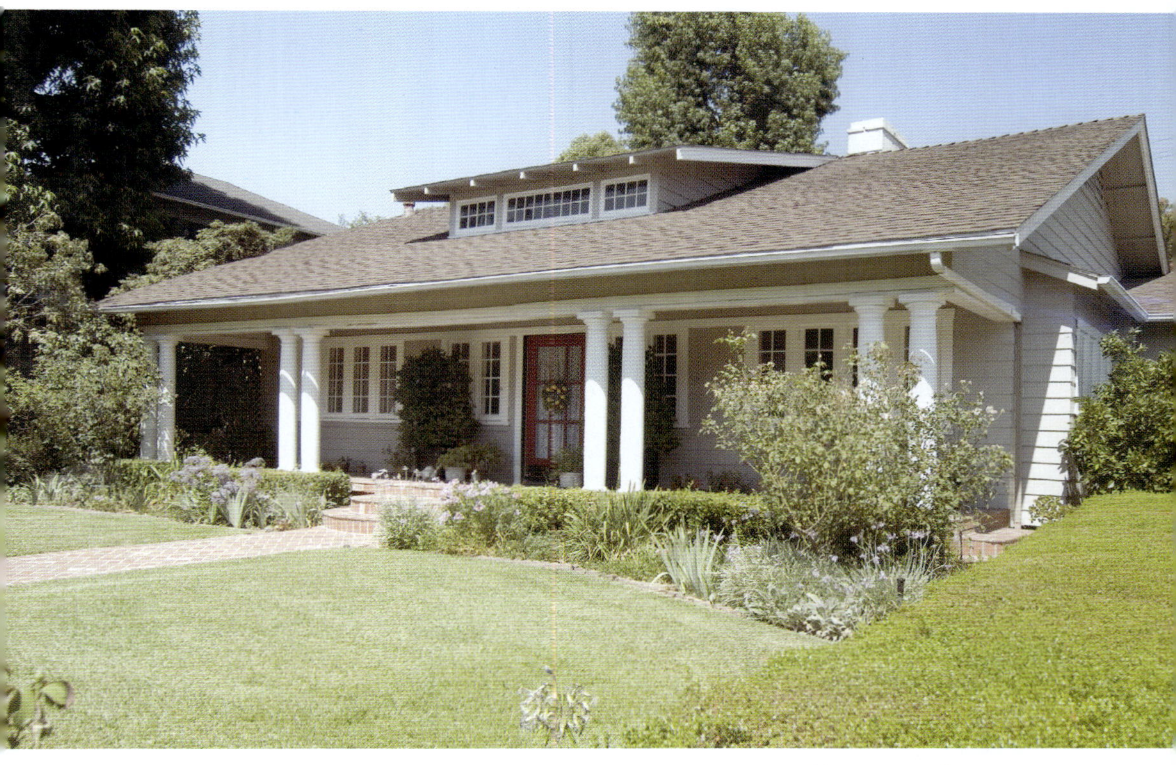

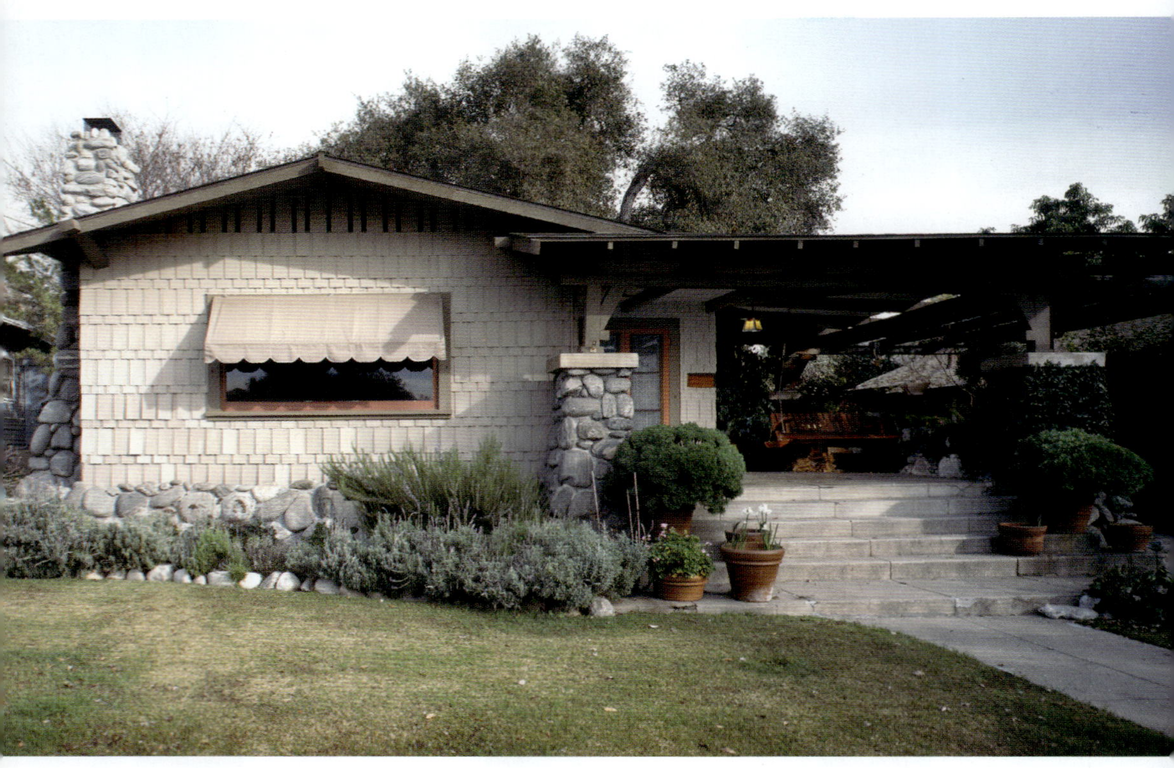

 Monrovia, California

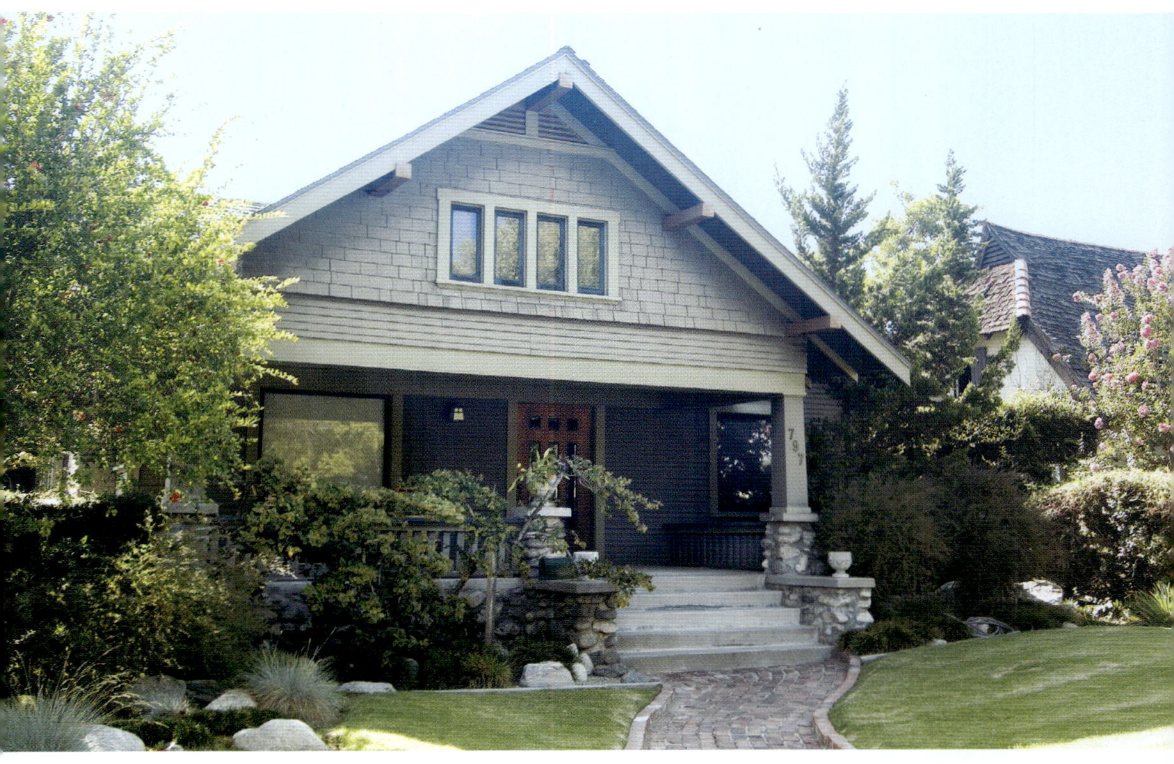


Pasadena, California

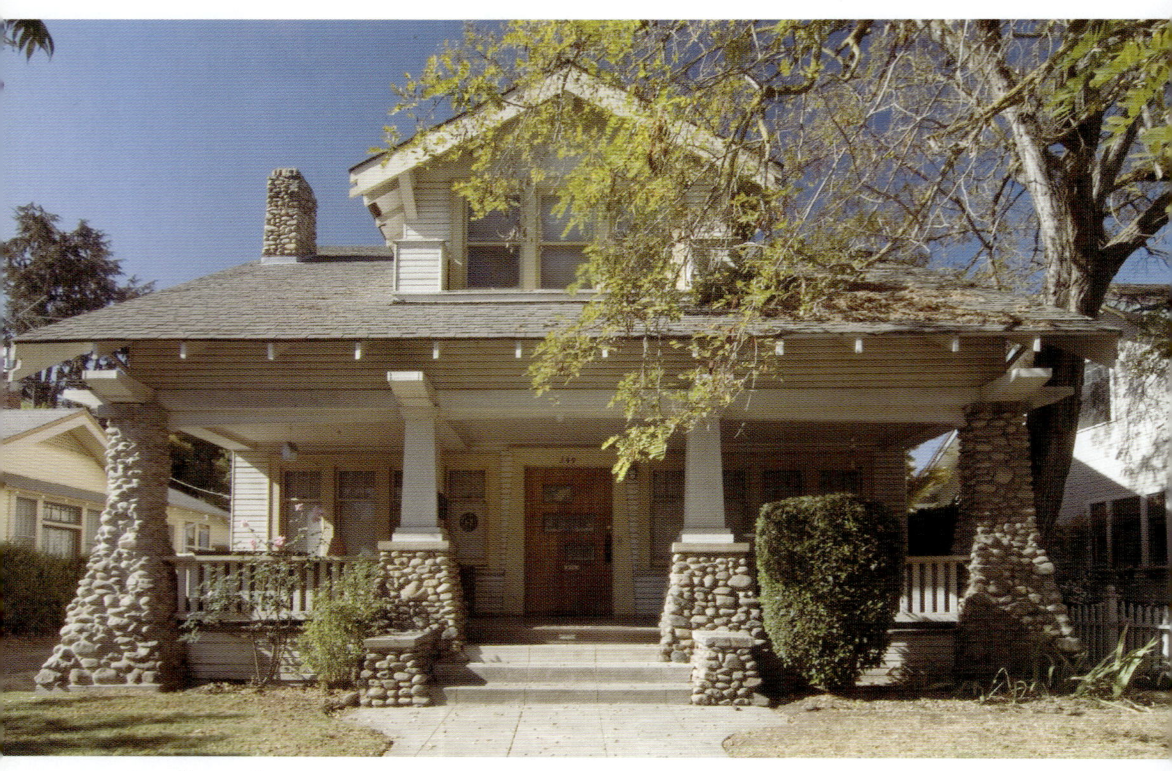

 San Jose, California

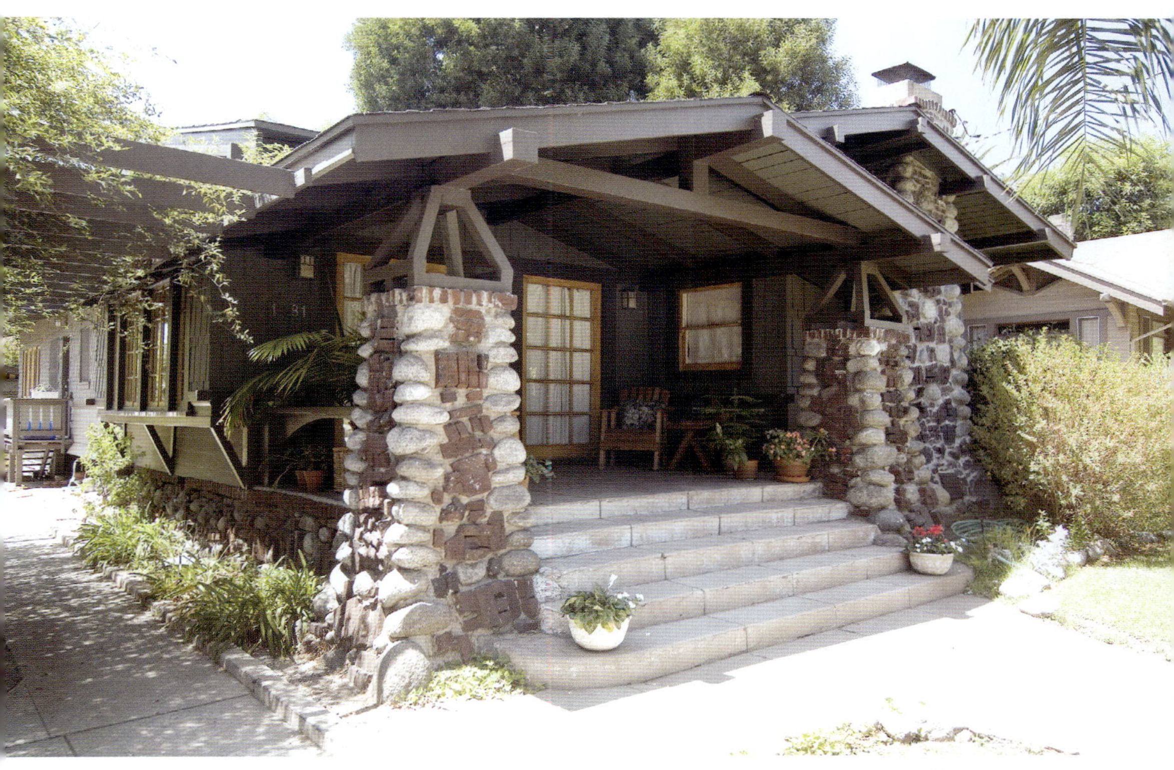

Pasadena, California 

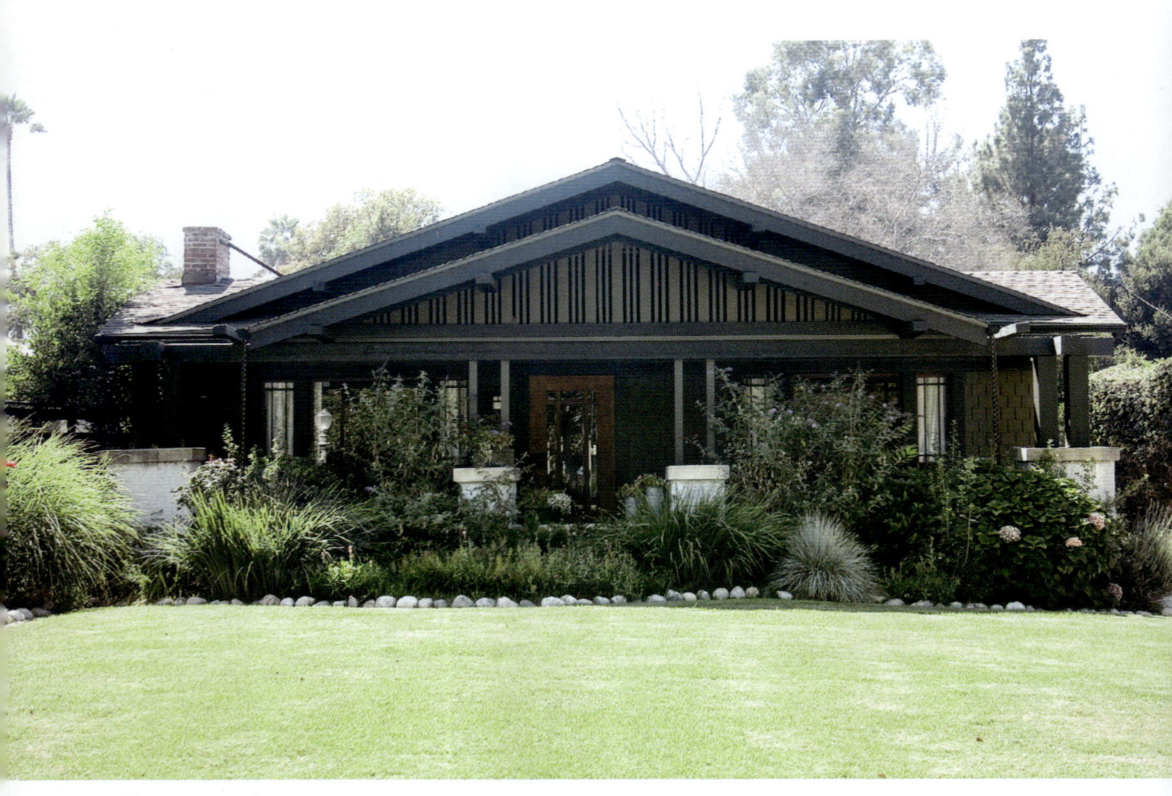

 Pasadena, California

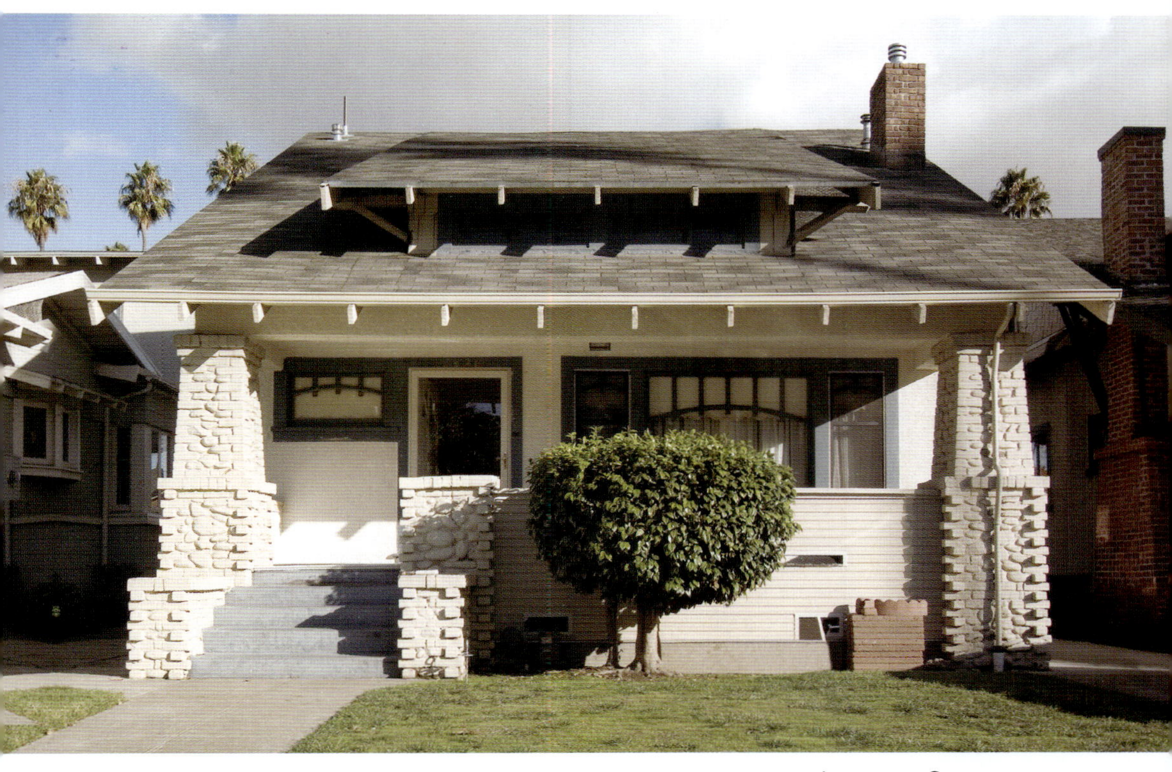

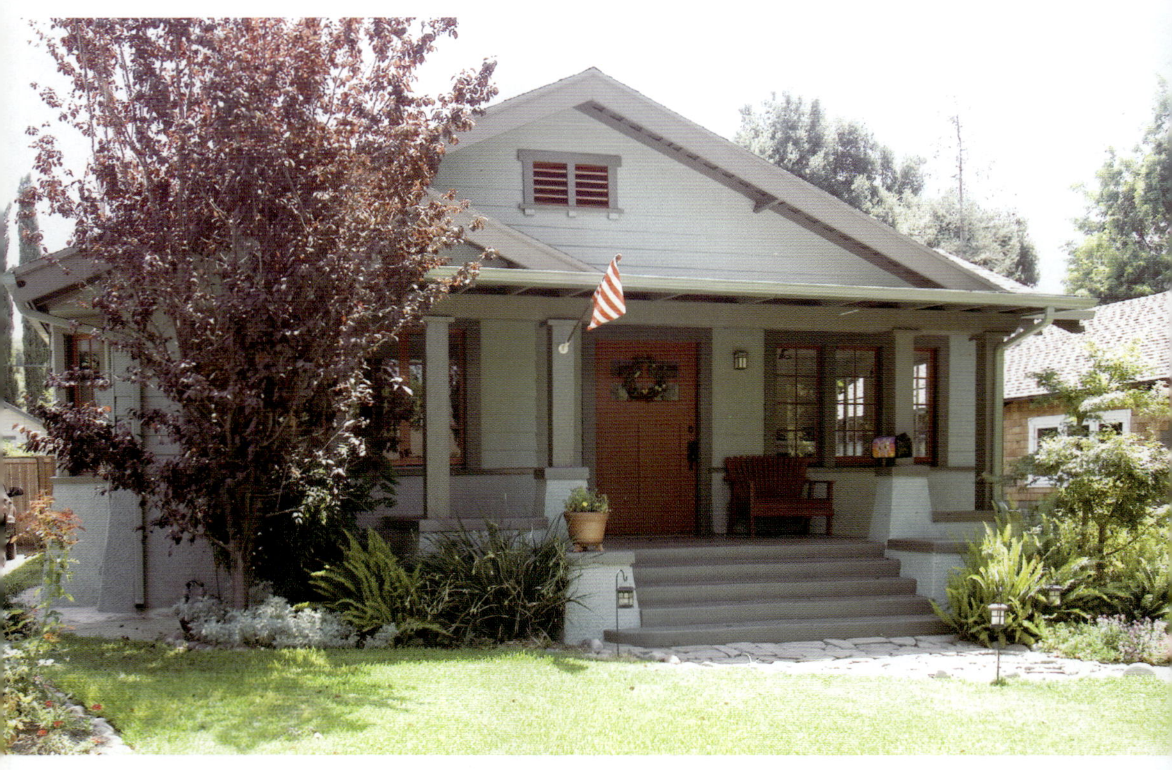

 Pasadena, California

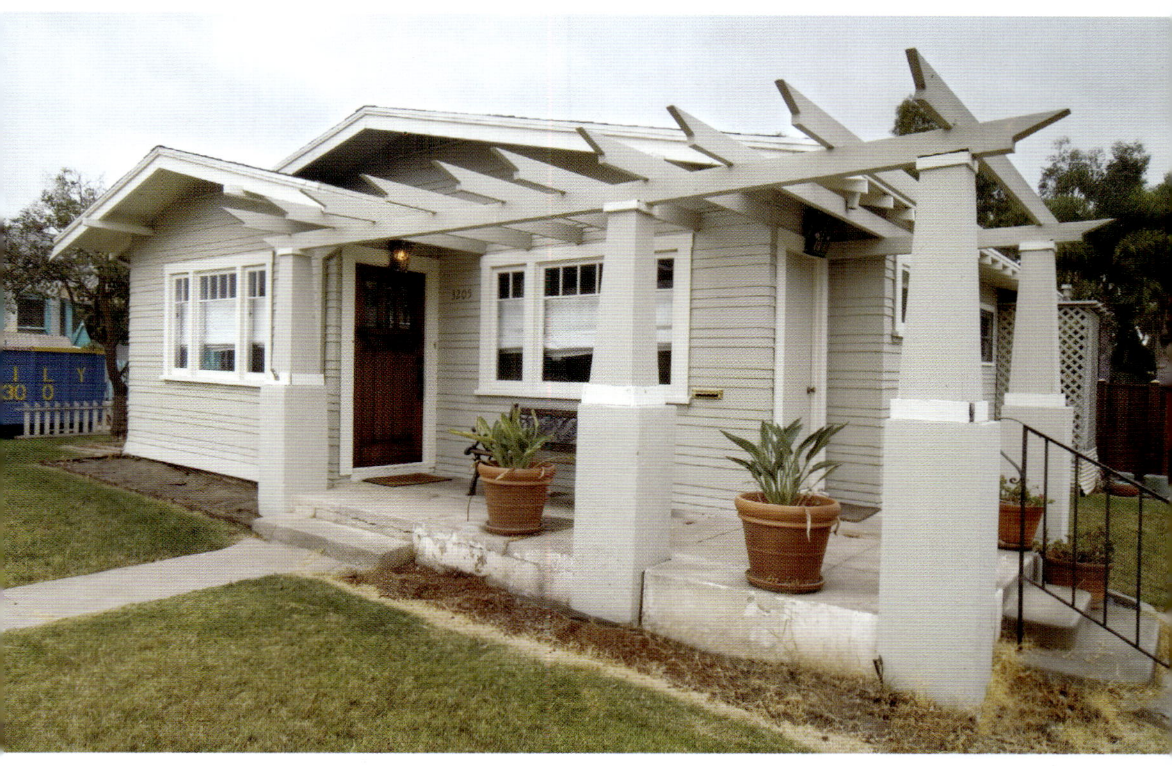

San Diego, California 

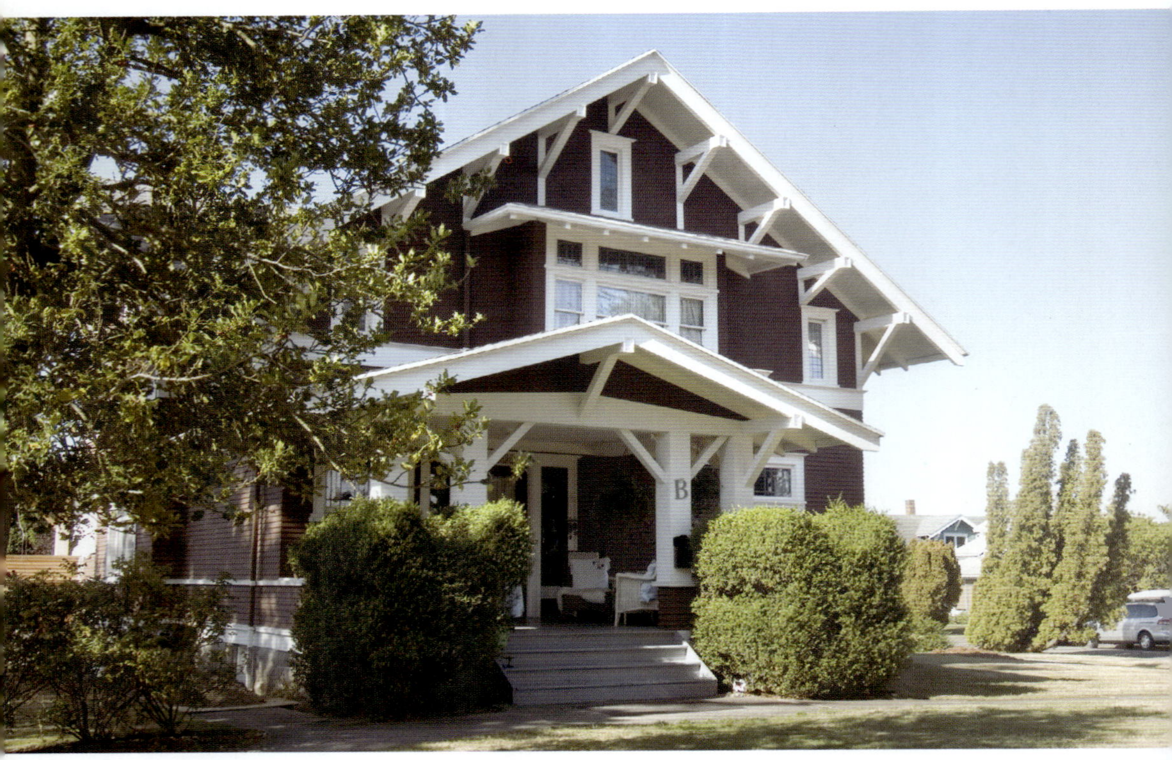


 Bellingham, Washington

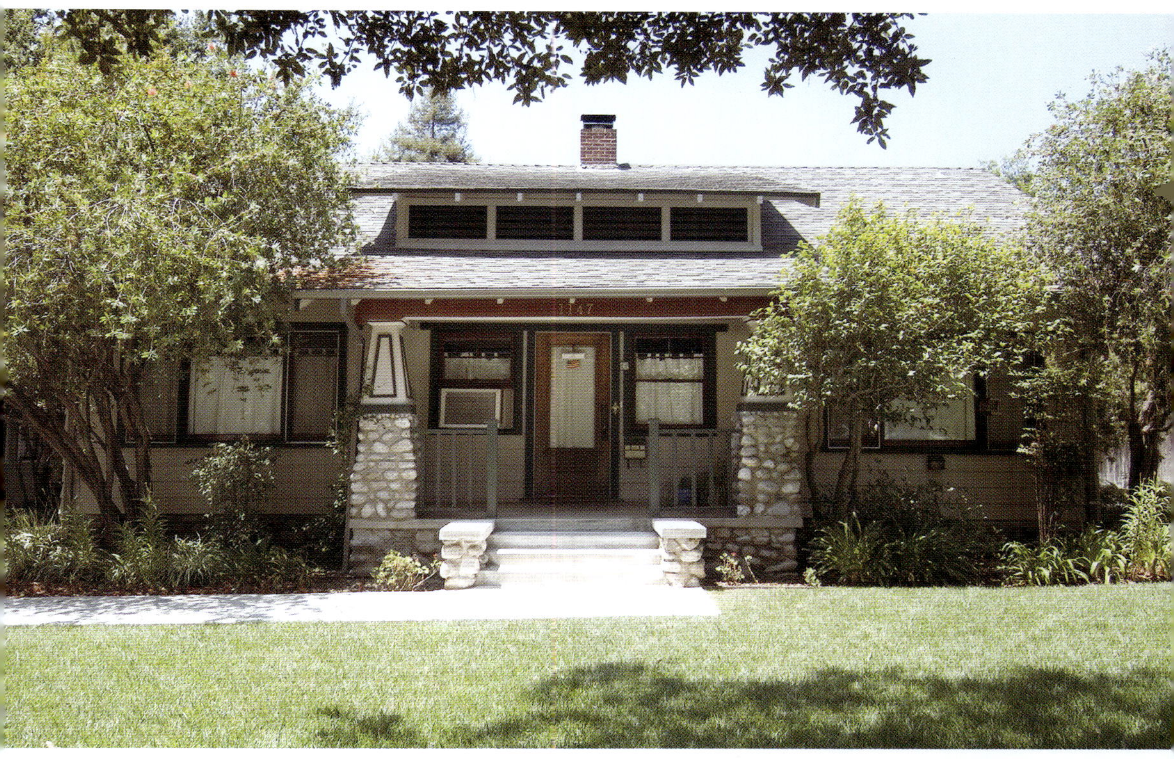

Pasadena, California

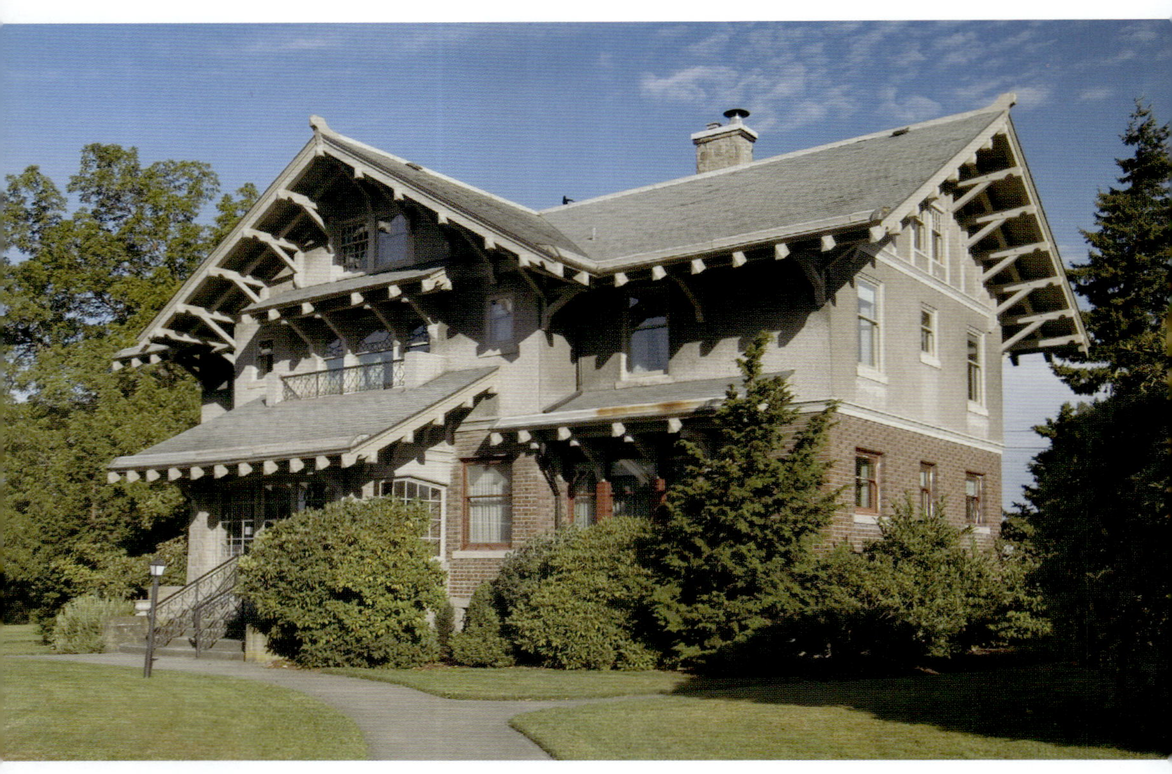



Bellingham, Washington

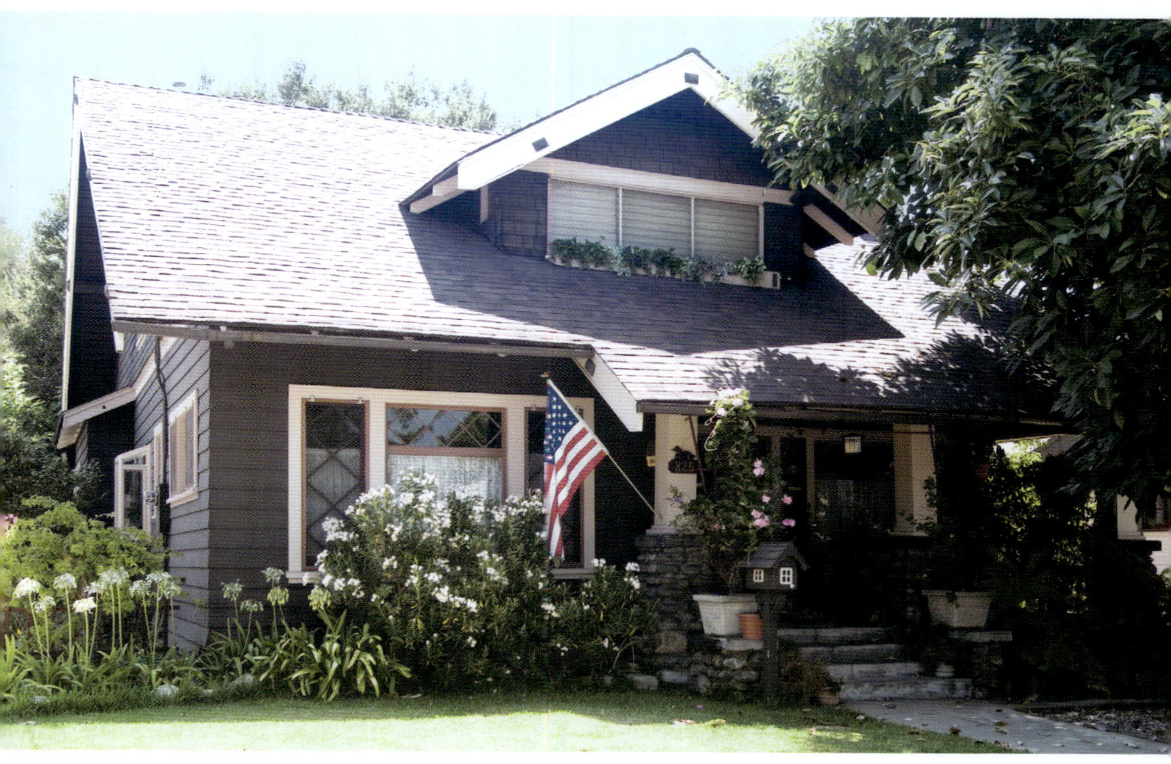

Pasadena, California

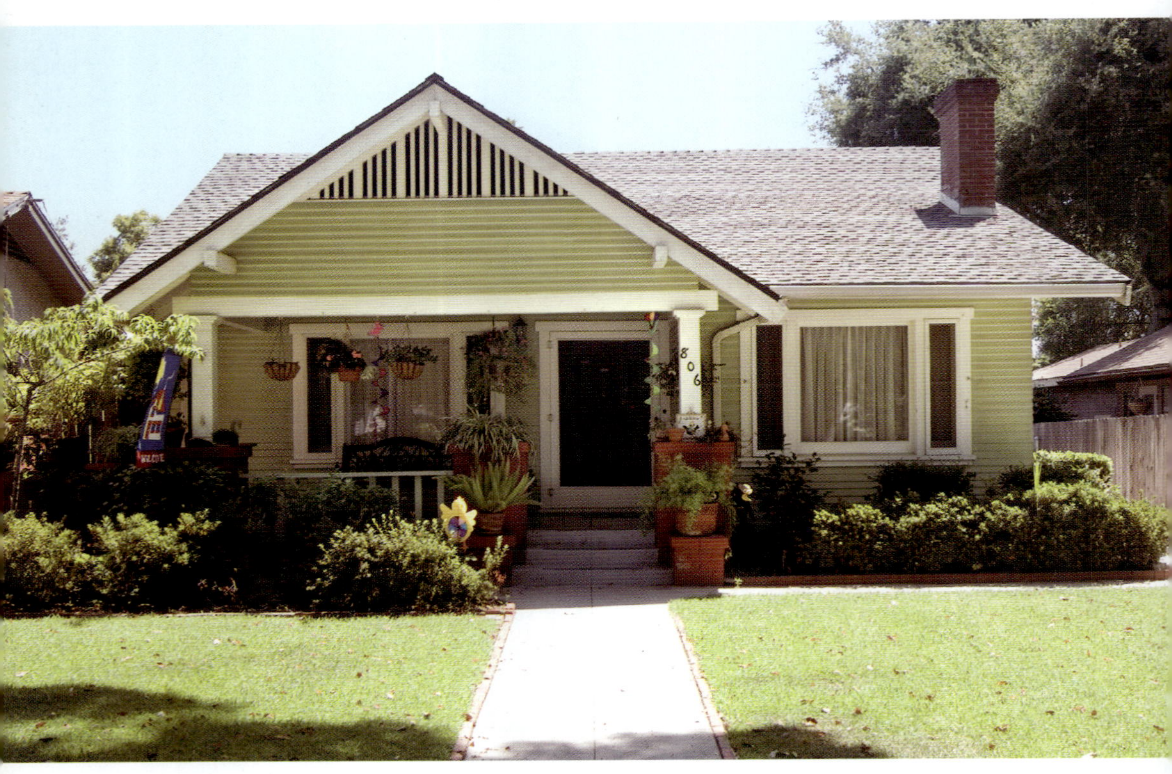


 Pasadena, California

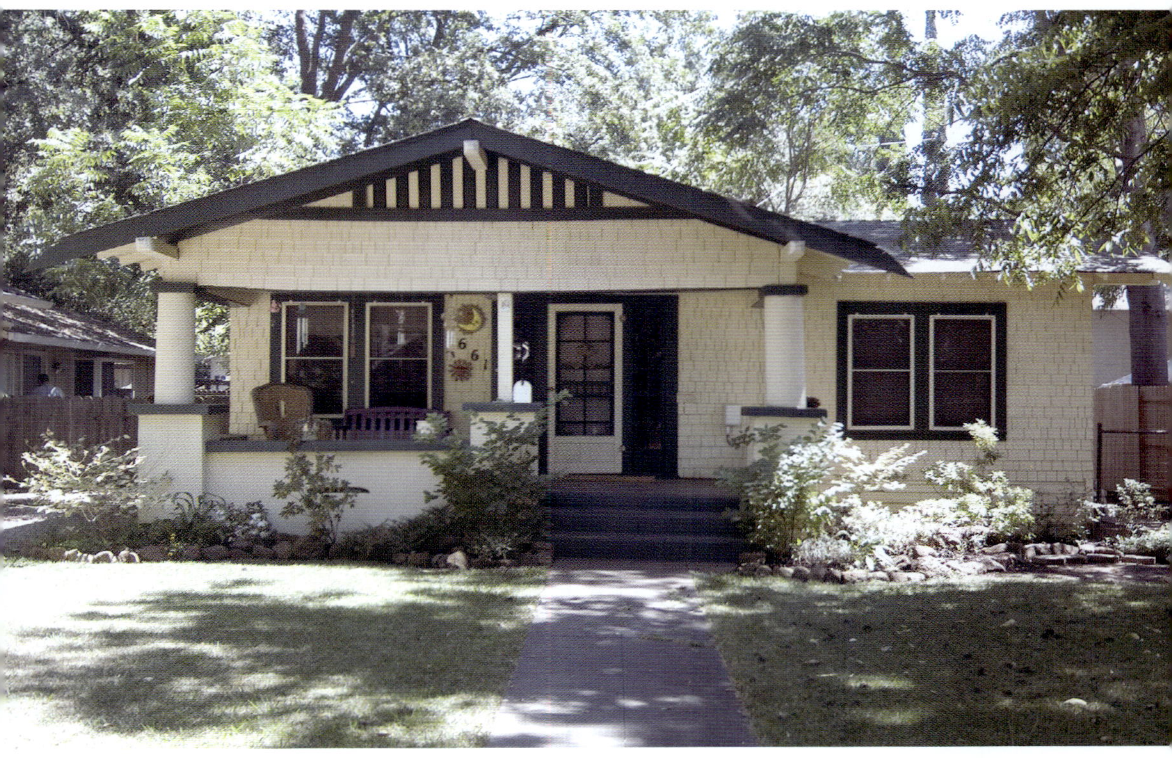

Chico, California

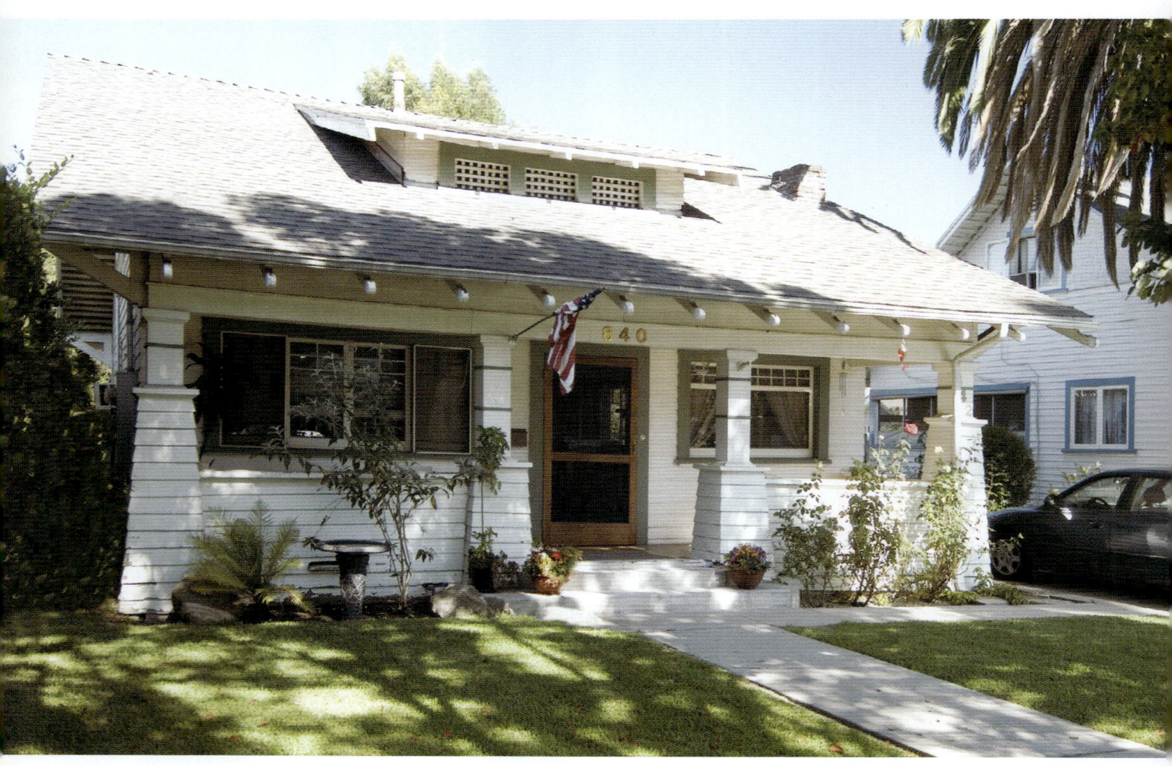


 Pasadena, California

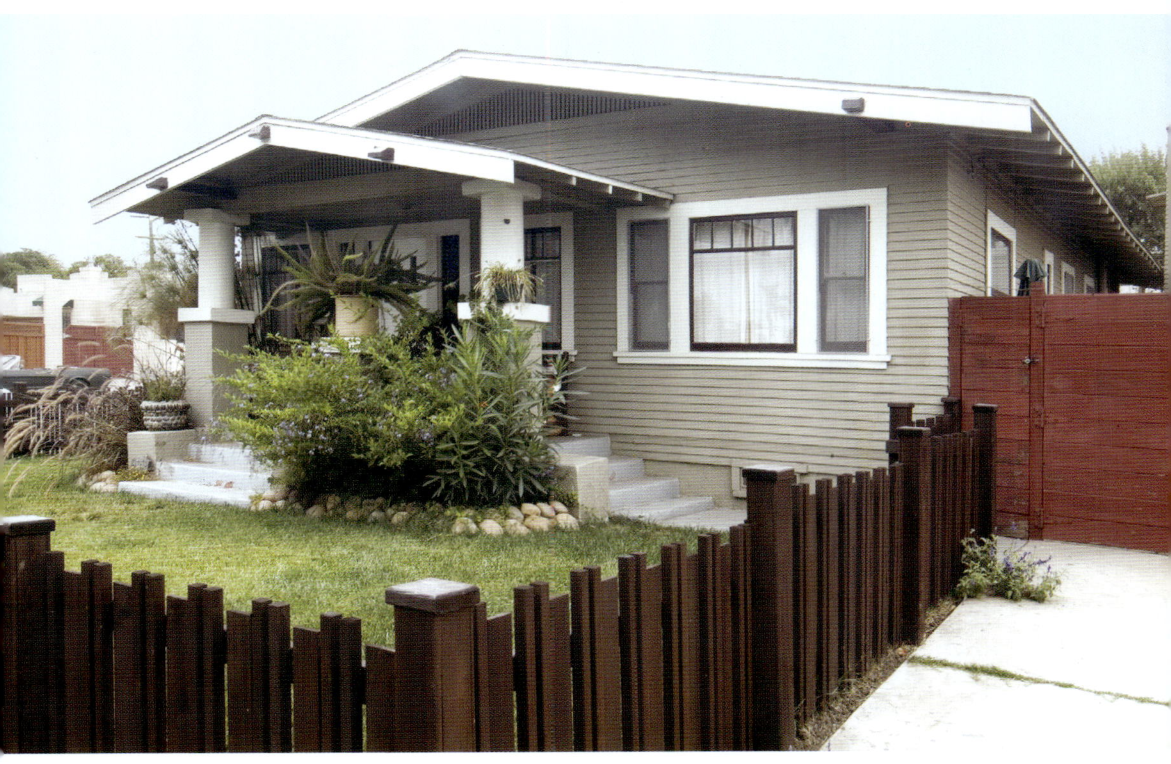

San Diego, California

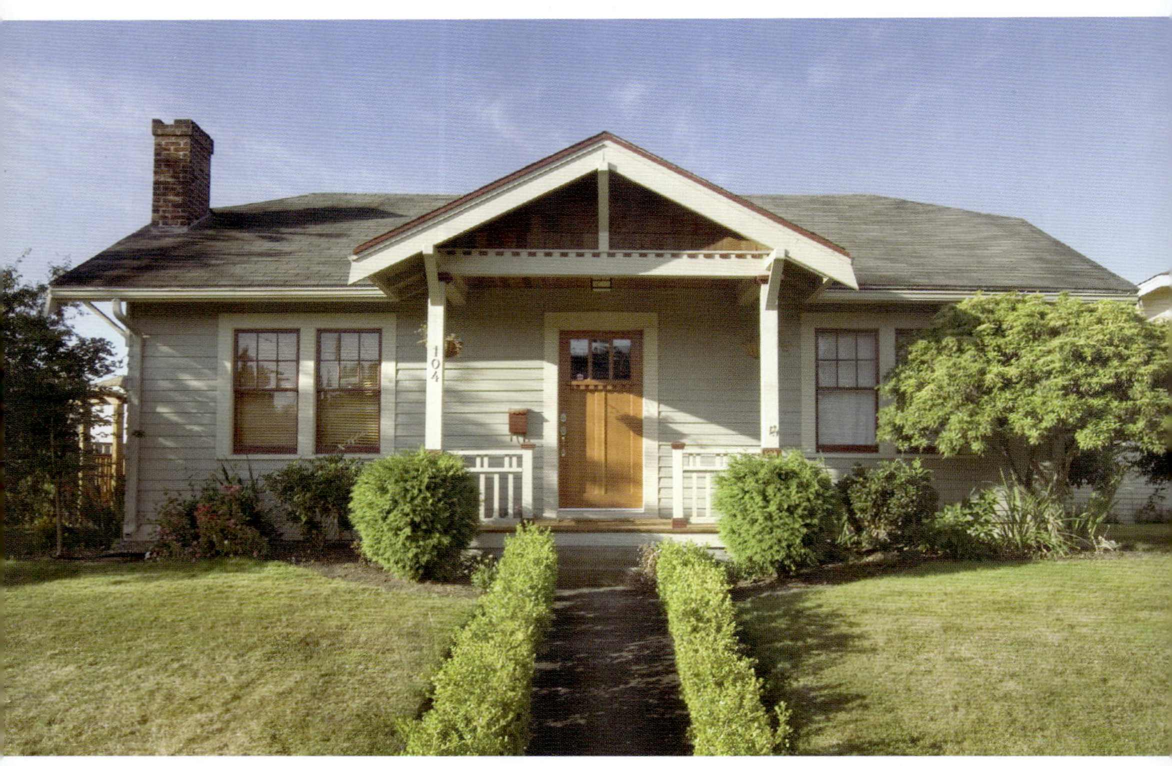


 Bellingham, Washington

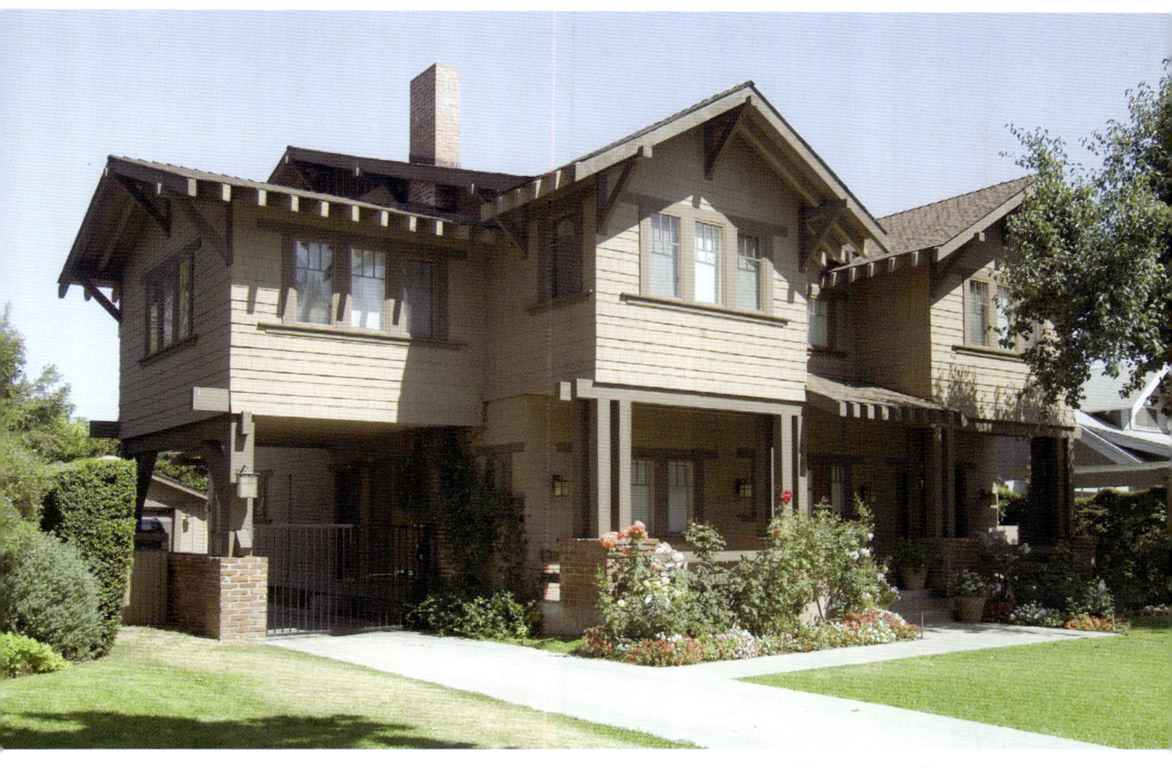

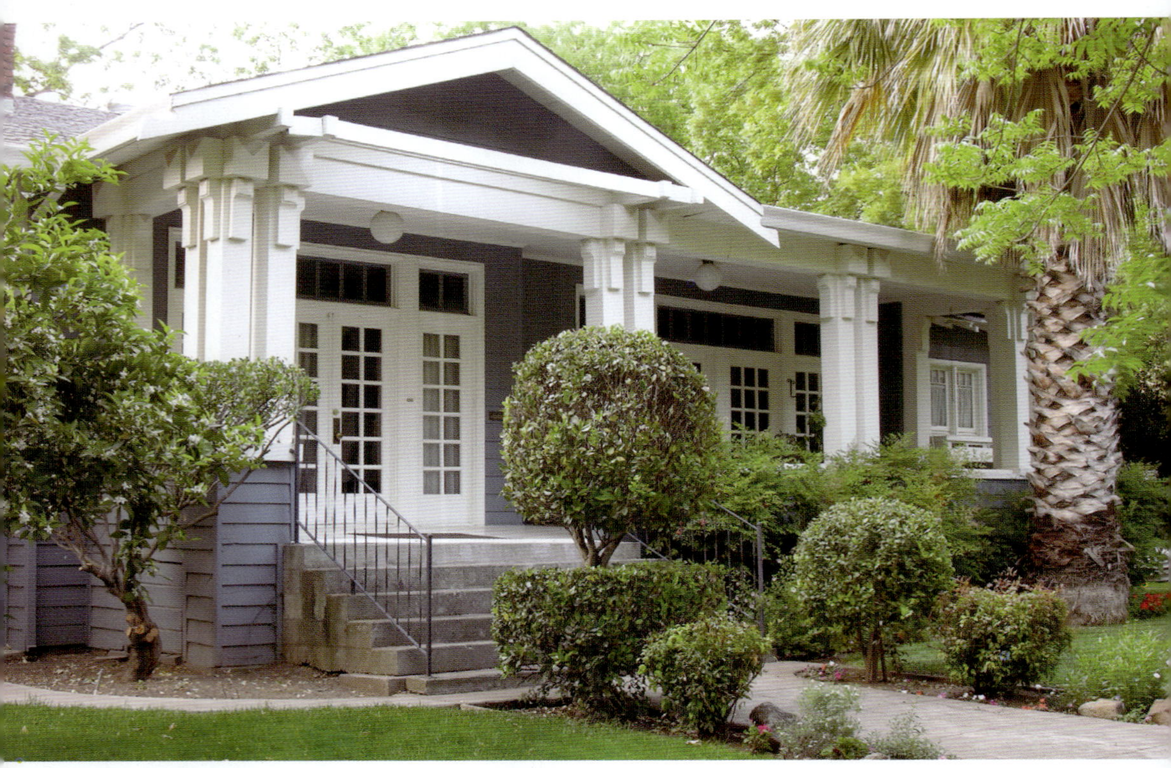

 Chico, California

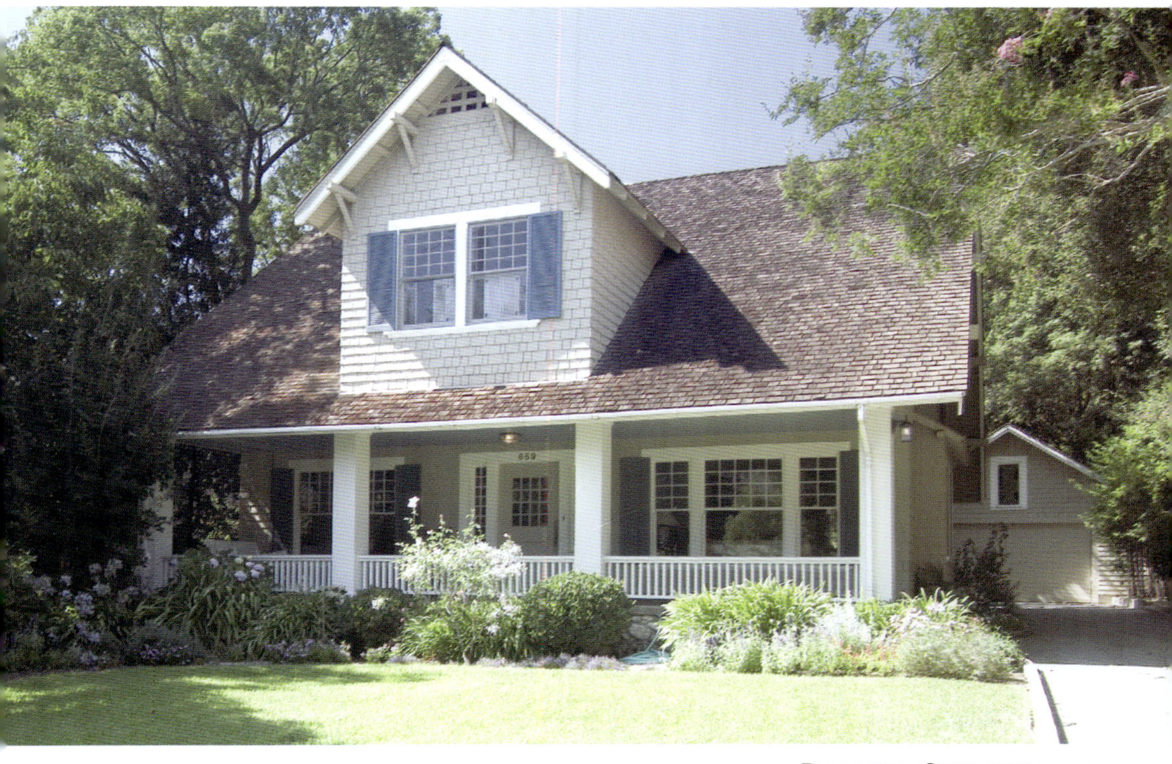

Pasadena, California

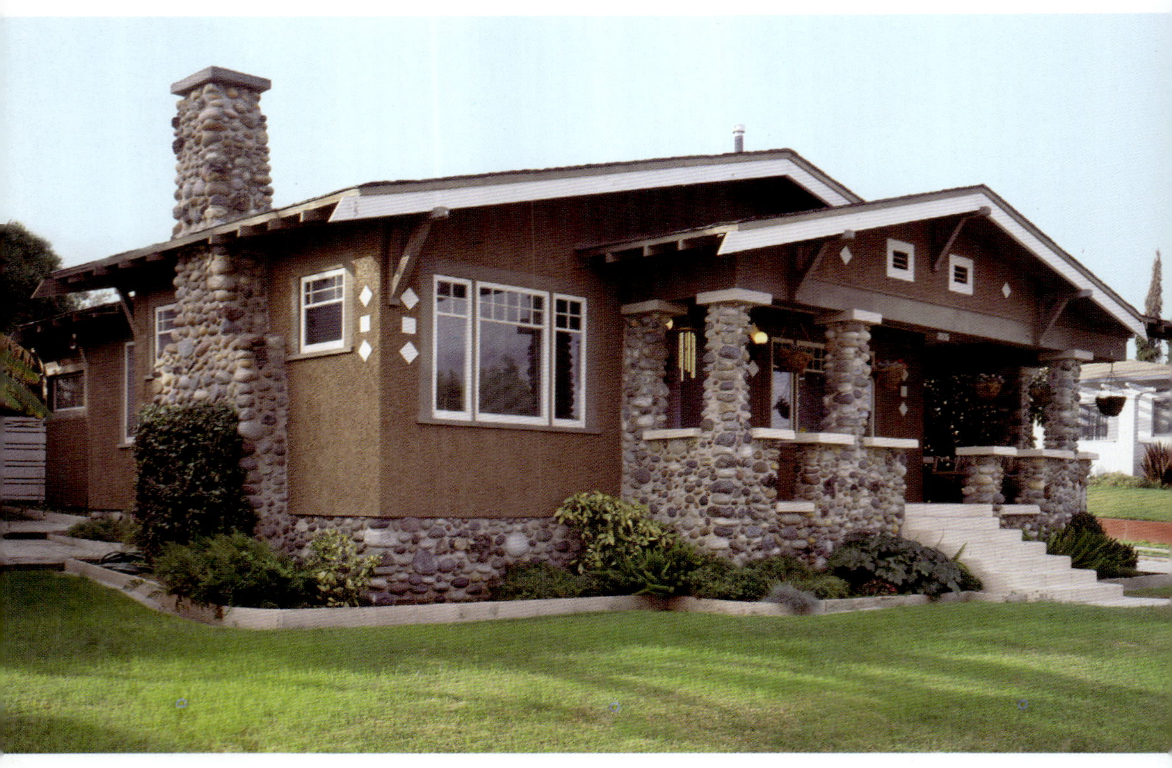

 San Diego, California

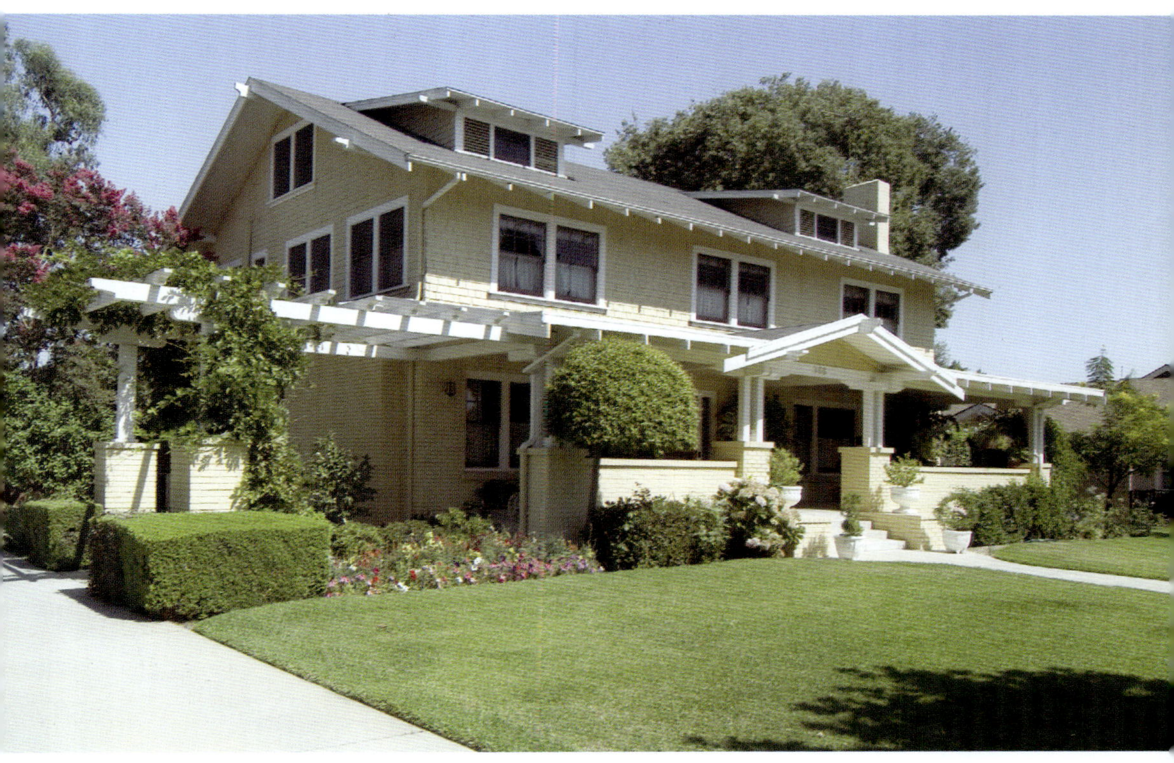

Pasadena, California

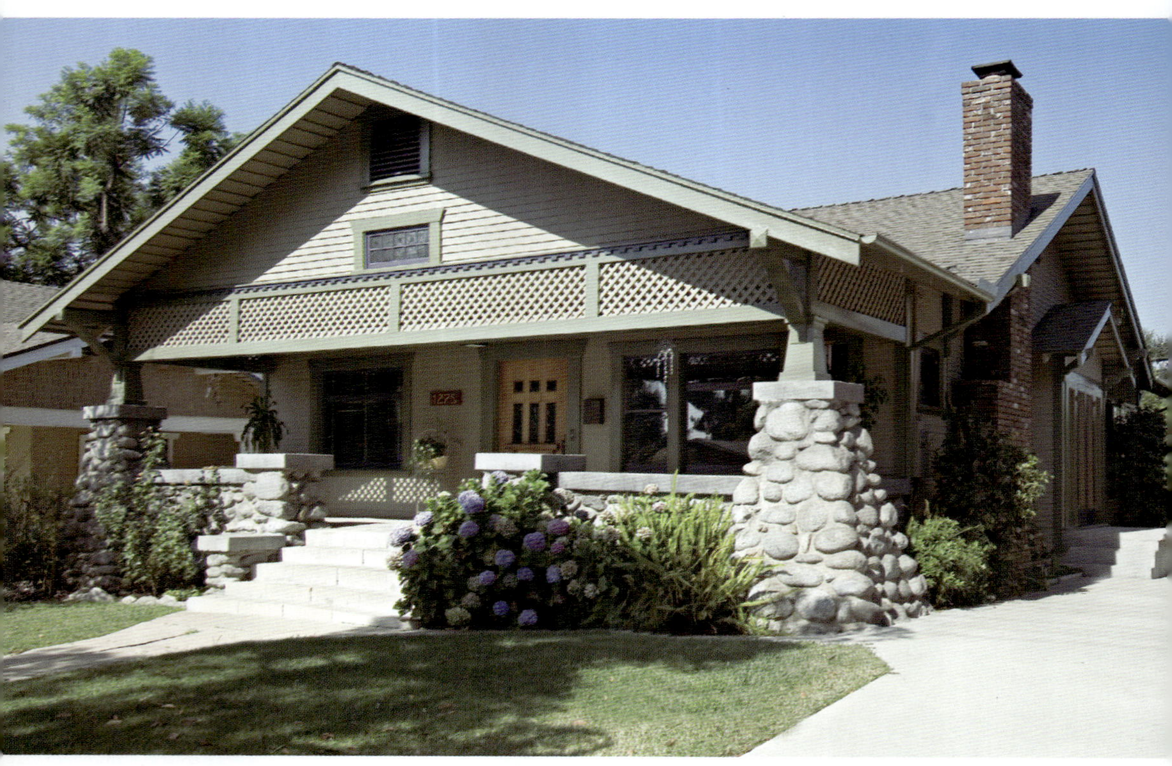

 PASADENA, CALIFORNIA

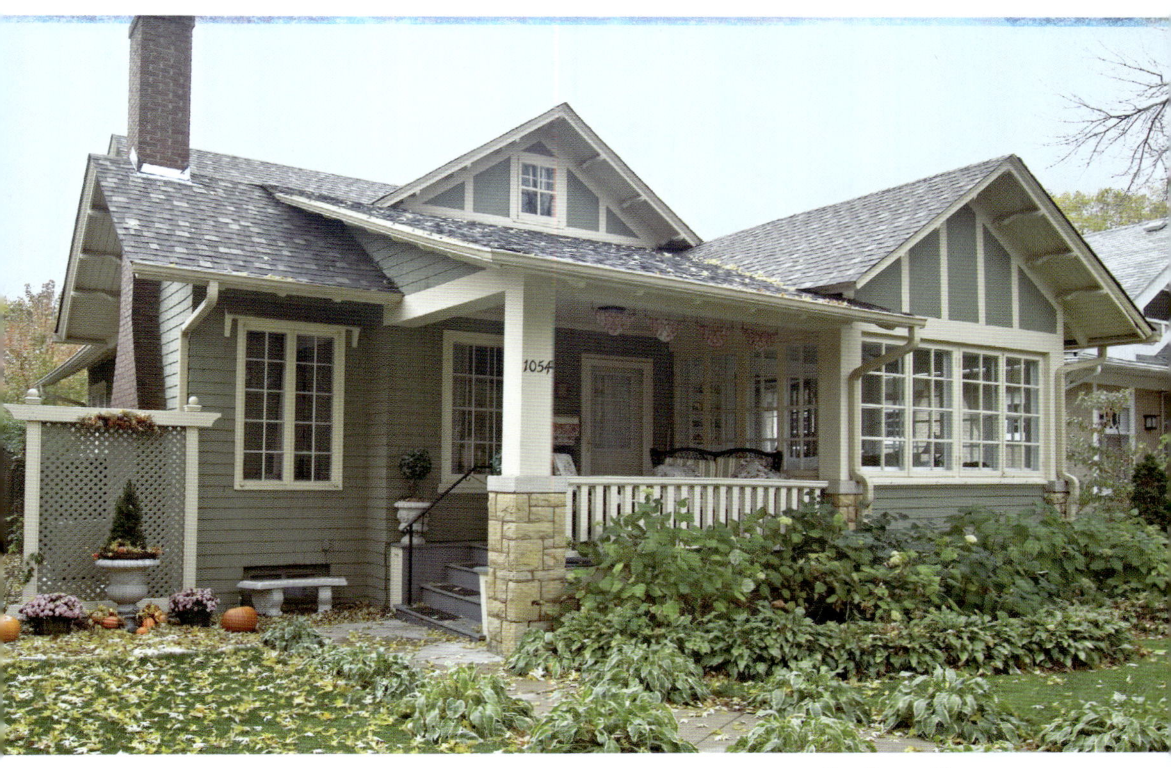


St. Paul, Minnesota

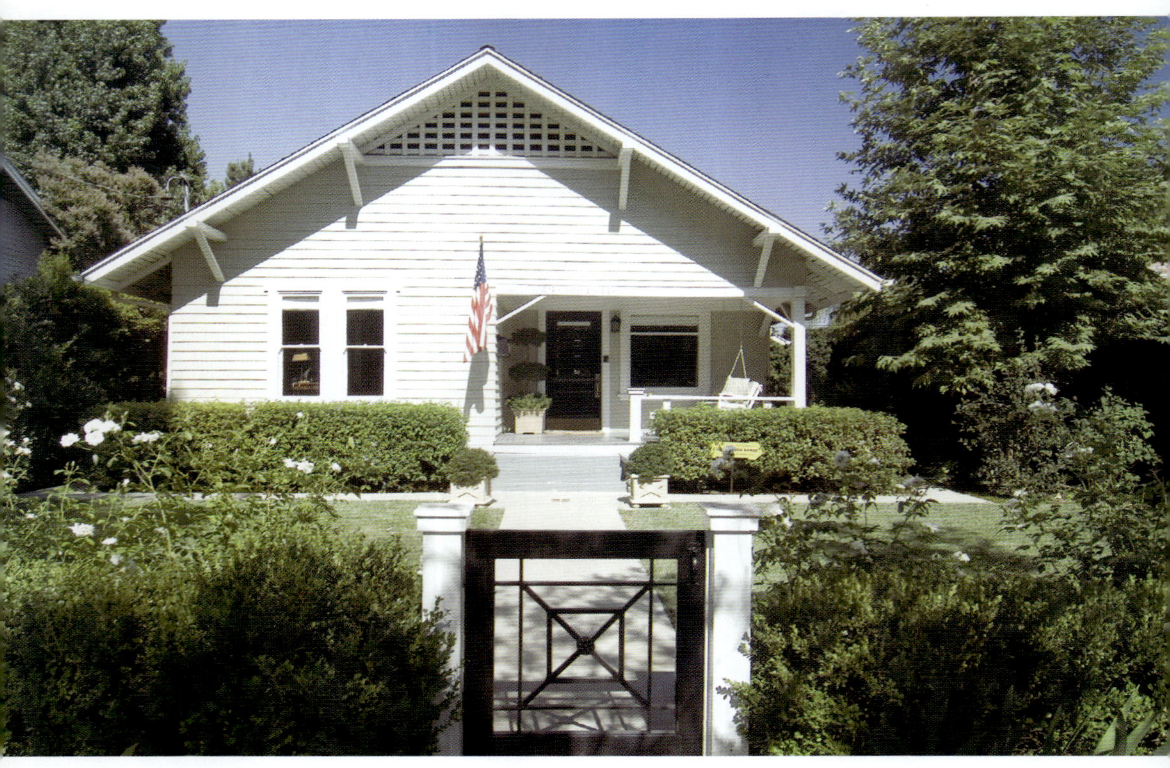

 Pasadena, California

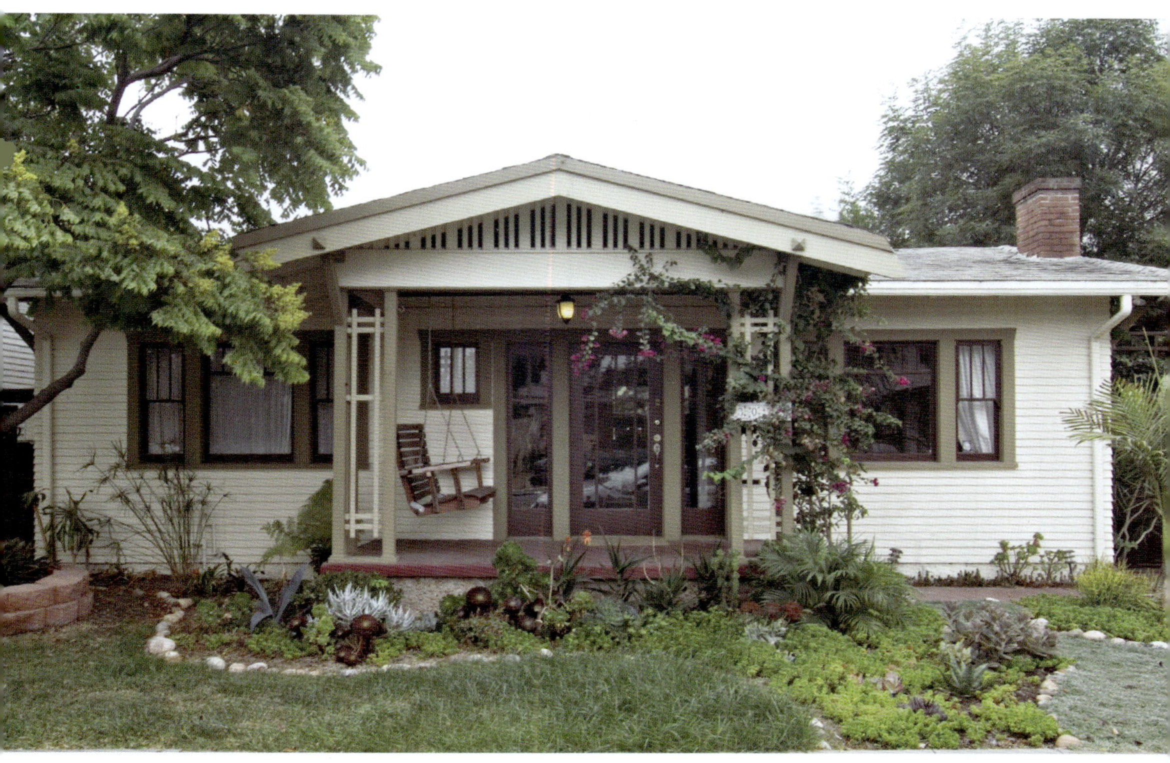

San Diego, California

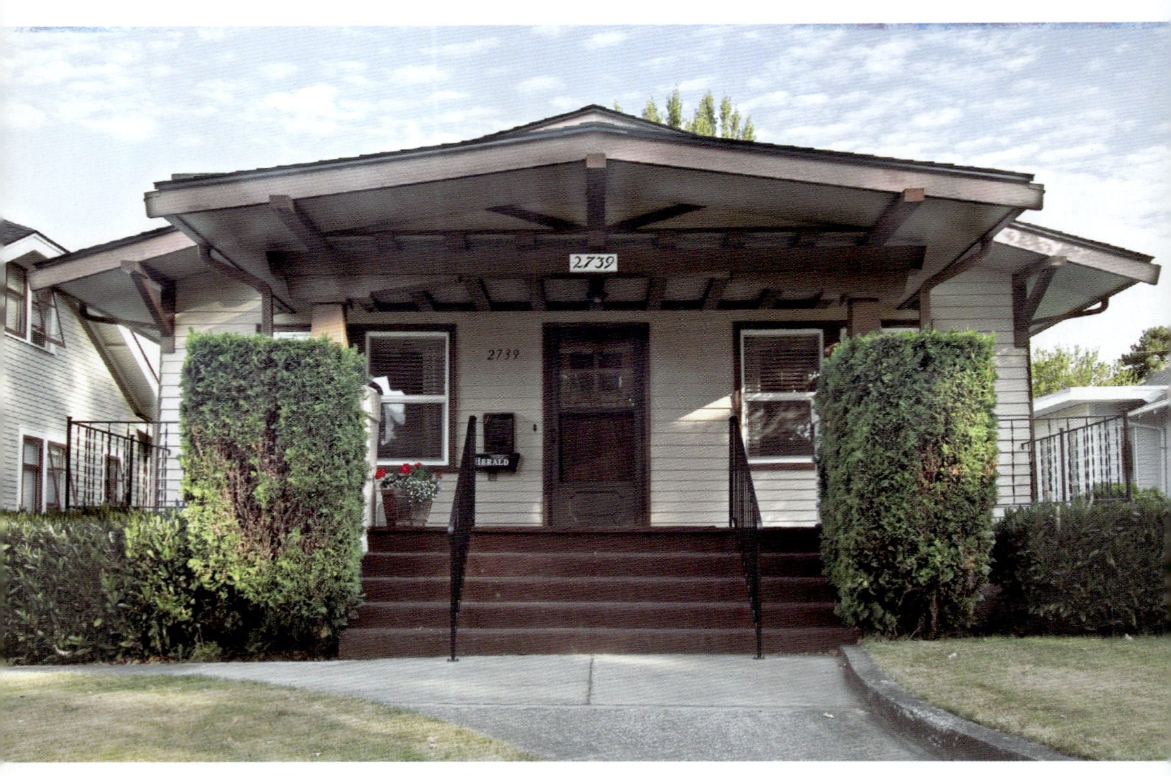


 Bellingham, Washington

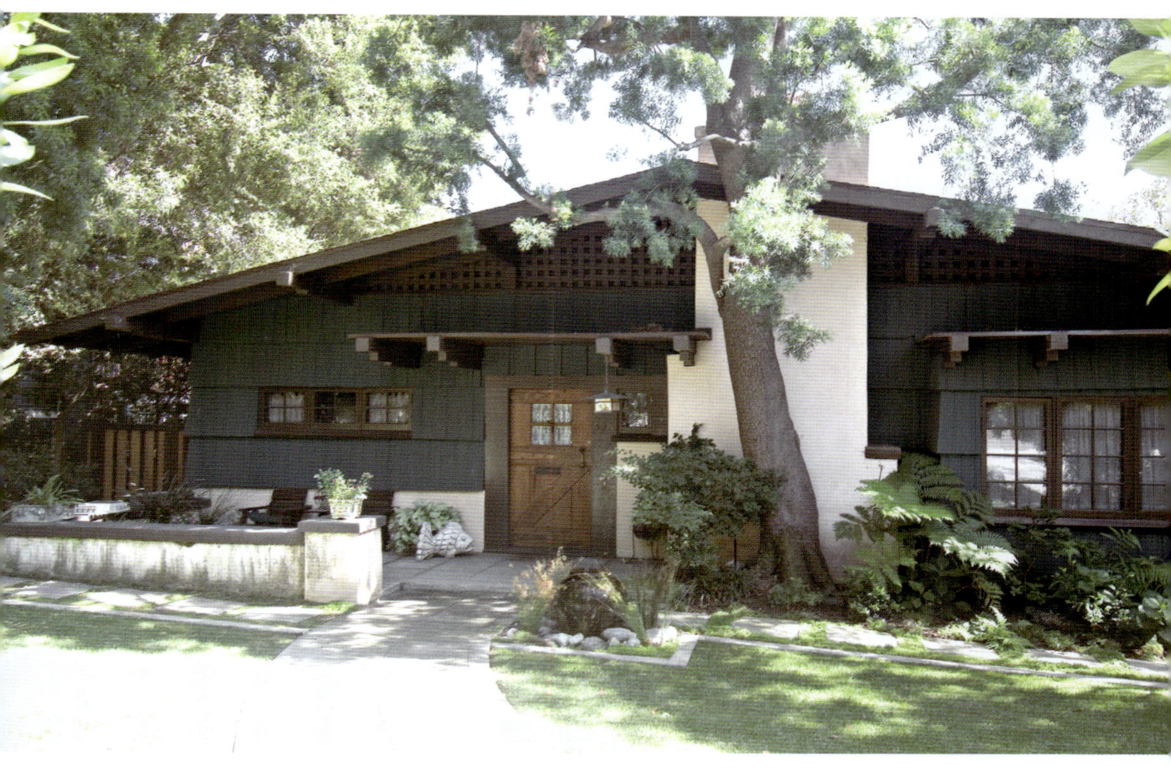

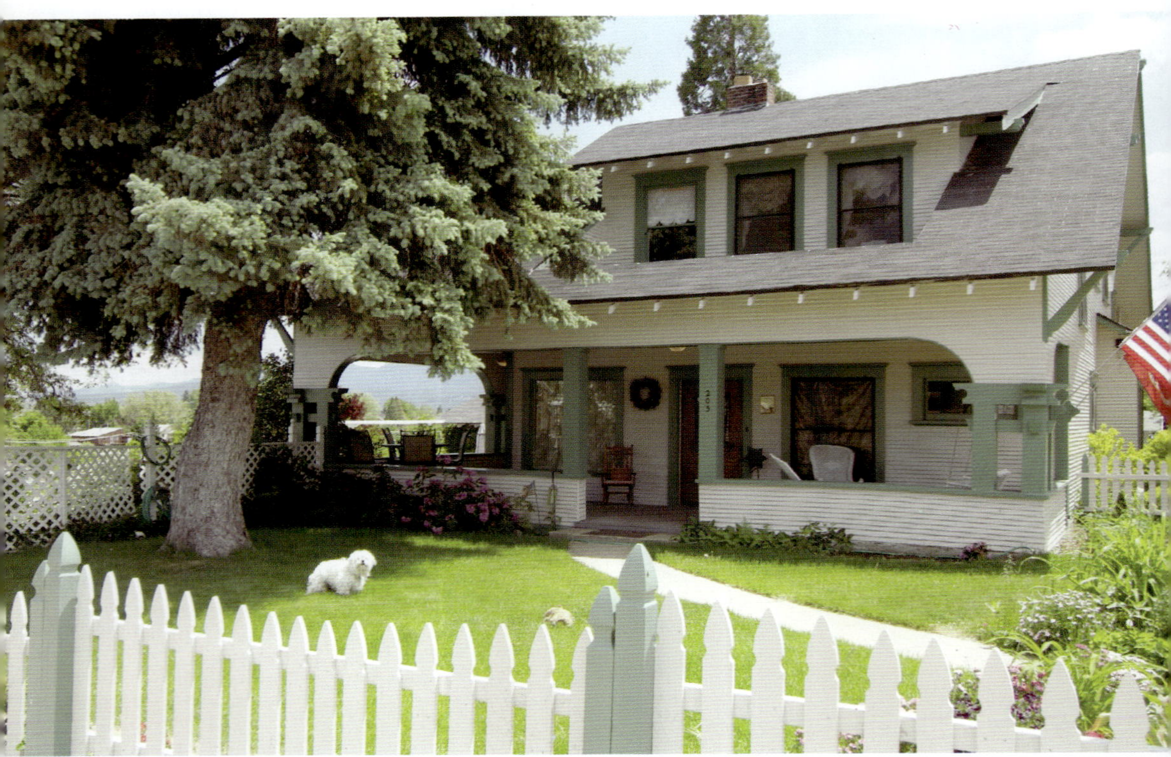

 Susanville, California

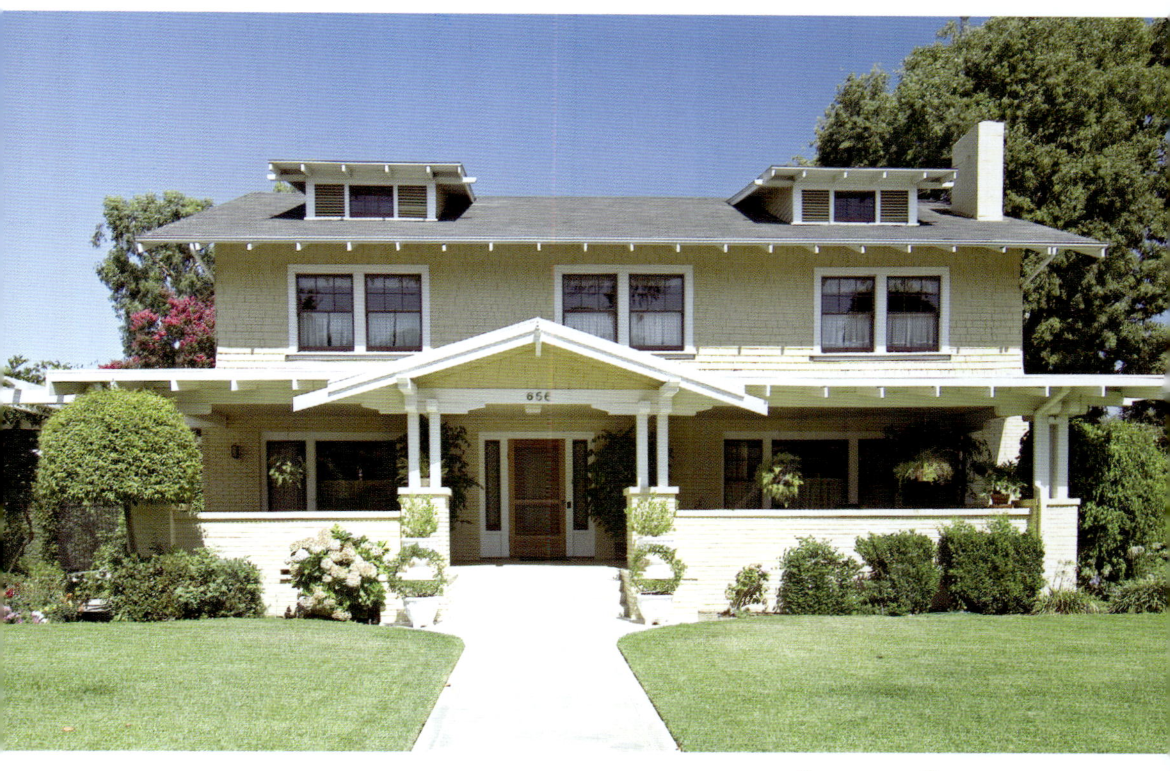

Pasadena, California

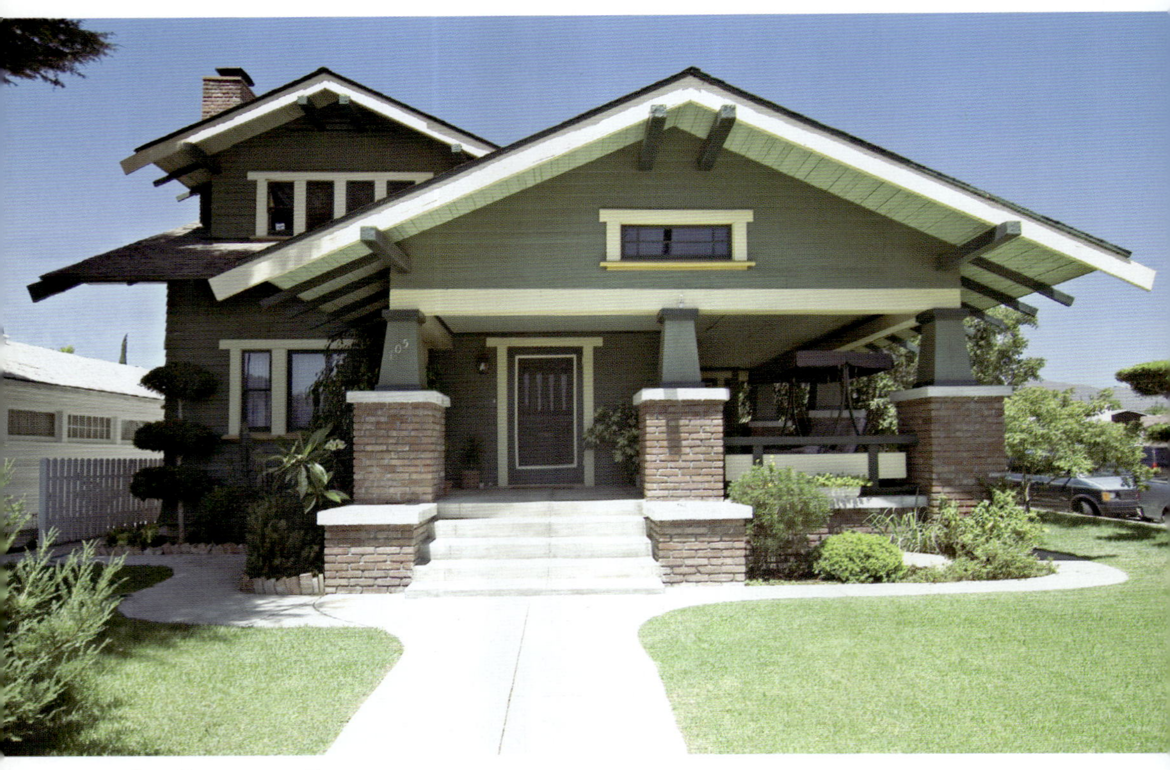

 San Fernando, California

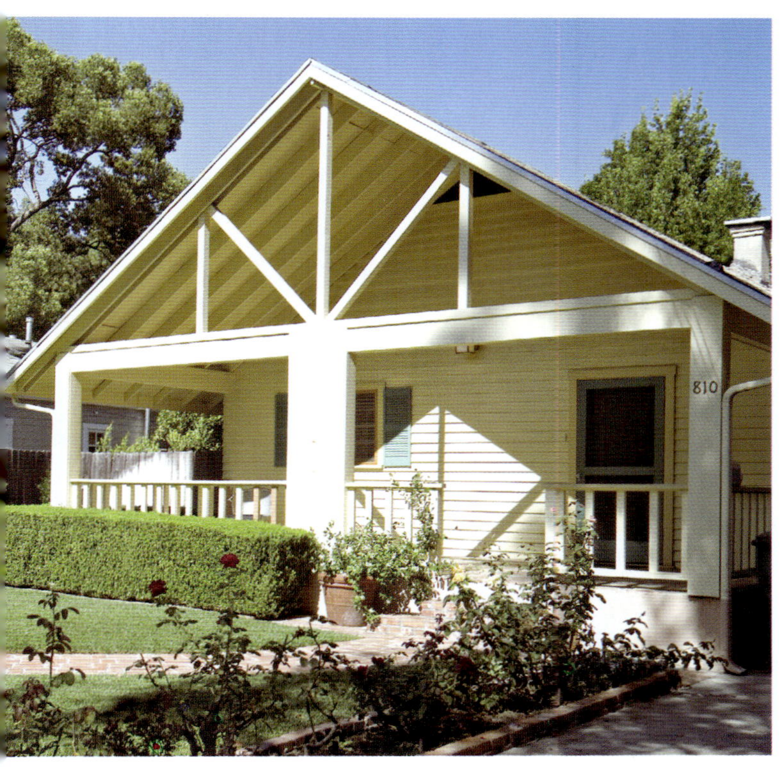
810

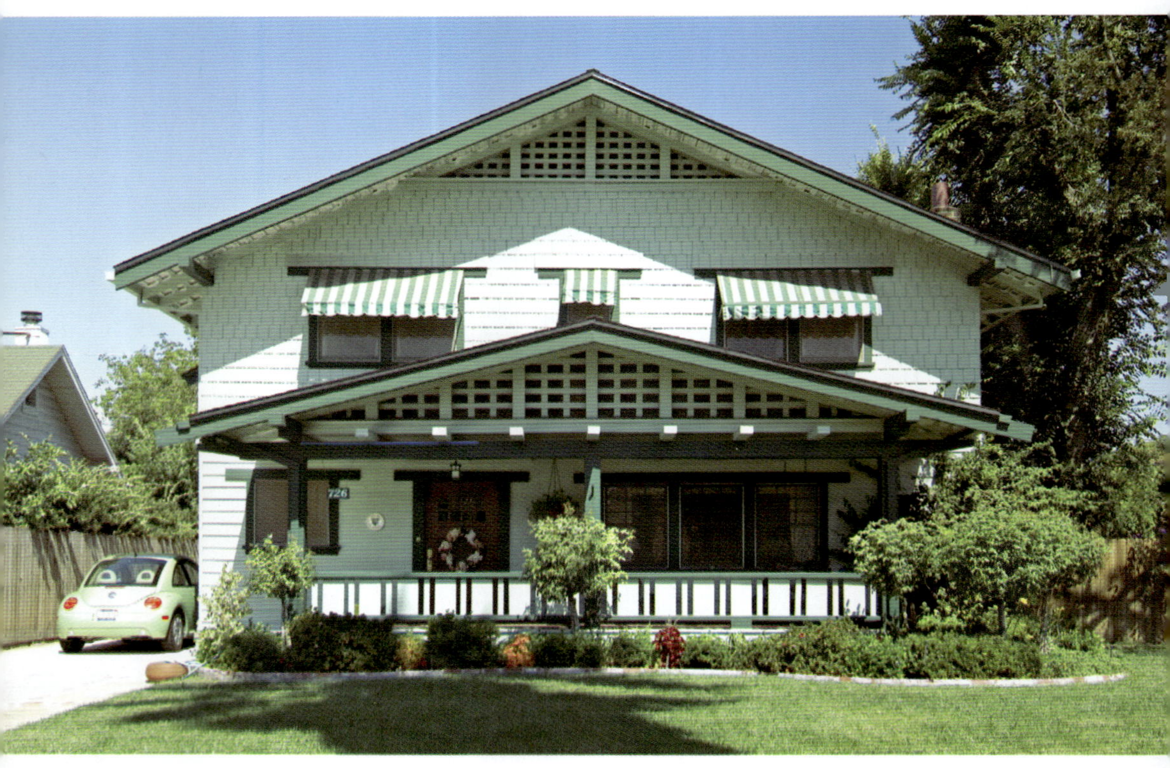


 Pasadena, California

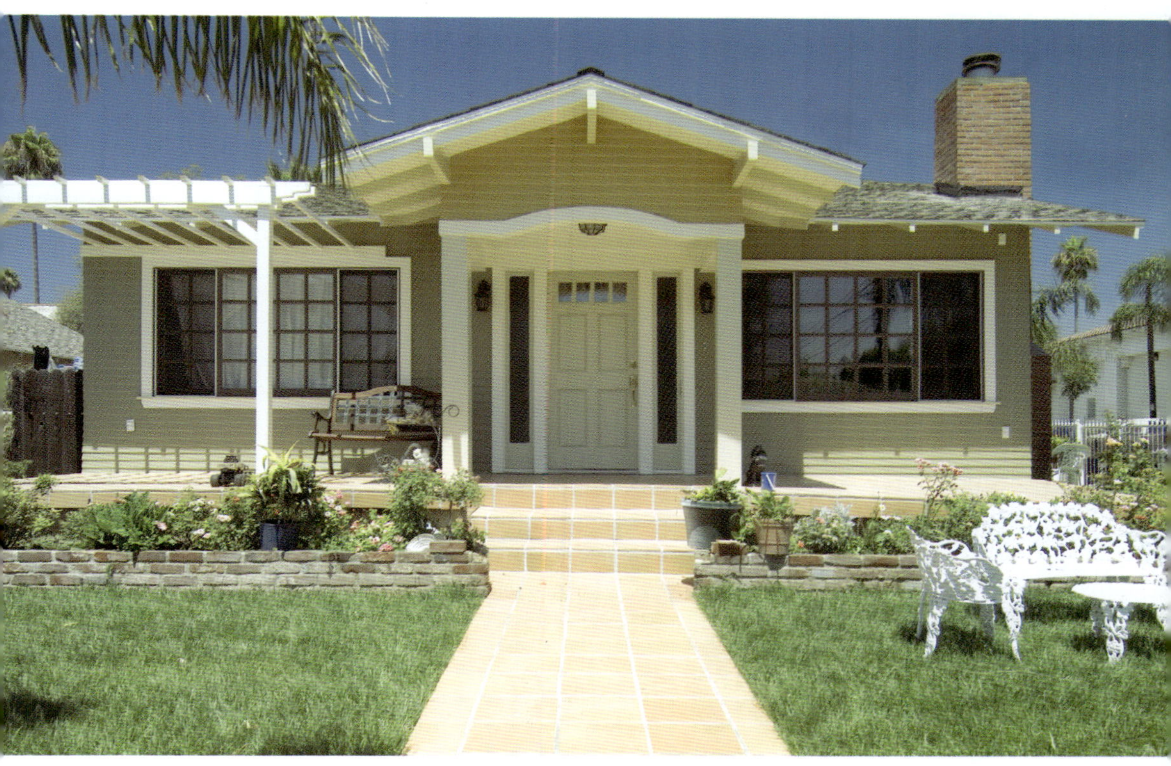

San Fernando, California

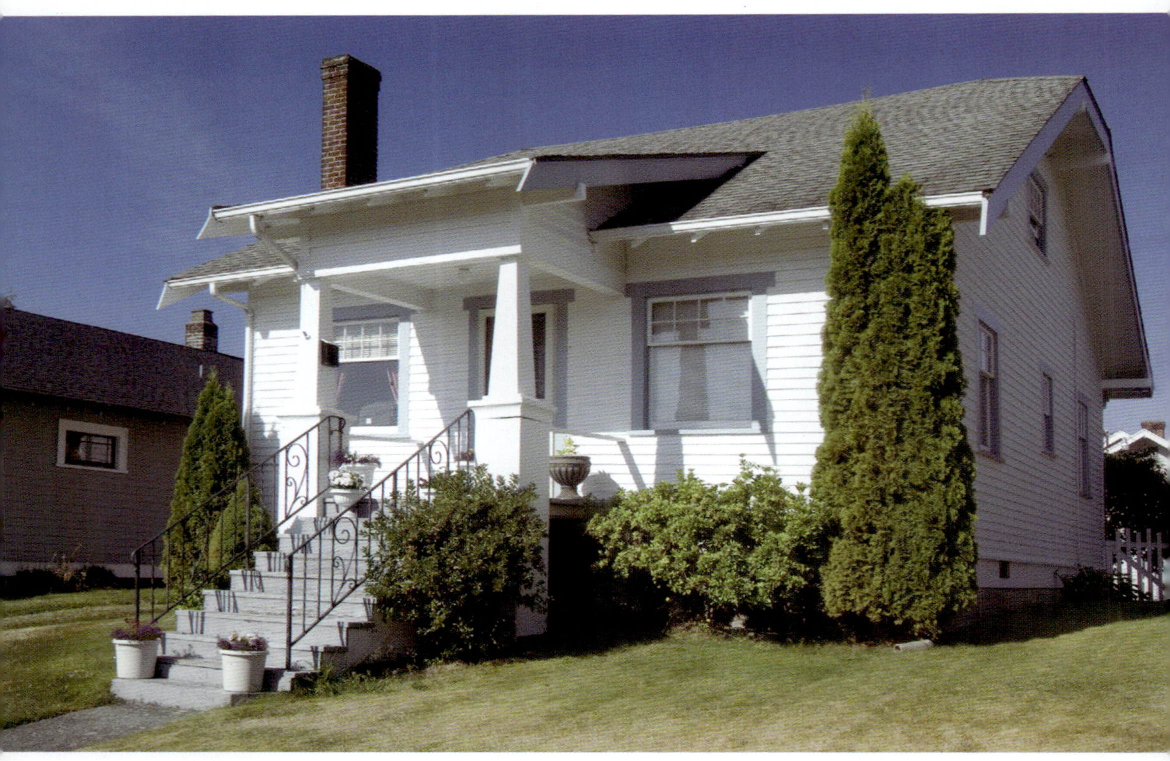

134 Bellingham, Washington

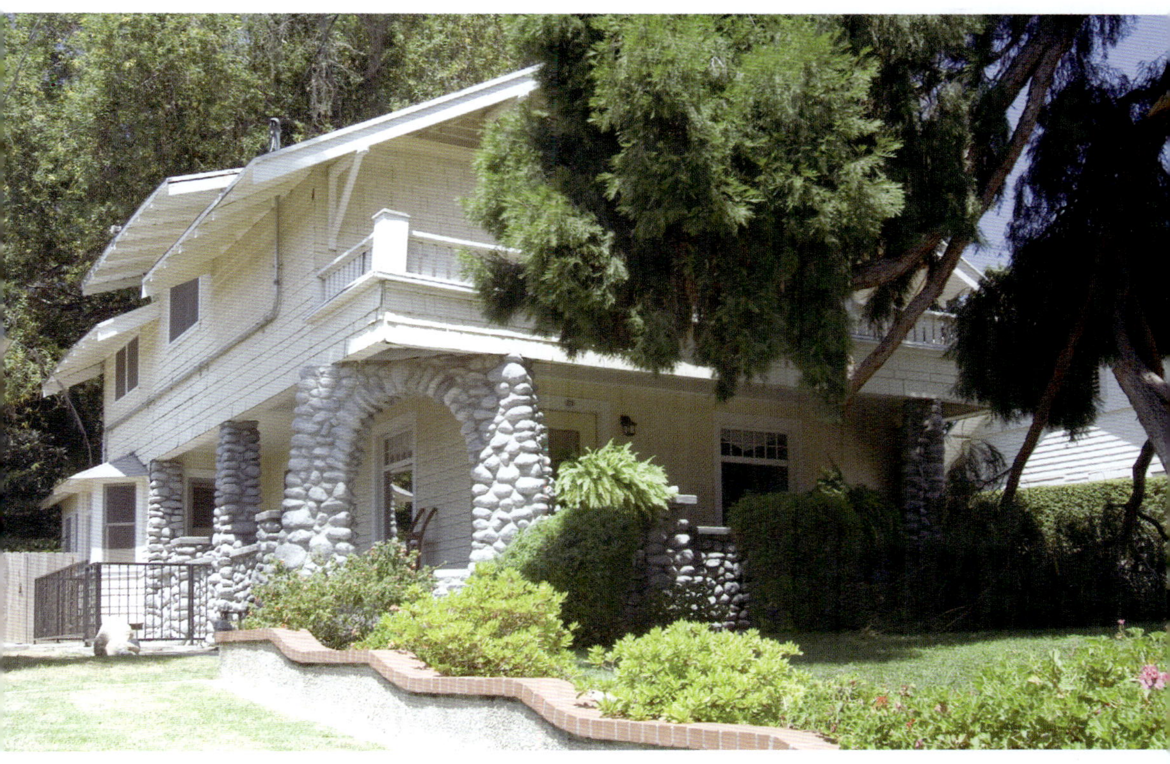

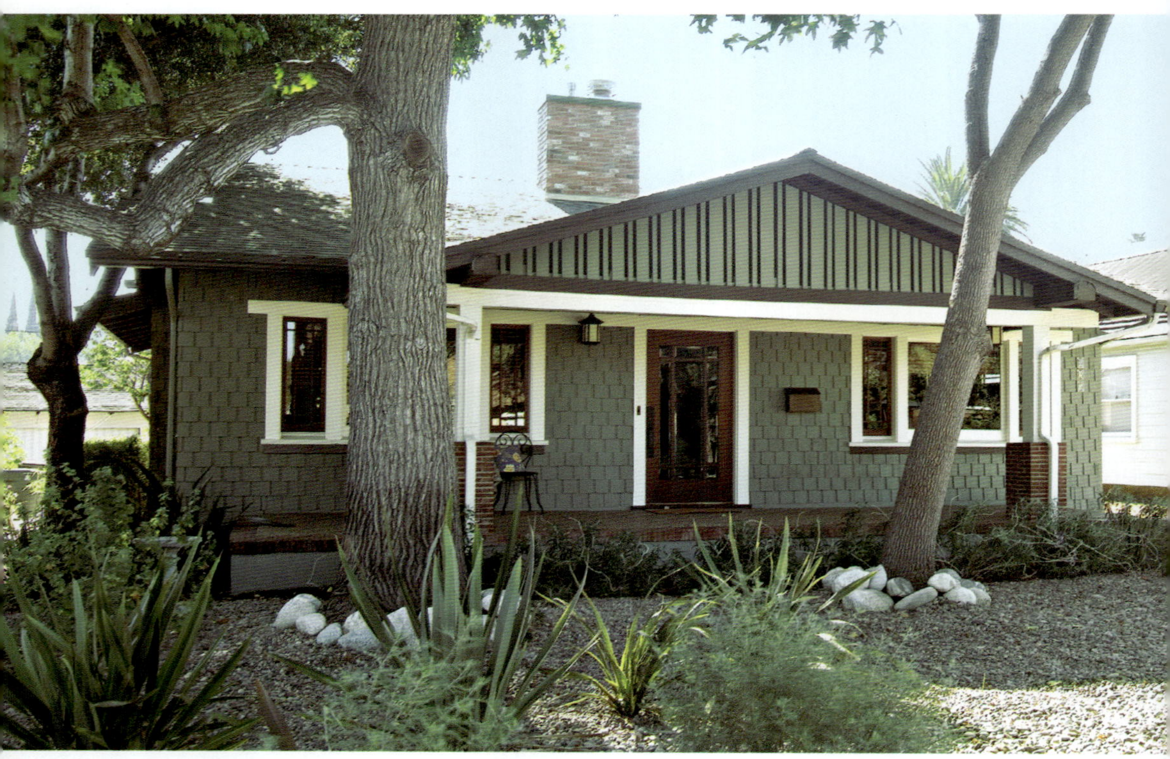

 Pasadena, California

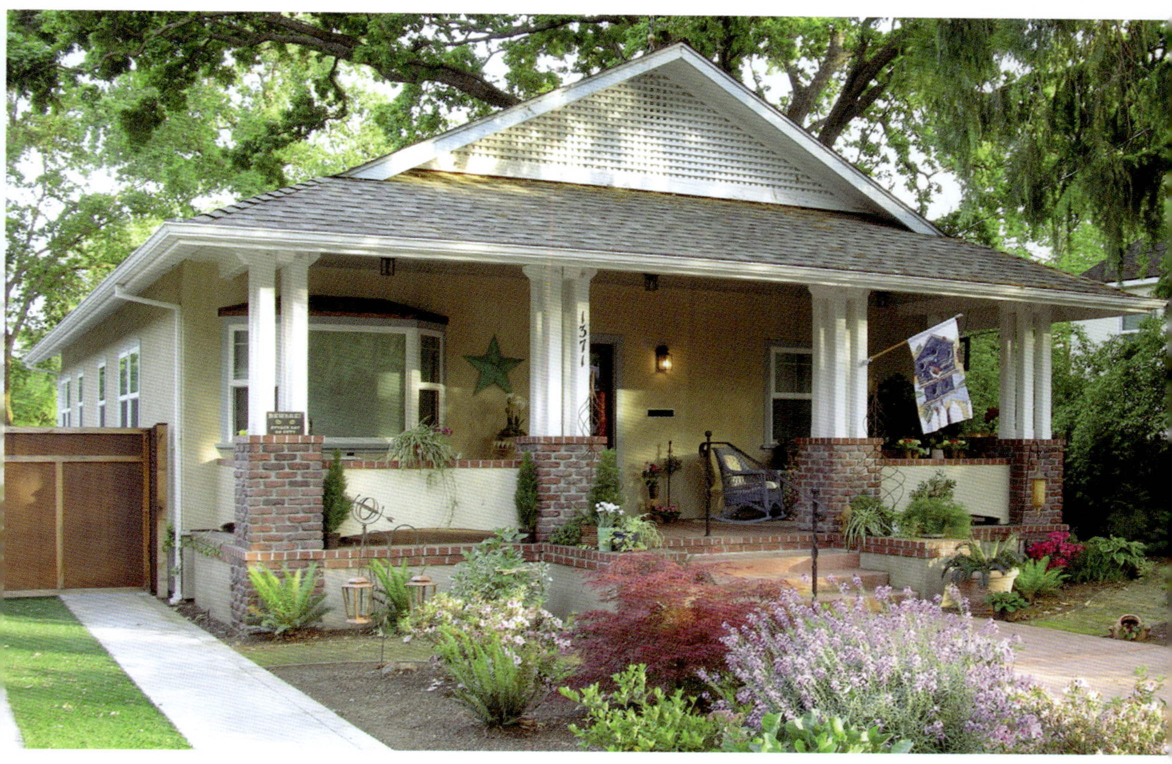


Chico, California

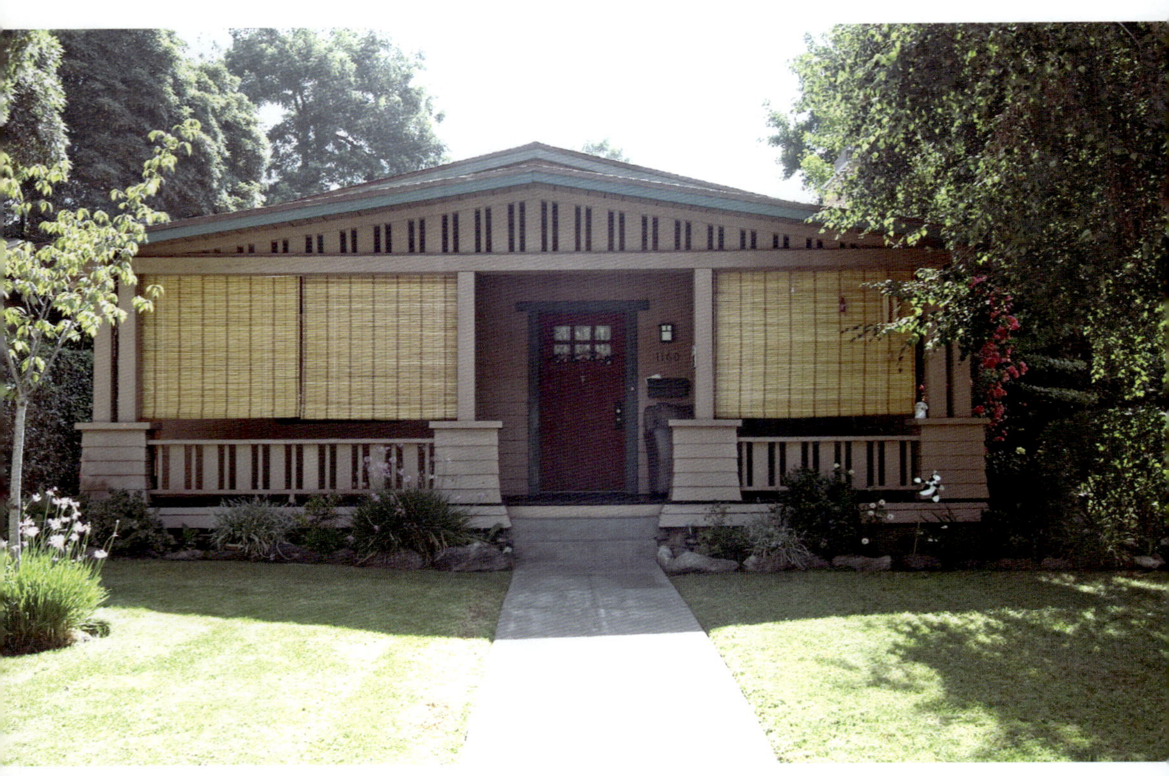

 Pasadena, California

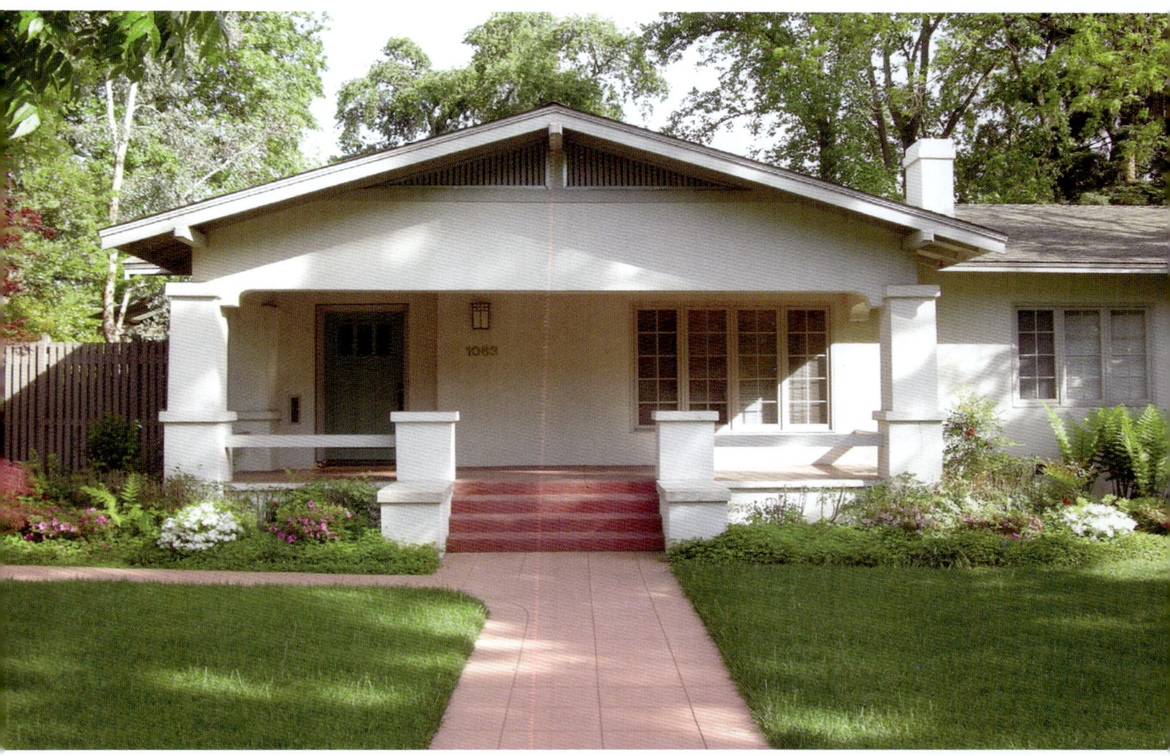

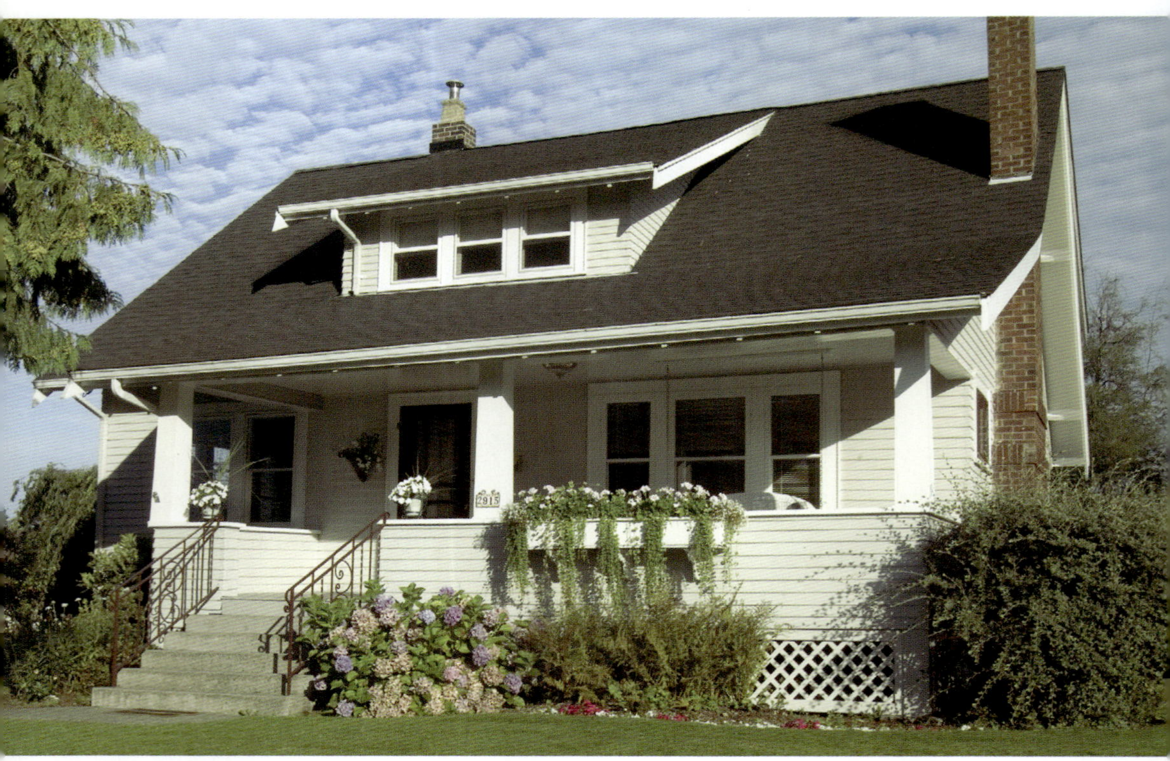


 BELLINGHAM, WASHINGTON

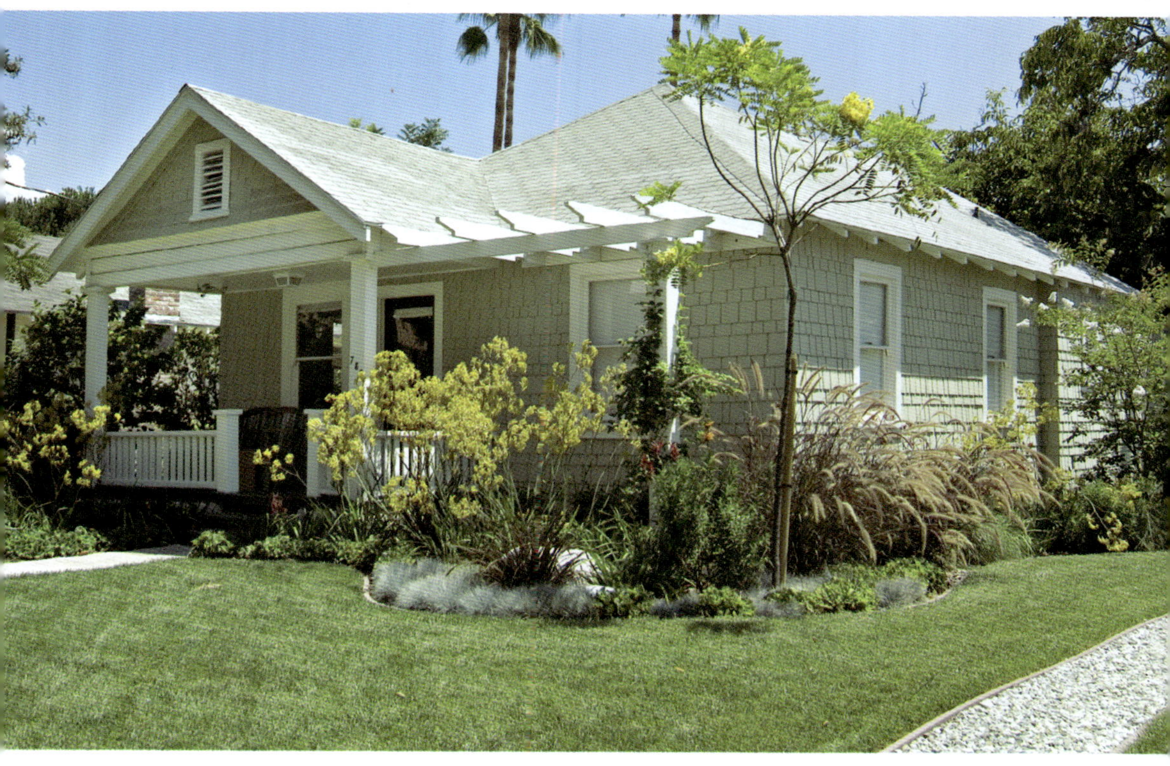

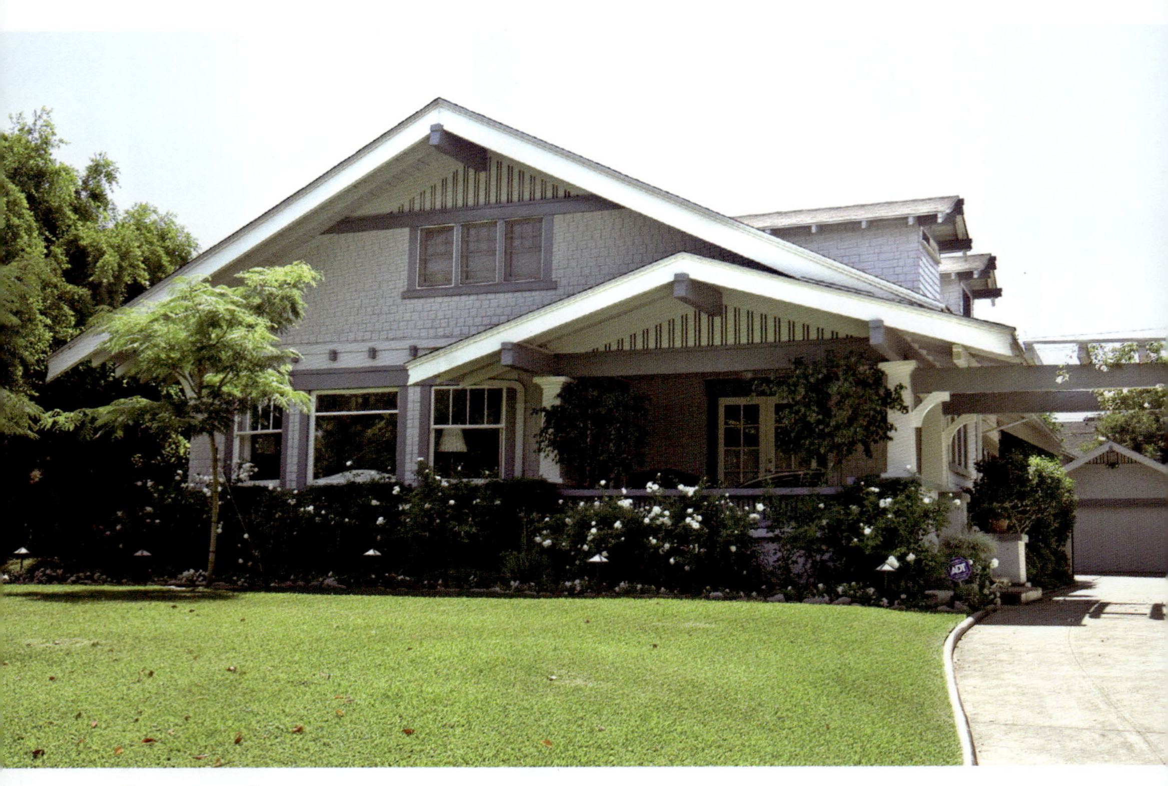


 PASADENA, CALIFORNIA

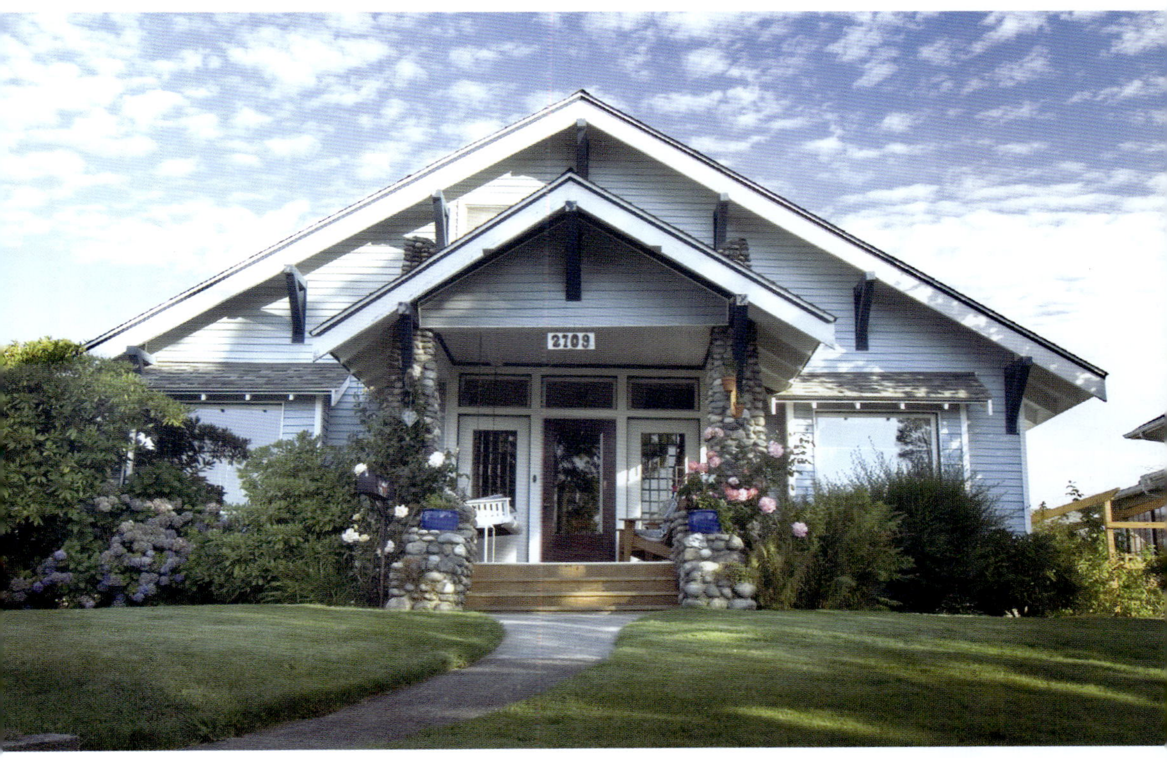


Bellingham, Washington

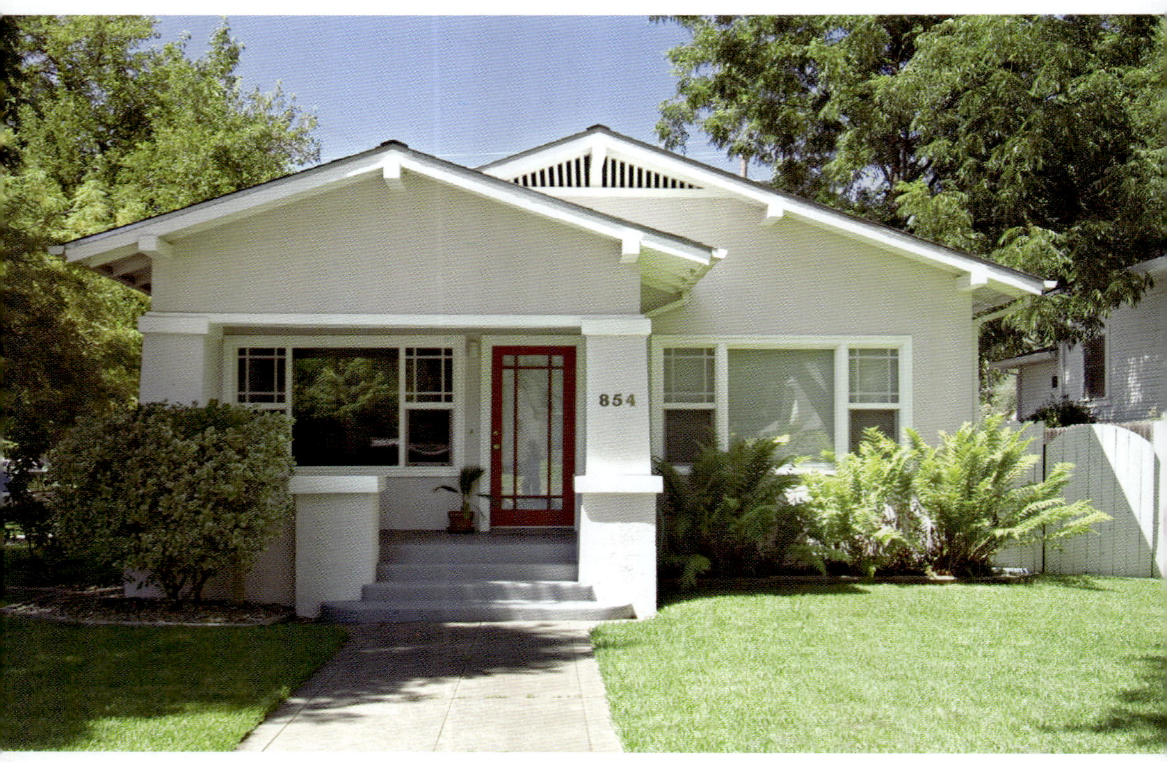


 Chico, California

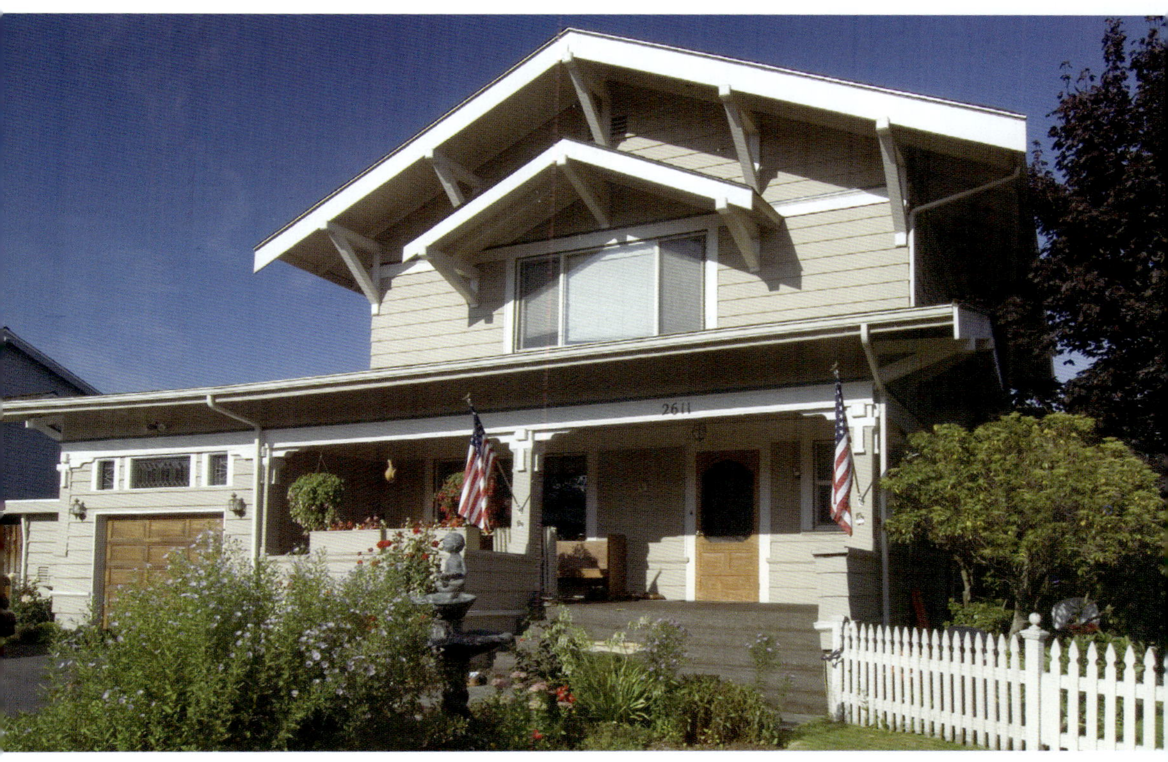
2611

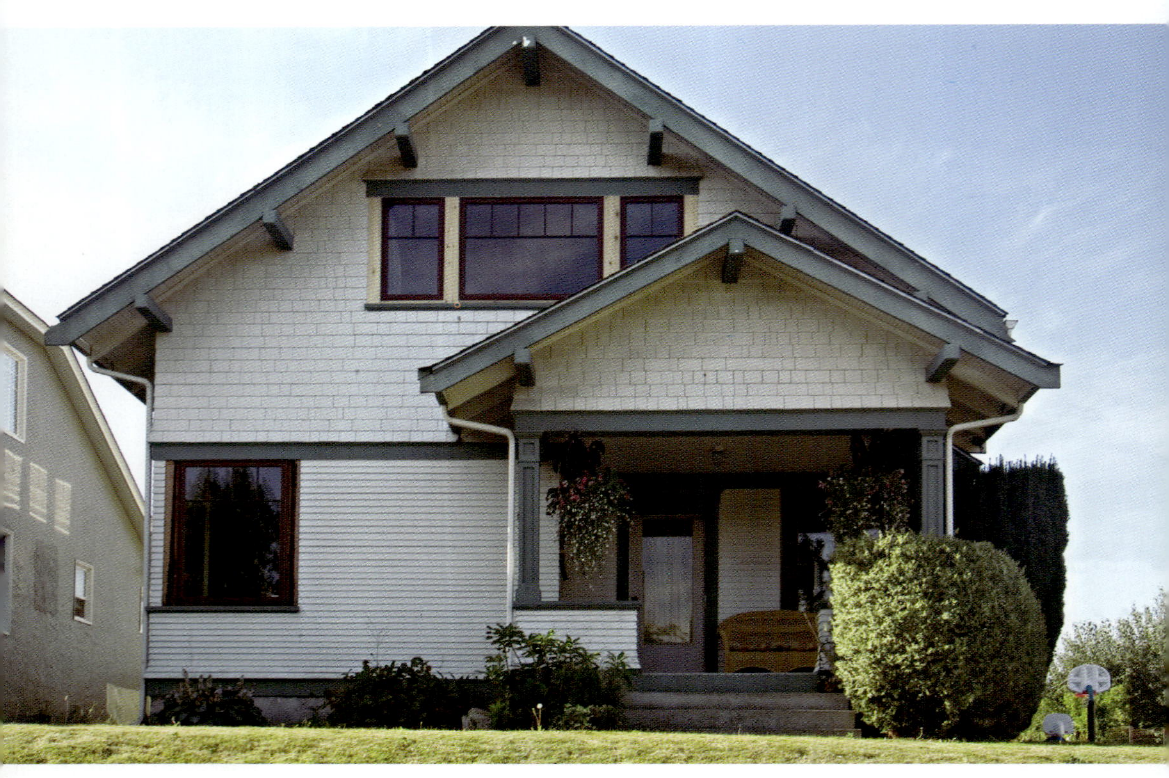

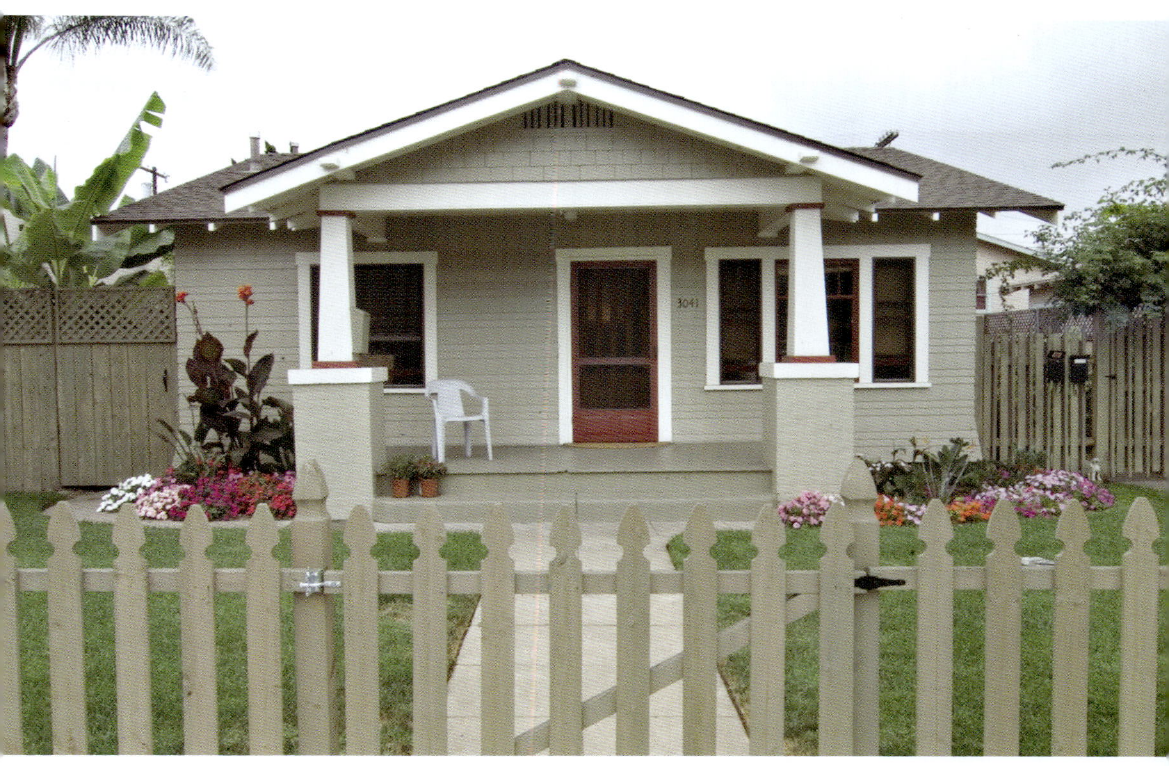


San Diego, California

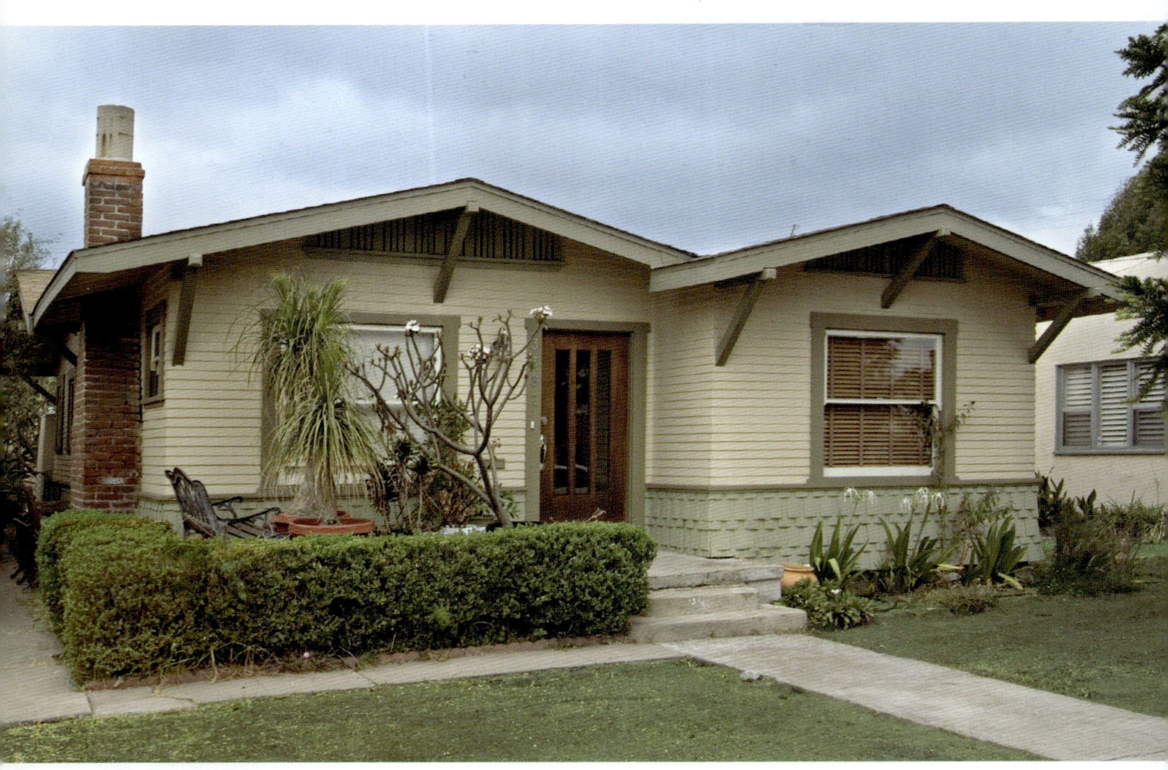

 San Diego, California

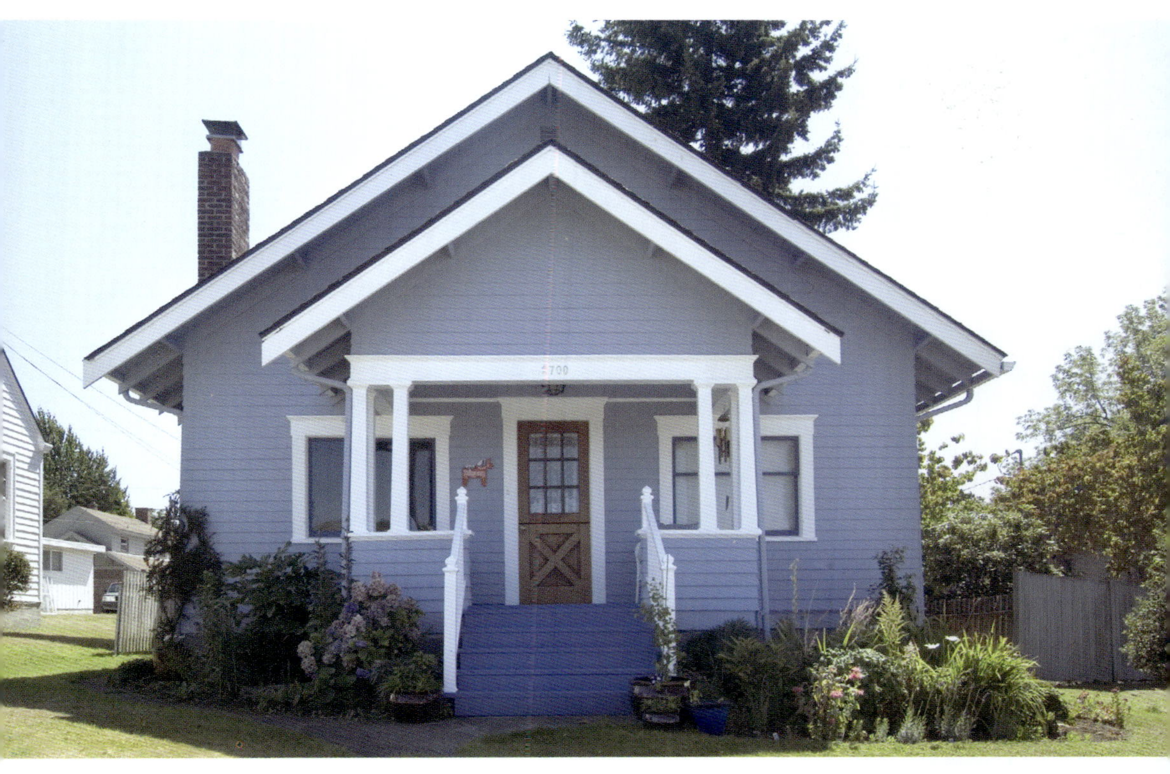

BELLINGHAM, WASHINGTON 

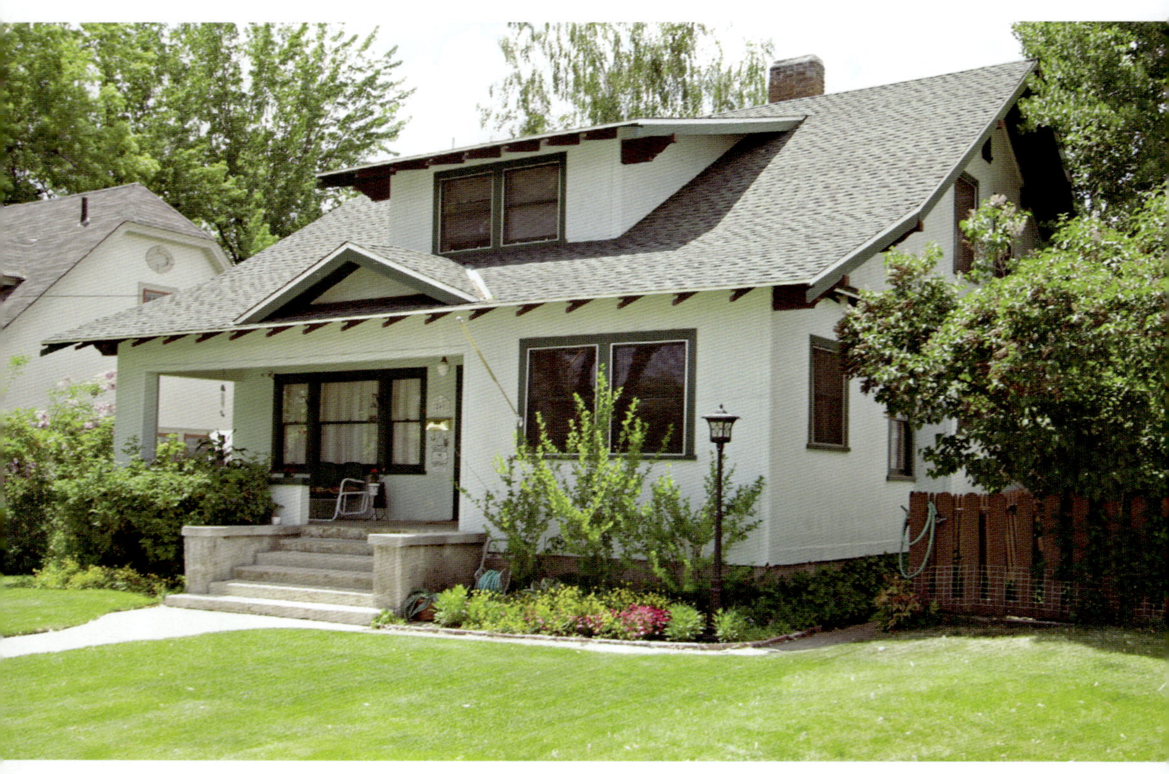

 Susanville, California

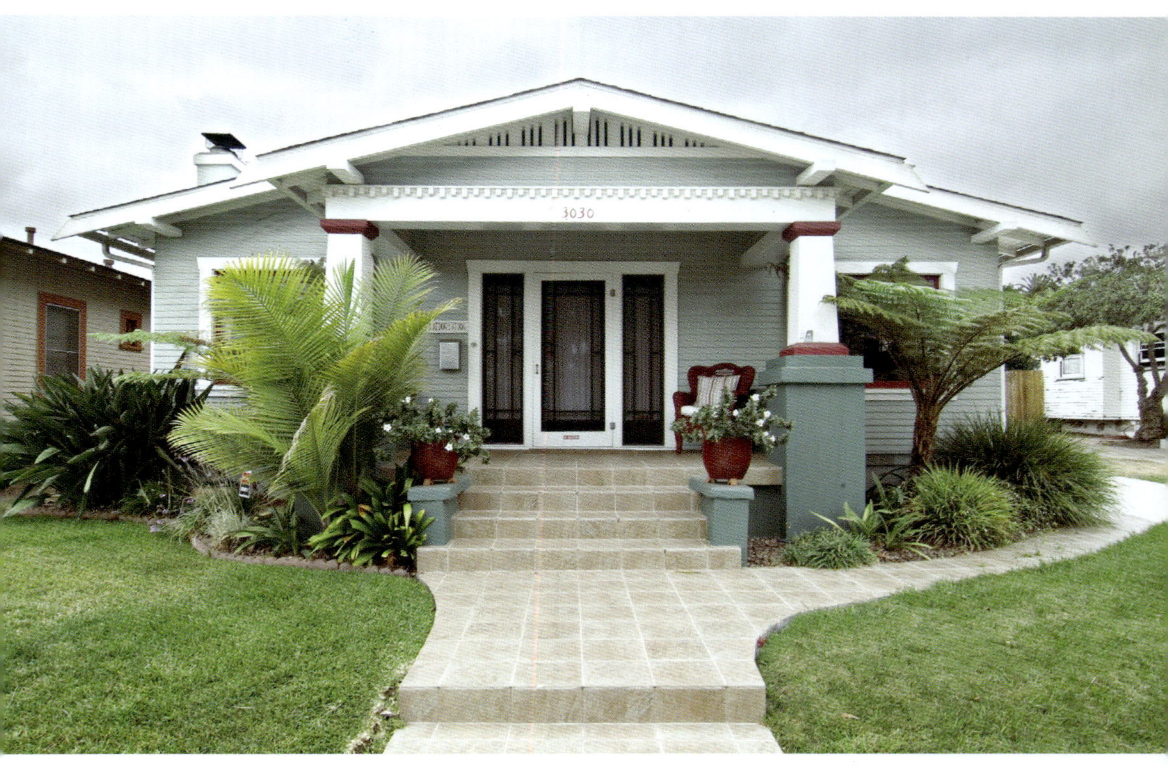


San Diego, California

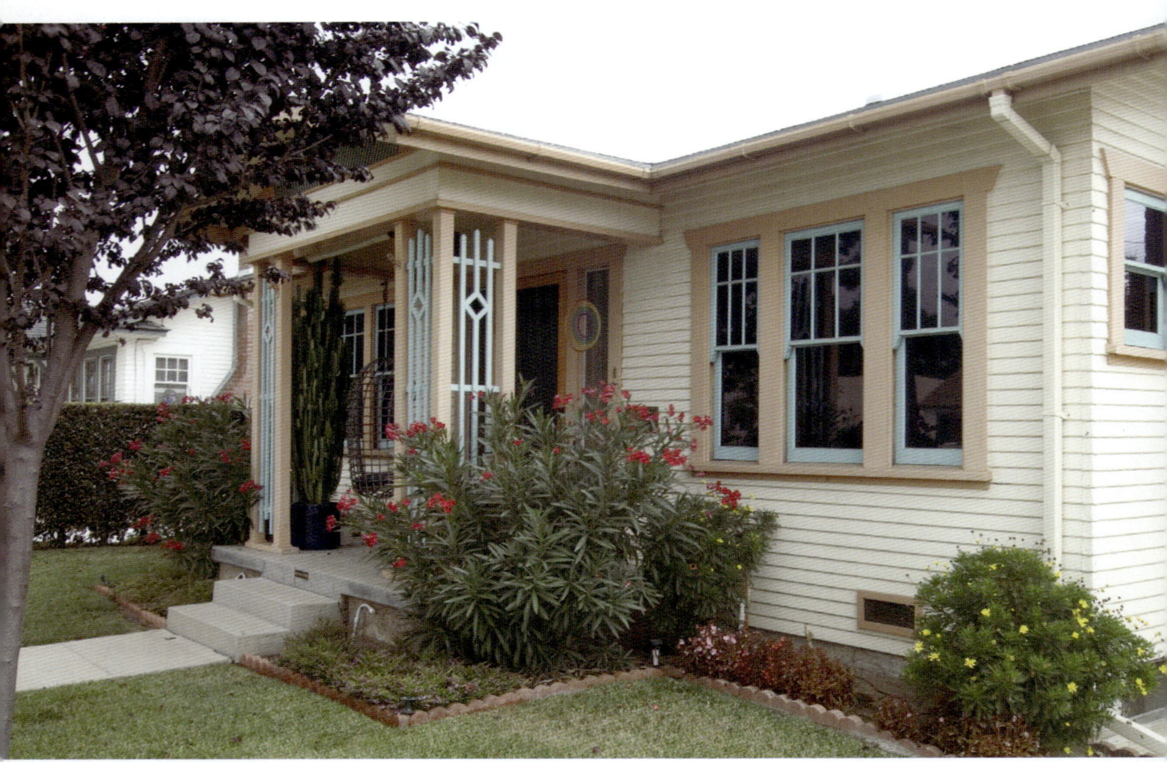

 San Diego, California

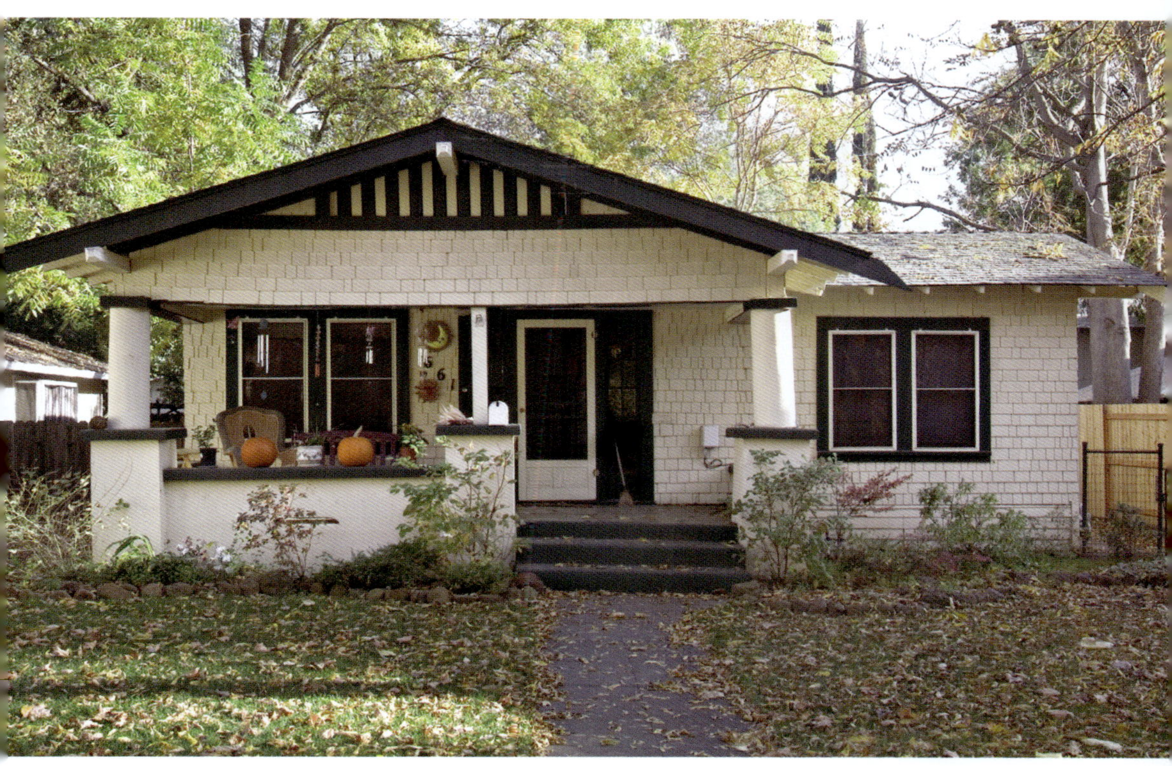

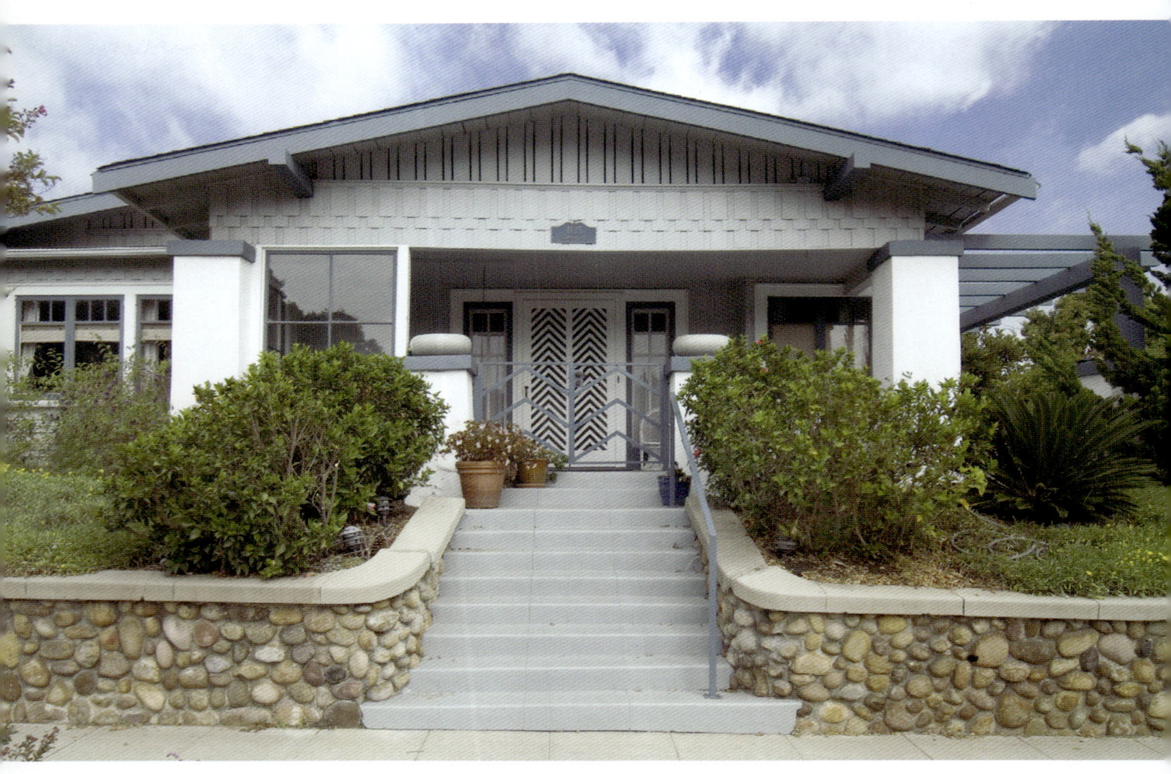

 San Diego, California

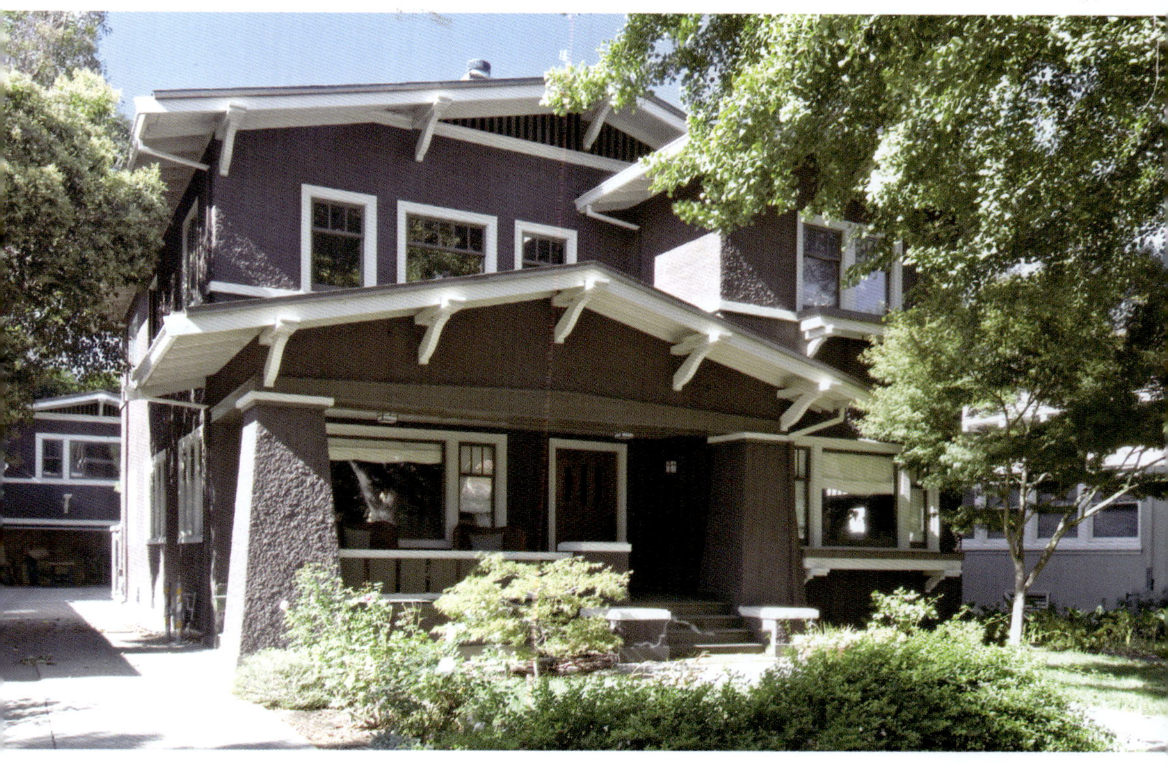

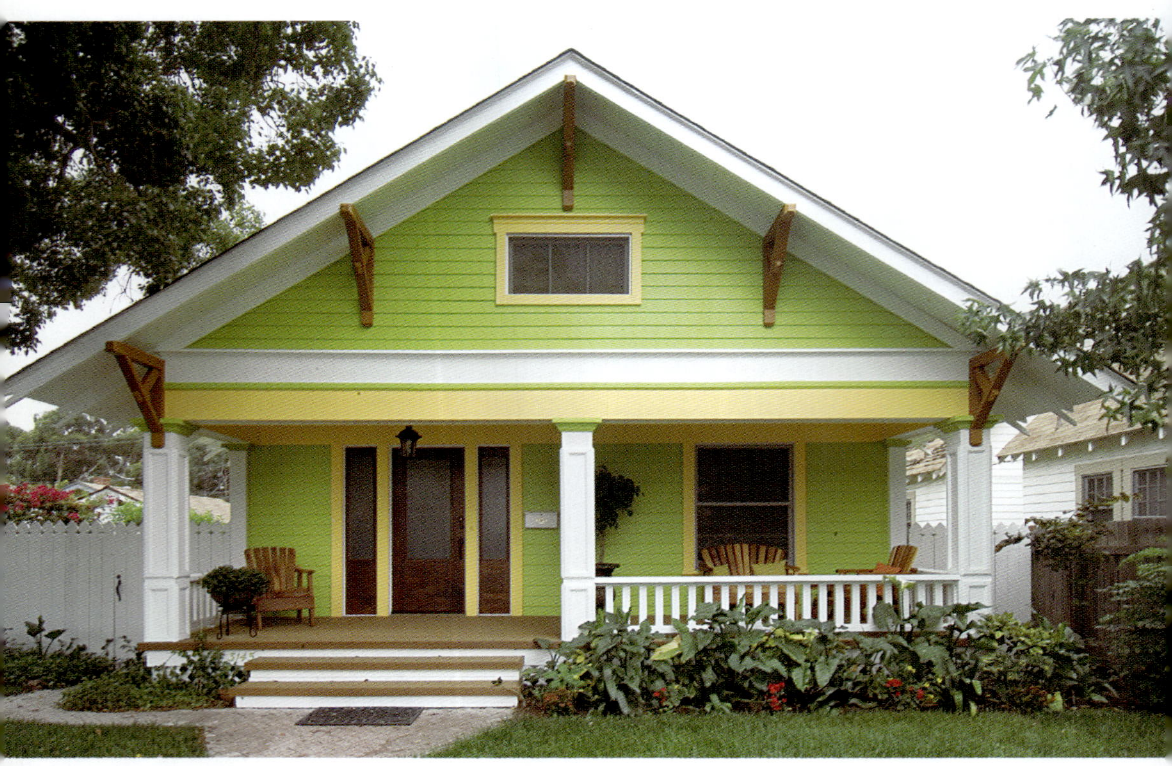

 San Diego, California

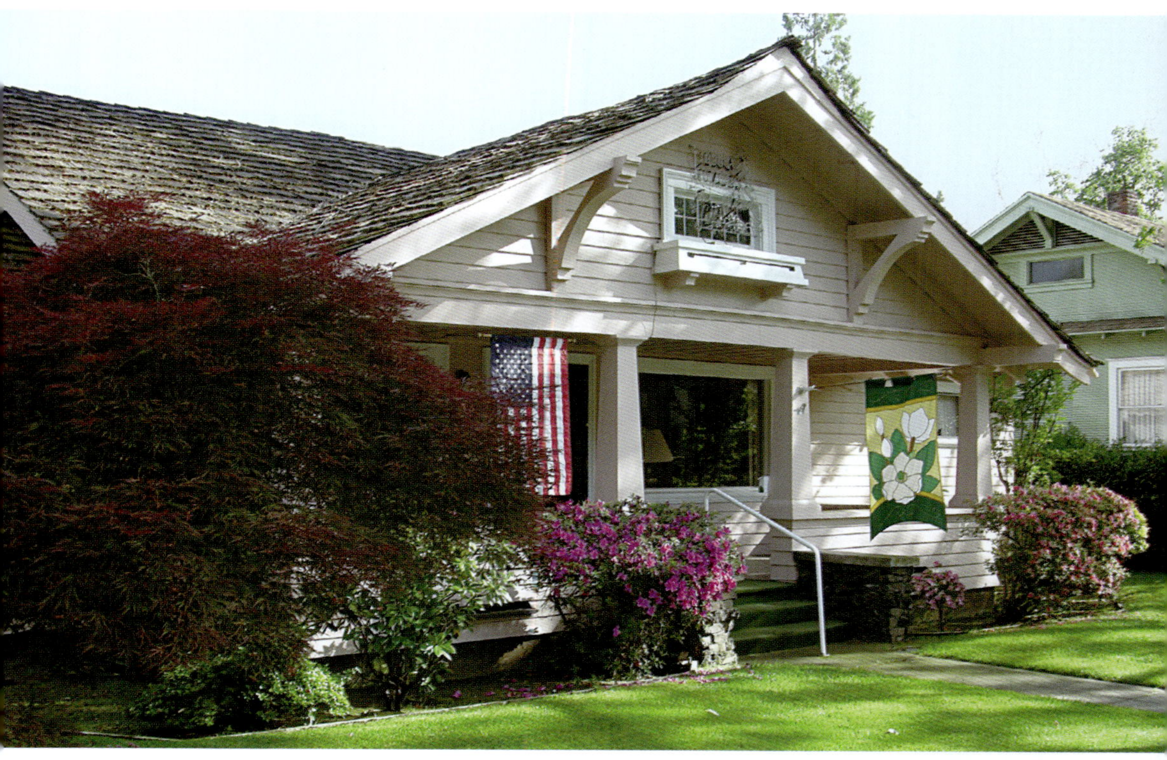

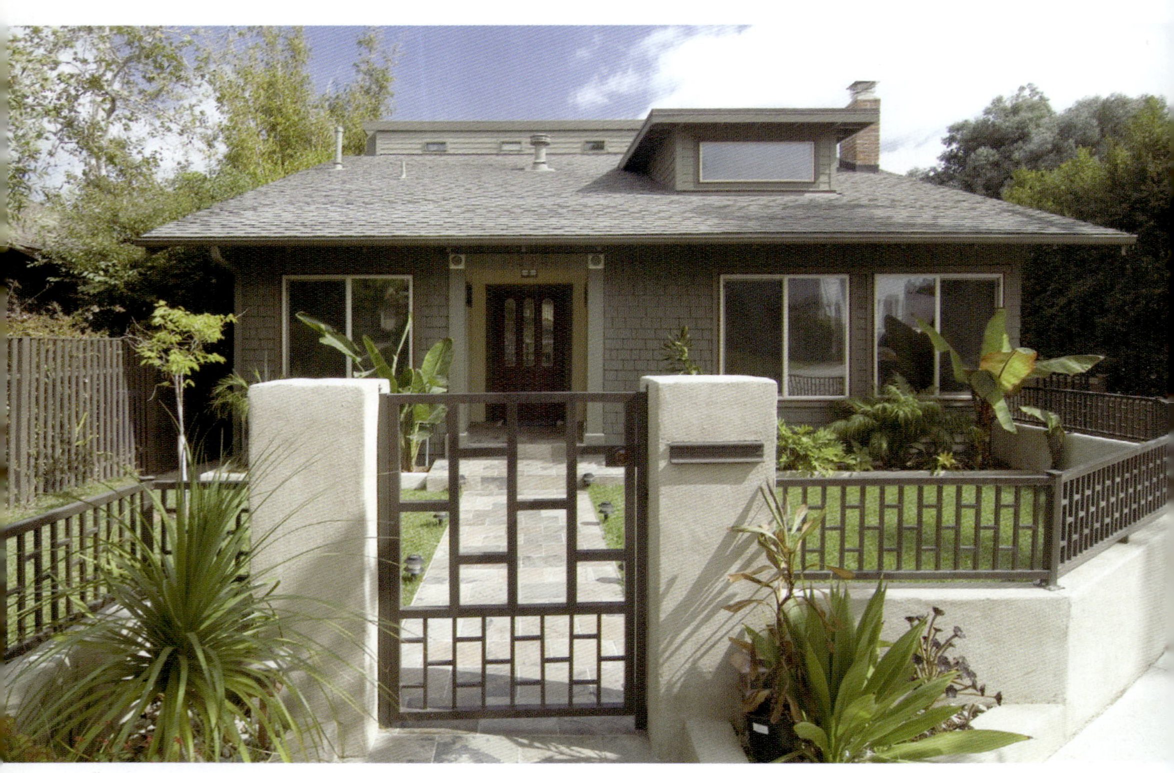

 San Diego, California

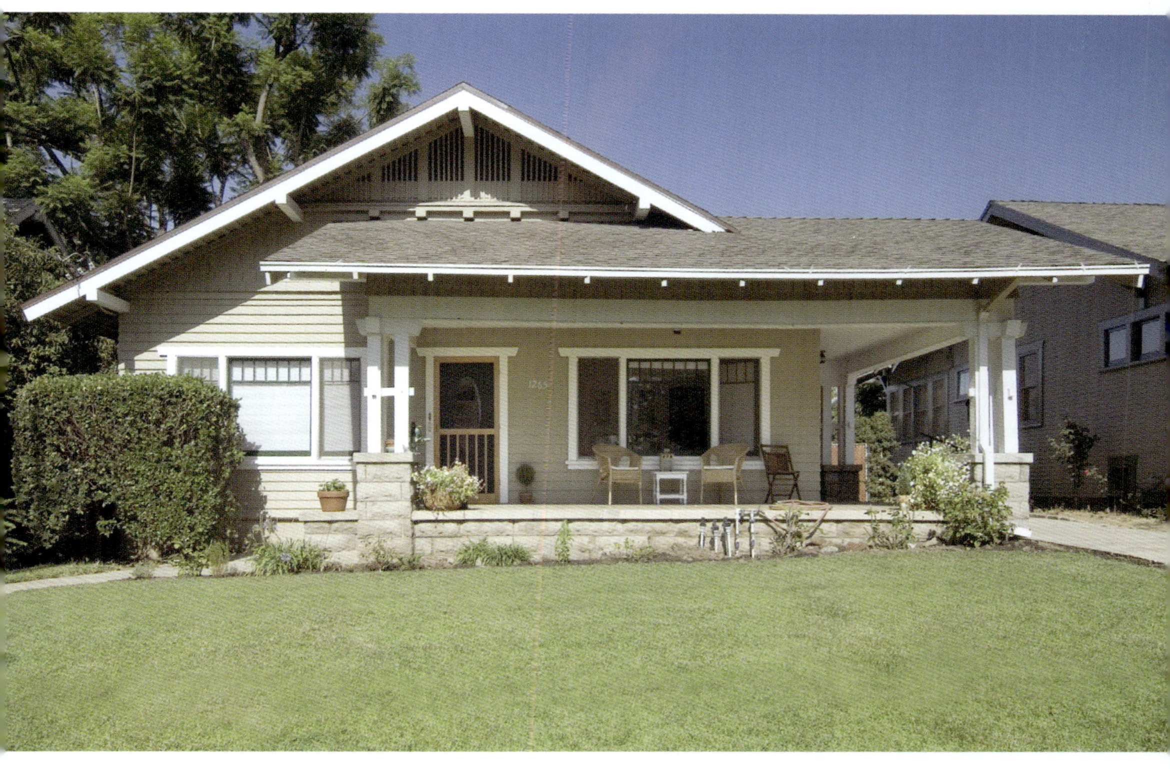

Pasadena, California

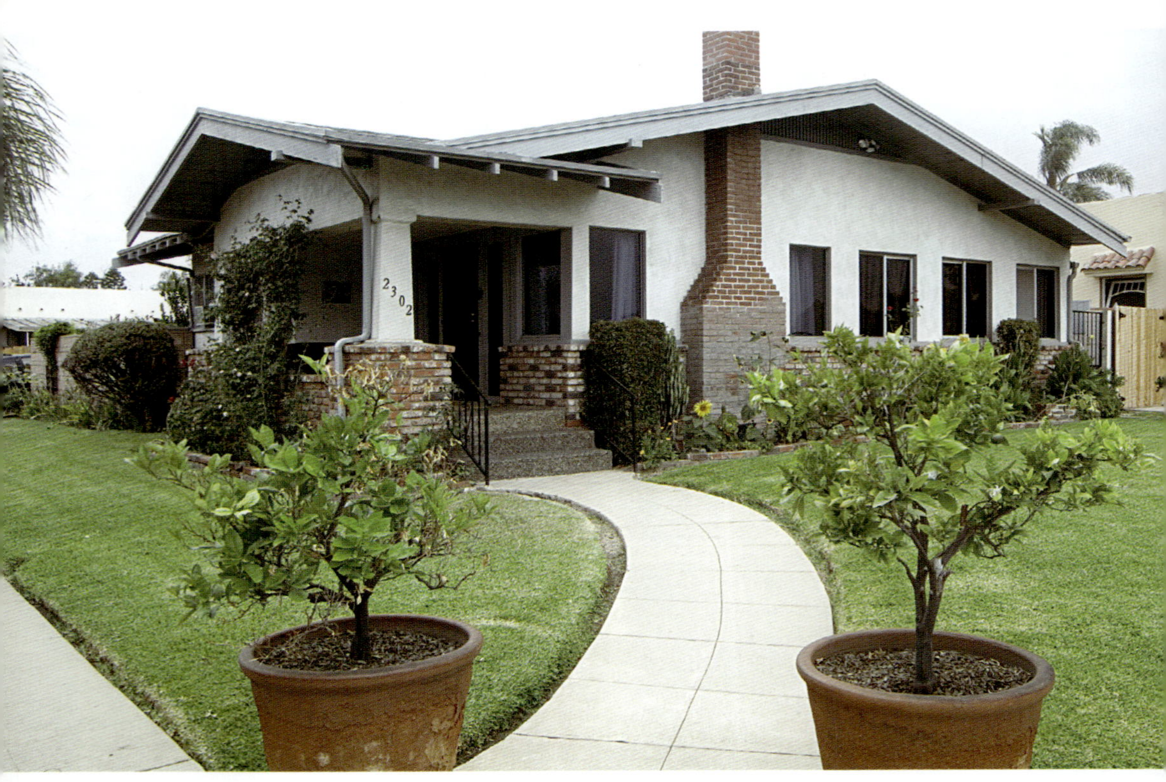


 San Diego, California

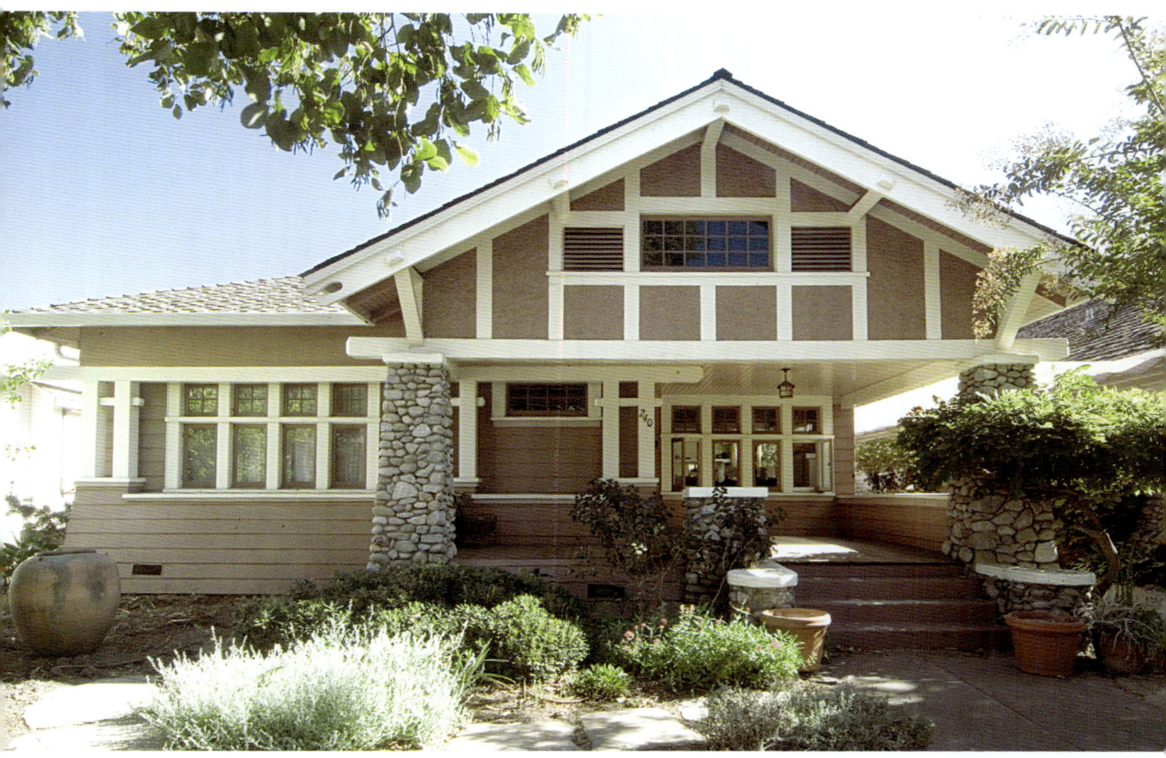


San Jose, California

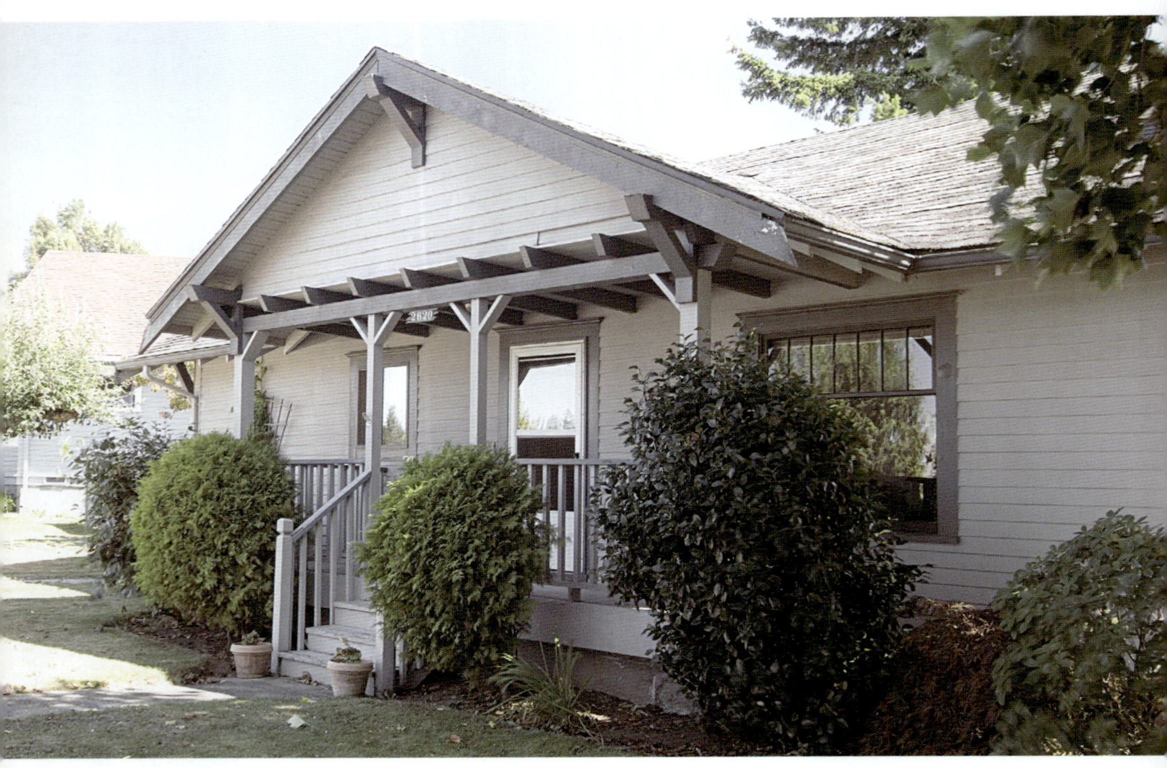


 Bellingham, Washington

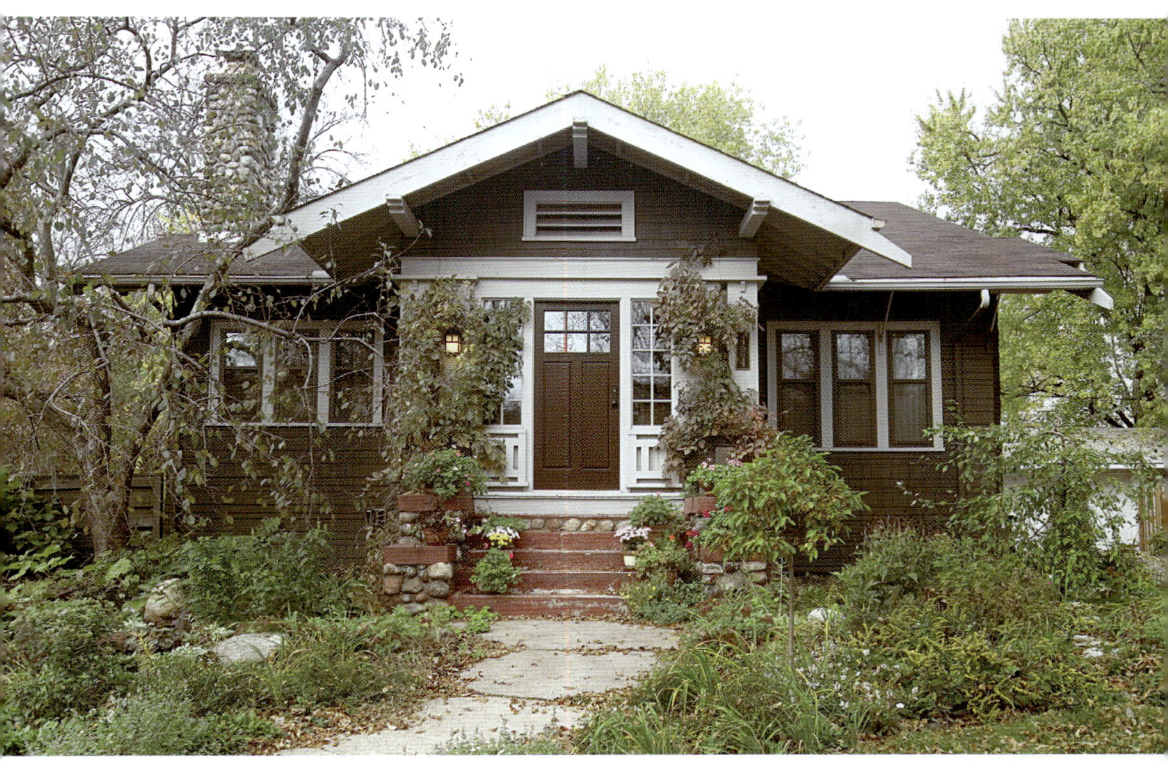

Minneapolis, Minnesota 

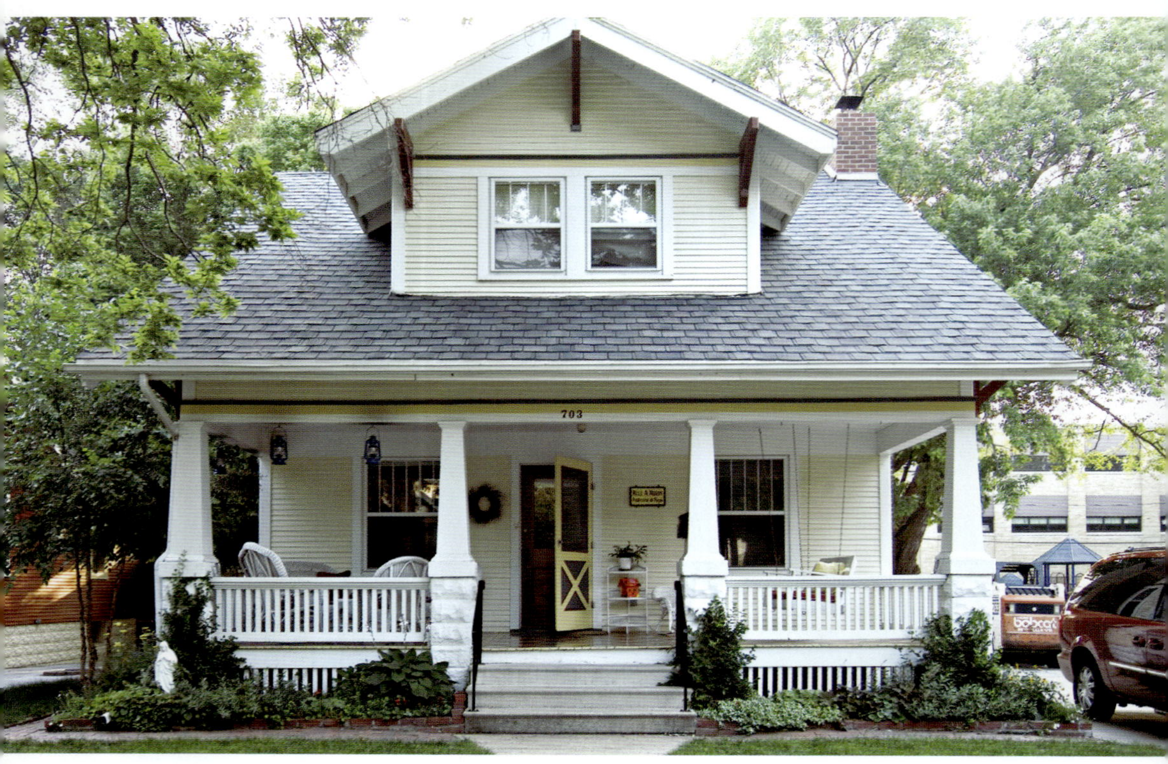
703

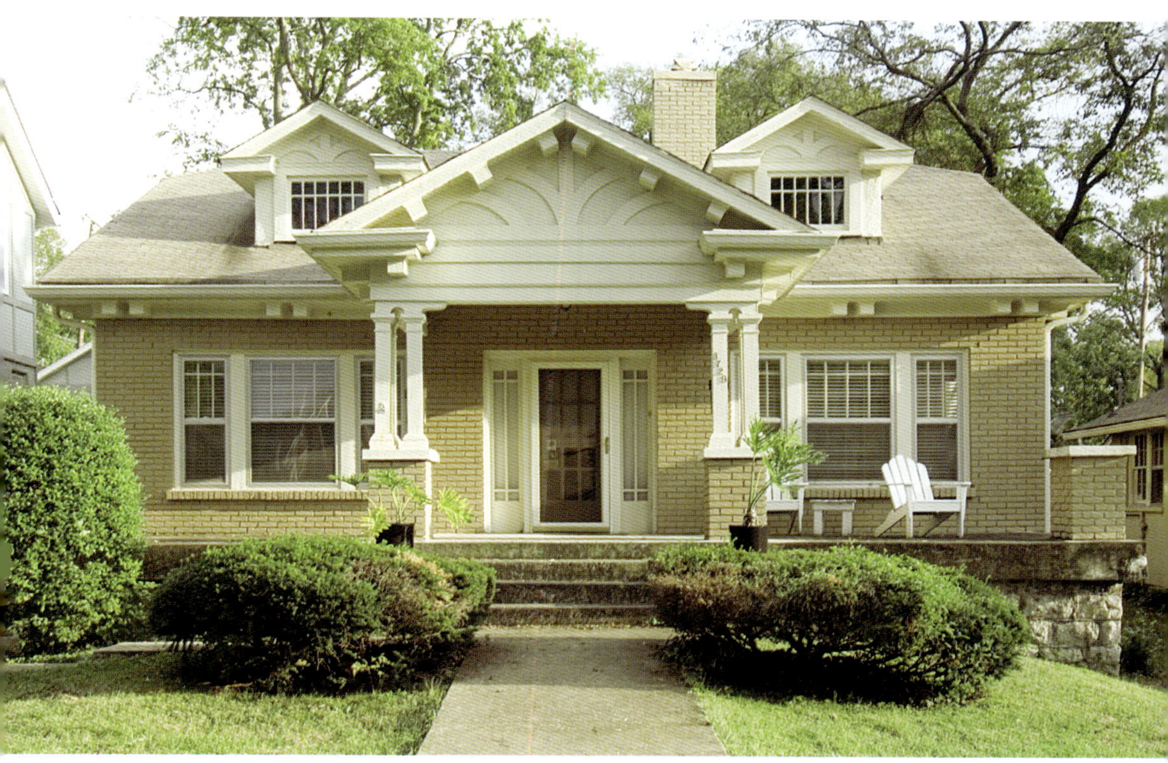

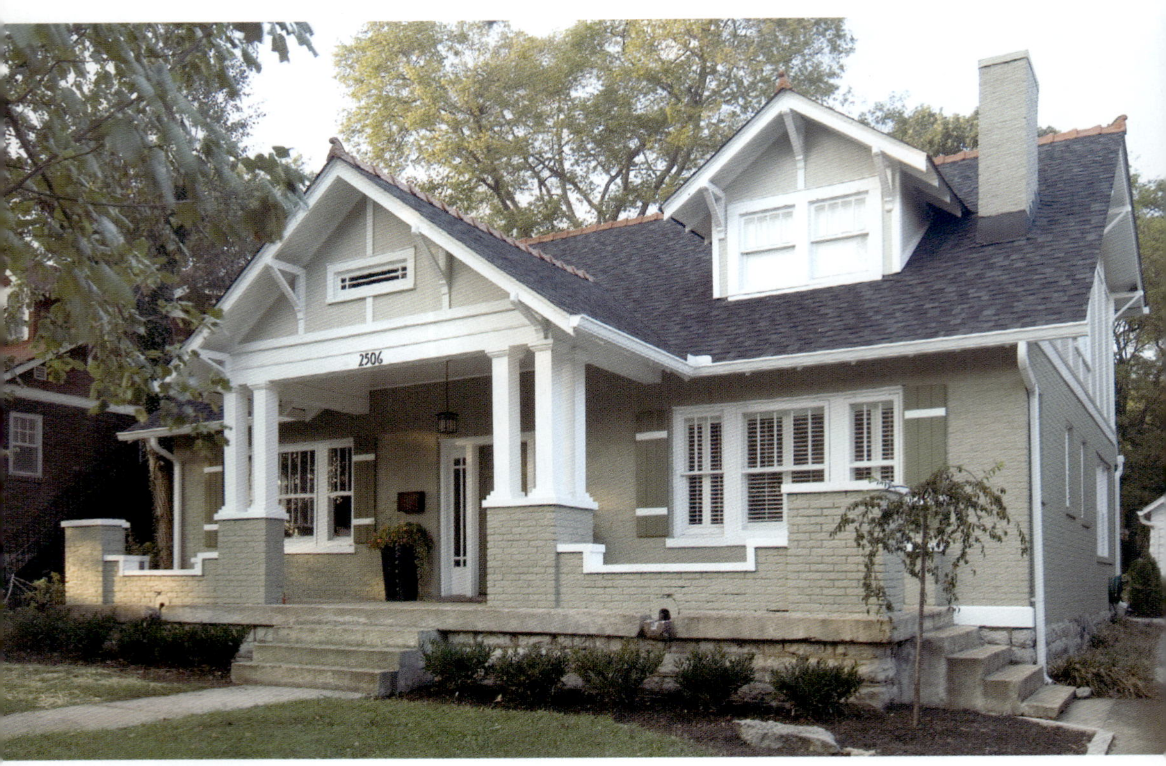
2506

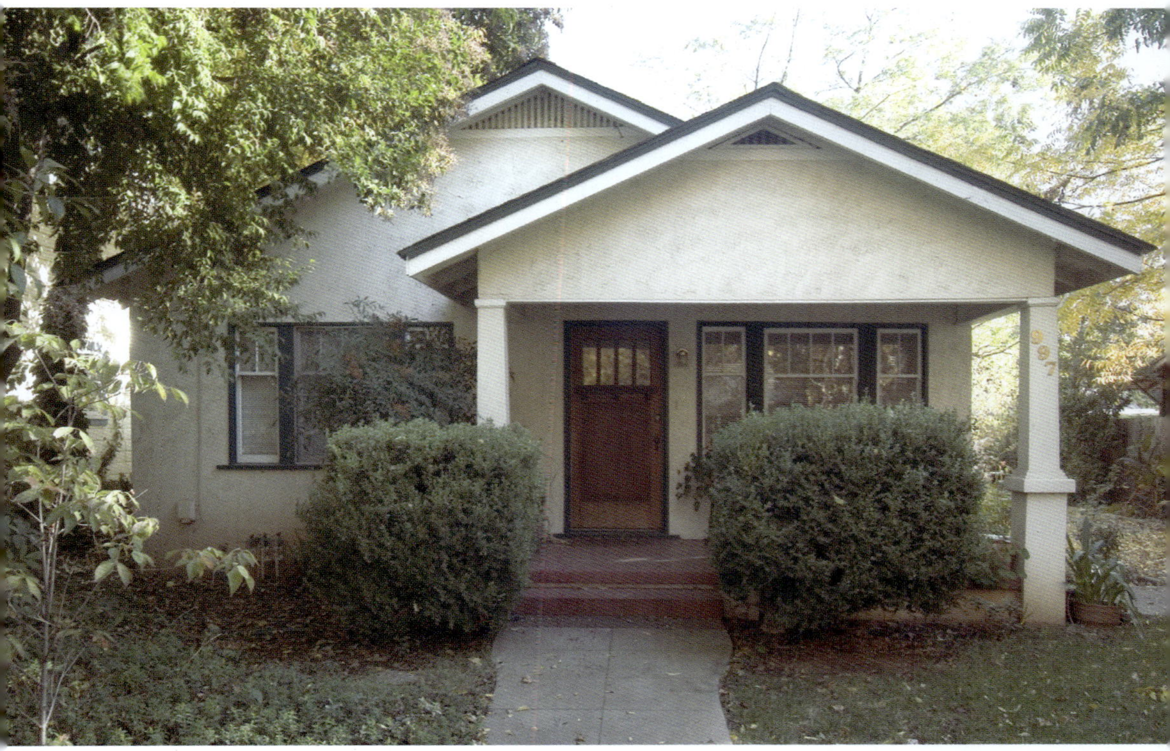


Chico, California

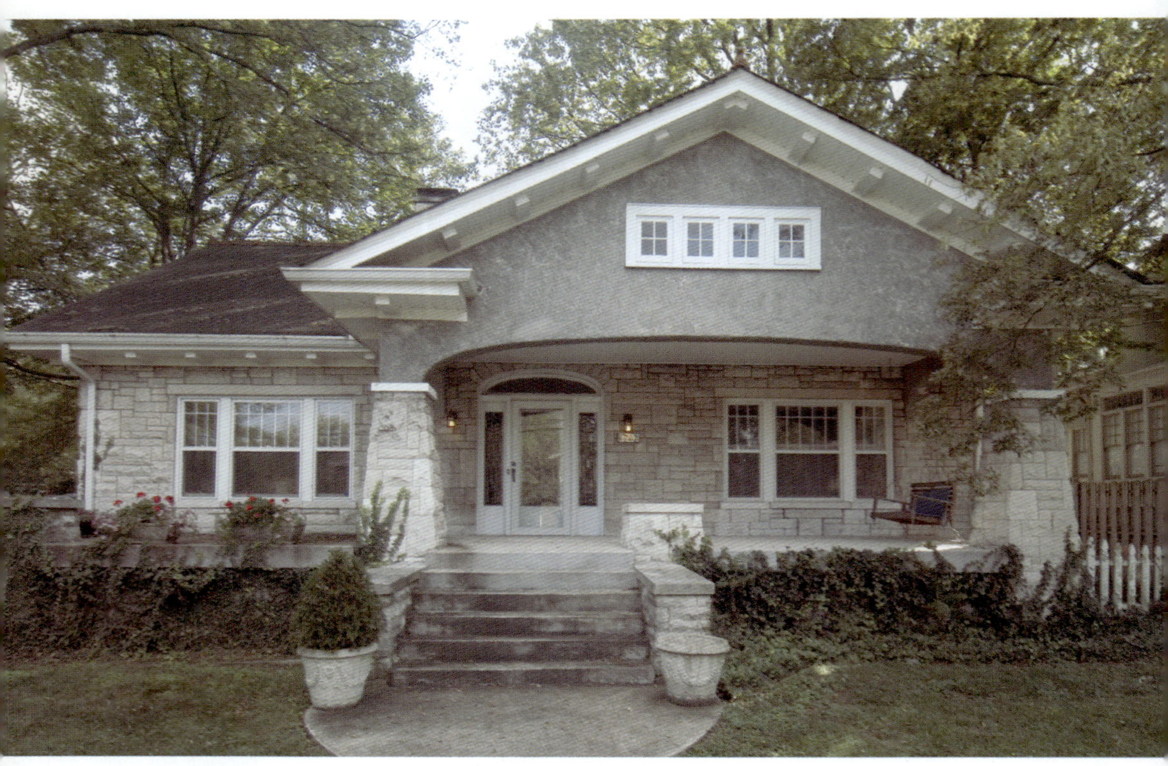

 Nashville, Tennessee

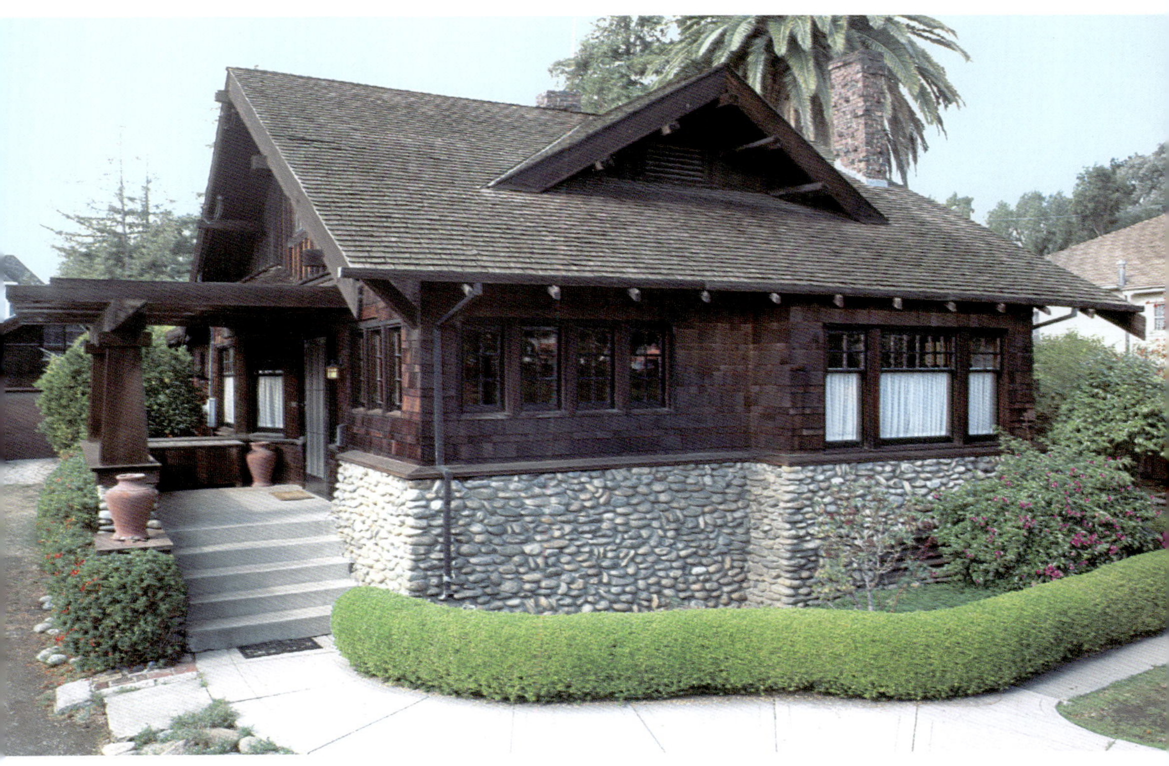

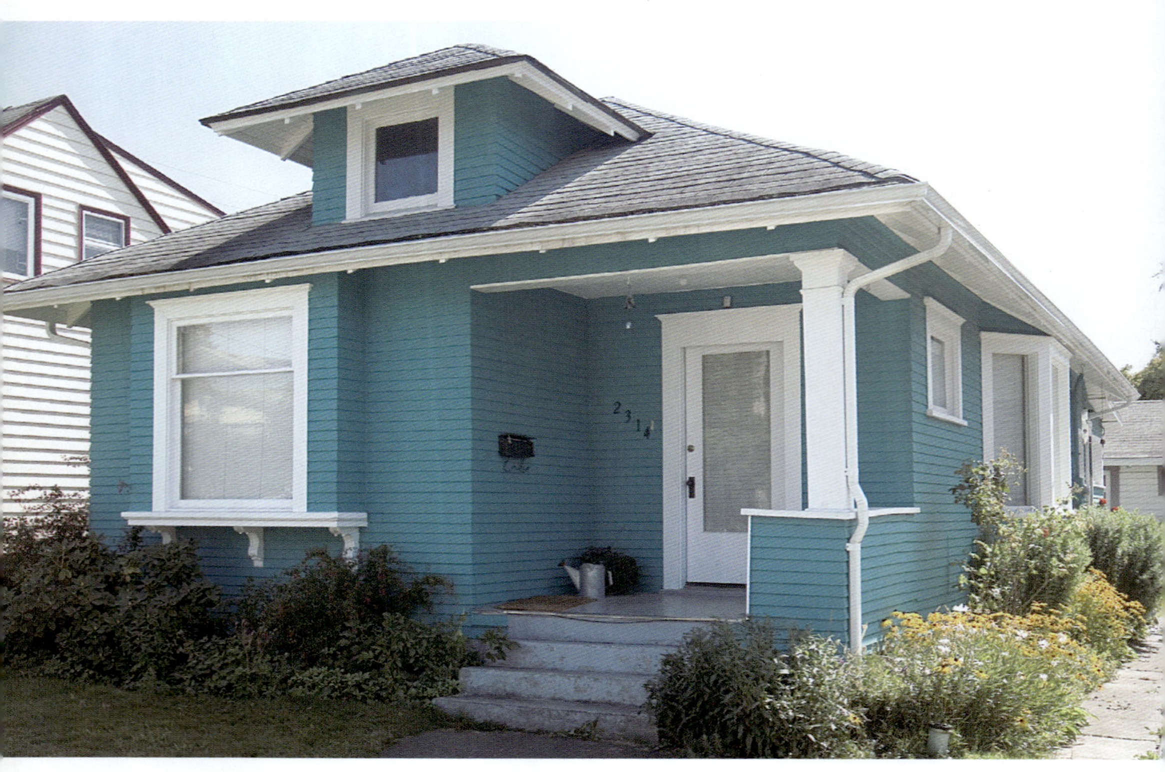


 Bellingham, Washington

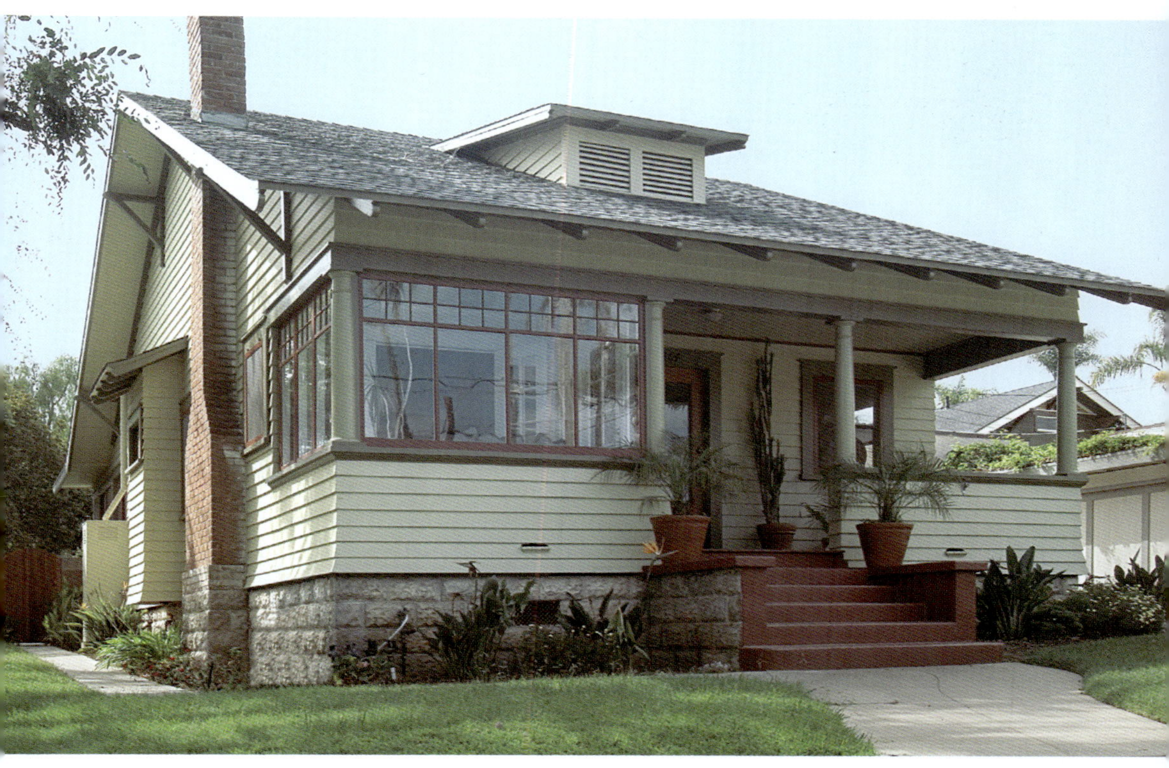

San Diego, California 

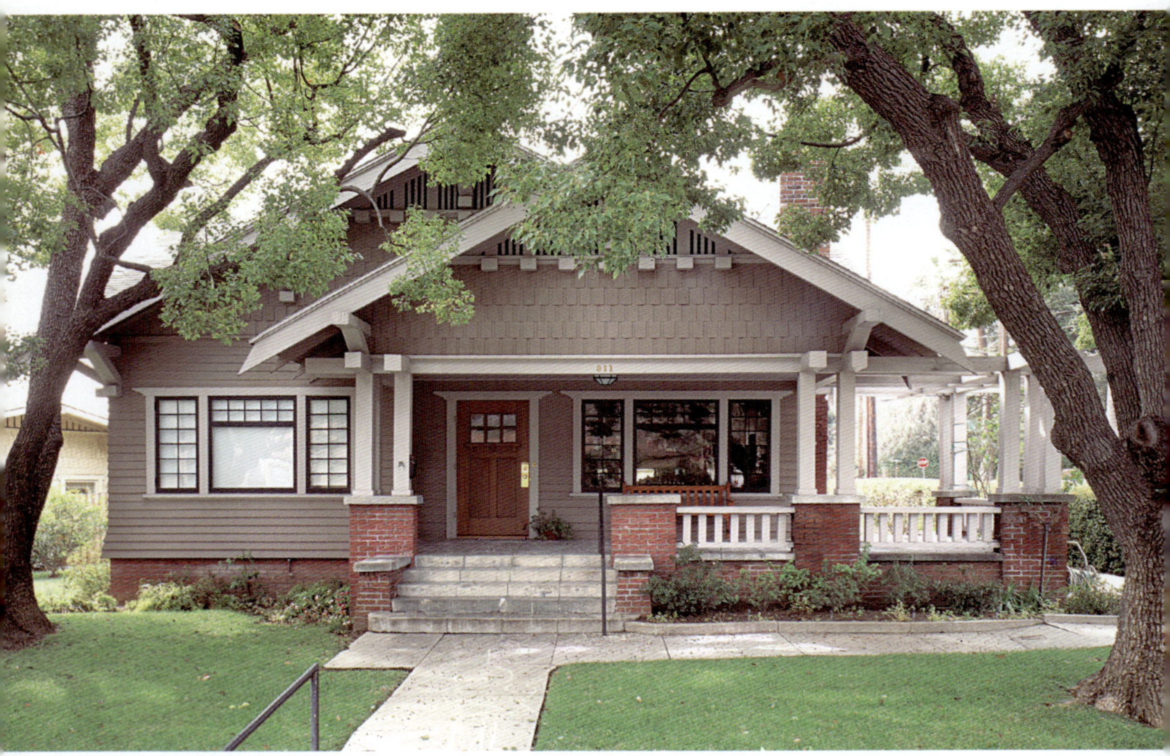

 Monrovia, California

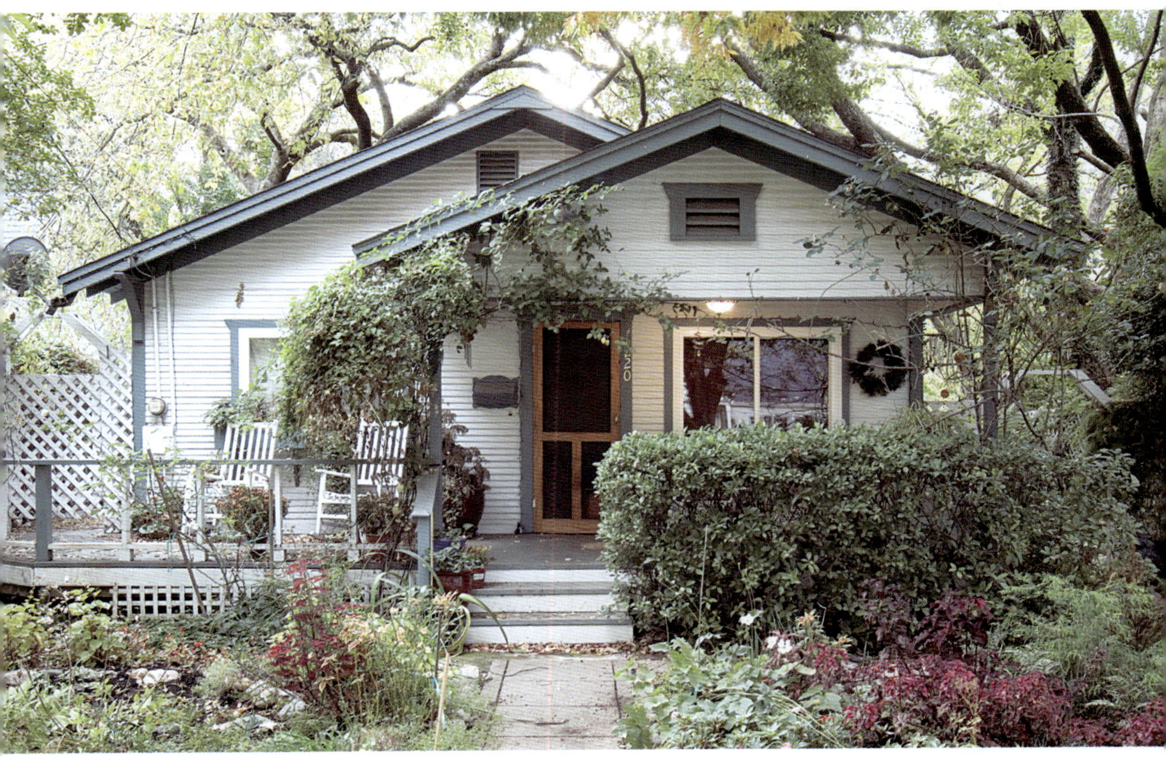

Chico, California

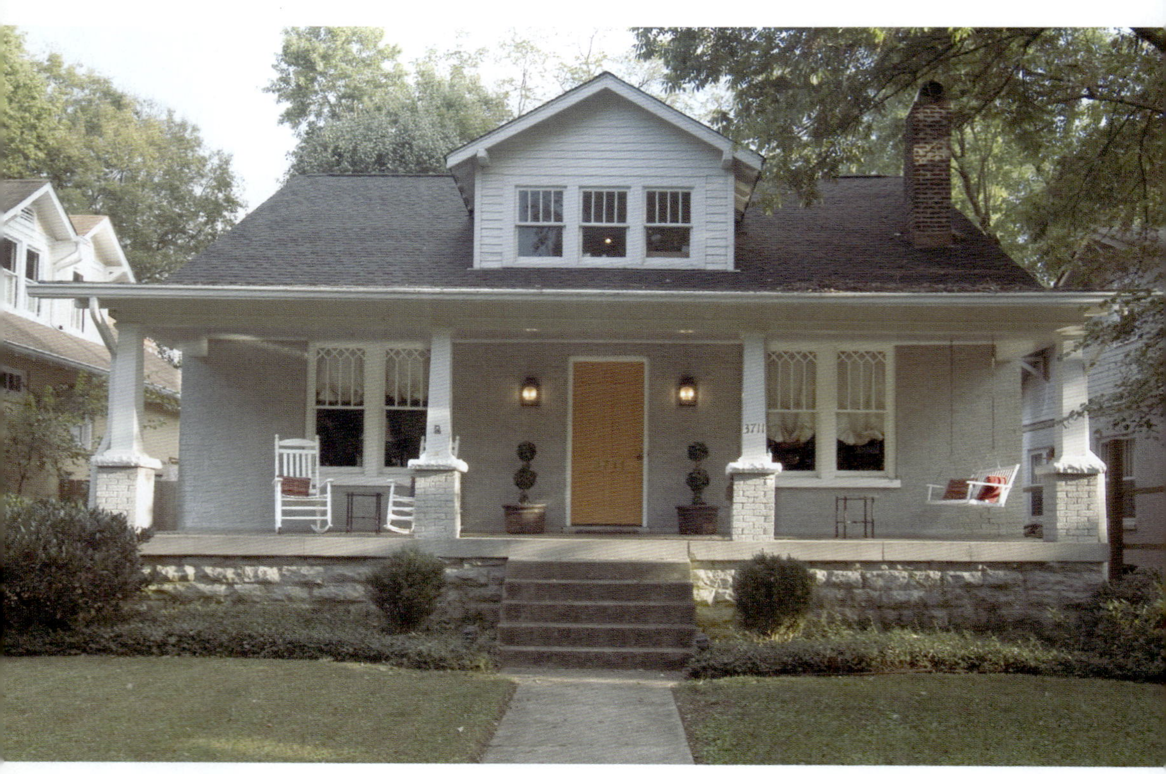
3711

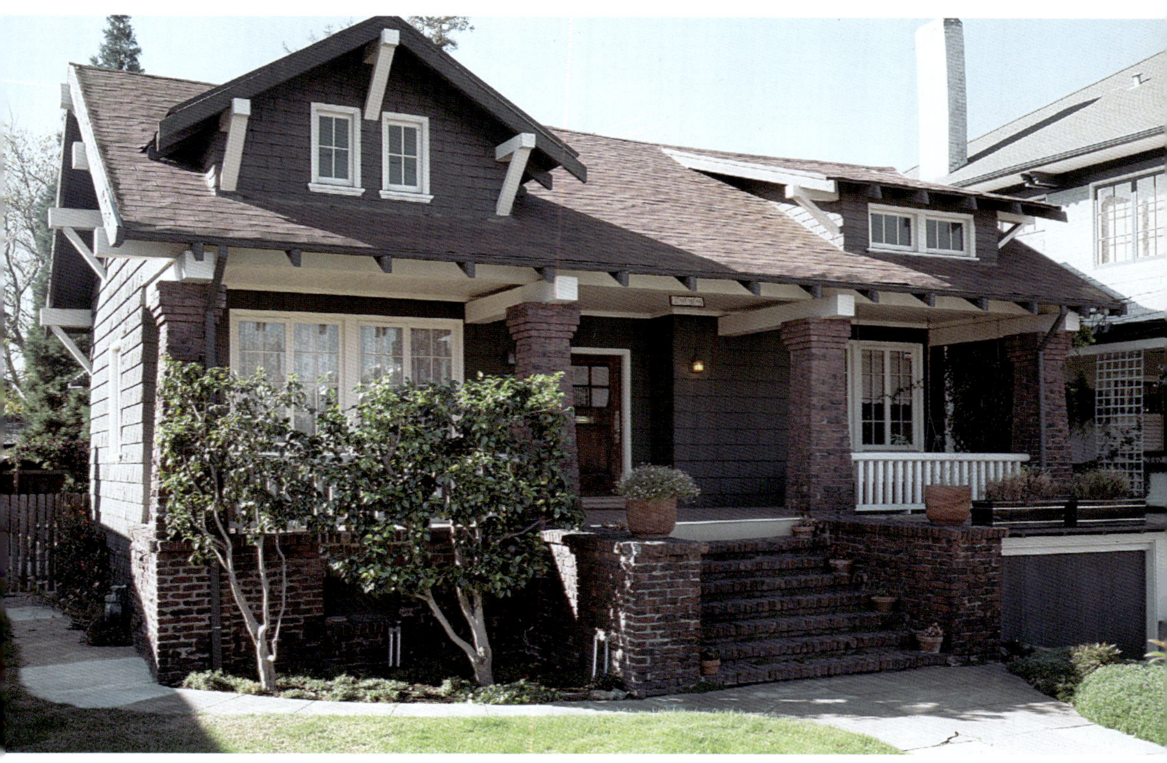

Alameda, California

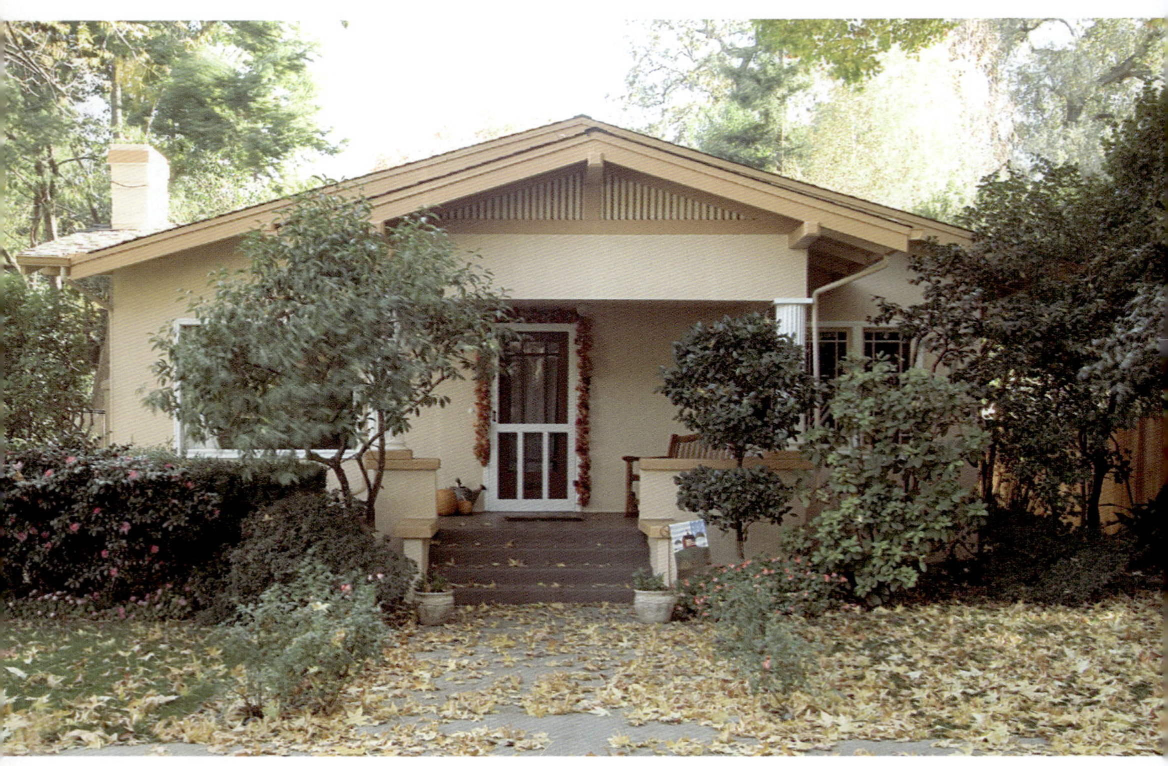

 Chico, California

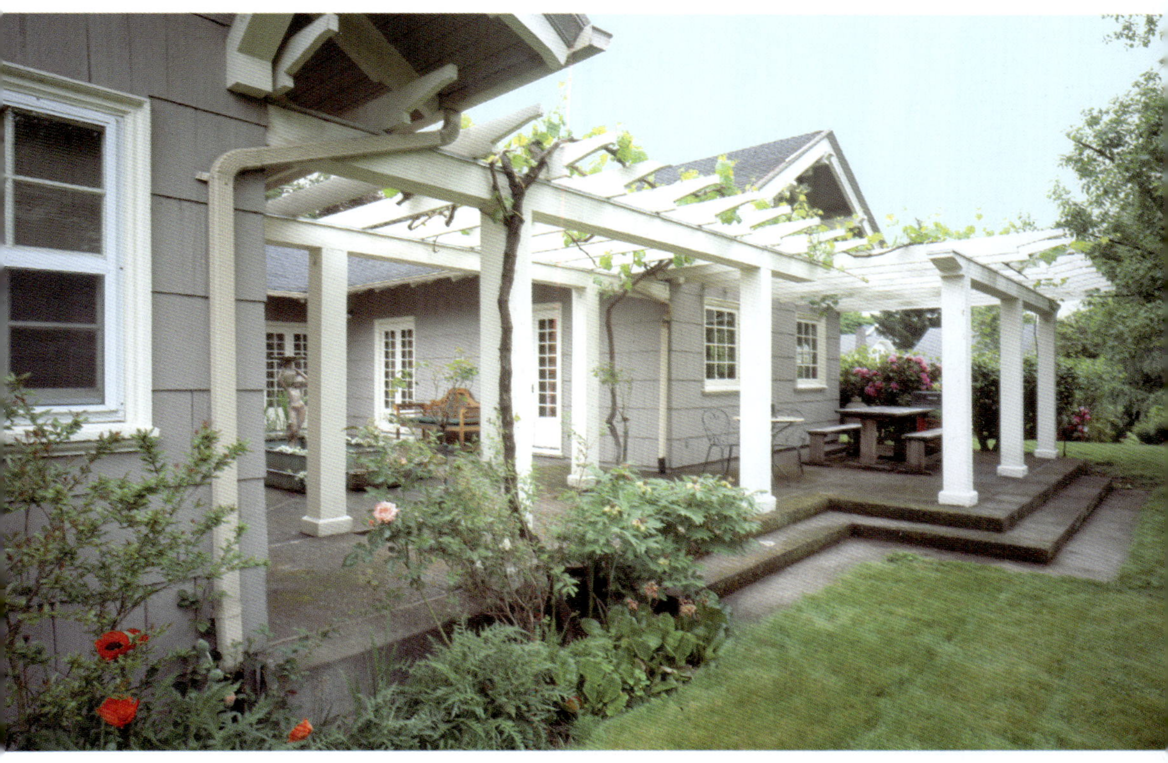

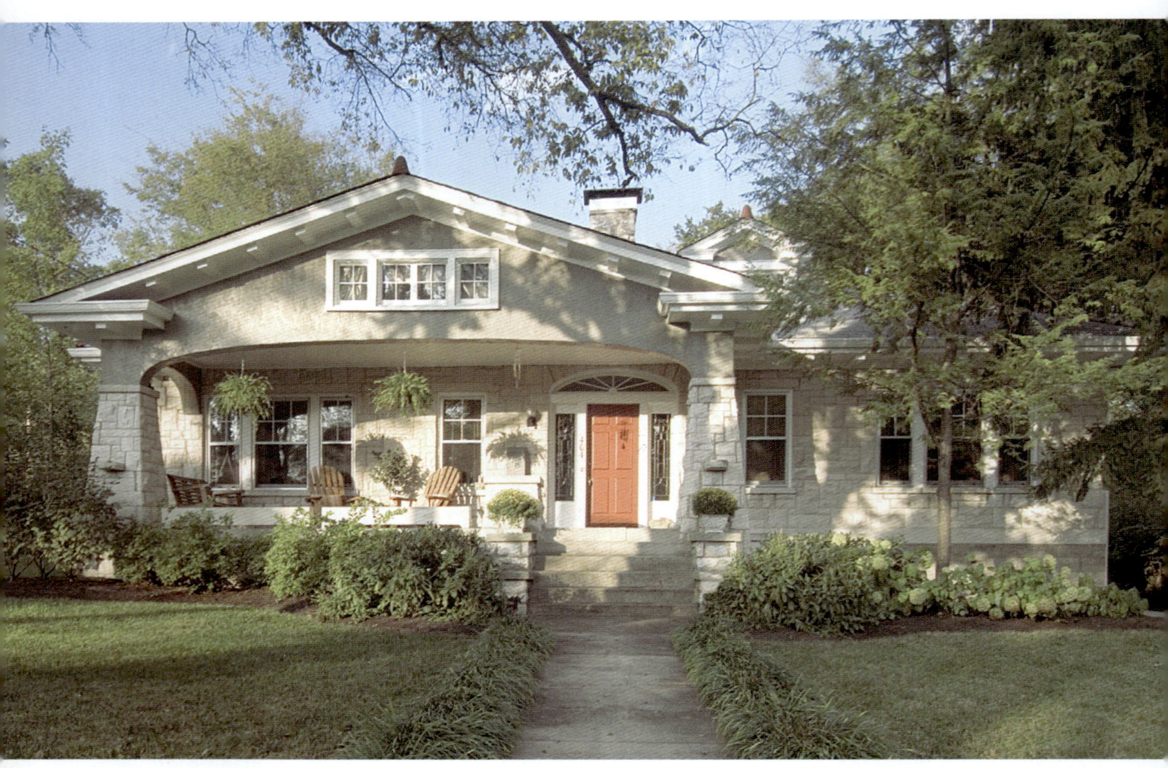

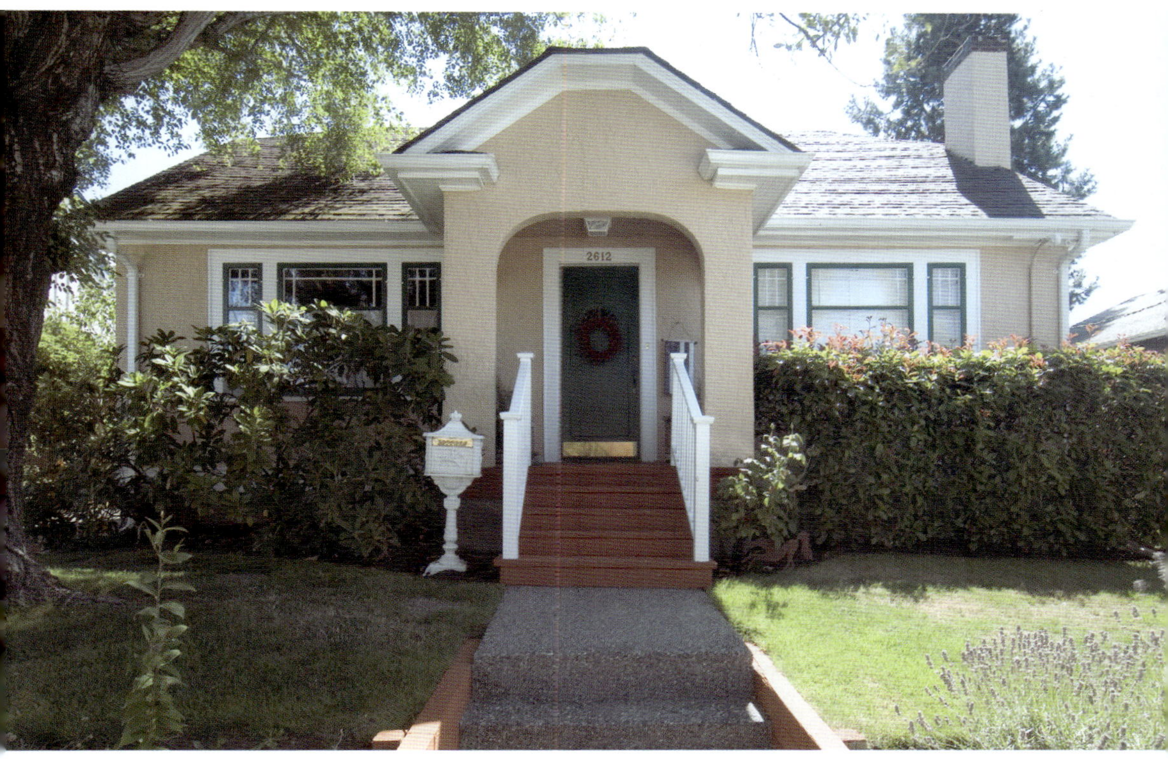


Bellingham, Washington

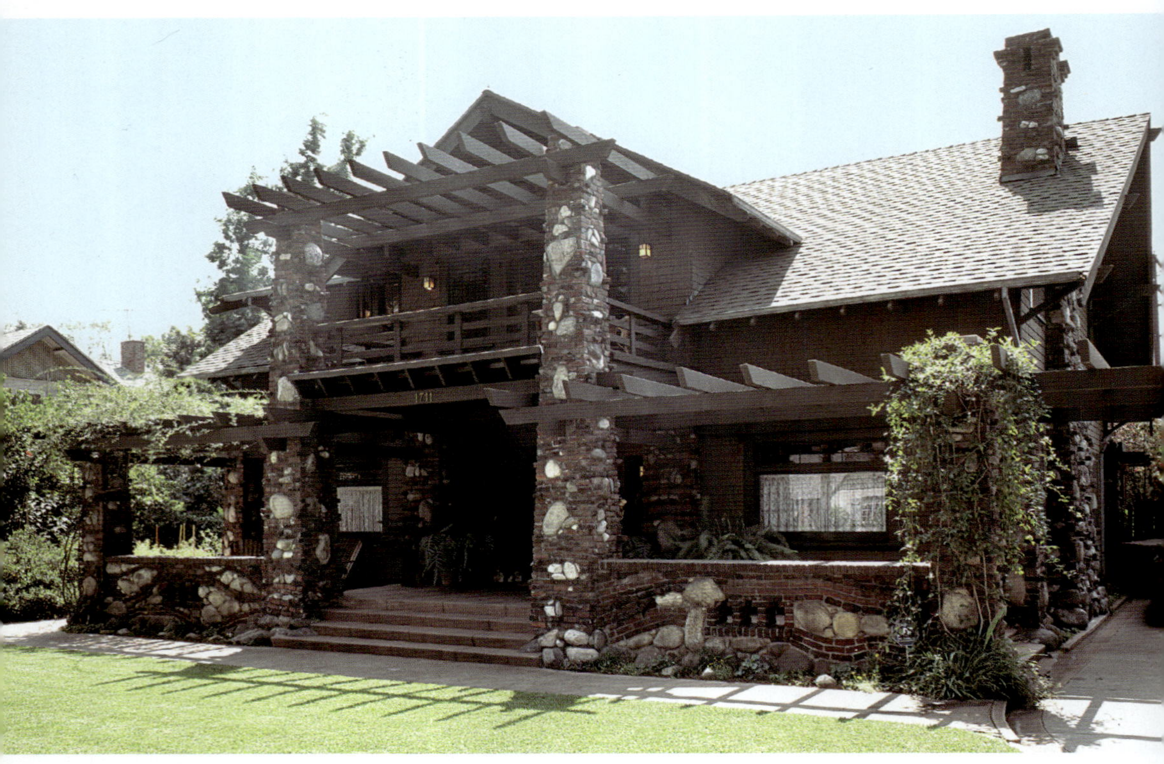
1711

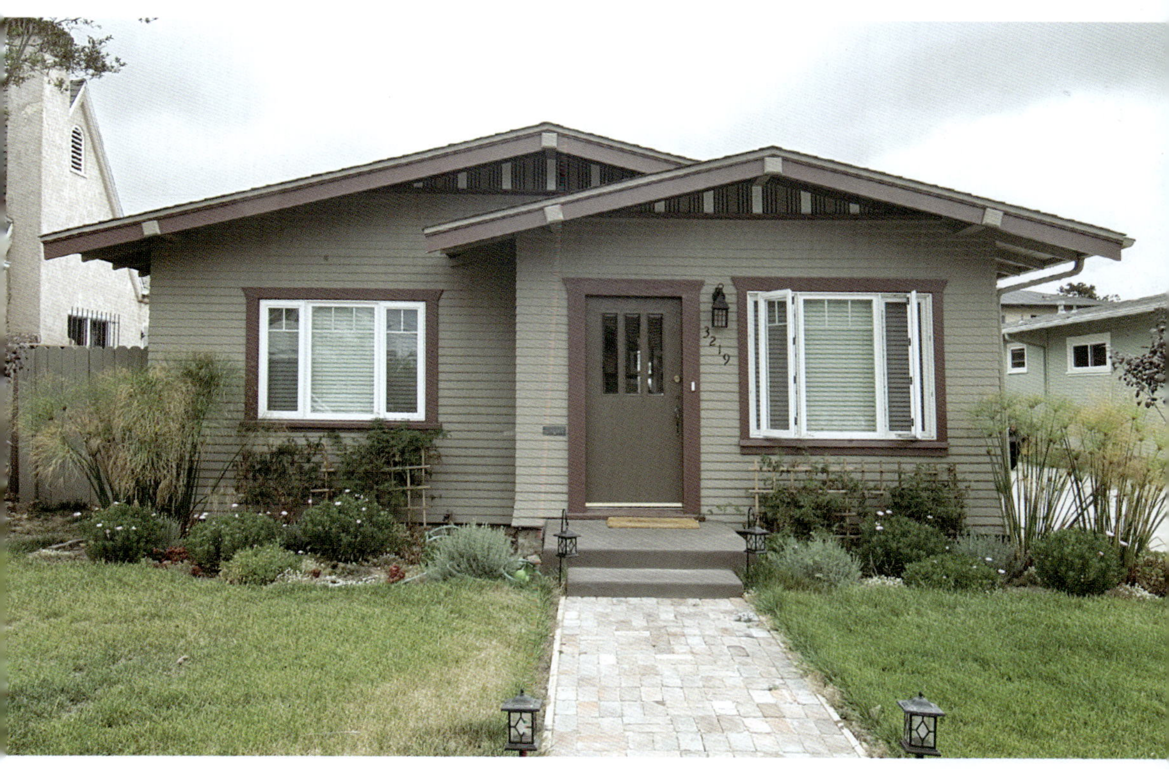


San Diego, California

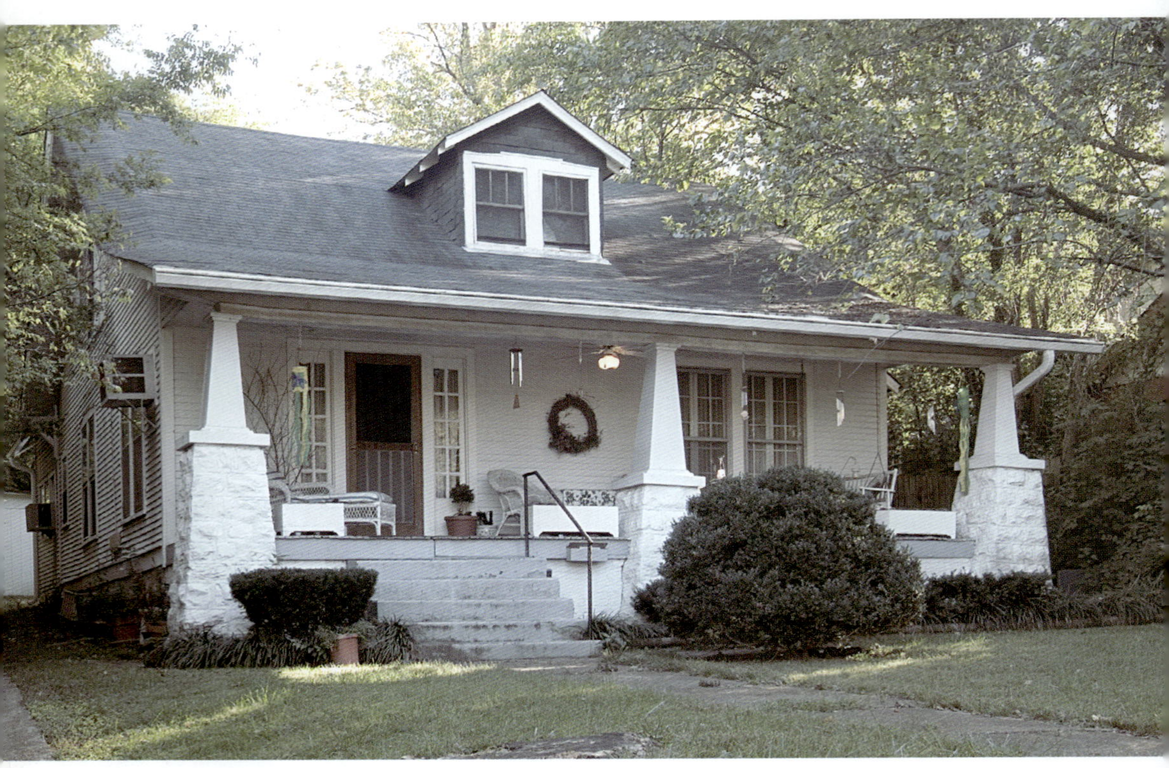

 Nashville, Tennessee

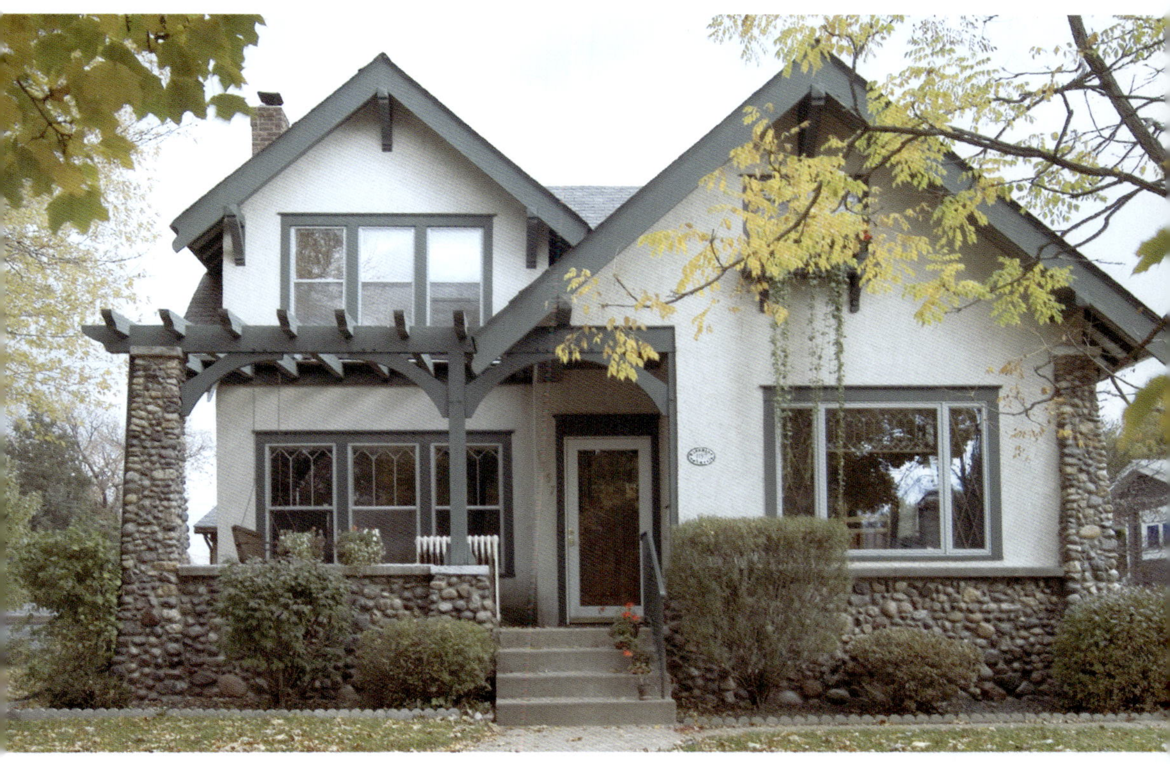

St. Paul, Minnesota

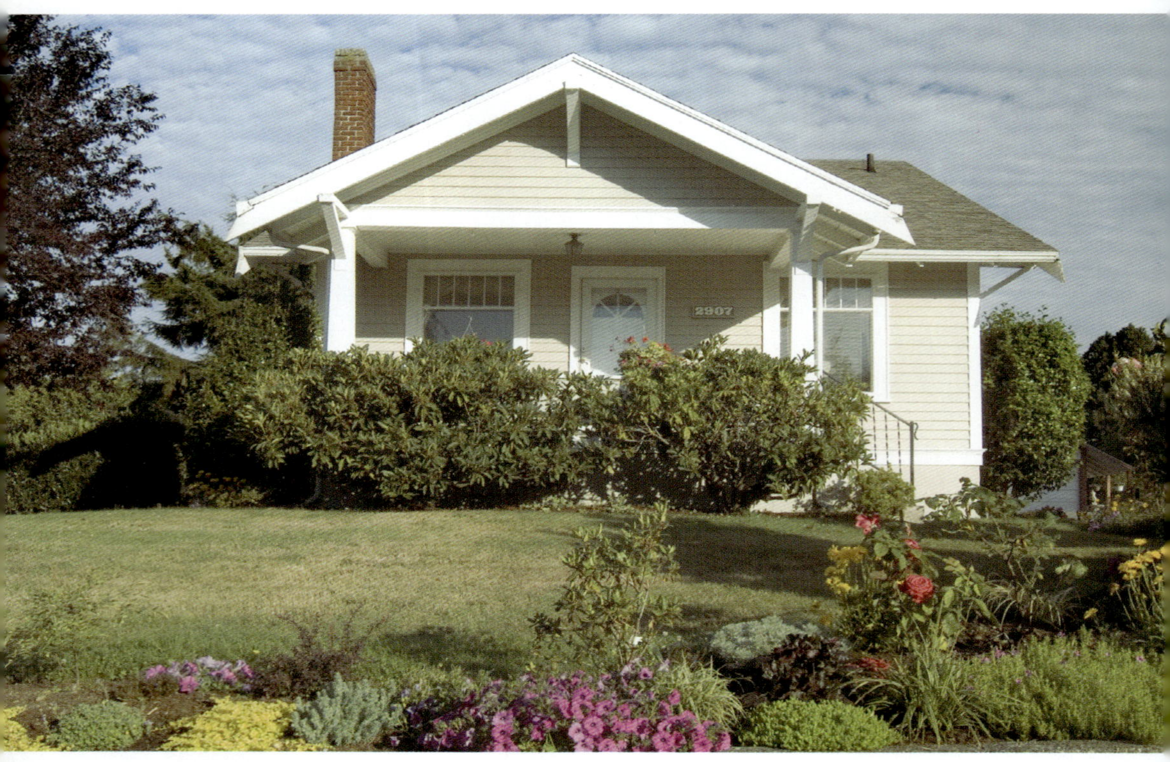


 Bellingham, Washington

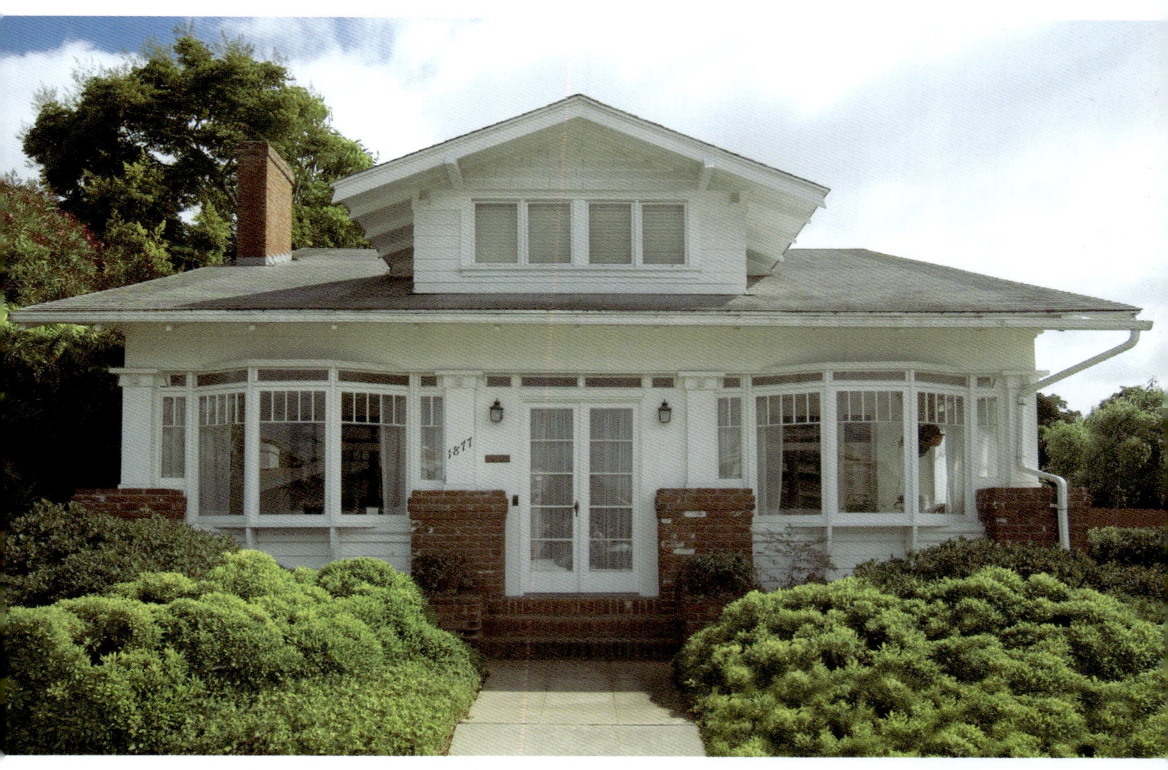


SAN DIEGO, CALIFORNIA

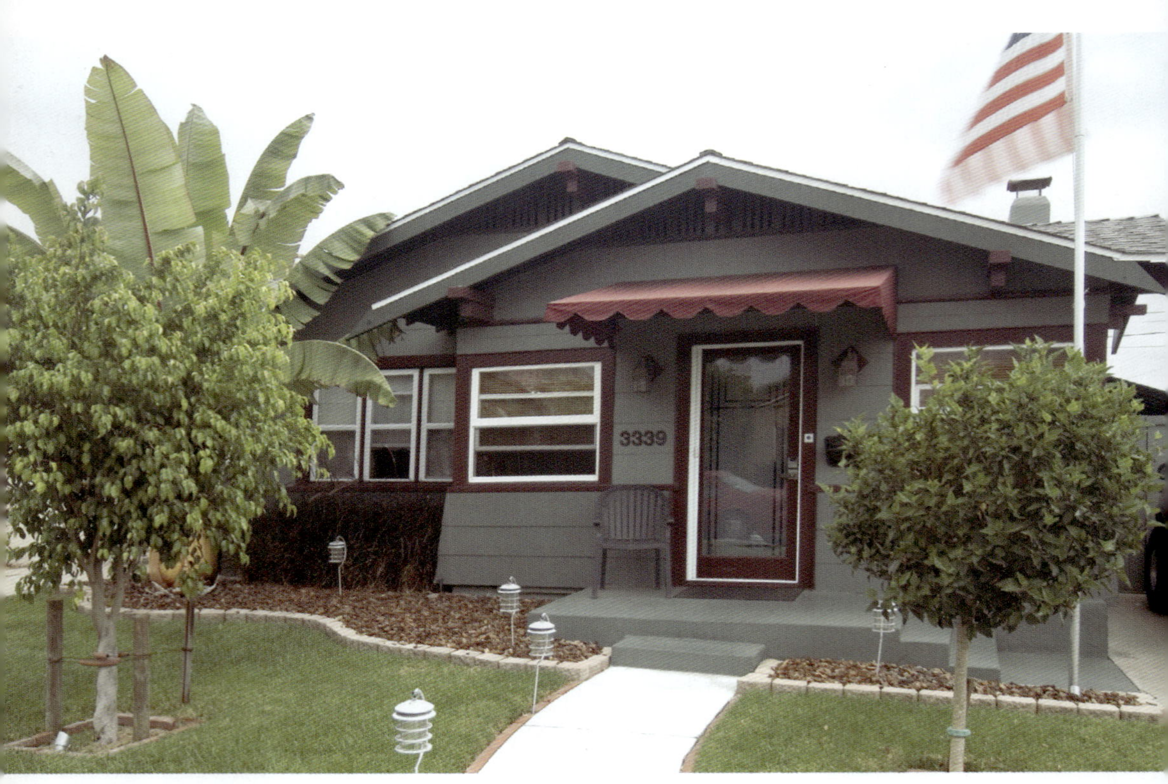


 San Diego, California

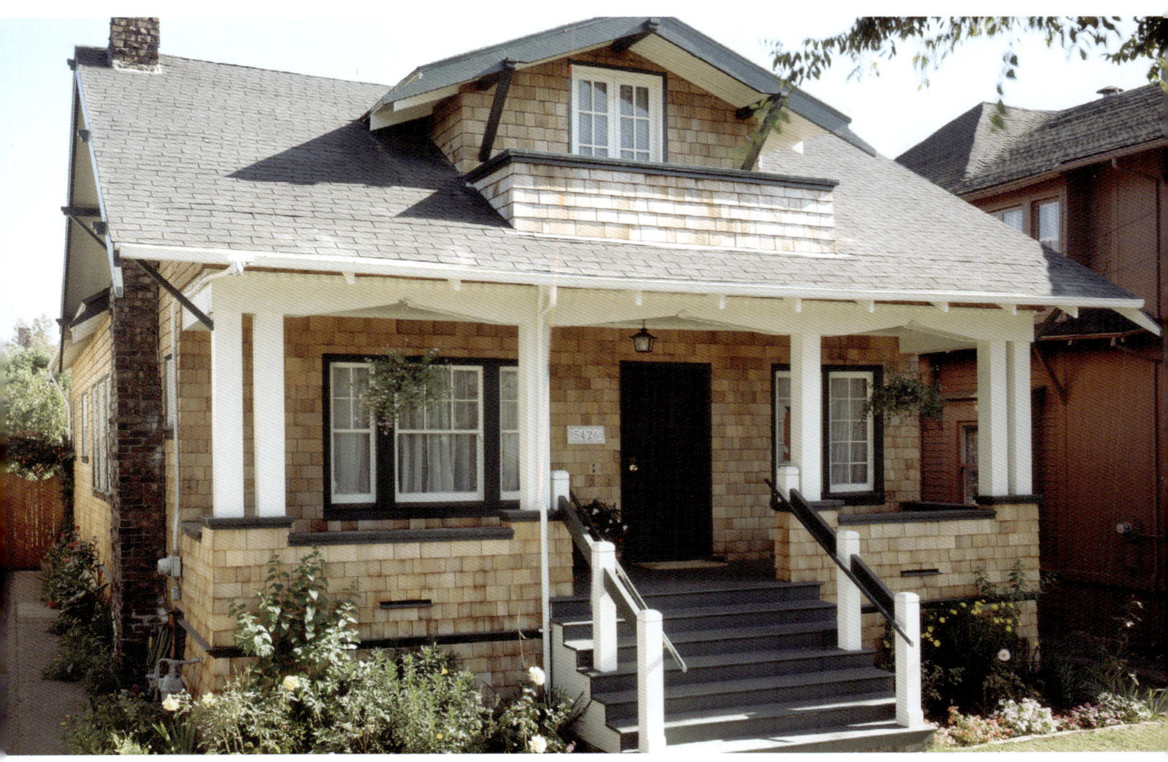


Oakland, California 

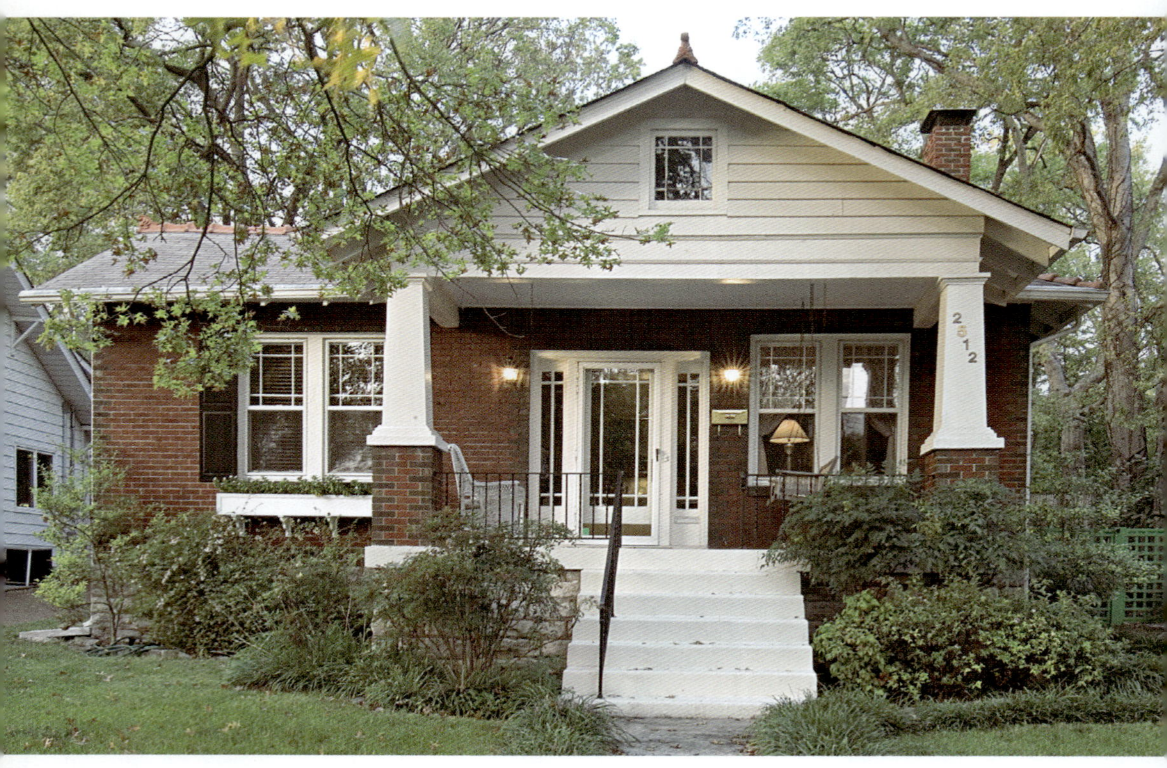


 Nashville, Tennessee

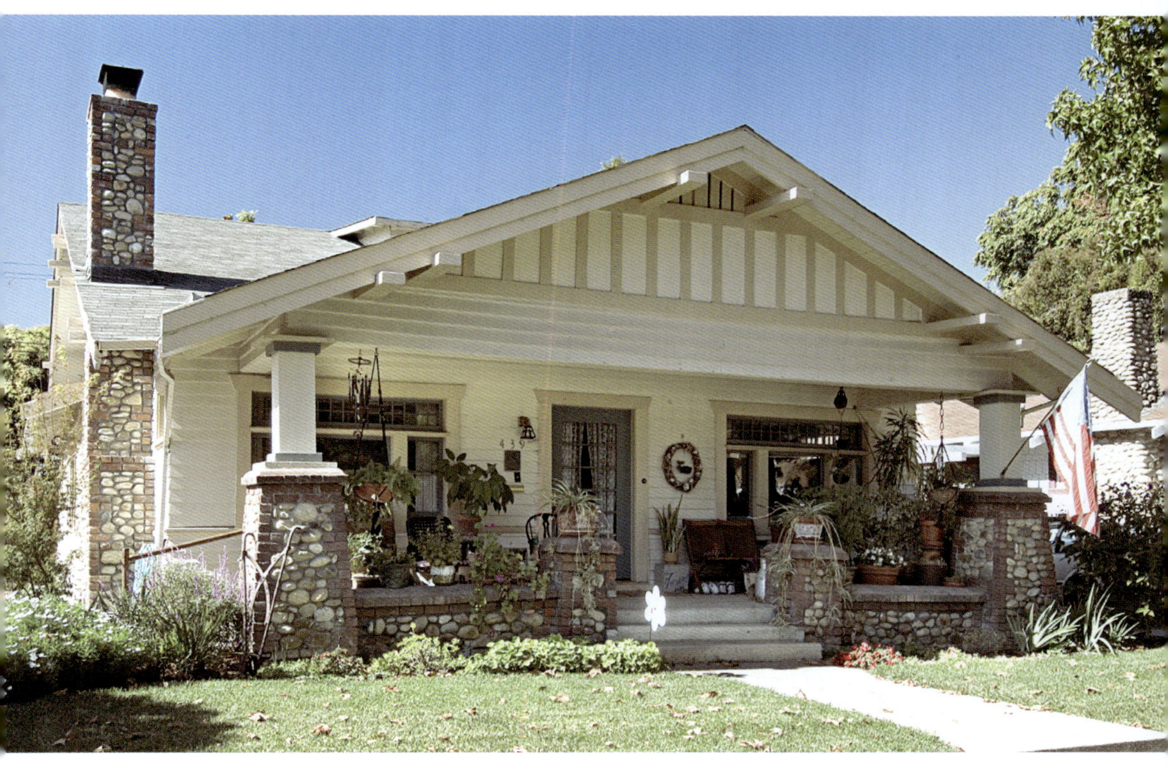

San Jose, California

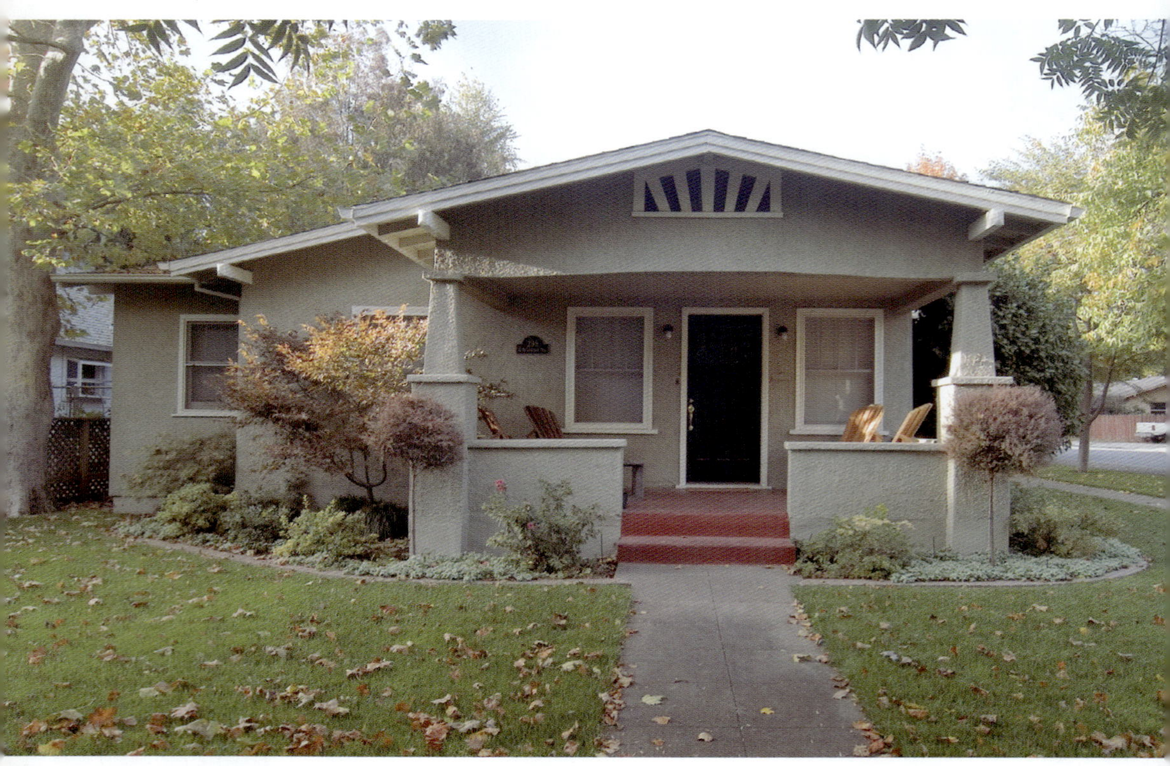

 Chico, California

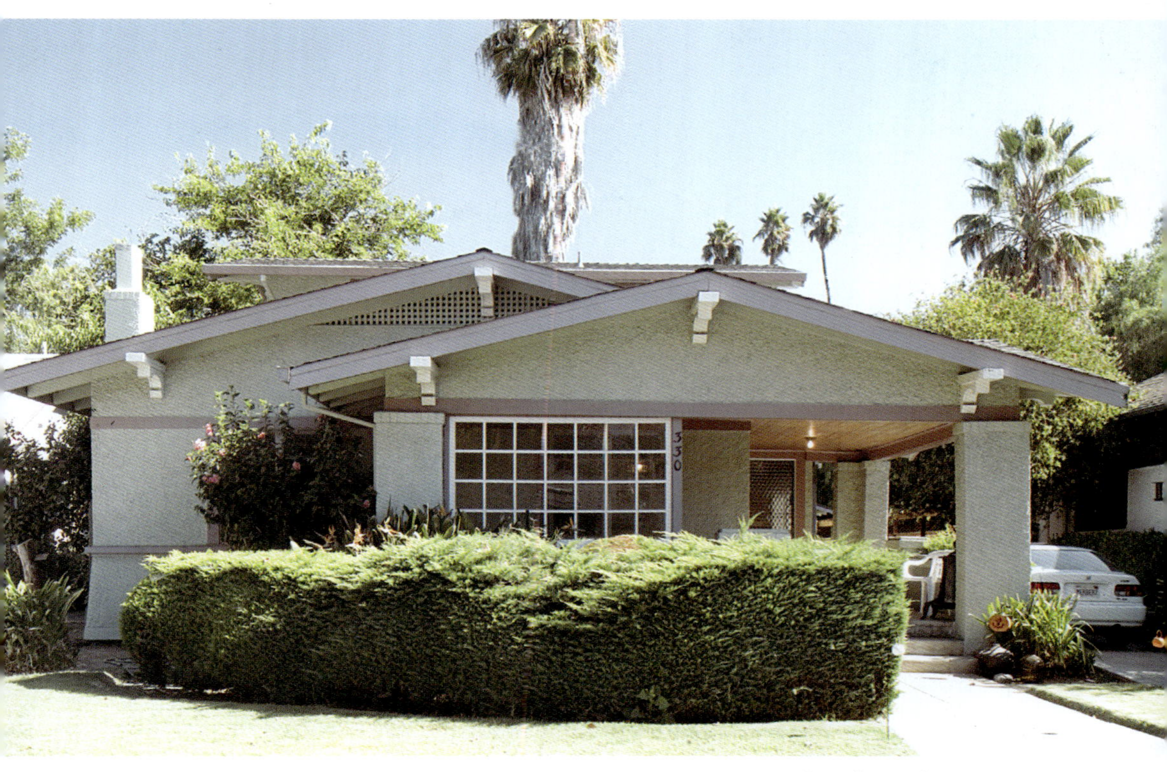


San Jose, California 

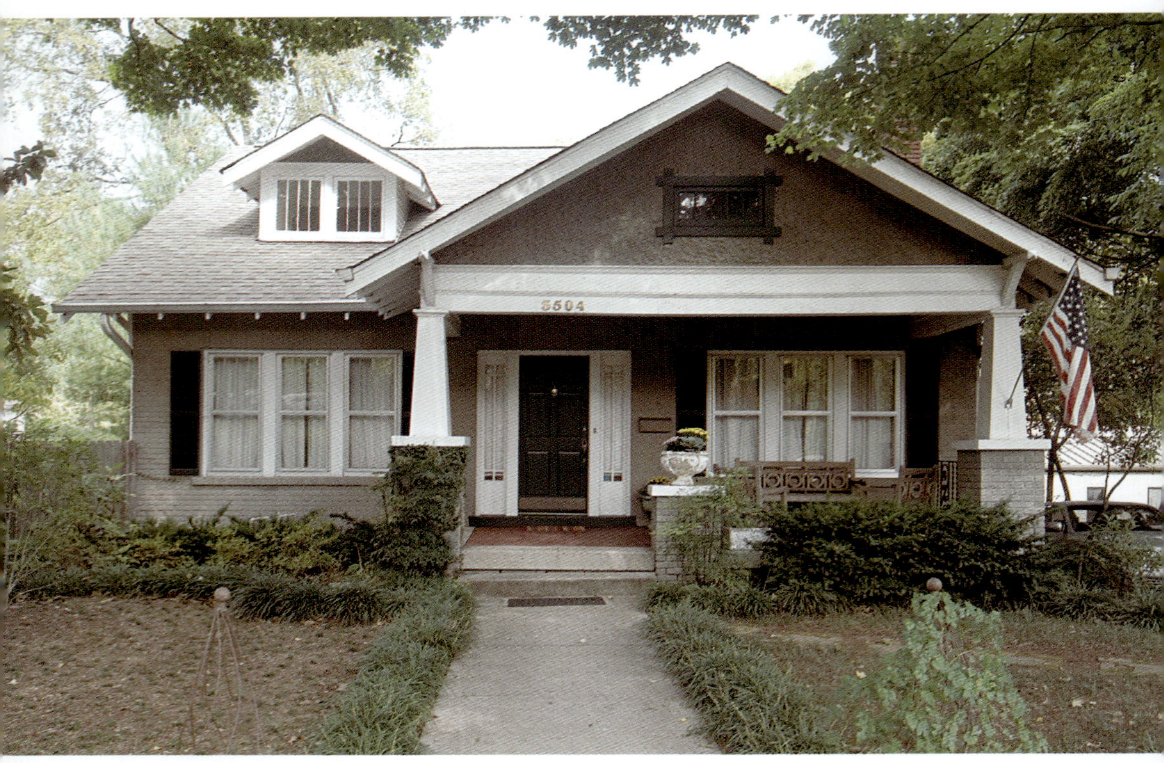


 Nashville, Tennessee

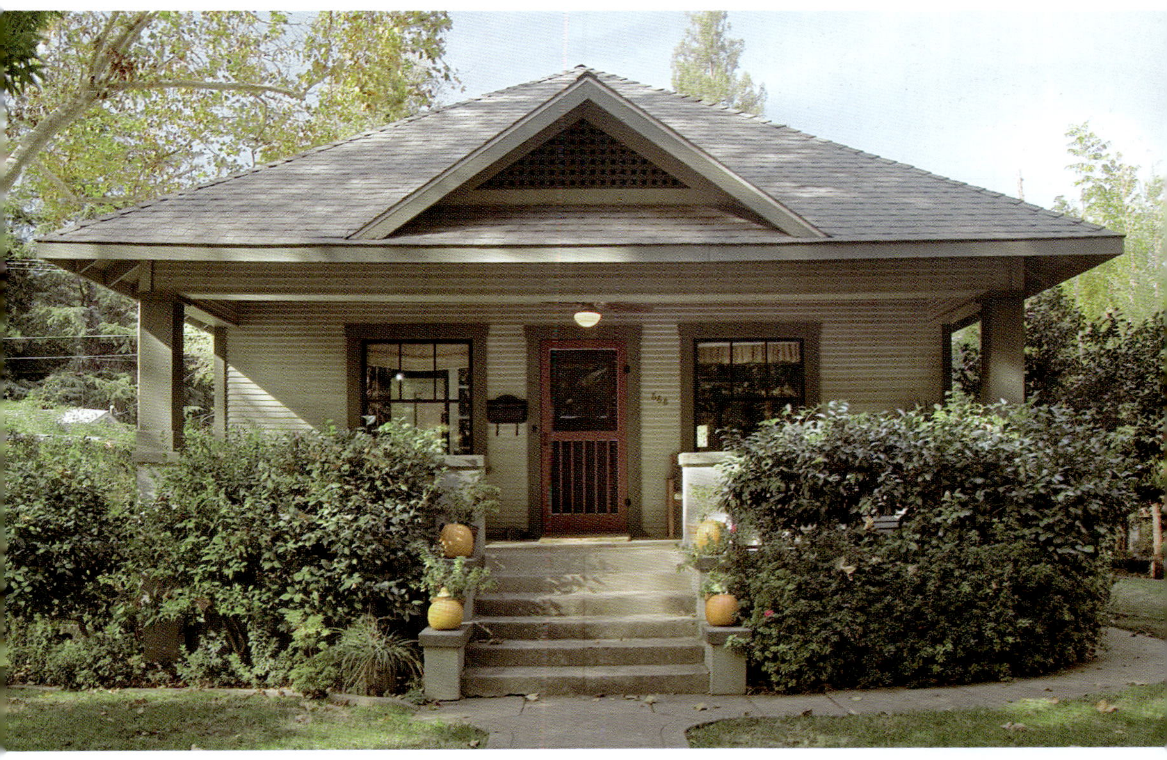

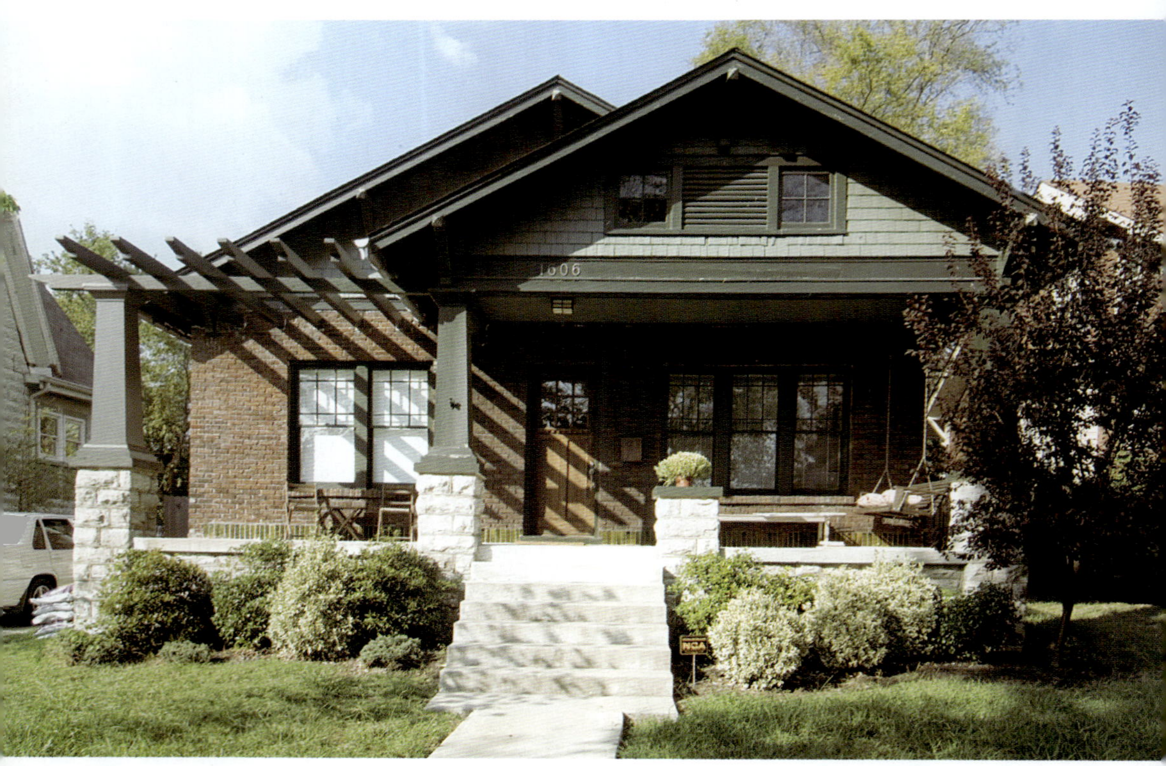

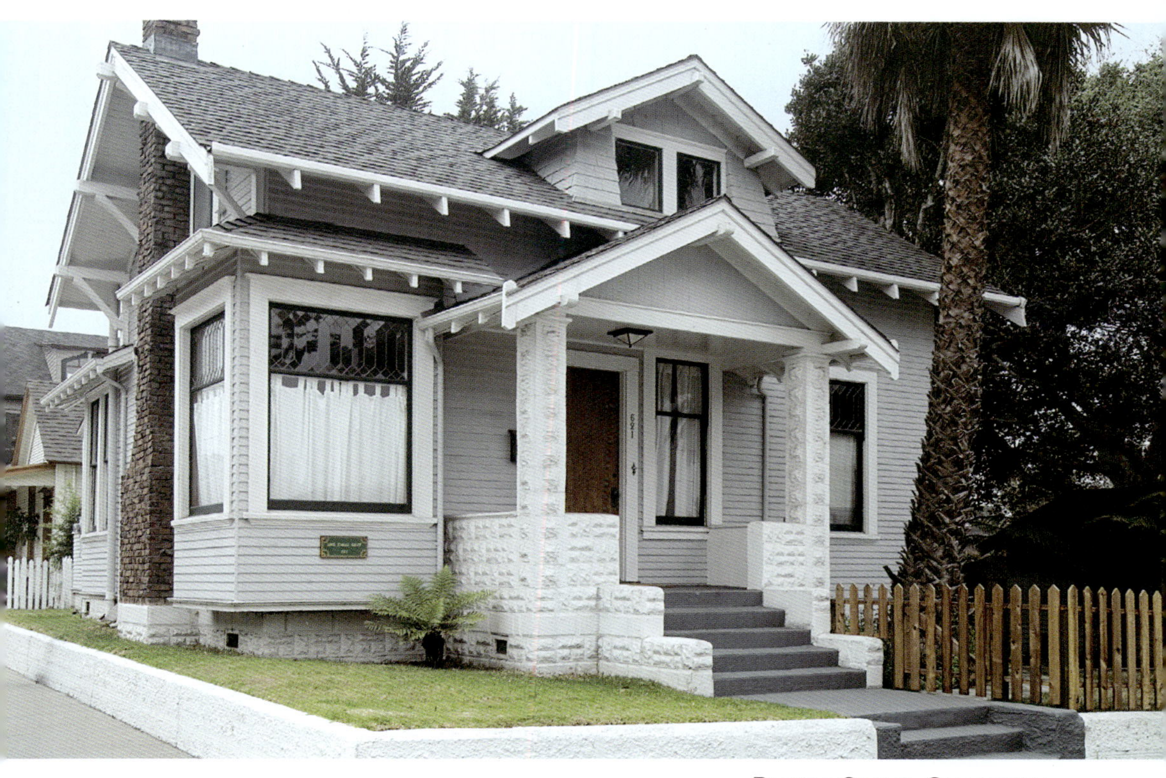

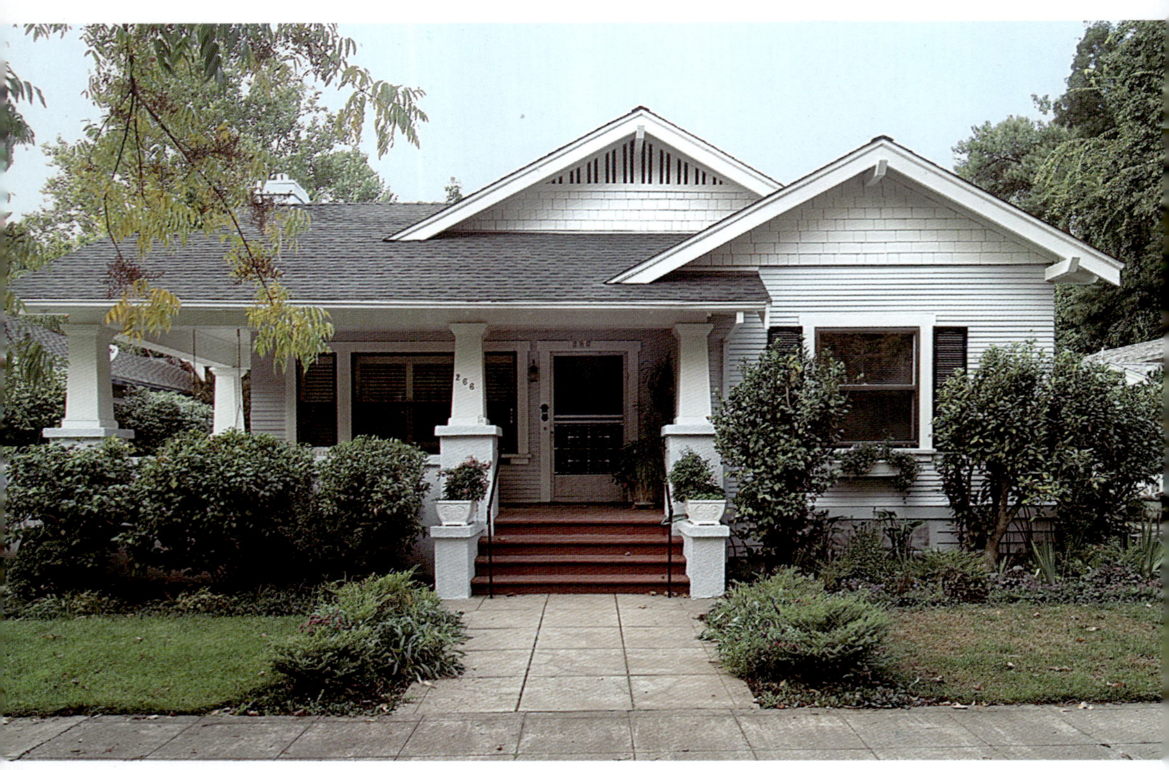


 Chico, California

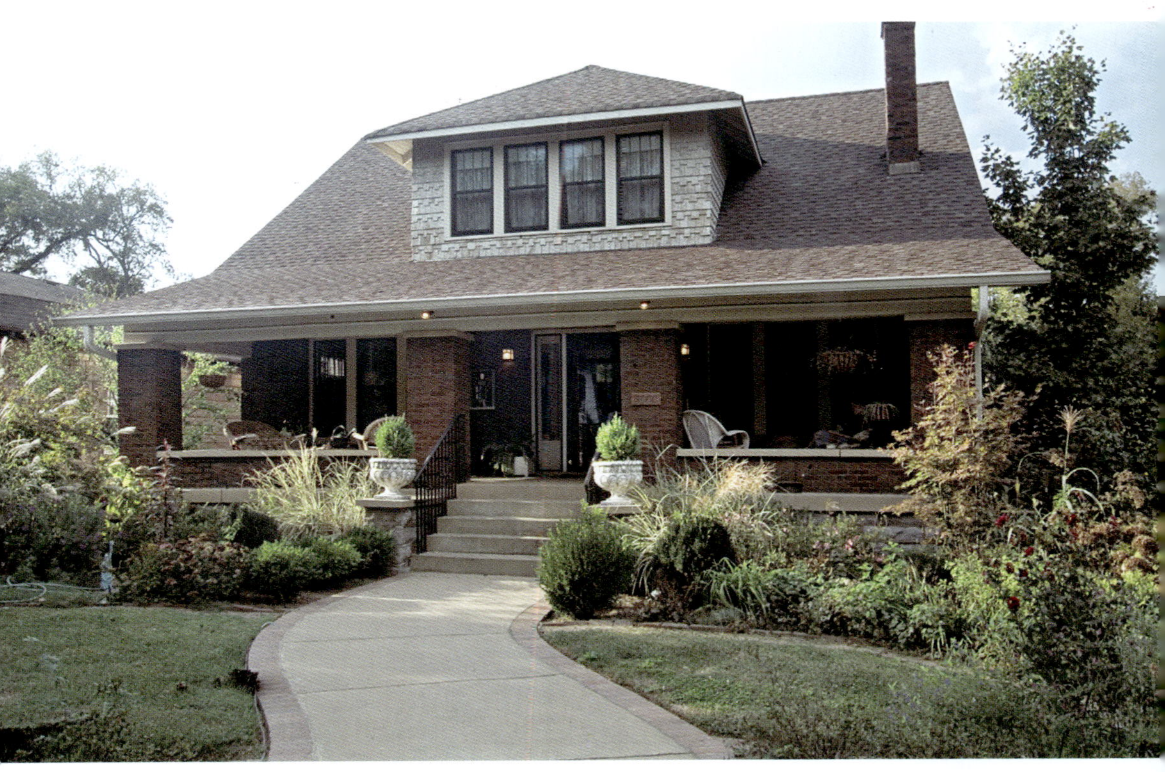

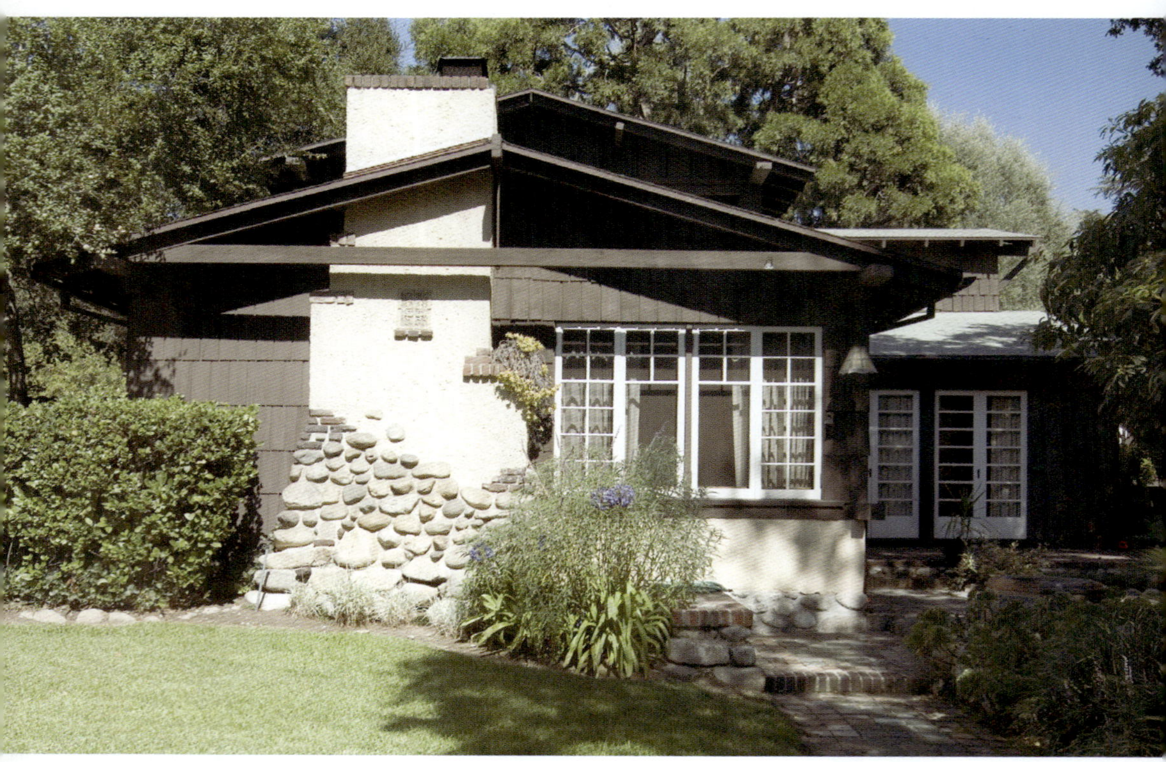

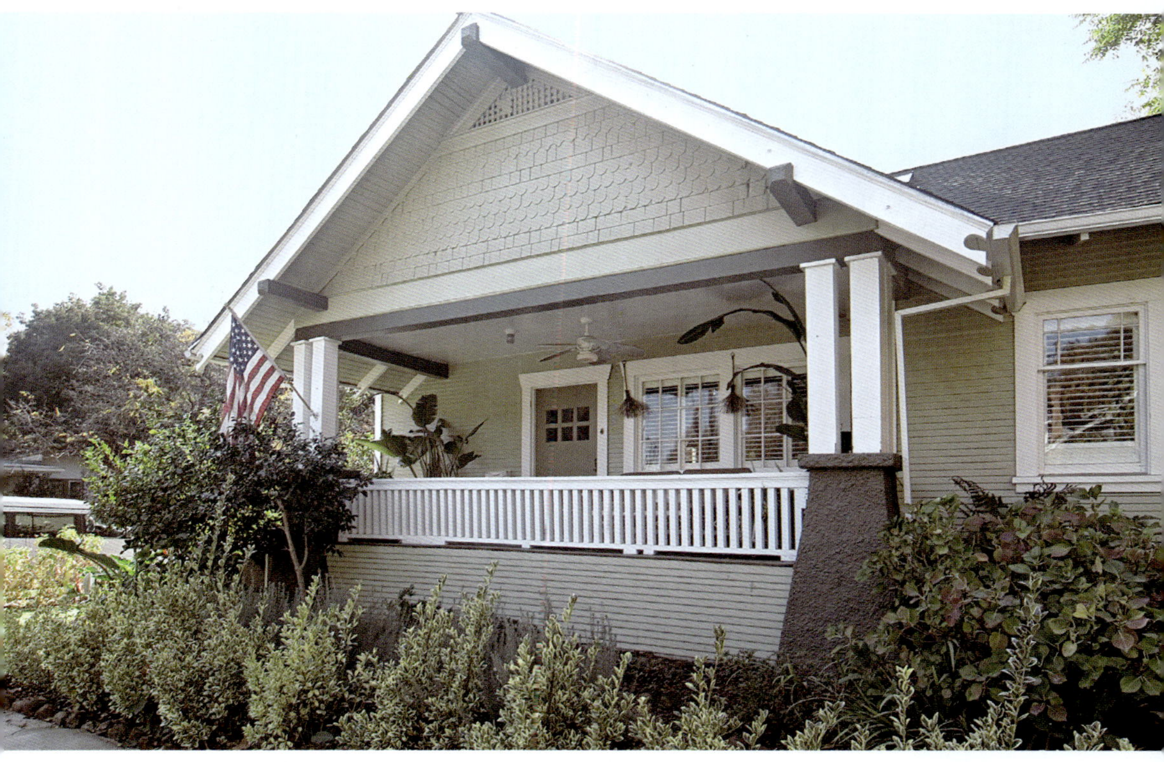

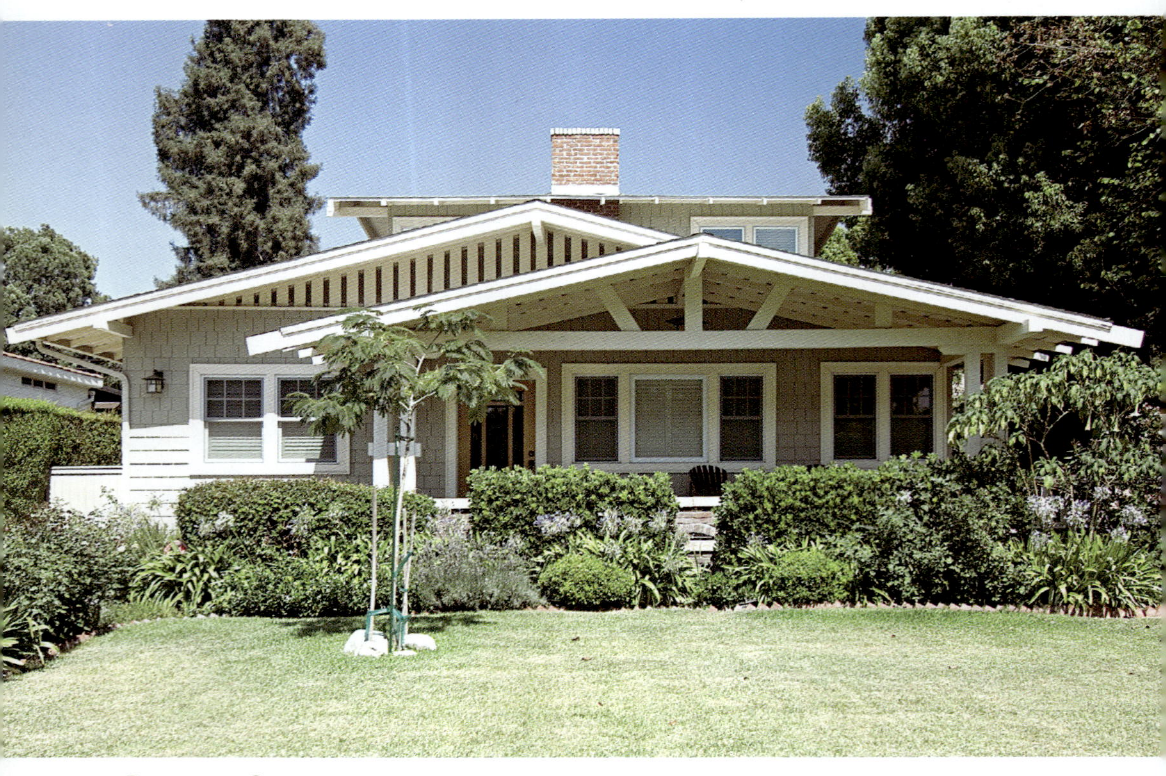

 Pasadena, California

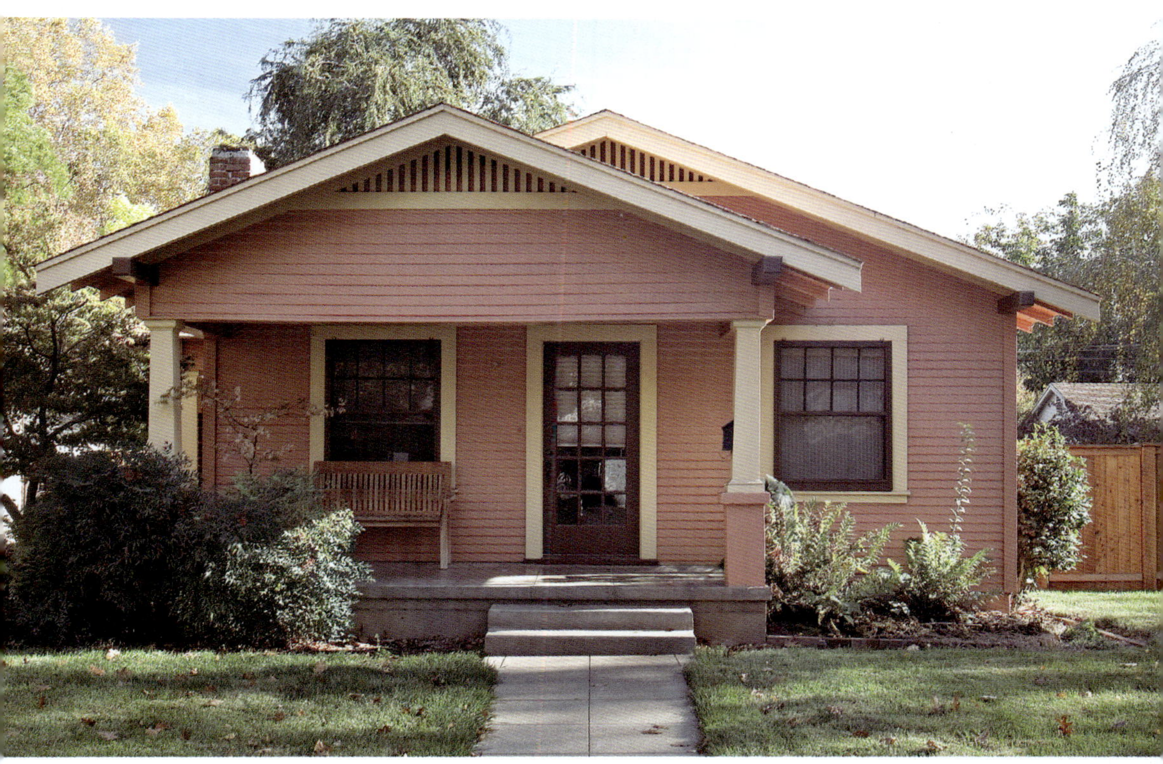

Chico, California

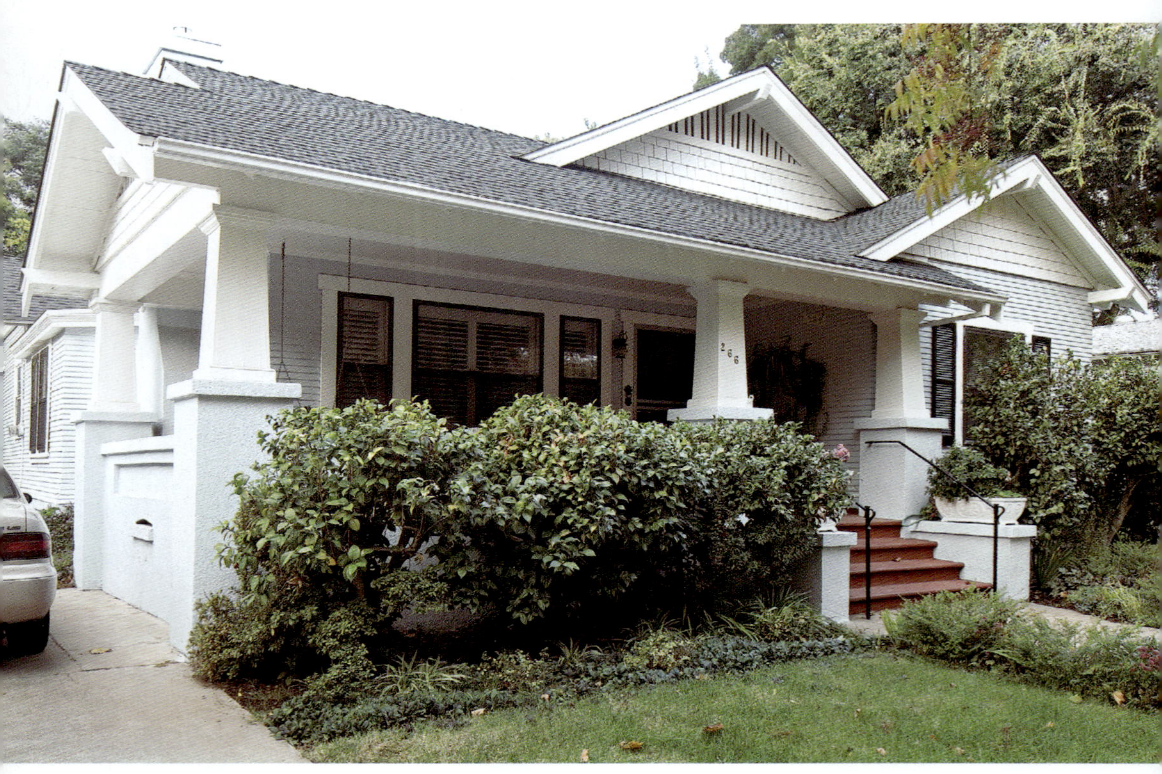


 CHICO, CALIFORNIA

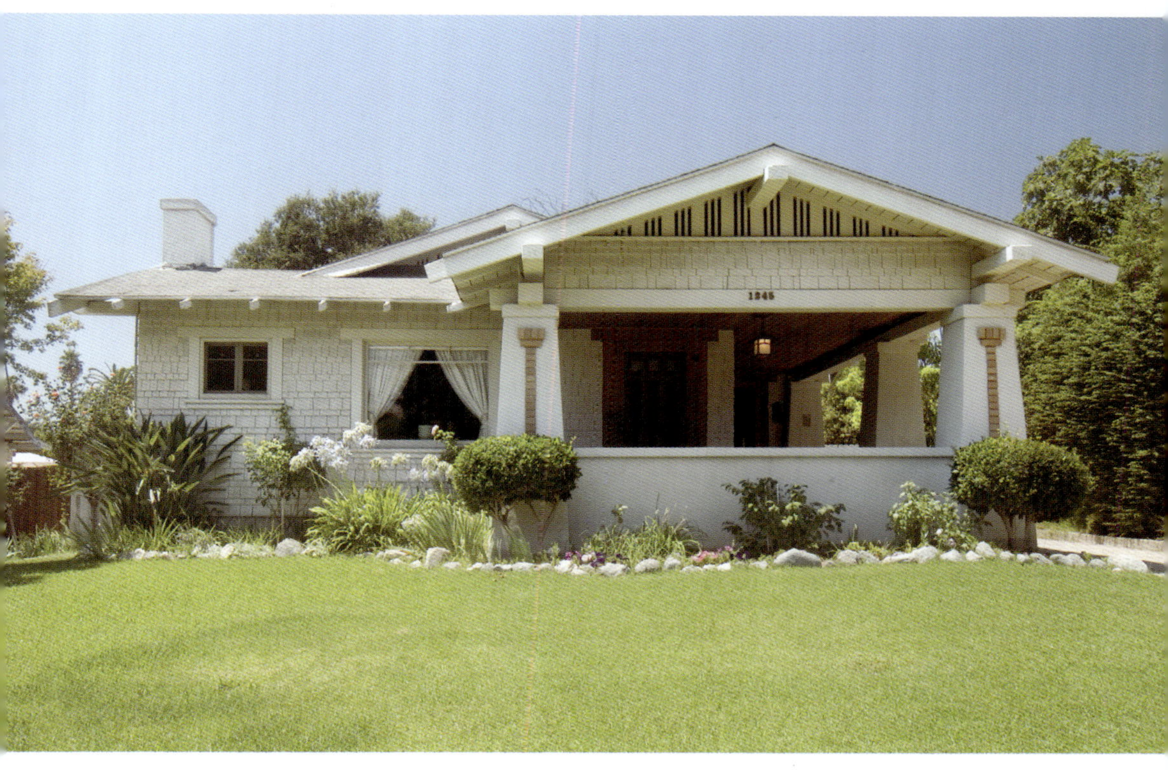

Pasadena, California 

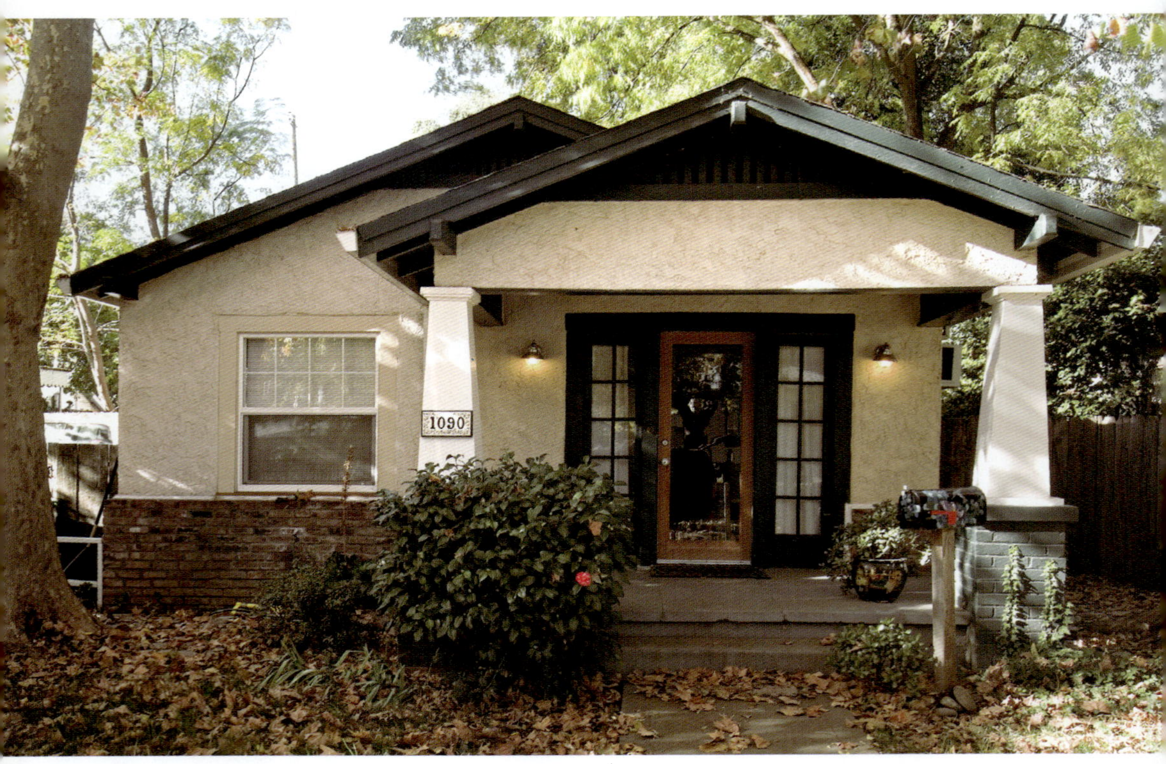
1090

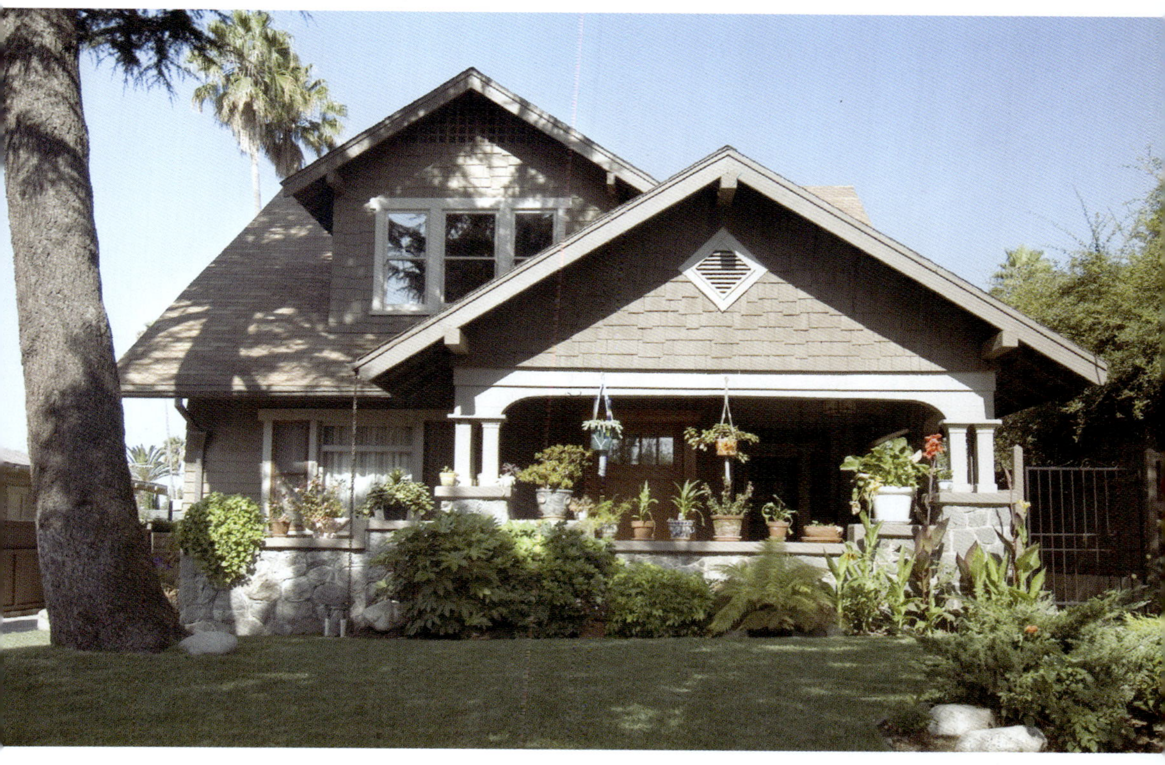

Pasadena, California 

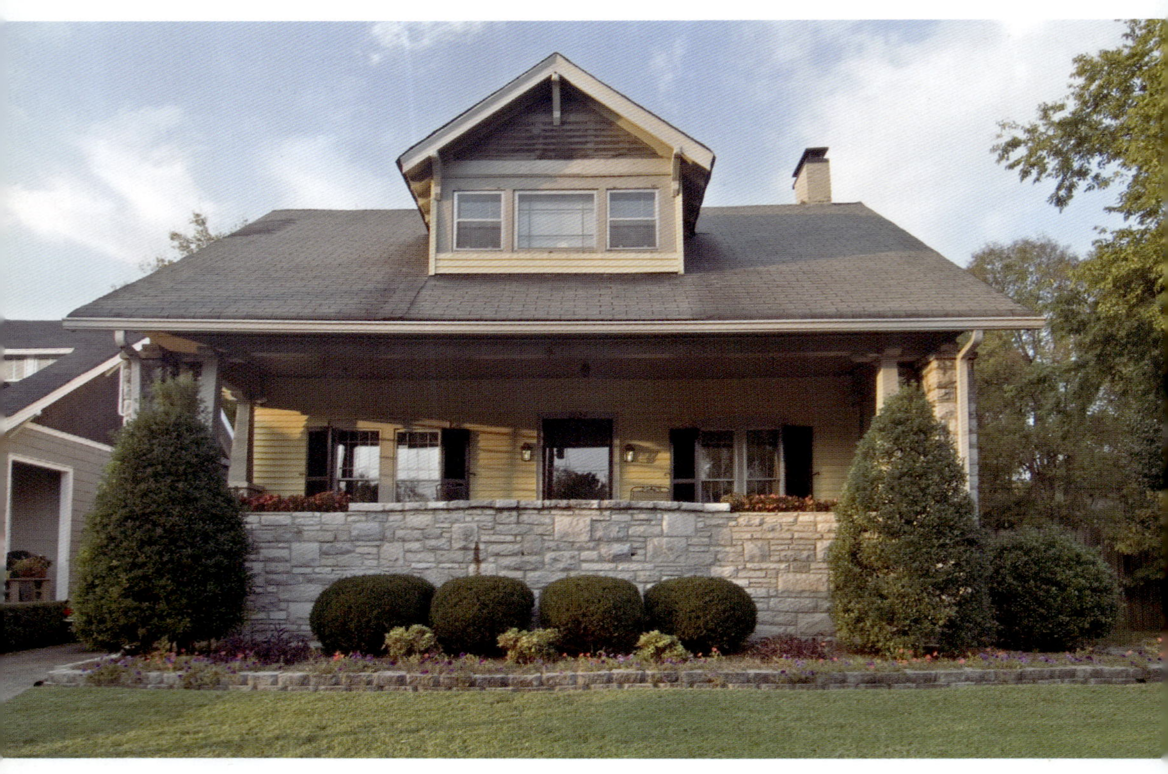

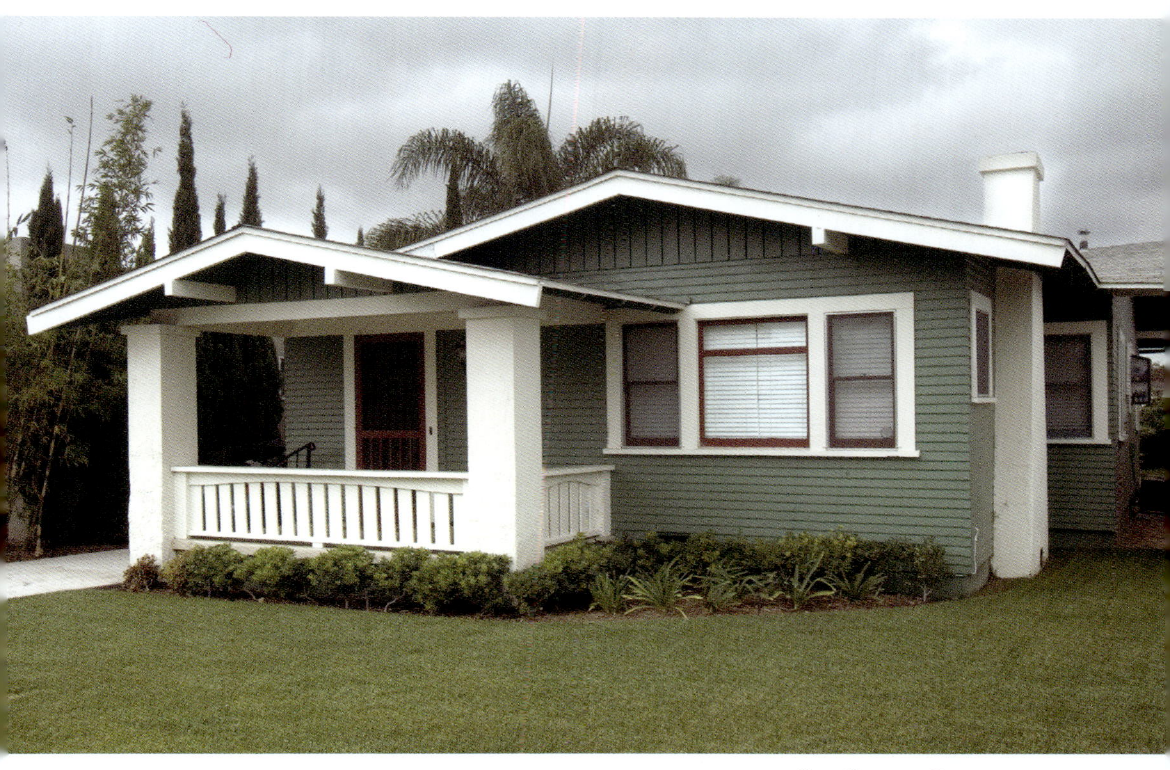

San Diego, California 

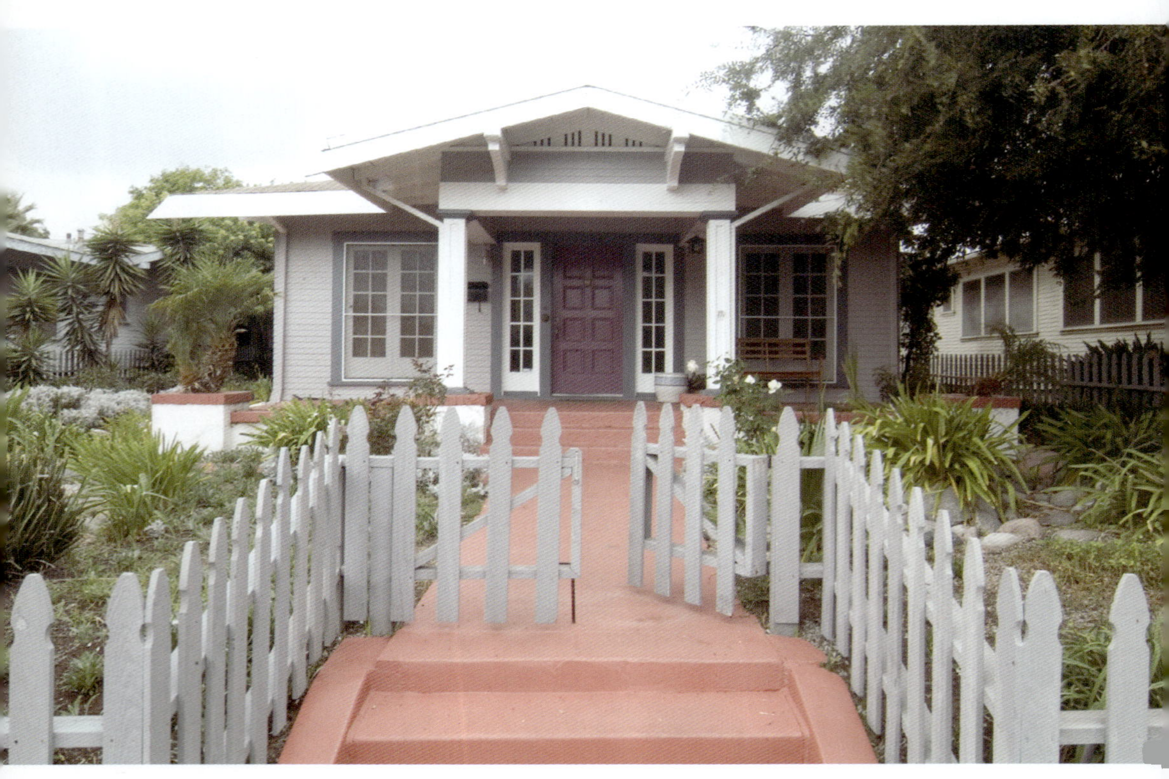

 San Diego, California

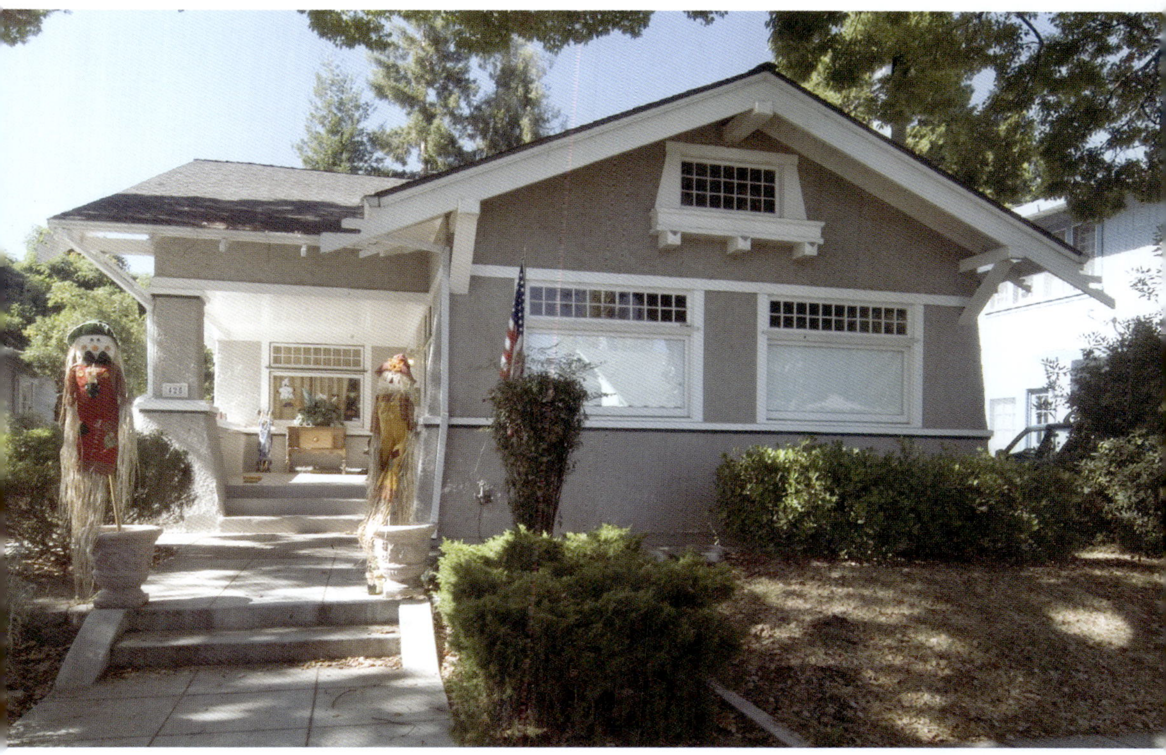

San Jose, California

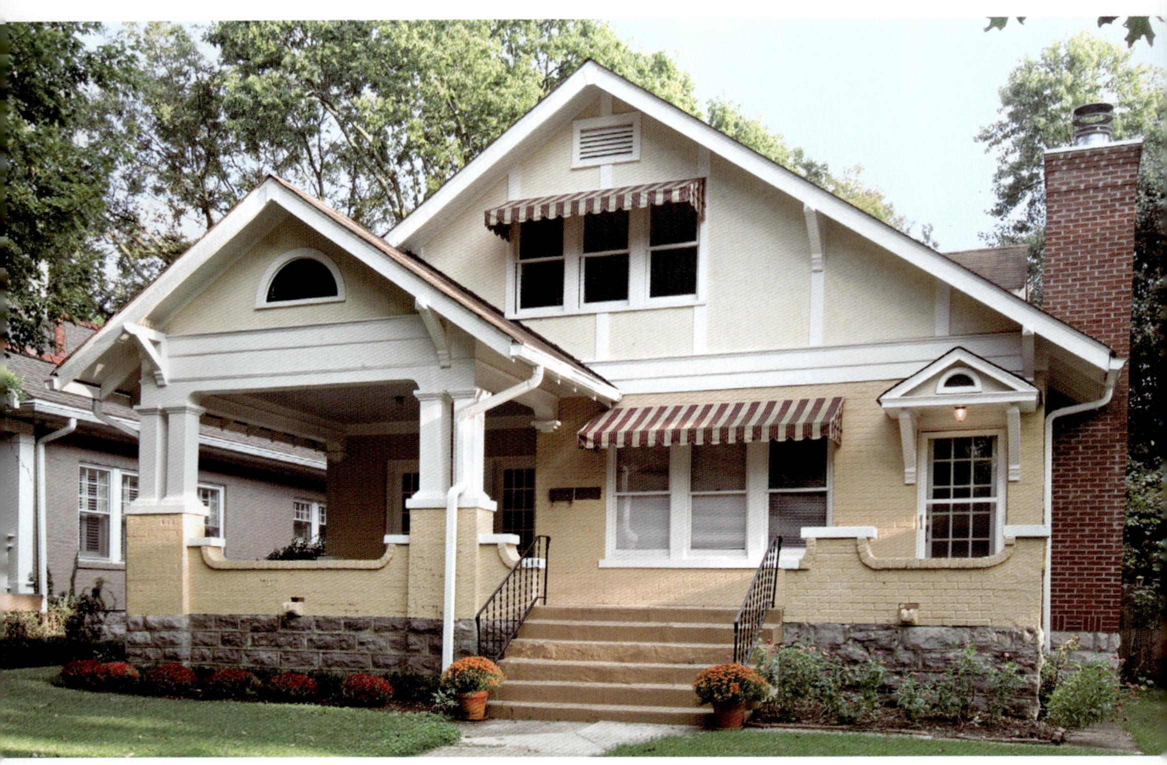

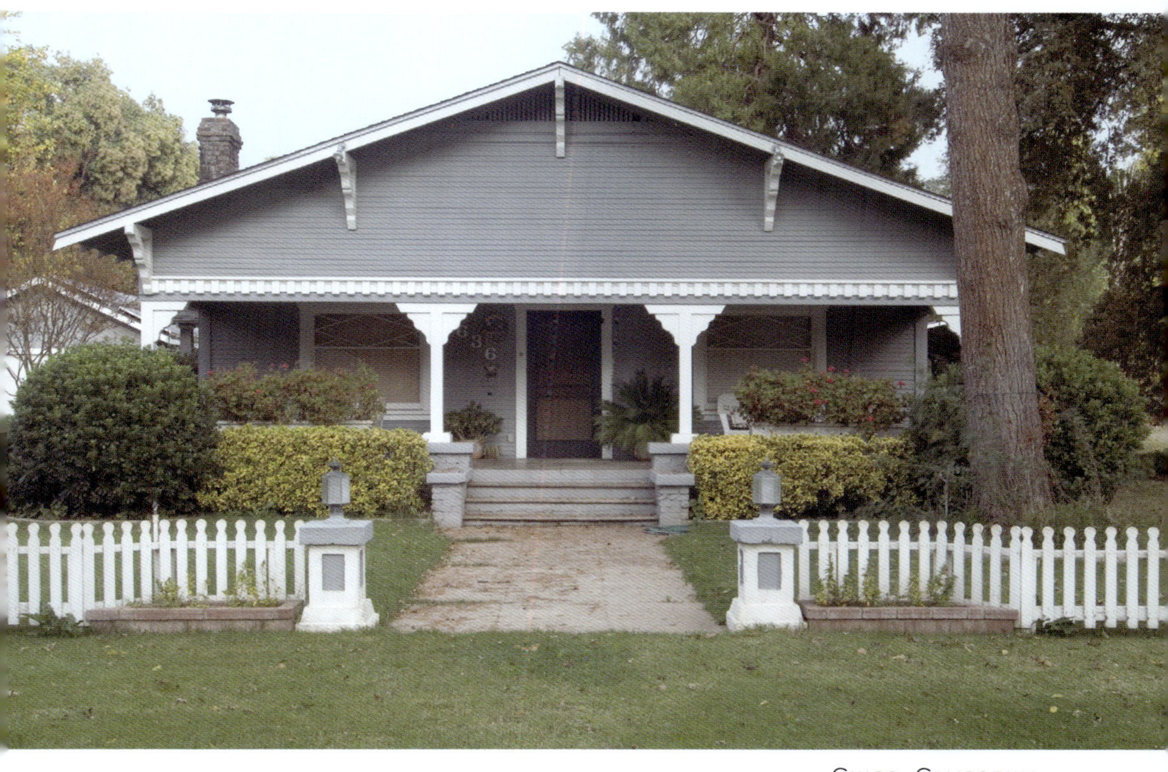

Chico, California

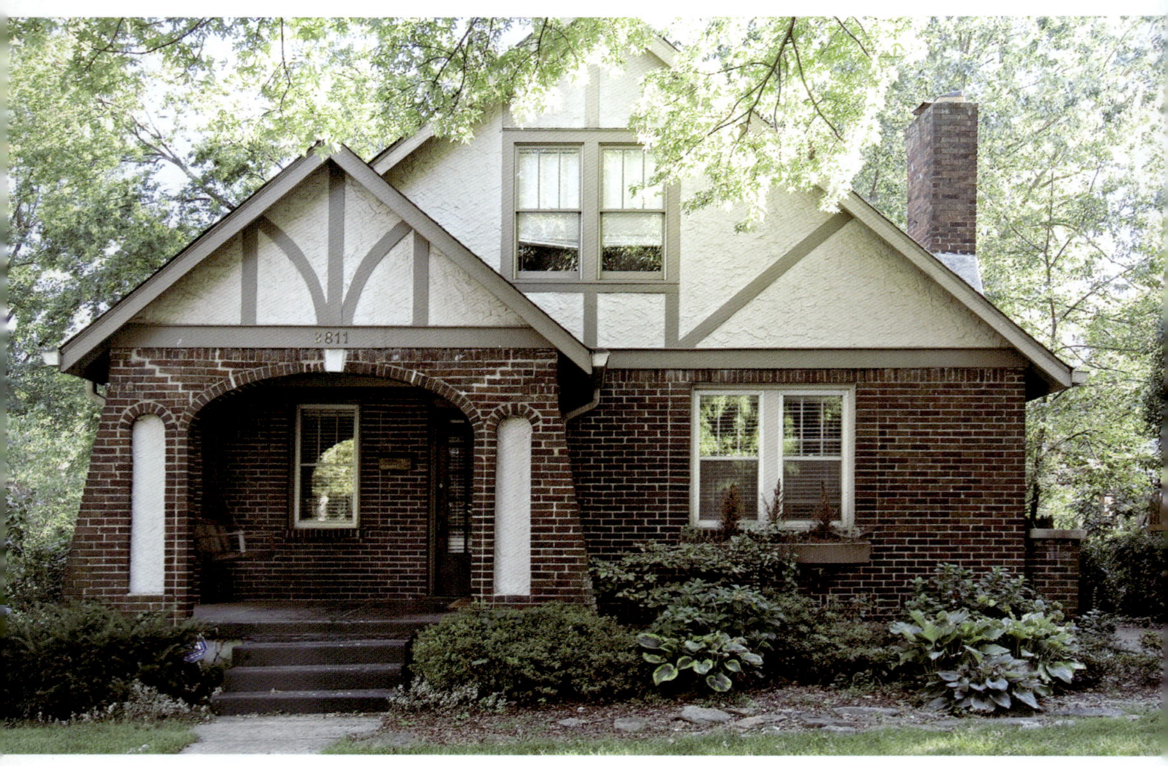
2811

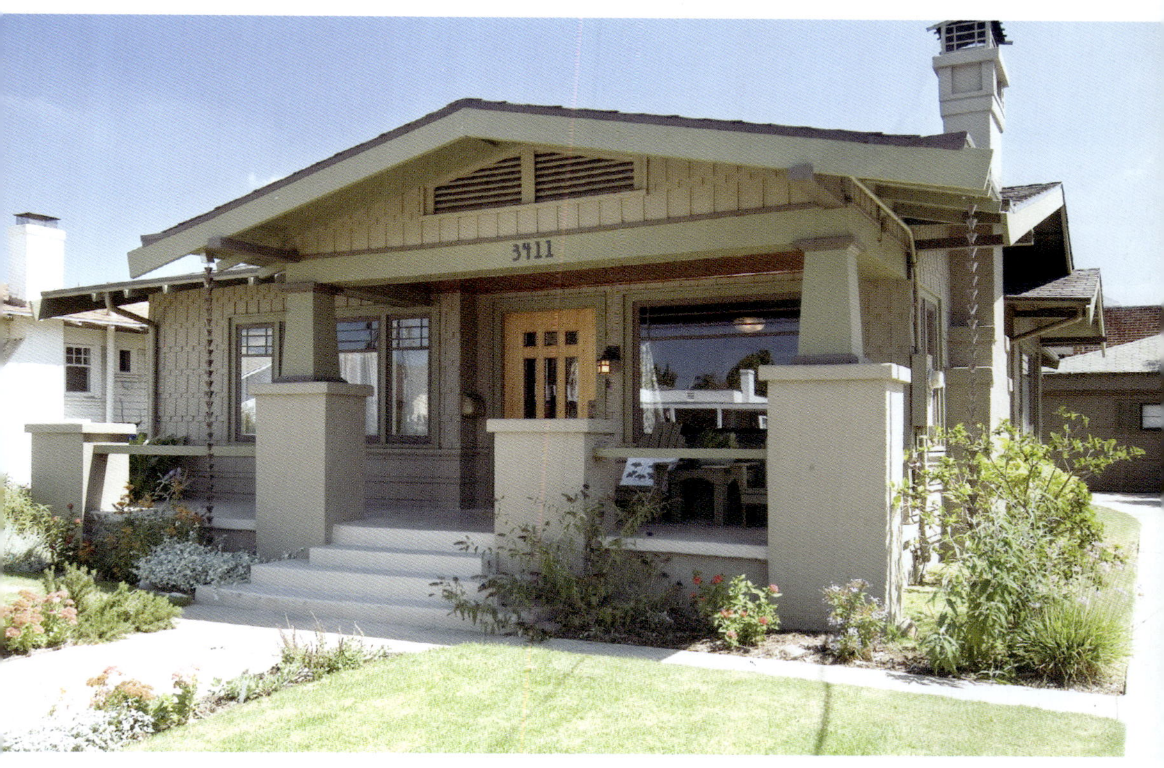
3411

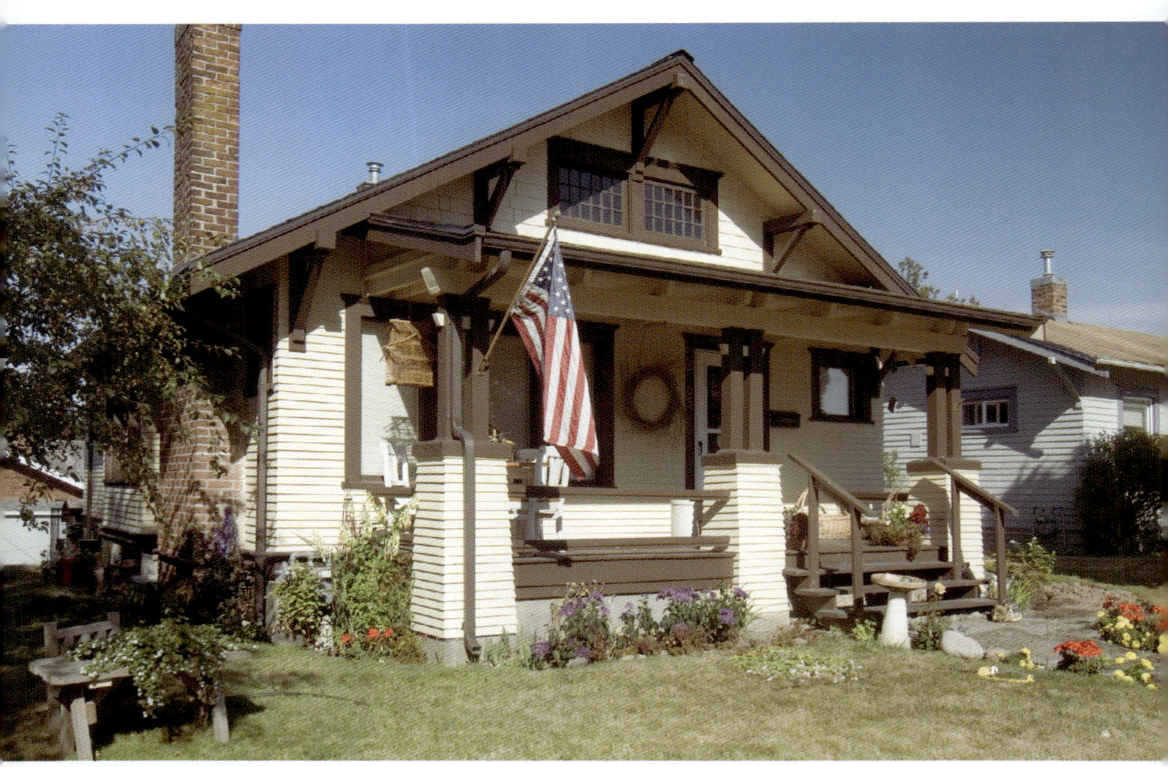

 Bellingham, Washington

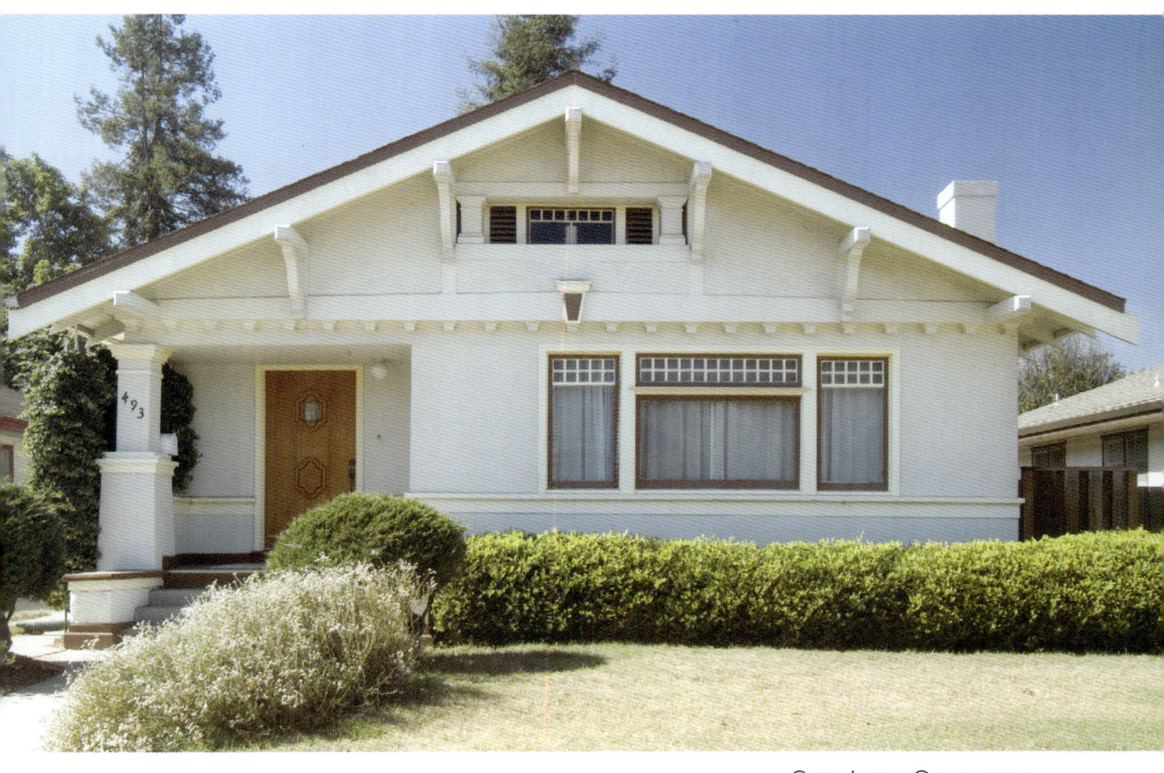


San Jose, California

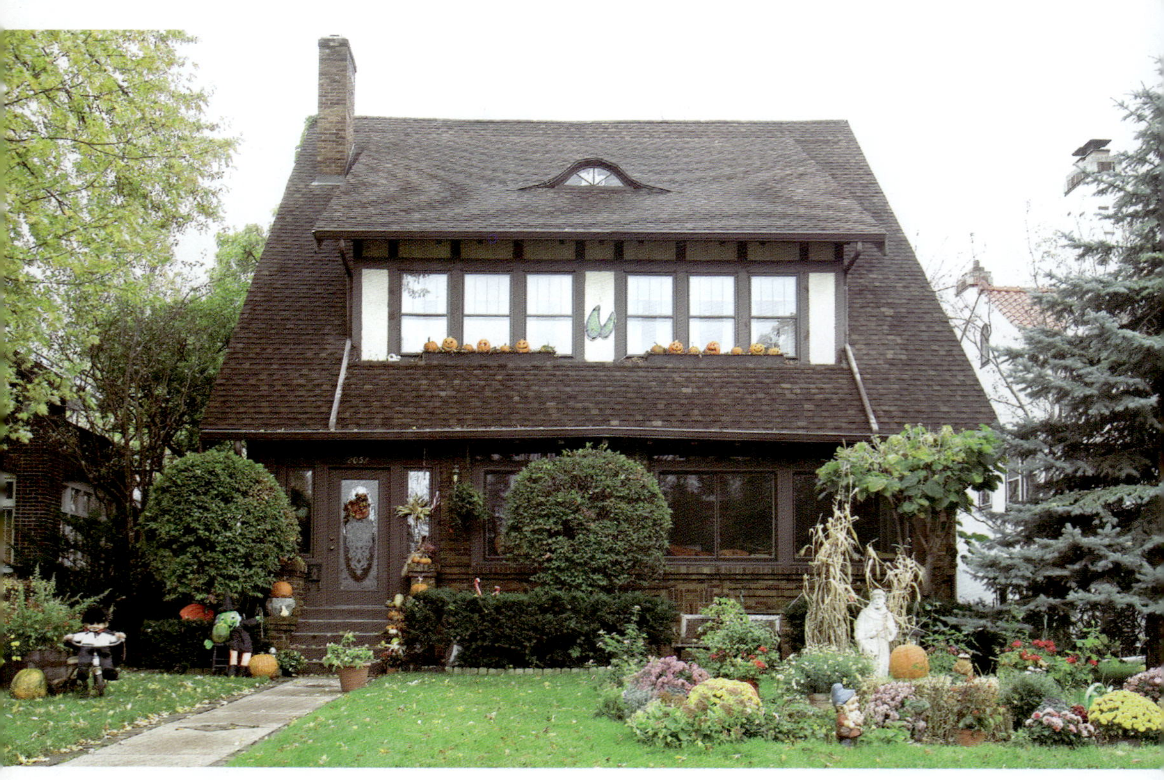

 St. Paul, Minnesota

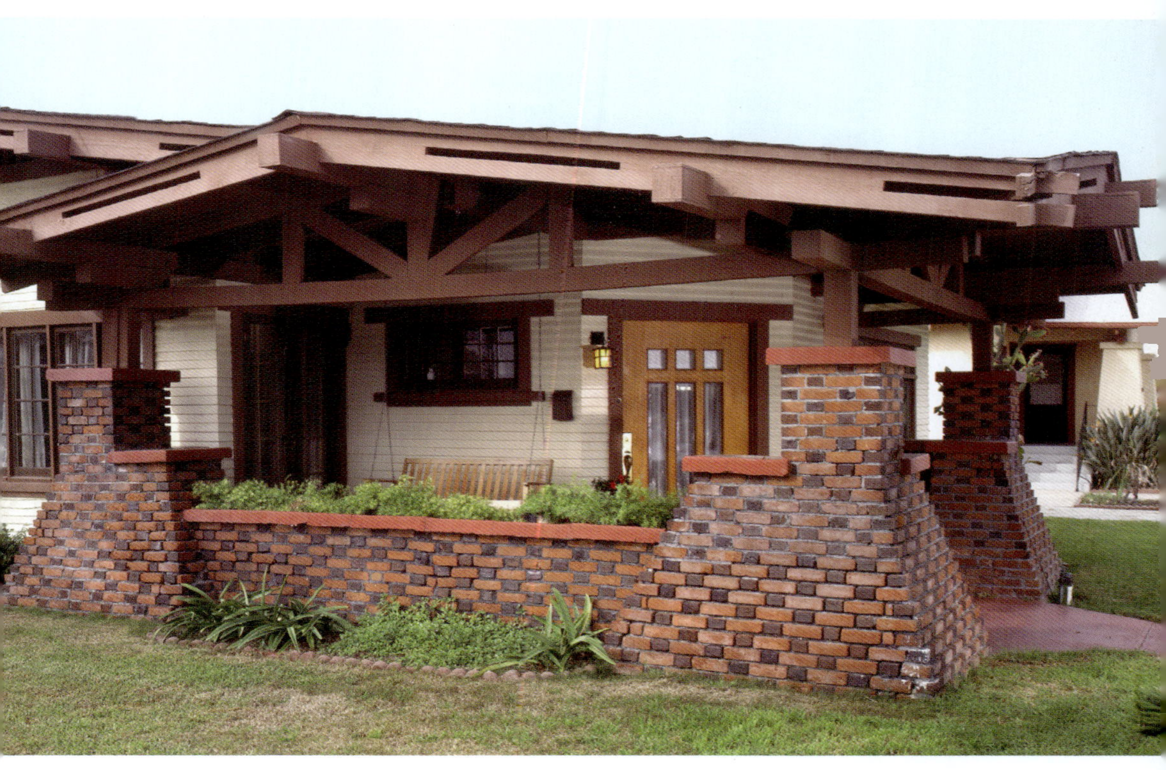

San Diego, California

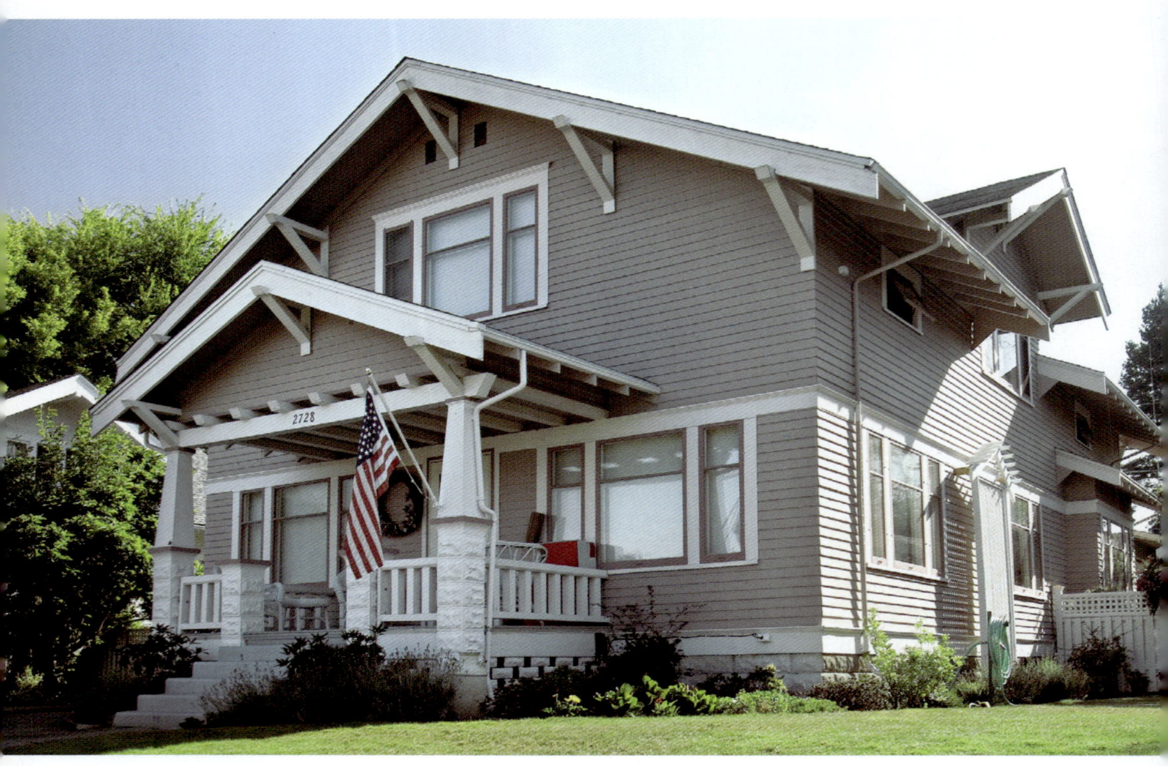


 Bellingham, Washington

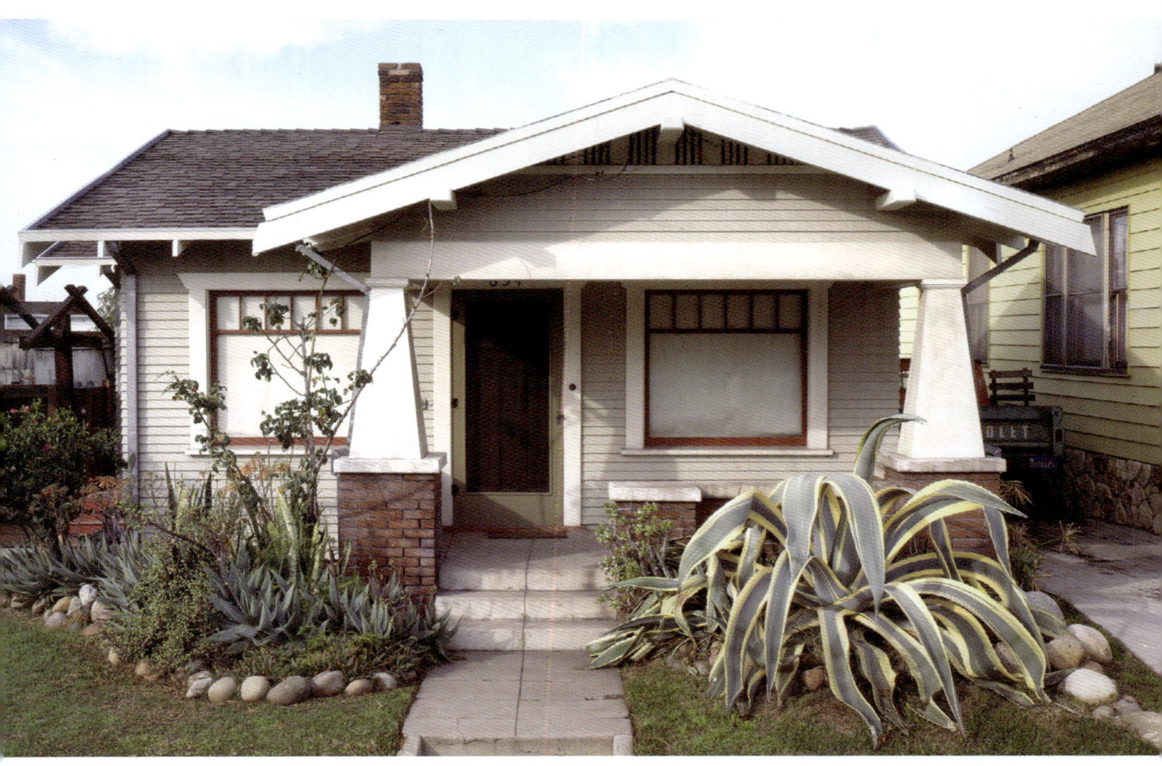

San Diego, California

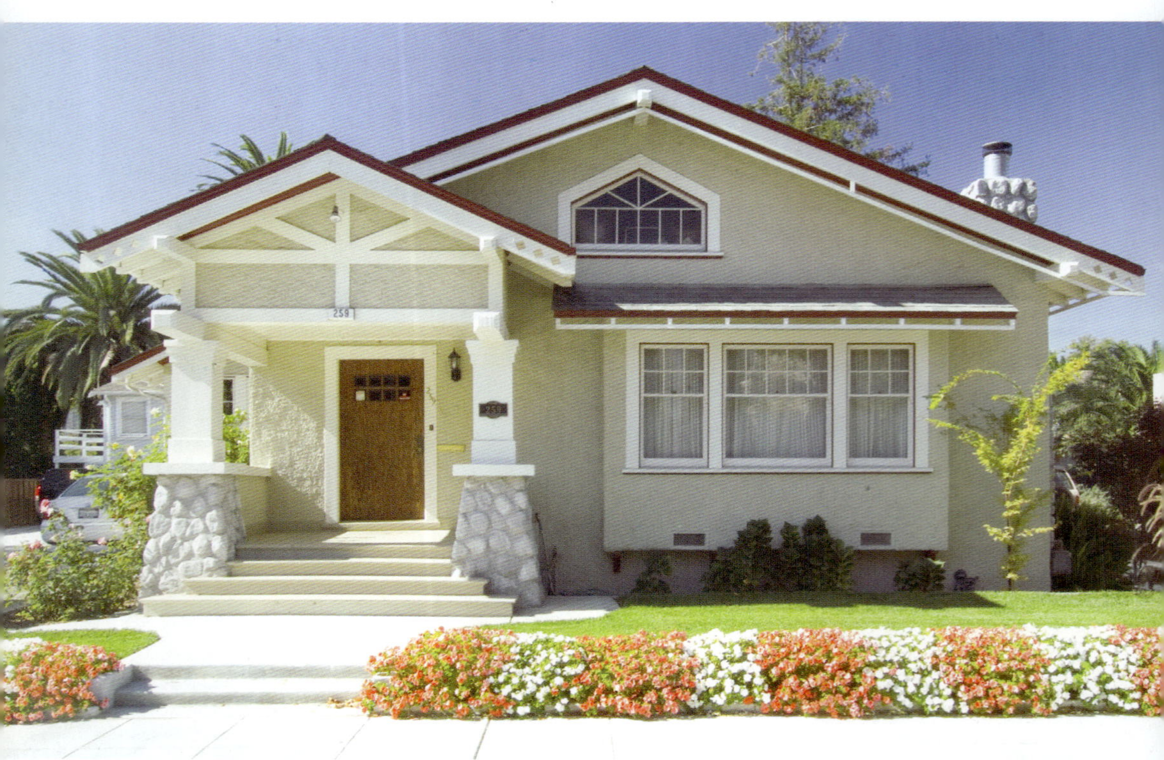

 San Jose, California

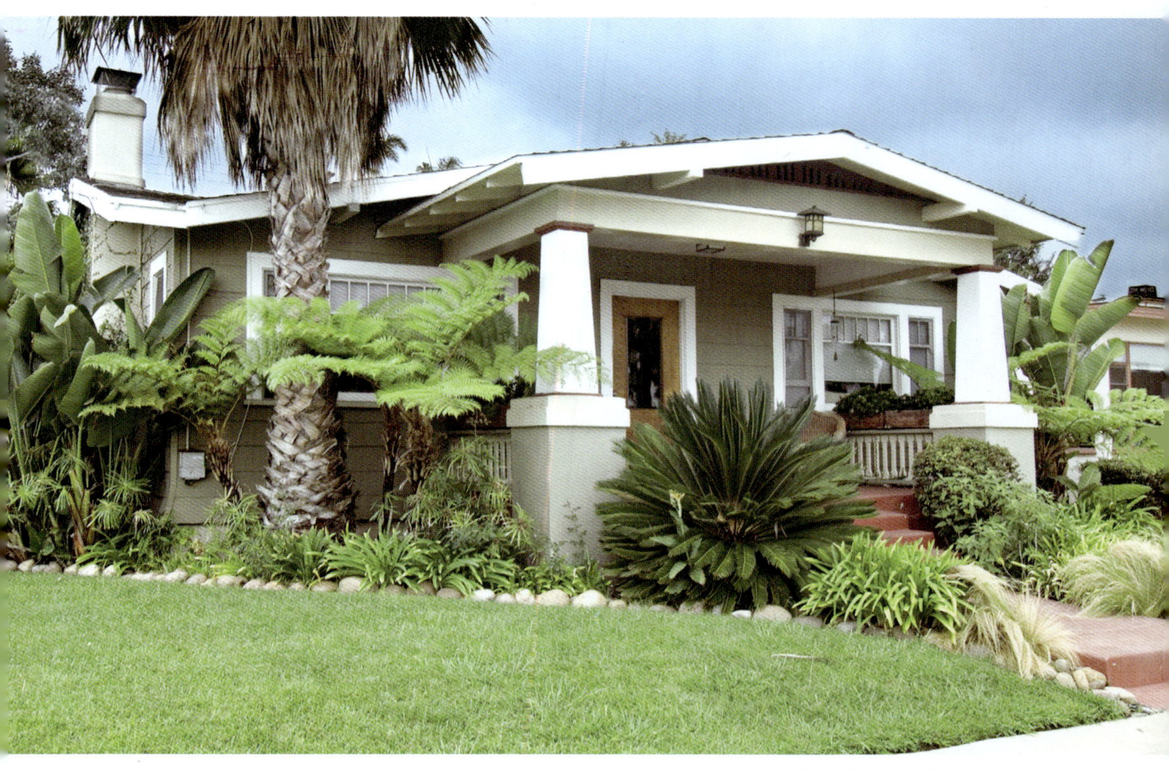

San Diego, California

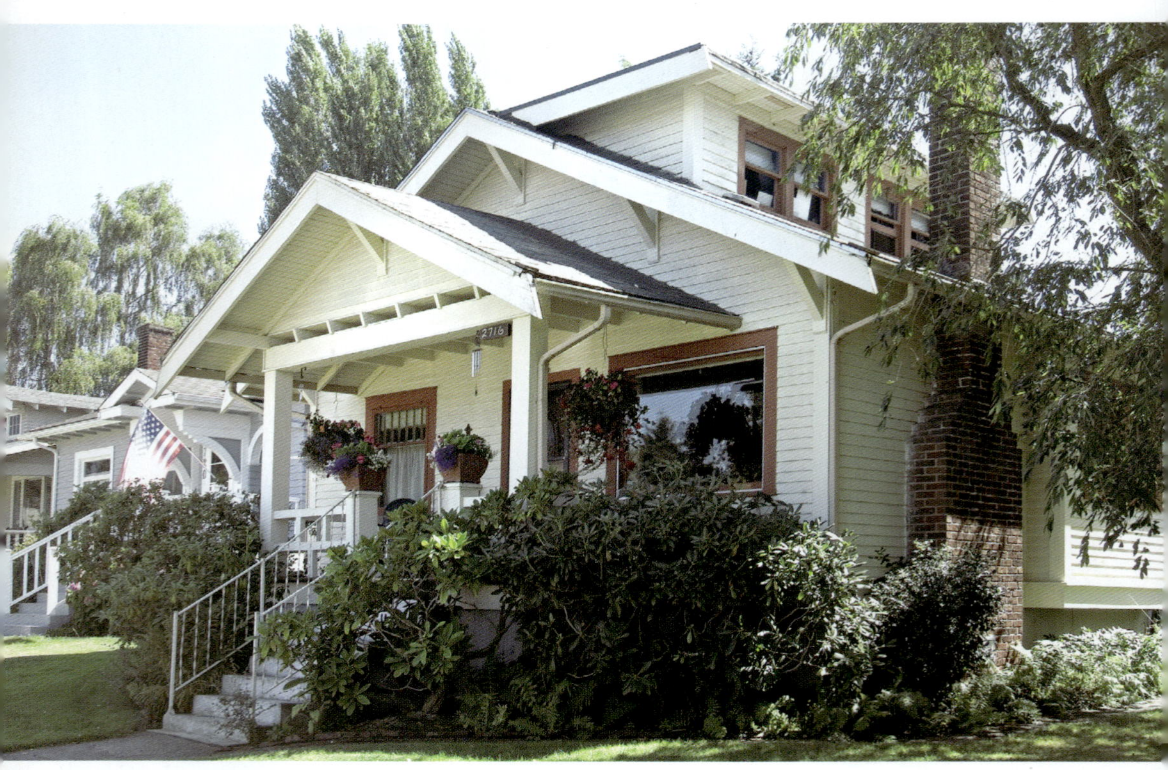


 Bellingham, Washington

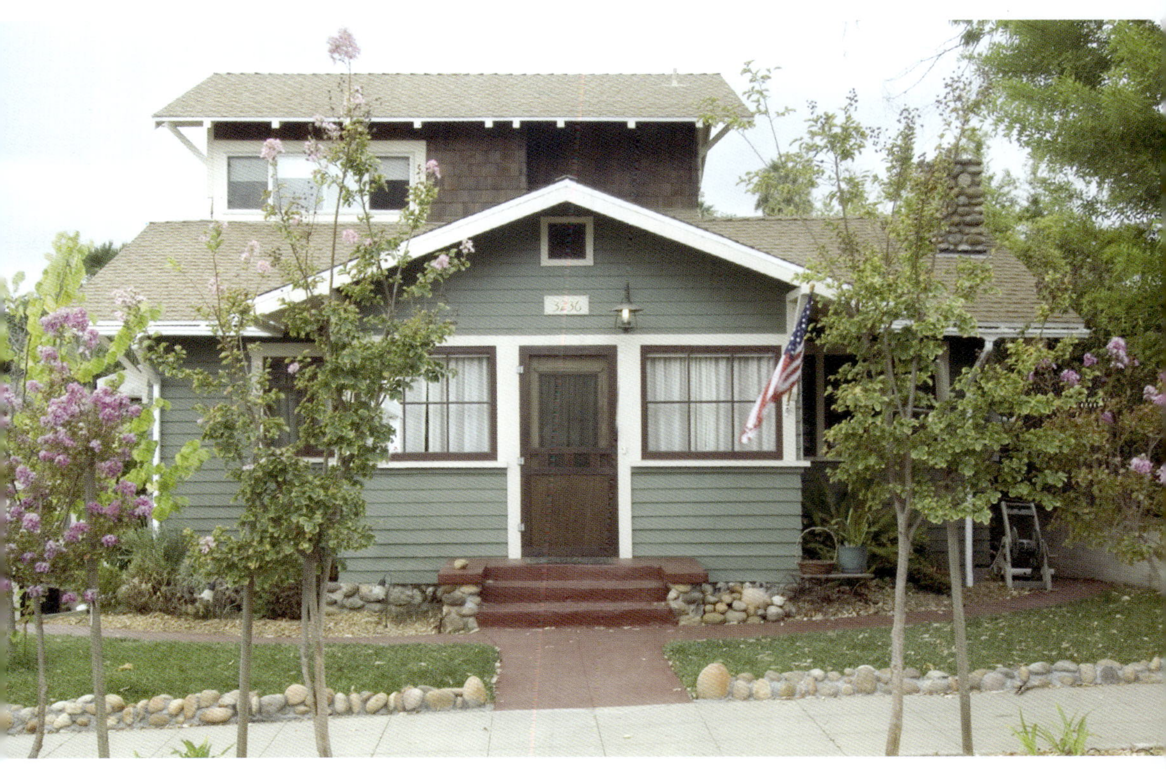

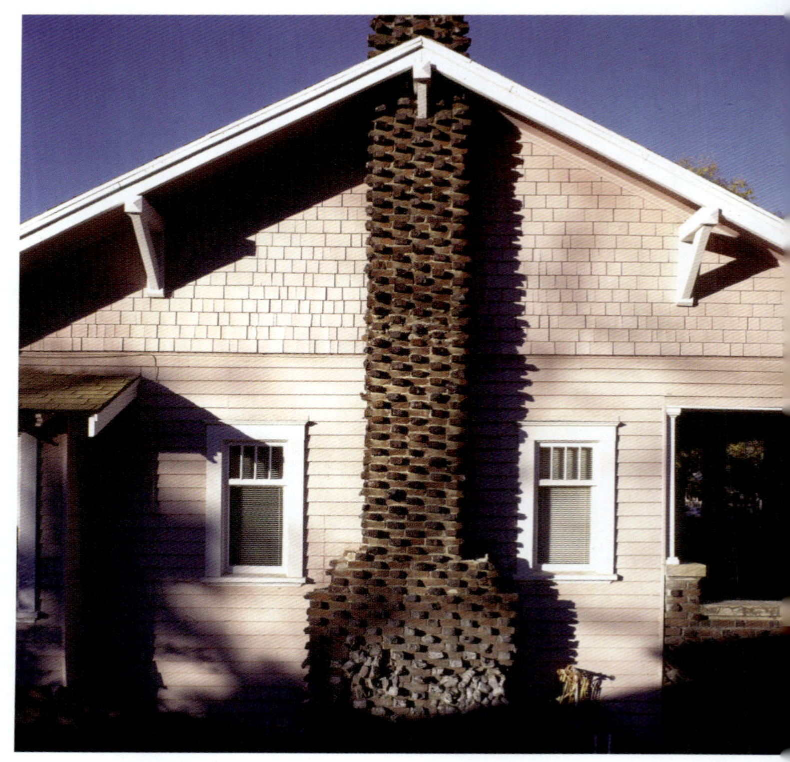

 MODESTO, CALIFORNIA

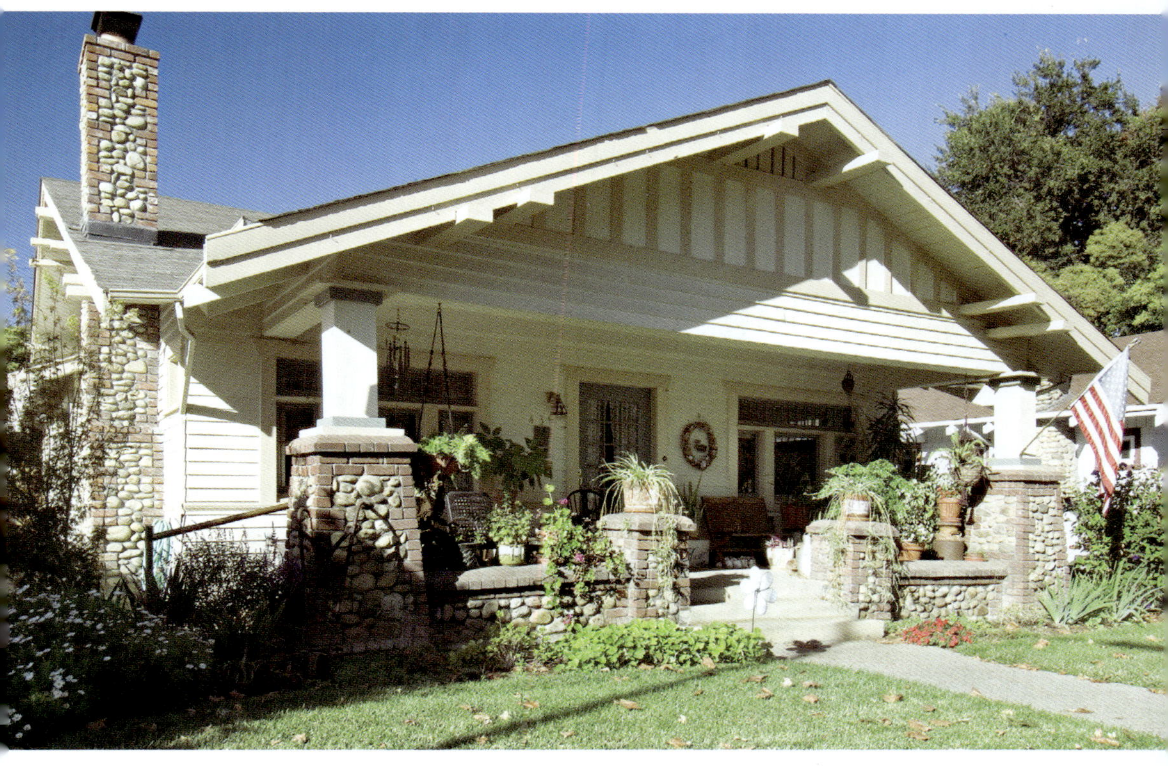

San Jose, California

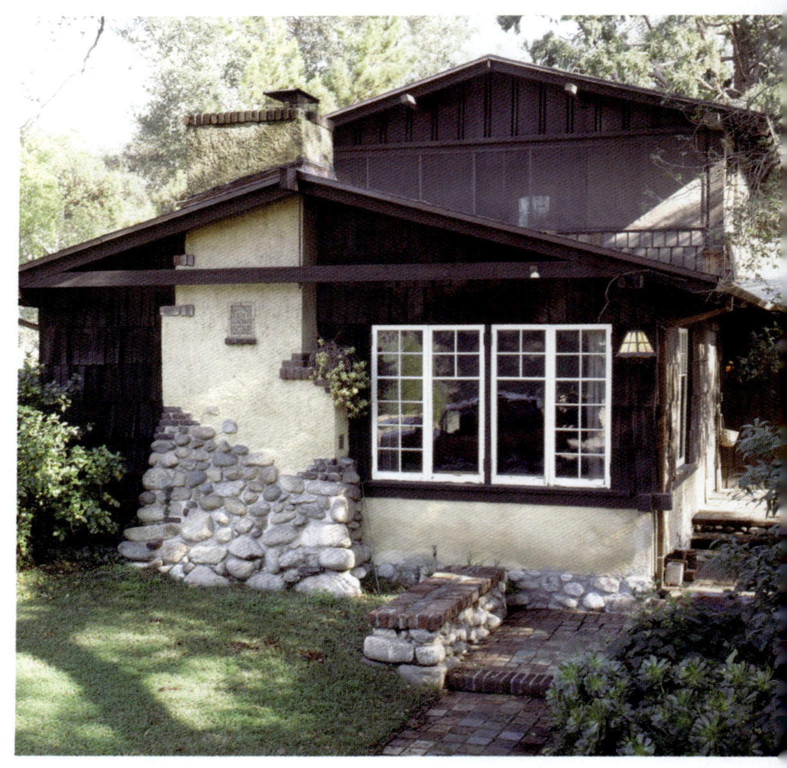

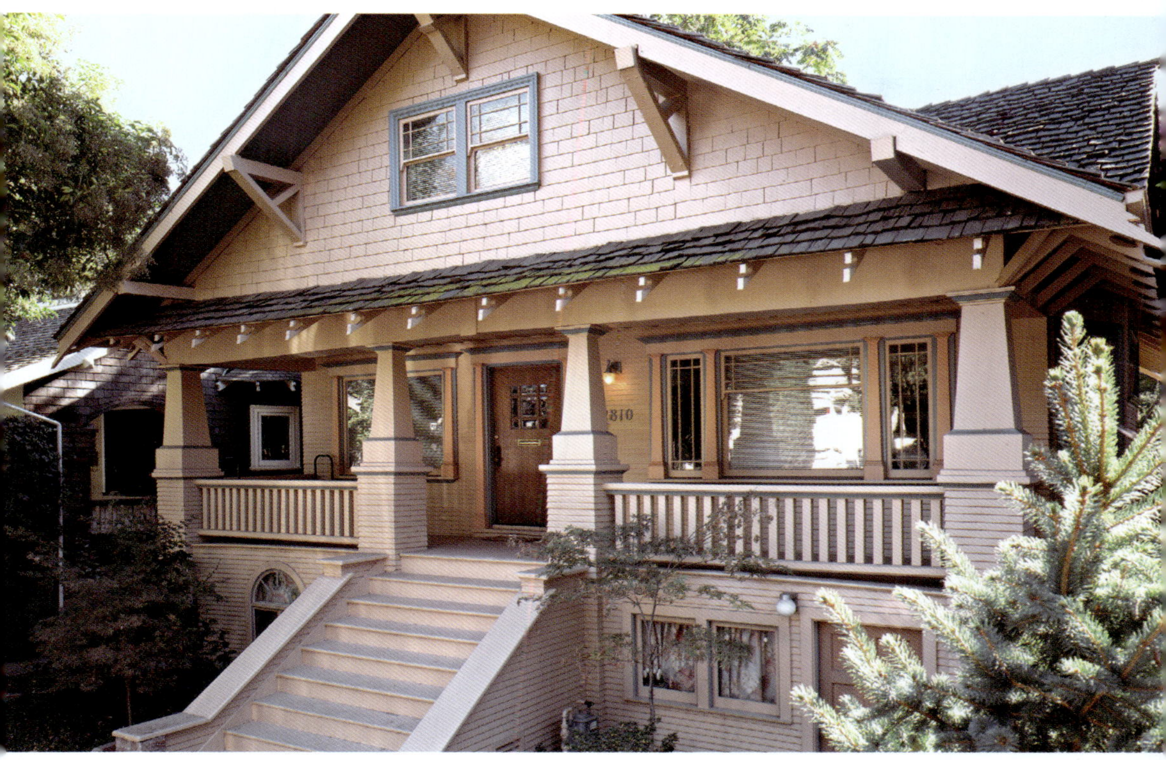
1810

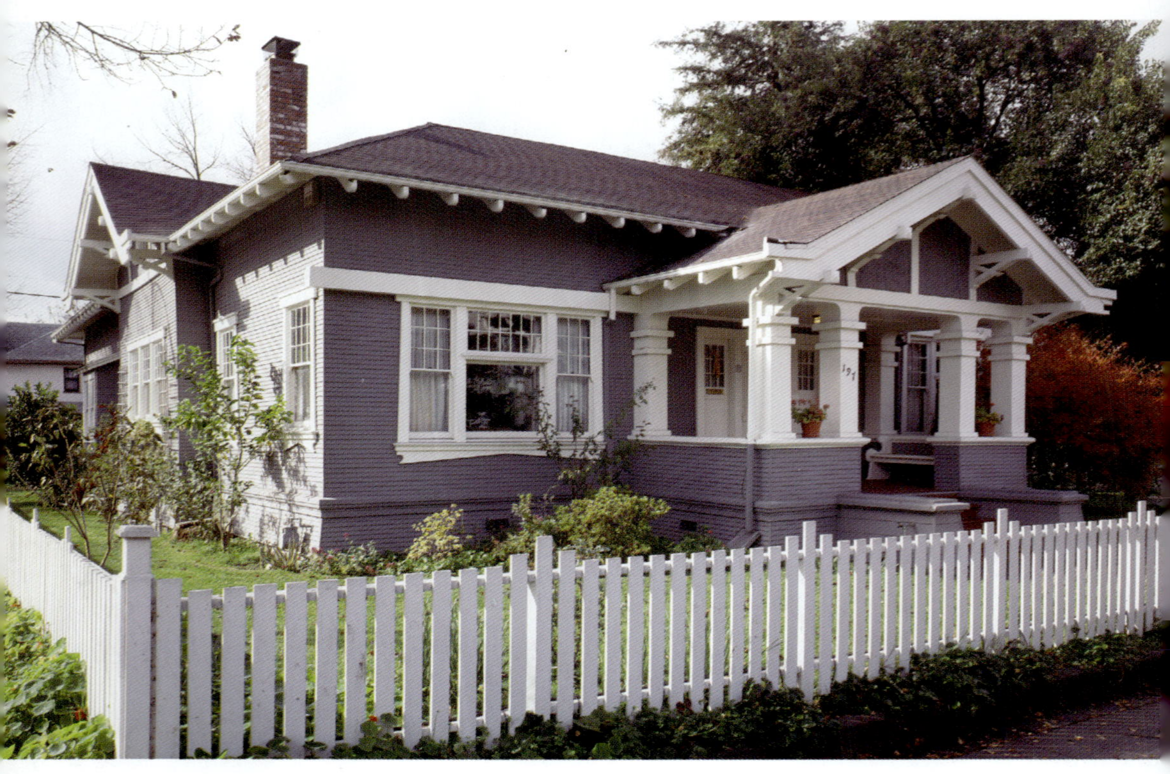

 SAN JOSE, CALIFORNIA

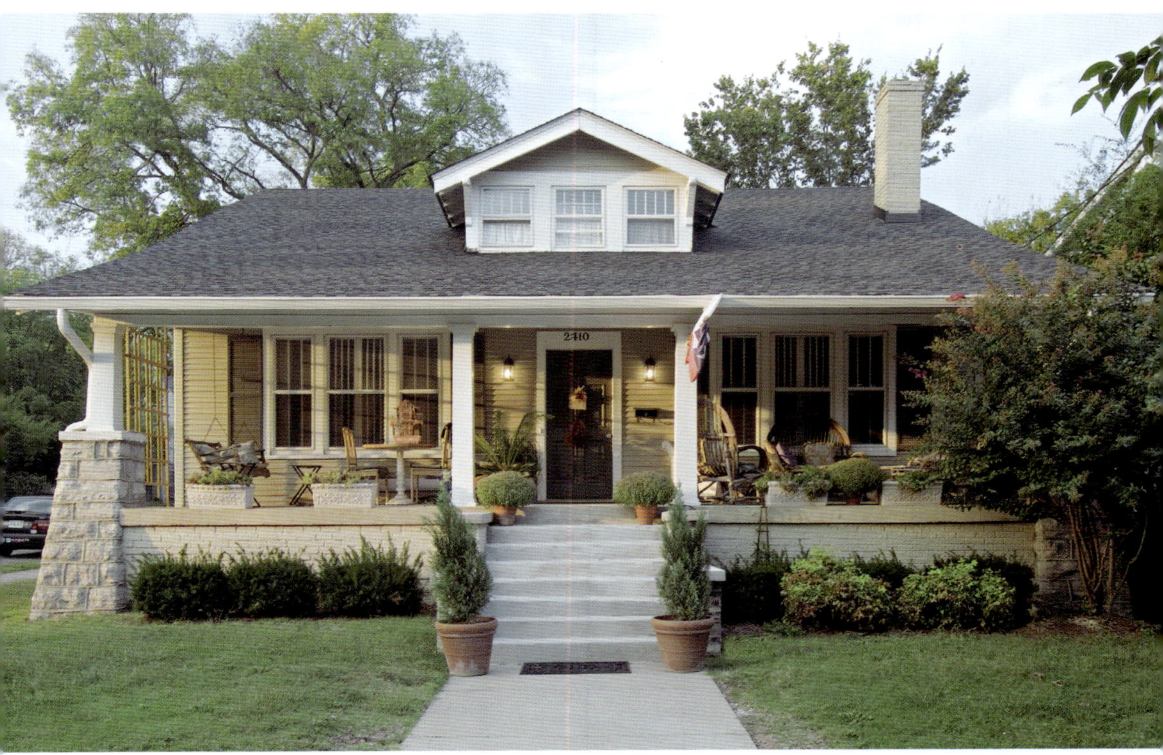
2410

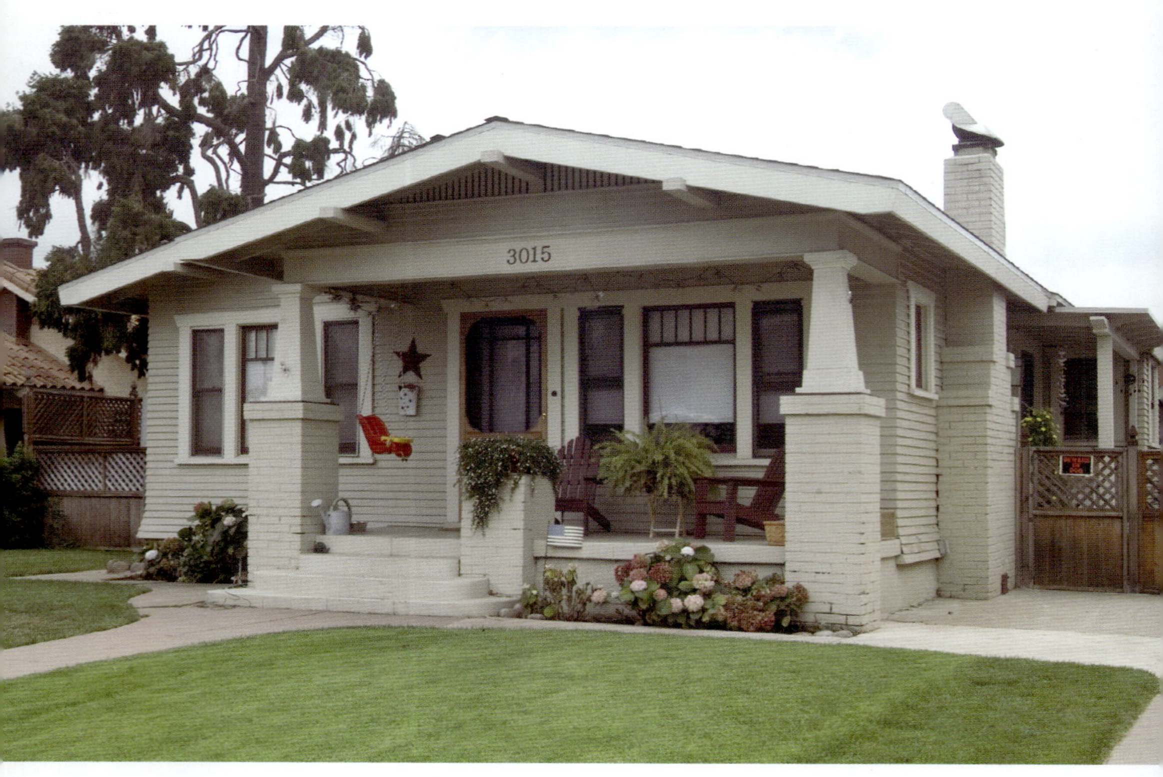


 San Diego, California

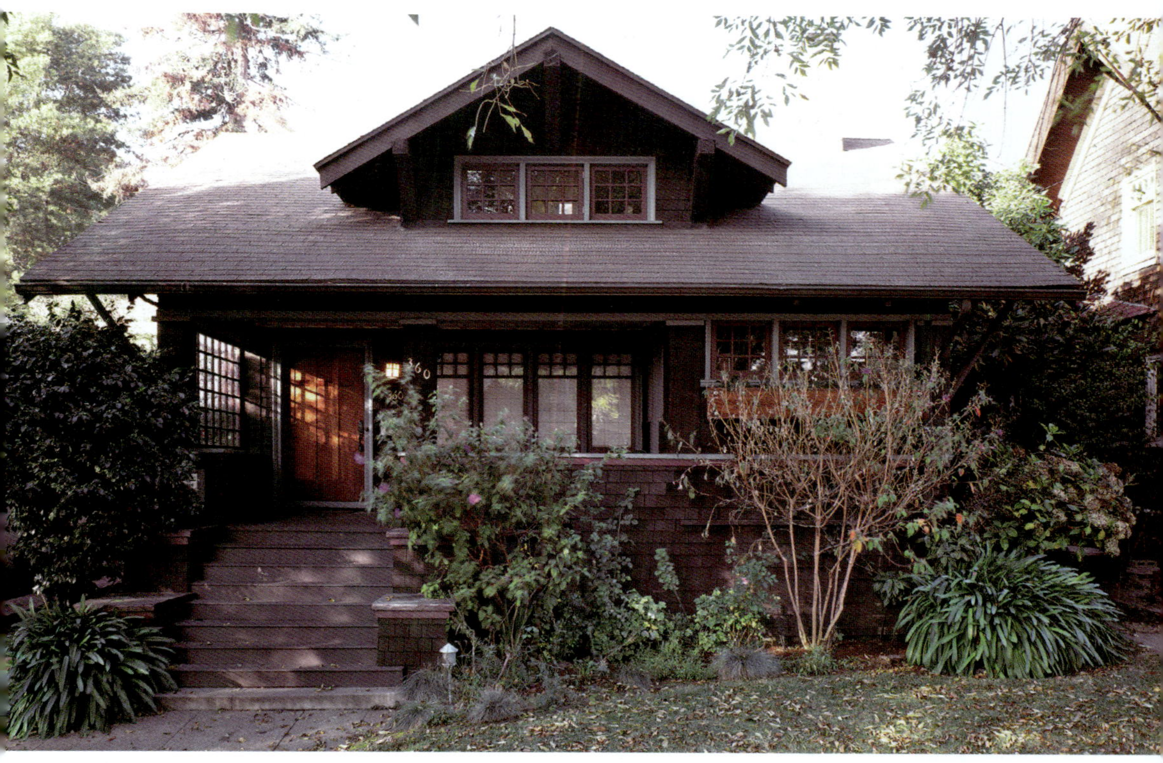
360

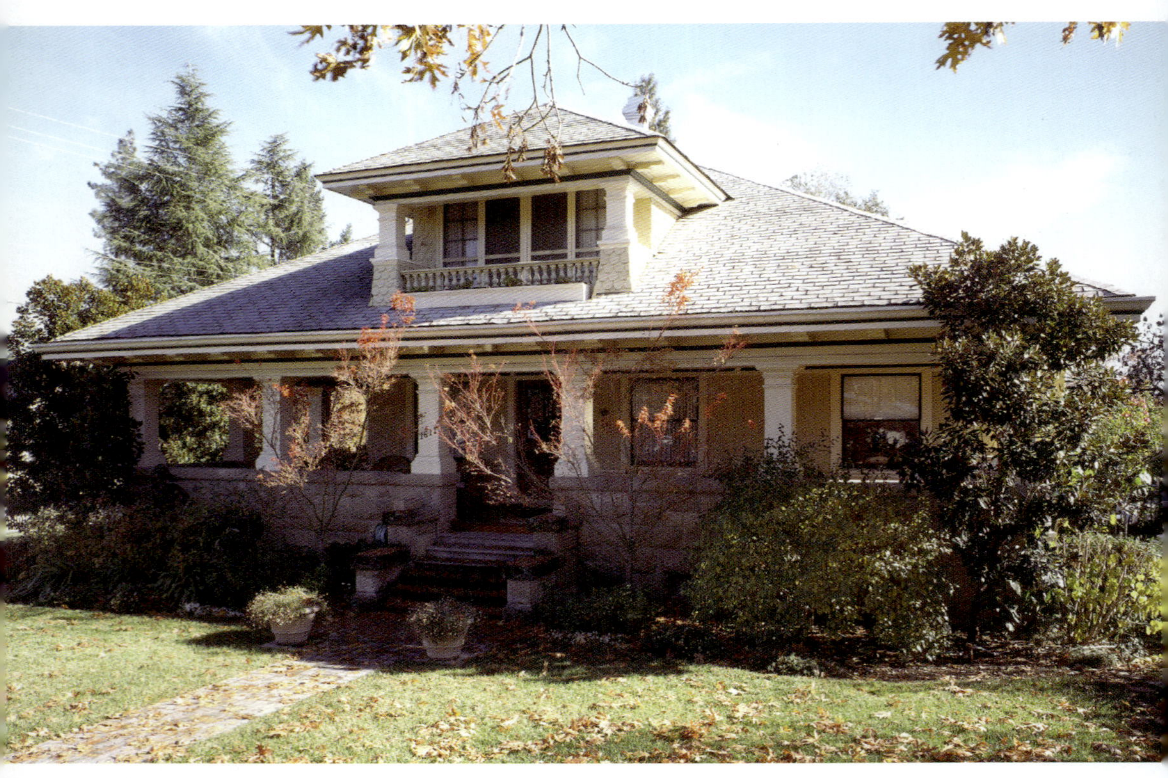

 St. Helena, California

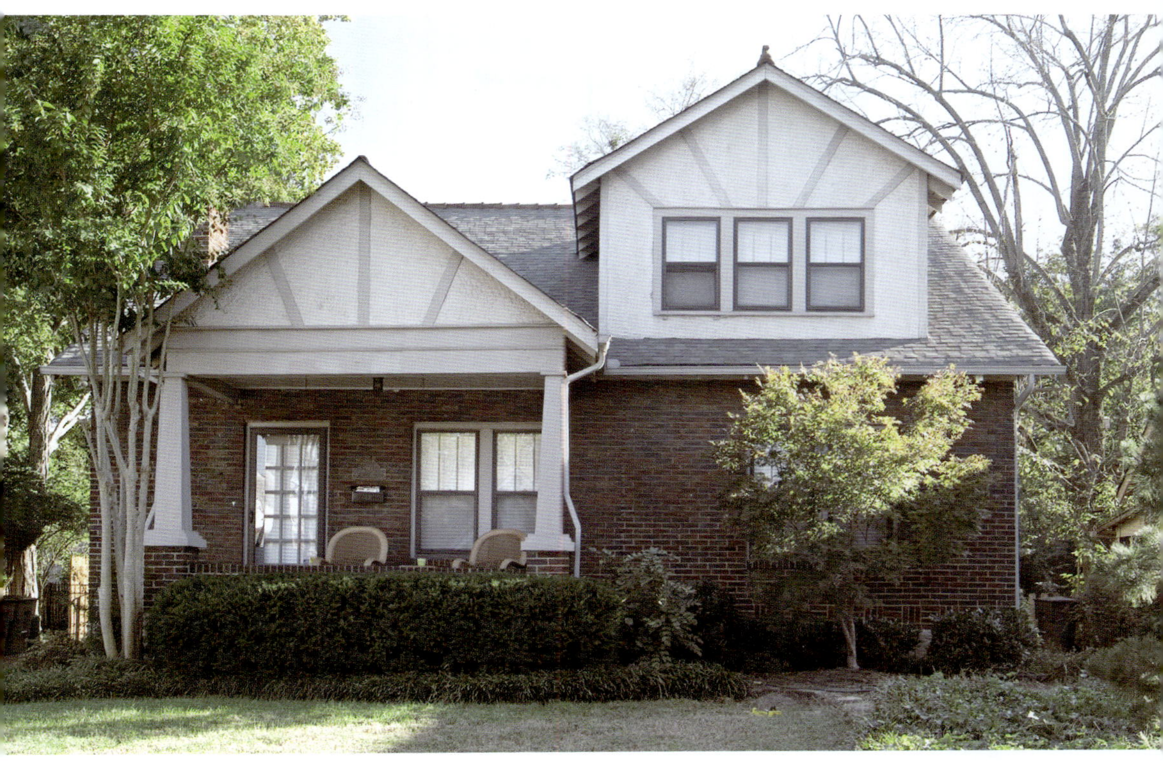

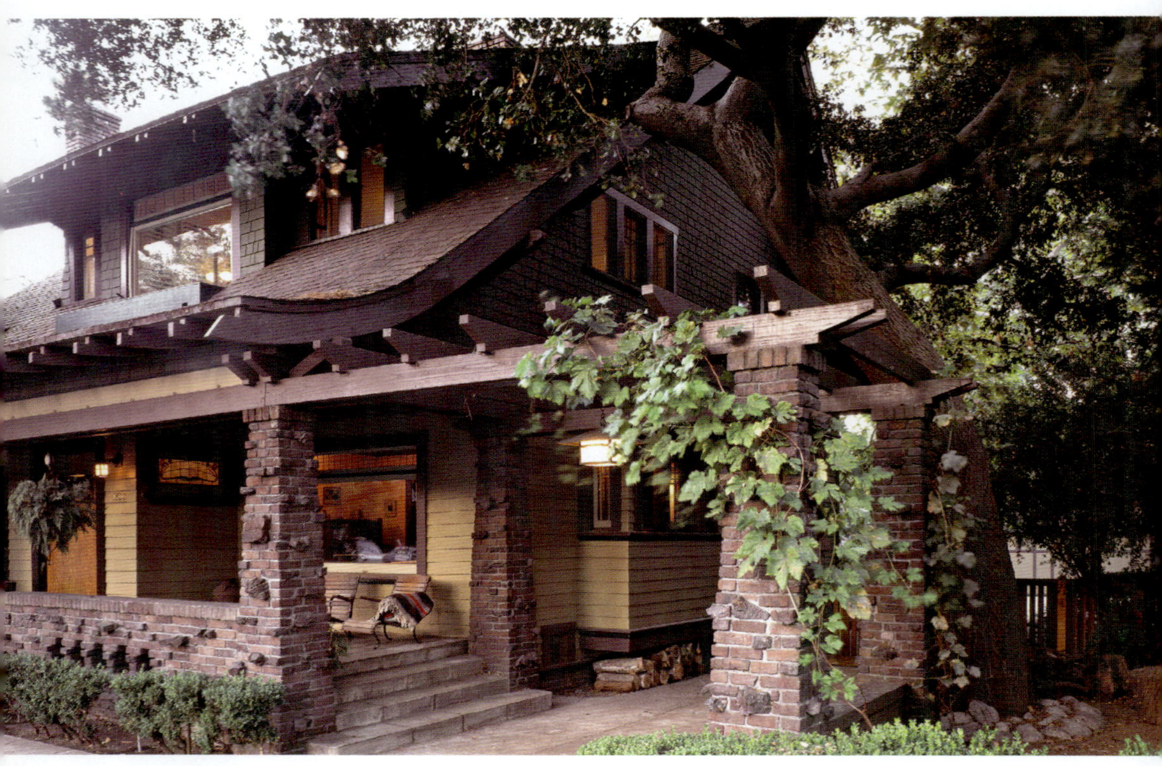

 PASADENA, CALIFORNIA

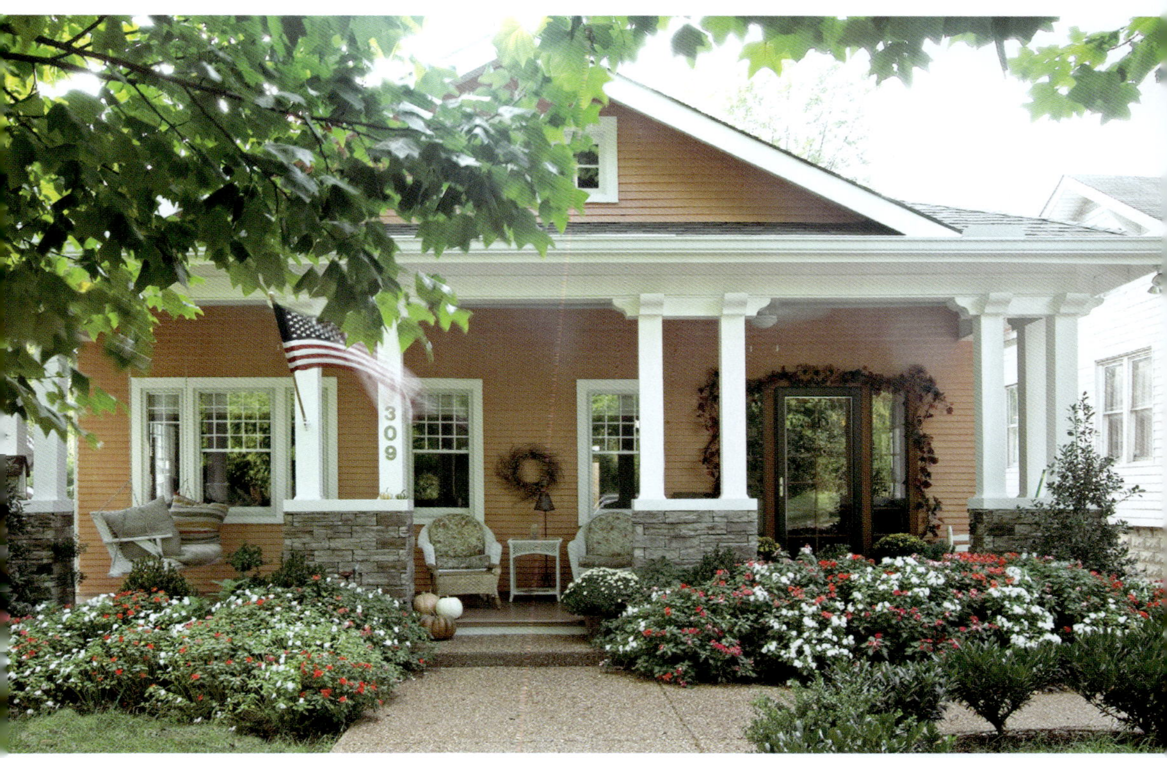
309

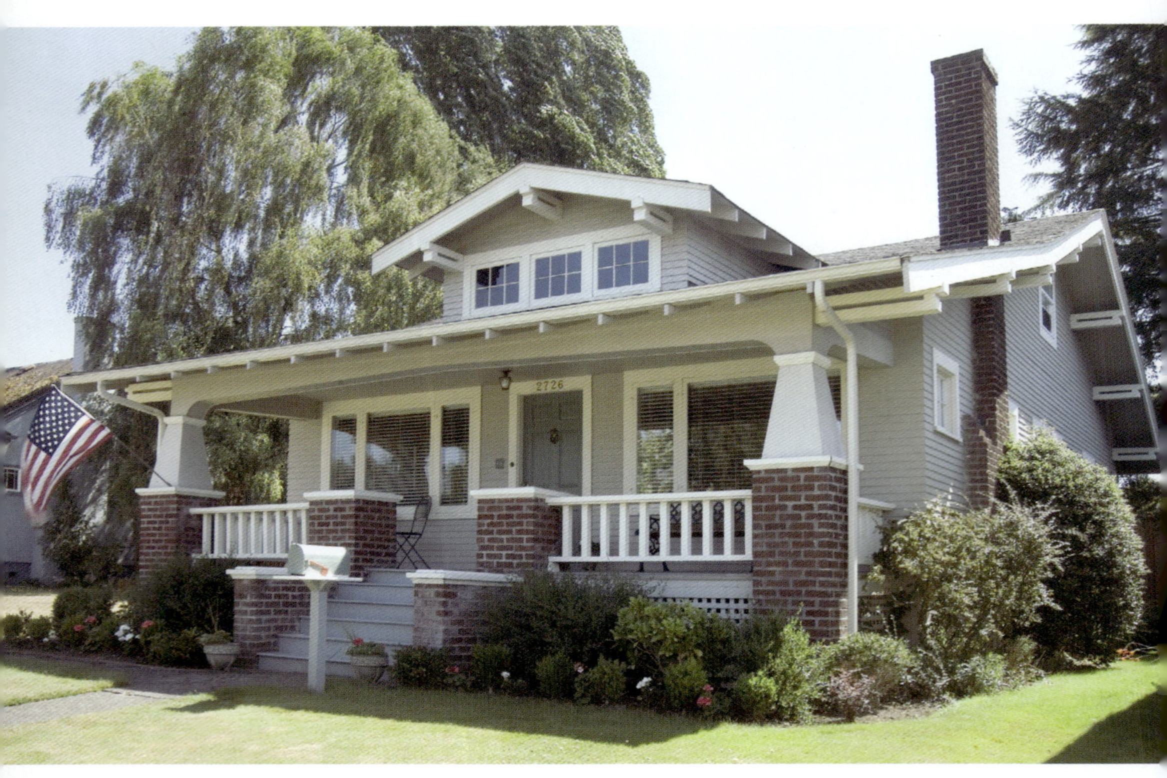


 Bellingham, Washington

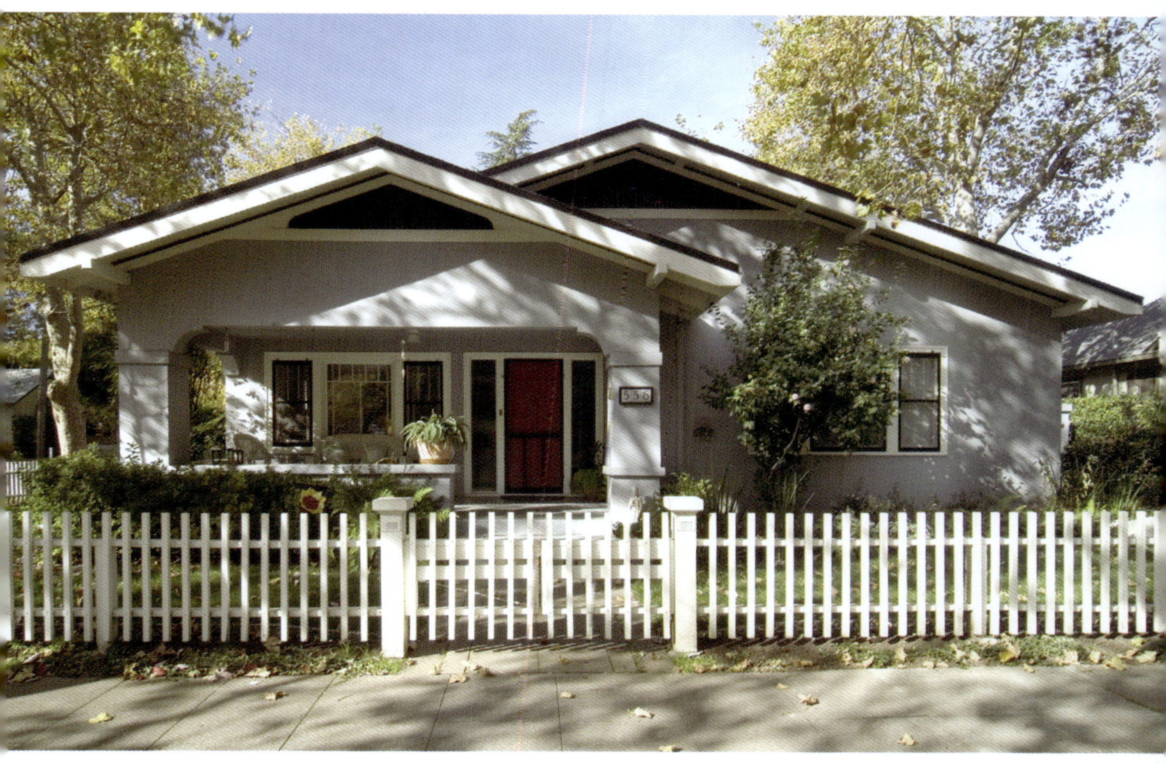


Chico, California

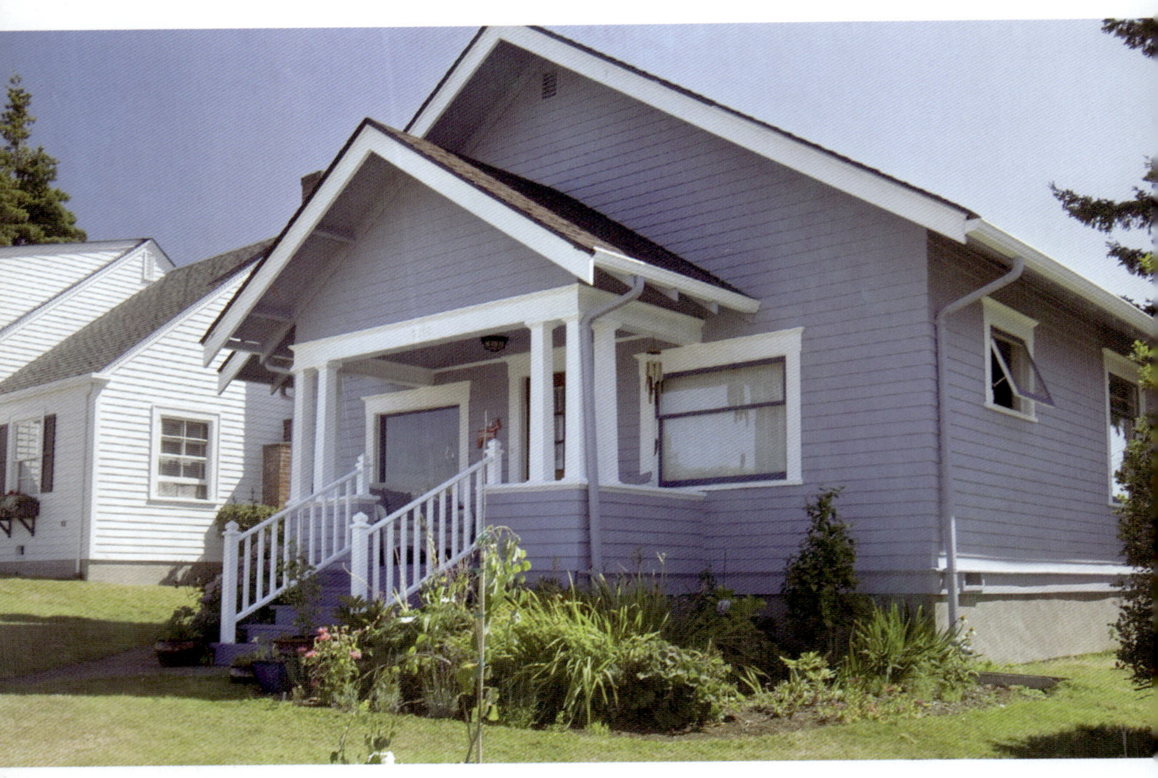

 Bellingham, Washington

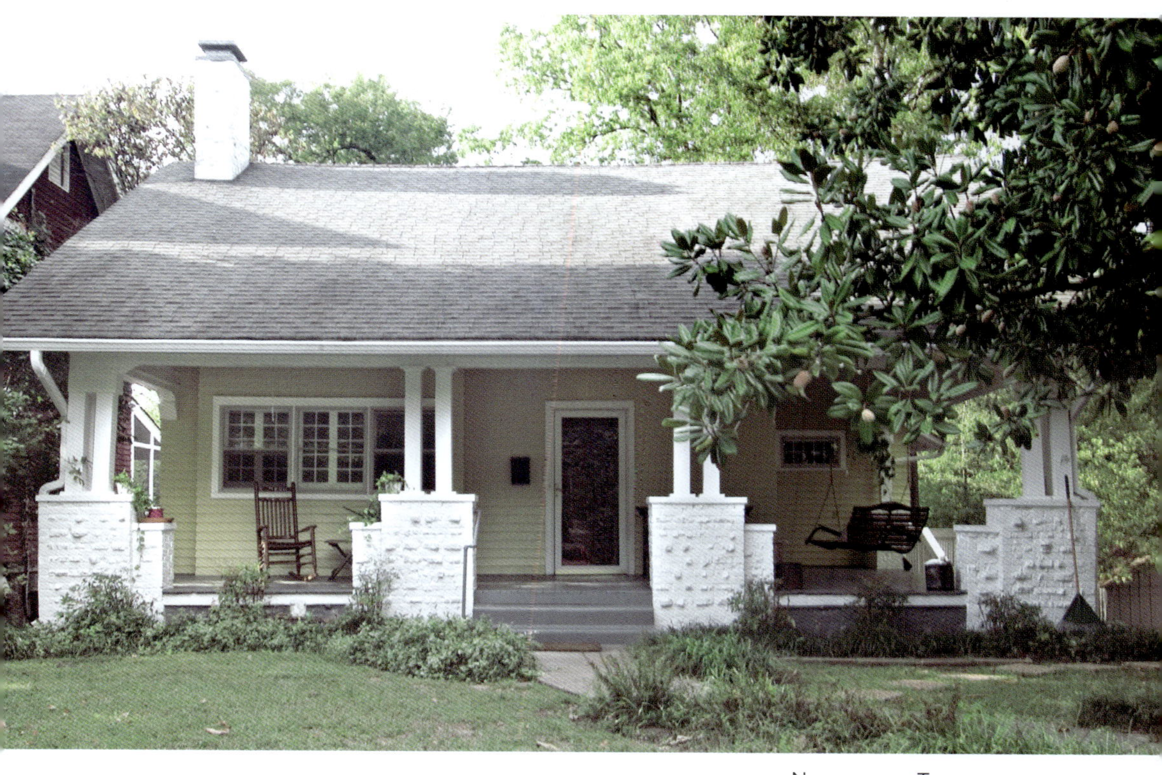

Nashville, Tennessee 

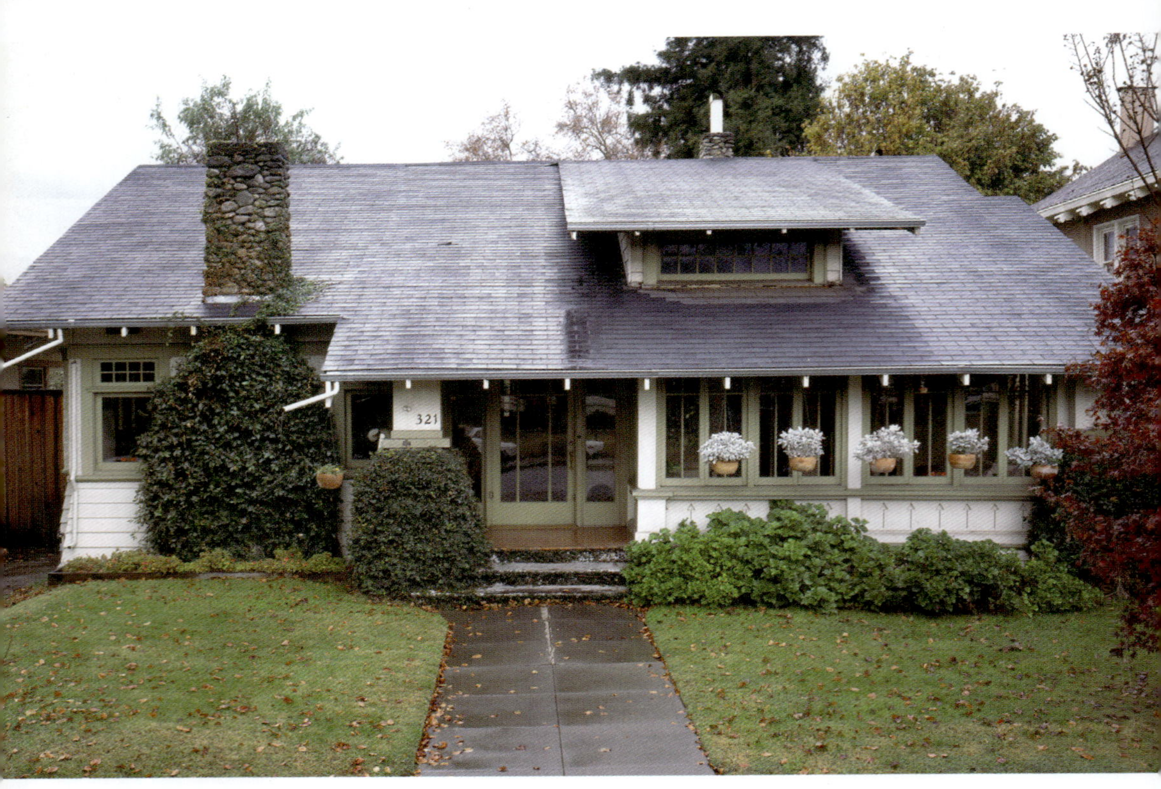


 San Jose, California

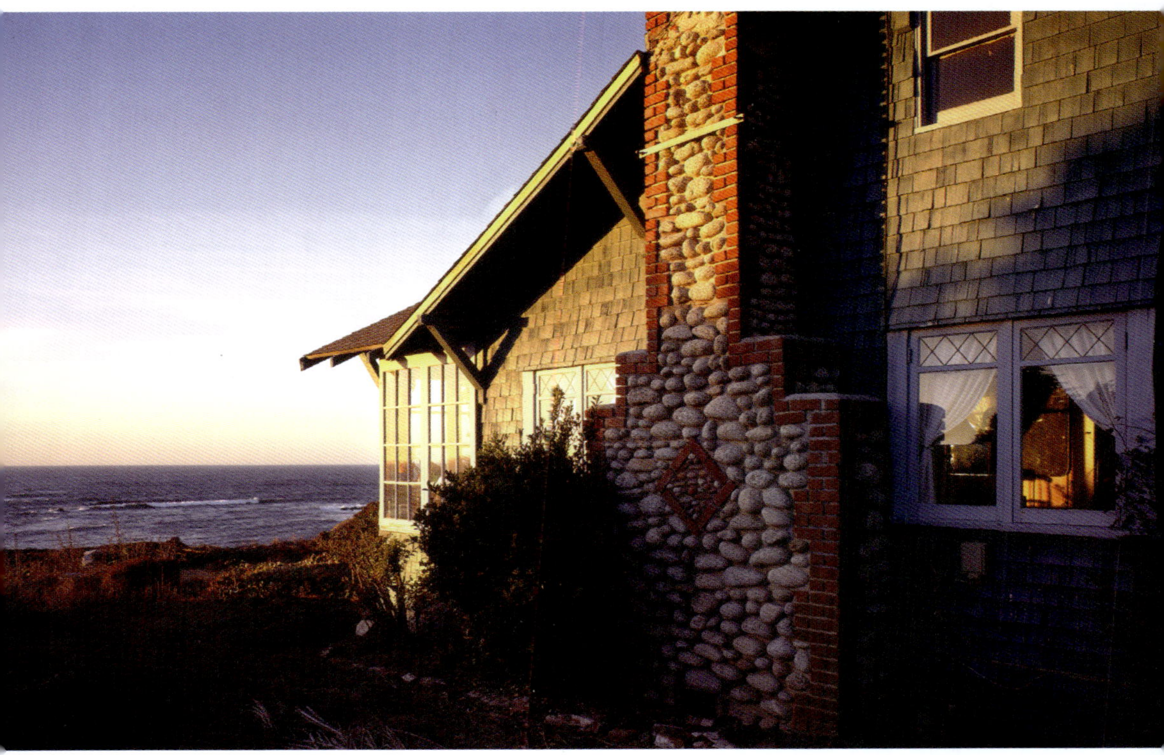

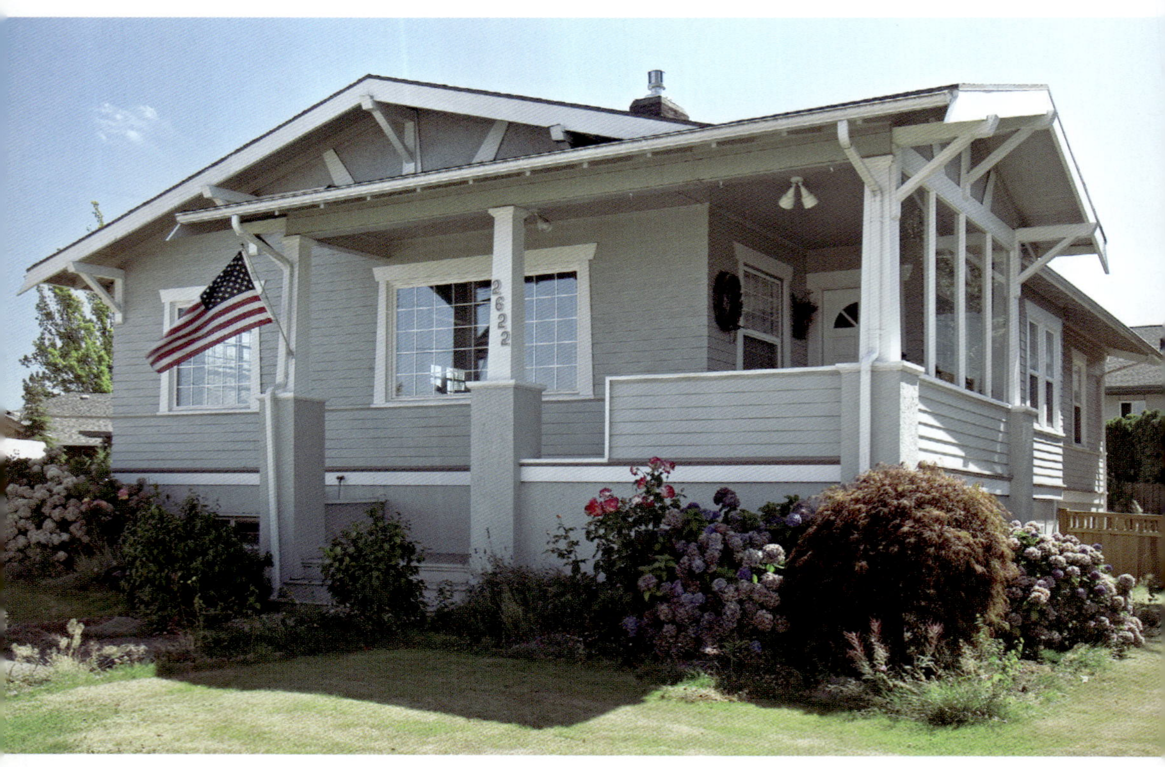


 BELLINGHAM, WASHINGTON

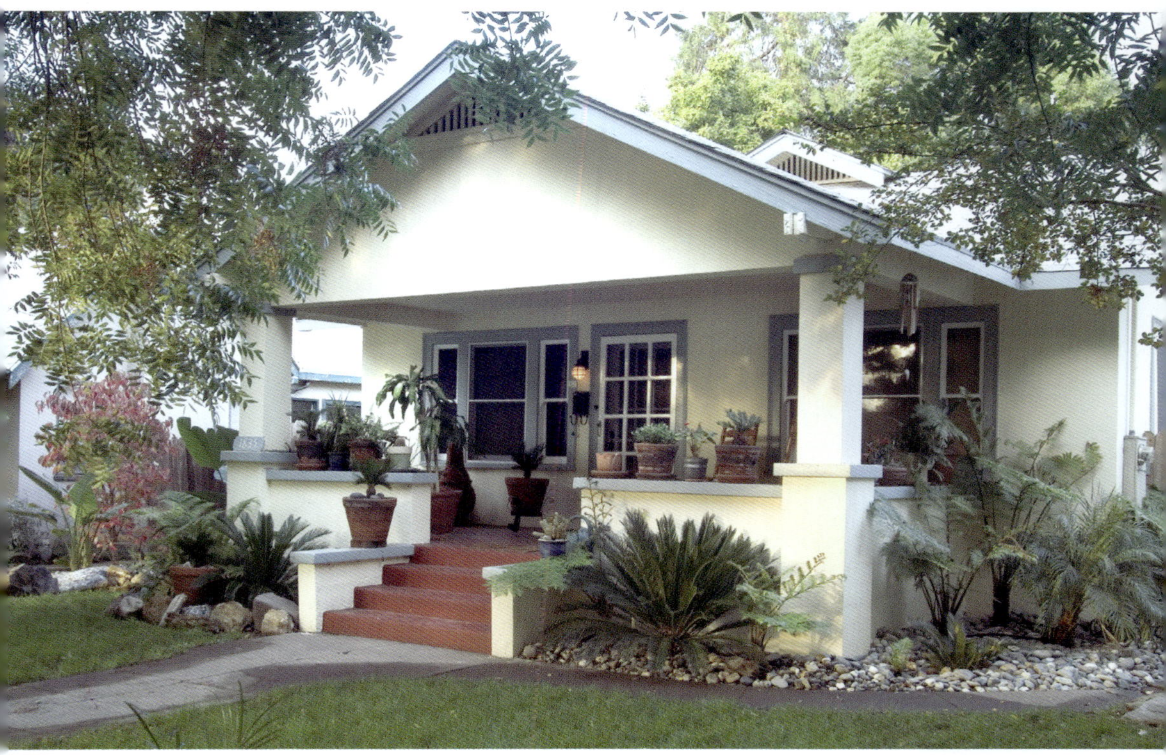

Chico, California 

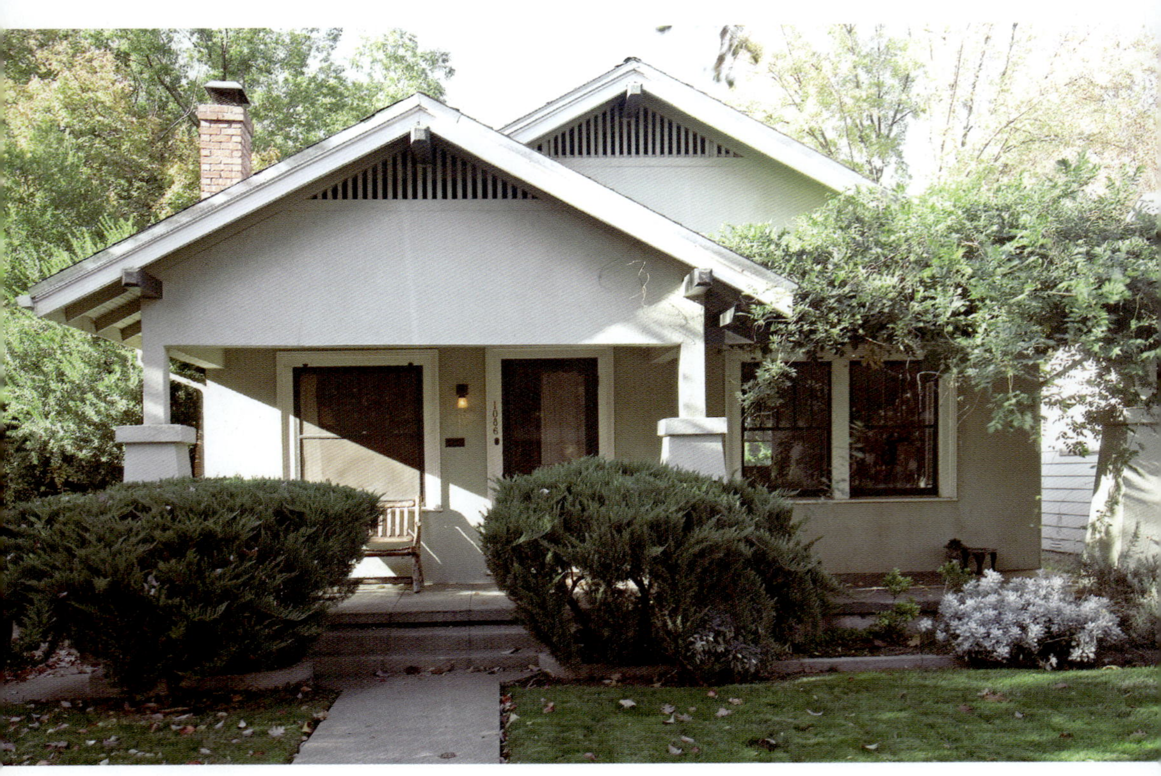

 CHICO, CALIFORNIA

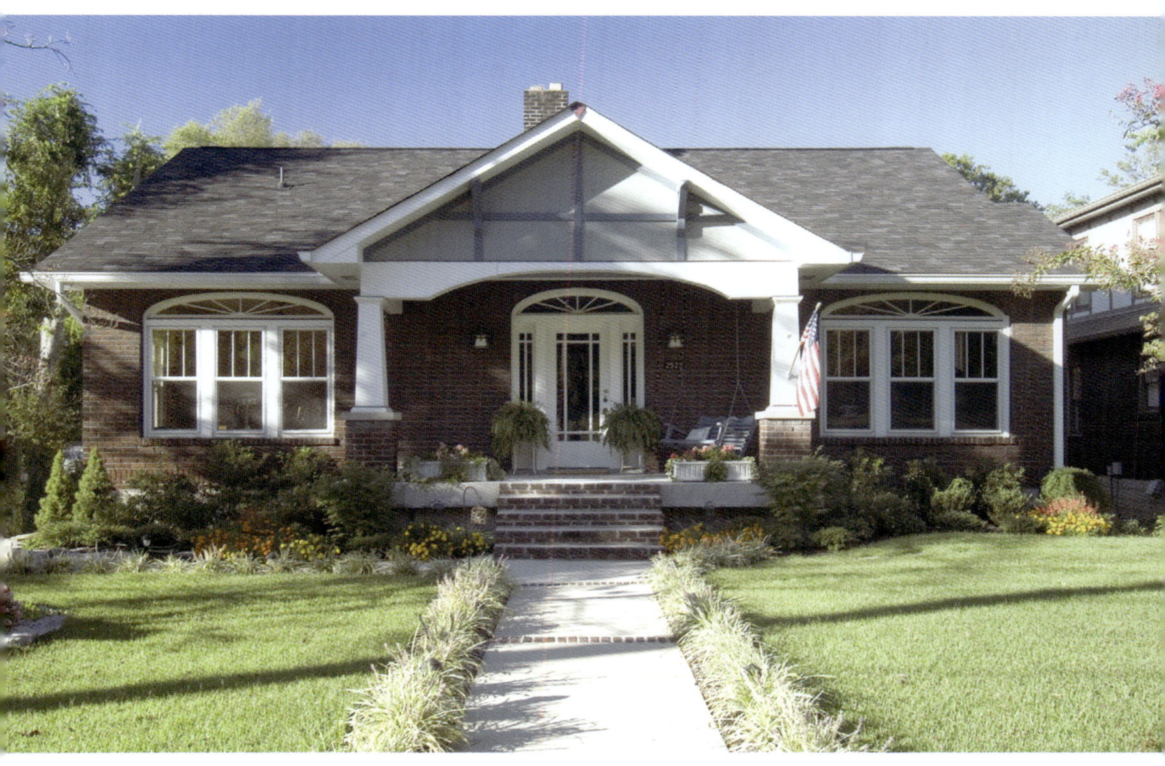

Nashville, Tennessee

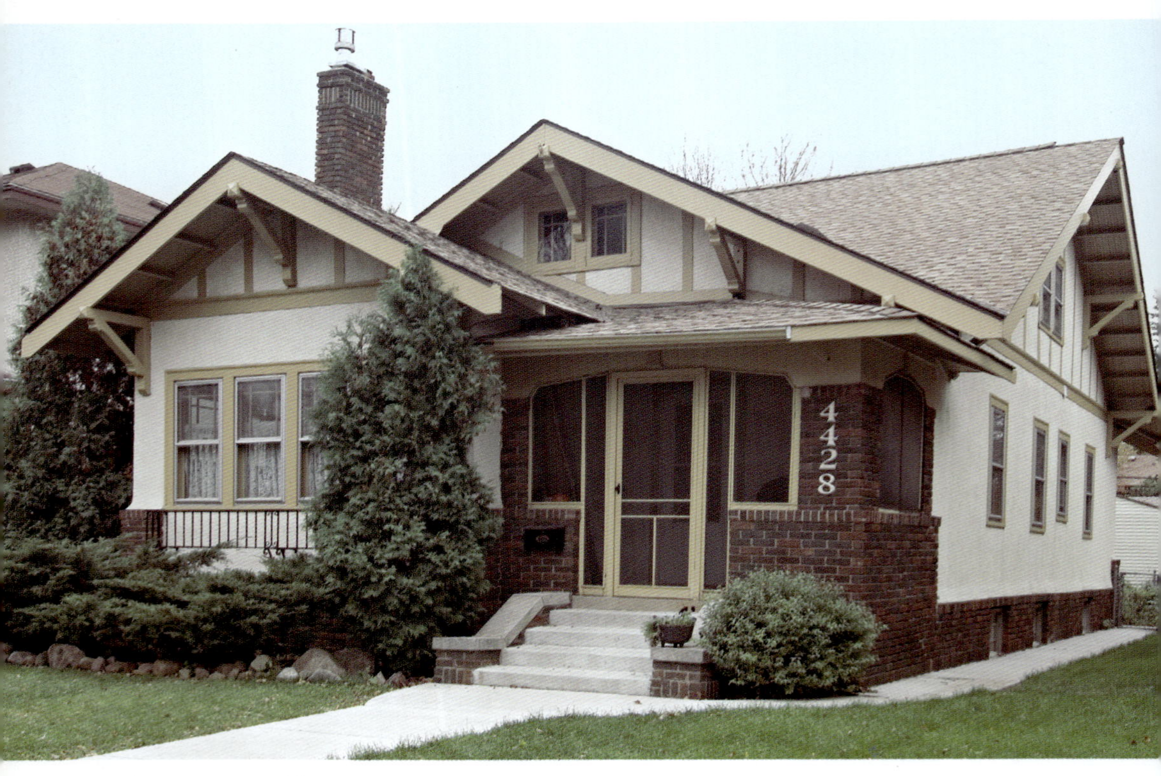


 MINNEAPOLIS, MINNESOTA

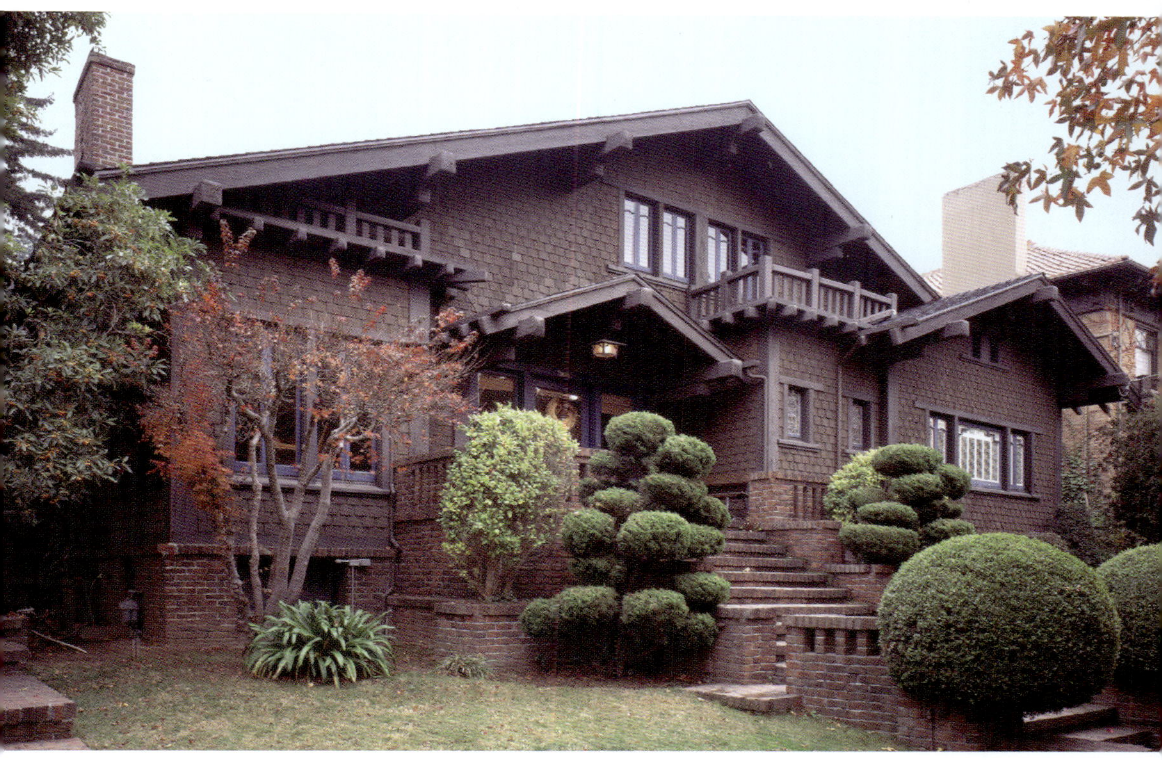

Piedmont, California

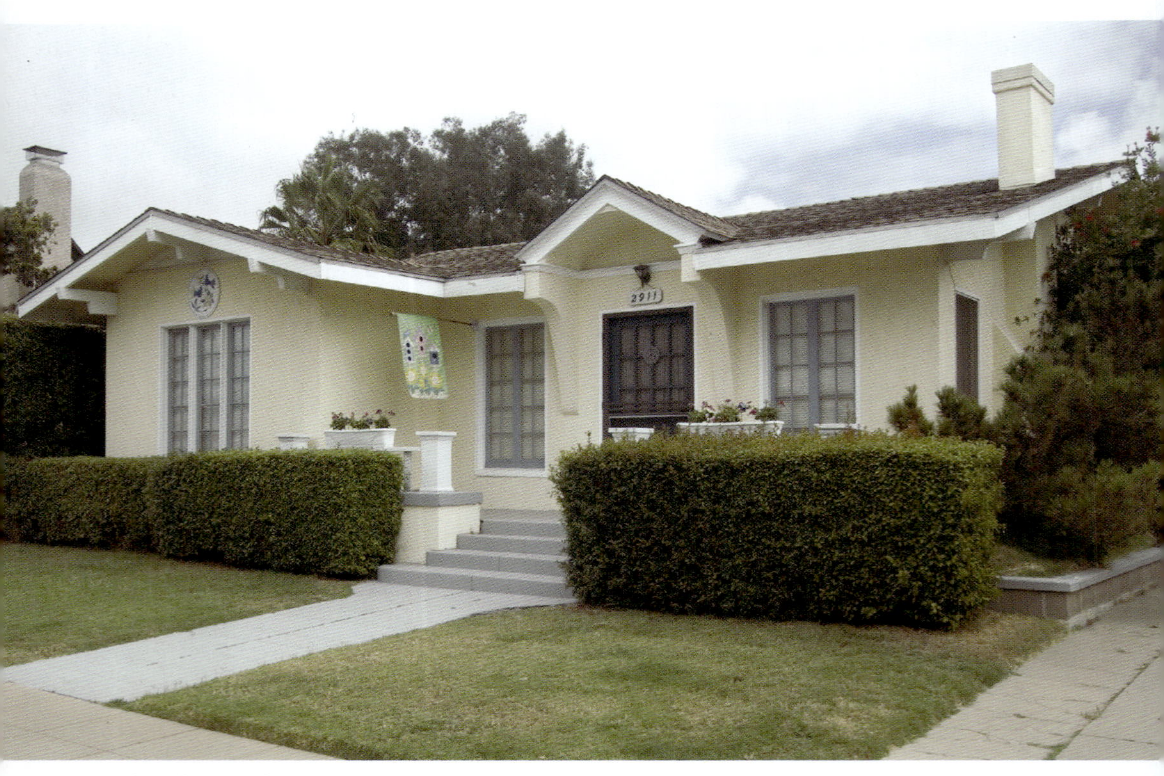


 San Diego, California

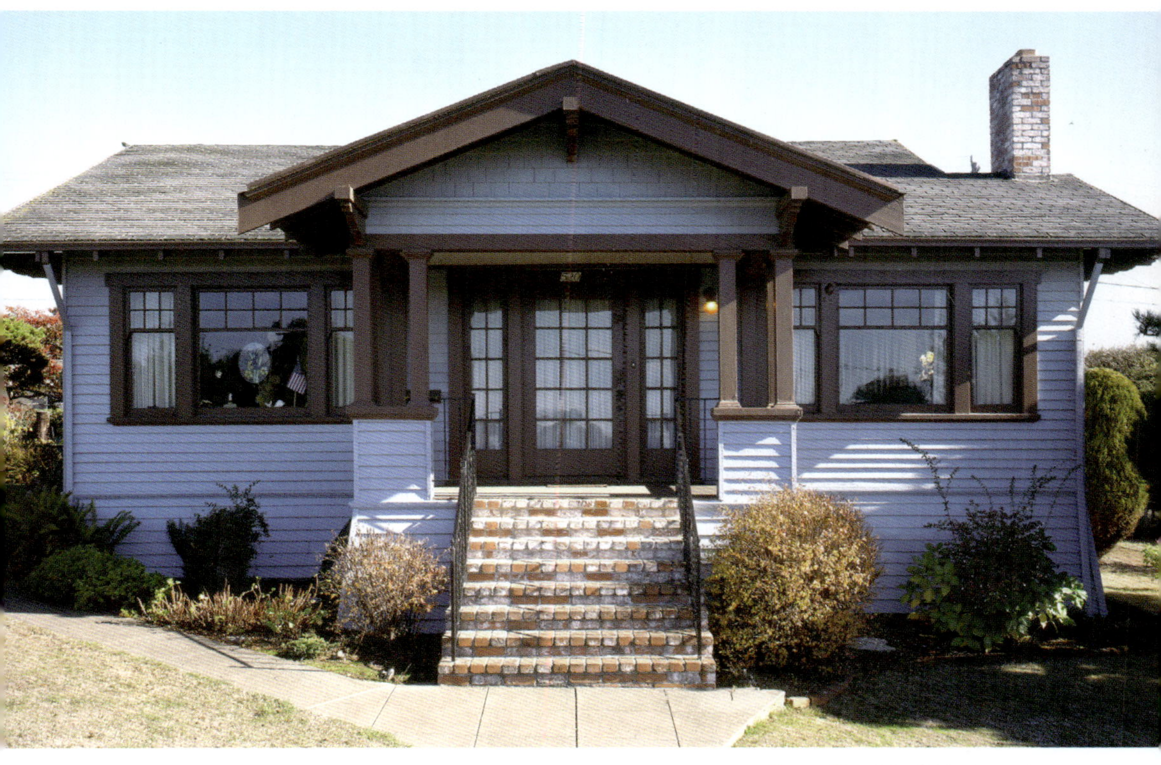

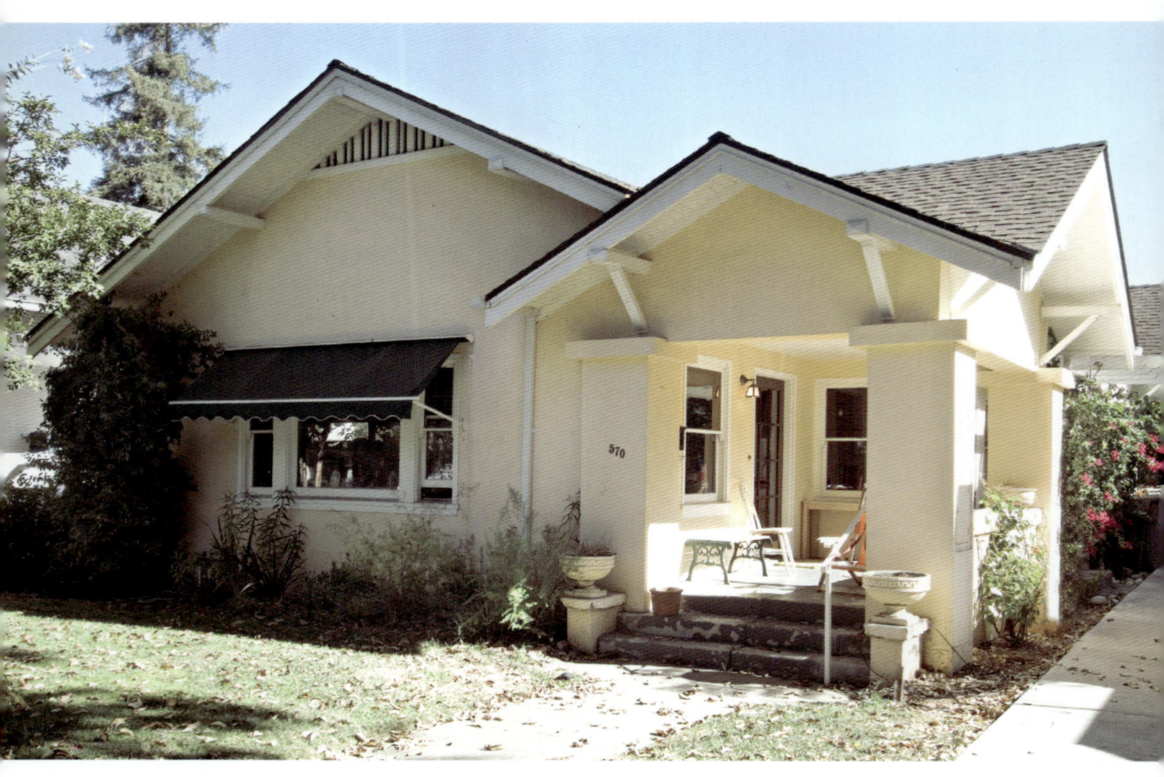


 San Jose, California

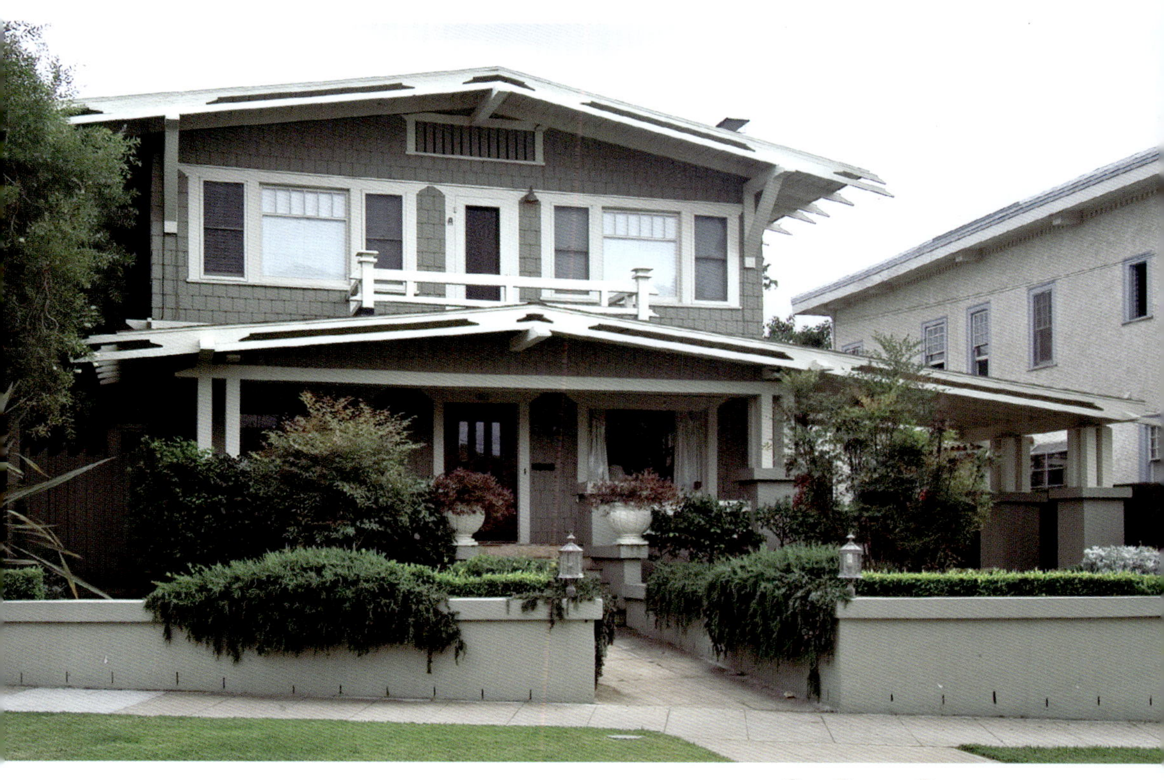

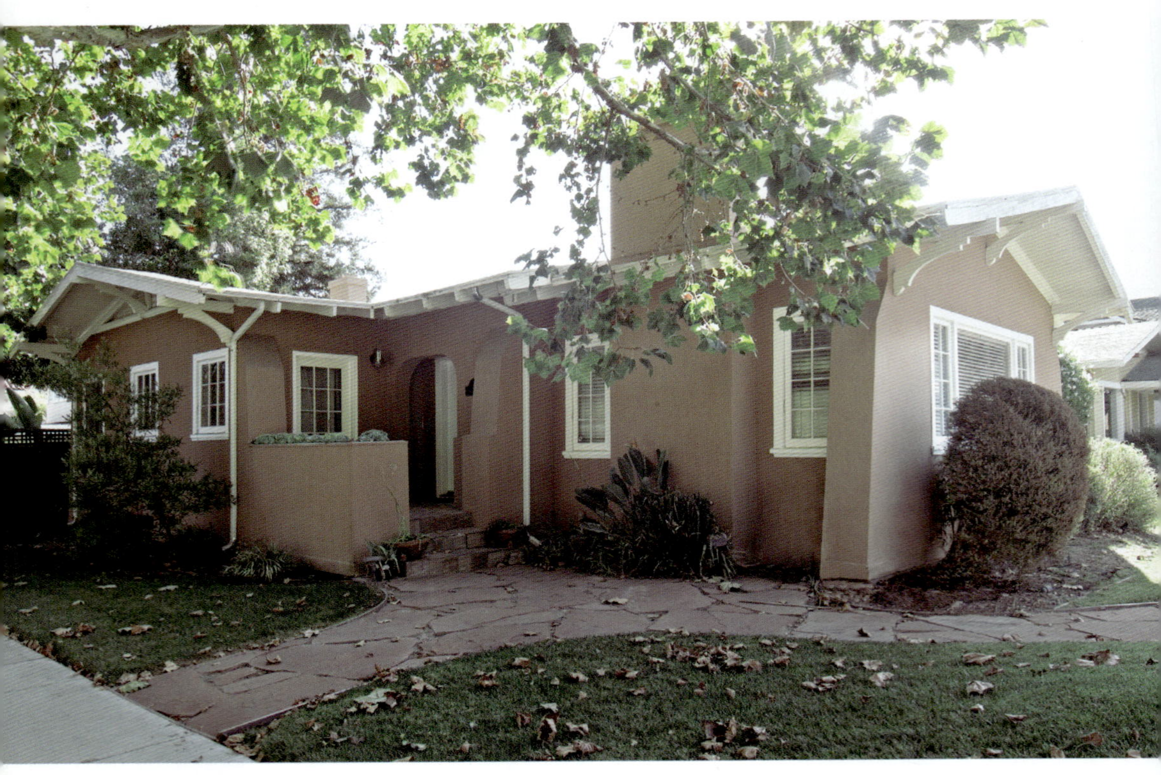

 San Jose, California

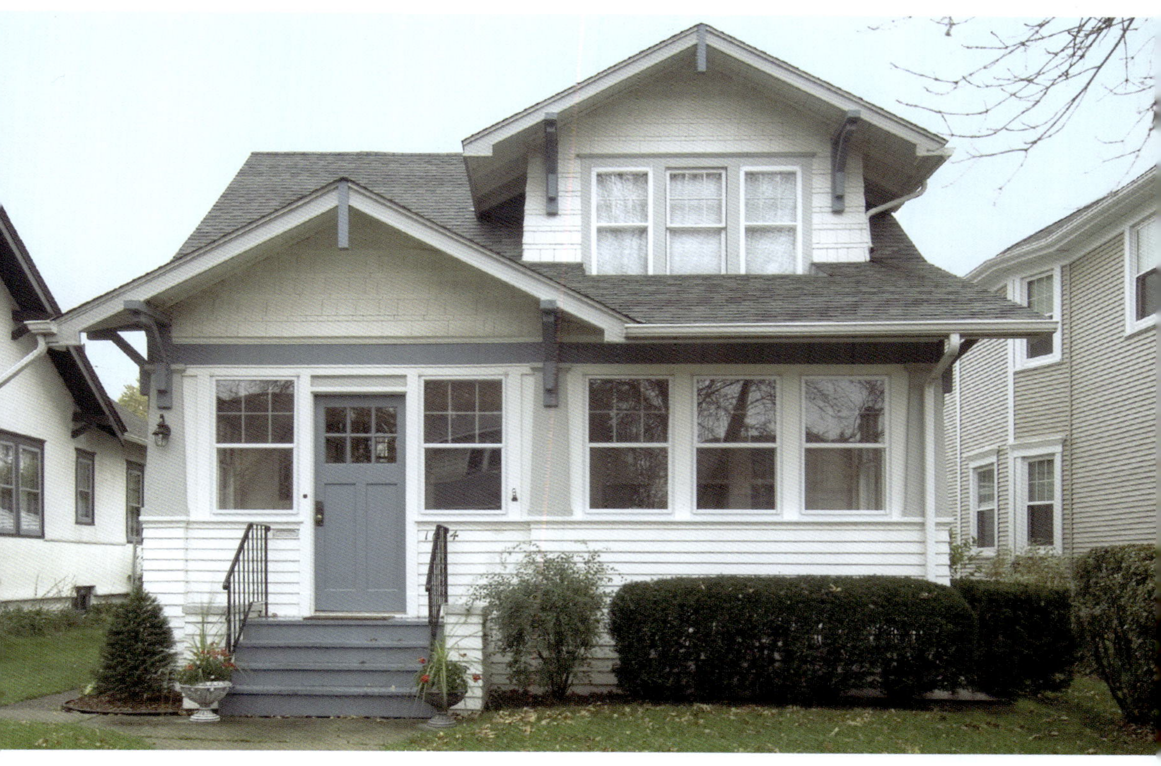

St. Paul, Minnesota

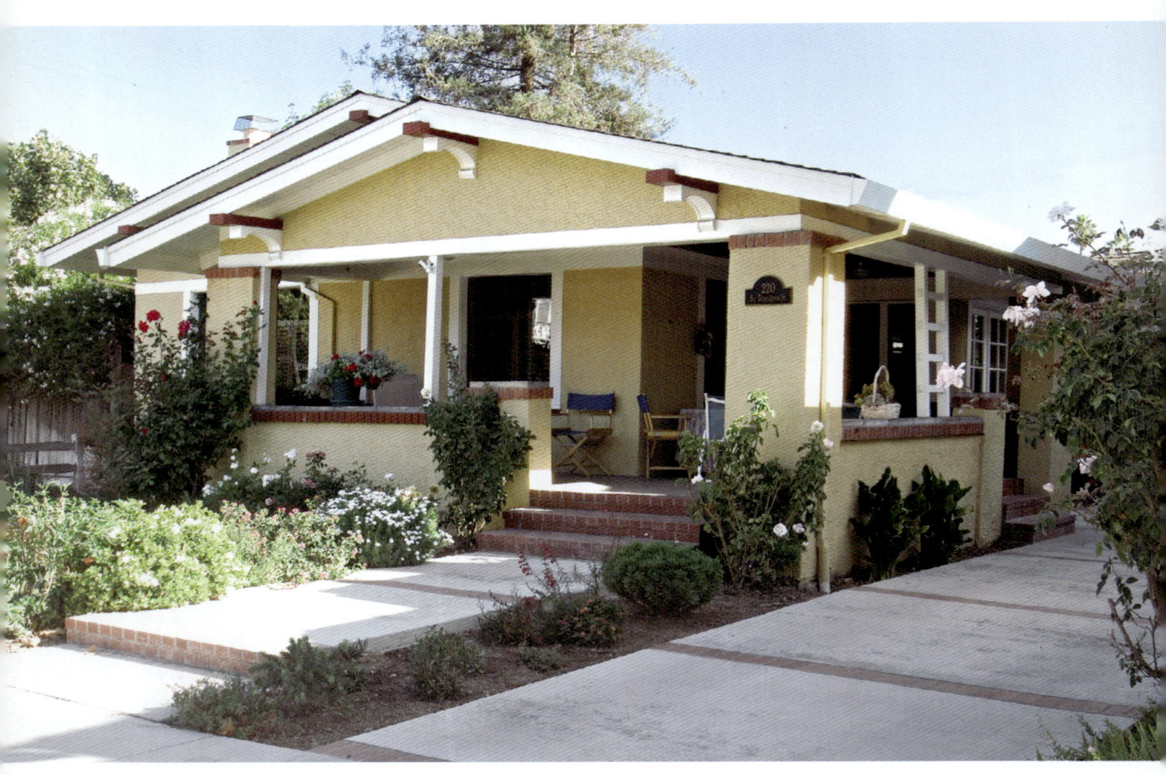


 San Jose, California

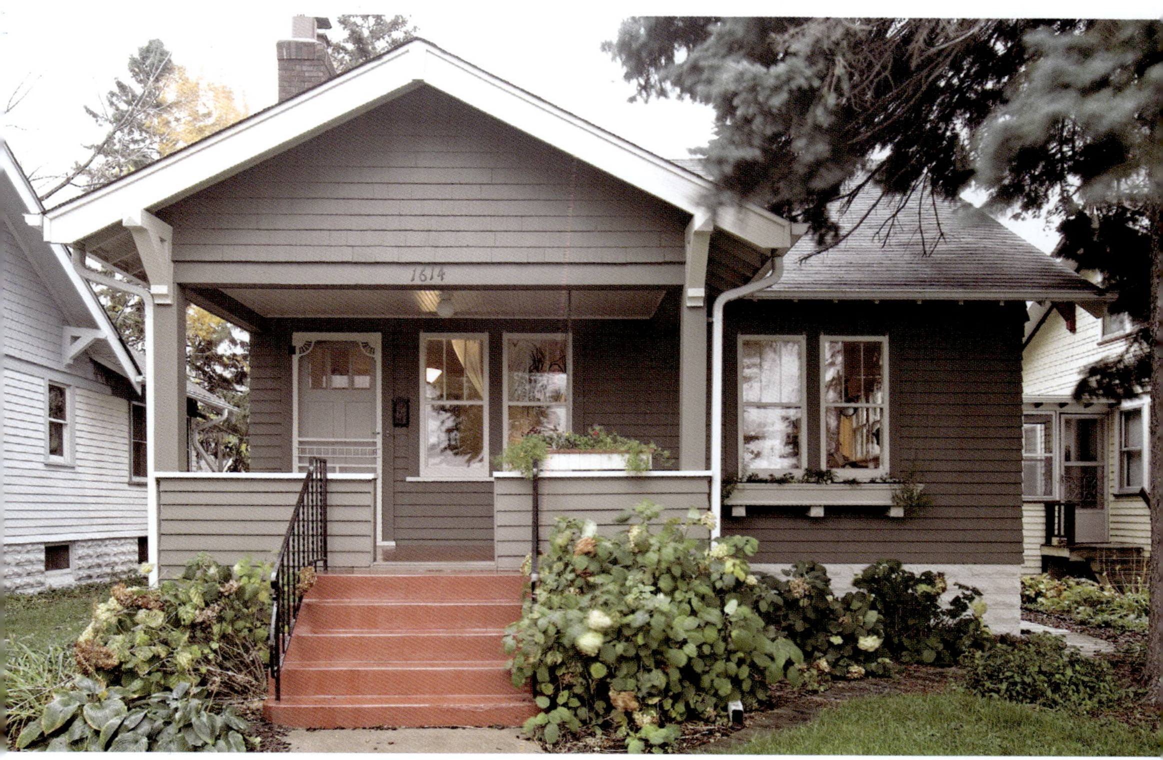


St. Paul, Minnesota 

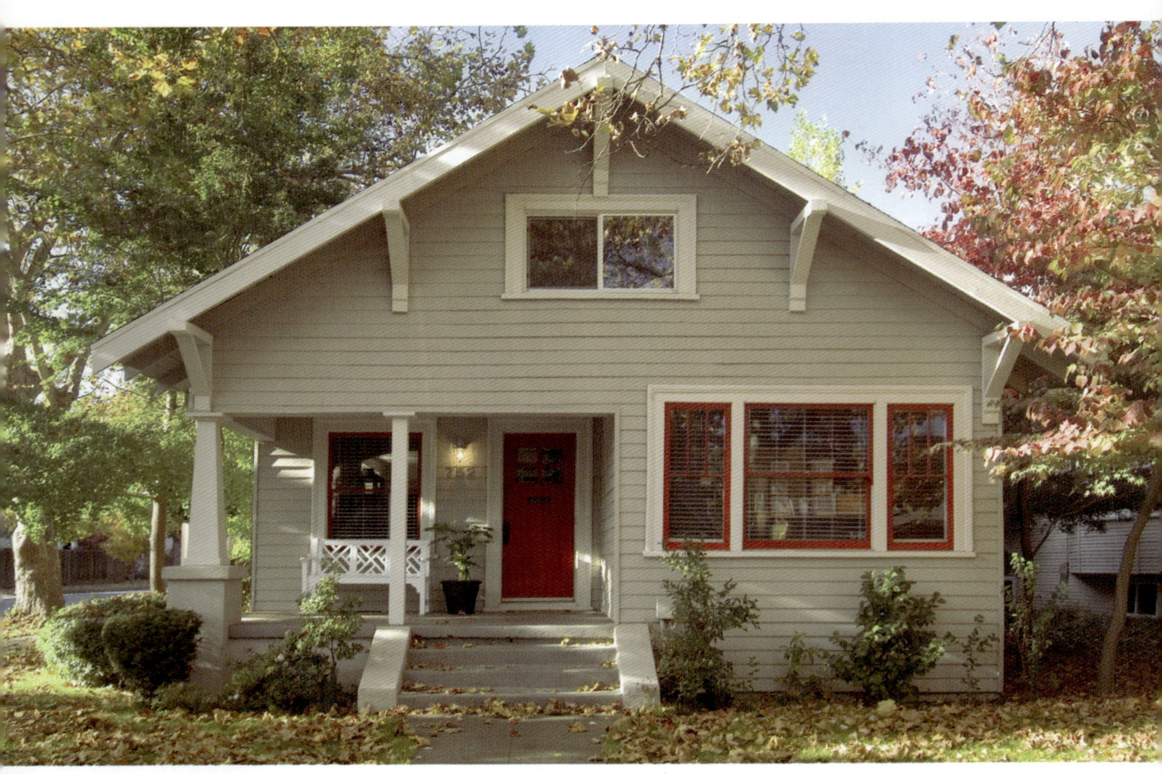

 Chico, California

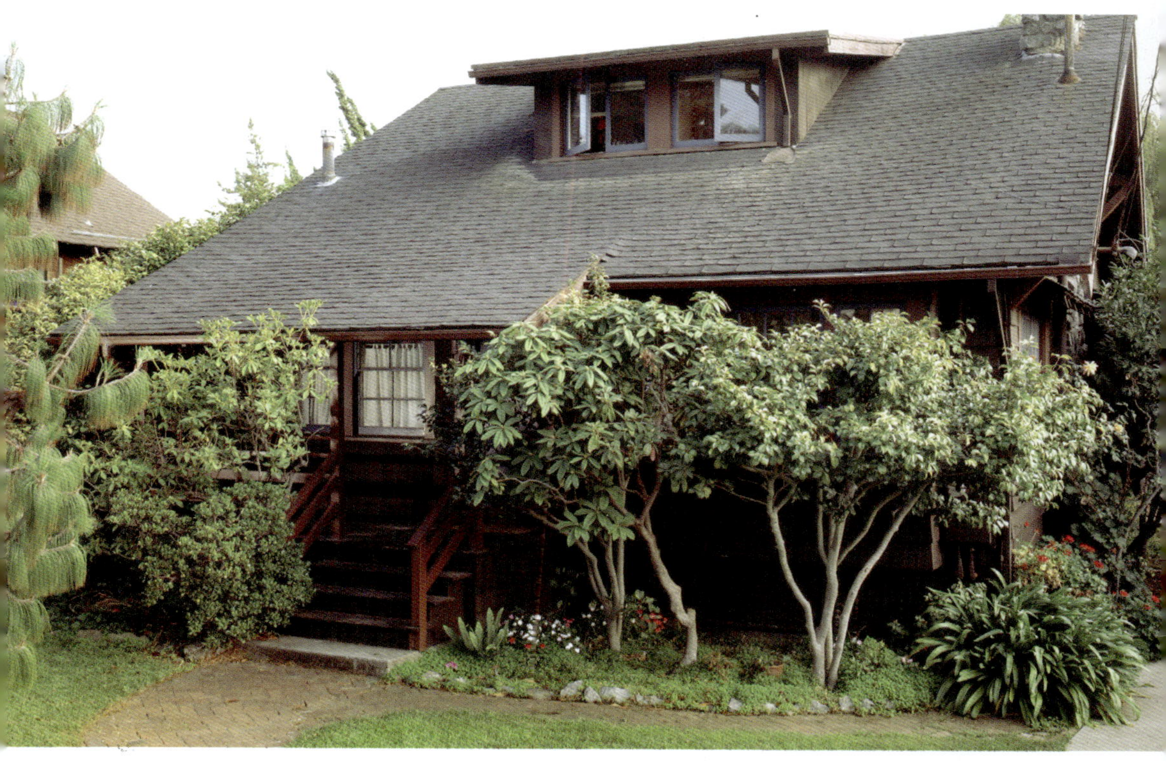

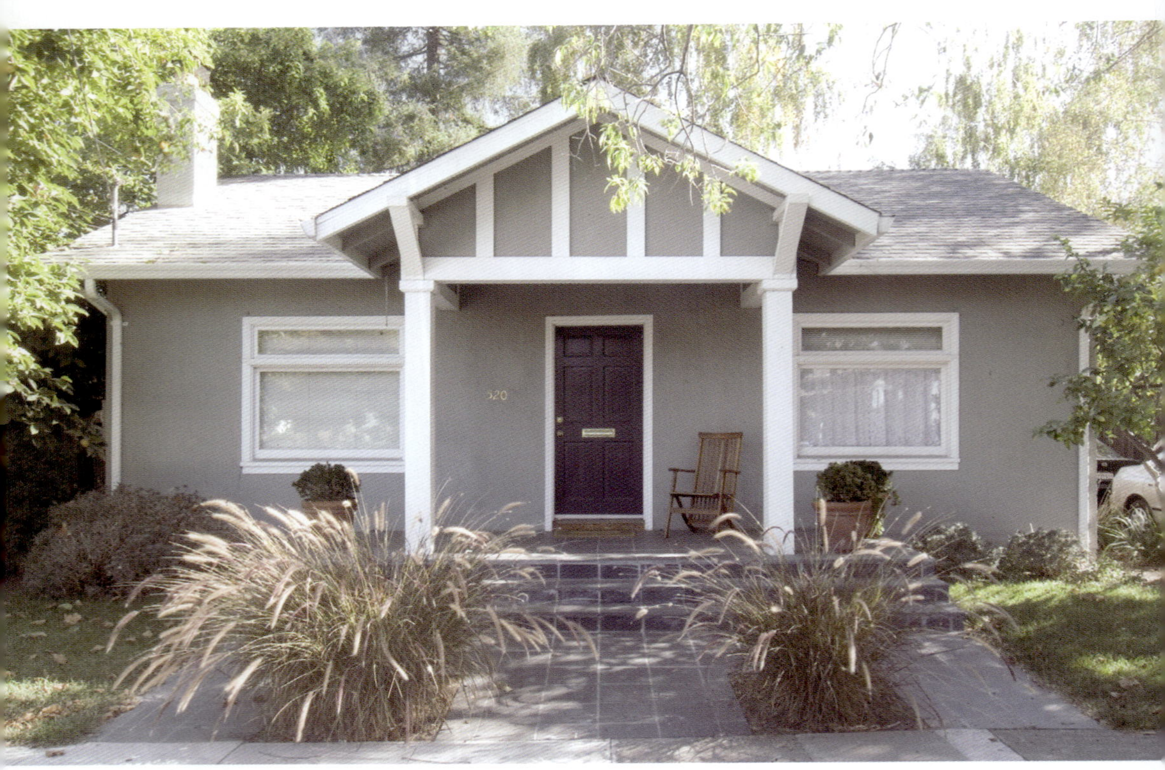

 San Jose, California

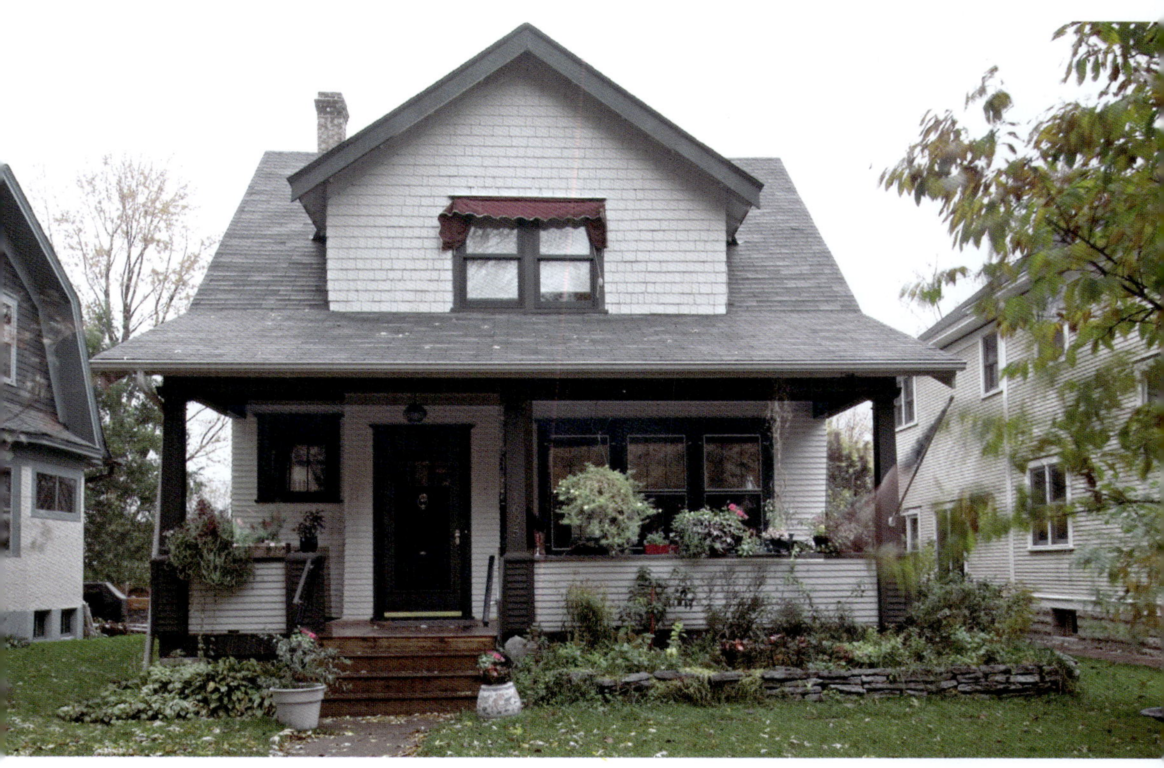

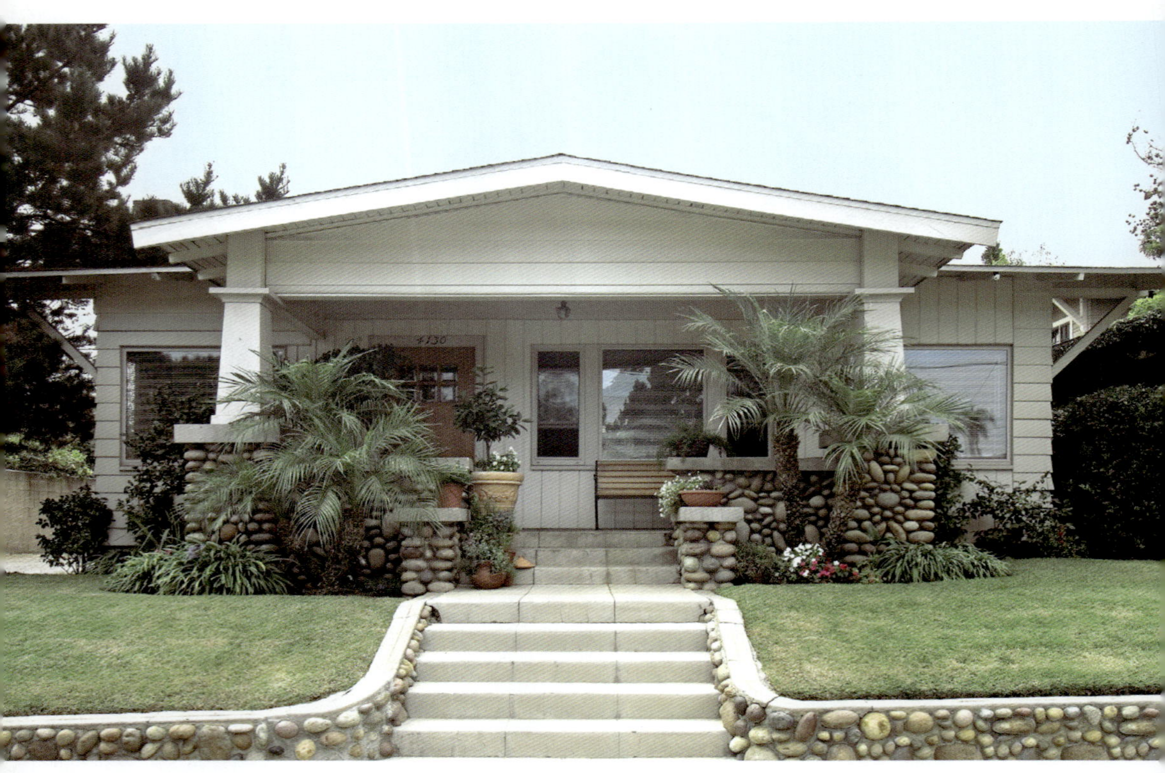


San Diego, California

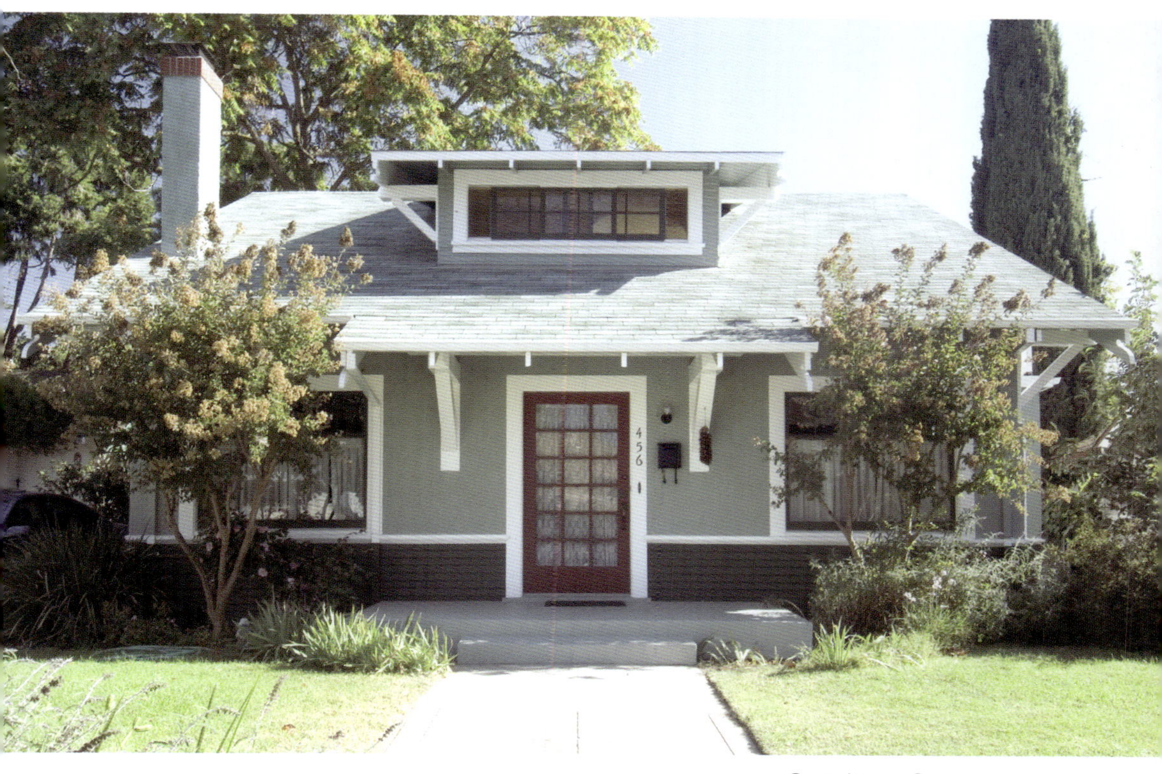


San Jose, California

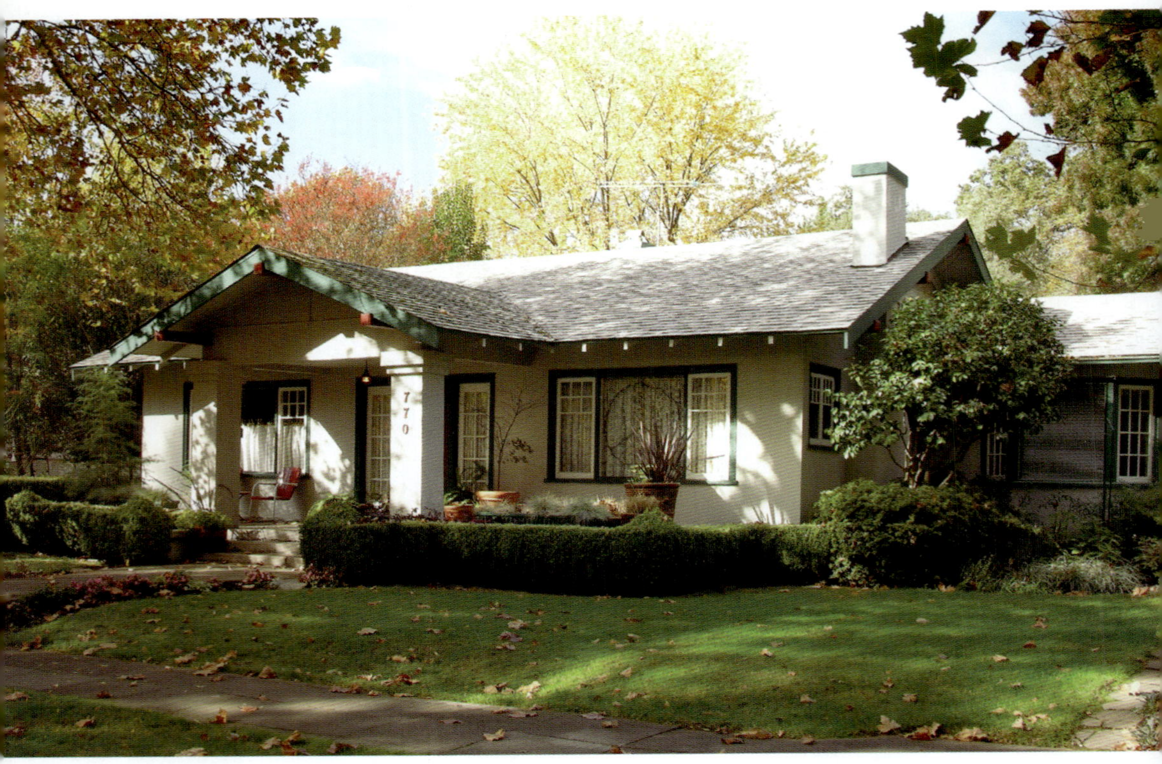


 Chico, California

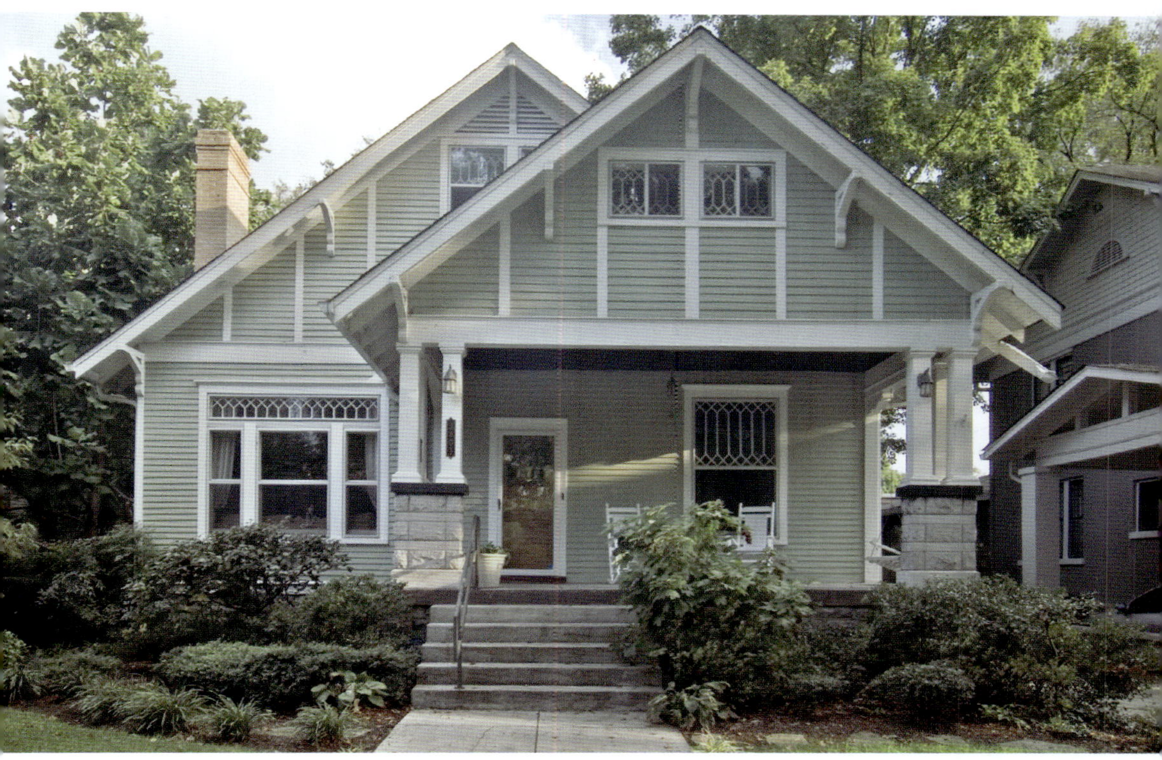

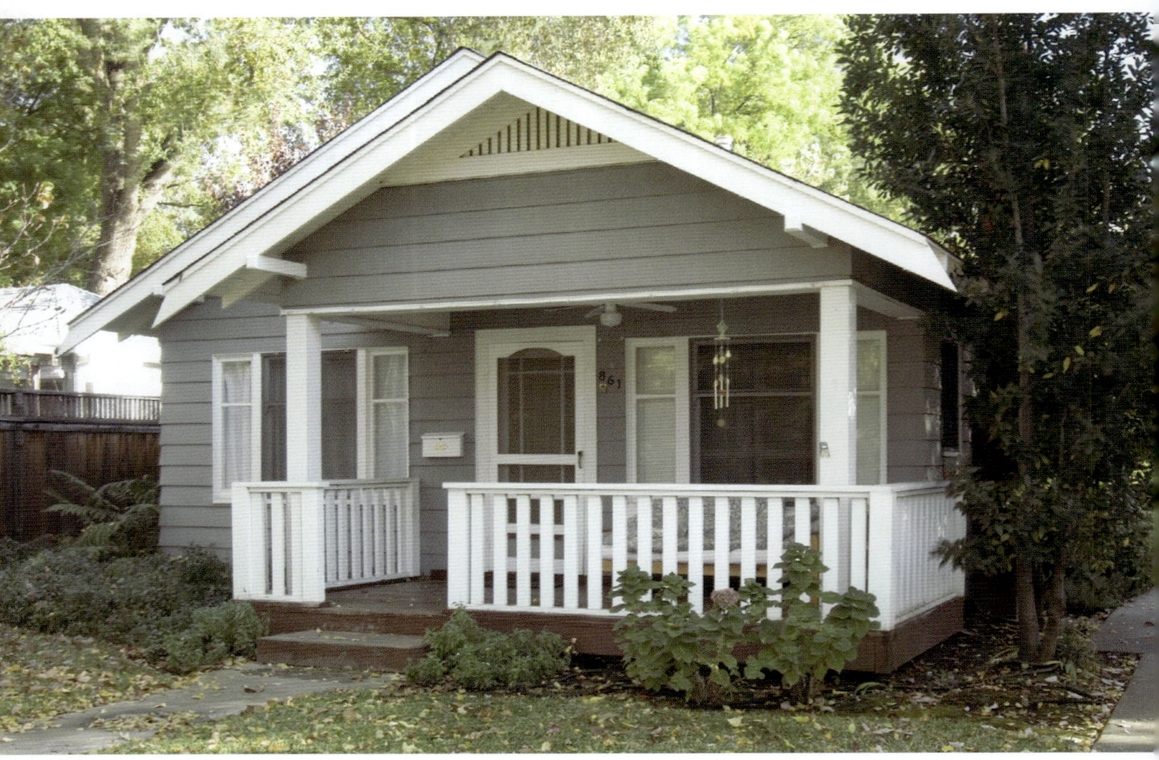


 Chico, California

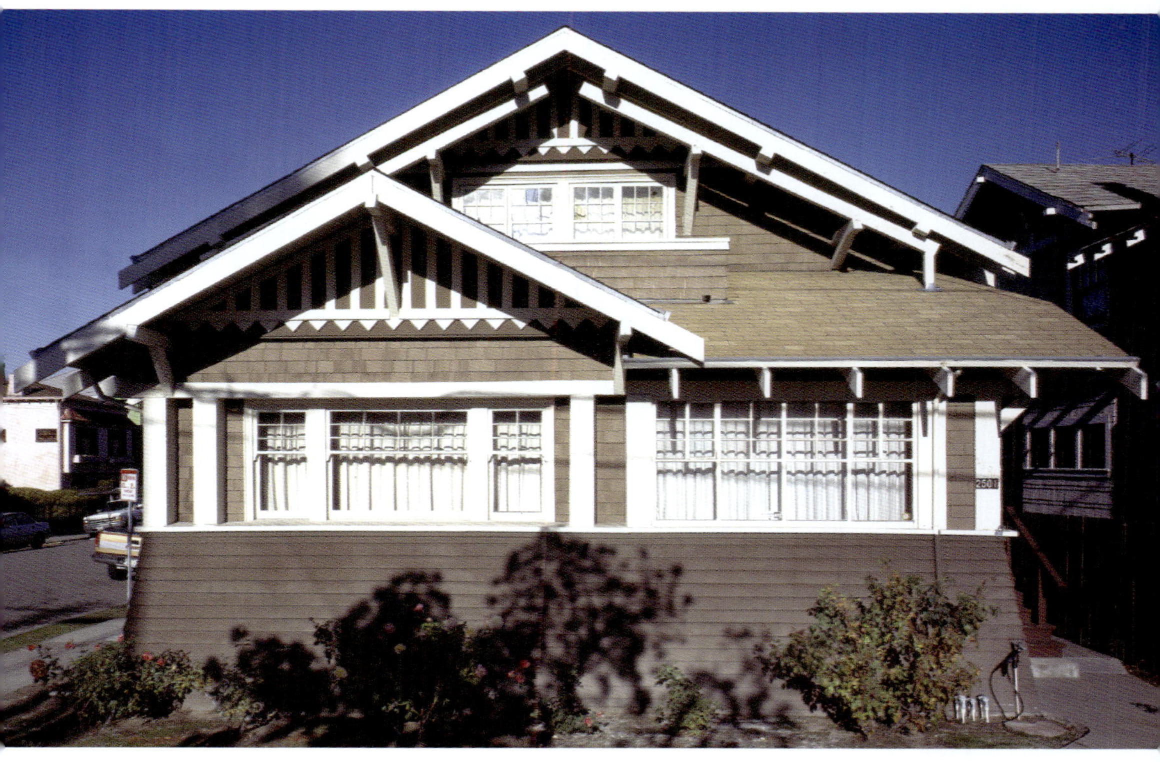


Alameda, California 

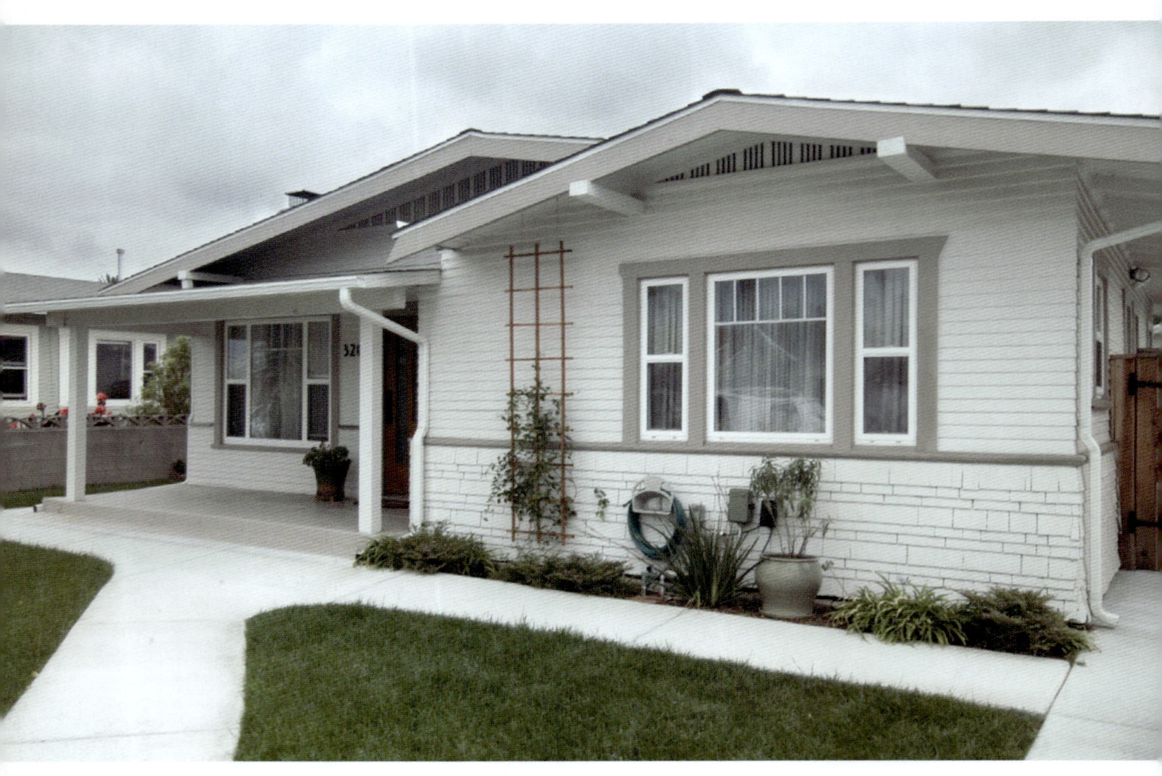

 San Diego, California

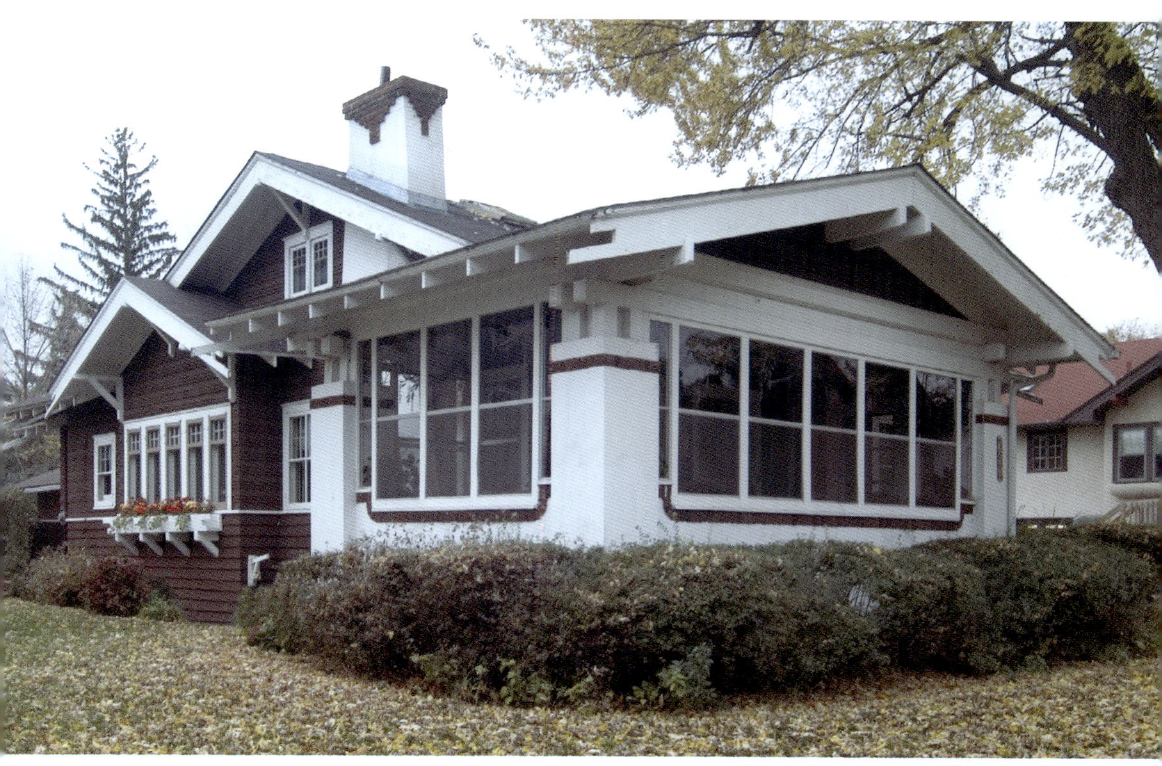

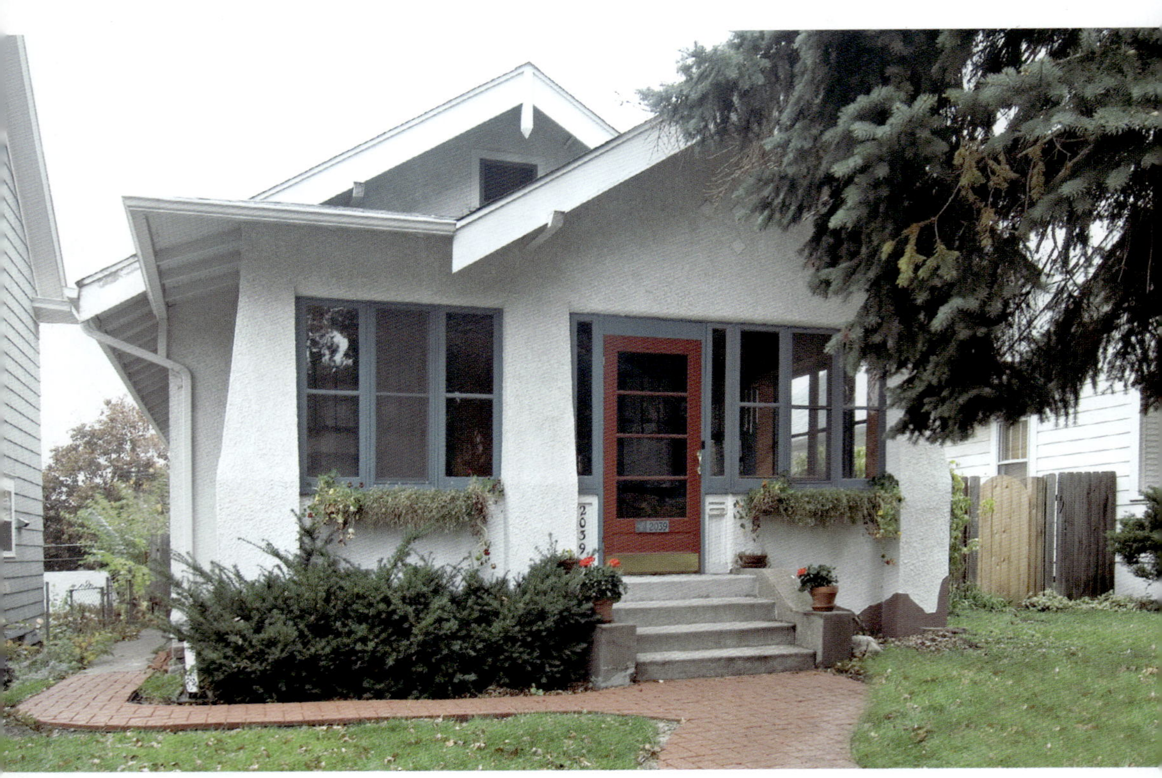
2039
2039

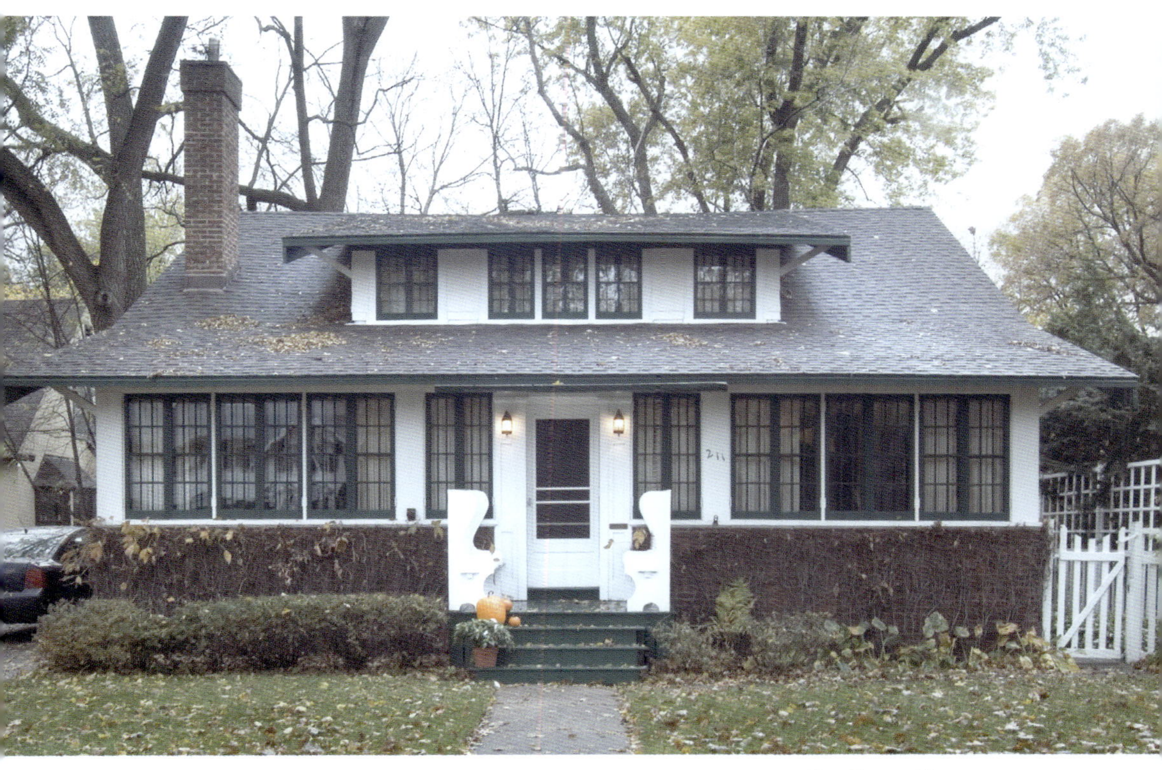

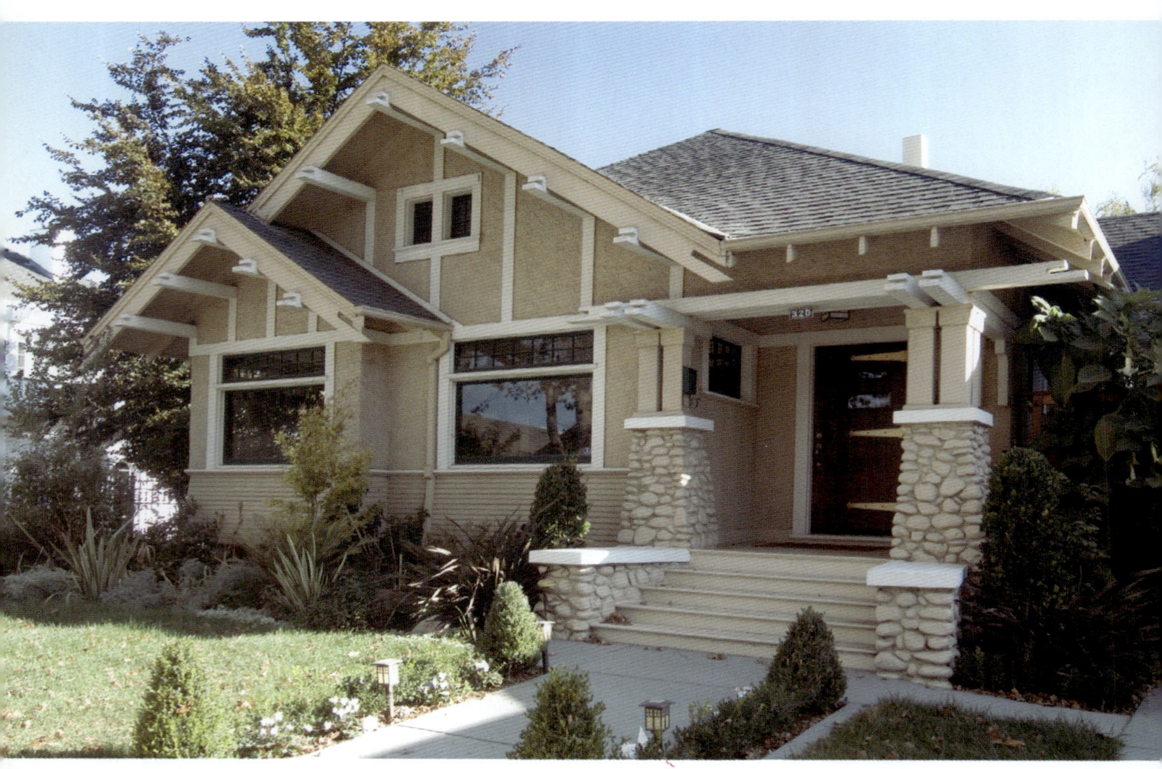

 San Jose, California

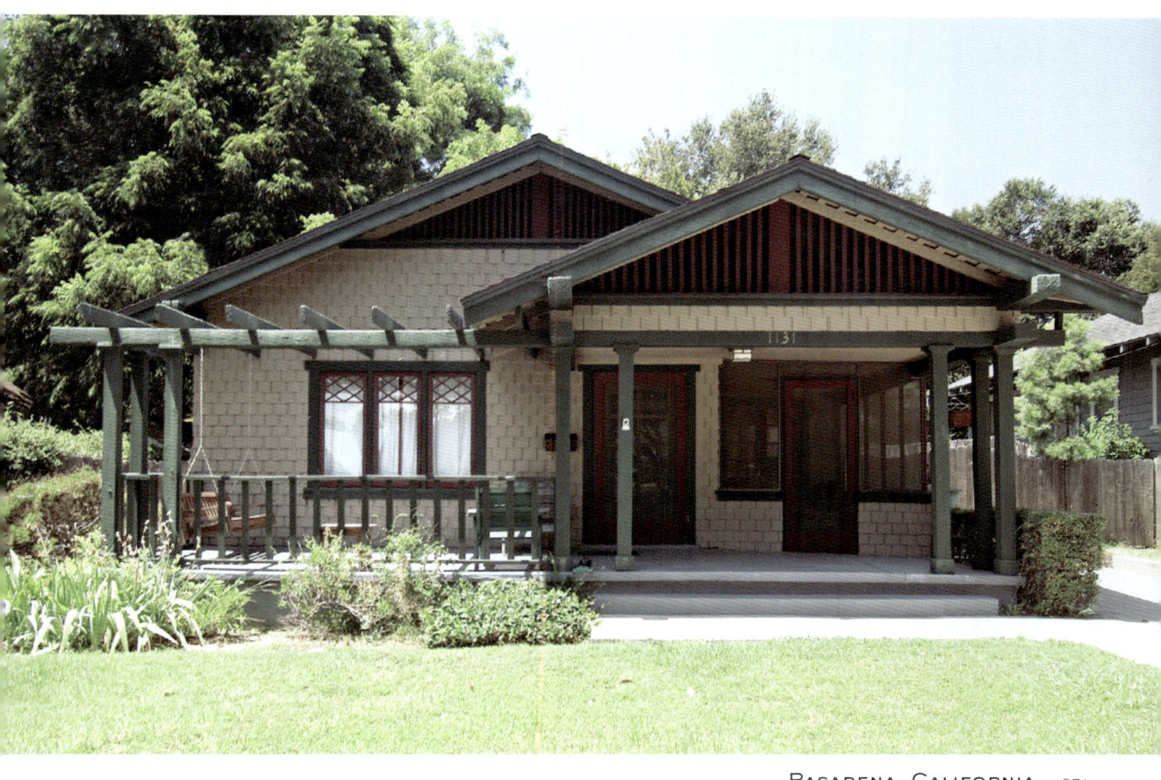

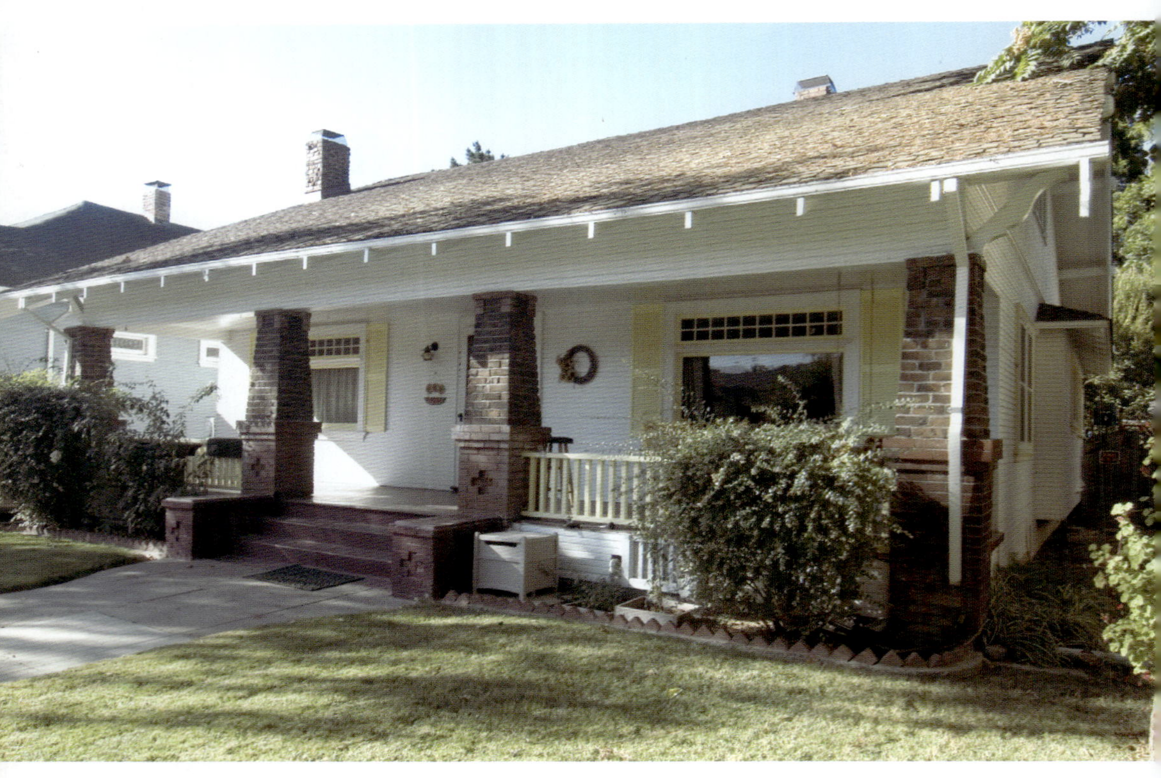

 San Jose, California

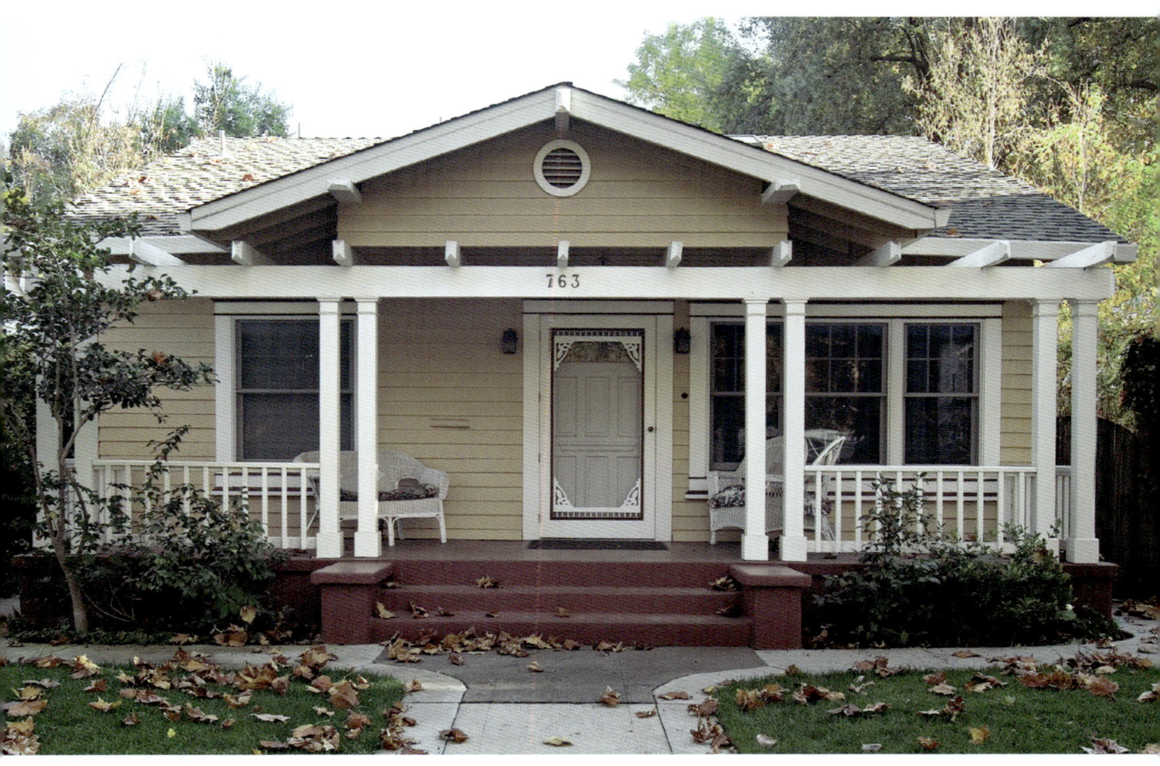


CHICO, CALIFORNIA 

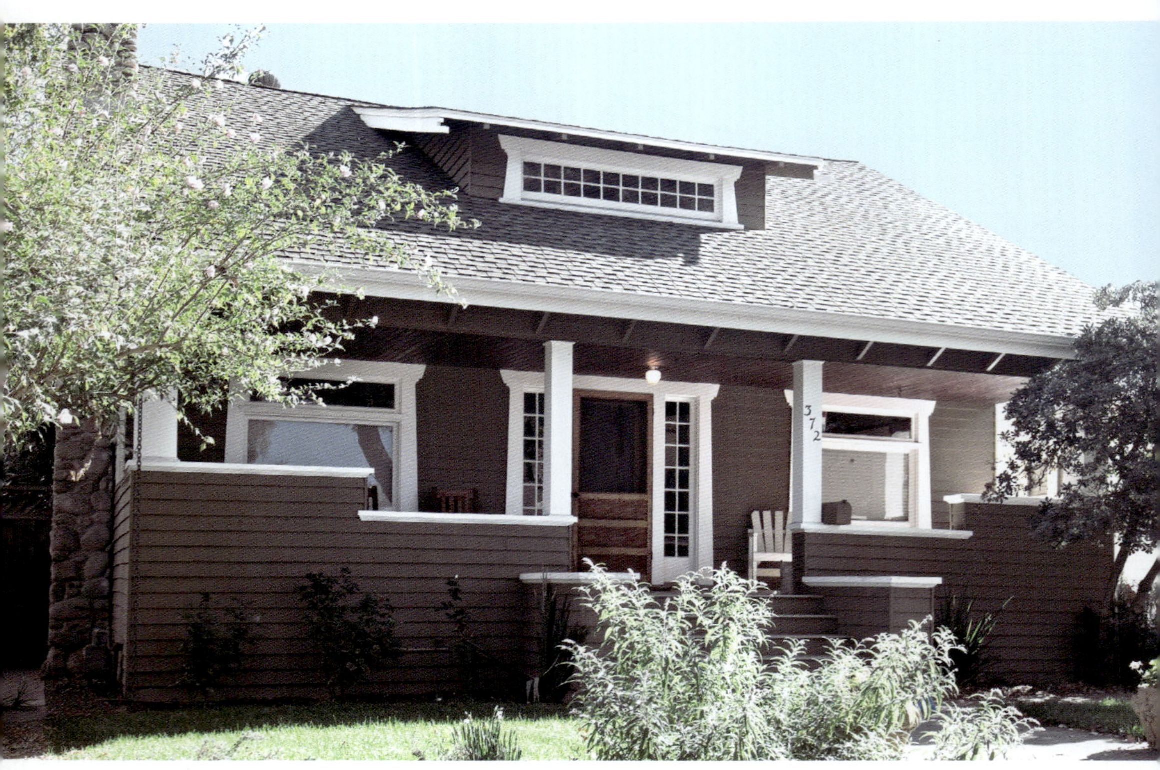


 San Jose, California

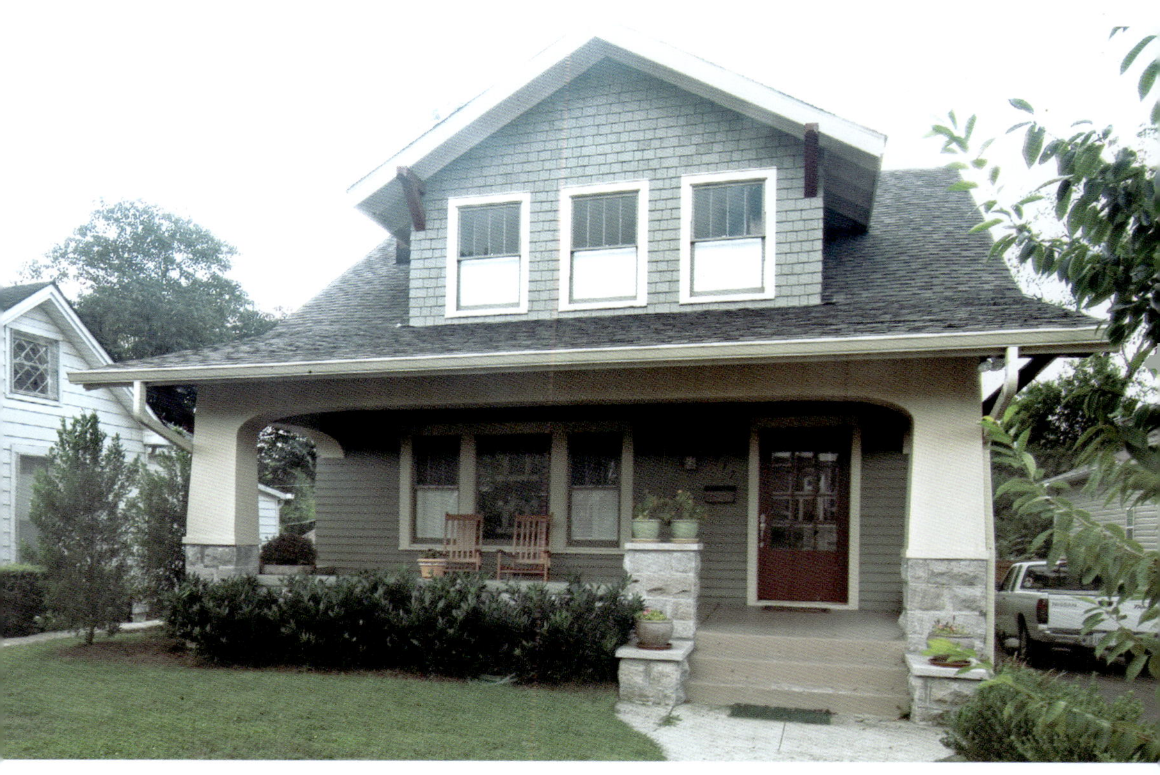

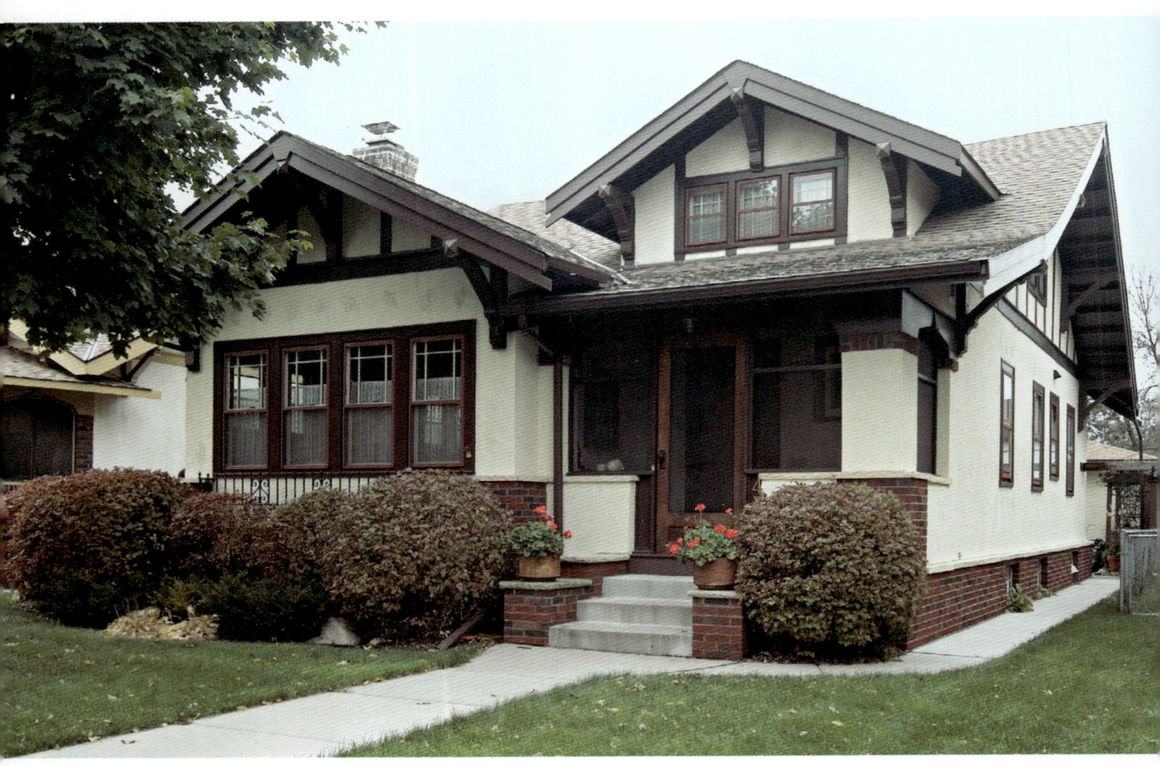

 Minneapolis, Minnesota

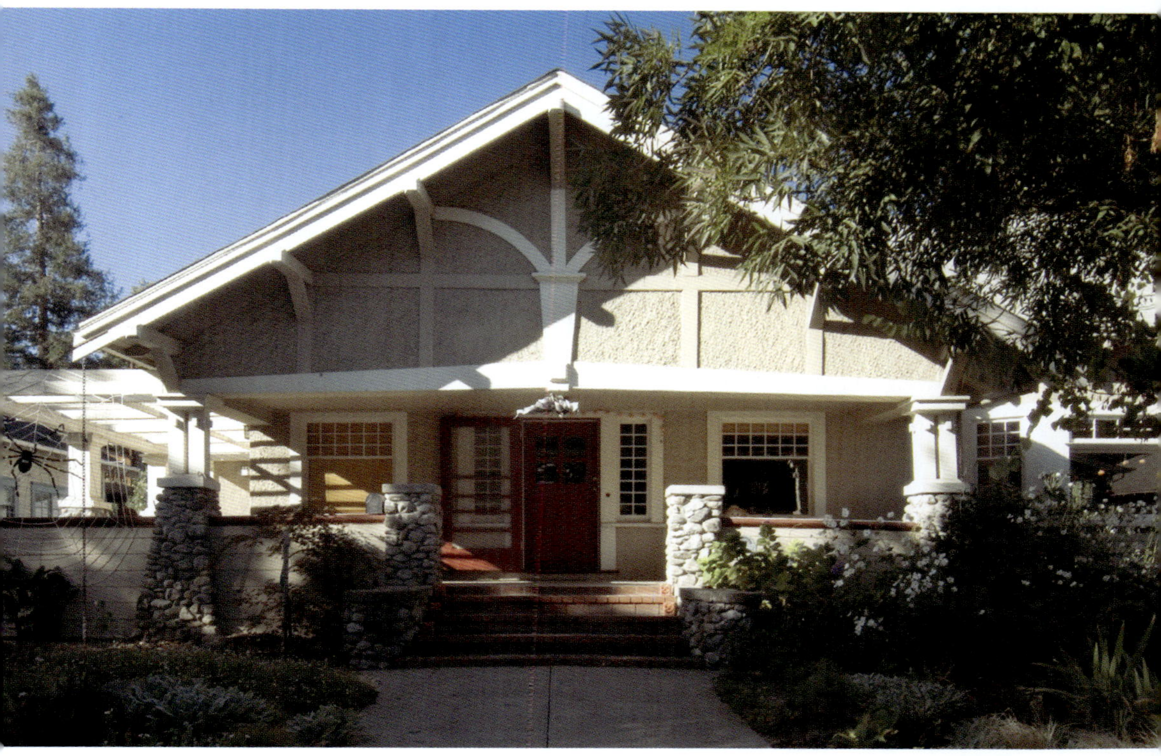

San Jose, California 

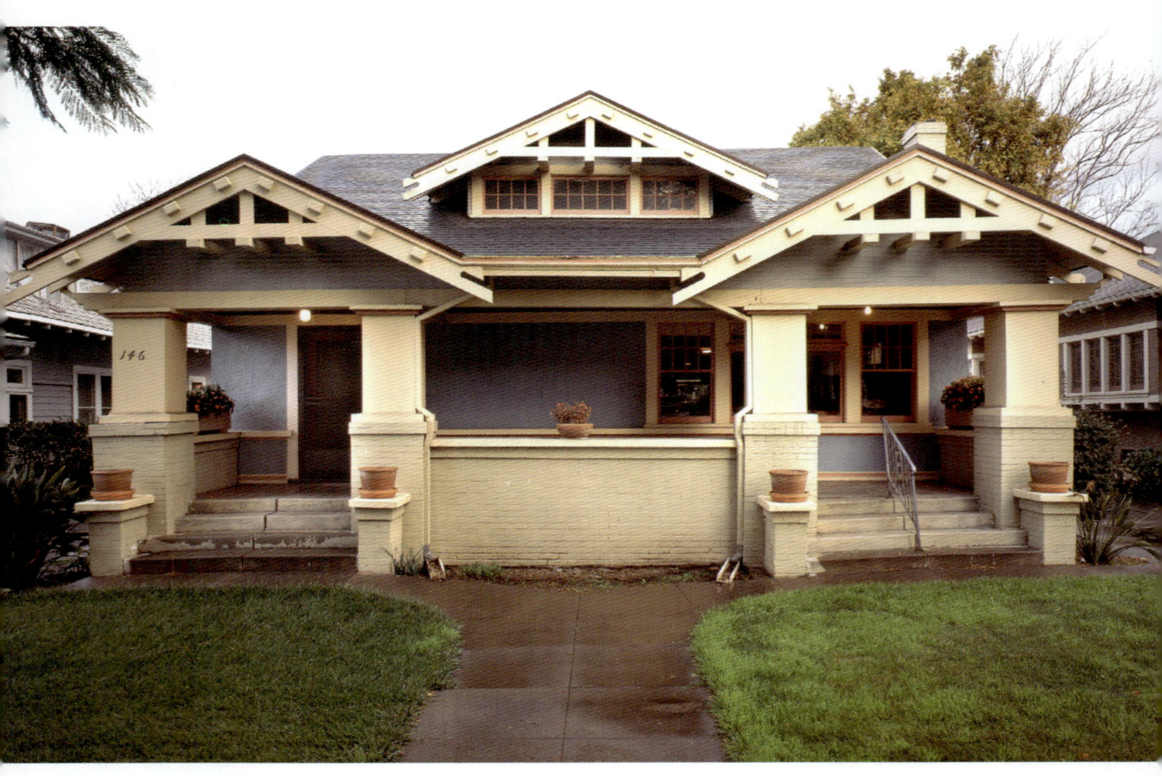


 San Jose, California

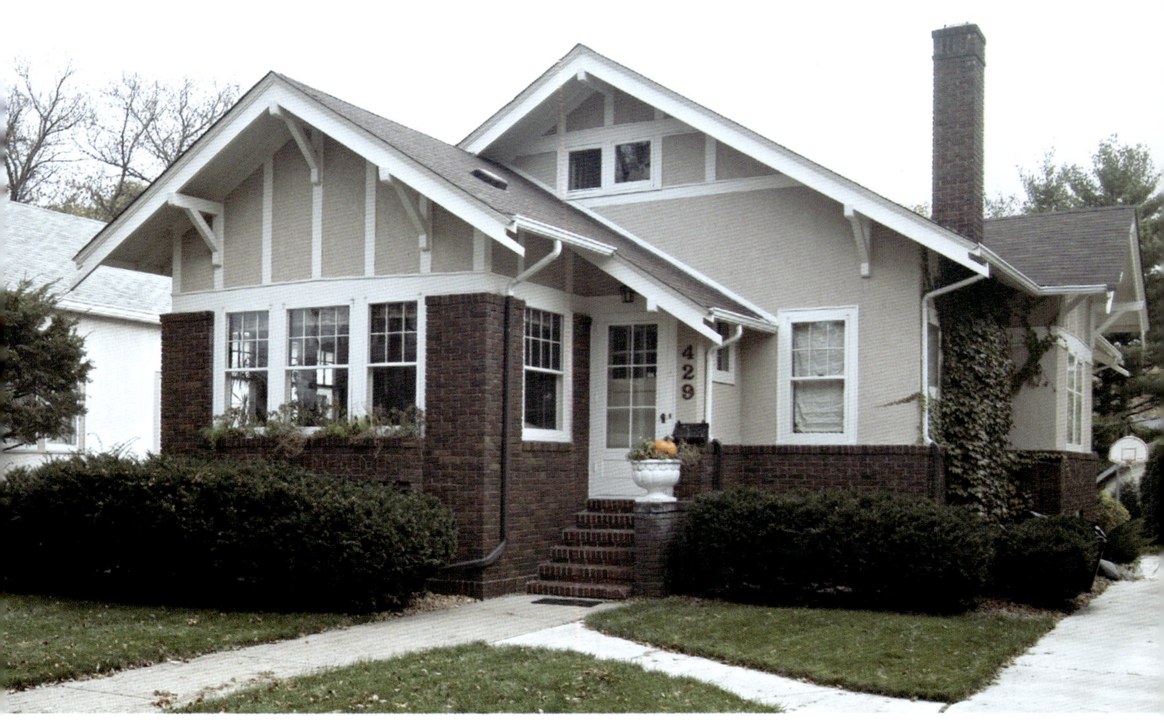


Minneapolis, Minnesota 

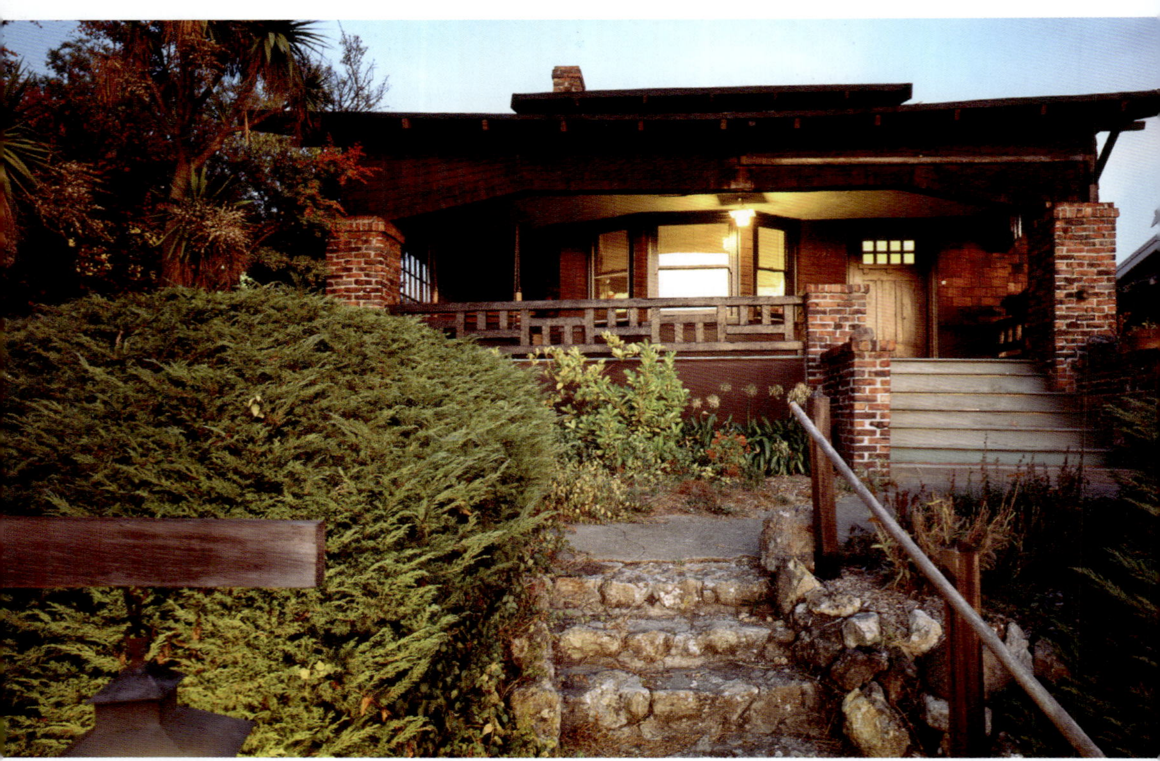

 Albany, California

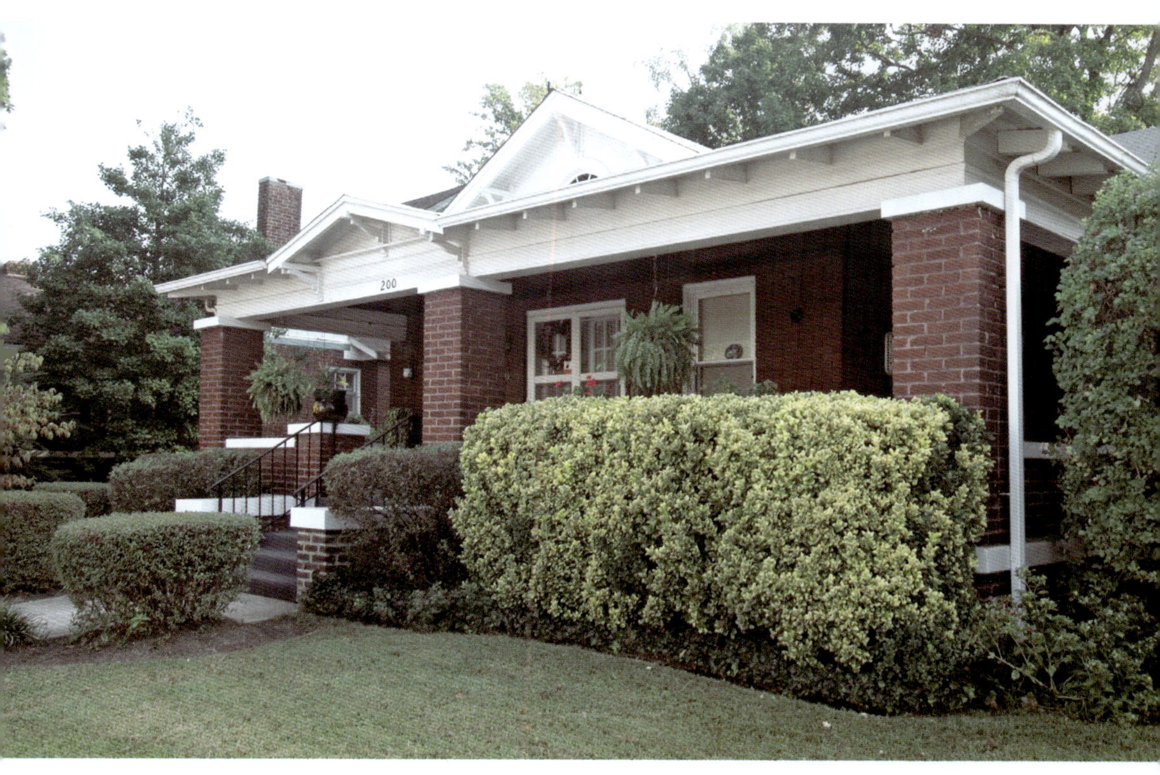
200

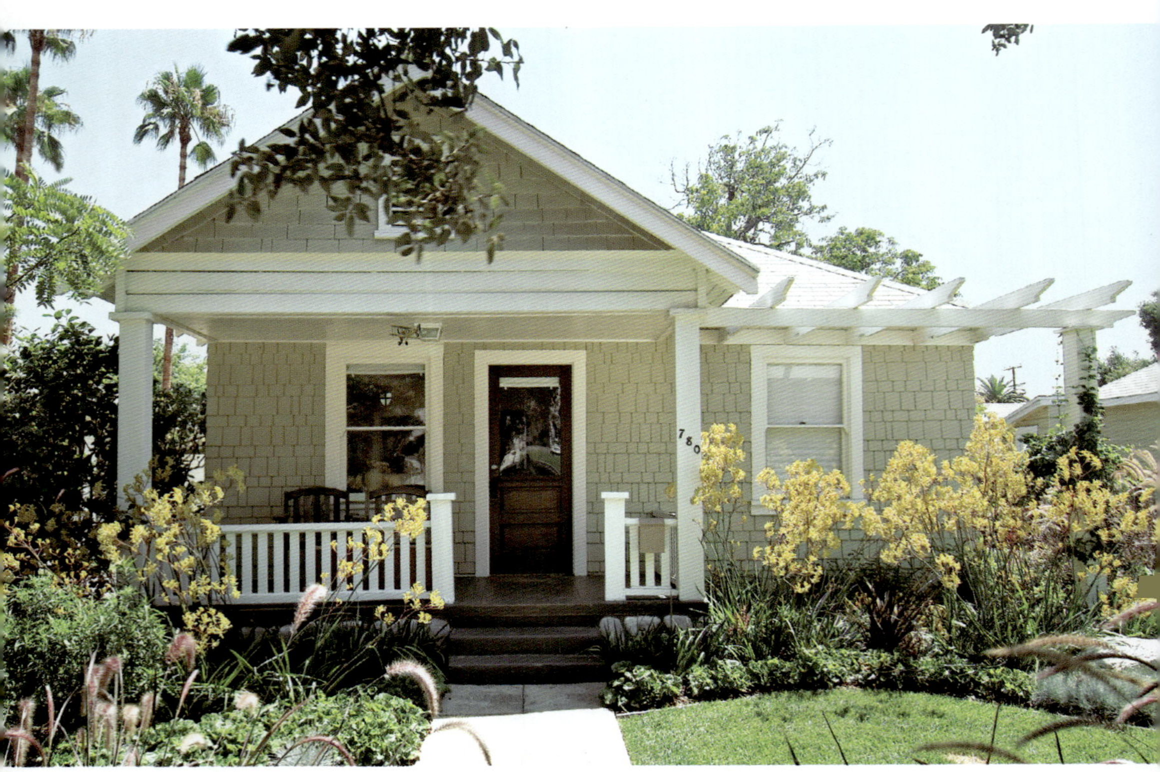


 PASADENA, CALIFORNIA

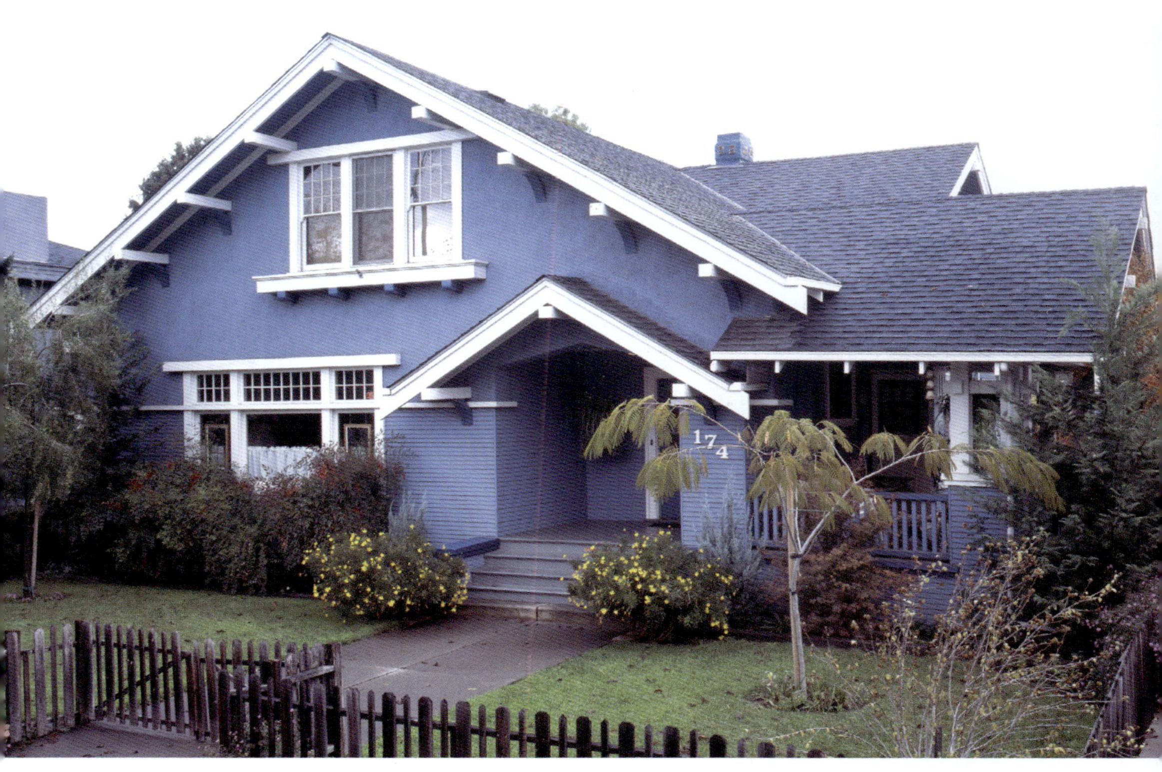


MODESTO, CALIFORNIA

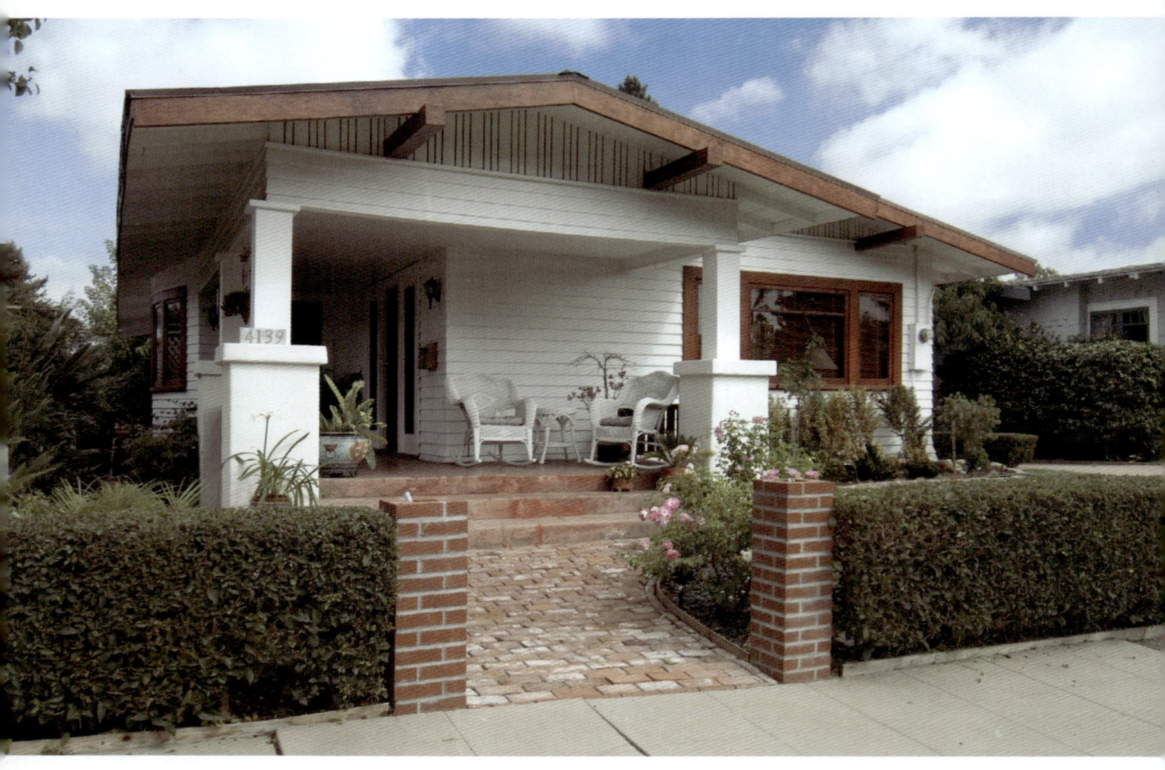


 San Diego, California

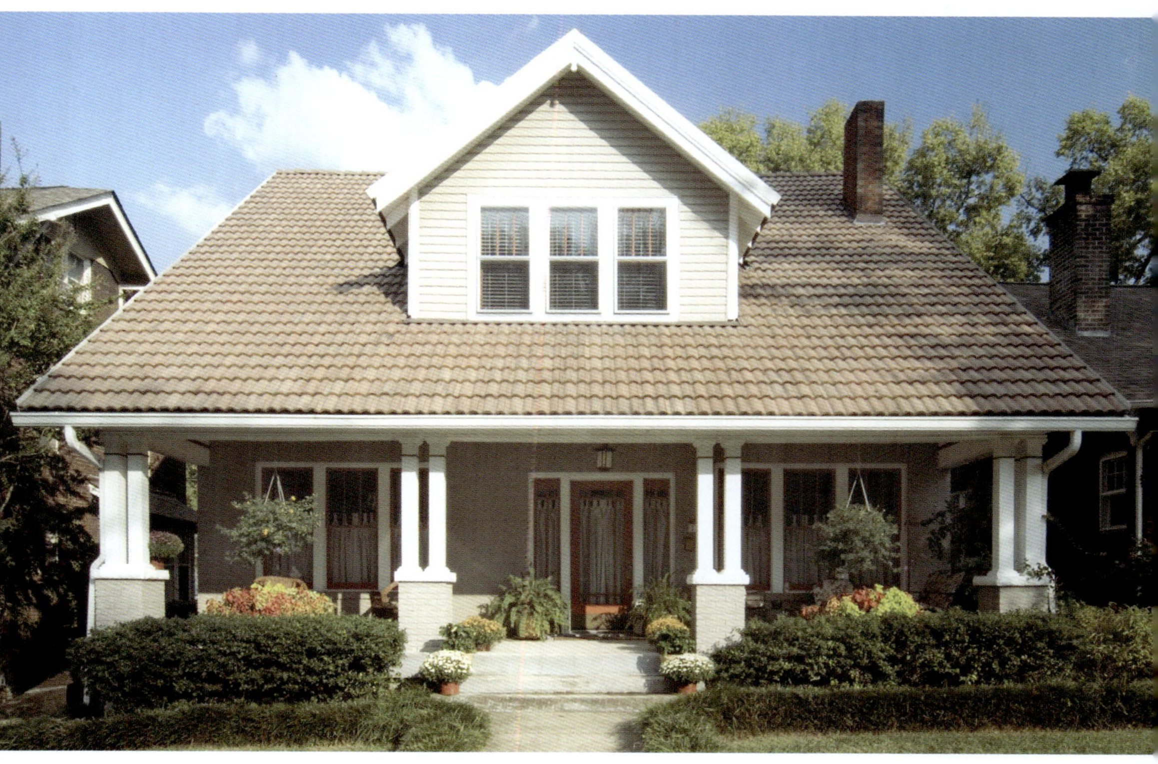

Nashville, Tennessee

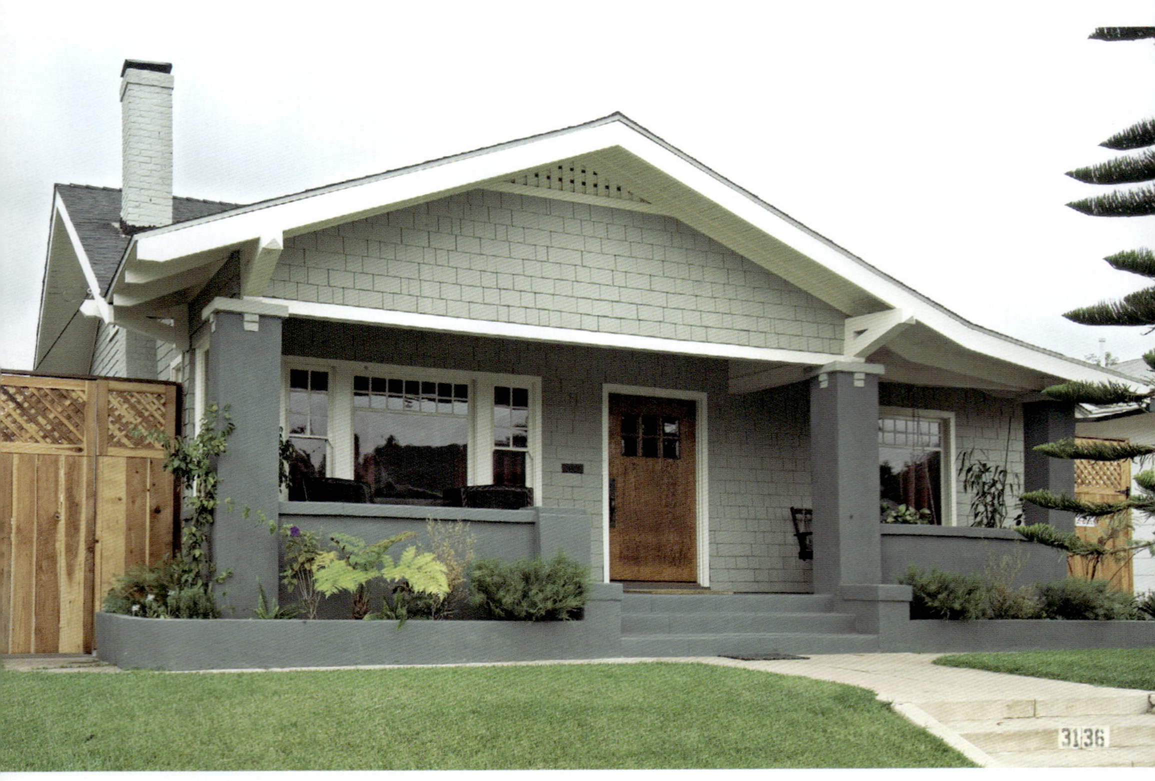



San Diego, California

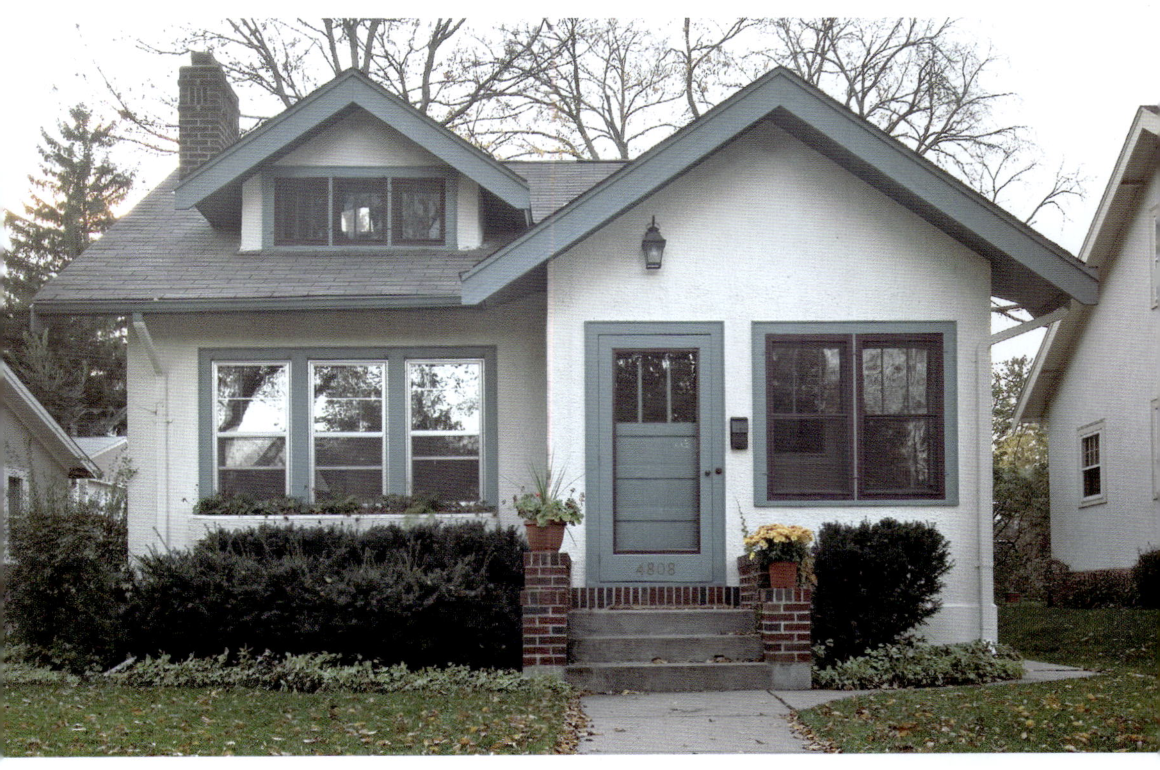
4808

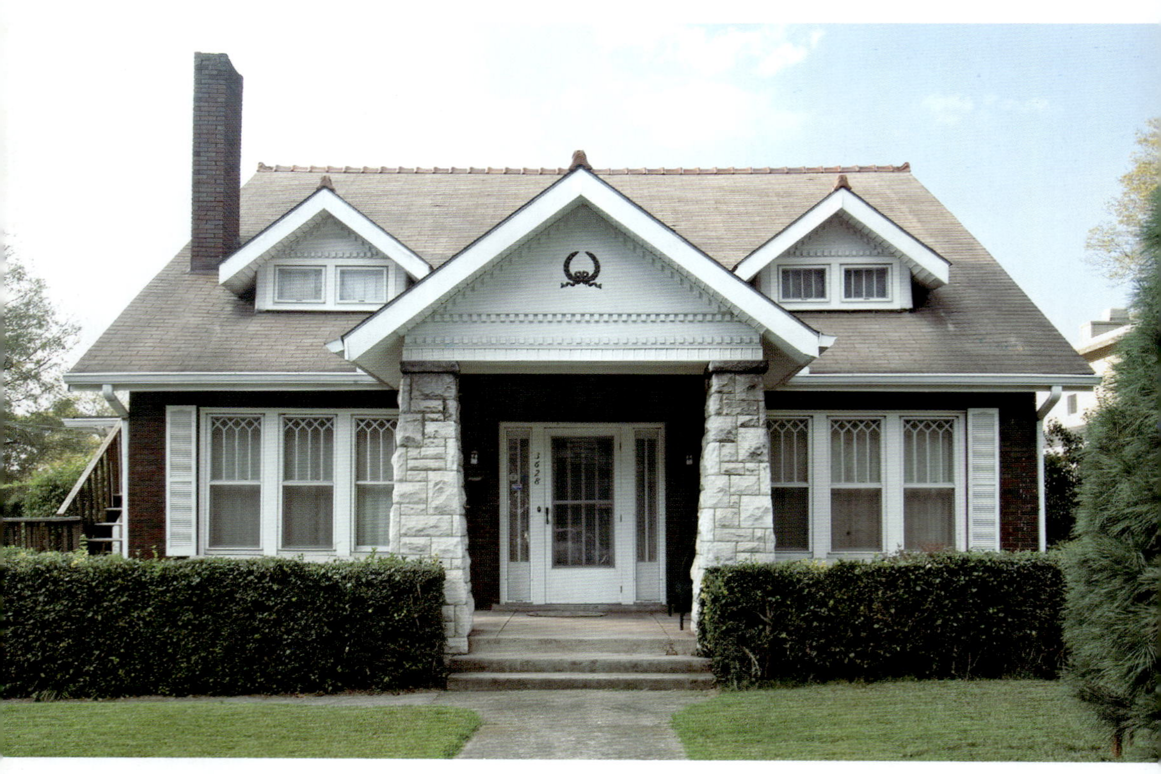


 Nashville, Tennessee

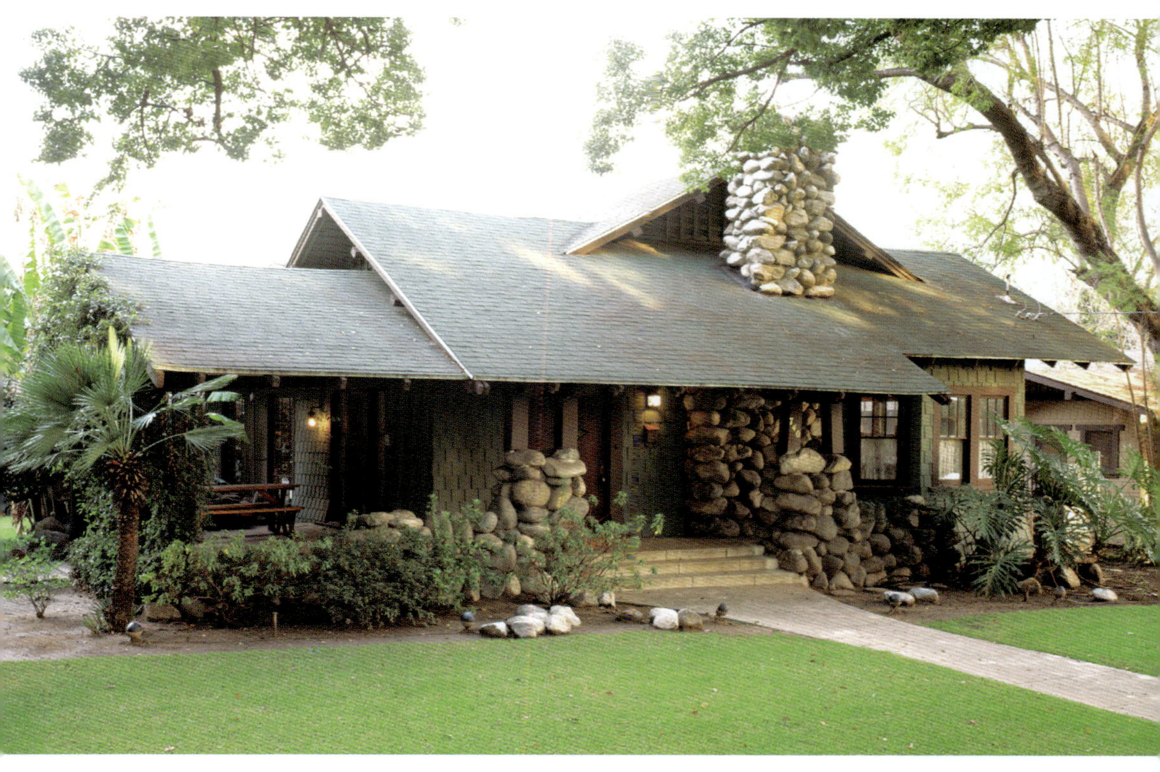

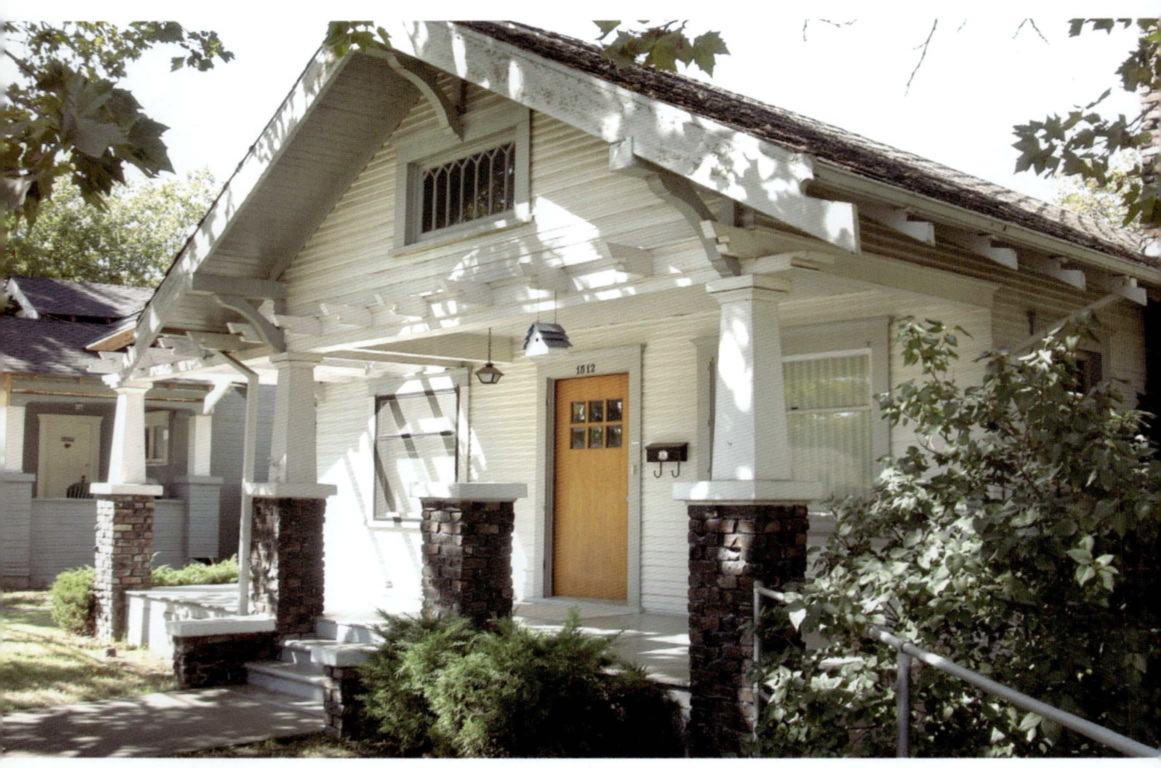


 GRIDLEY, CALIFORNIA

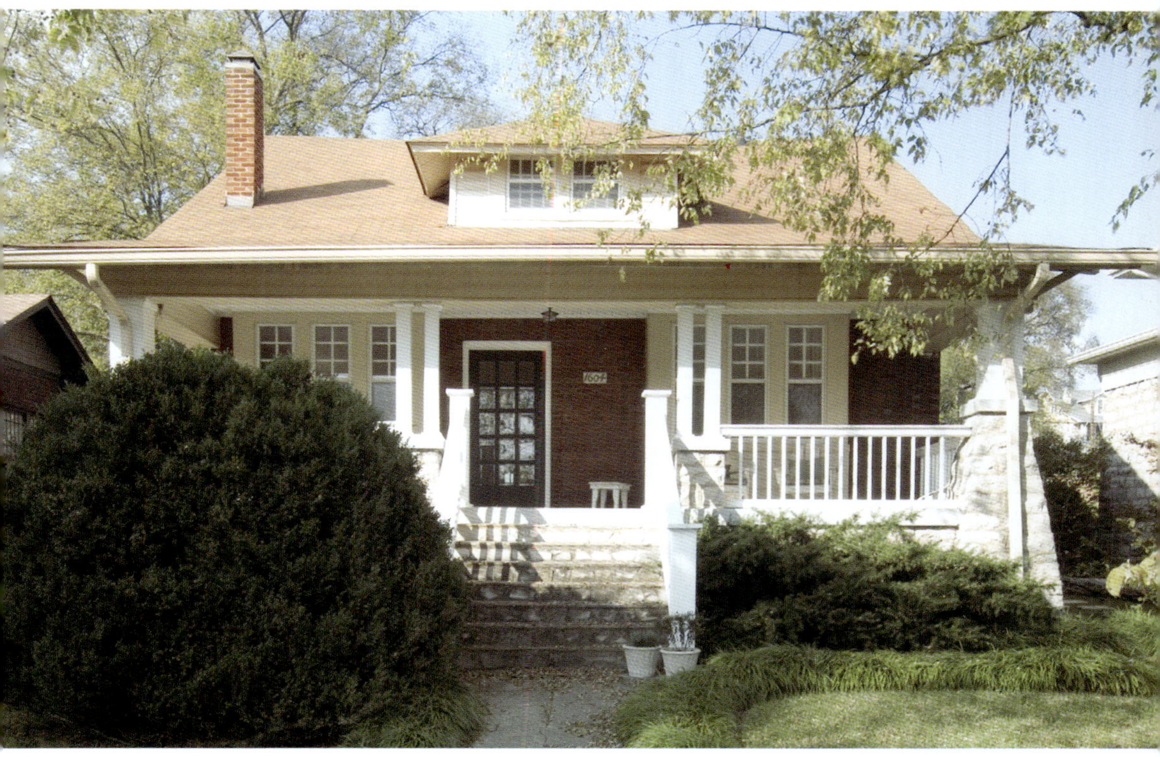
1604

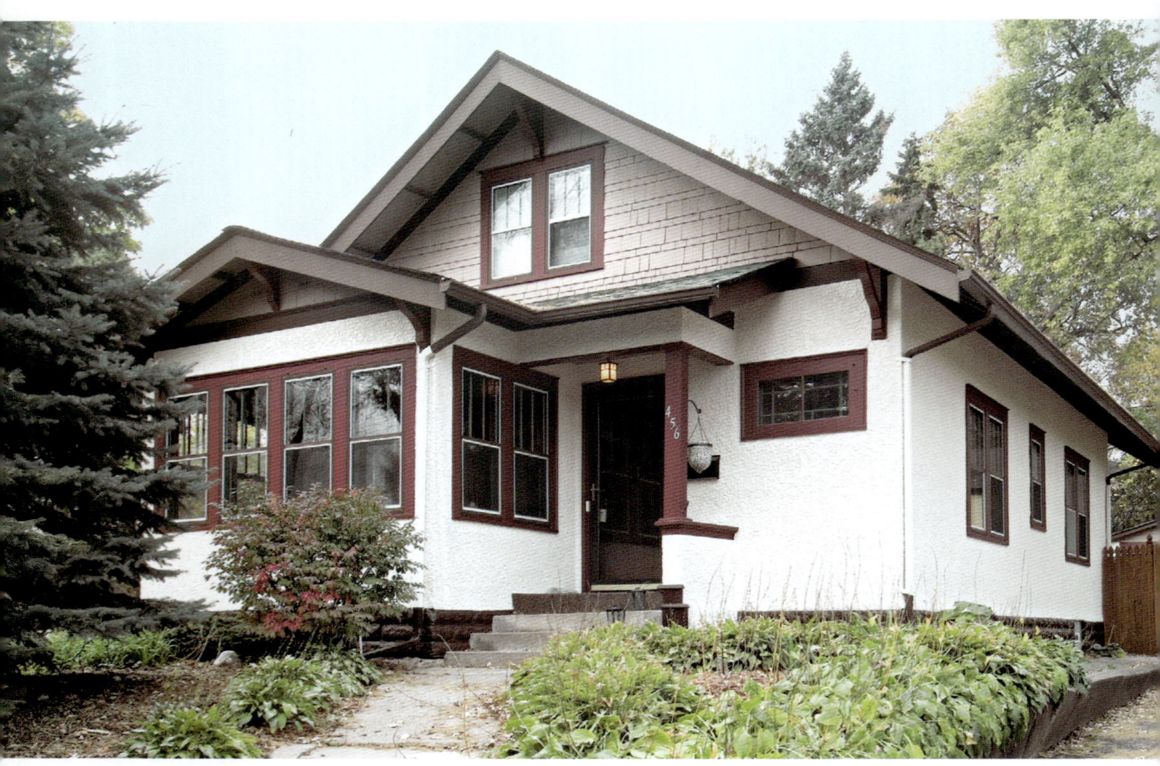


 Minneapolis, Minnesota

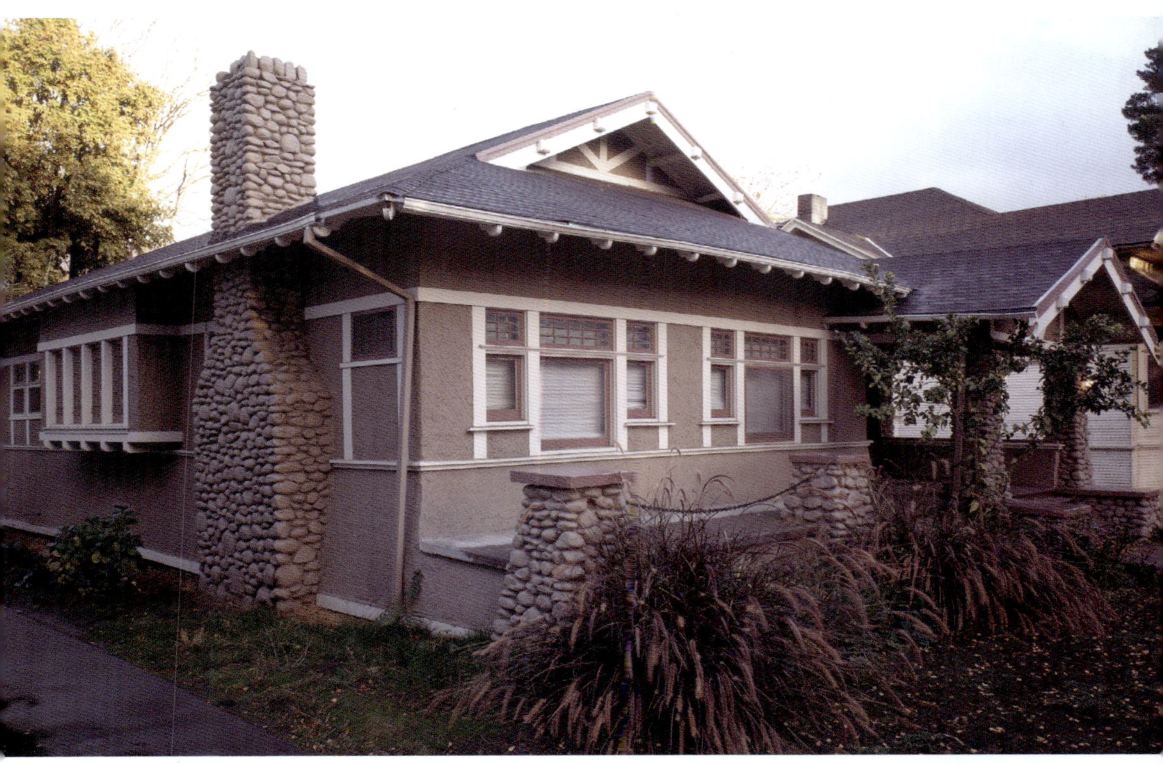

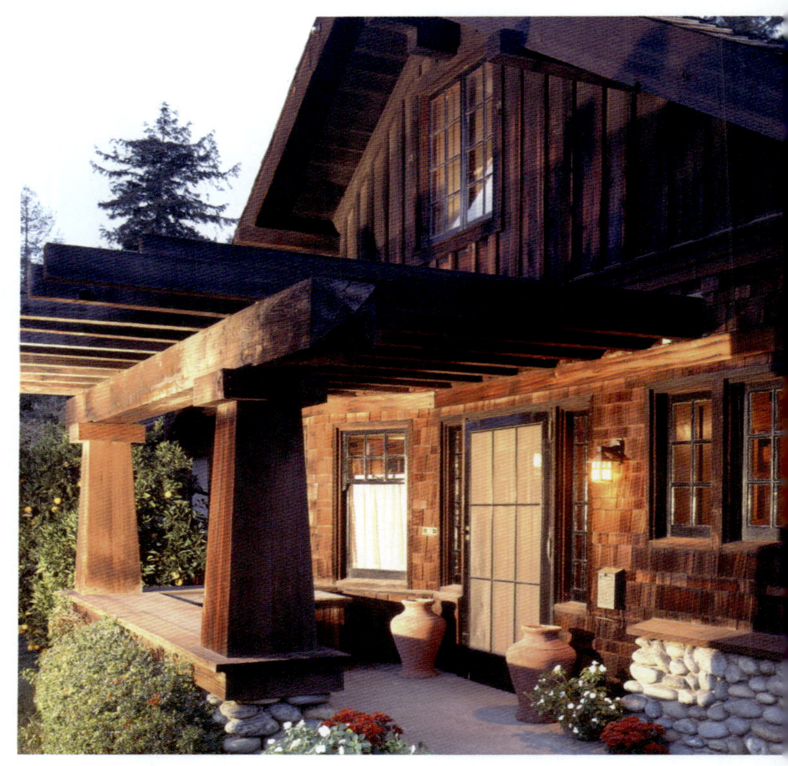

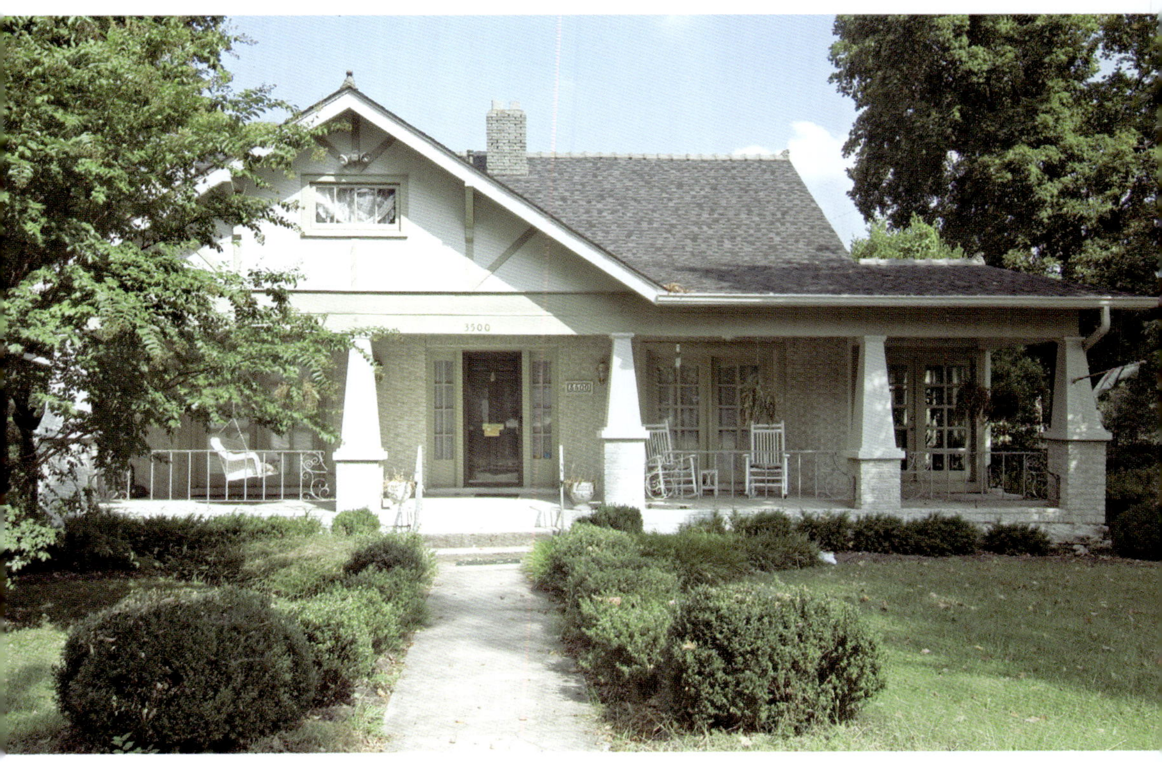
3500

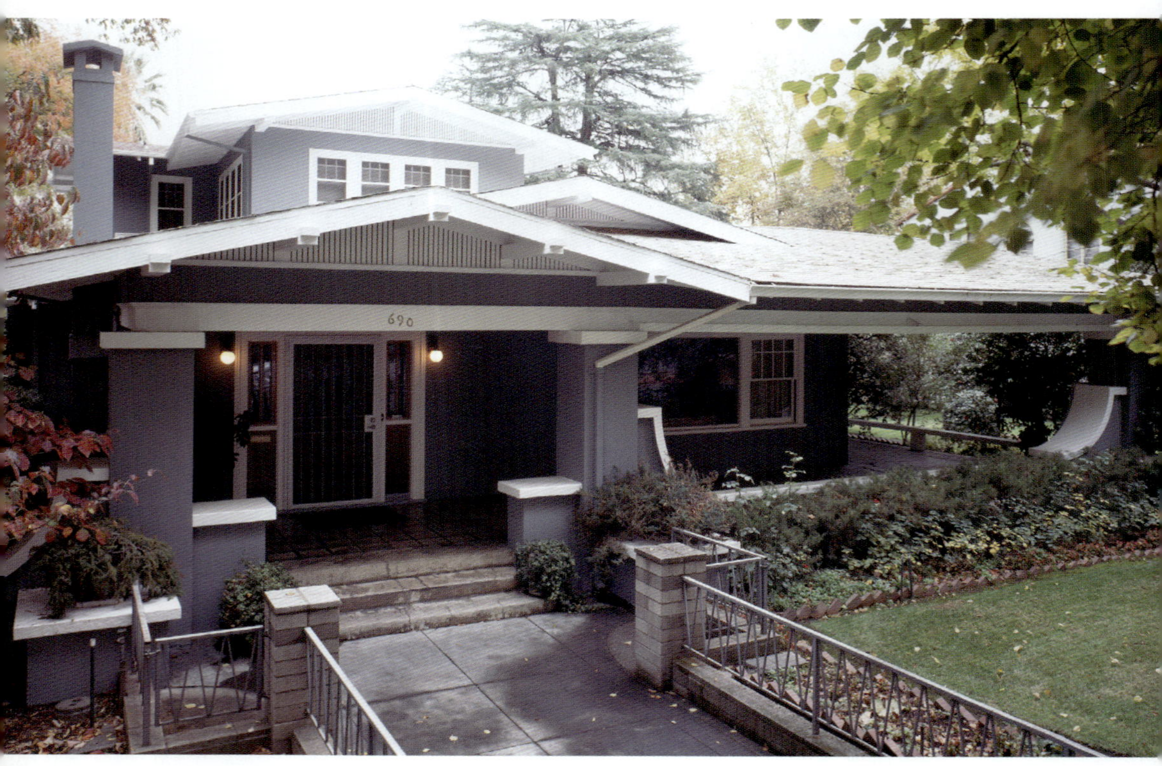


 Chico, California

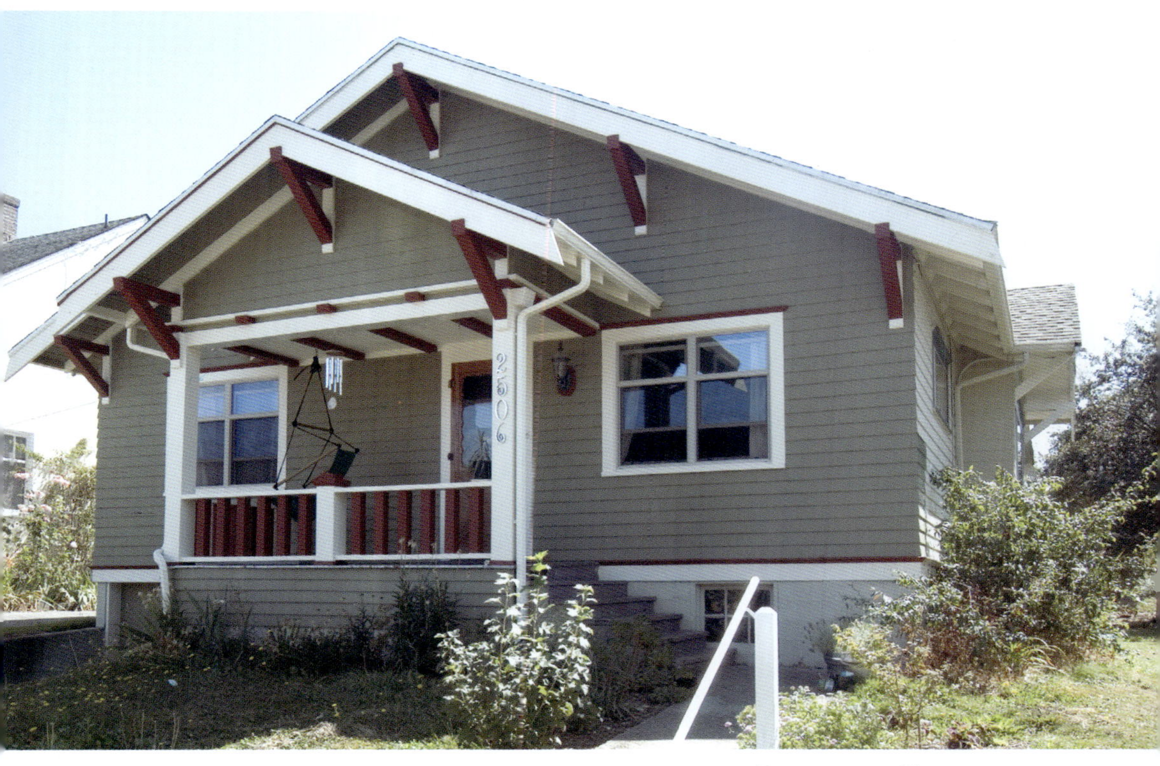


Bellingham, Washington

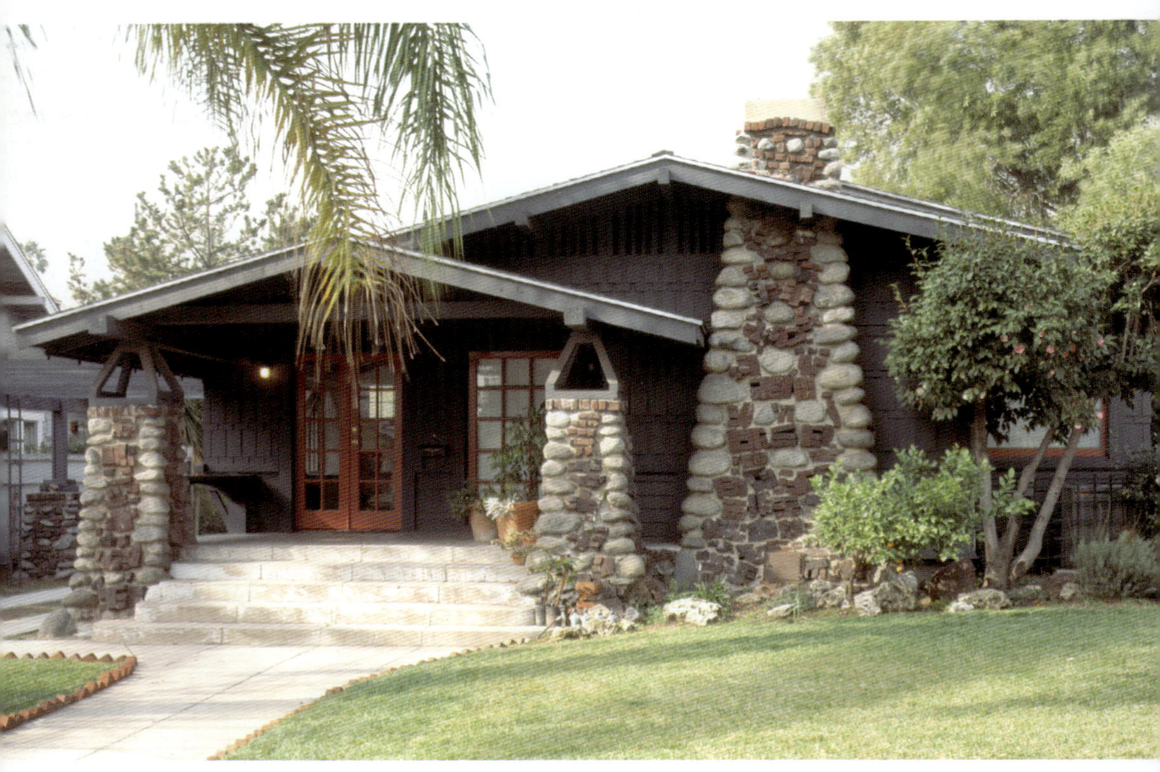

 Pasadena, California

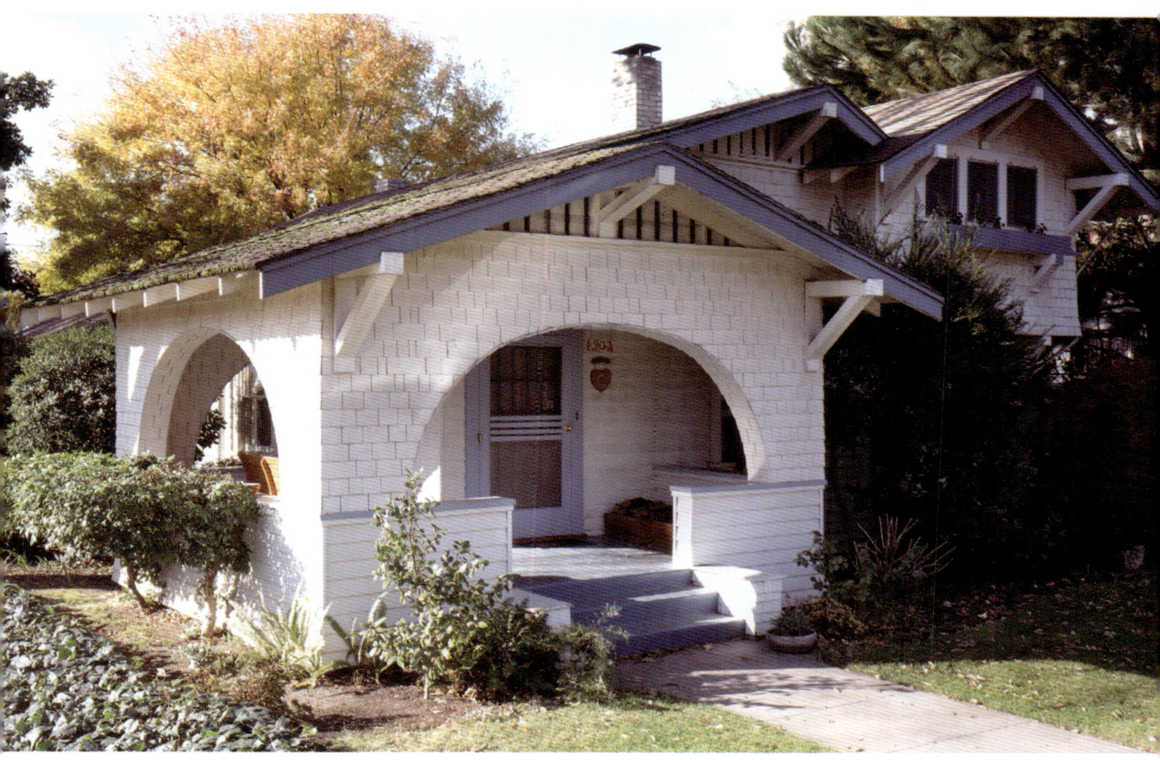

Modesto, California 

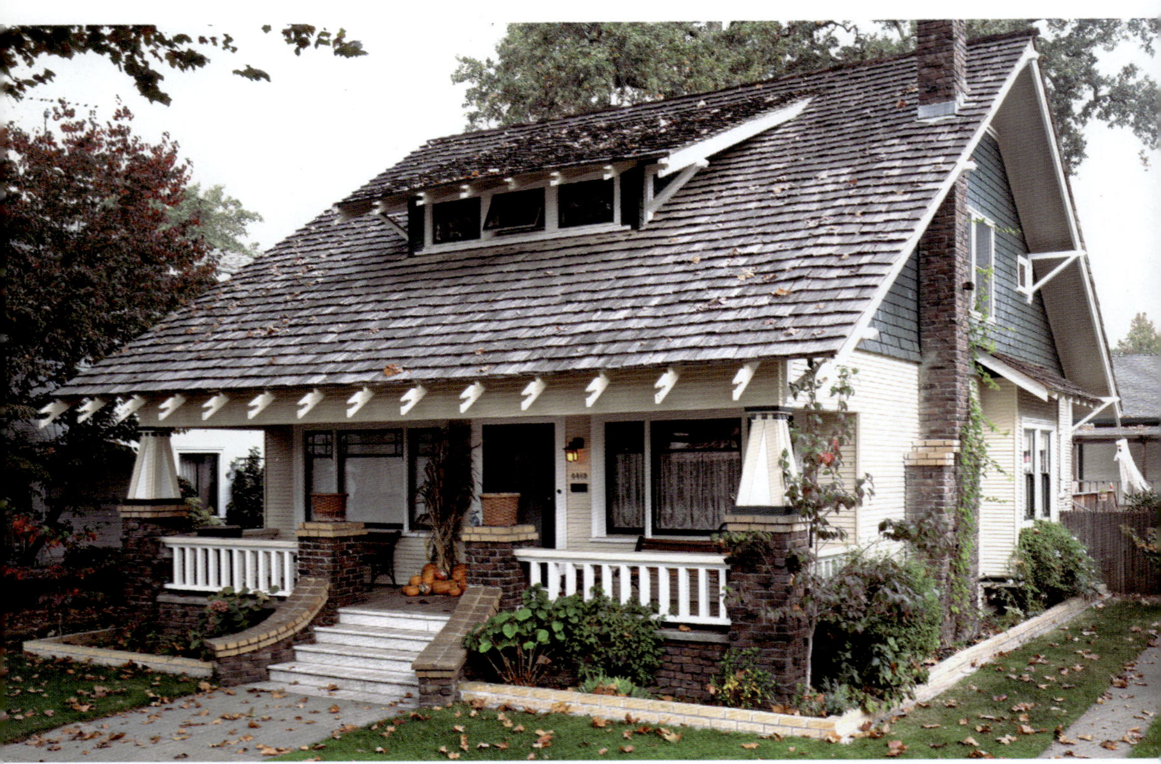

 Sacramento, California

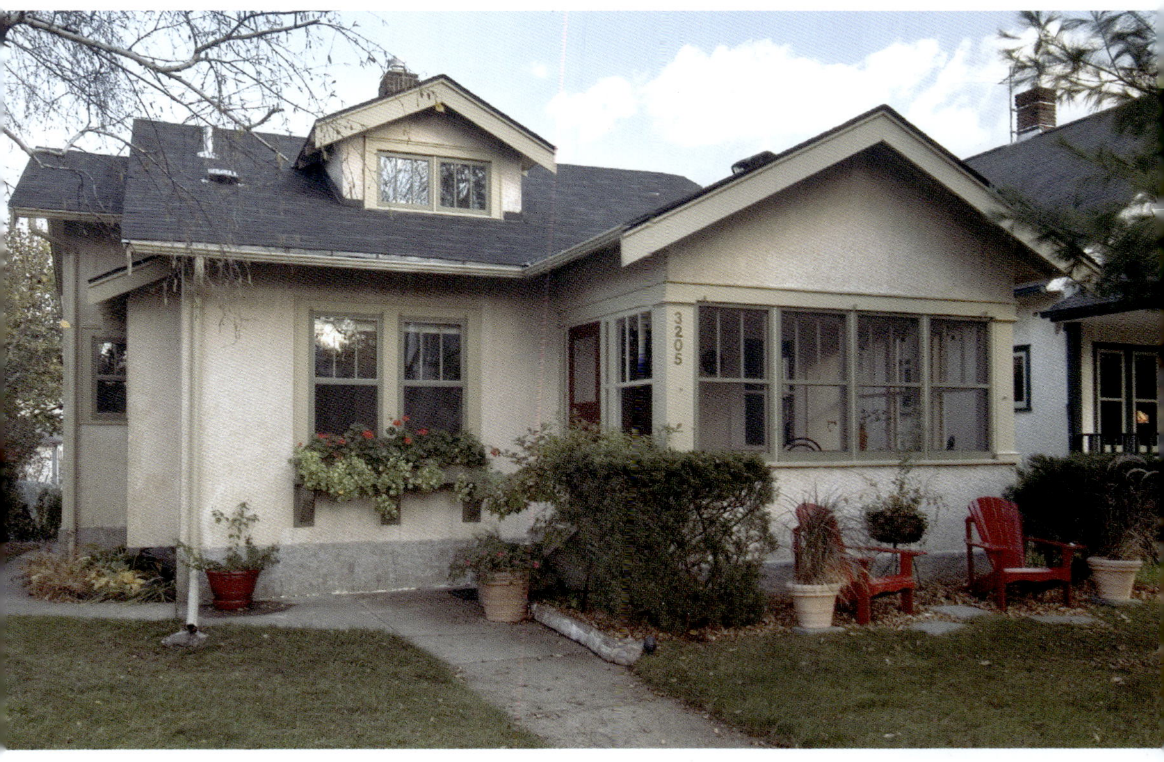
3205

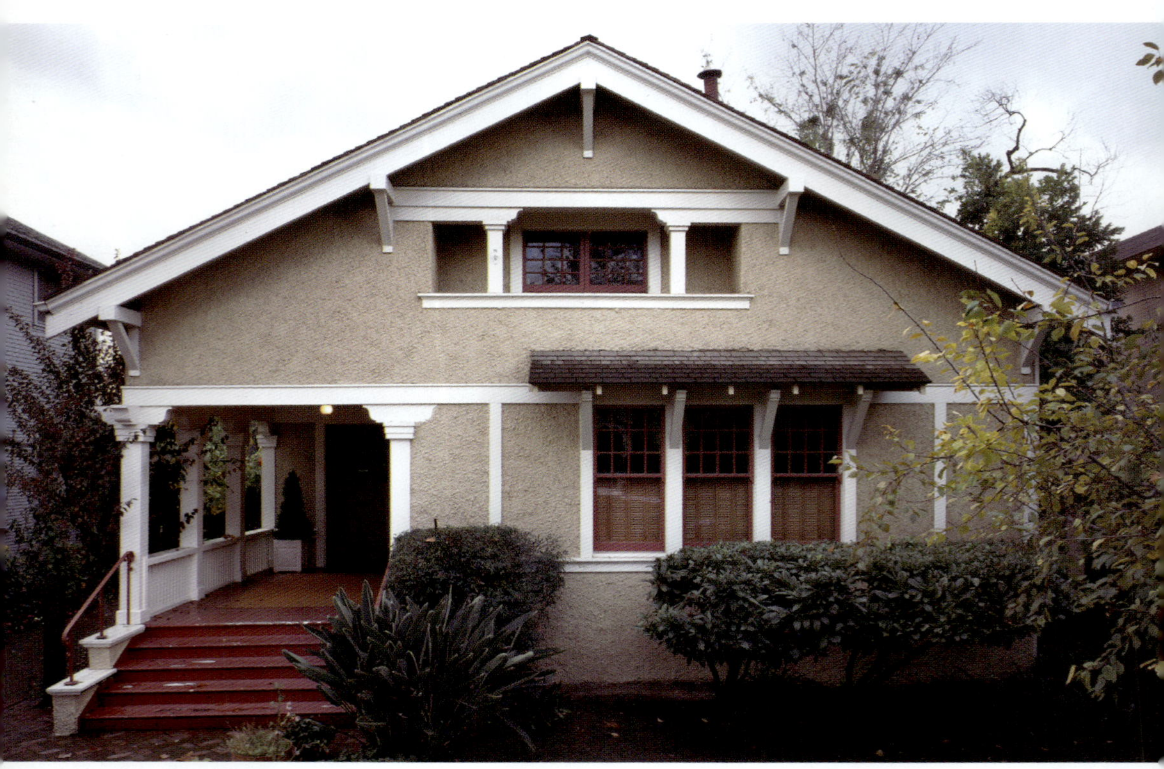

 San Jose, California

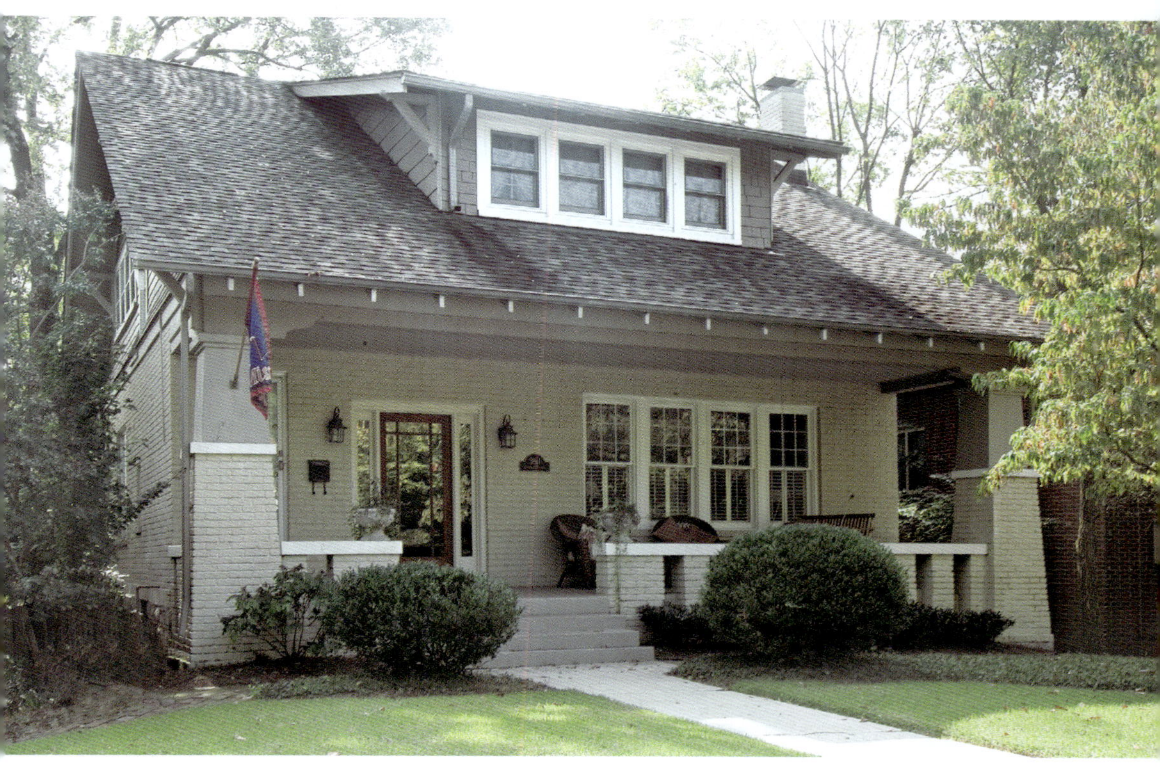

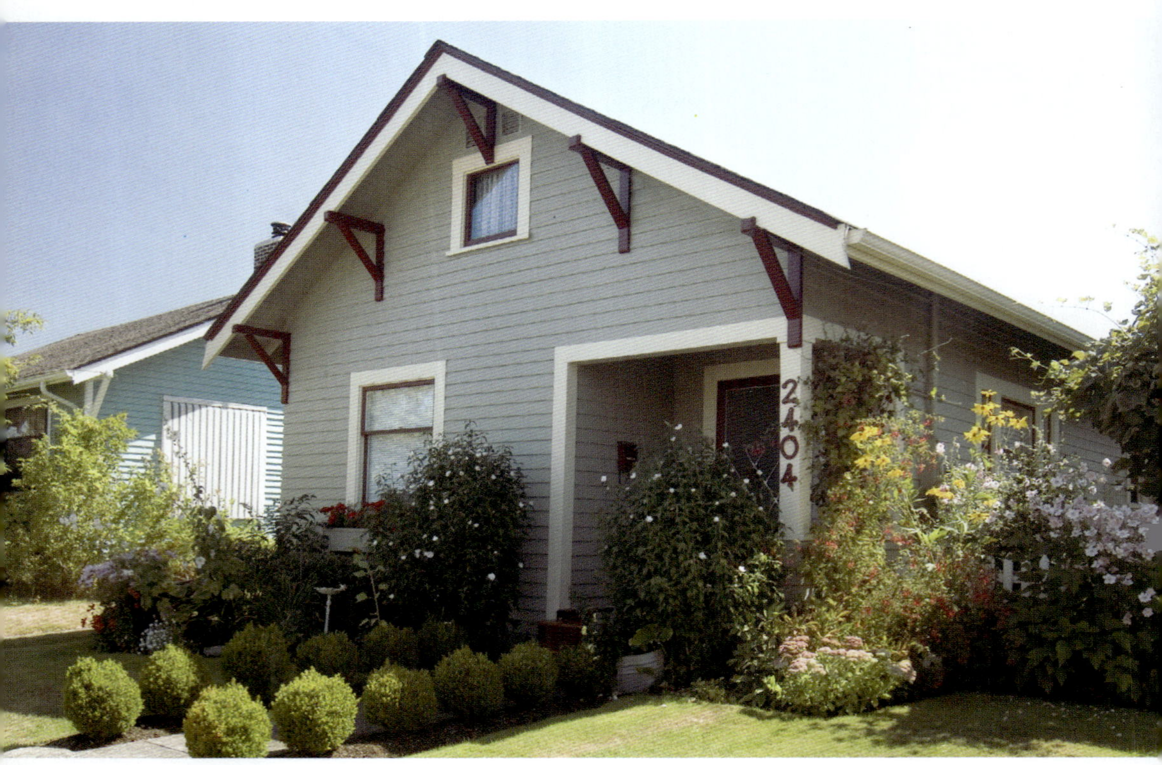


 Bellingham, Washington

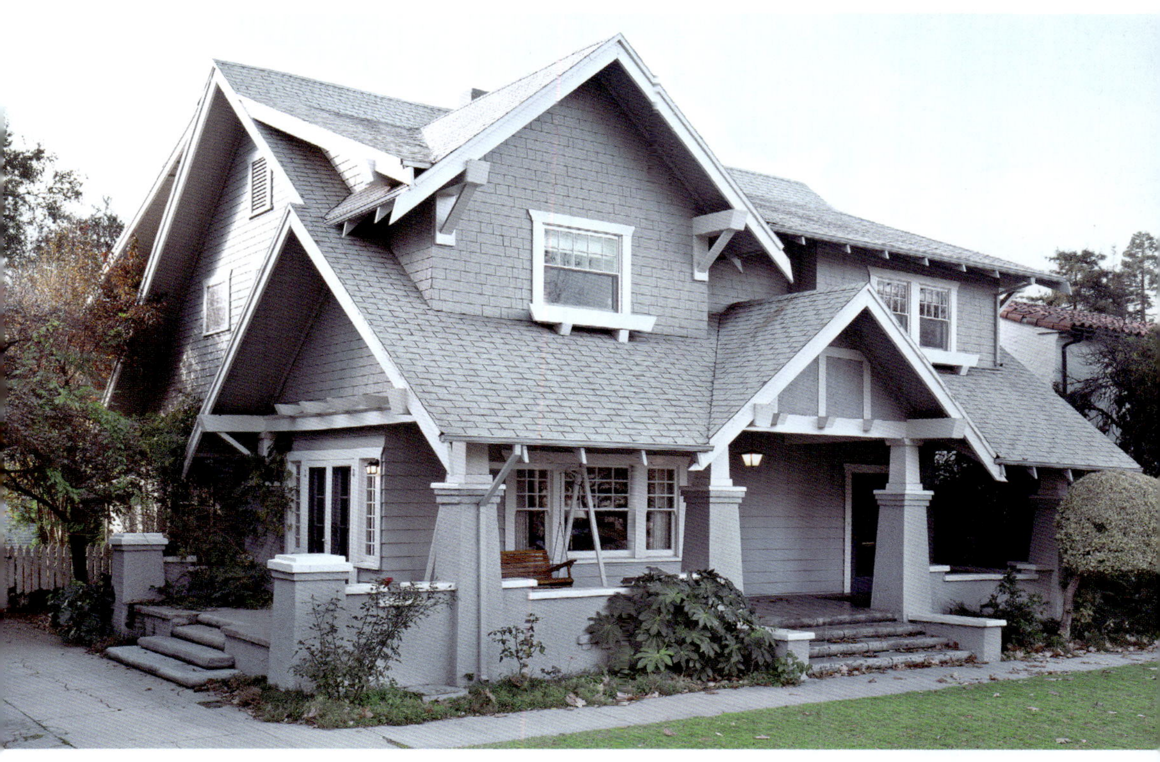

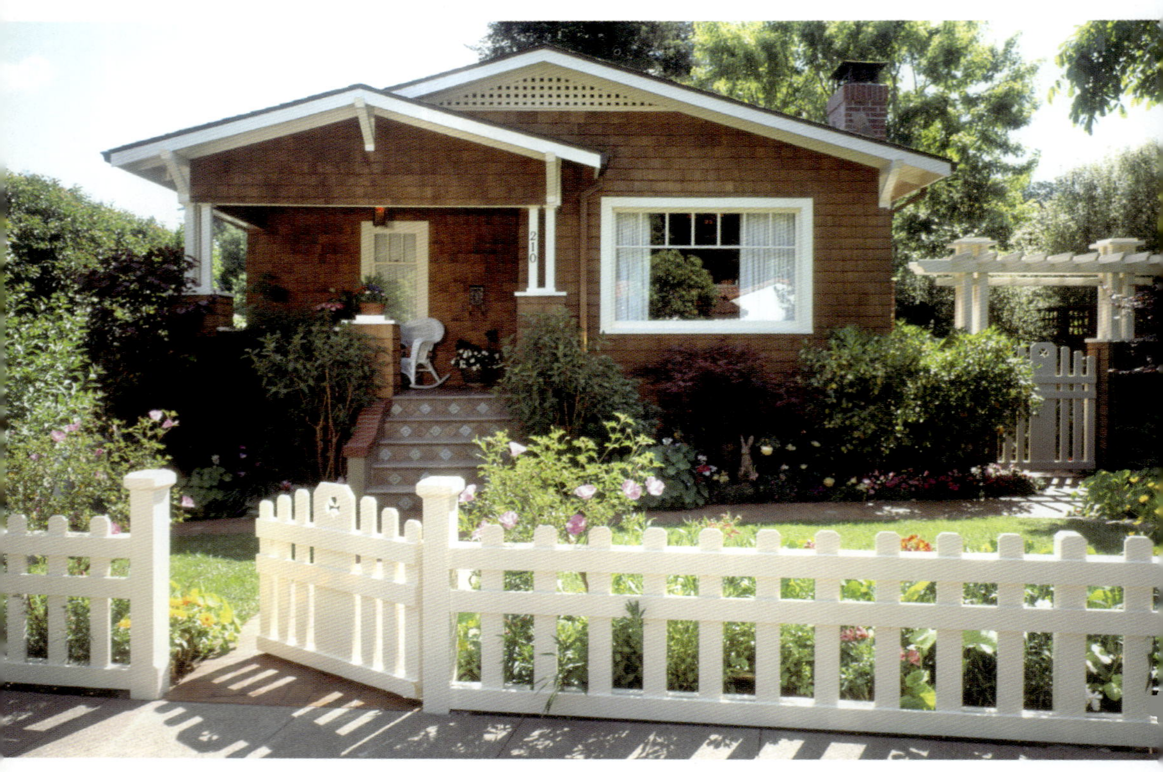


 Marin County, California

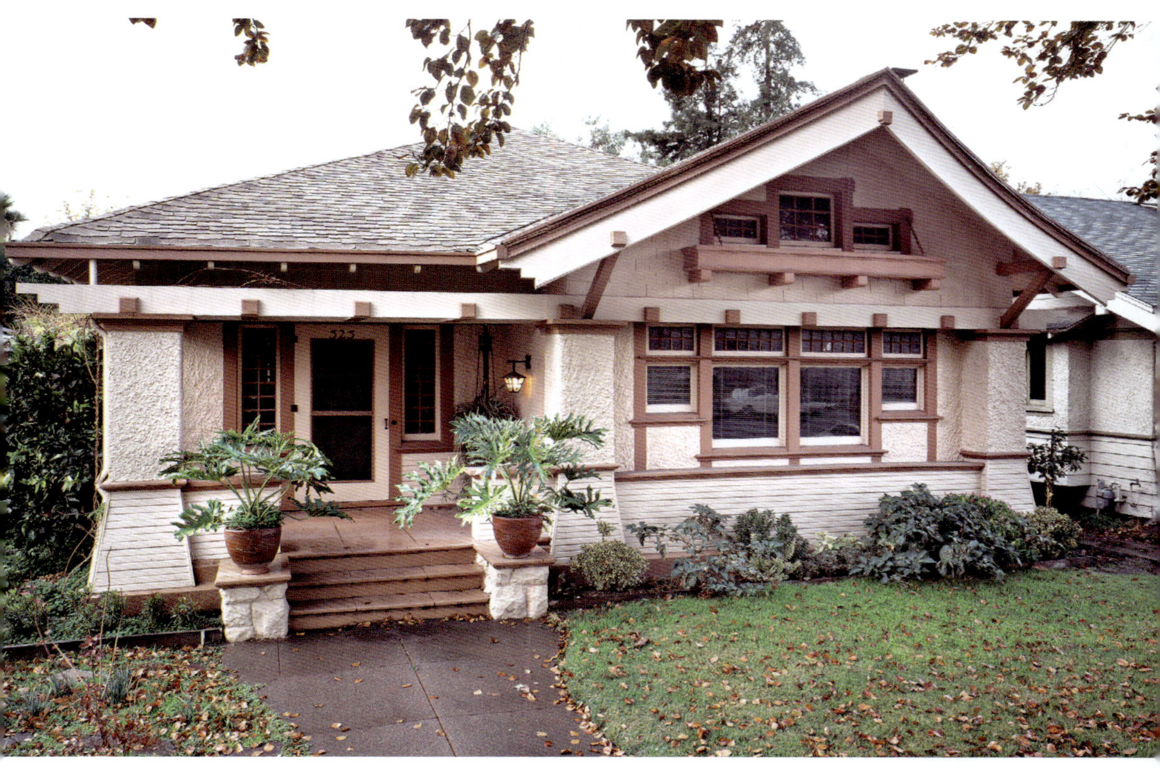

San Jose, California

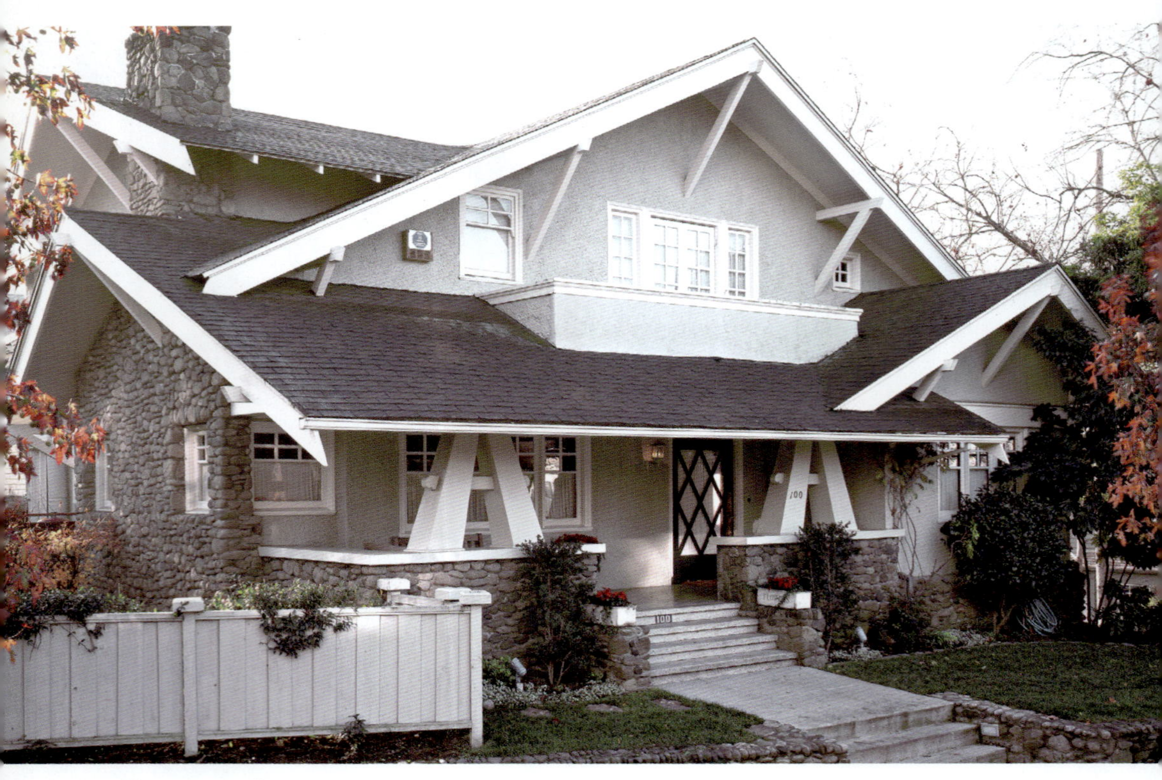
100

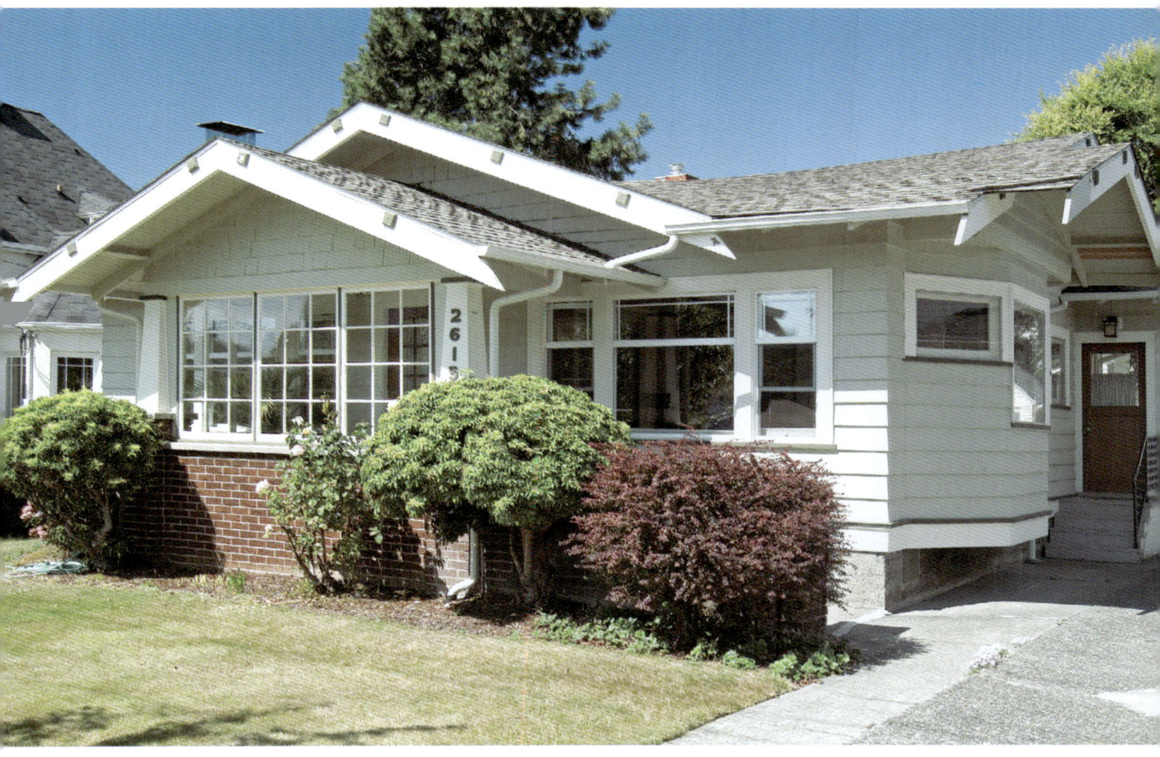

Bellingham, Washington

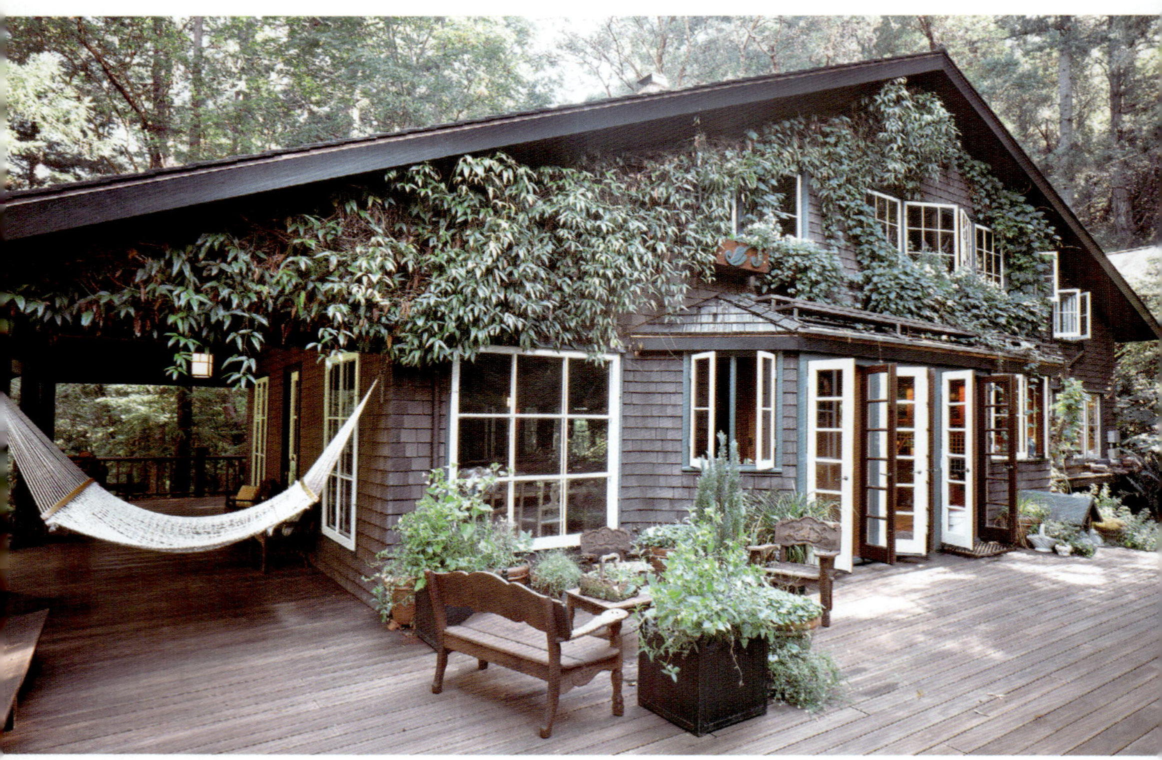

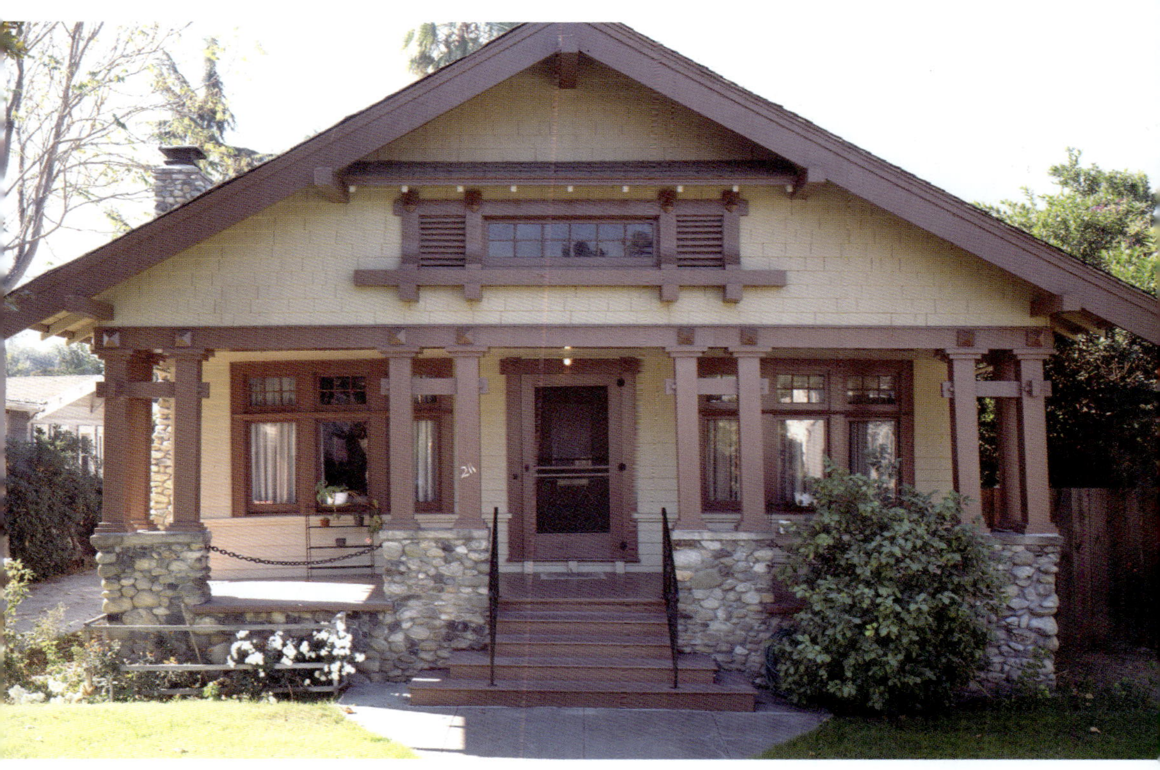

San Jose, California

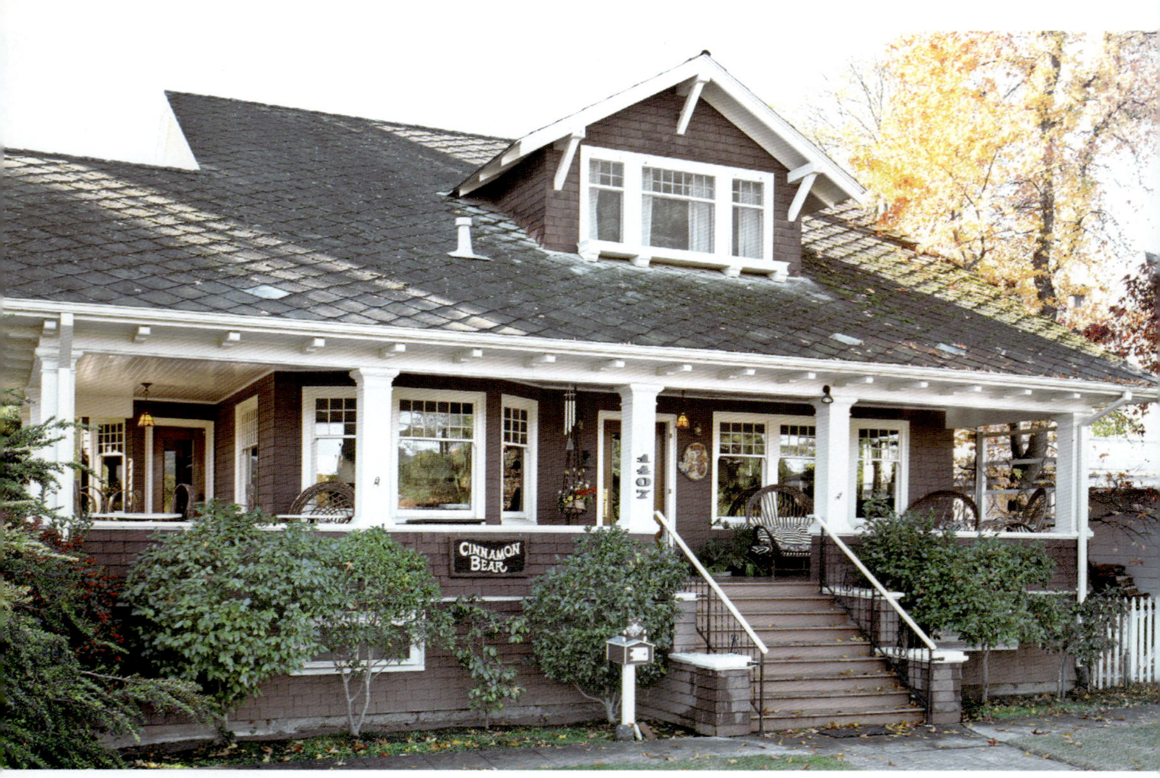
CINNAMON
BEAR
1407

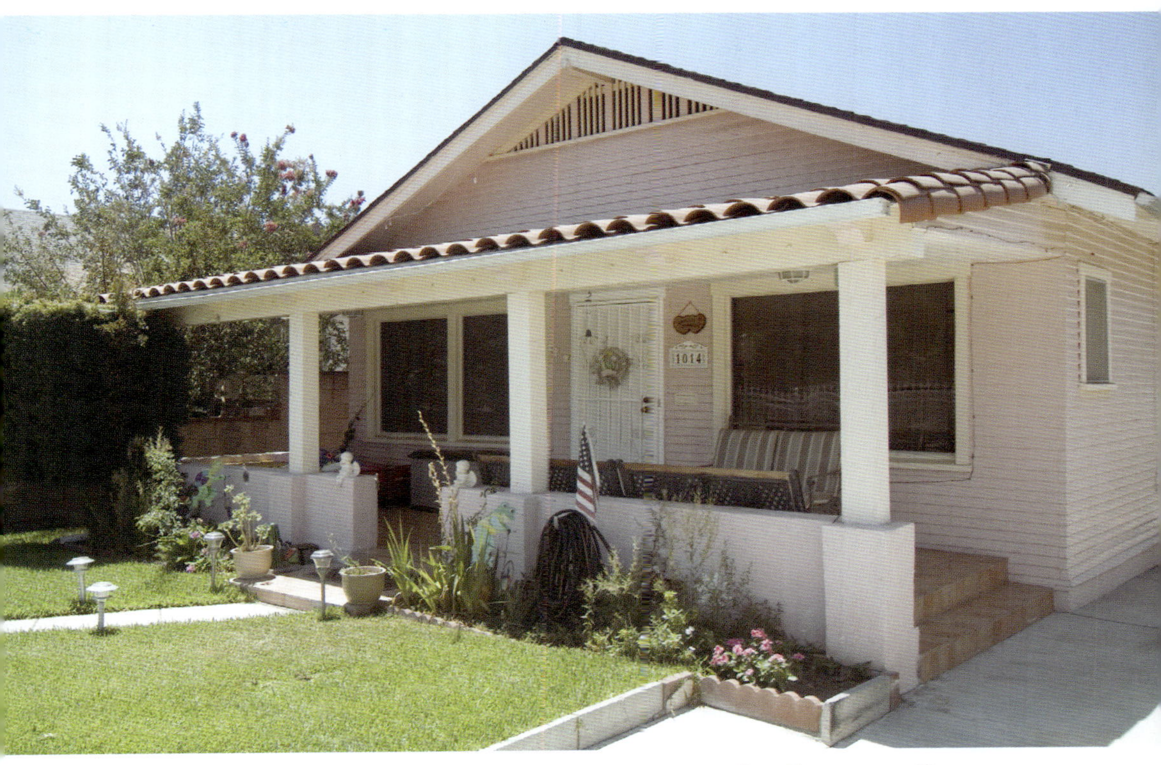


San Fernando, California

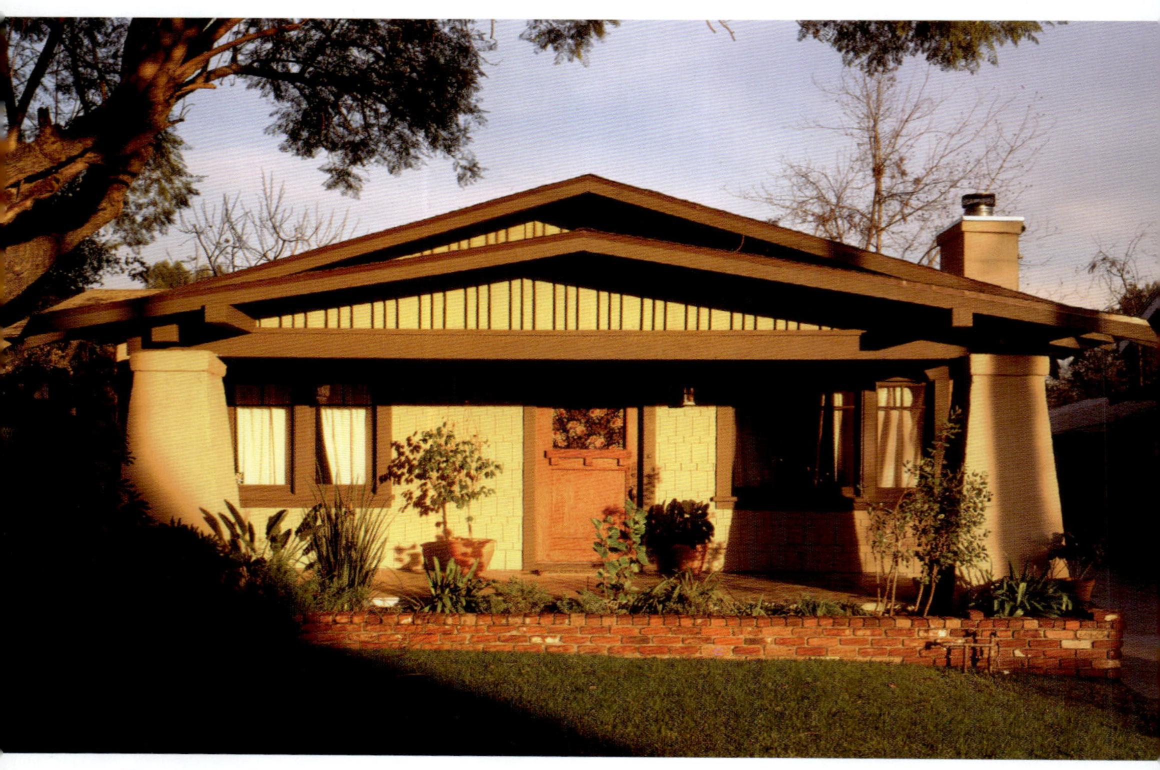

 PASADENA, CALIFORNIA

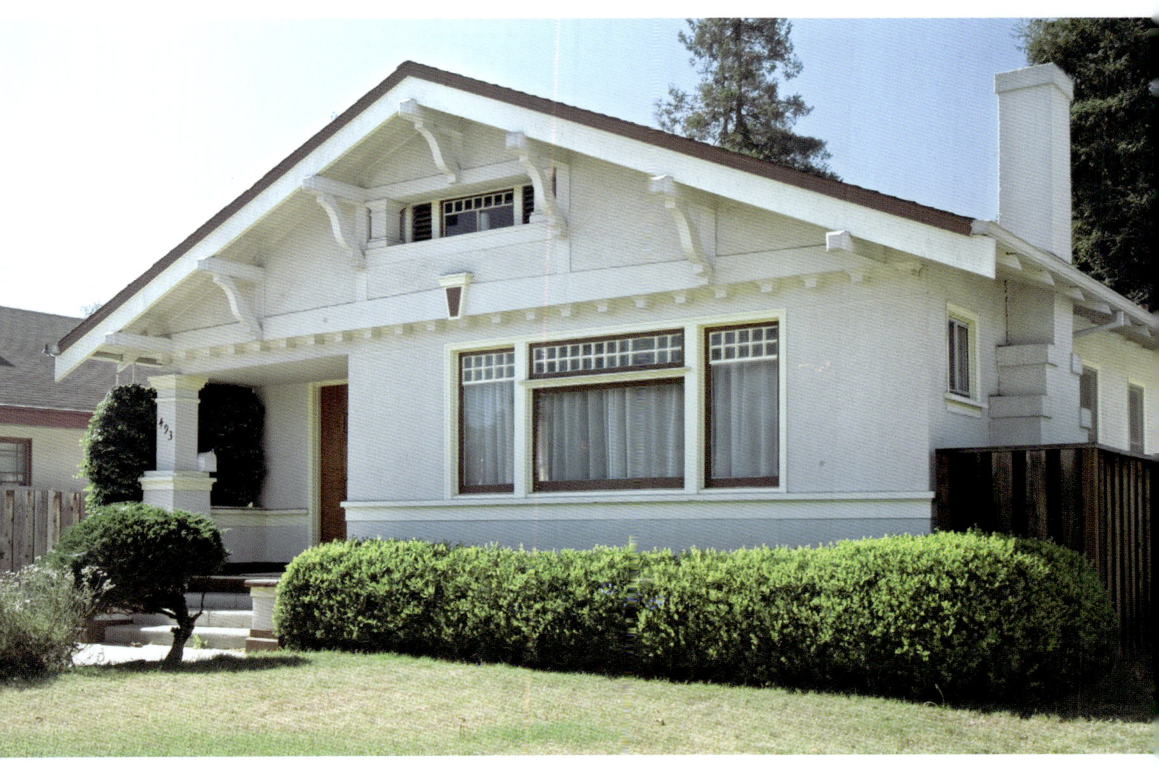
493

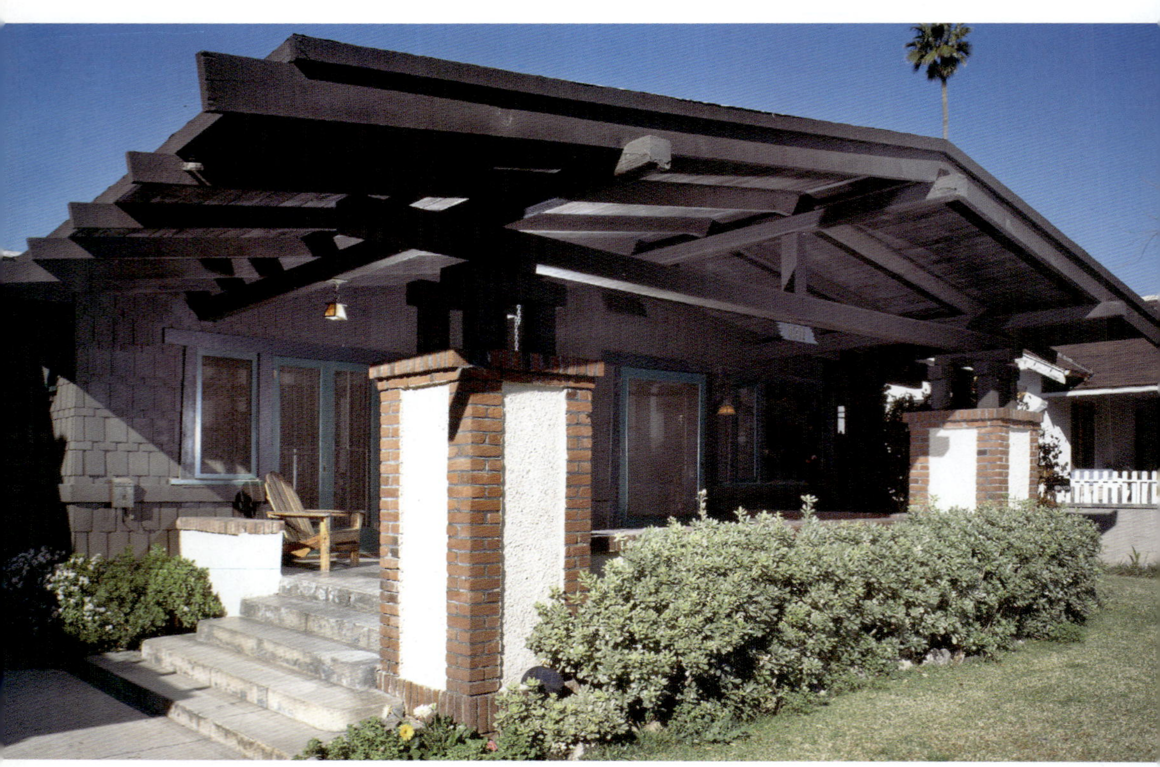

 Pasadena, California

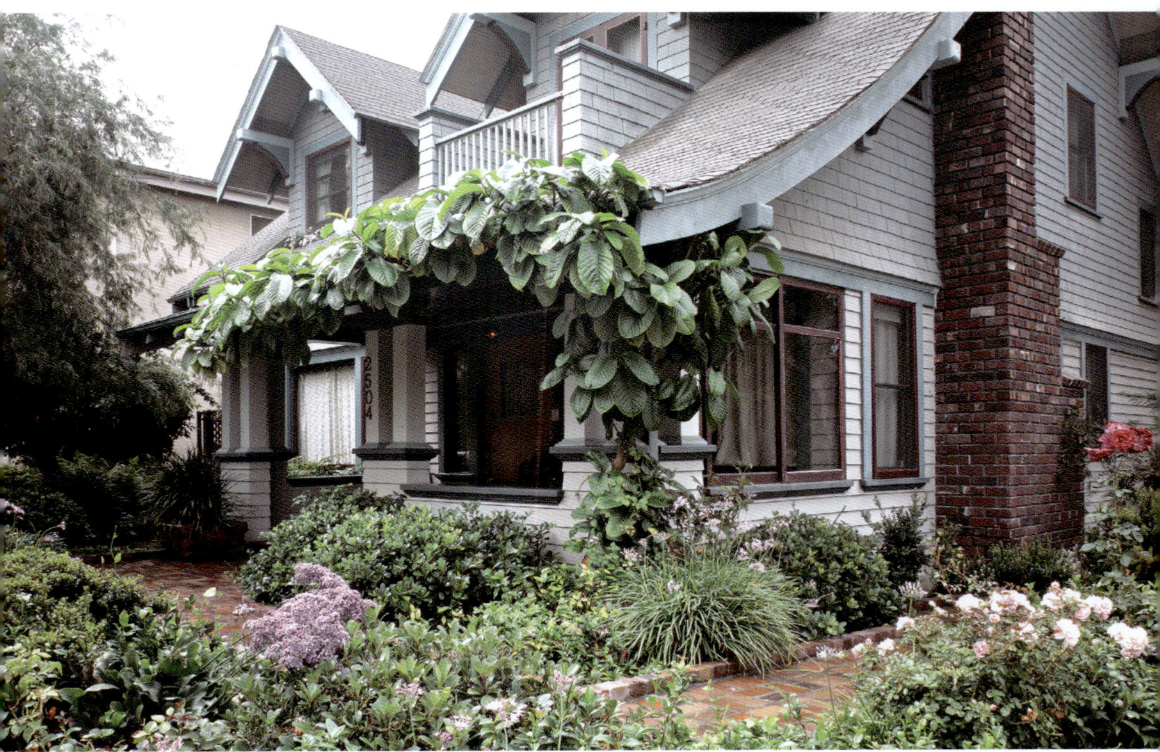


Santa Monica, California 

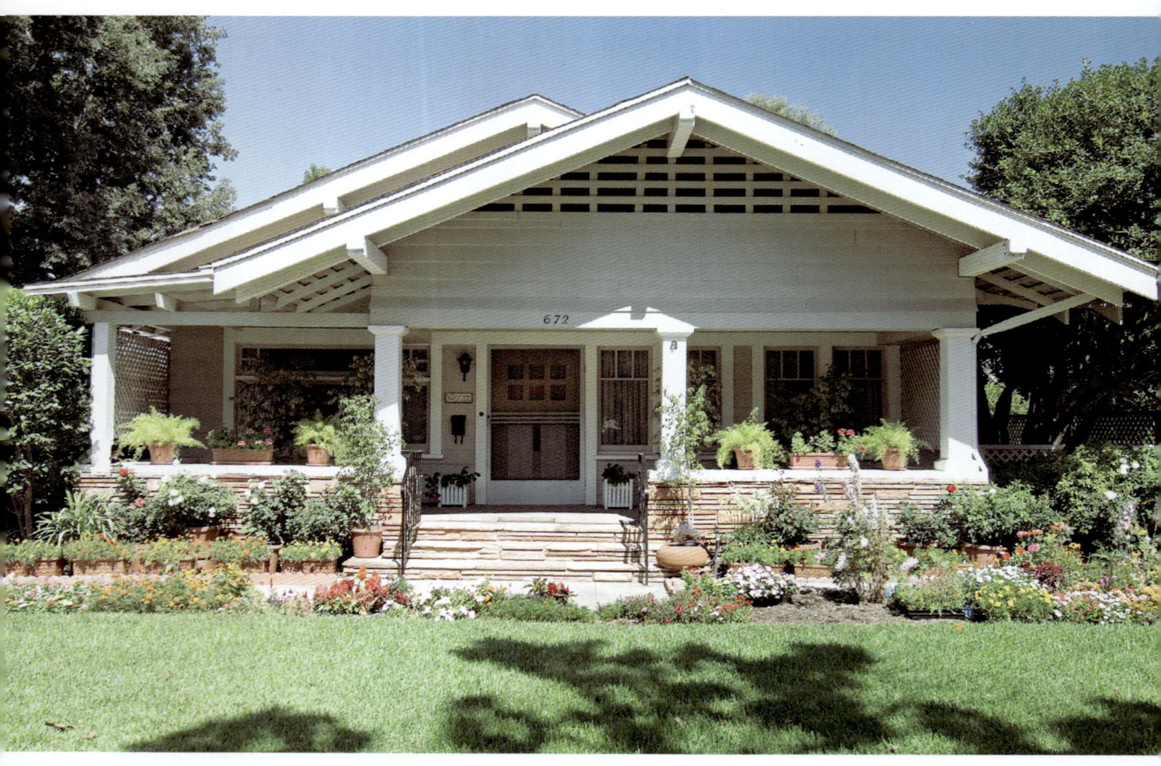


 Pasadena, California

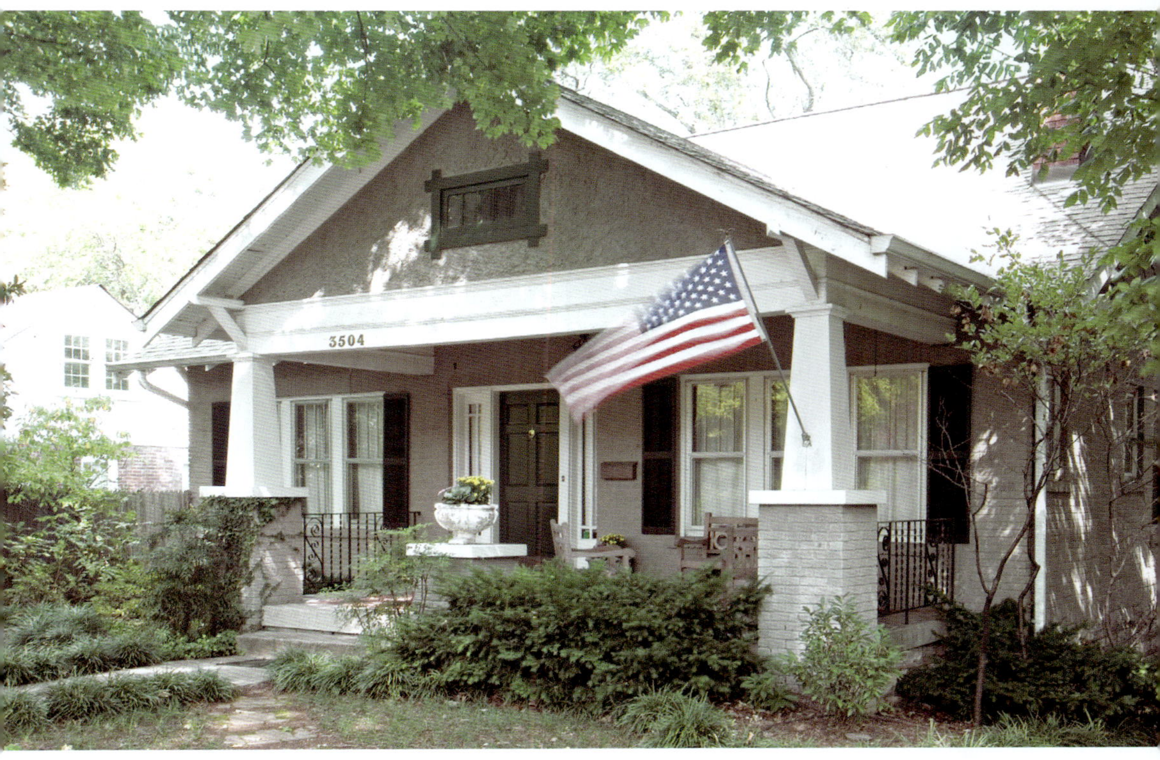


NASHVILLE, TENNESSEE

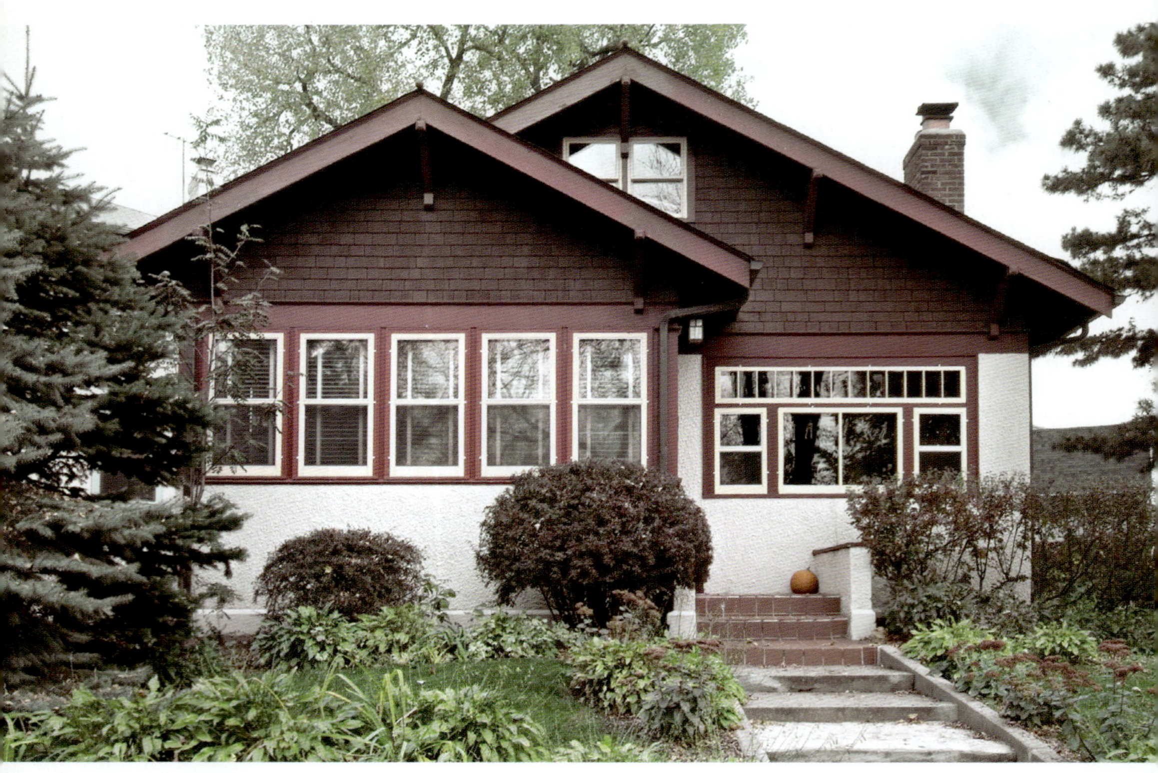

 MINNEAPOLIS, MINNESOTA

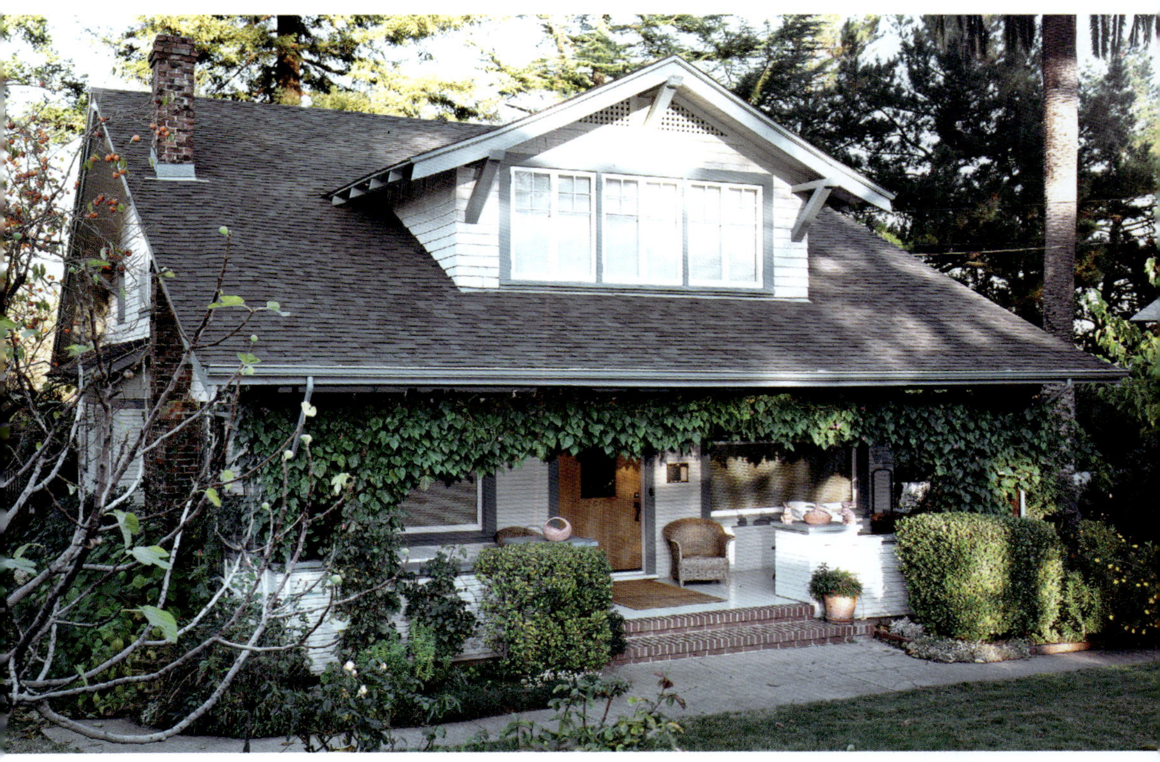

ST. HELENA, CALIFORNIA

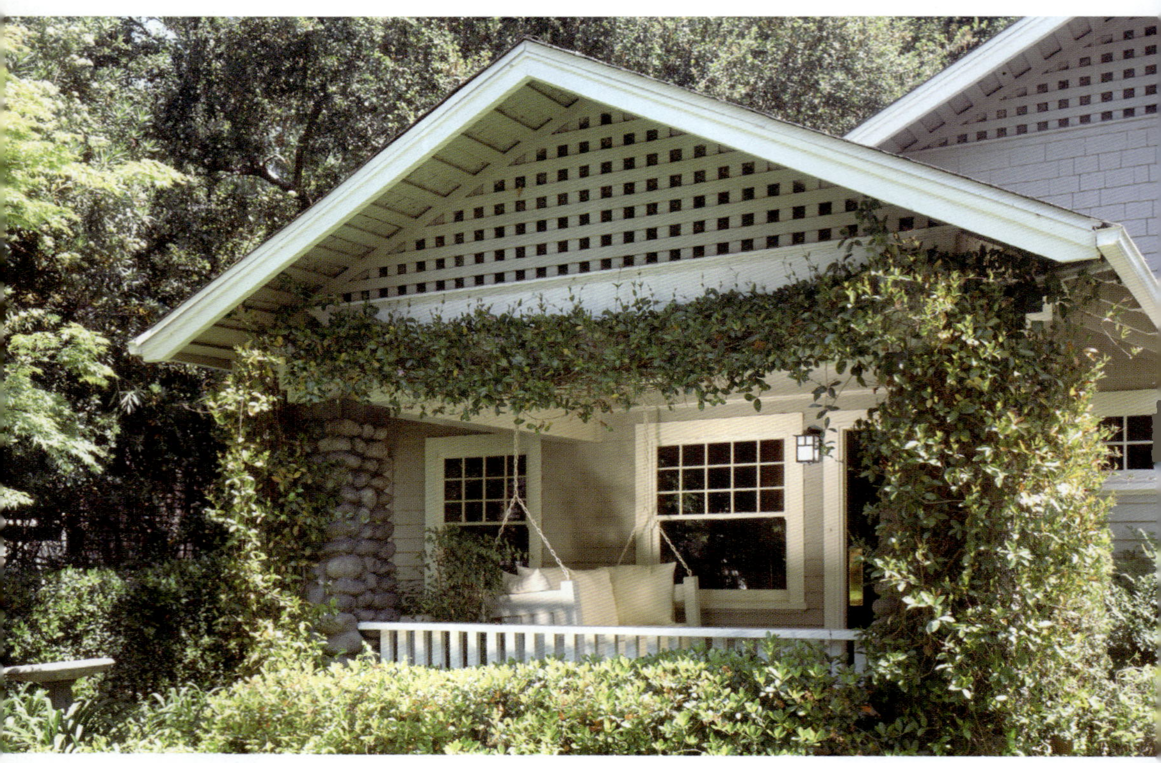

 Pasadena, California

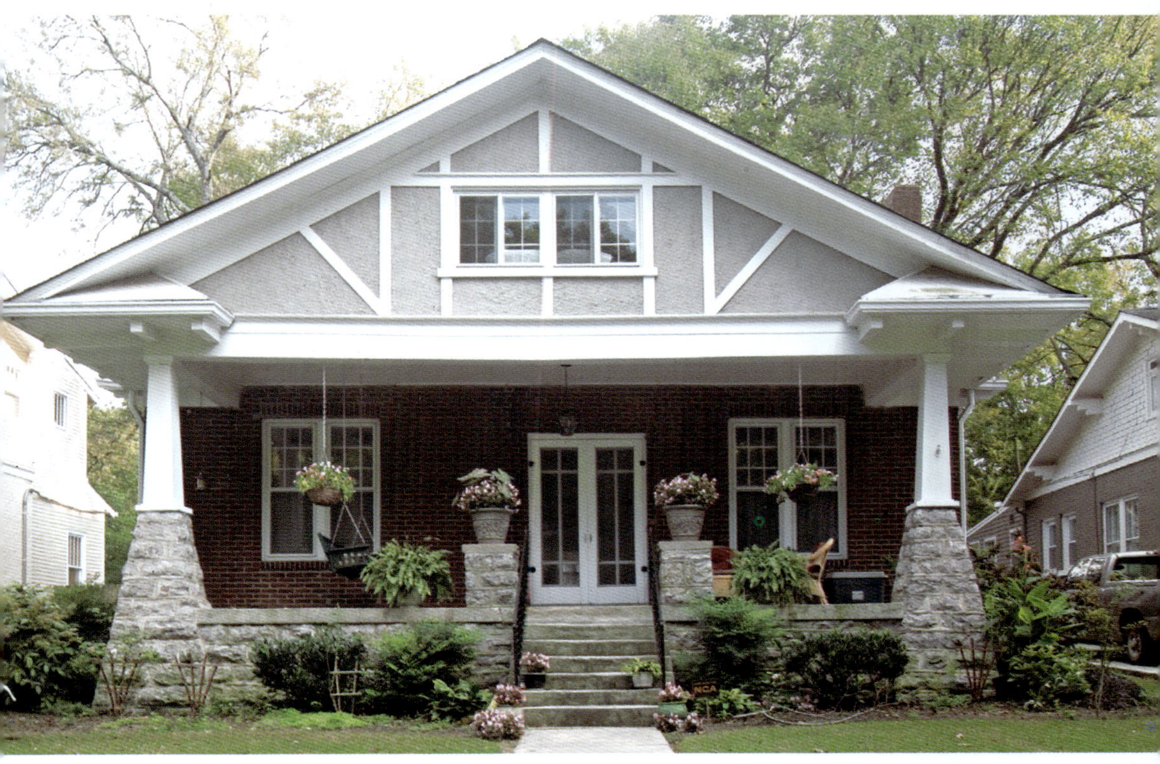

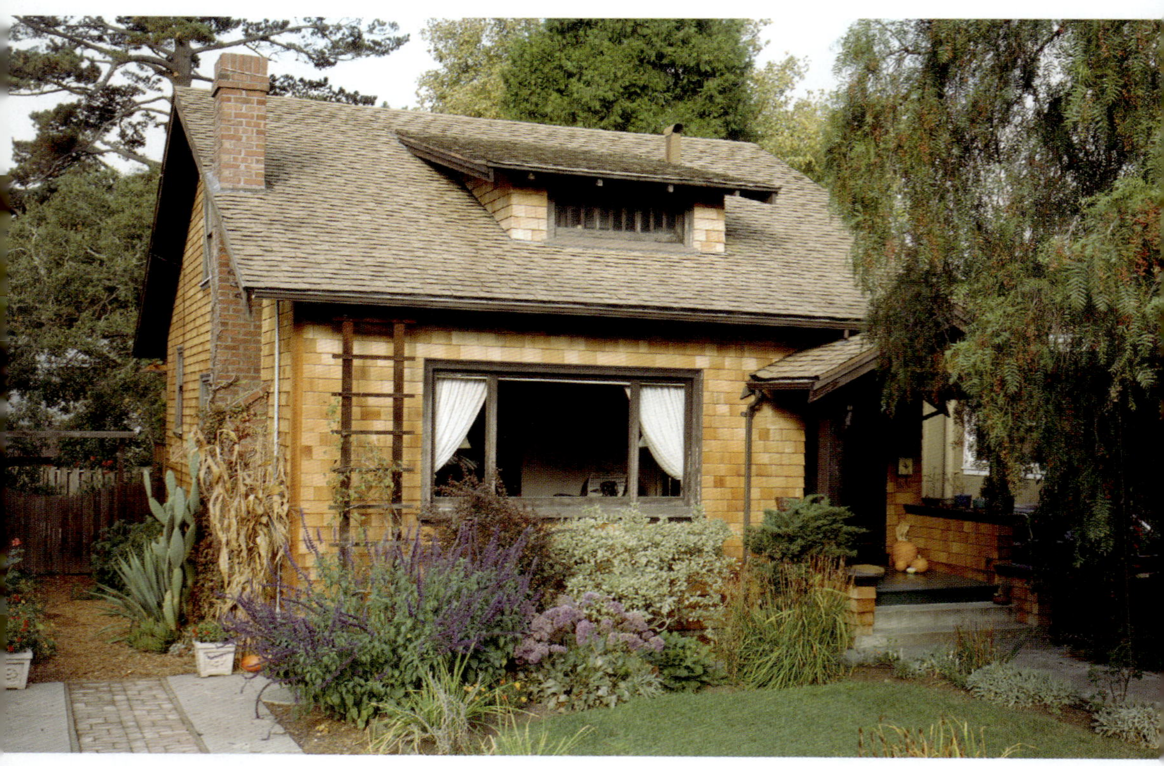

 Berkeley, California

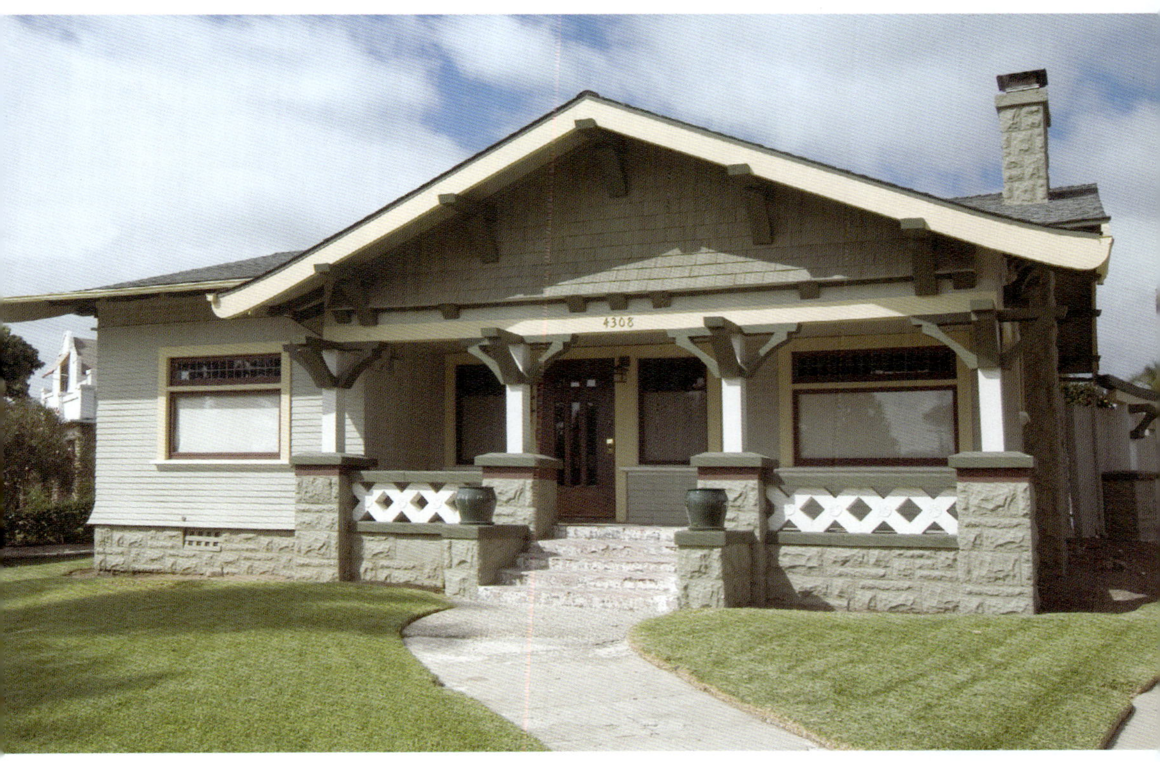


San Diego, California

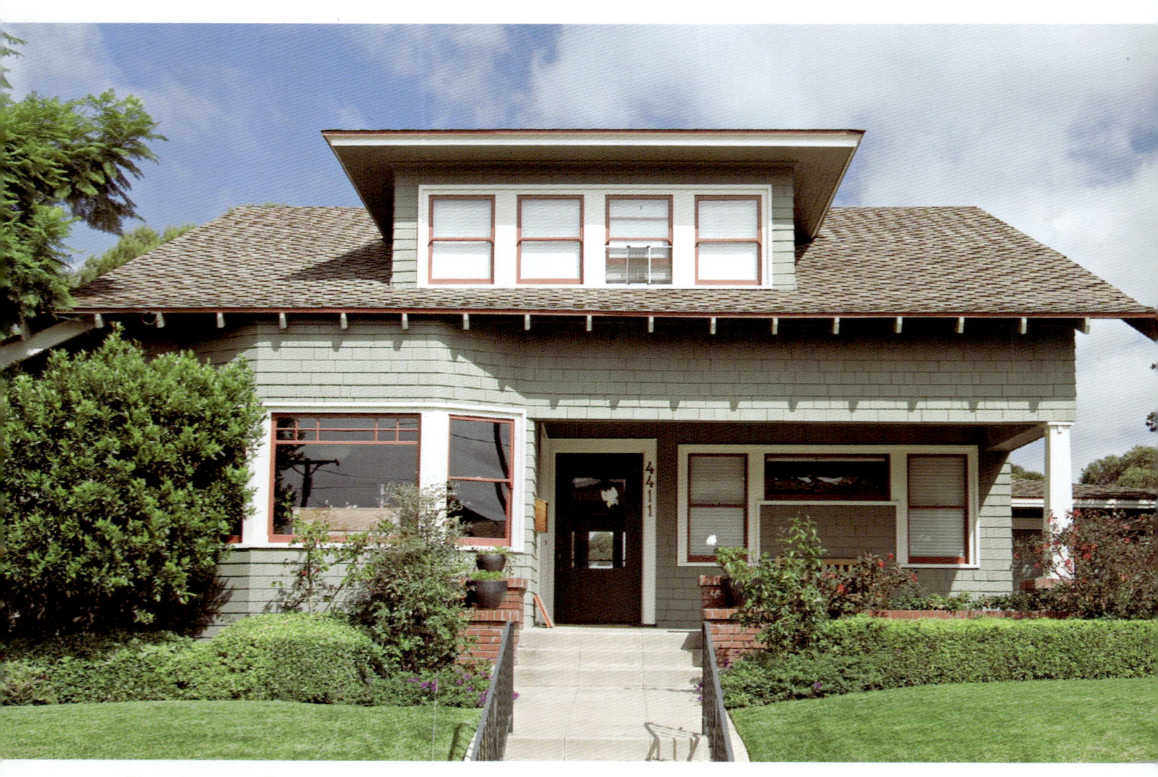


 San Diego, California

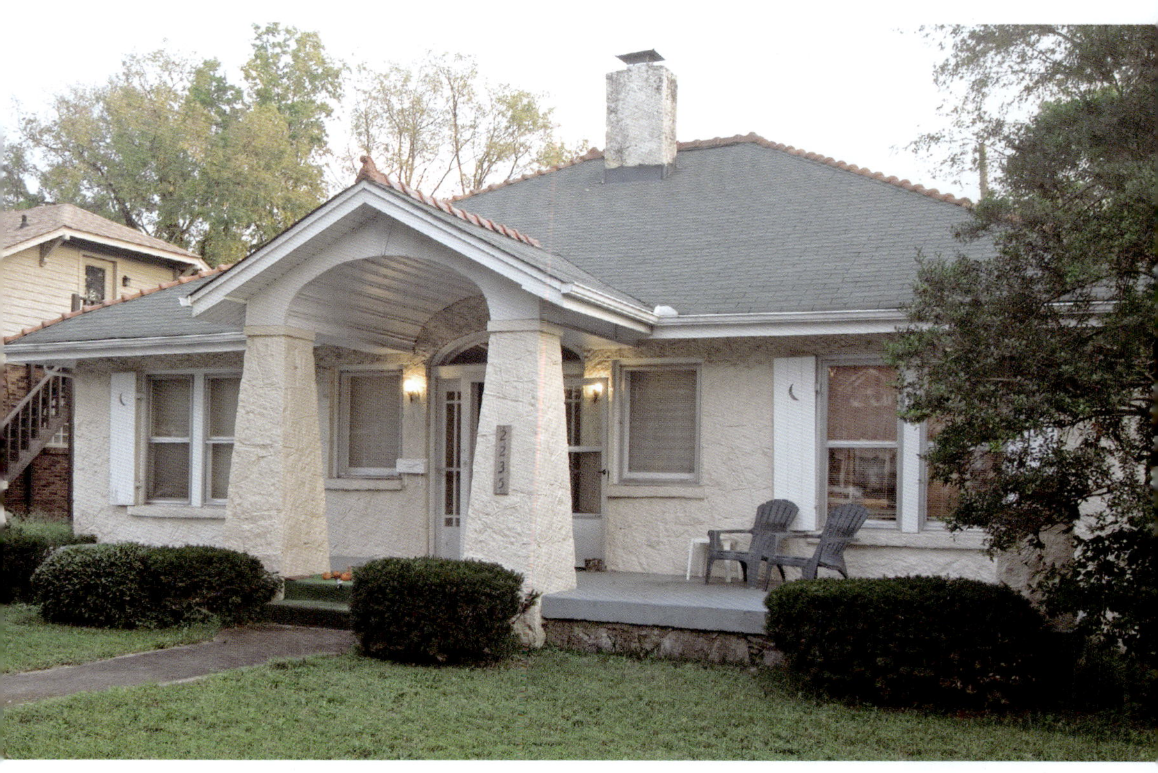
2235

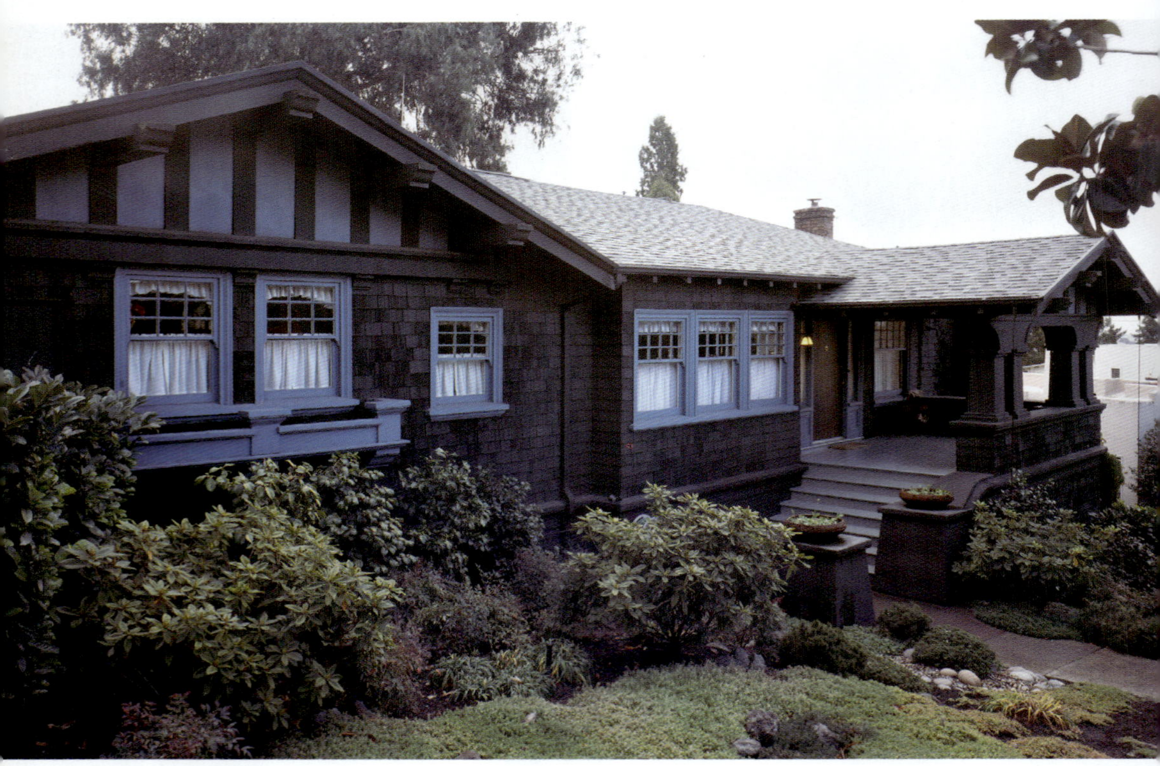

 Piedmont, California

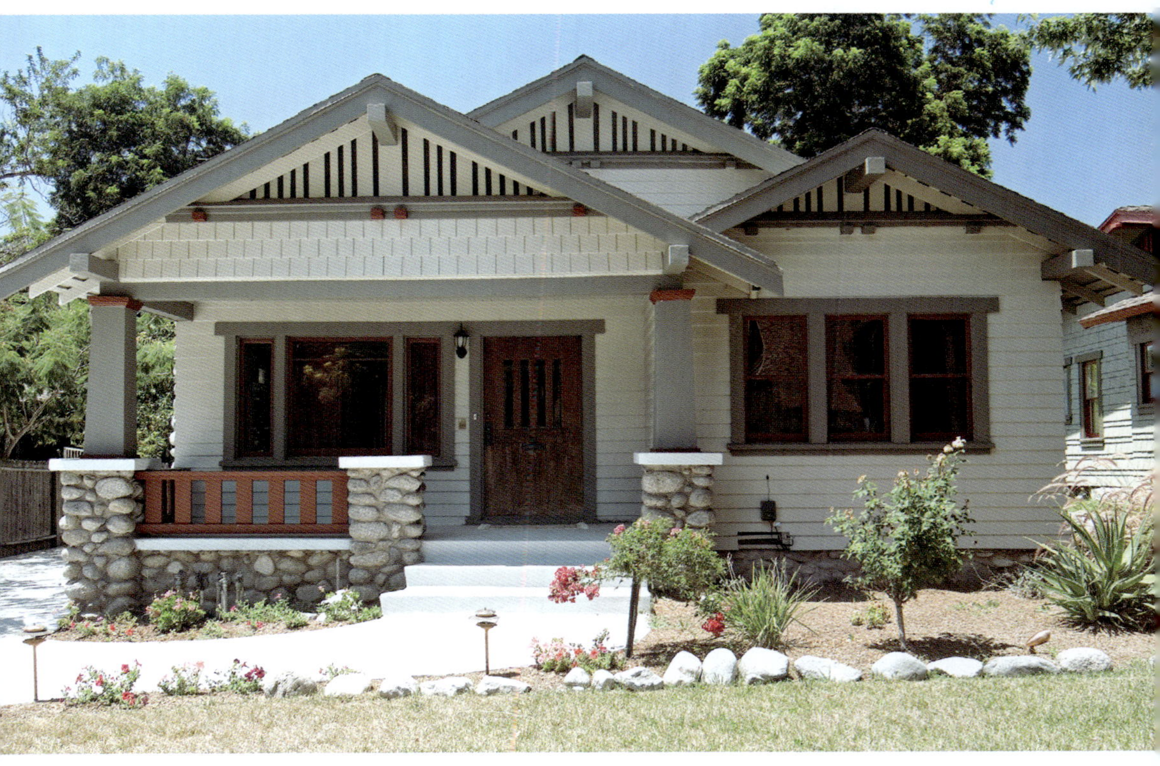

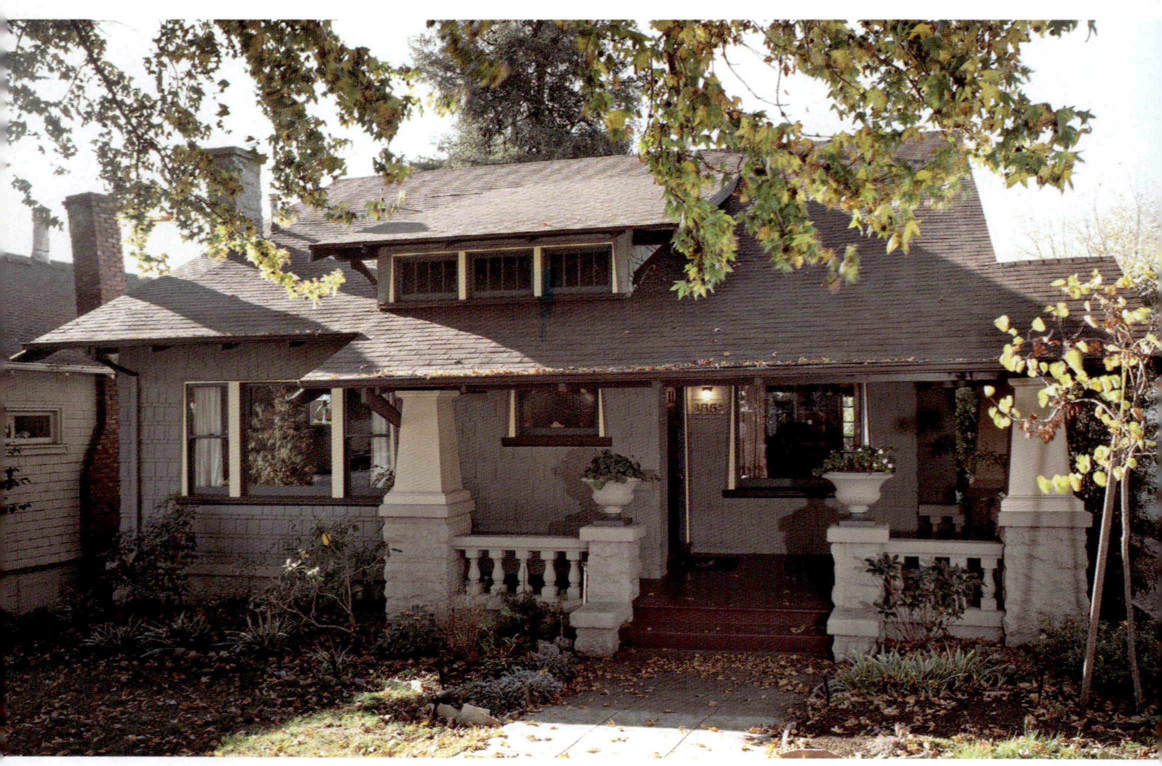

 ALAMEDA, CALIFORNIA

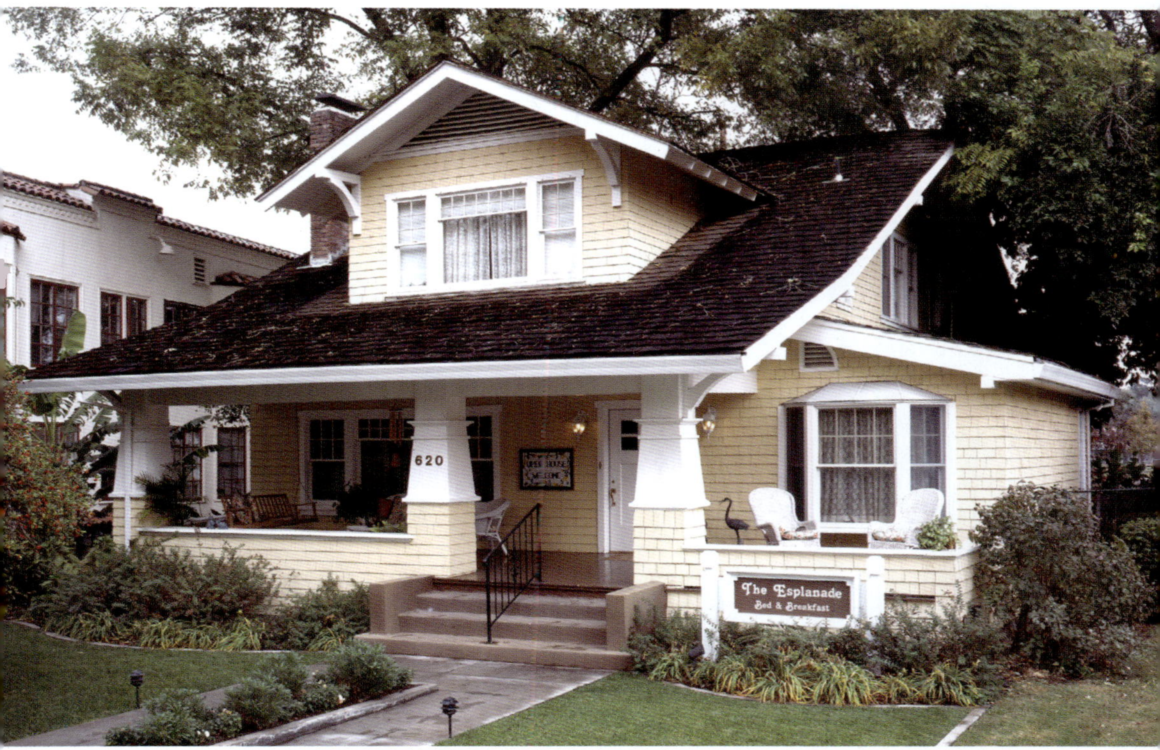
620
The Esplanade
Bed & Breakfast

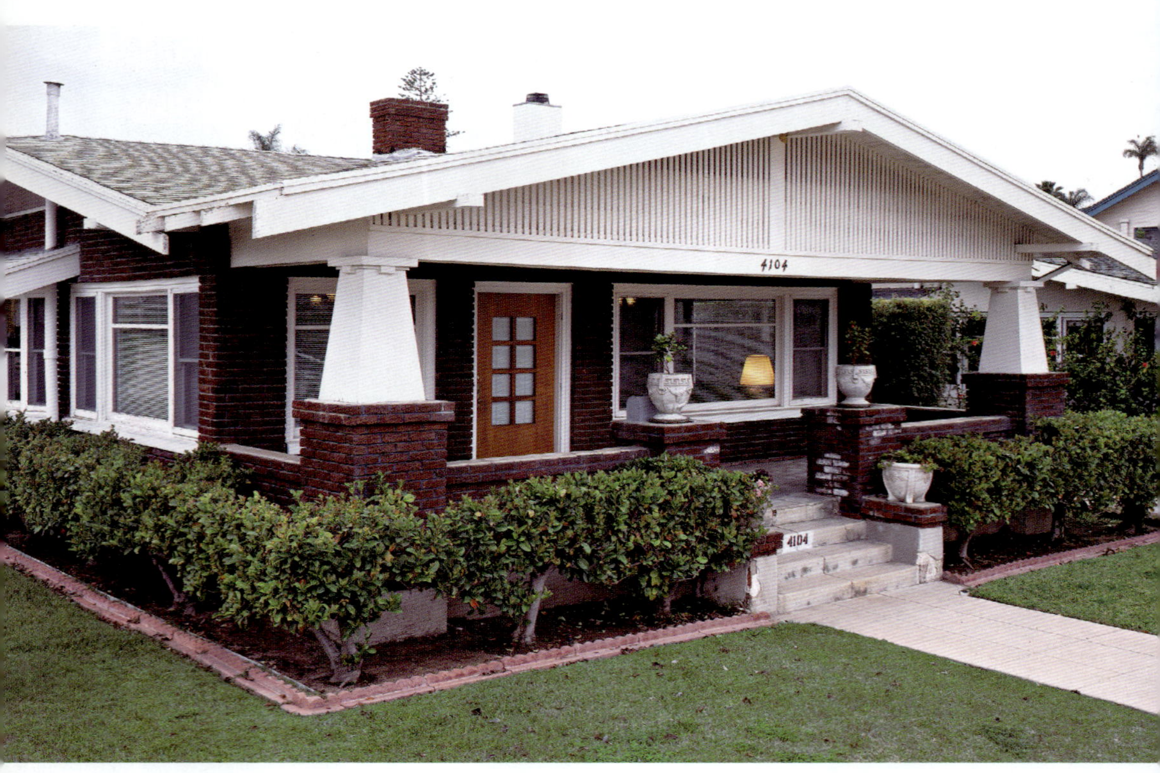


 Alameda, California

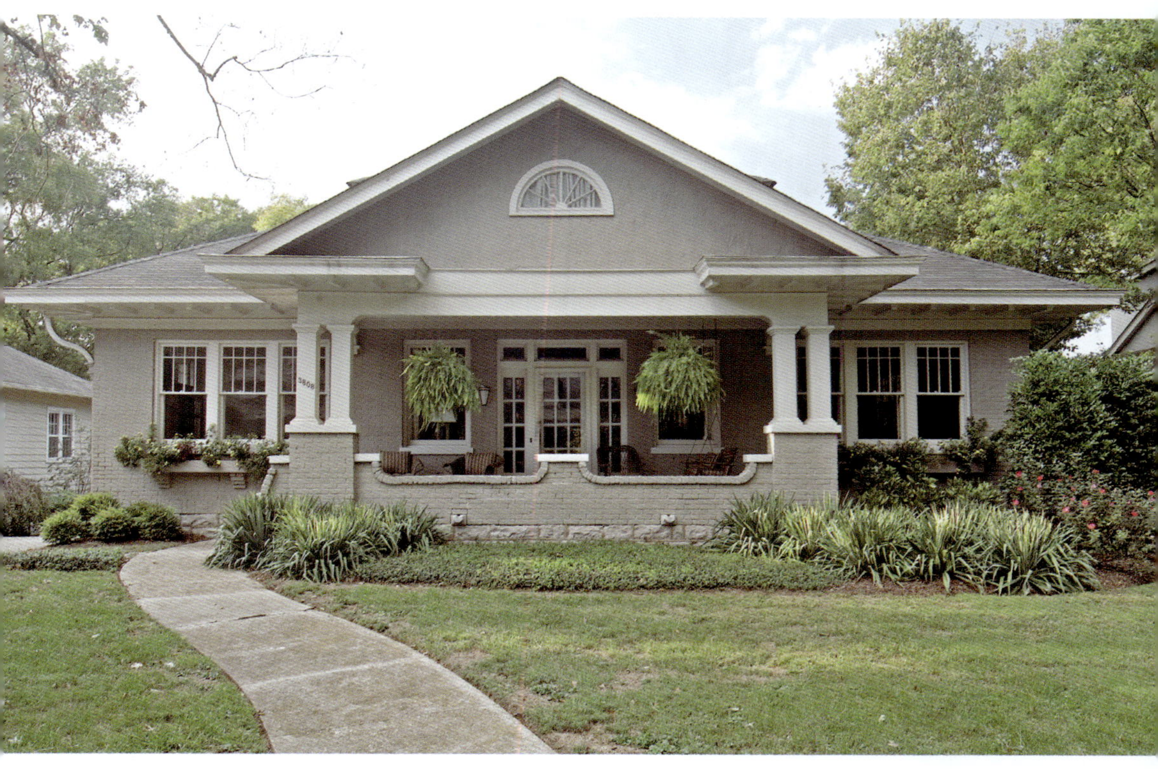

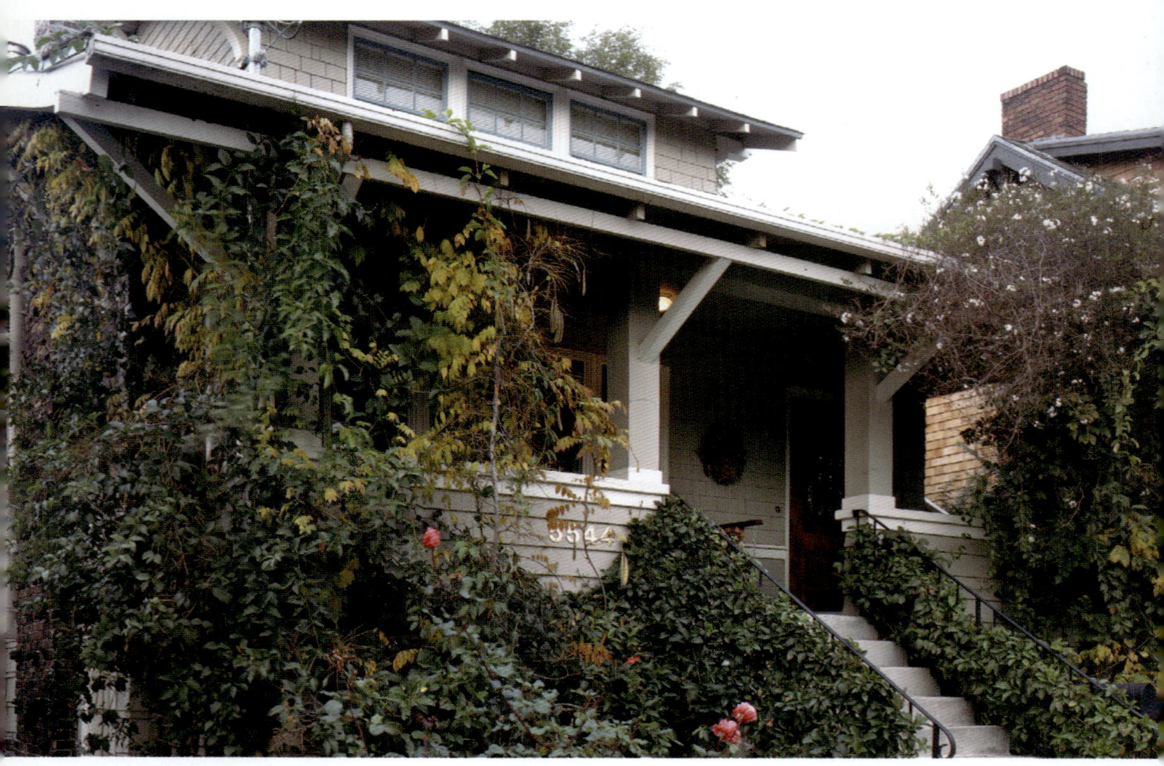

 Oakland, California

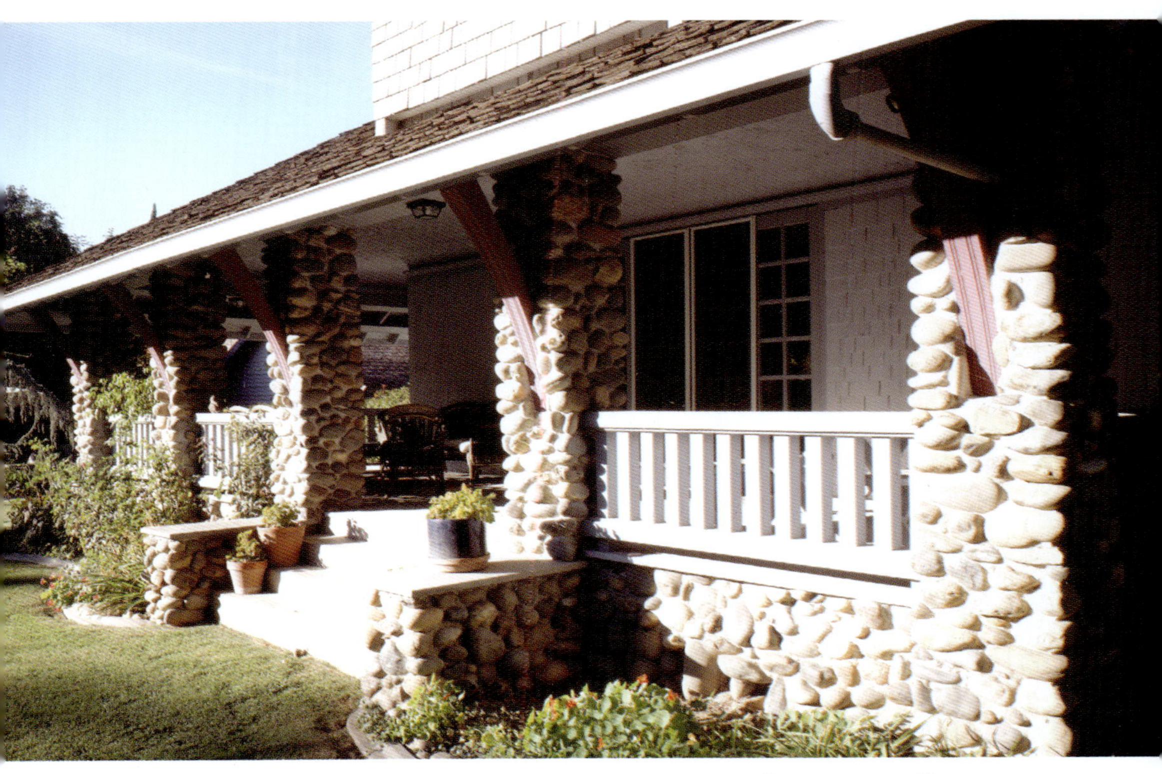

Sacramento, California 

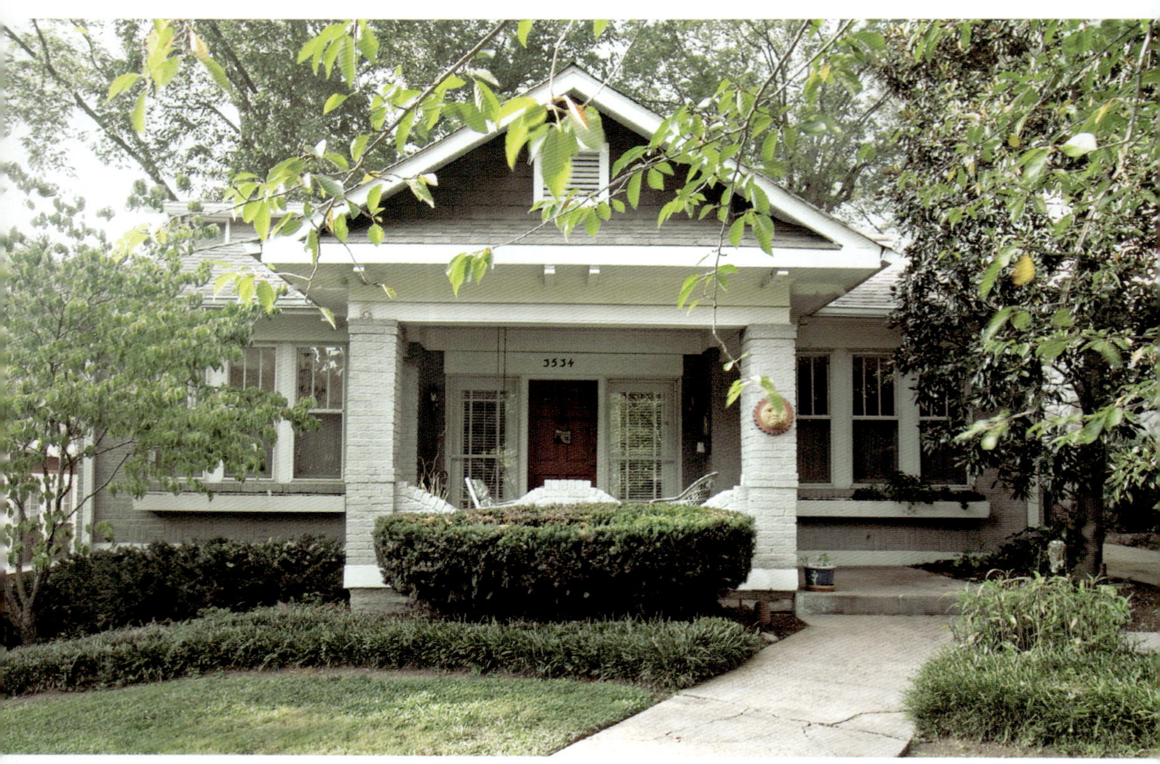


 Nashville, Tennessee

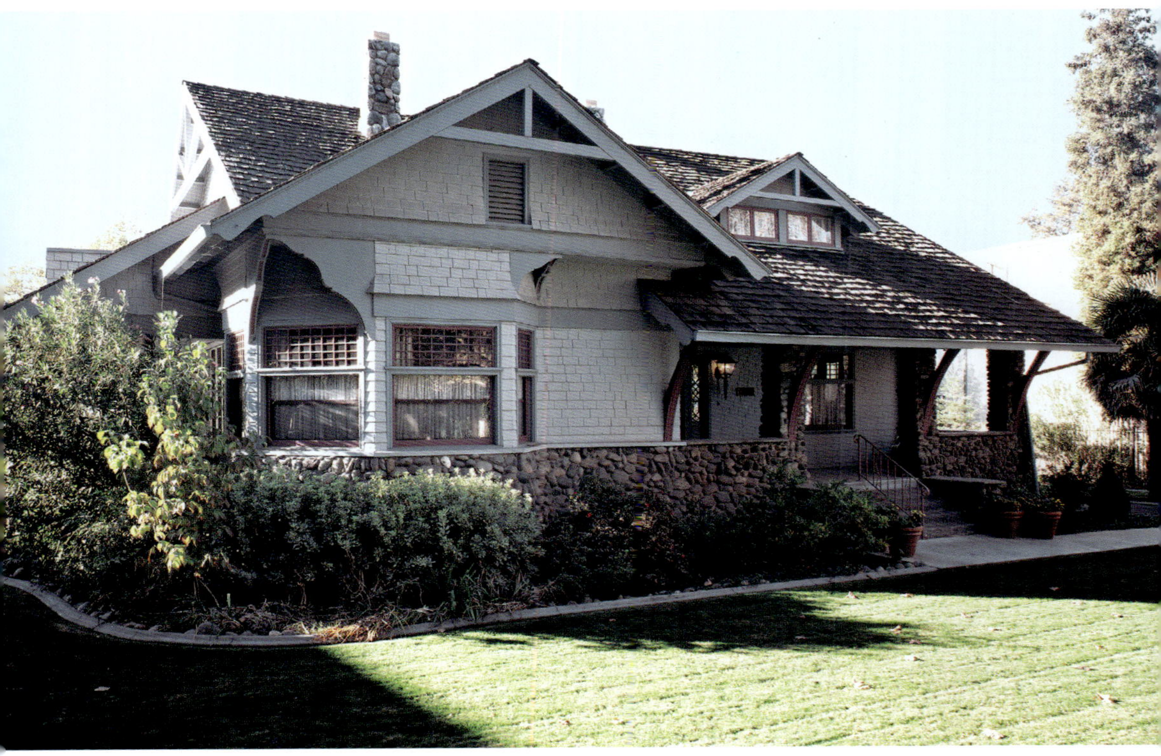

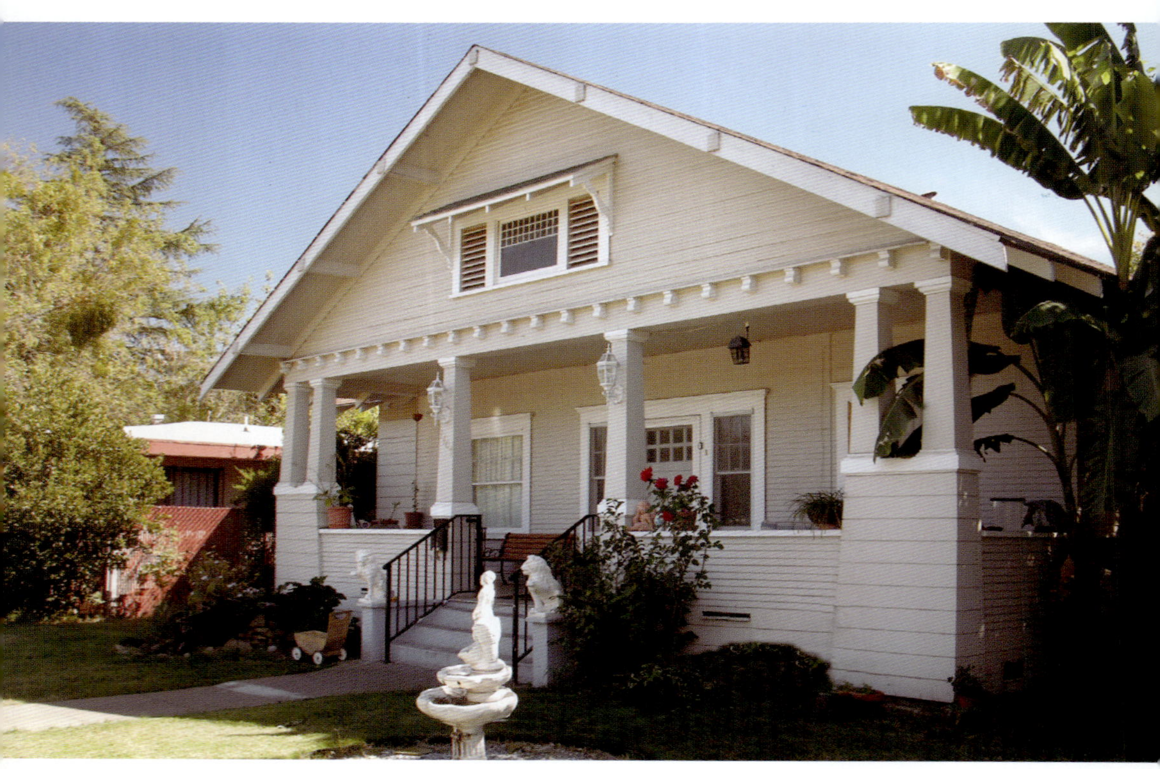

 GRIDLEY, CALIFORNIA

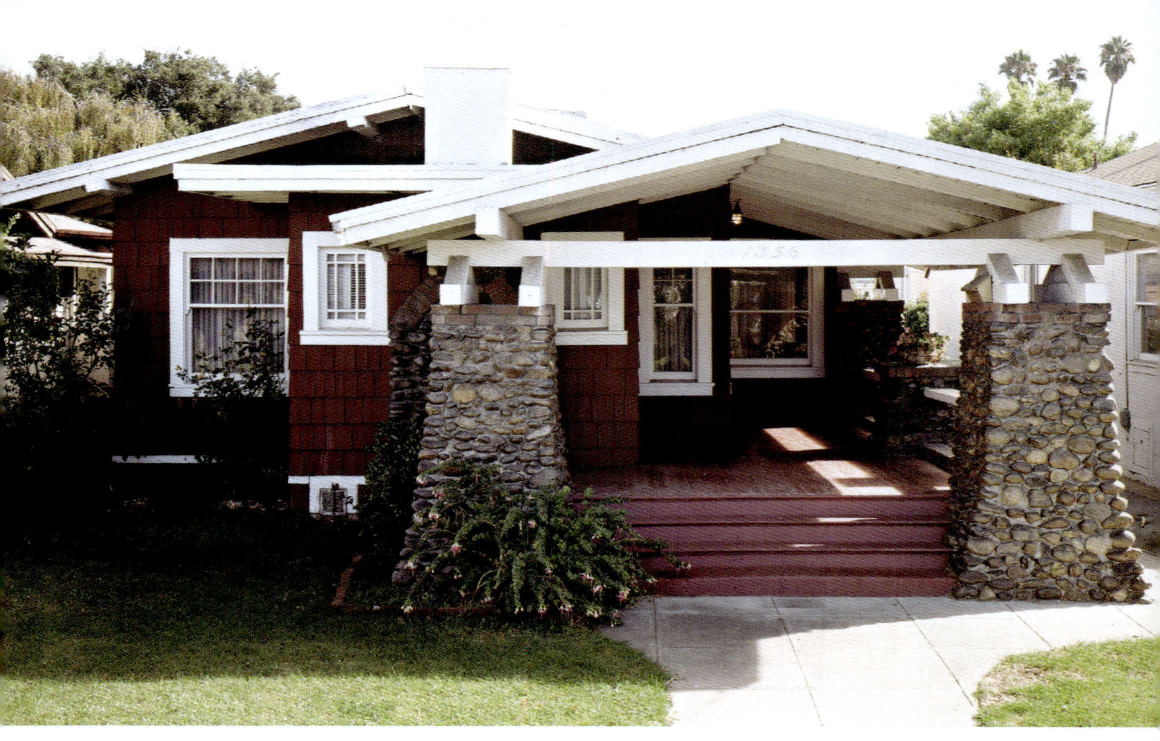


Alameda, California

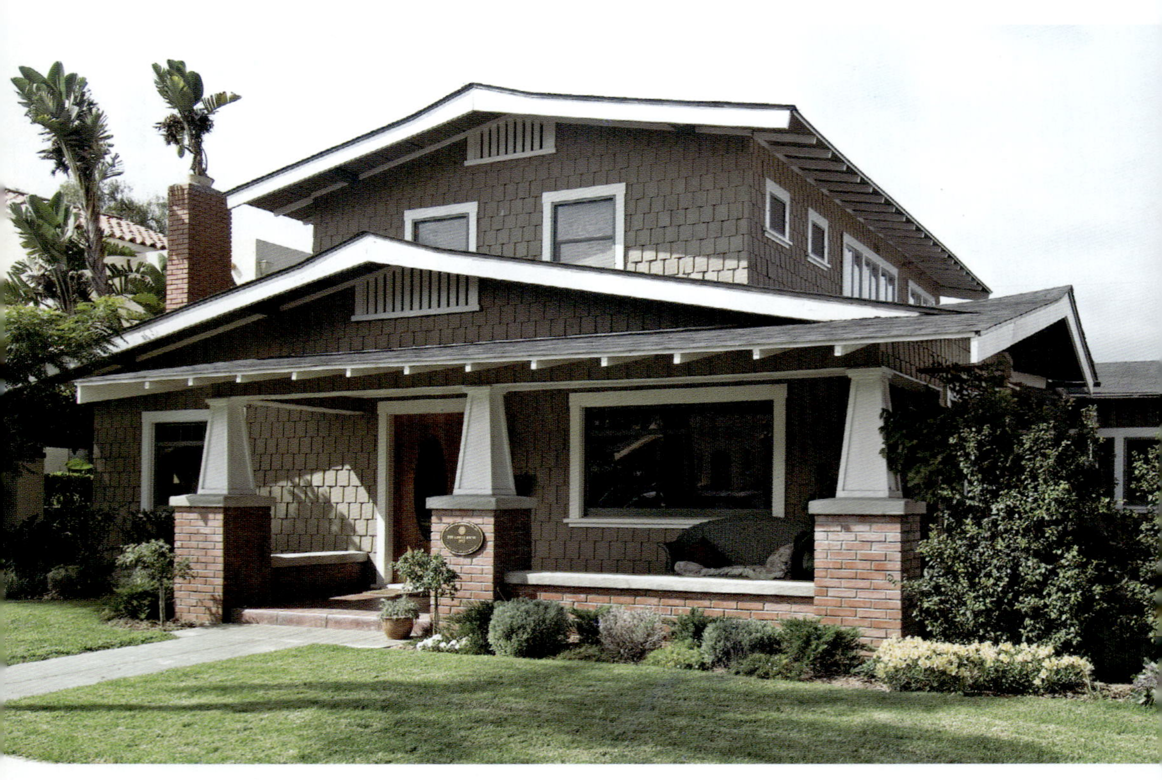

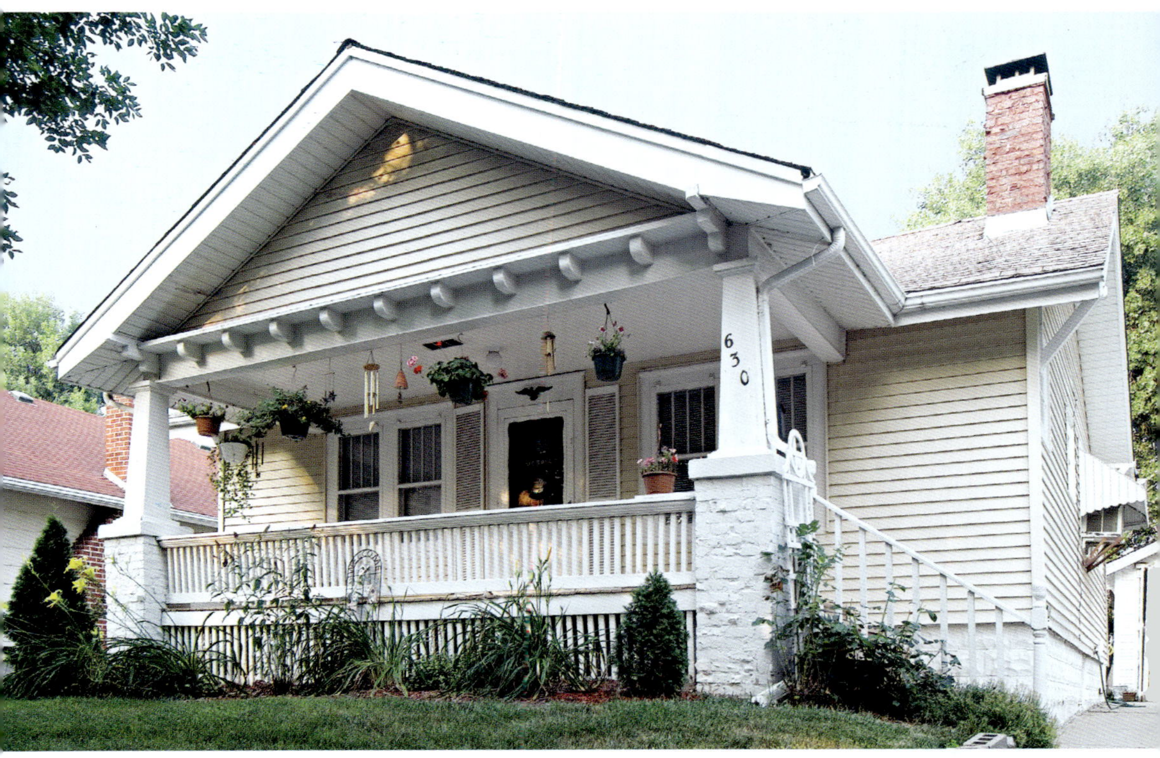
630

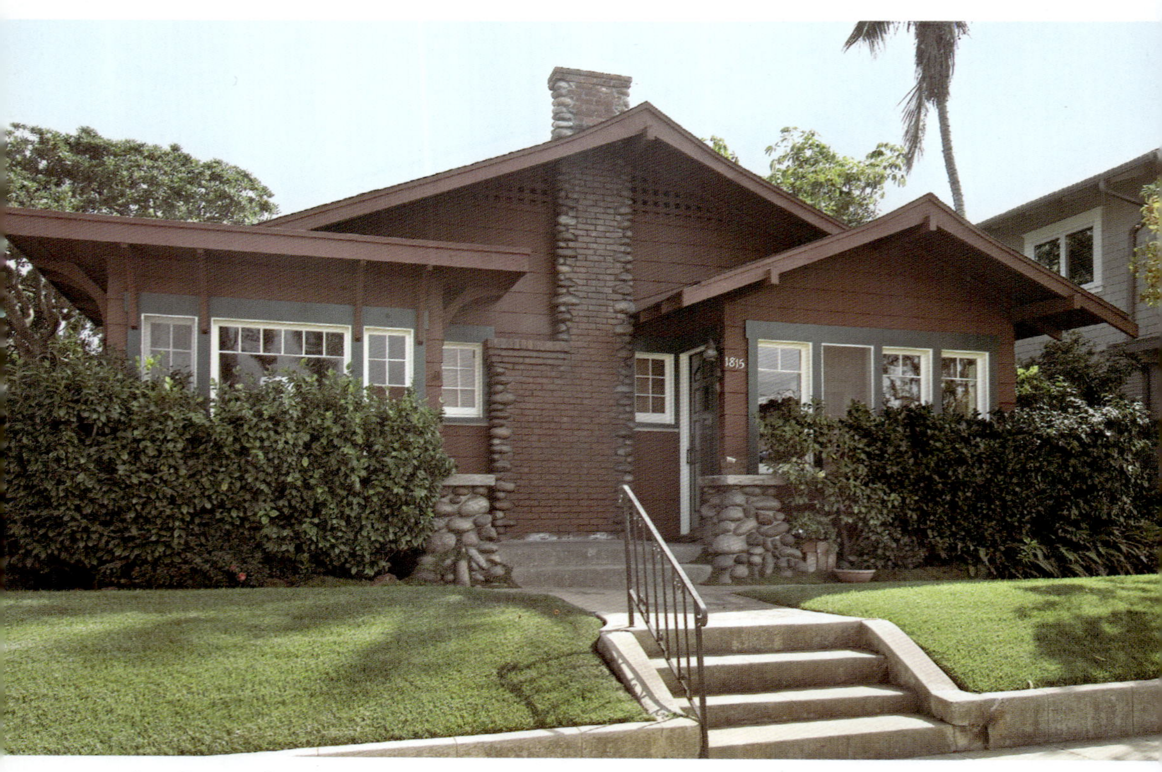
1815

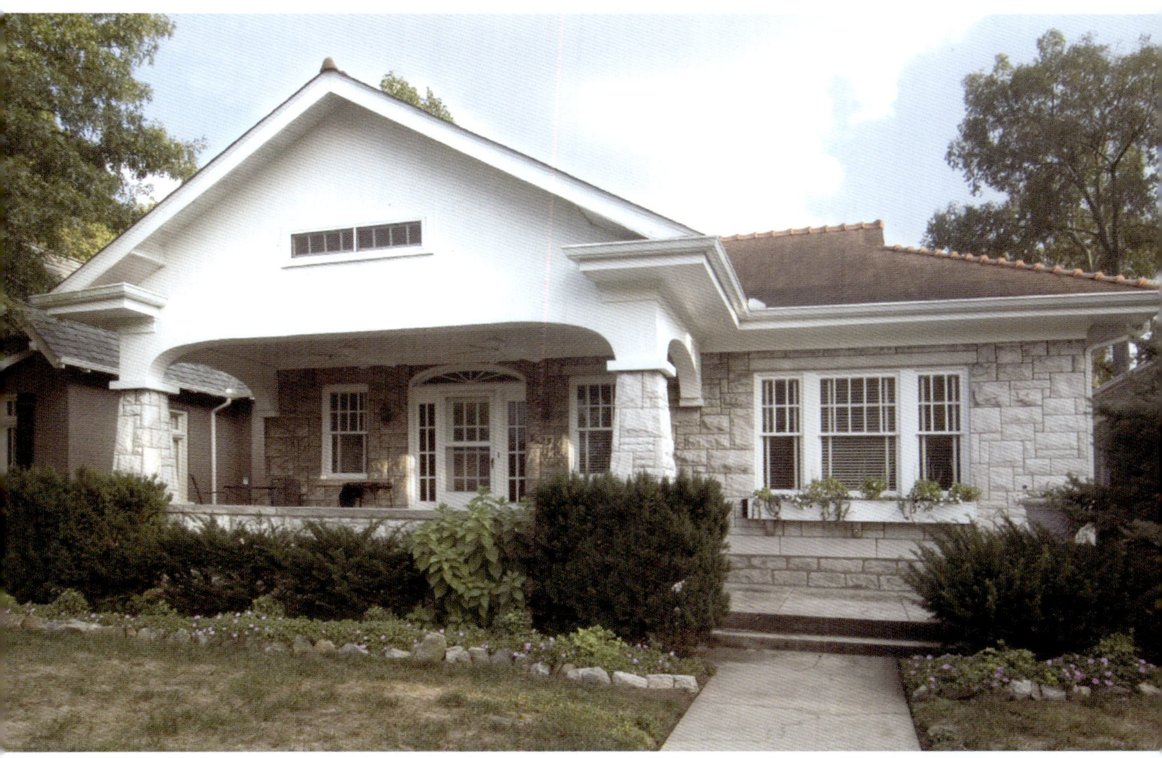

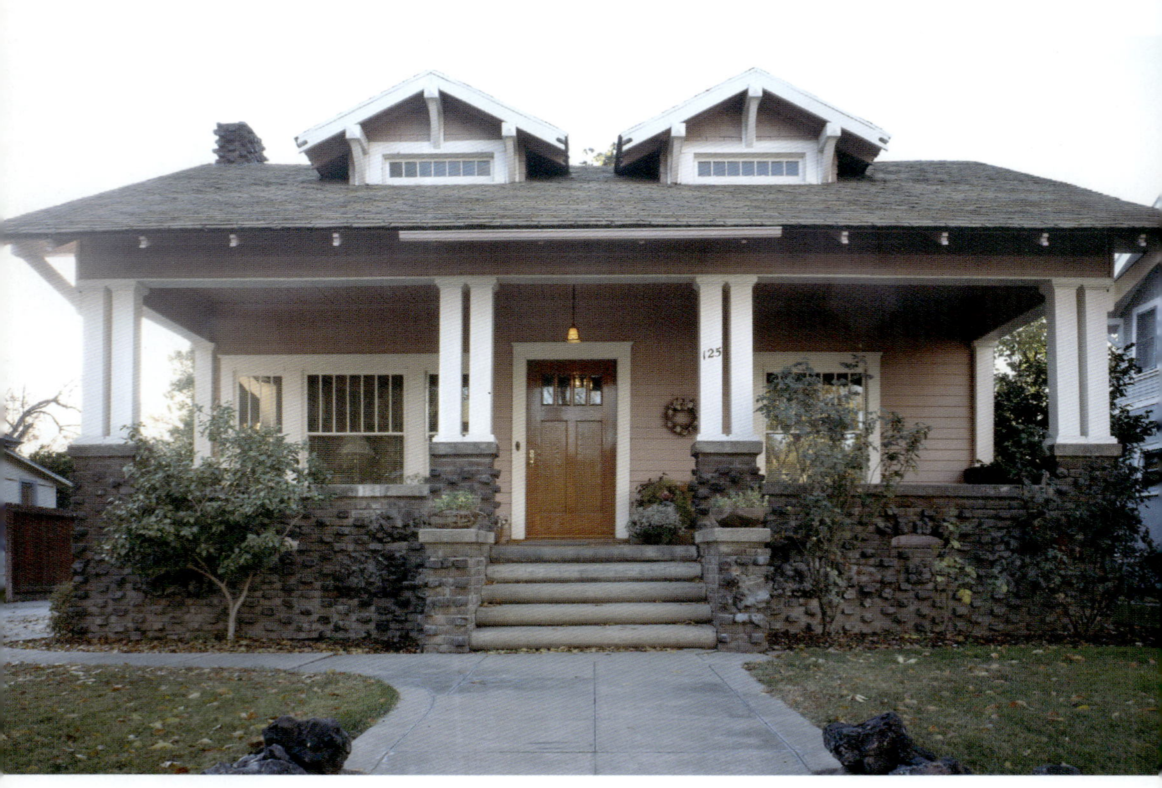


 Modesto, California

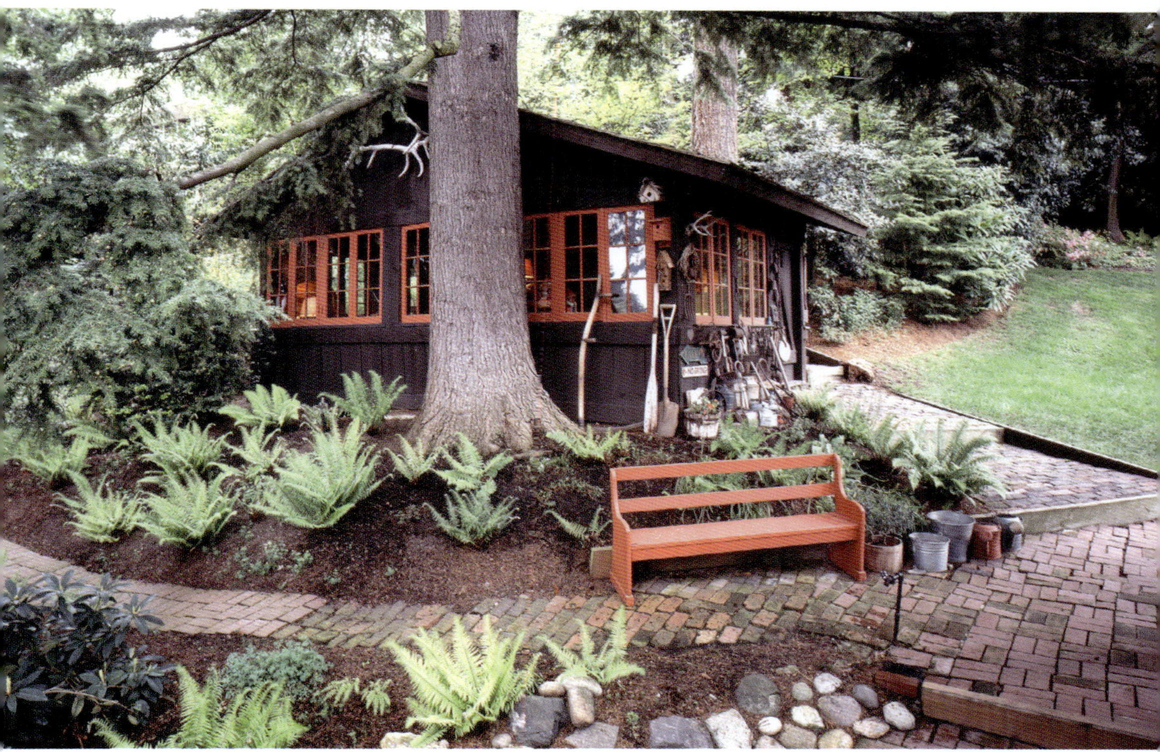

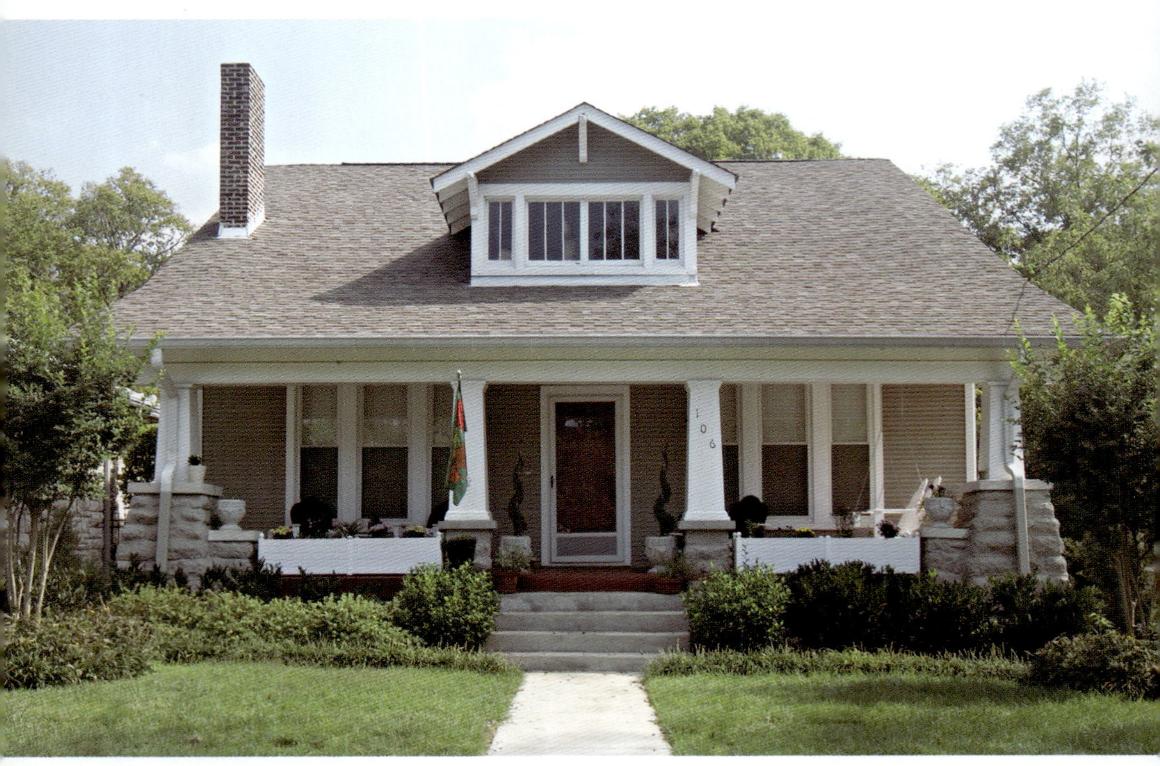


 Nashville, Tennessee

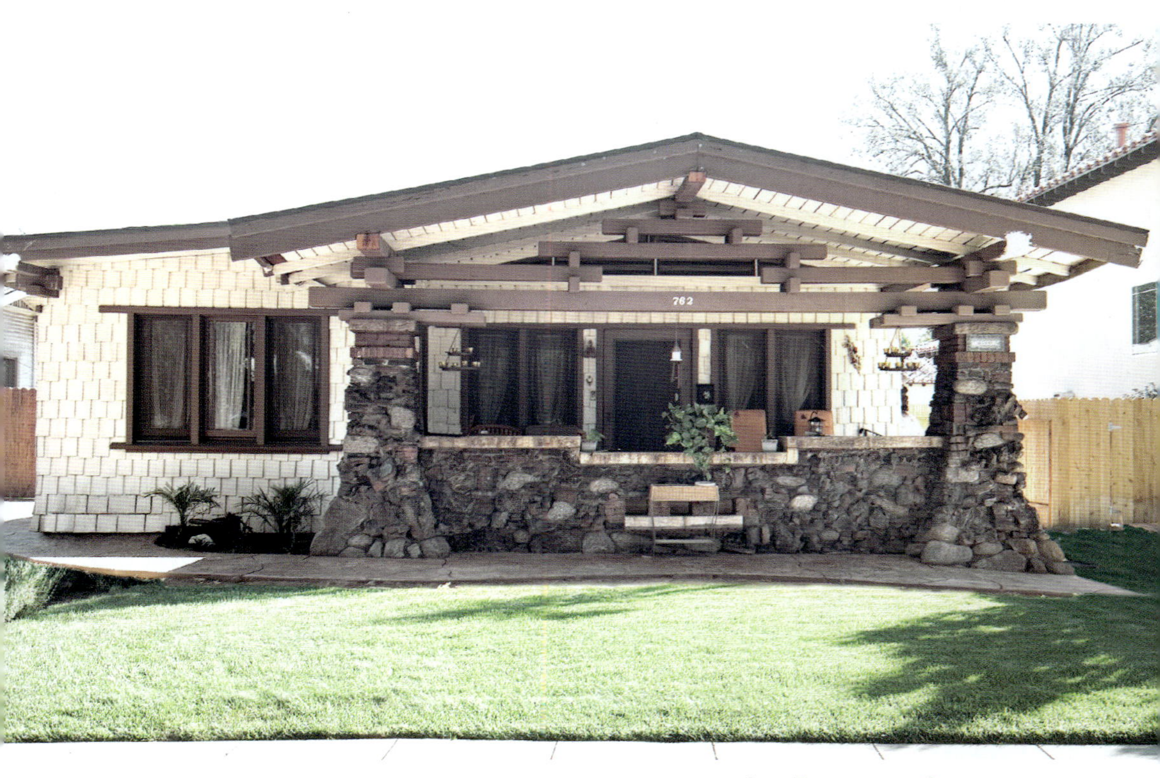


San Fernando, California 

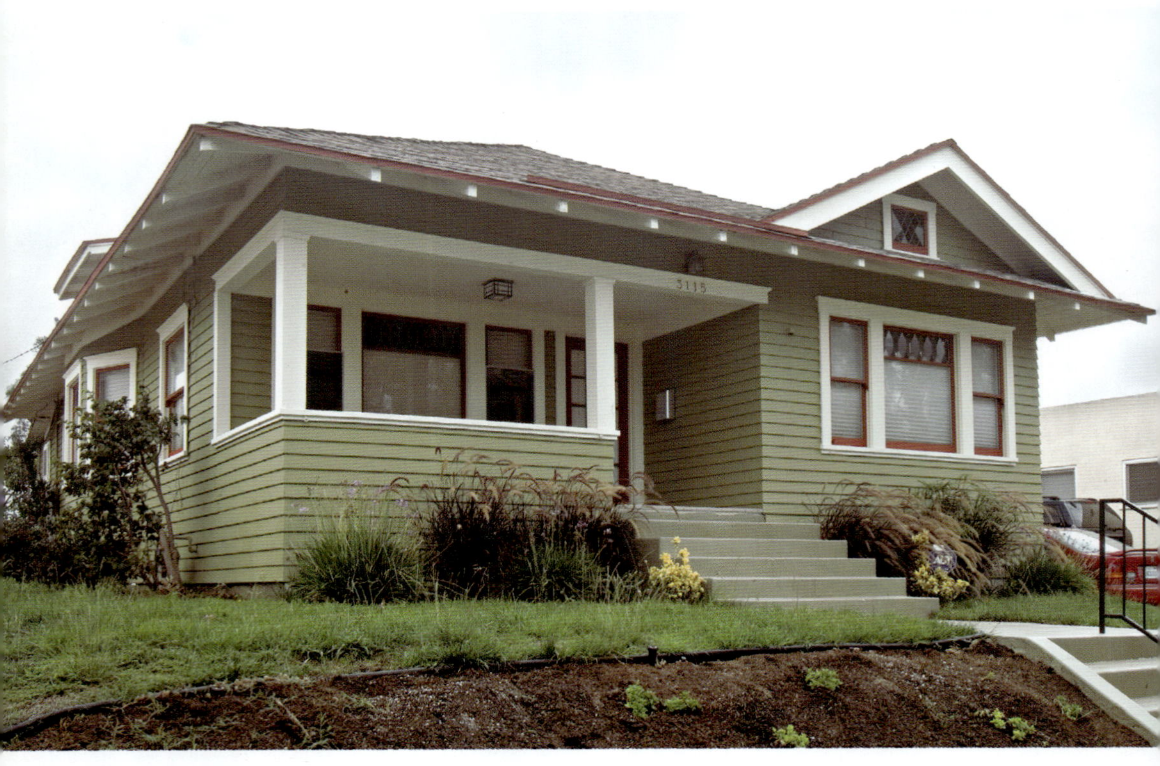


 San Diego, California

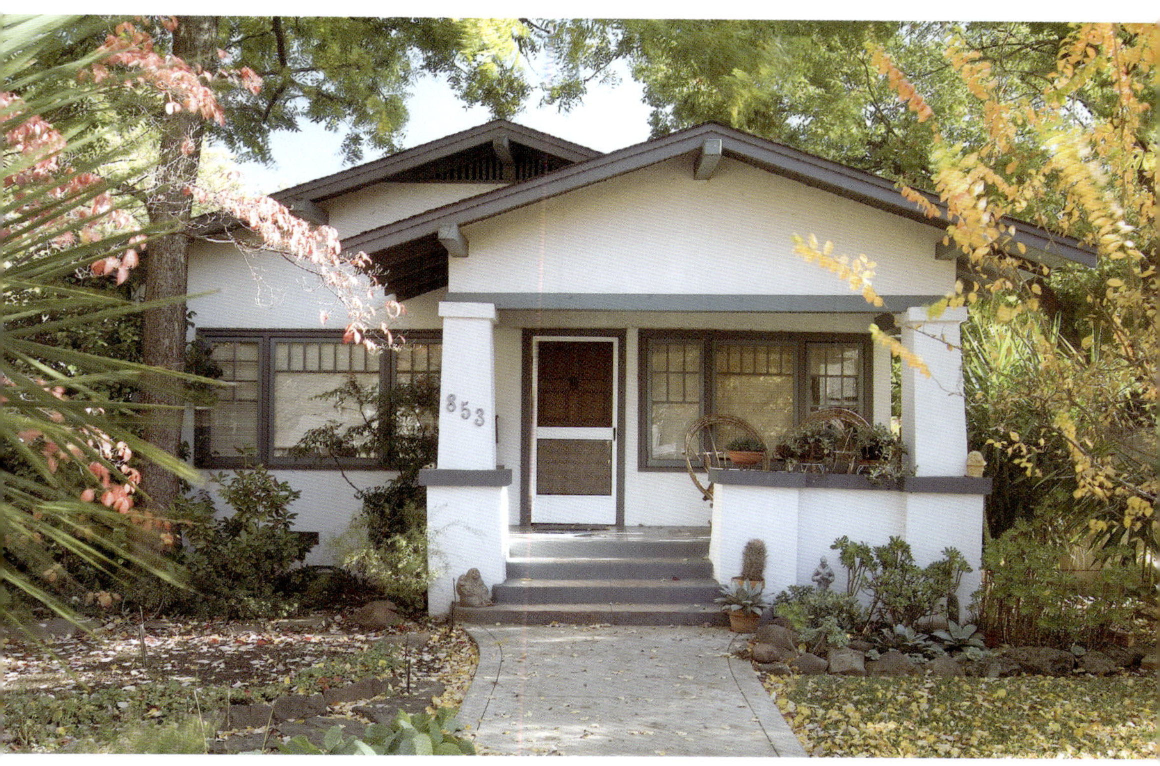


Chico, California 

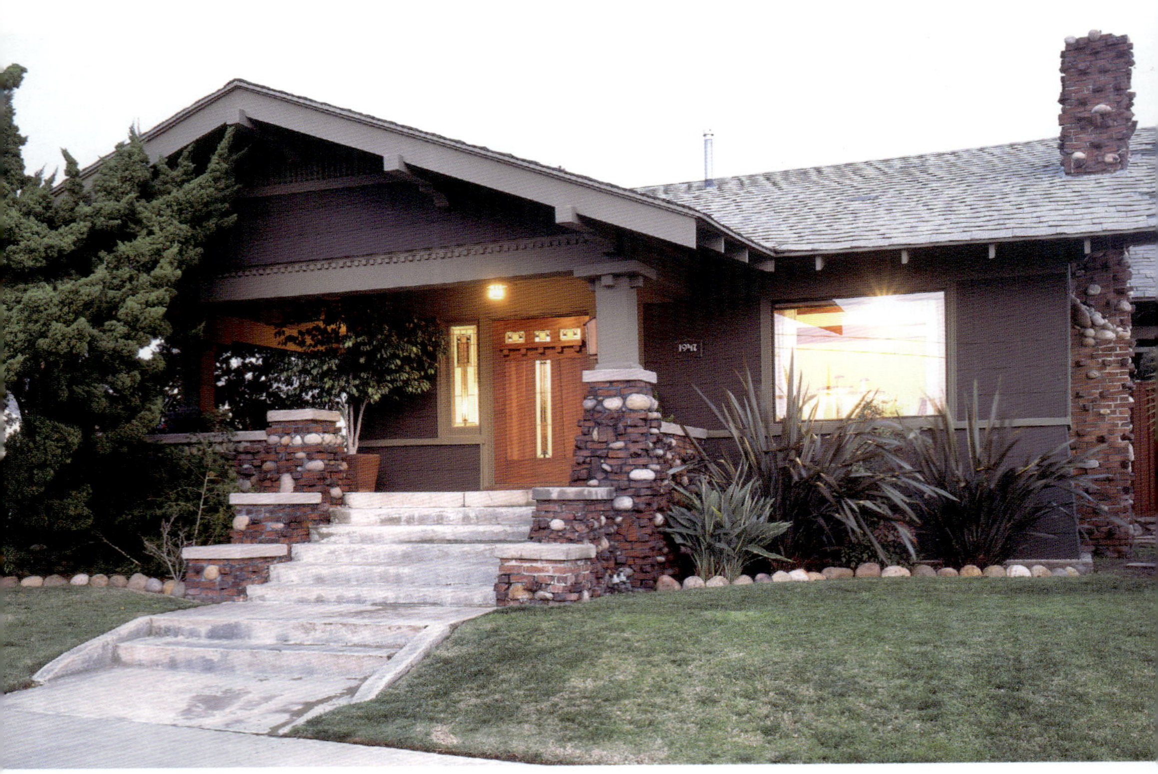

 San Diego, California

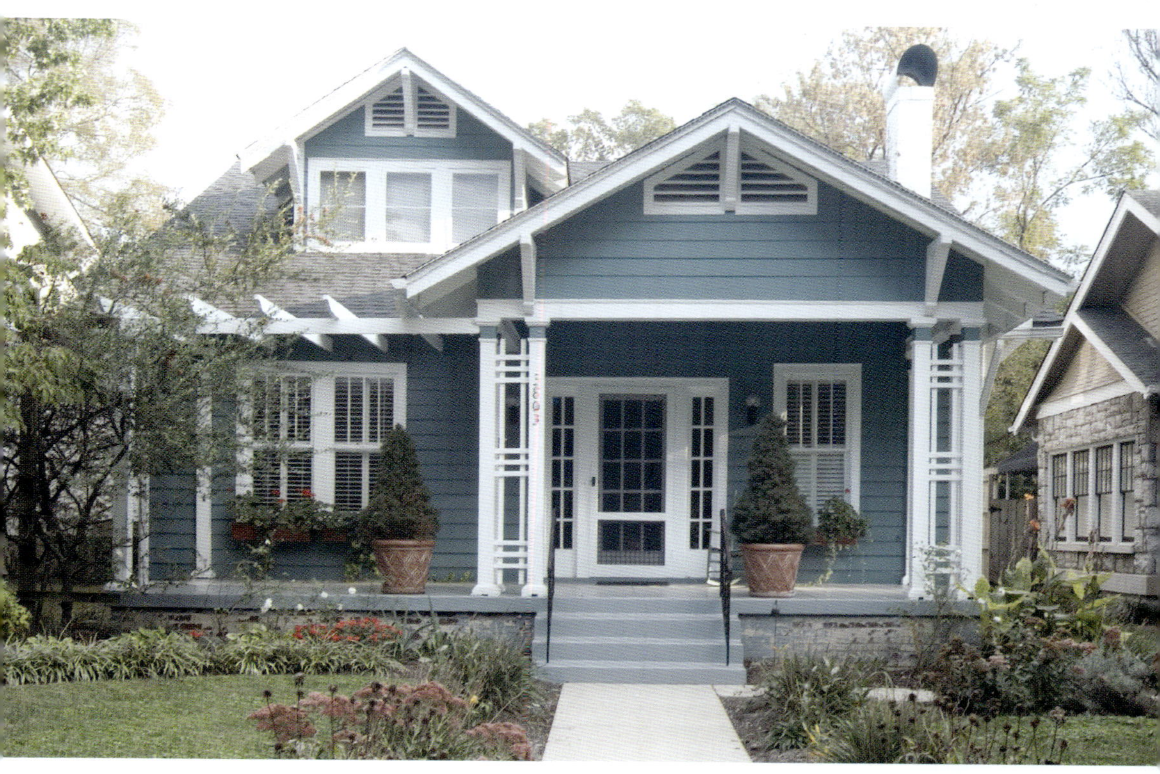

Nashville, Tennessee

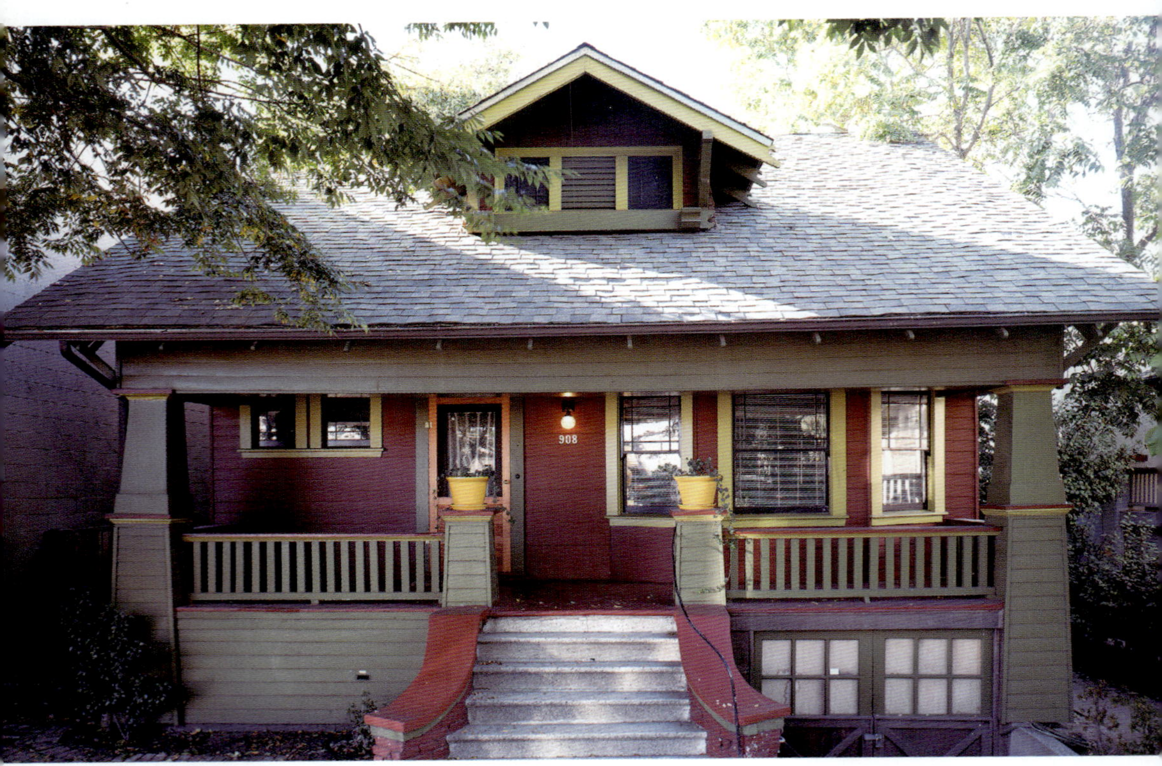


 Sacramento, California

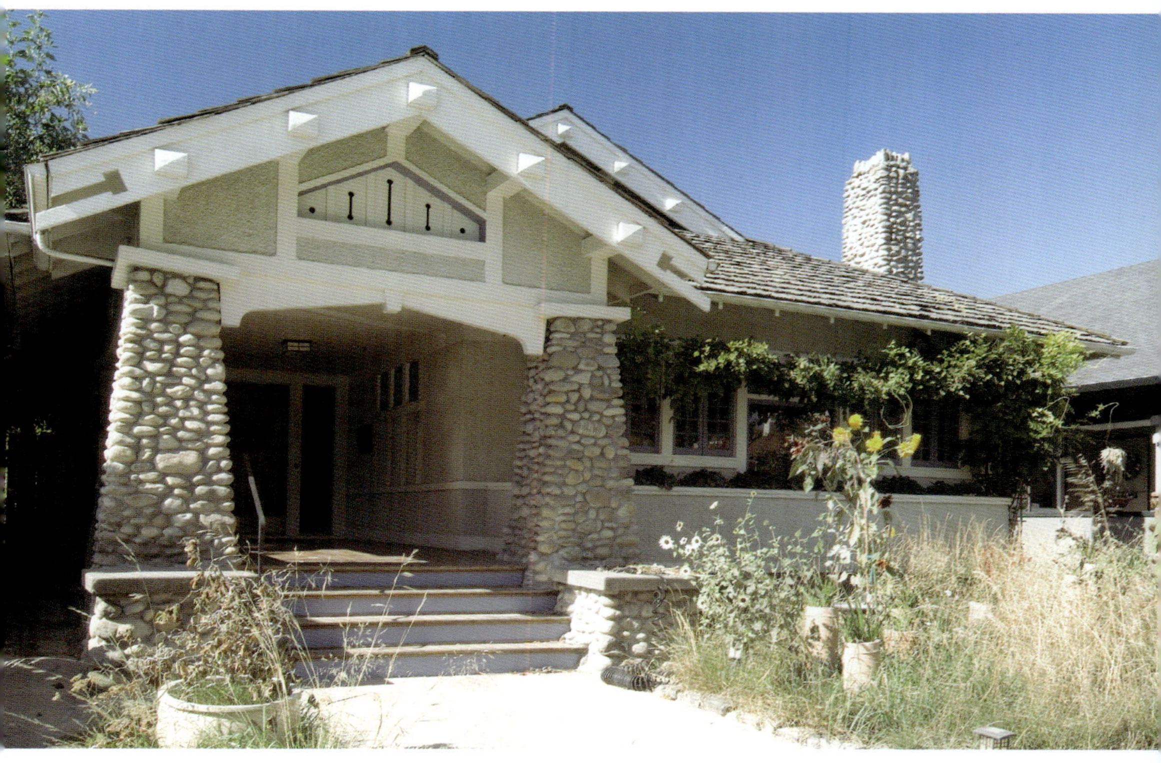

San Jose, California 

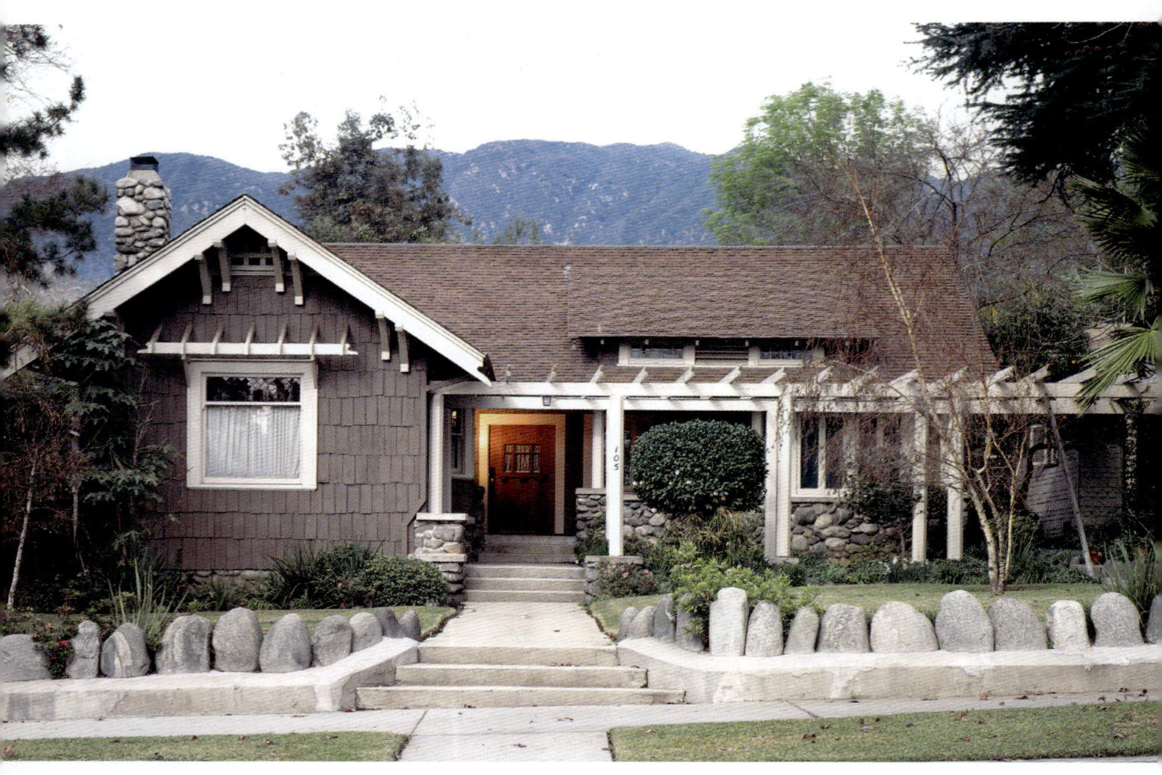


 Monrovia, California

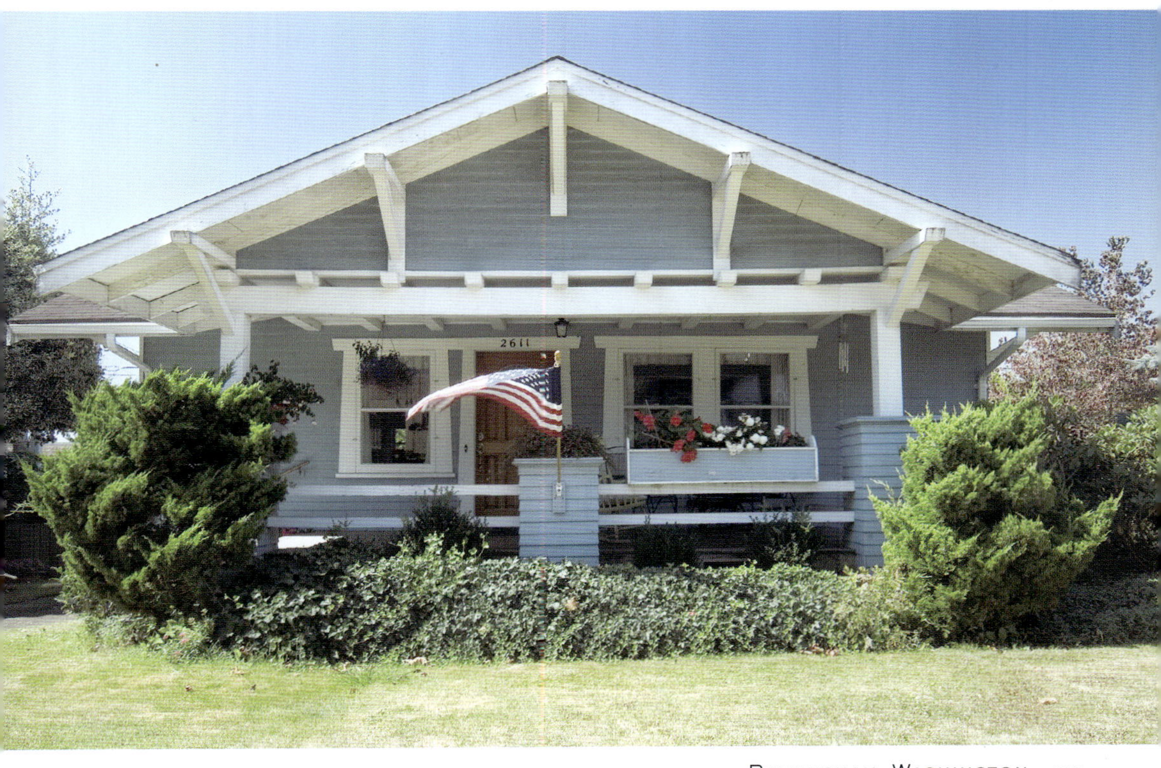


Bellingham, Washington

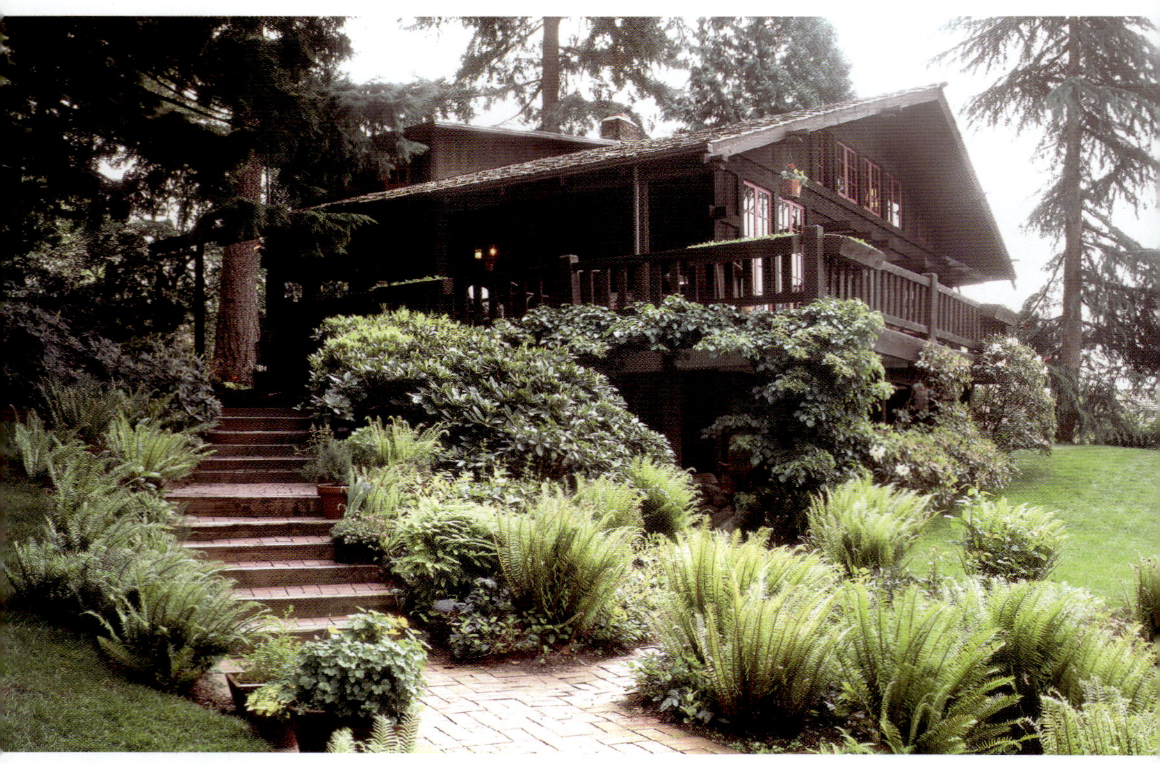

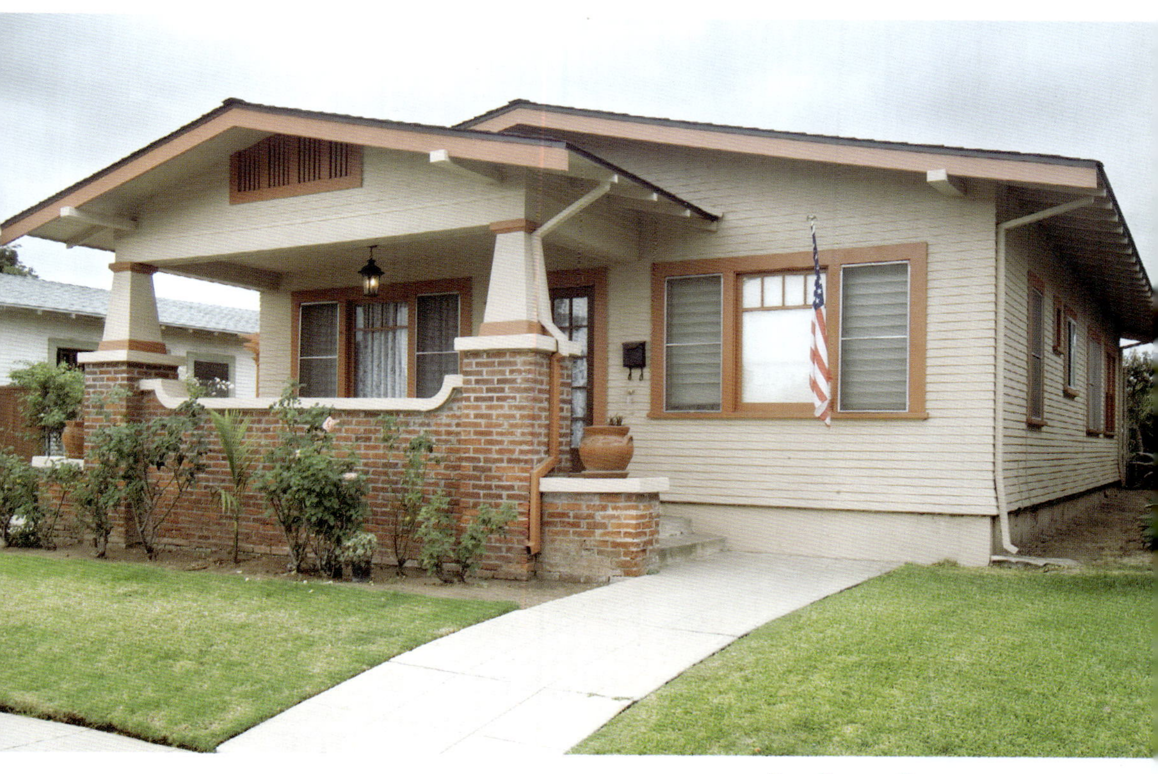

San Diego, California

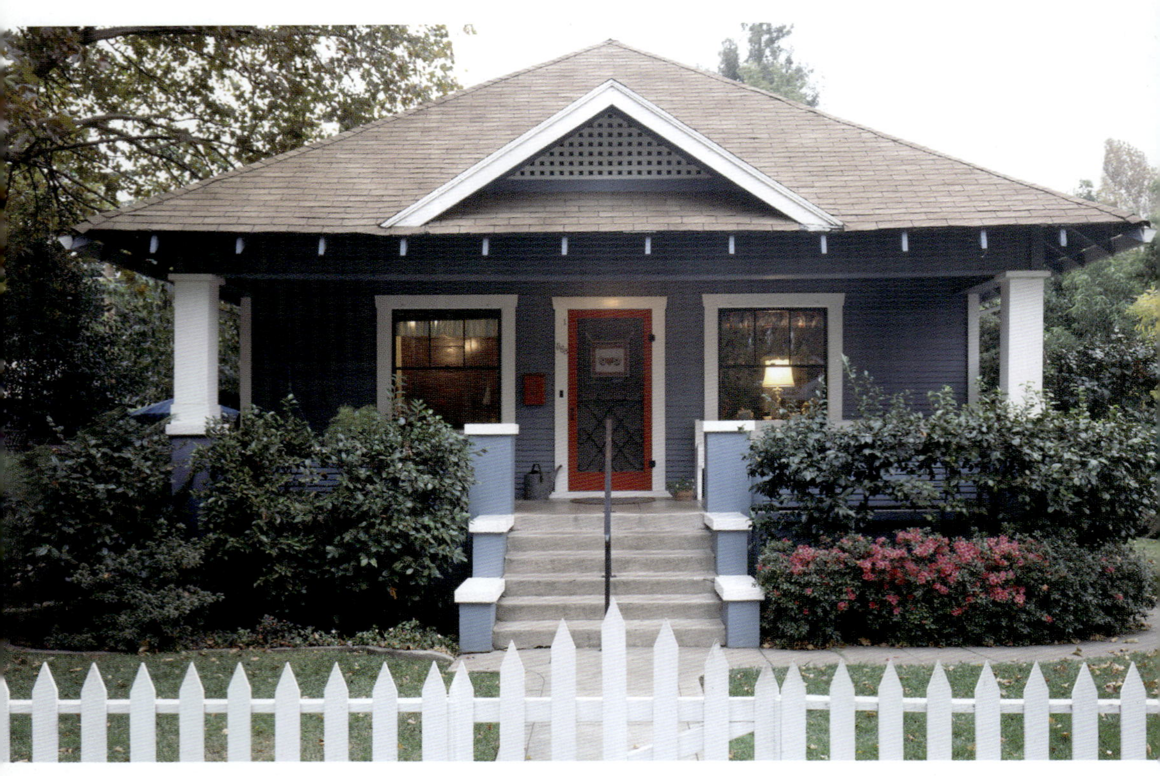

 CHICO, CALIFORNIA

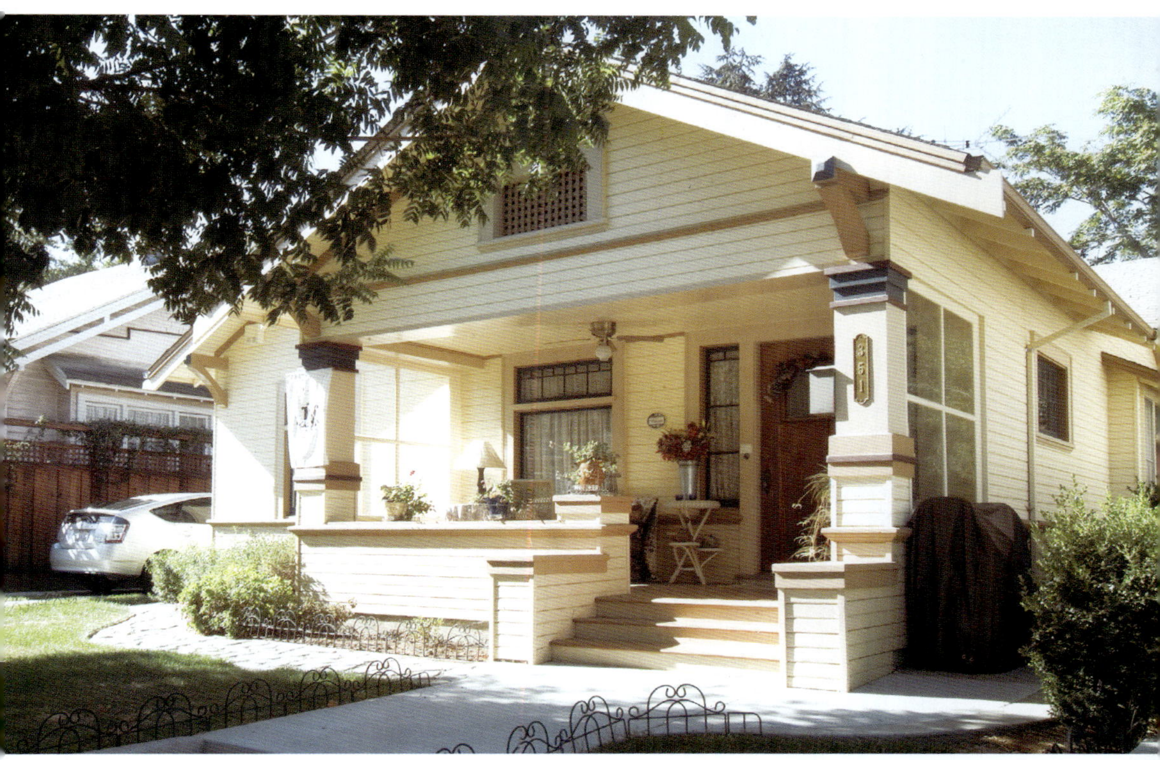
351

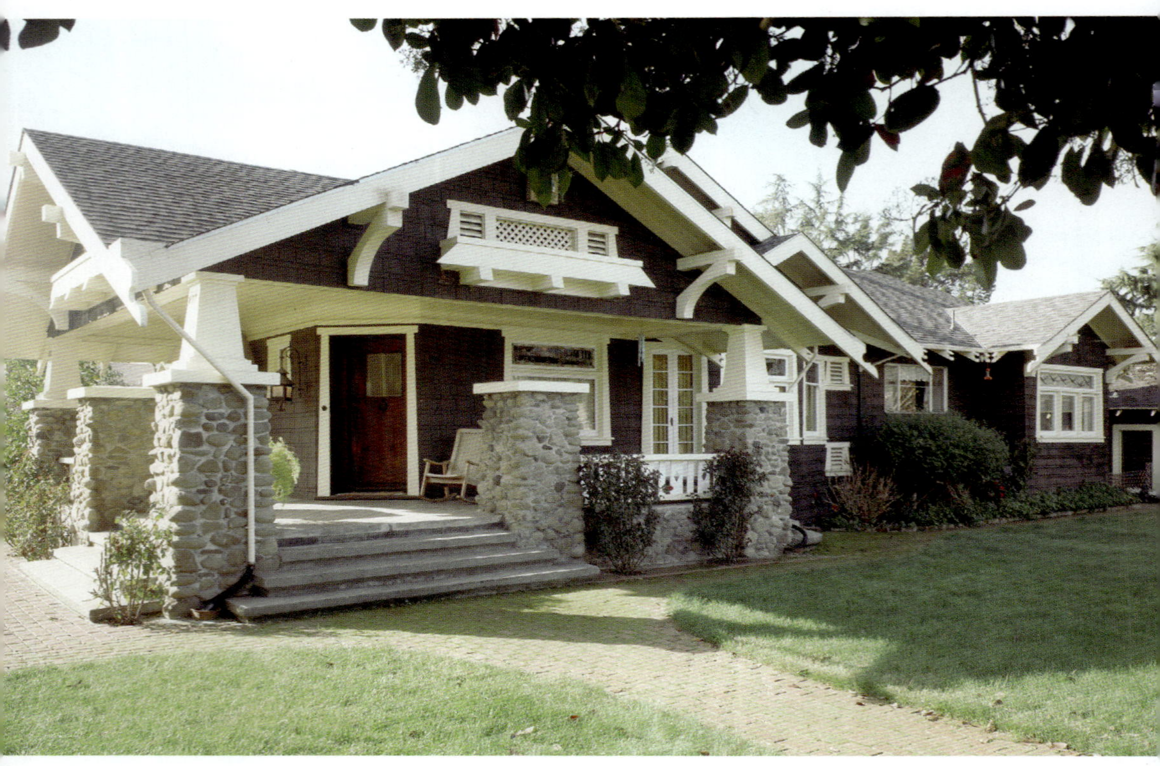

 San Leandro, California

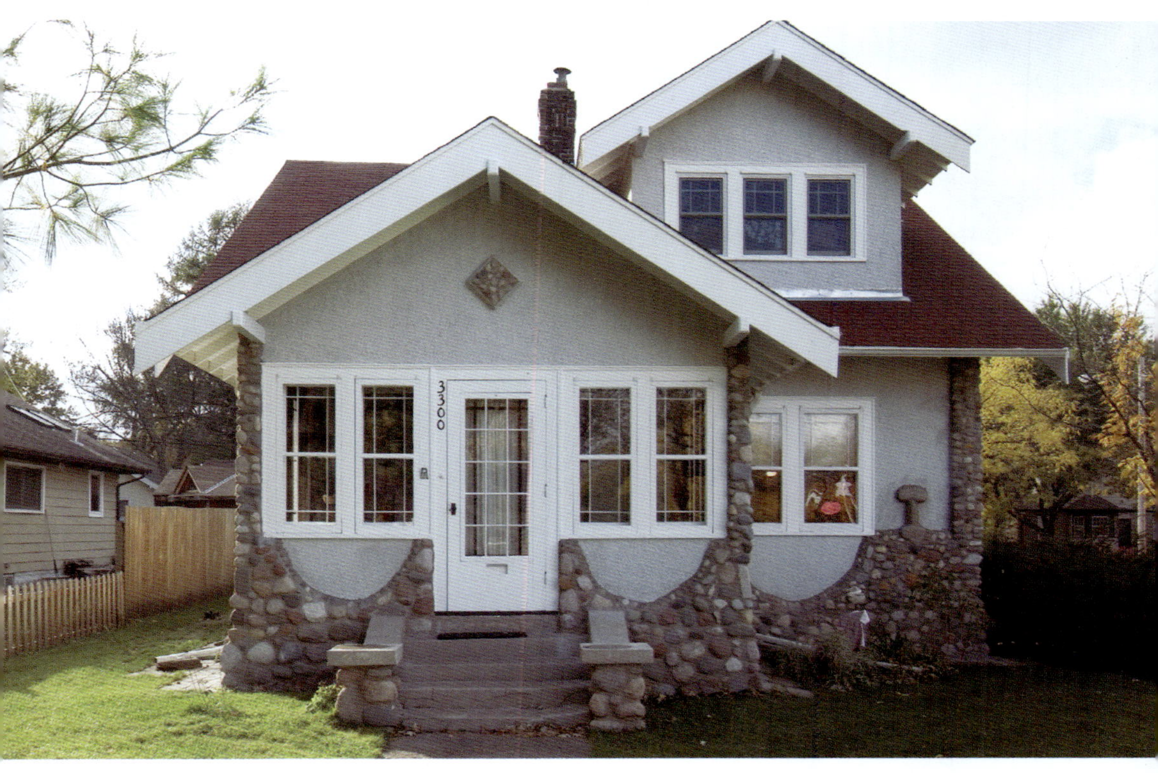
3300

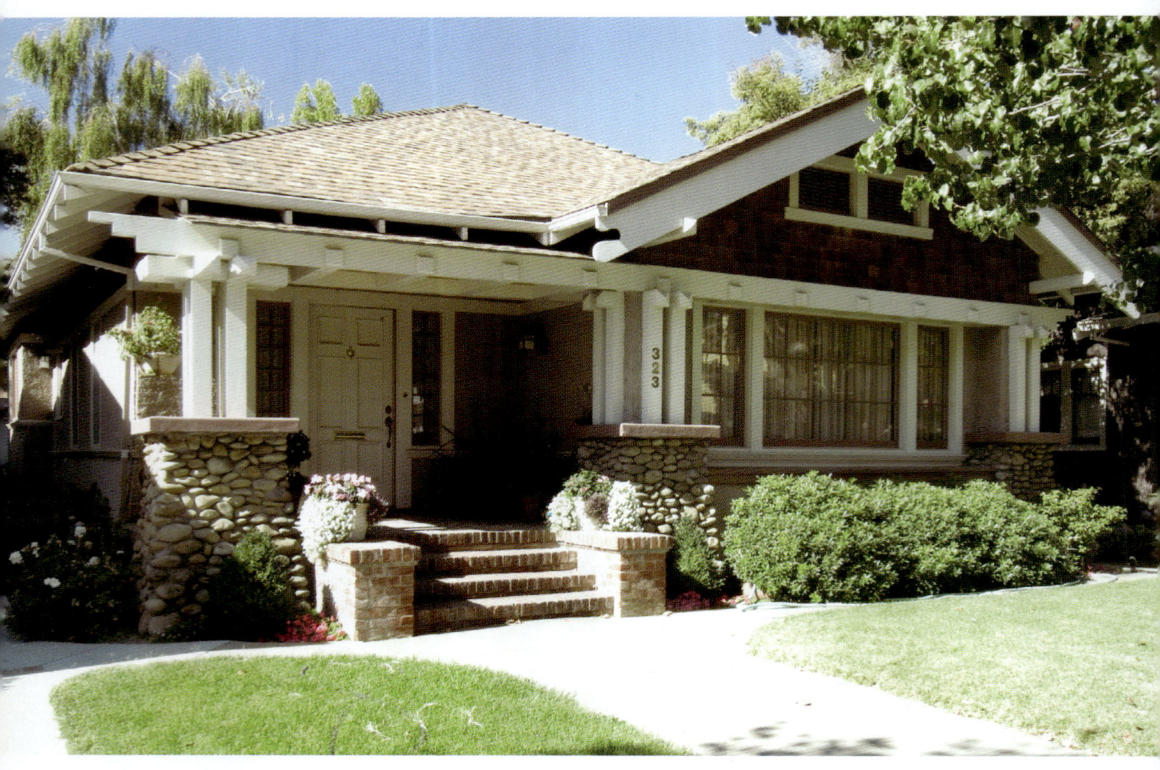


 San Jose, California

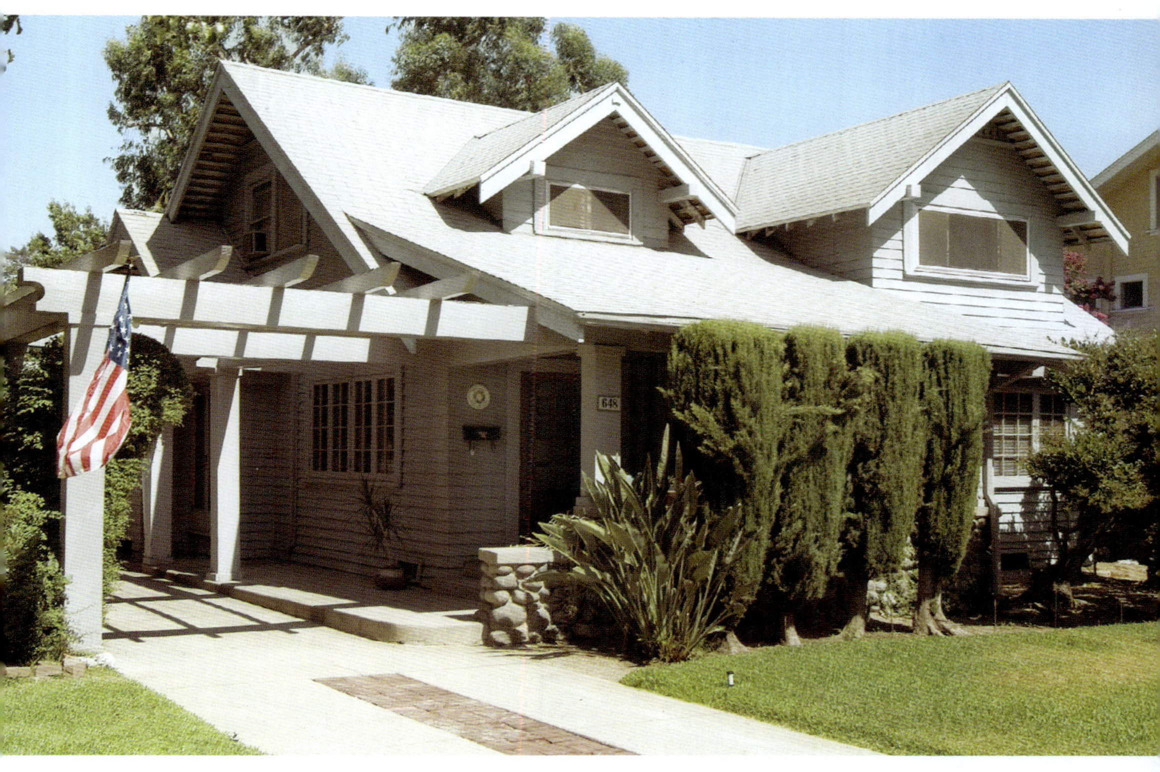
648

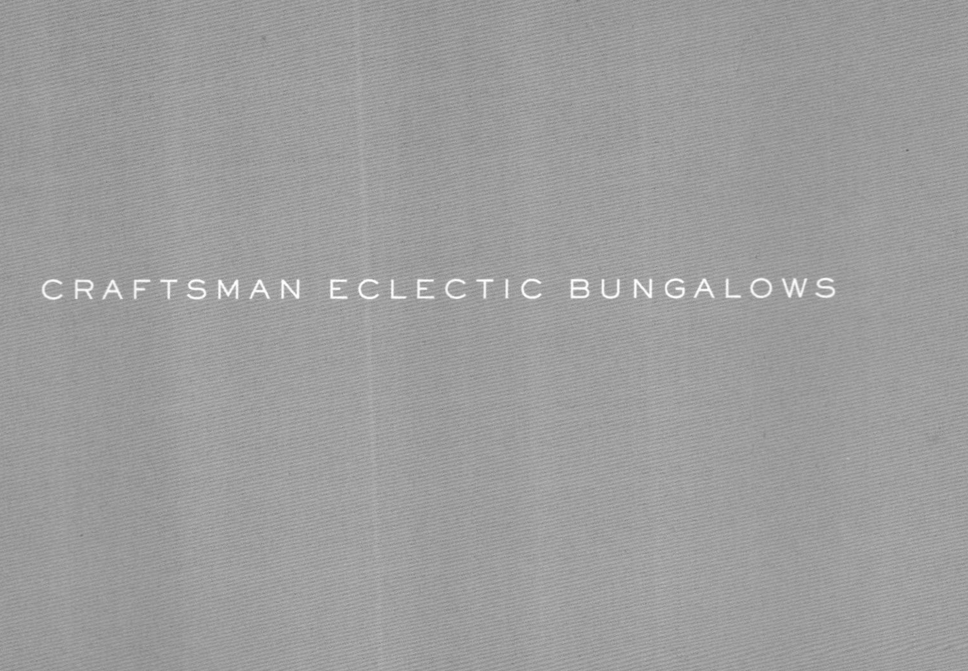

# CRAFTSMAN ECLECTIC BUNGALOWS

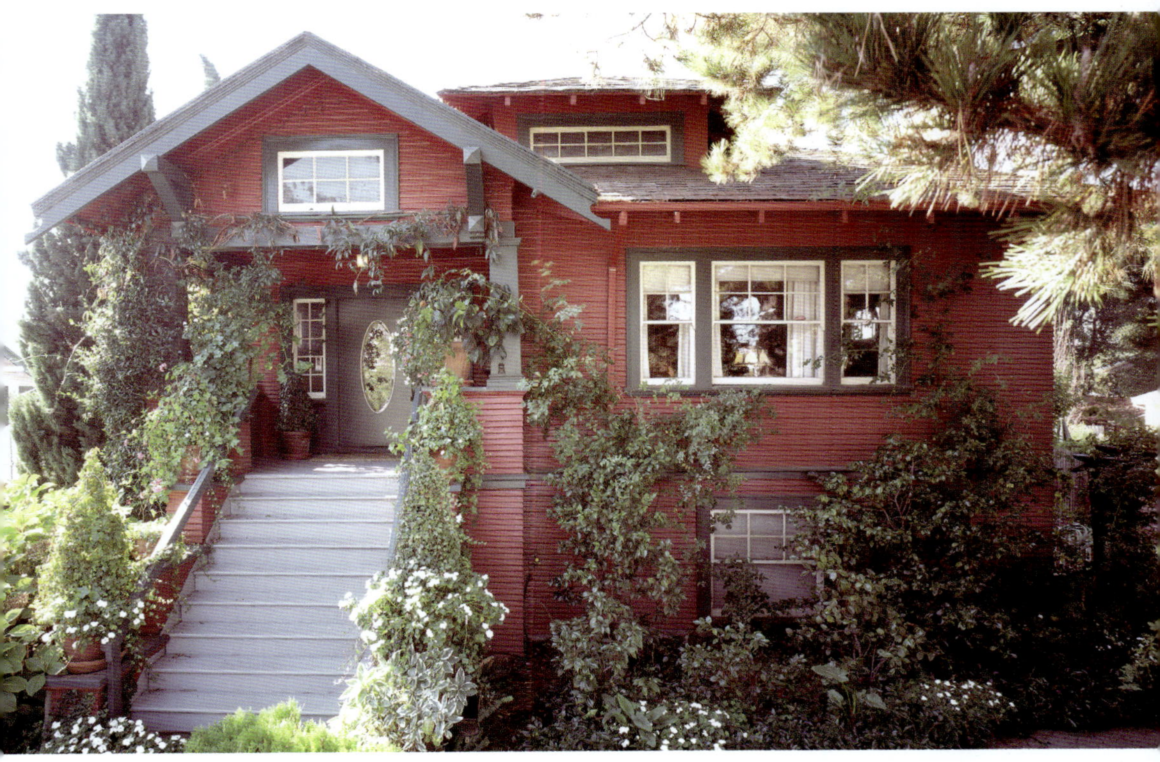

Benicia, California

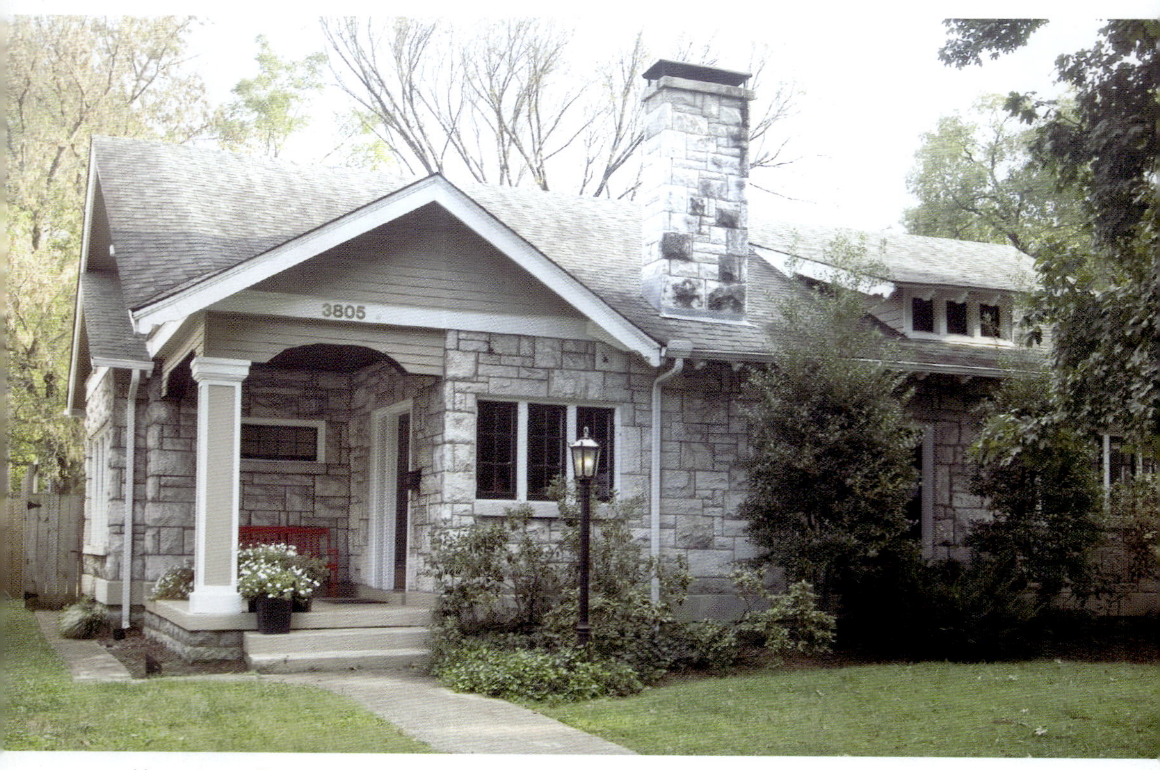
3805

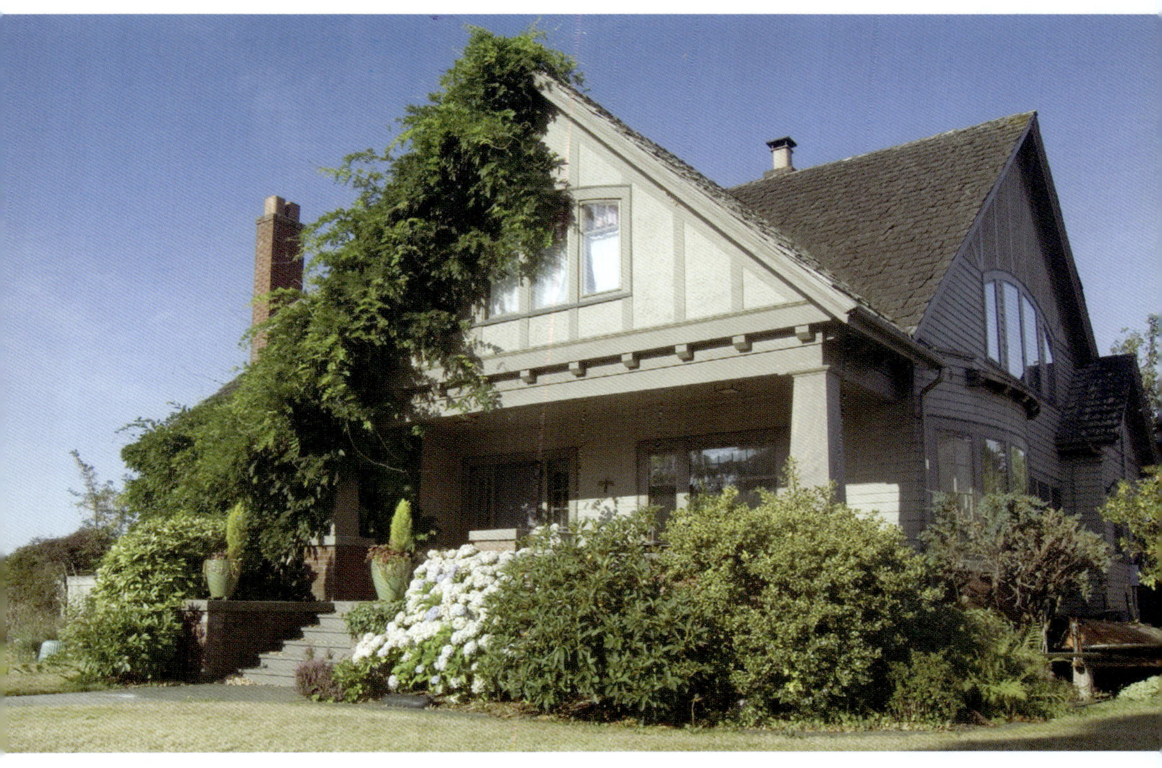

CHALET BUNGALOW | BELLINGHAM, WASHINGTON

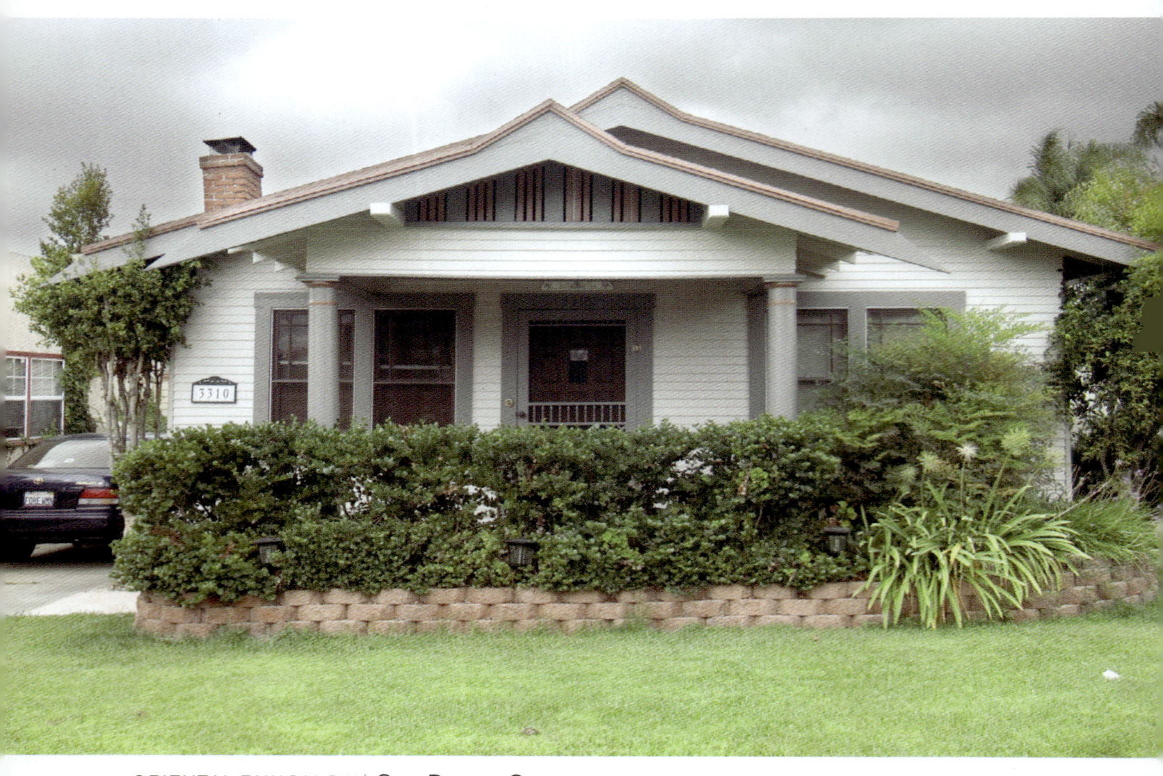


 ORIENTAL BUNGALOW | San Diego, California

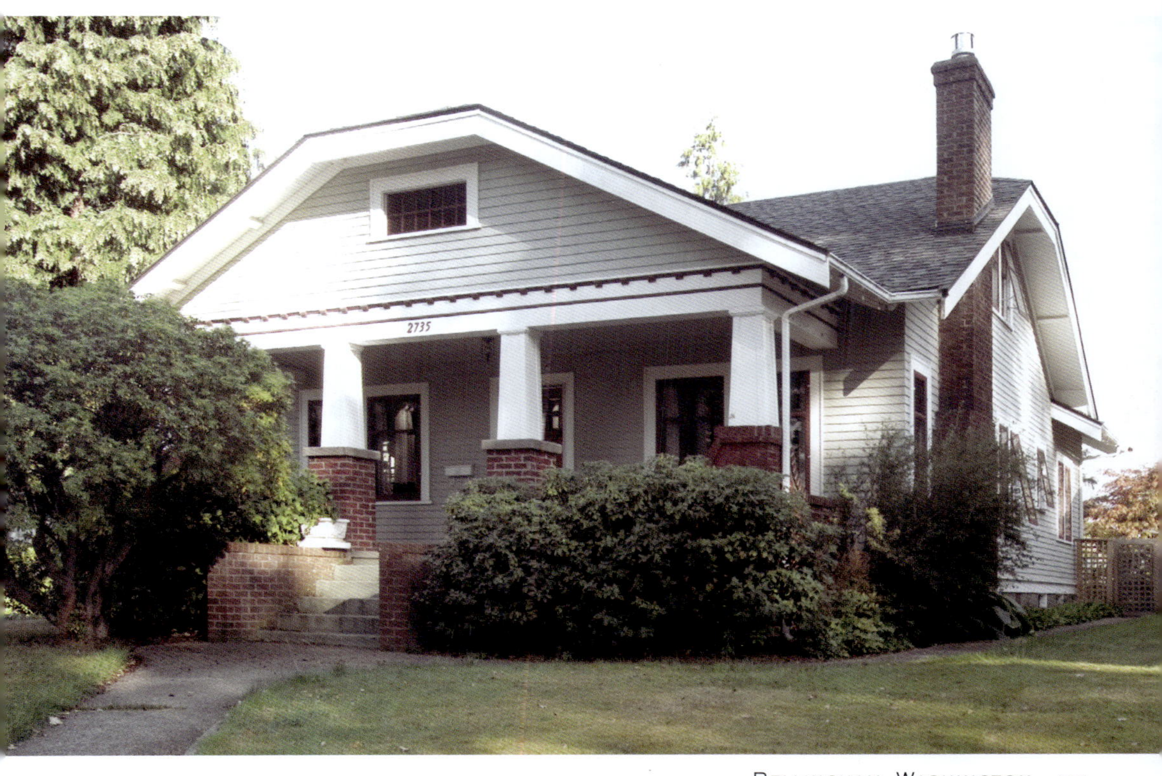


Bellingham, Washington 

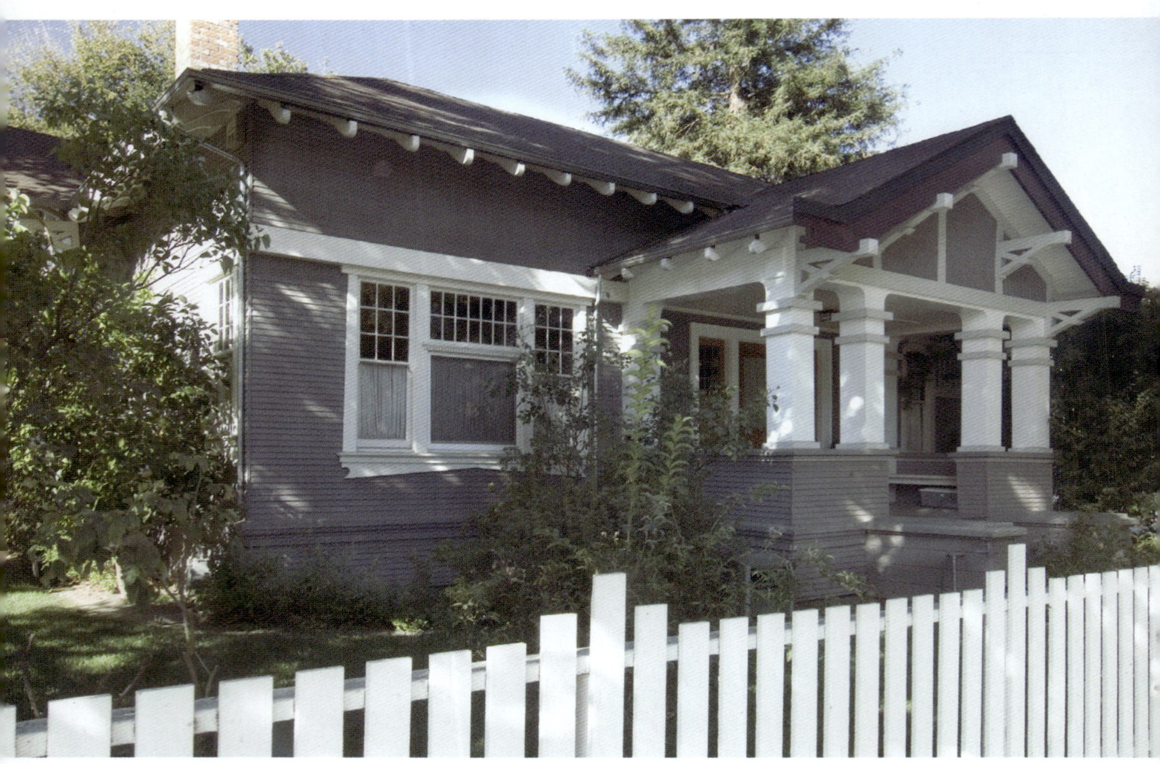

 San Jose, California

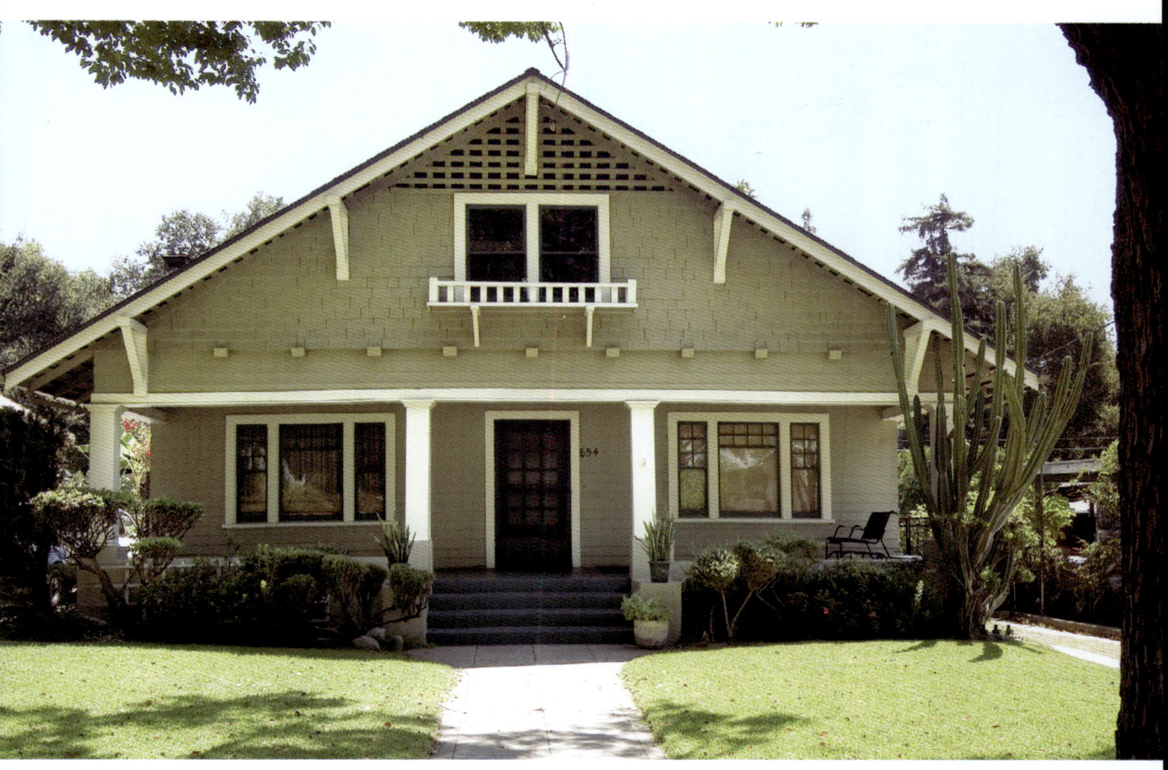

CHALET BUNGALOW | PASADENA, CALIFORNIA

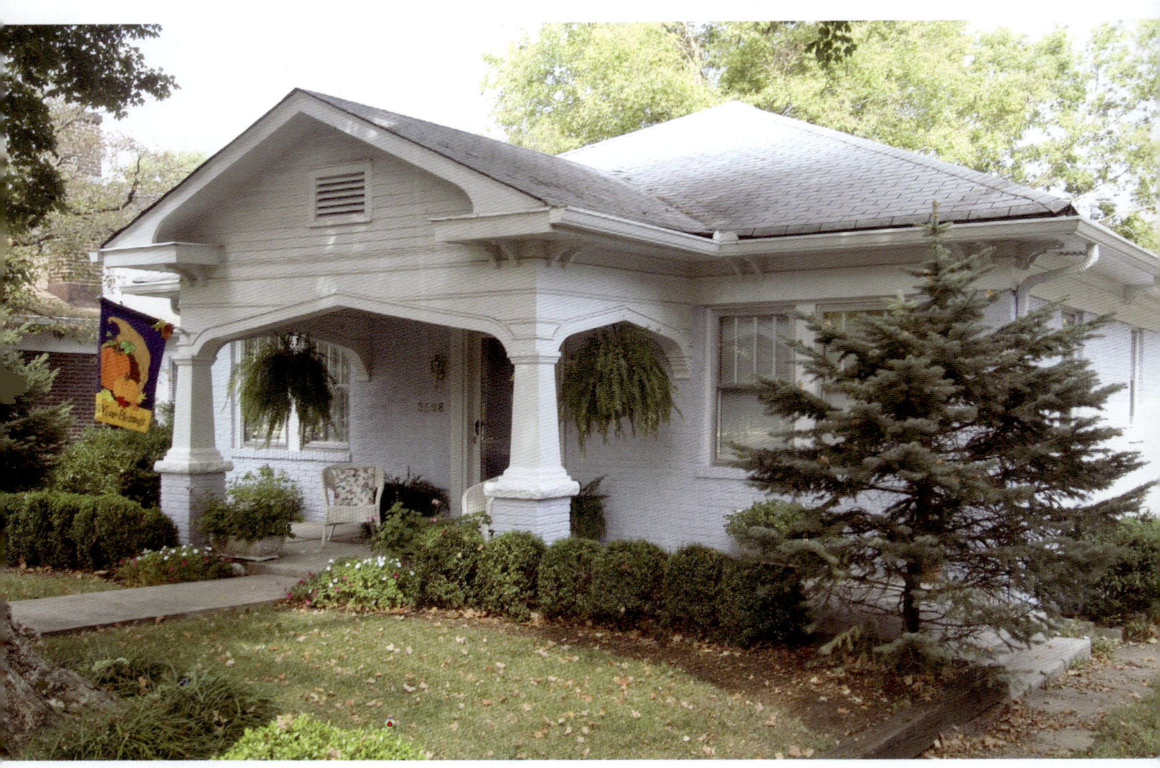

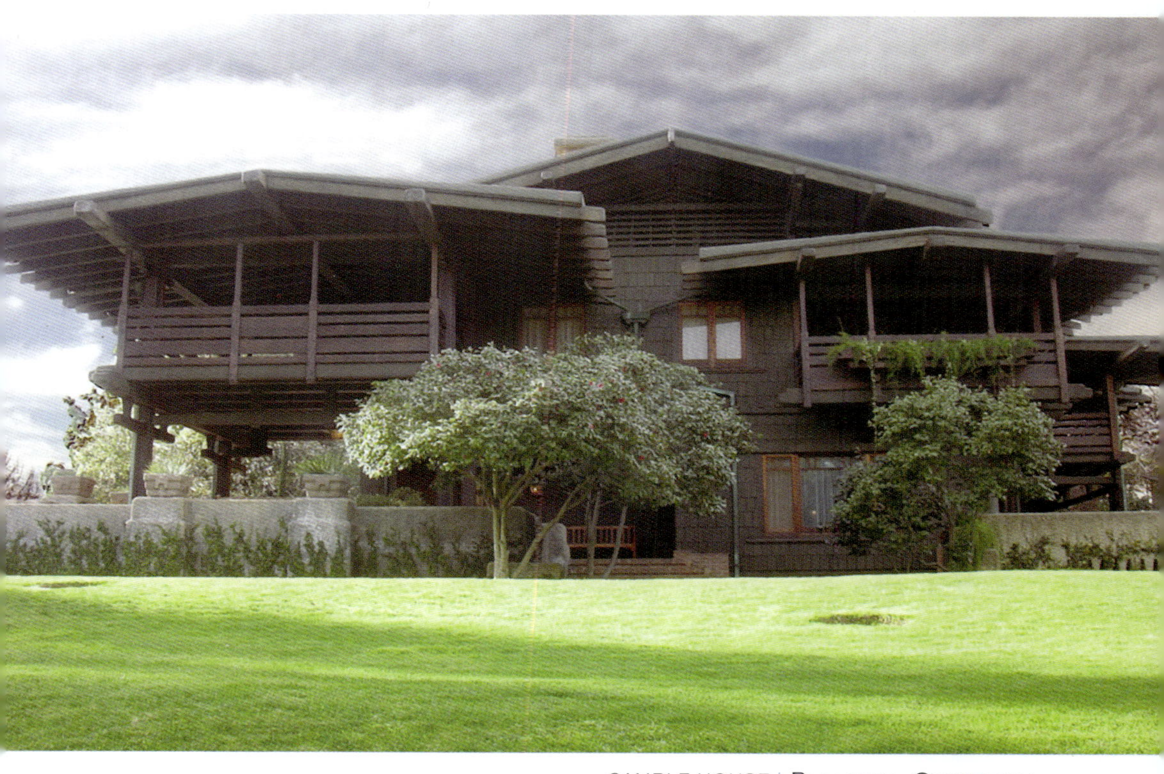

GAMBLE HOUSE | PASADENA, CALIFORNIA

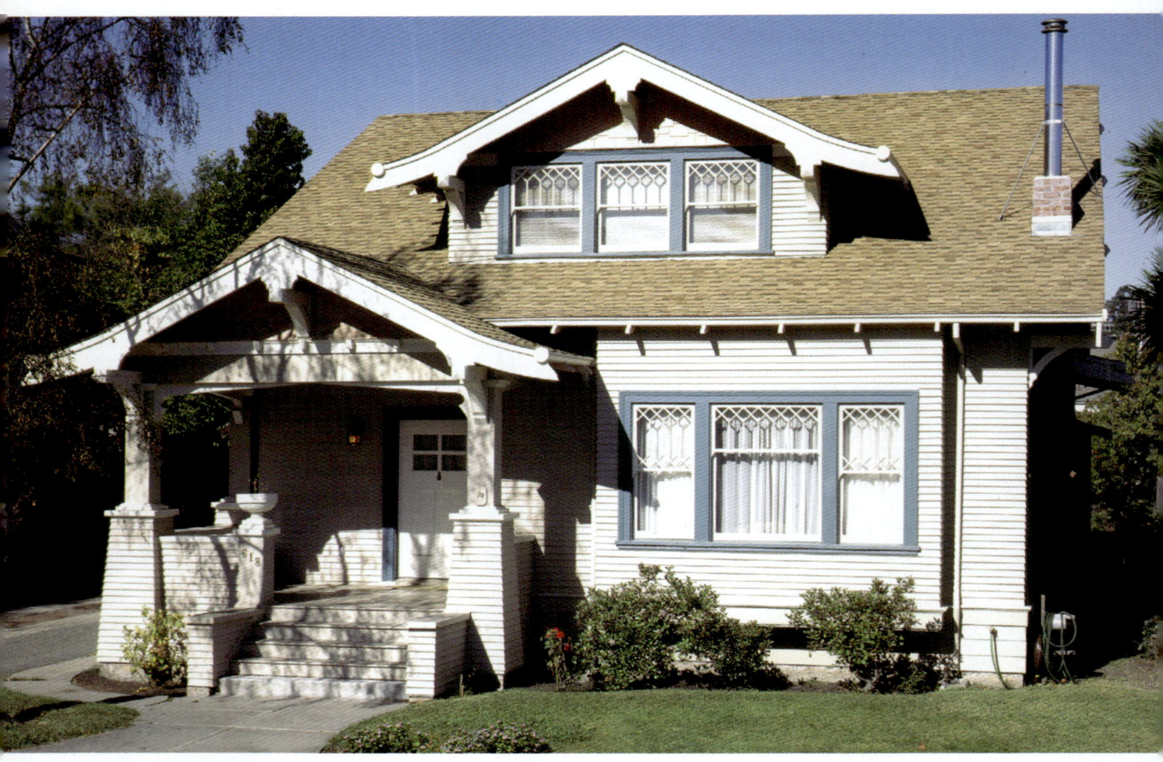


 Oakland, California

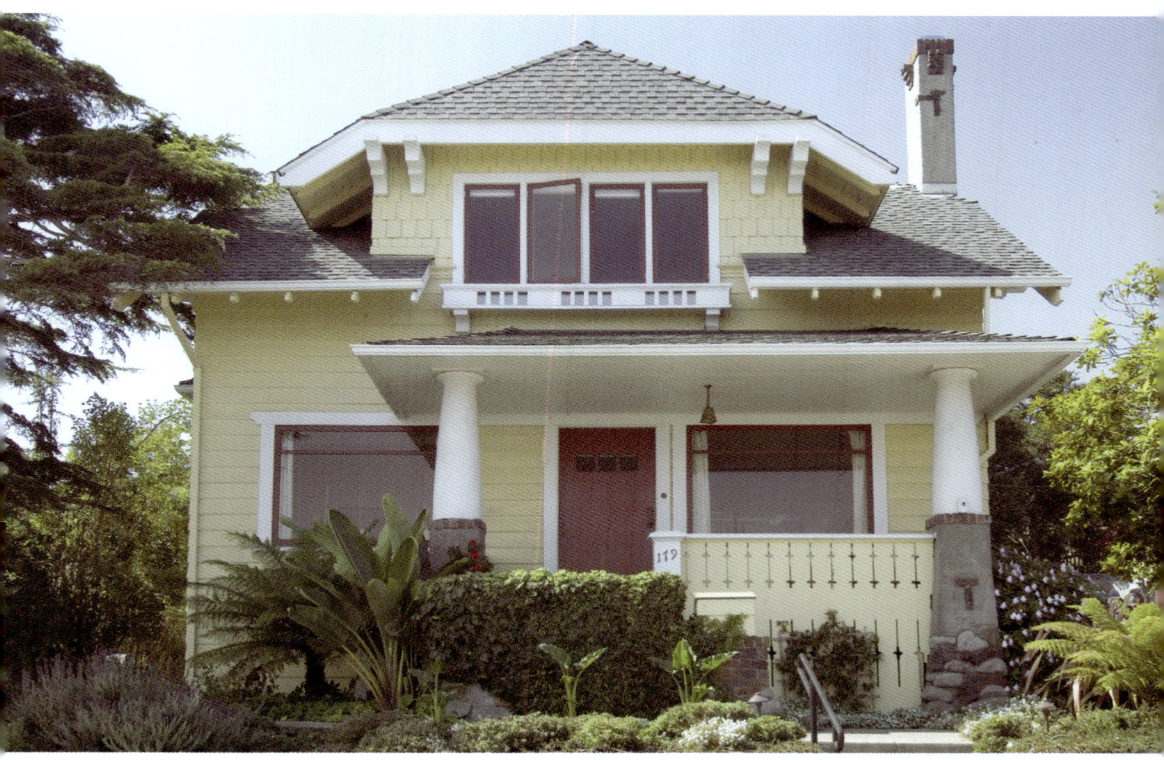
179

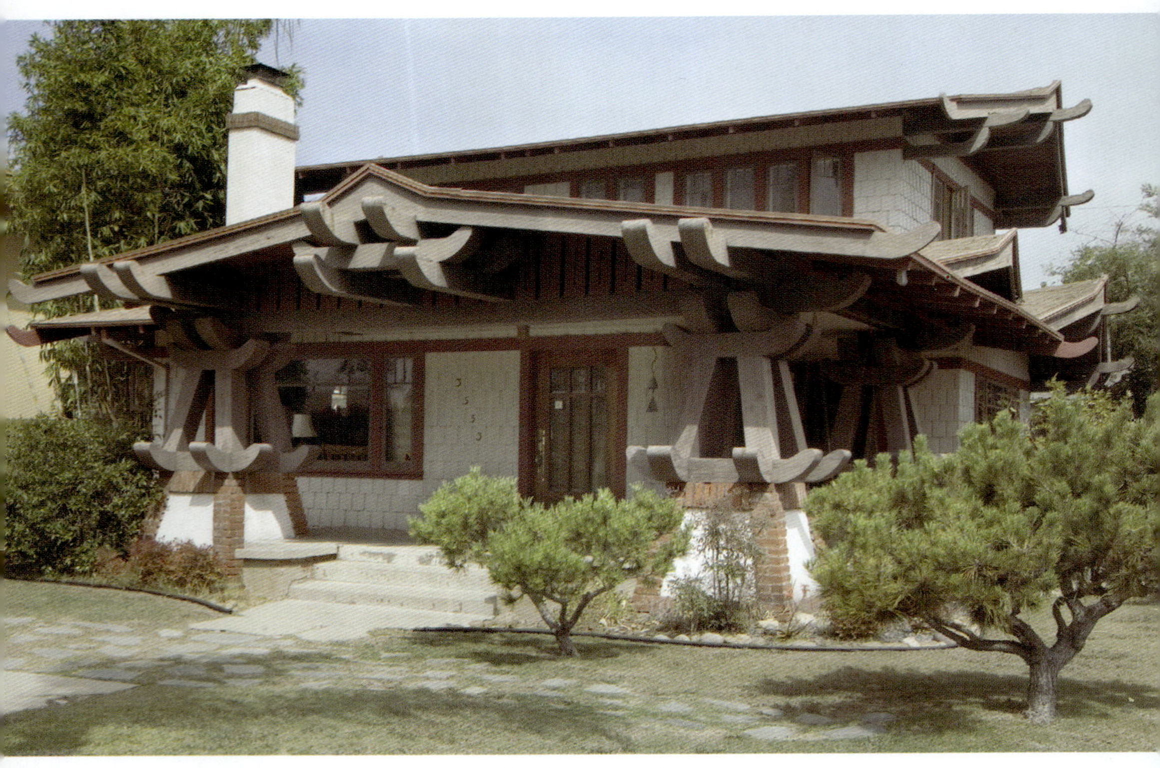

 ORIENTAL BUNGALOW | SAN DIEGO, CALIFORNIA

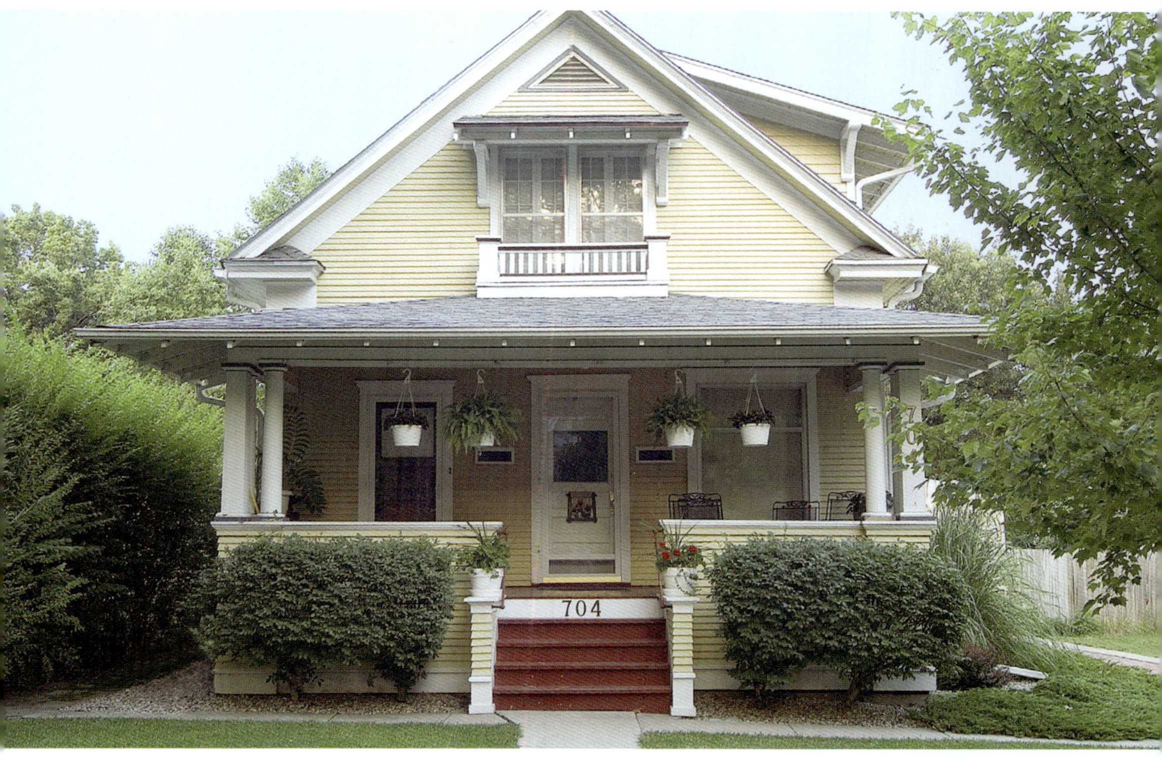


Lincoln, Nebraska

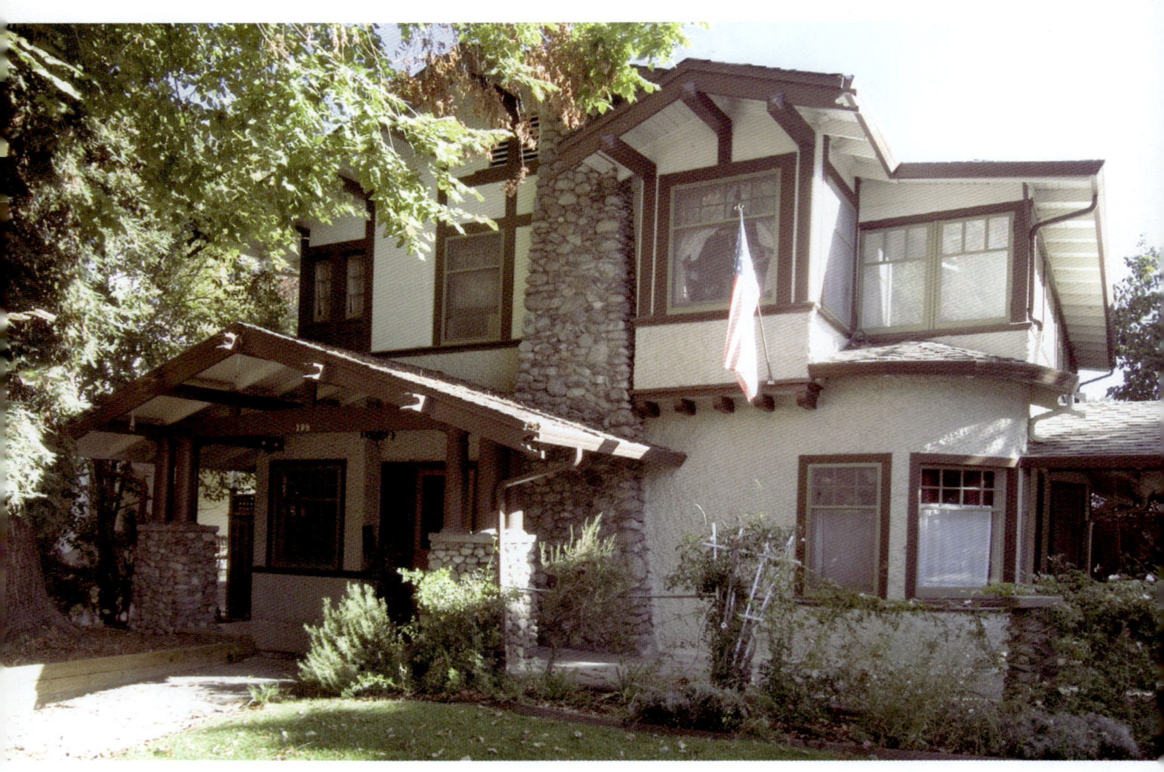

 San Jose, California

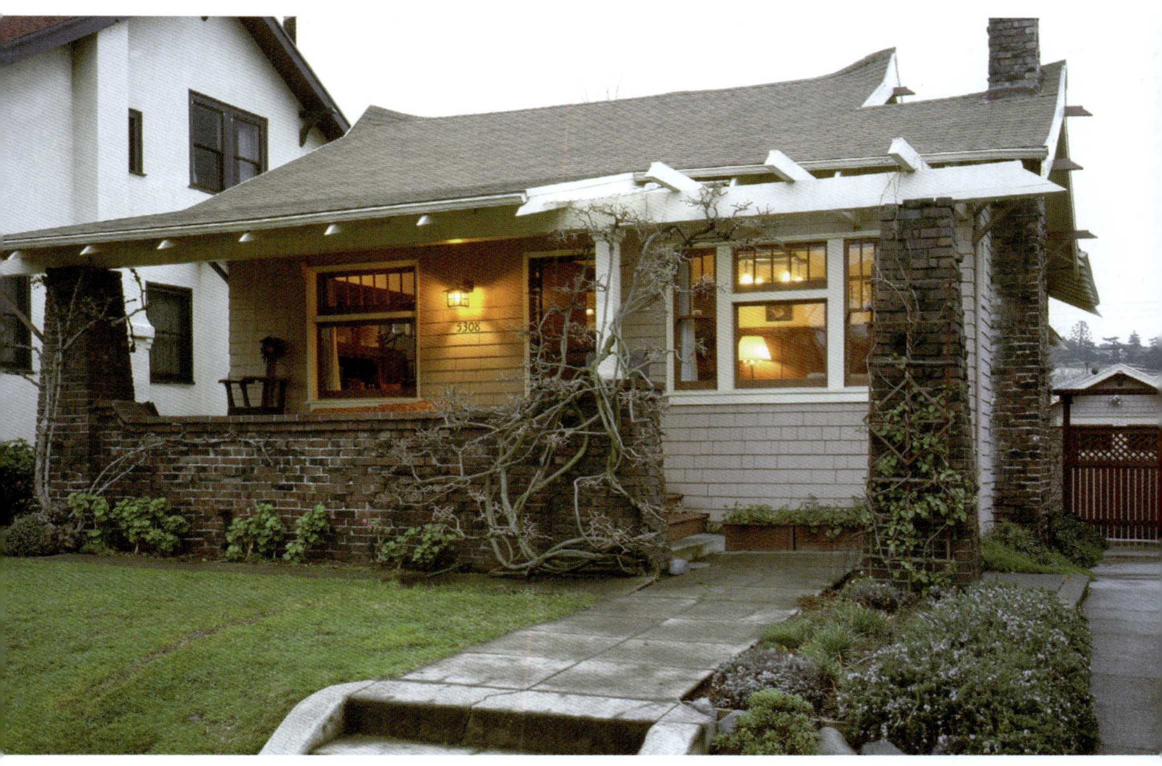


ORIENTAL BUNGALOW | OAKLAND, CALIFORNIA

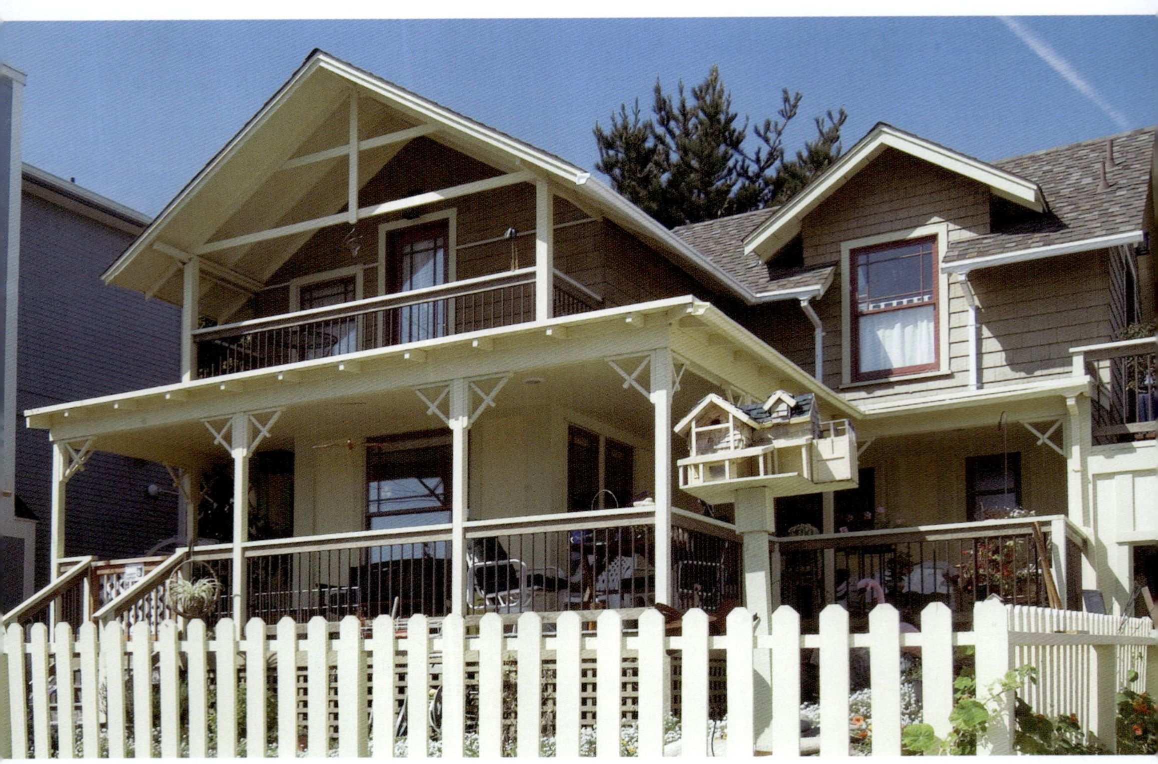

 Pacific Grove, California

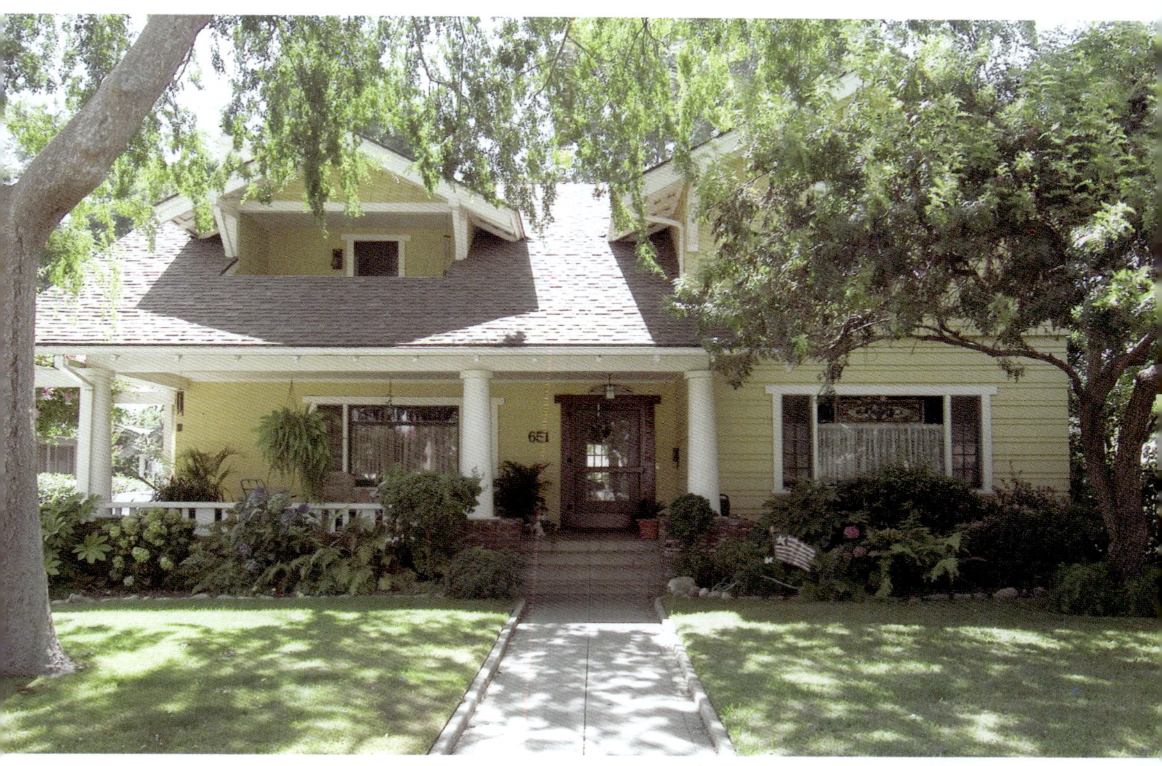


Pasadena, California 

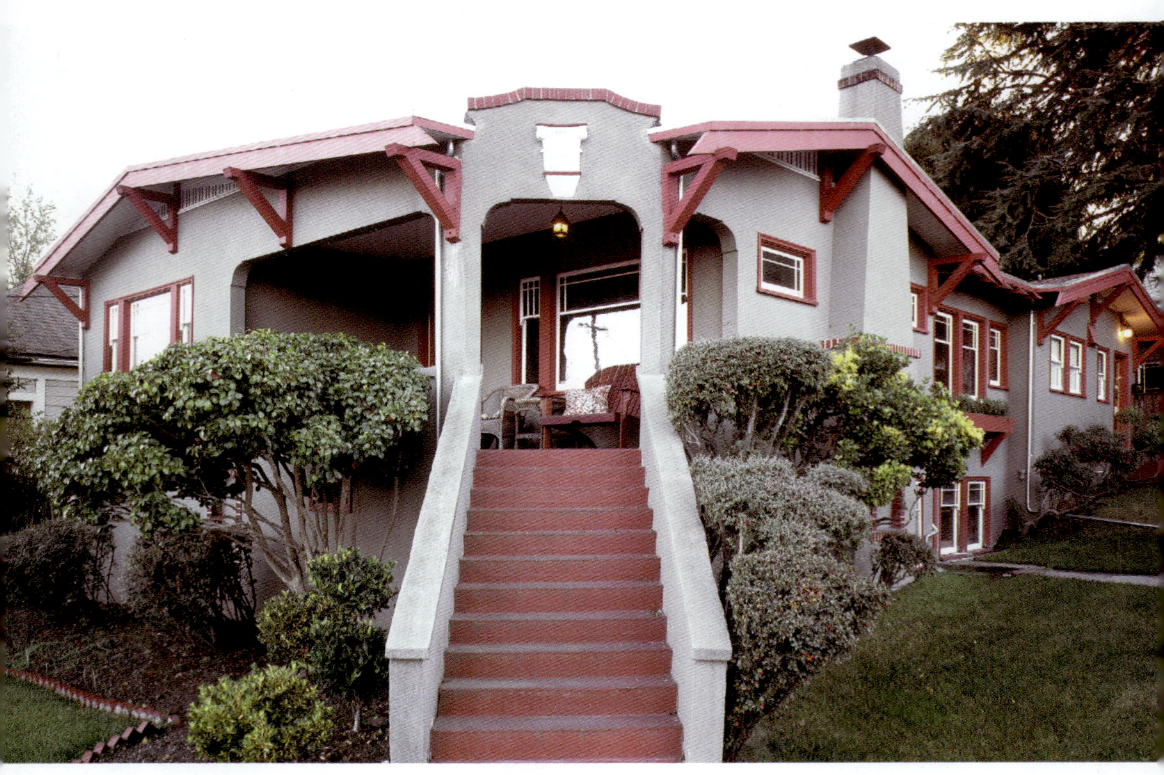

 CALIFORNIA BUNGALOW | PETALUMA, CALIFORNIA

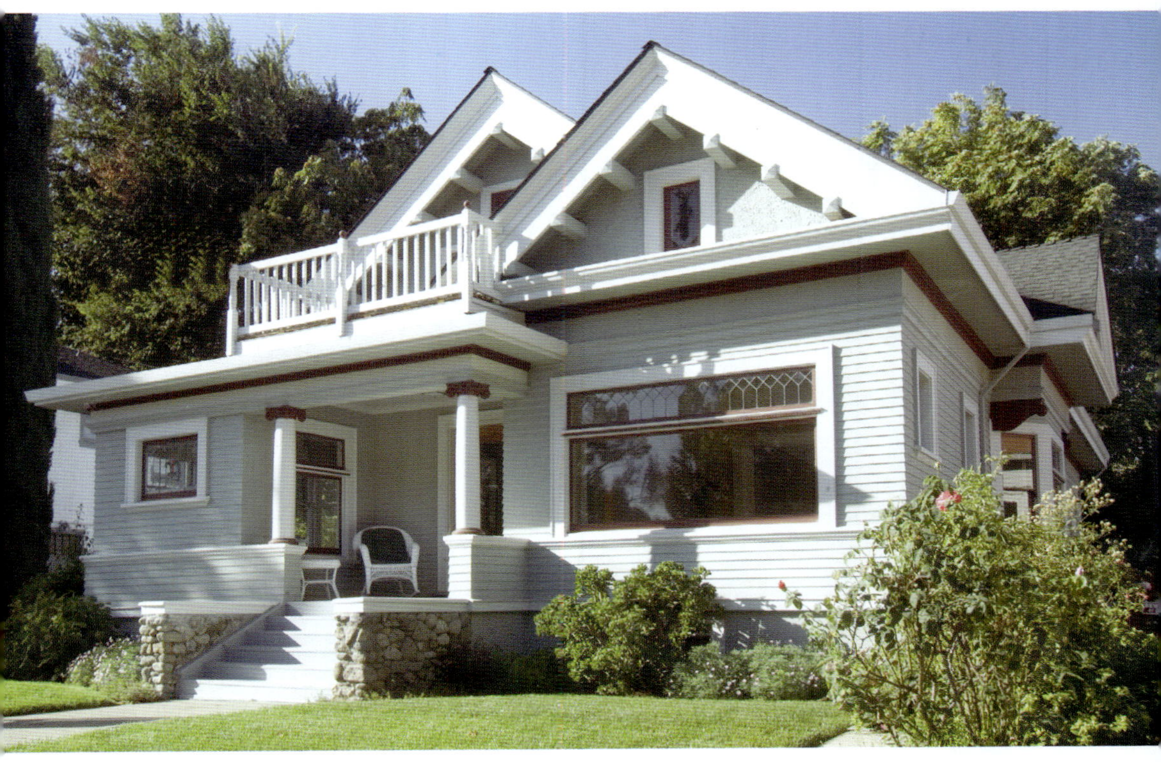

COLONIAL REVIVAL BUNGALOW | SAN JOSE, CALIFORNIA 

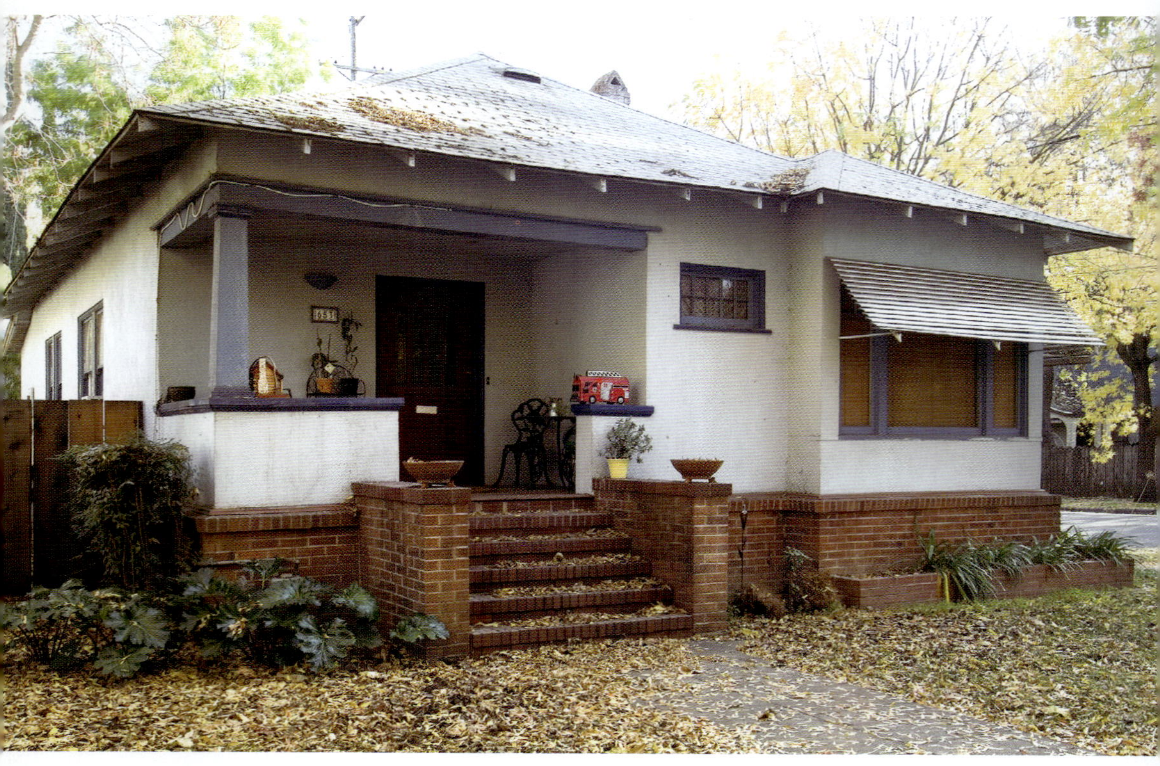


 Chico, California

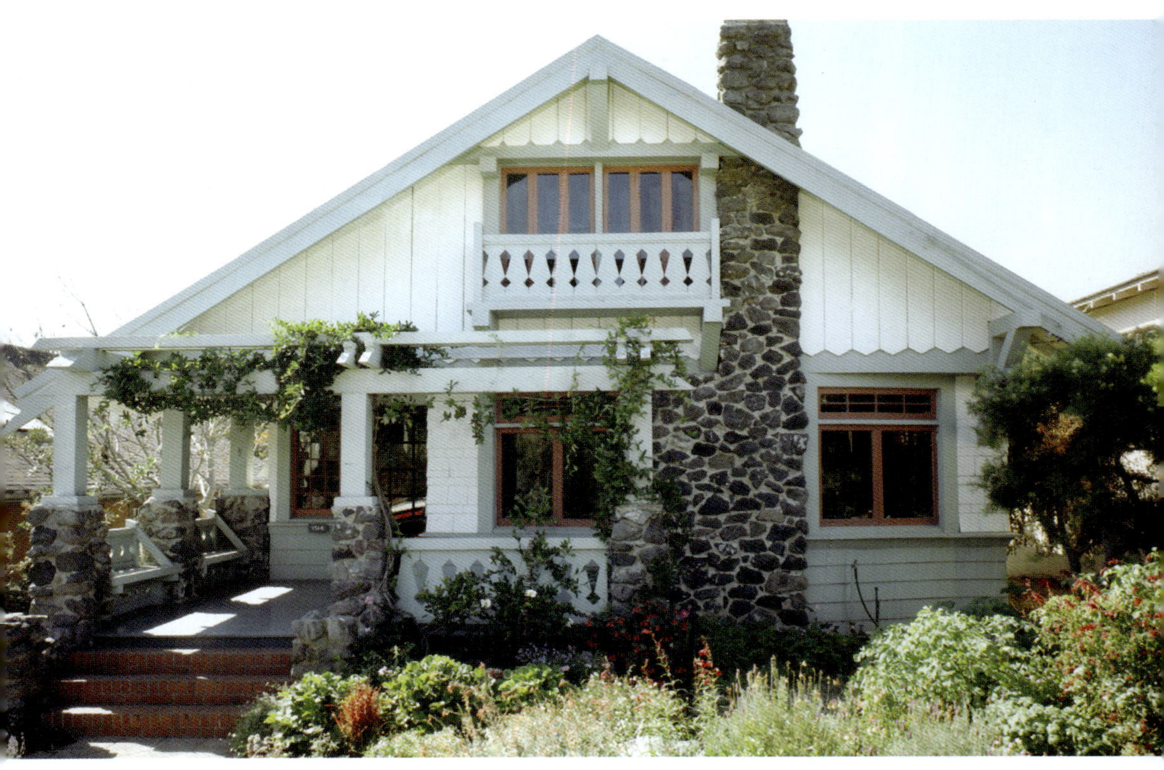

CHALET BUNGALOW | BERKELEY, CALIFORNIA

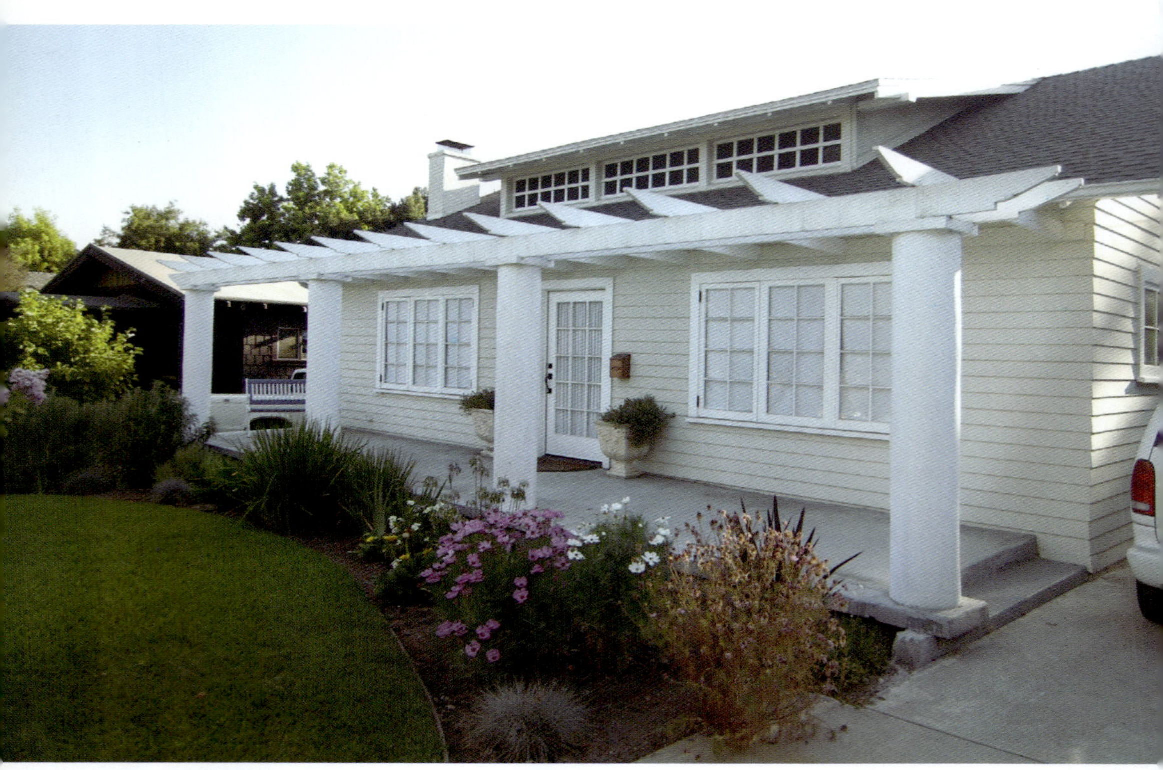

 Pasadena, California

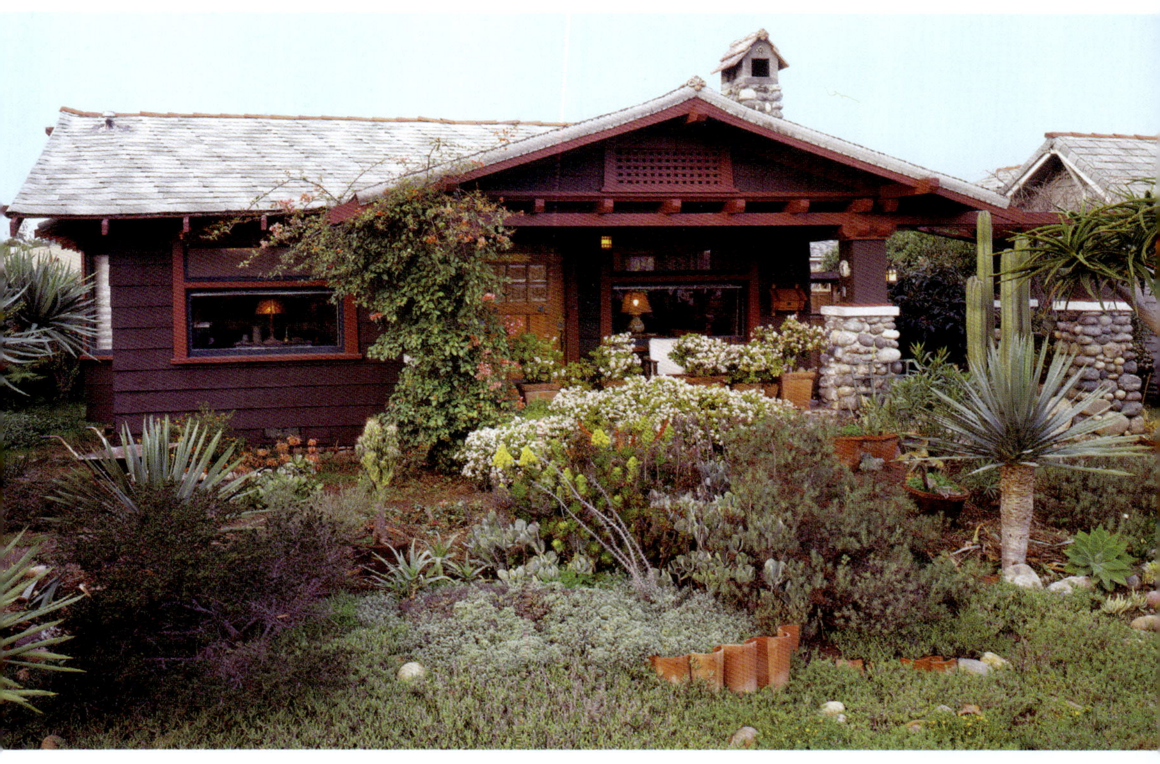

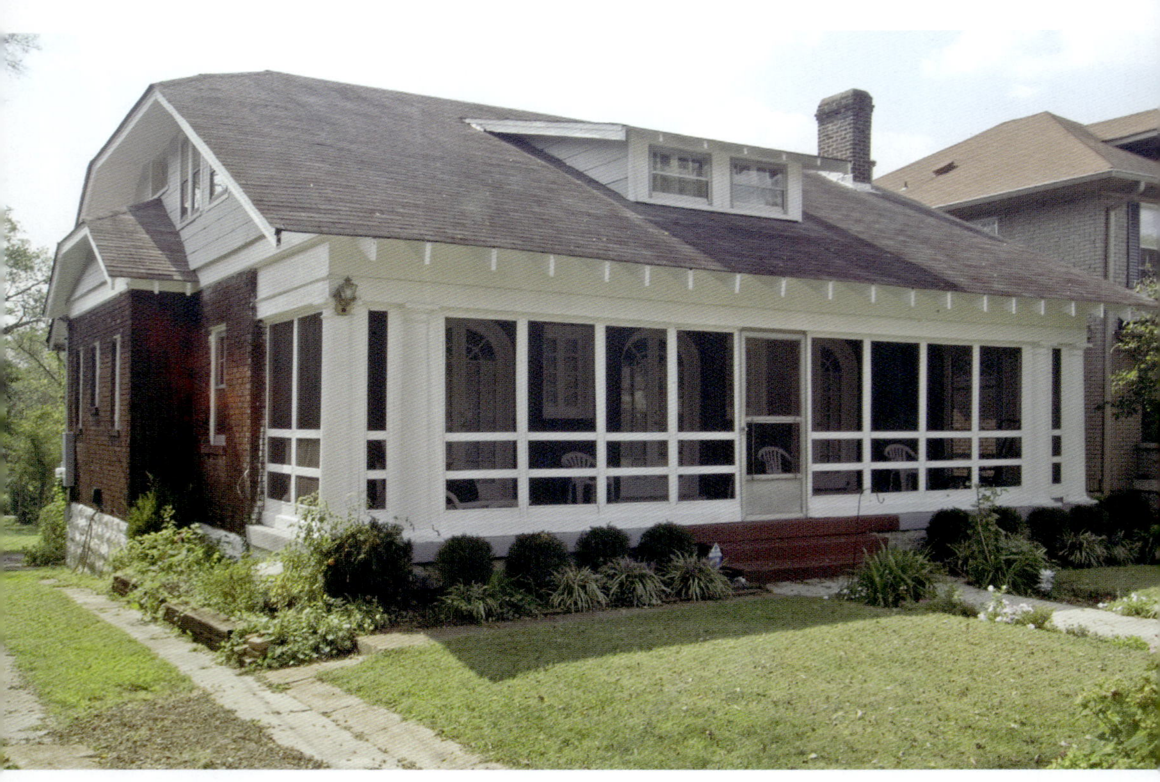

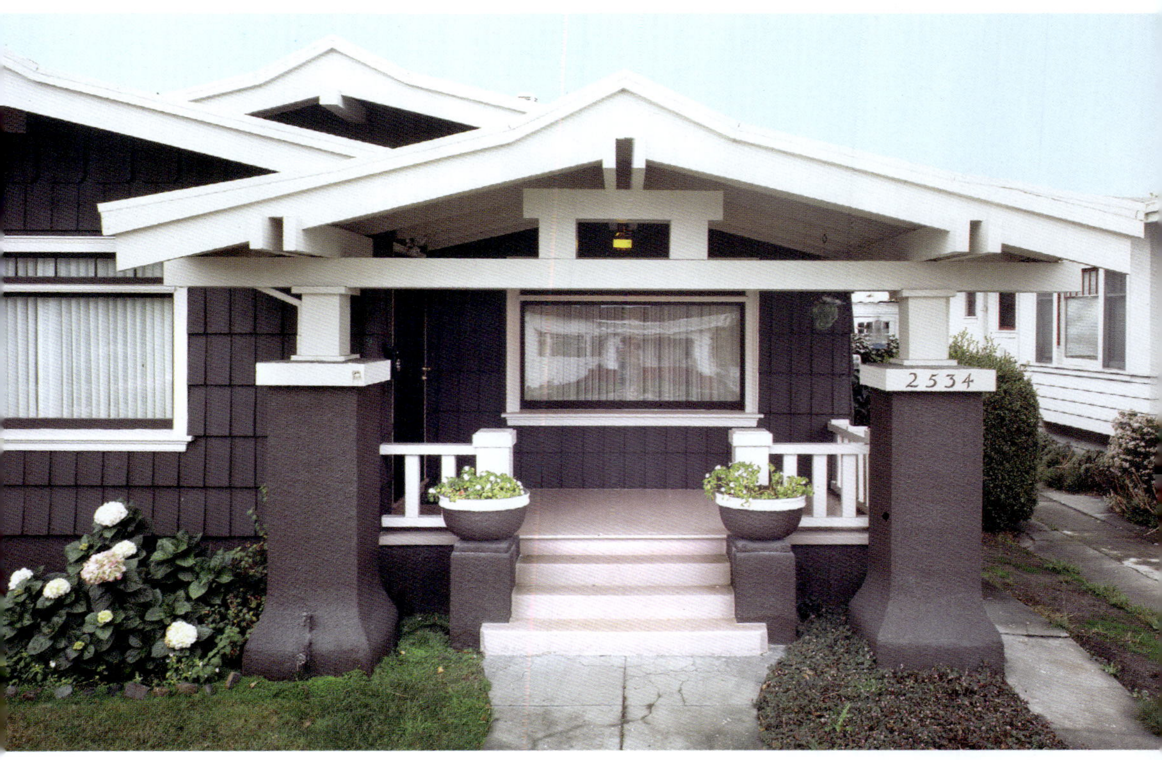
2534

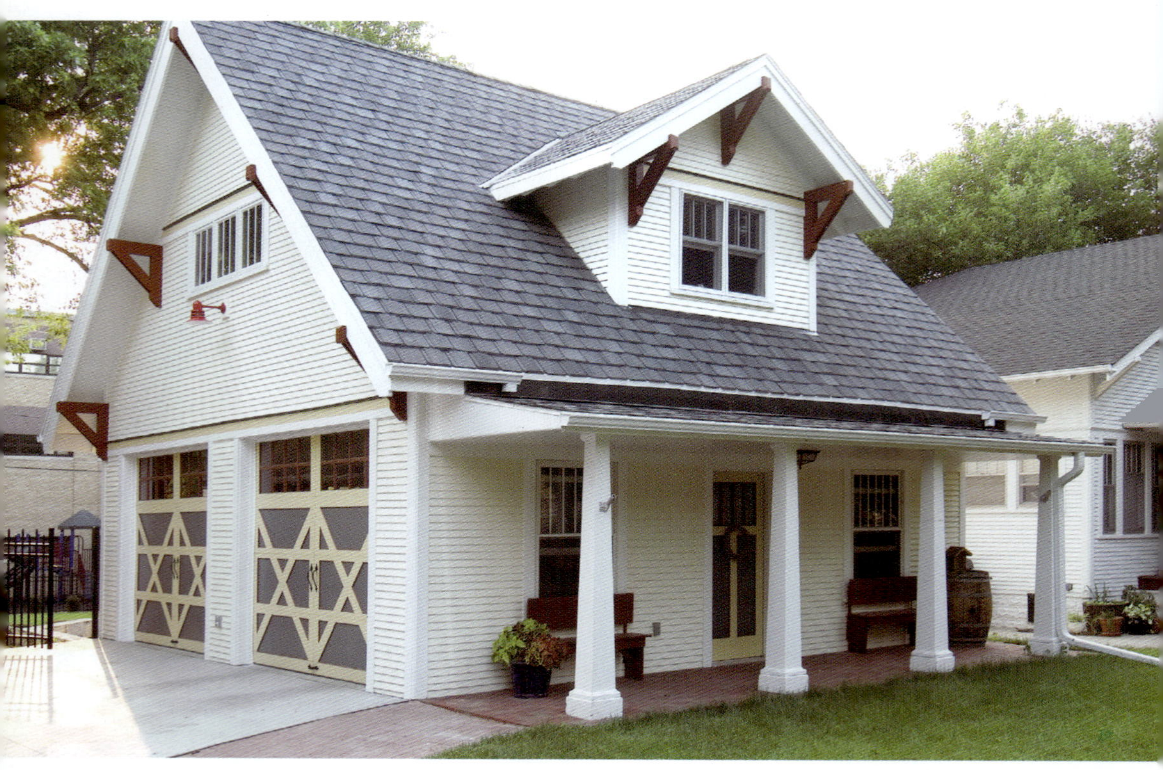

 Lincoln, Nebraska

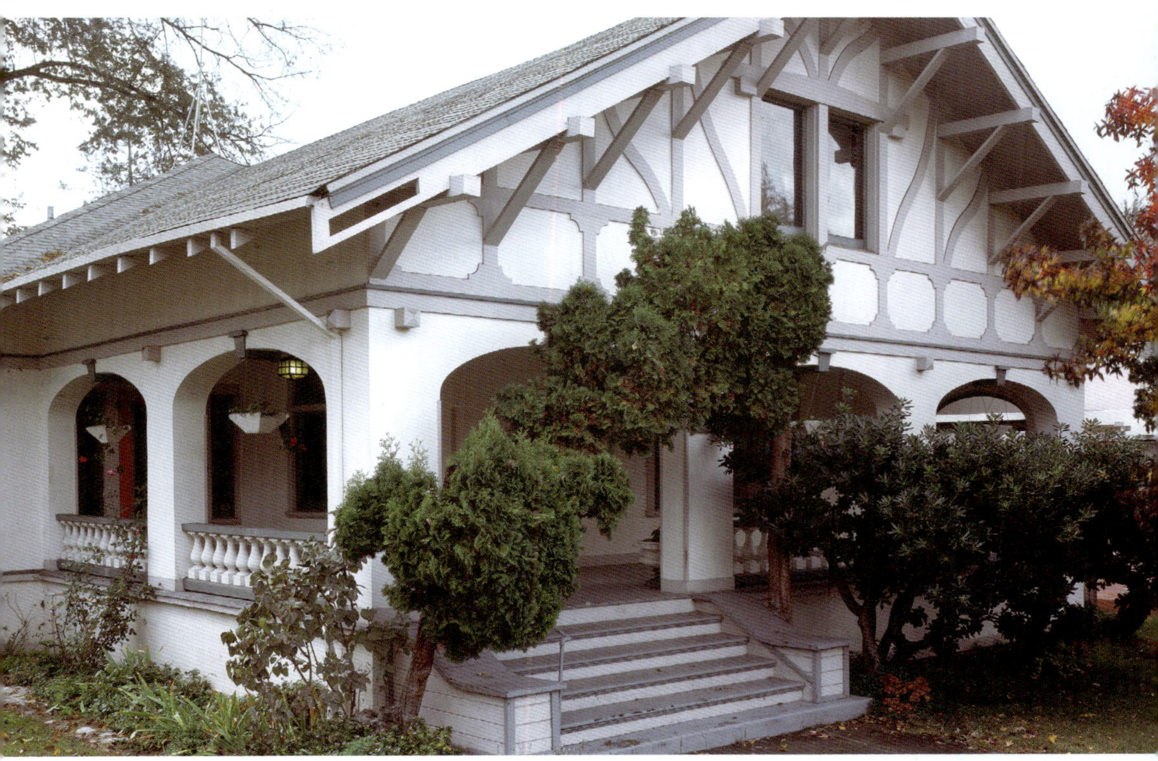

CHALET BUNGALOW | SAN JOSE, CALIFORNIA

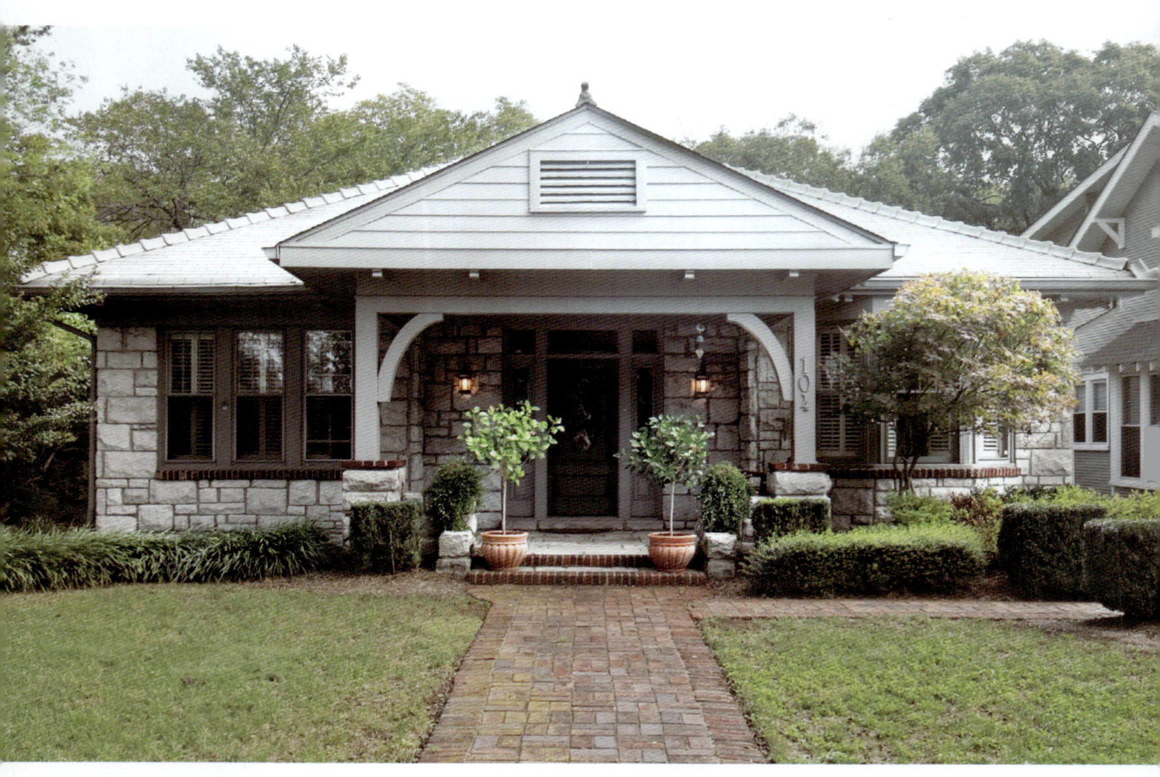

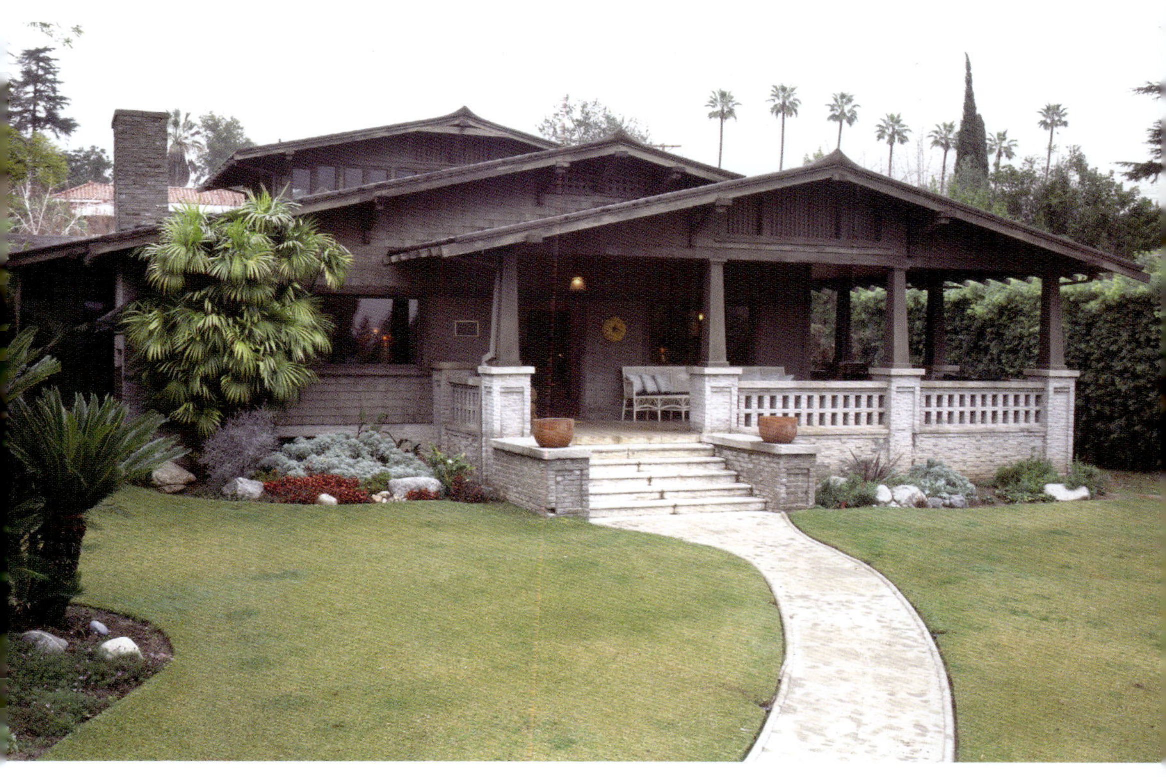

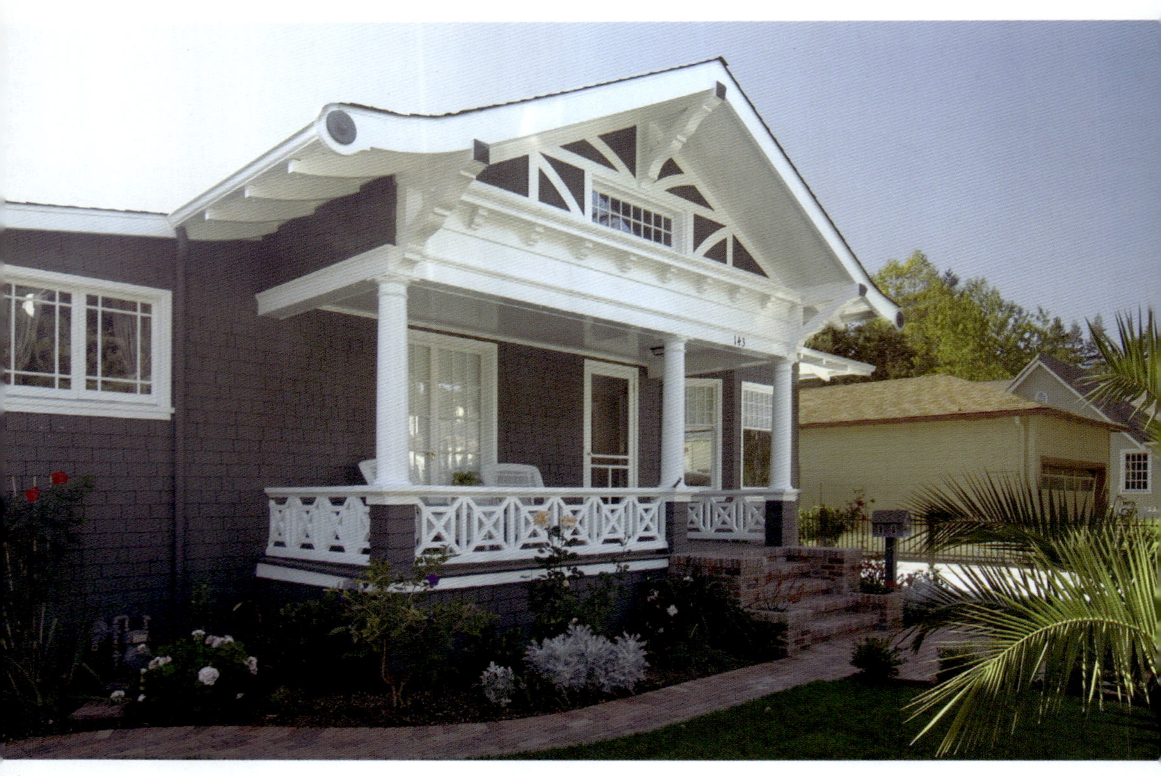

 ORIENTAL BUNGALOW | REDWOOD CITY, CALIFORNIA

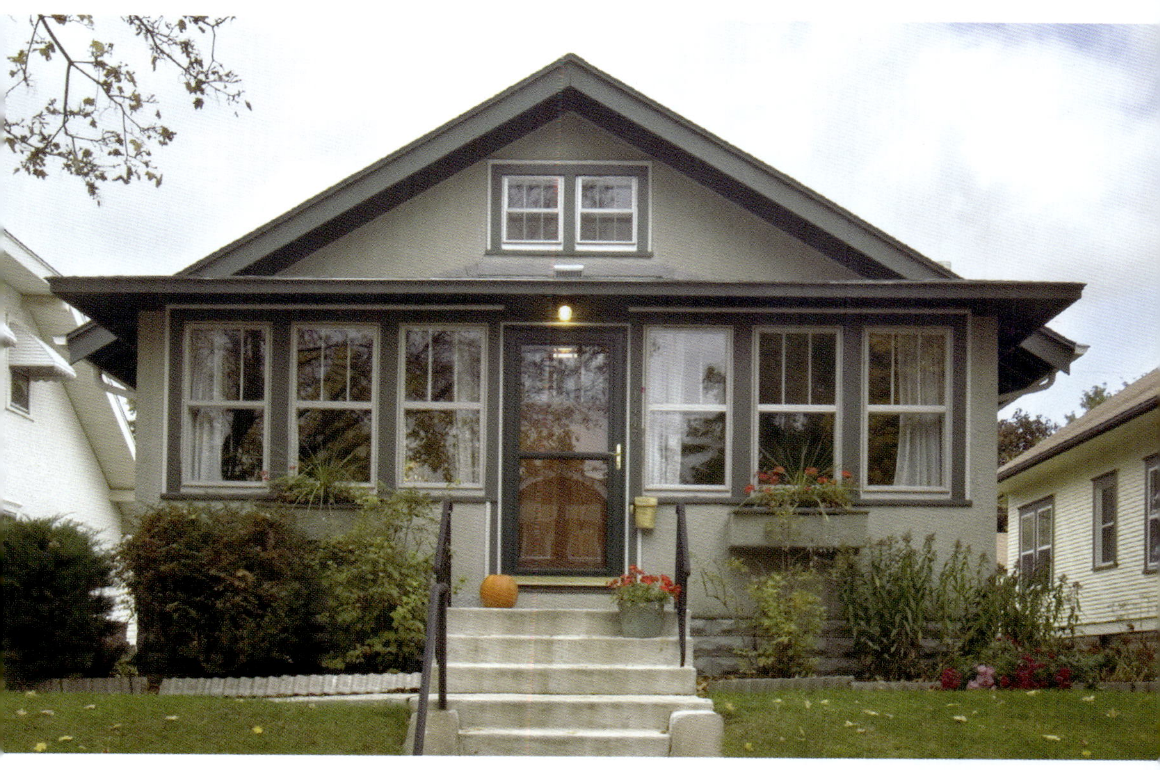

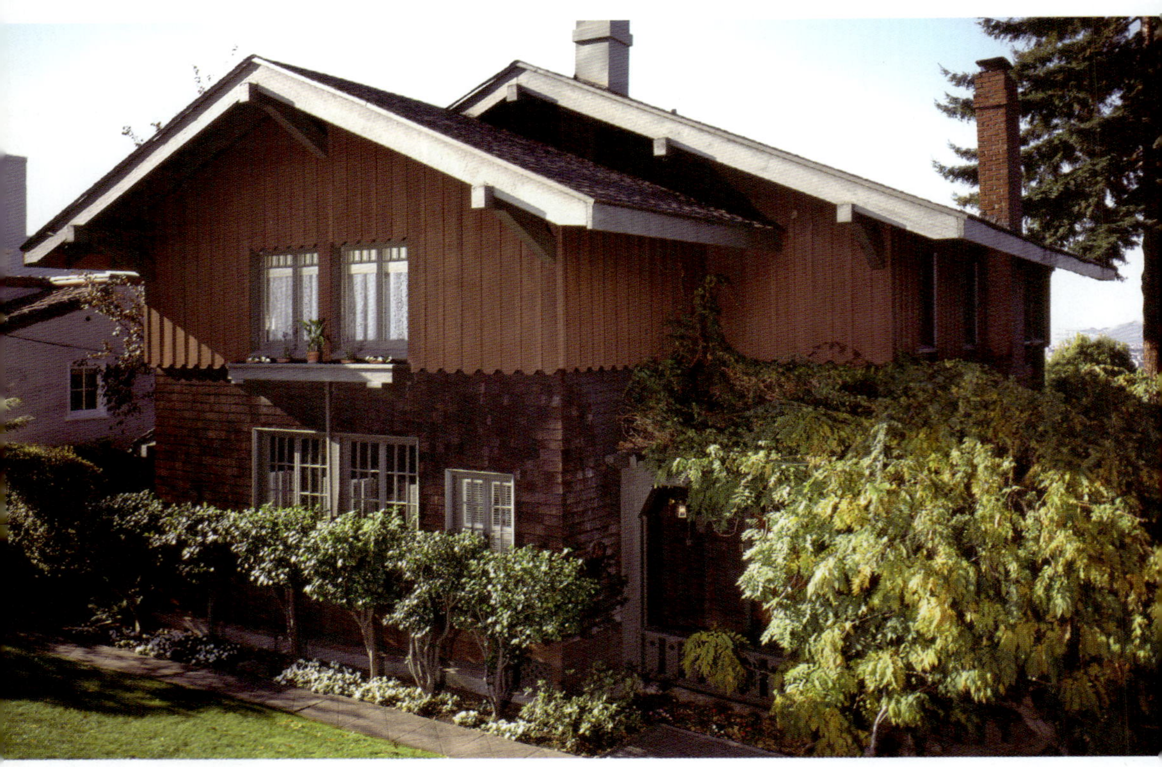

 CHALET BUNGALOW | PIEDMONT, CALIFORNIA

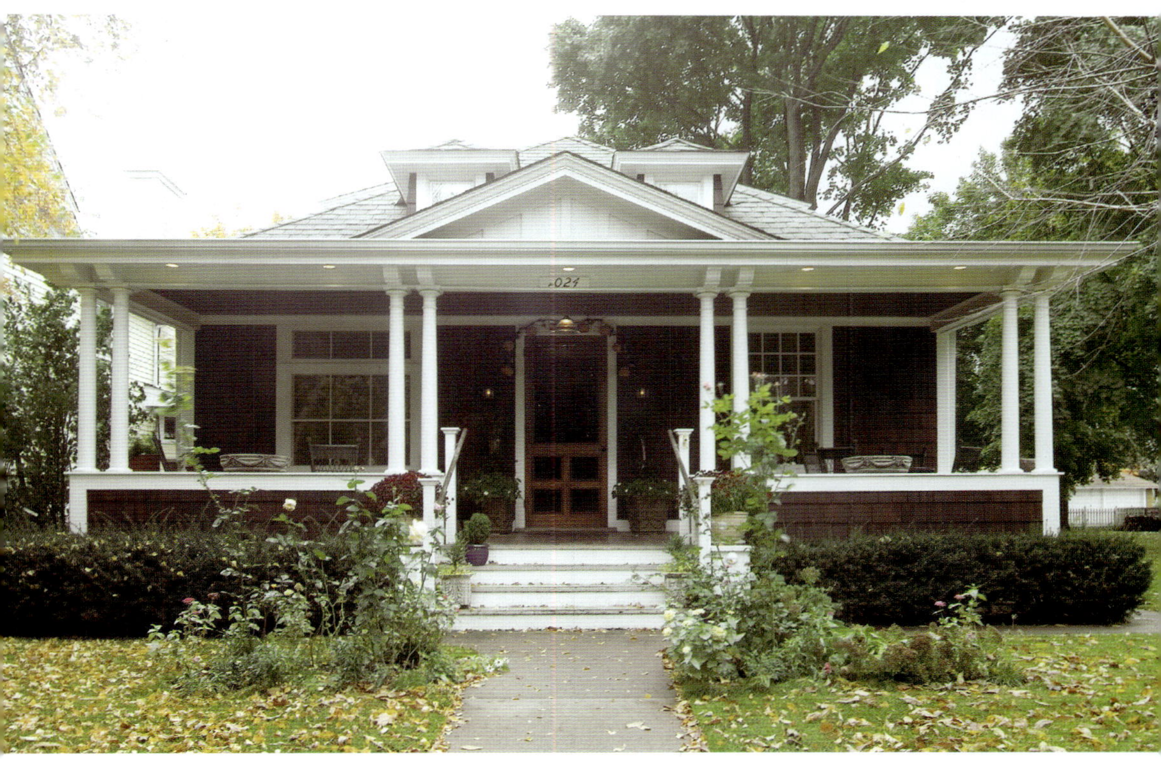

St. Paul, Minnesota

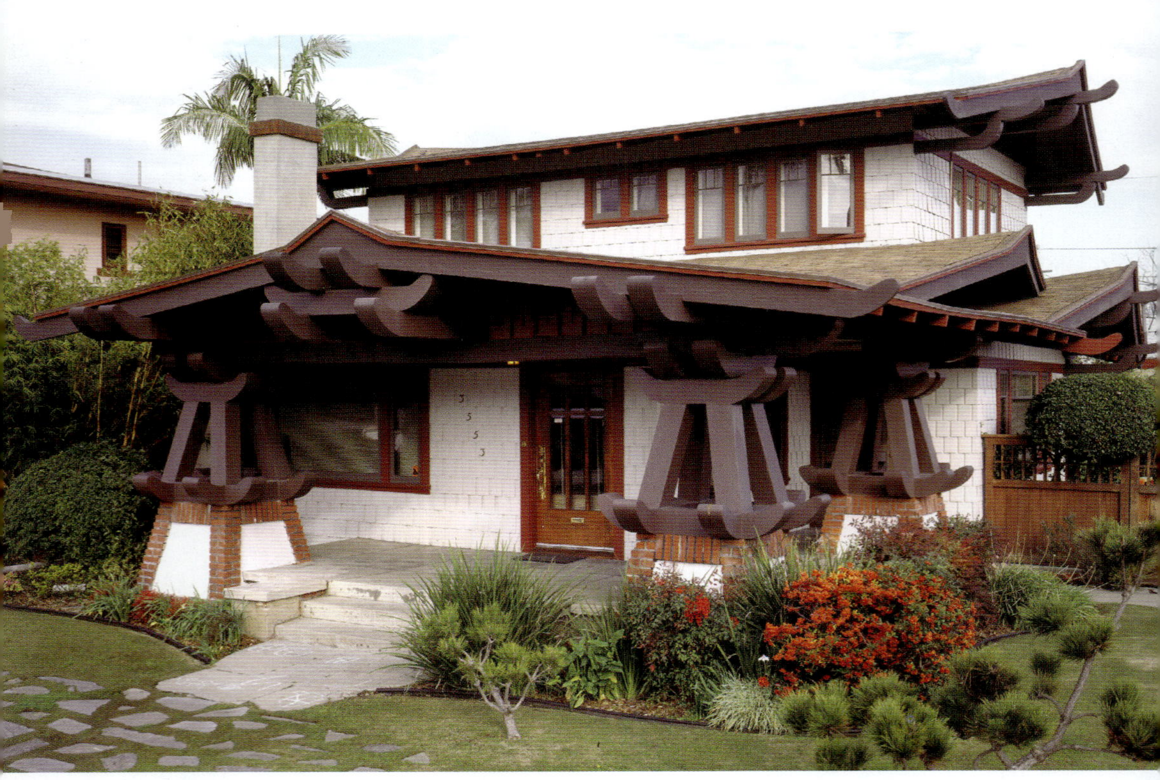


 CHALET BUNGALOW | SAN DIEGO, CALIFORNIA

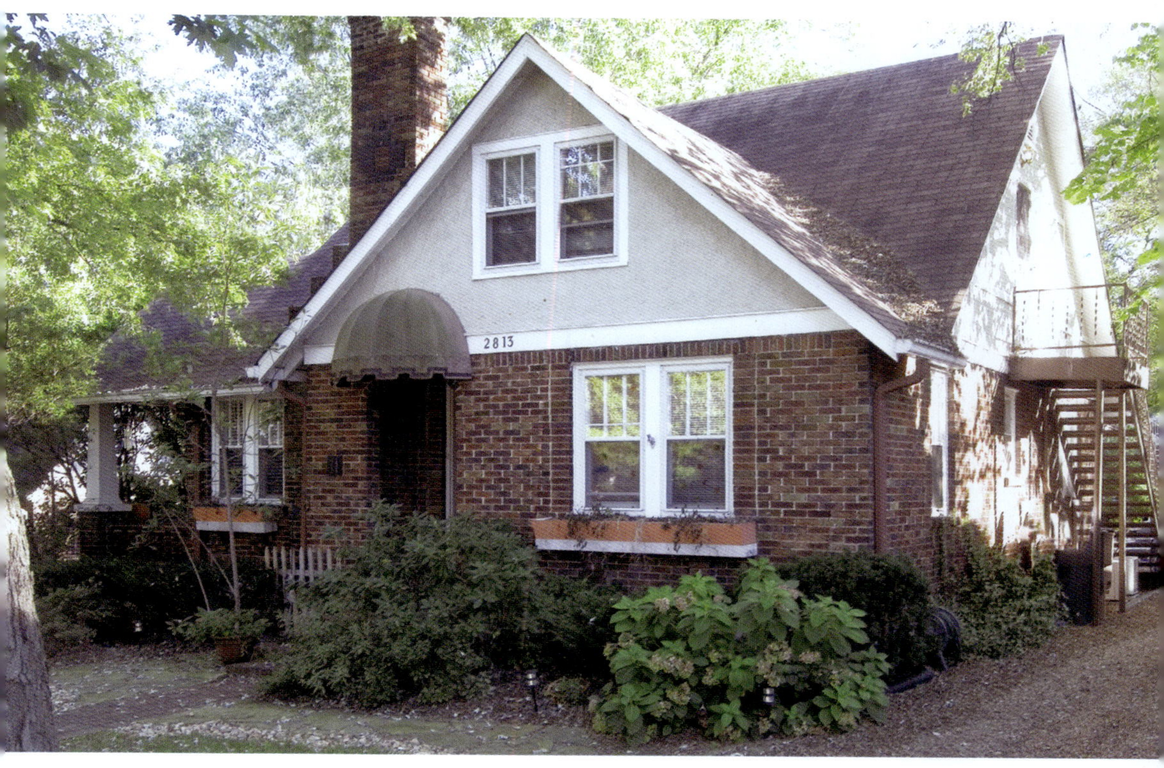
2813

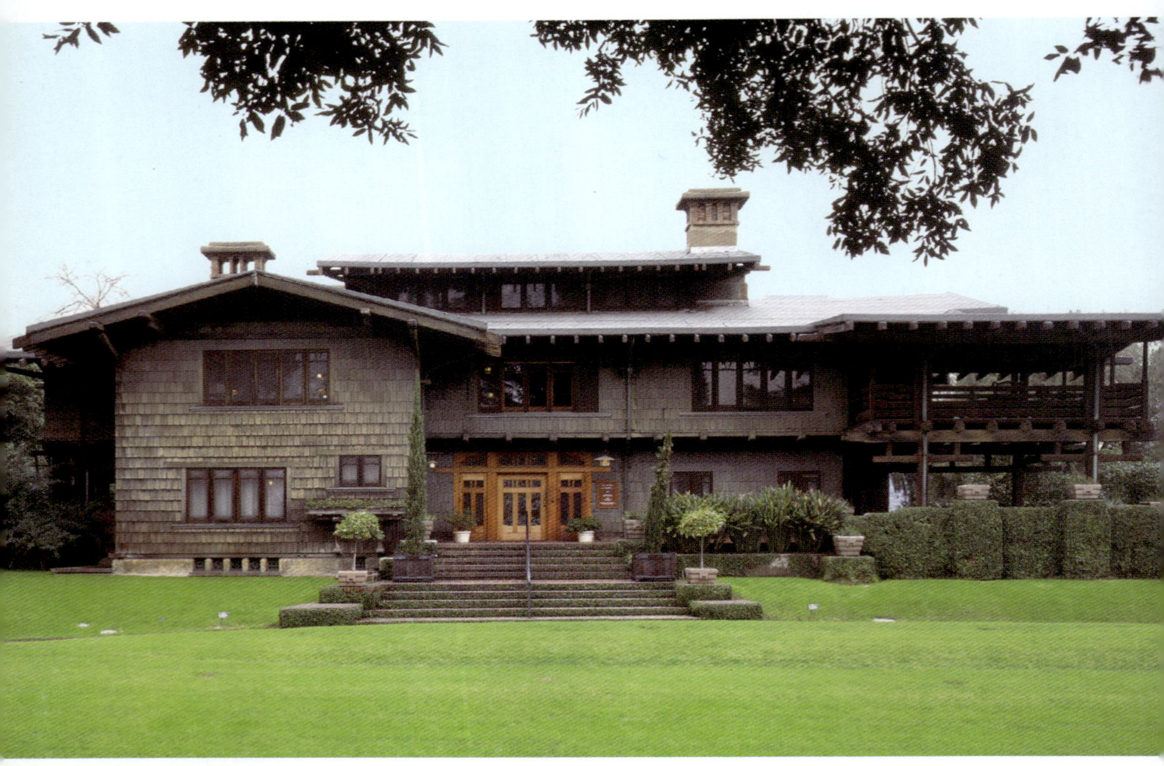

 GAMBLE HOUSE | PASADENA, CALIFORNIA

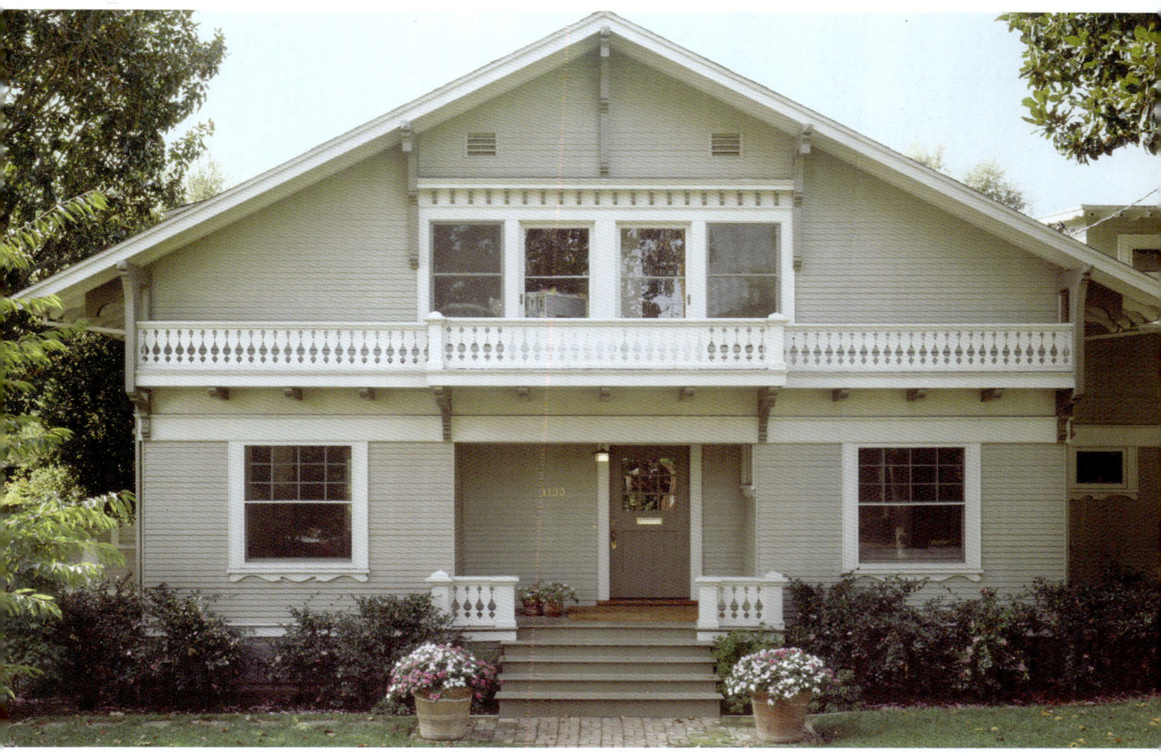

CHALET BUNGALOW | SAN JOSE, CALIFORNIA

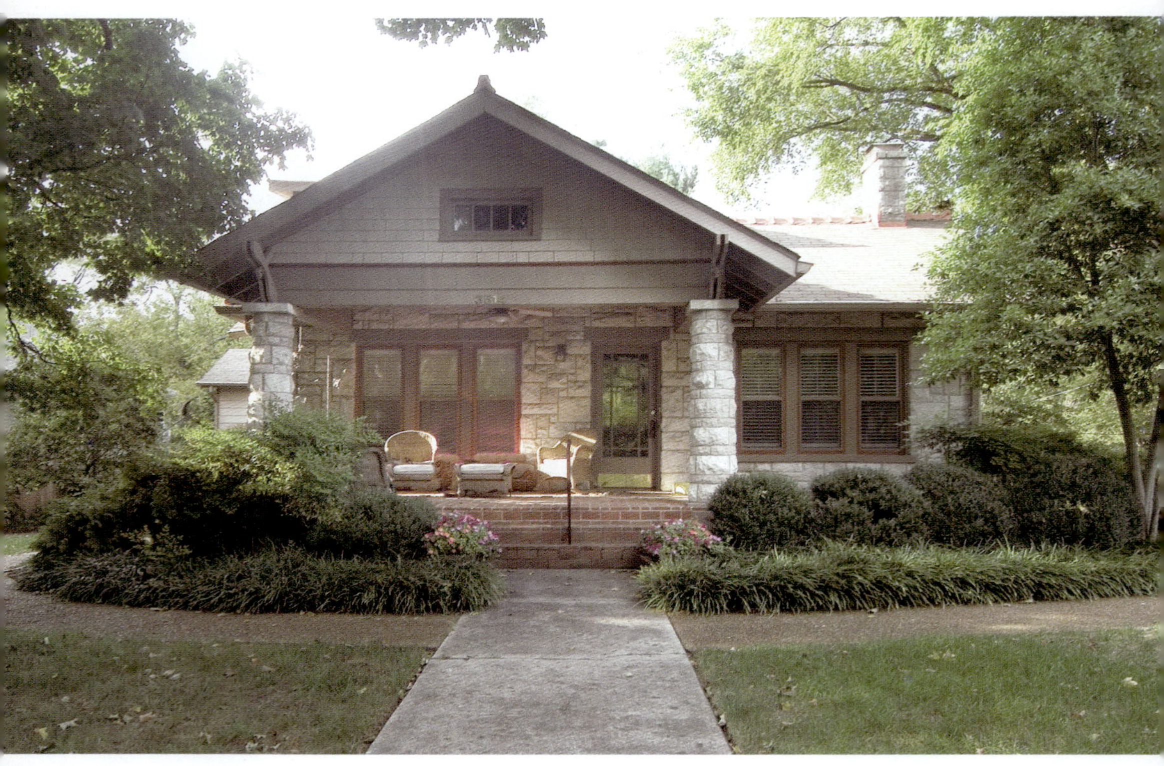

 Nashville, Tennessee

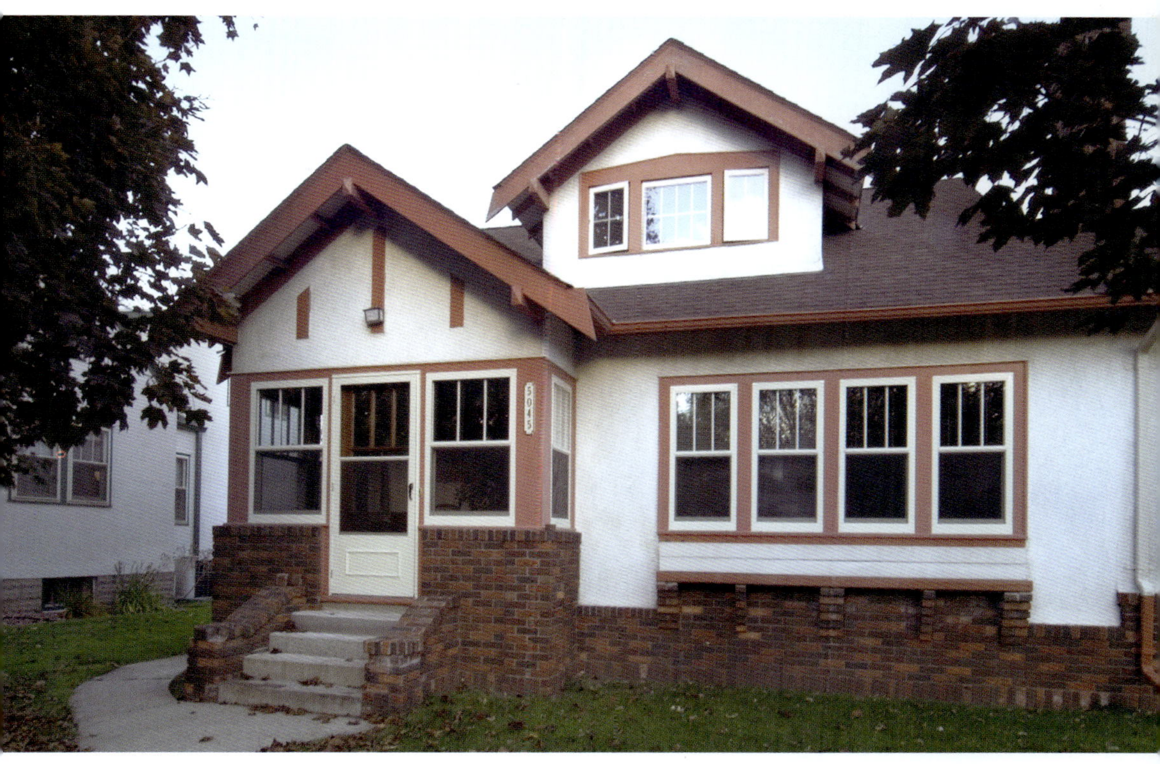
5045

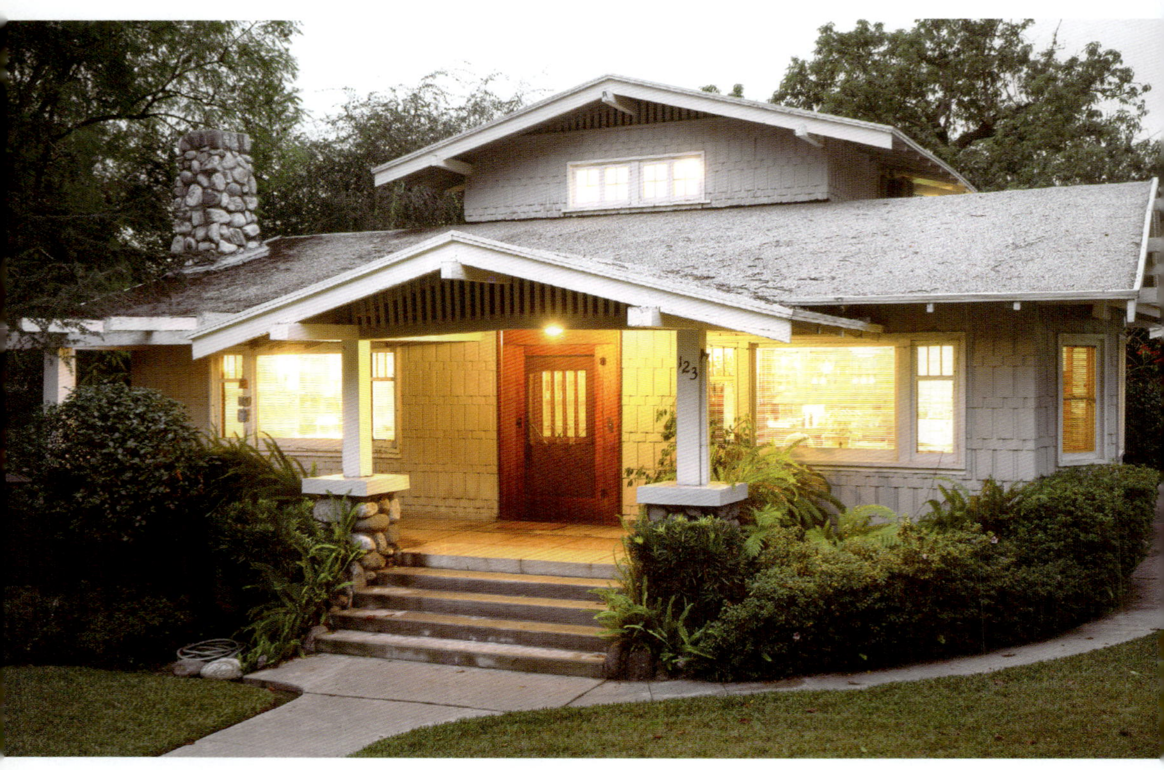


 AIRPLANE BUNGALOW | SIERRA MADRE, CALIFORNIA

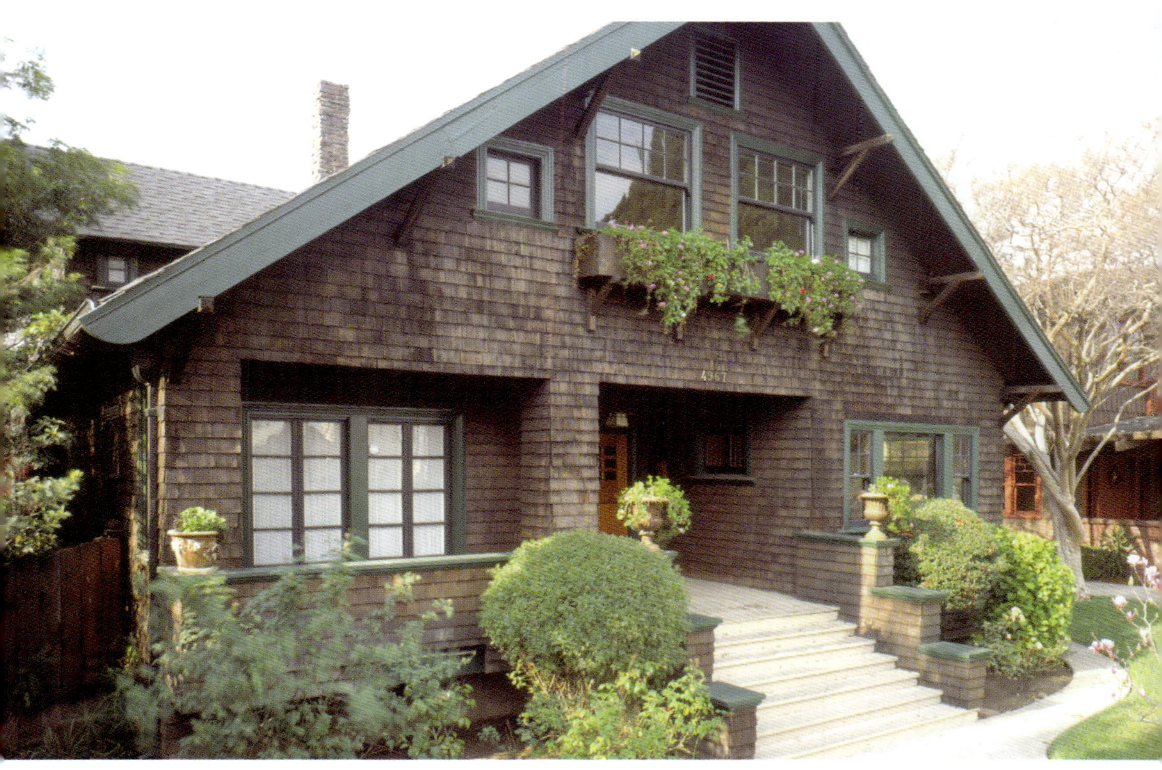

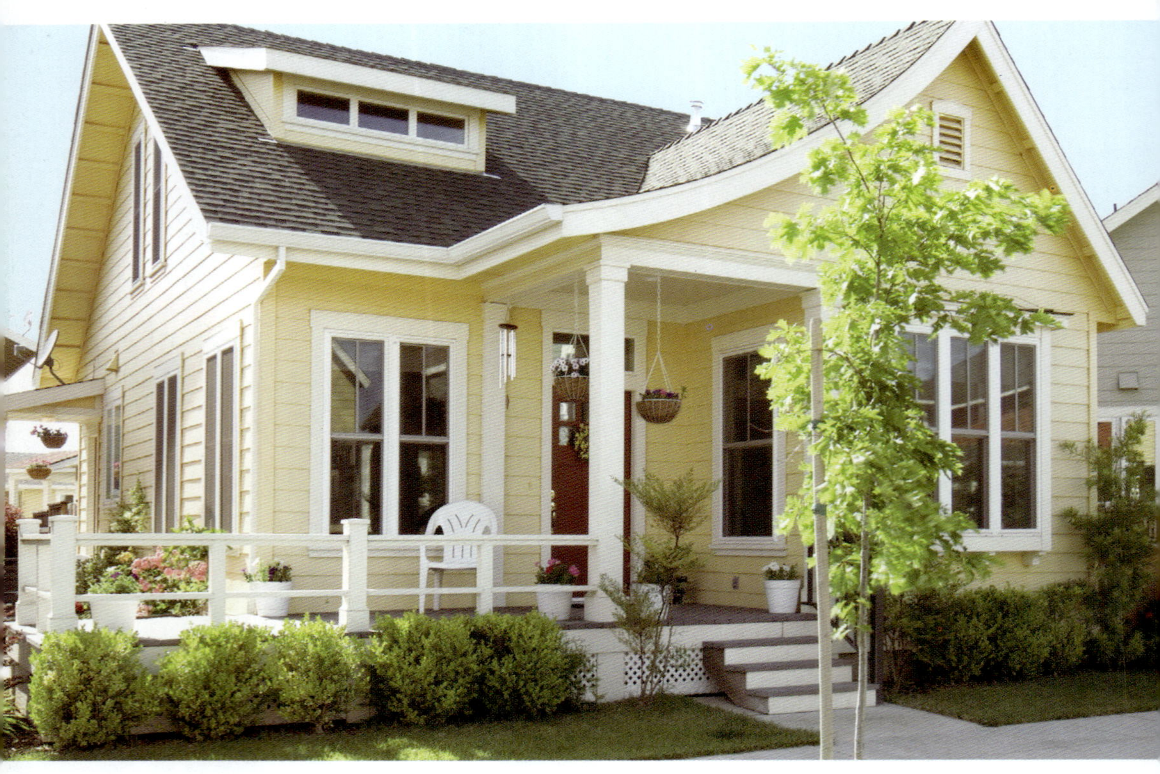

 Chico, California

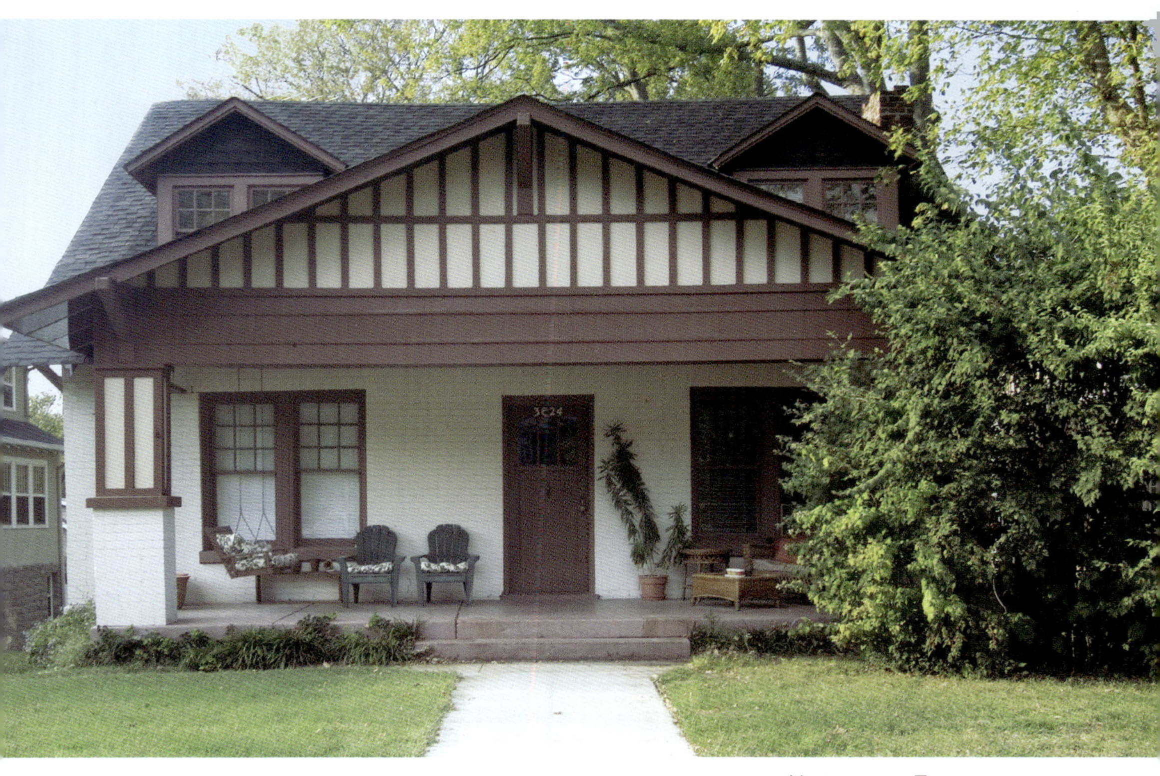


Nashville, Tennessee 

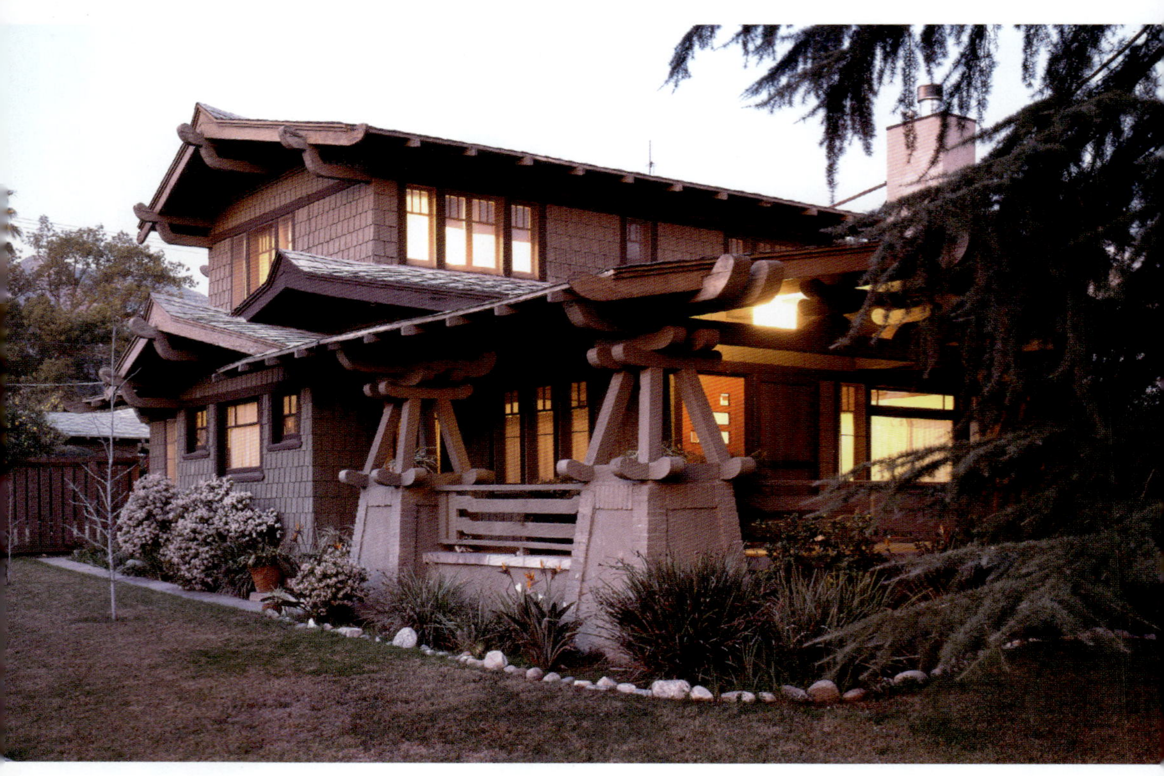

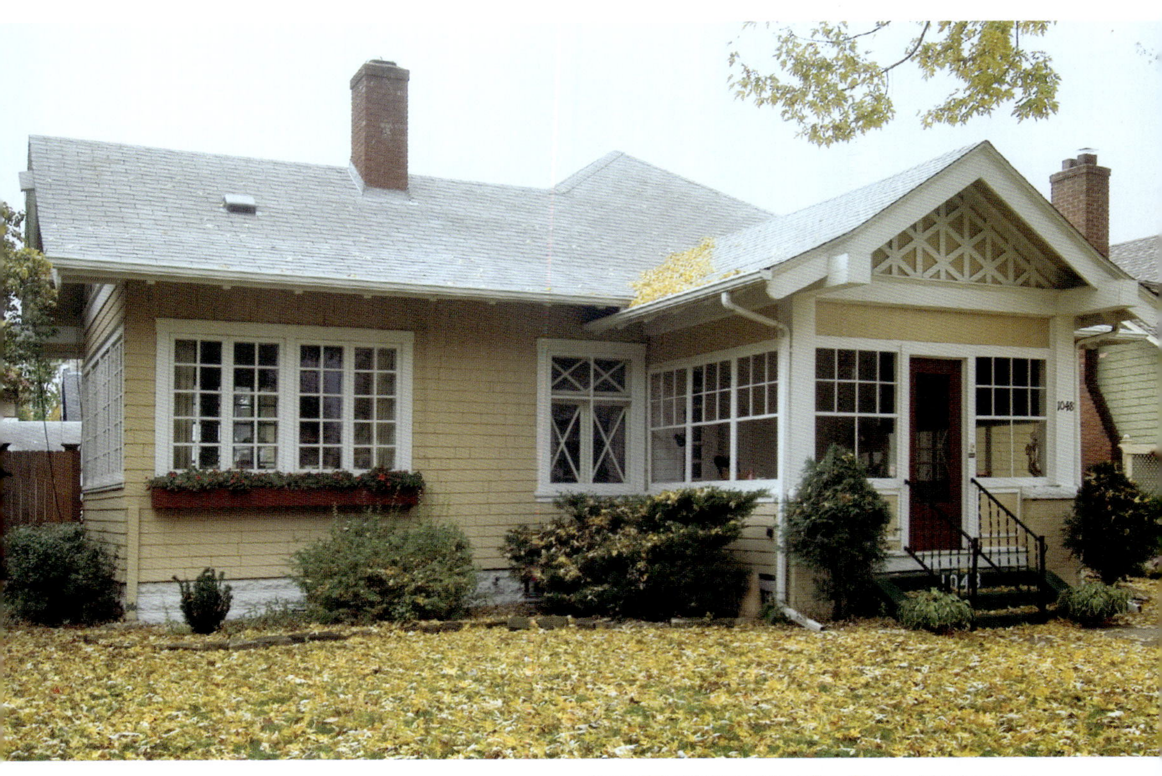


CHALET BUNGALOW | ST. PAUL, MINNESOTA 

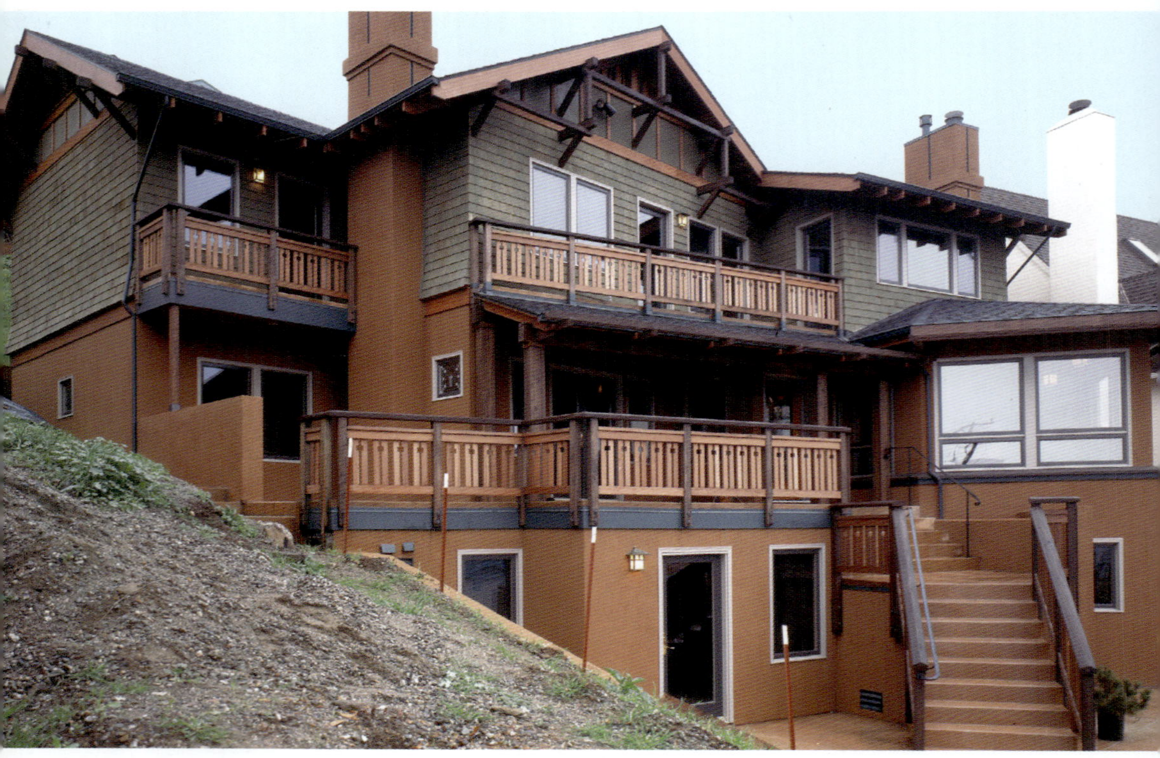

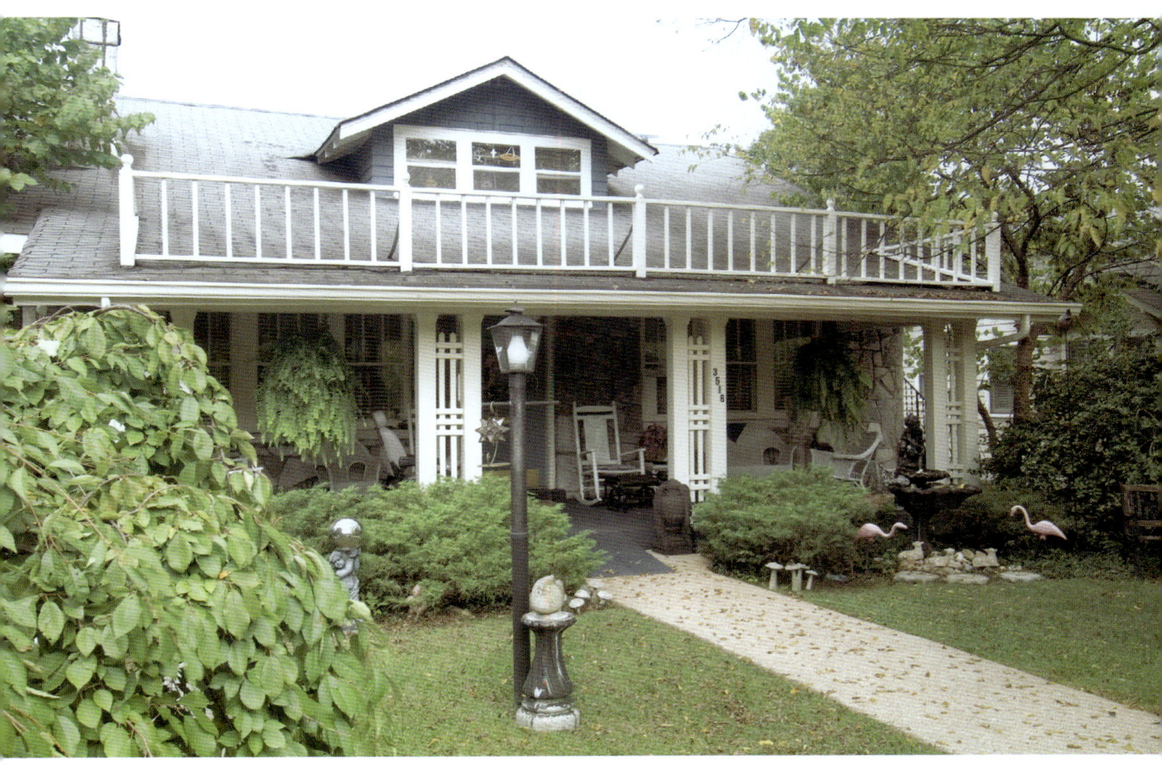
3518

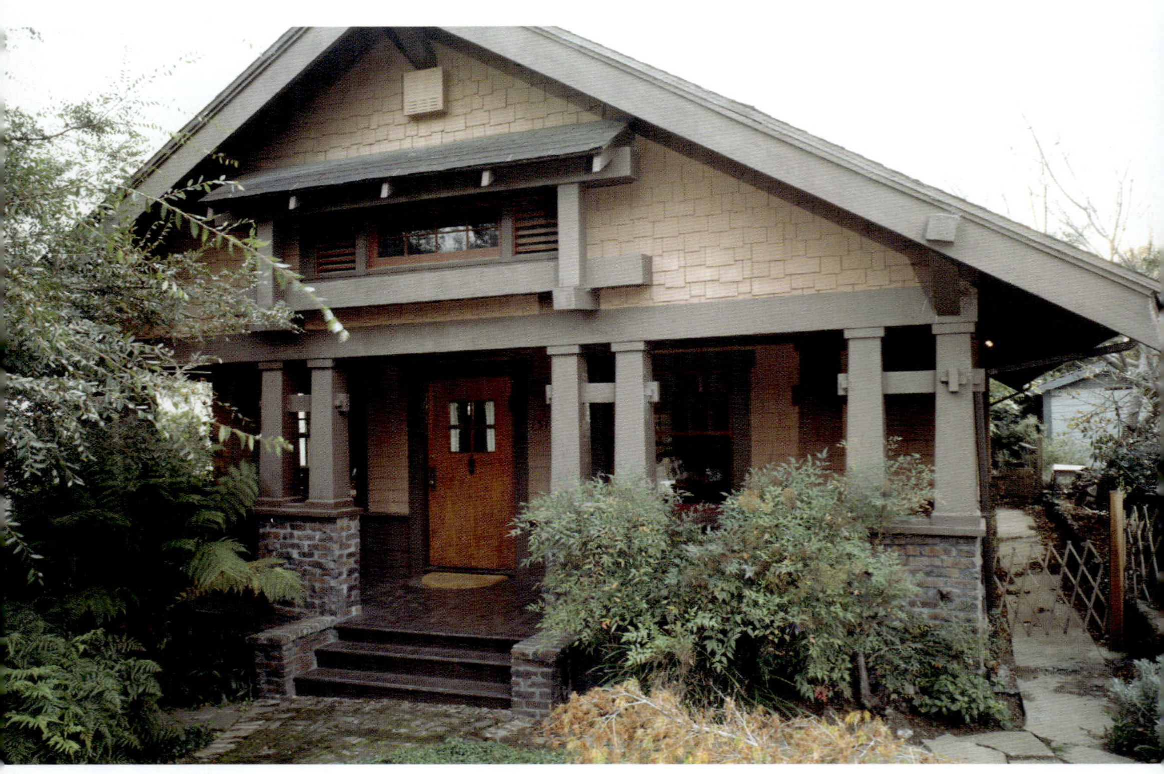

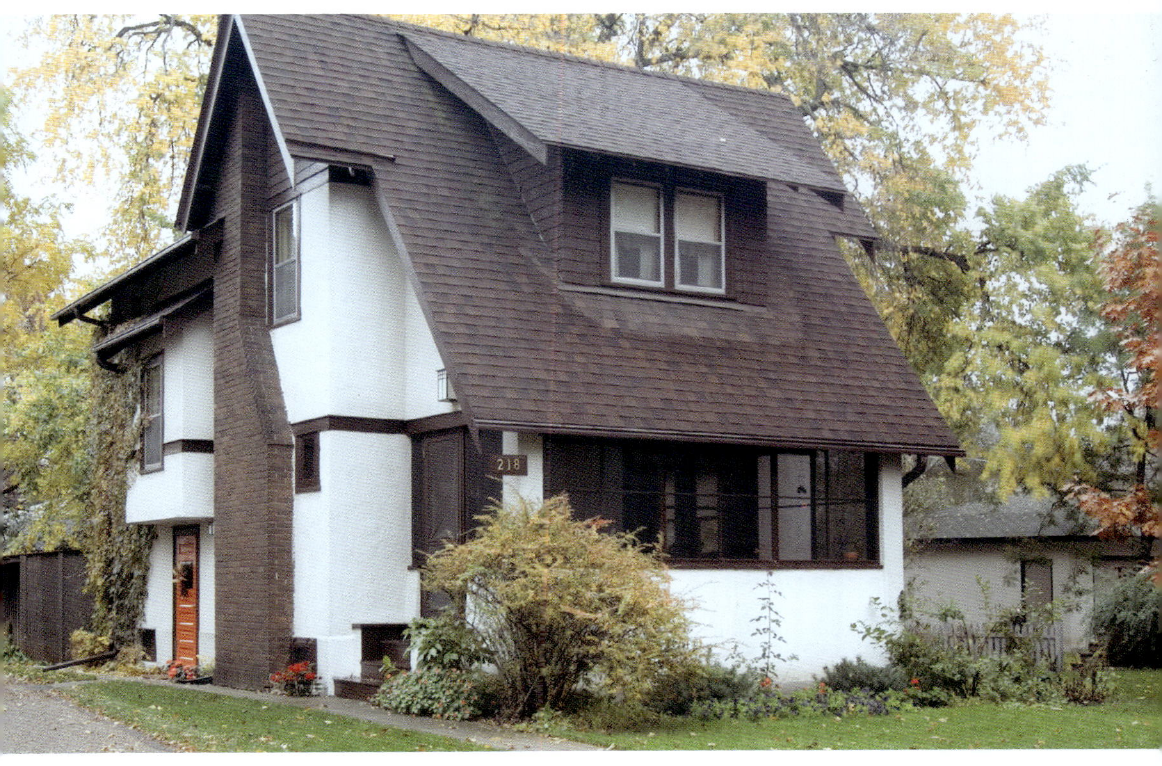
218

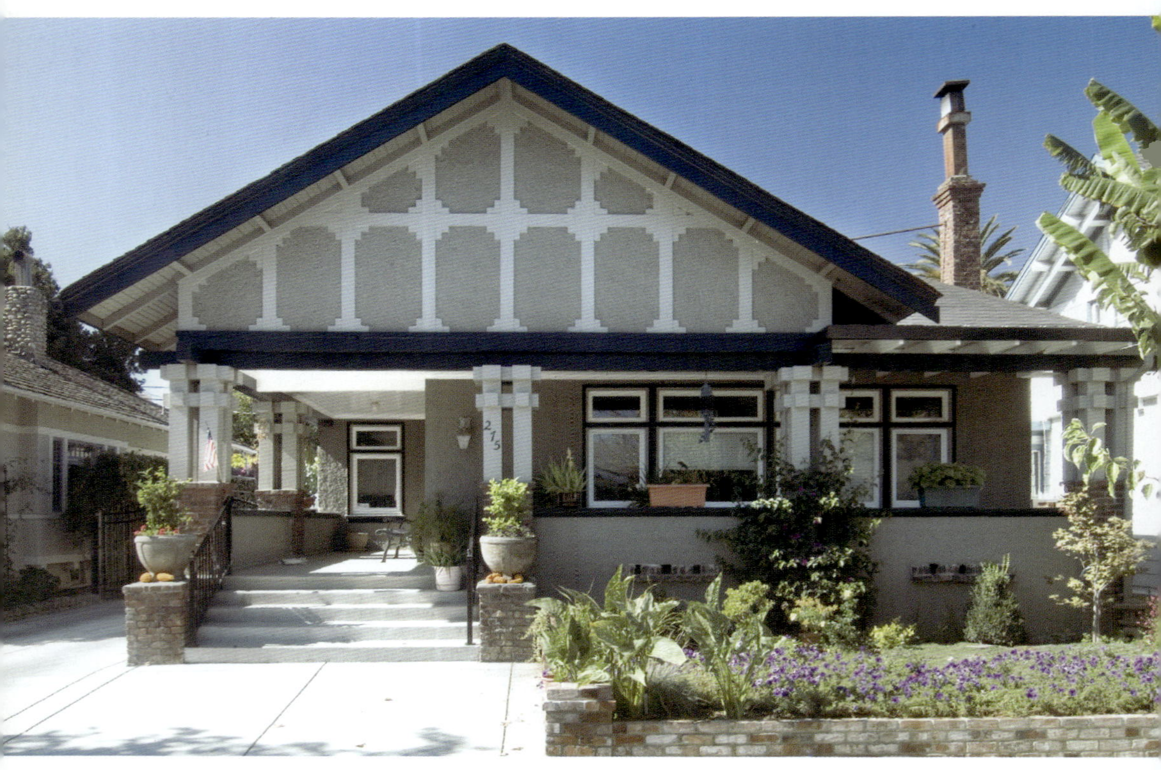


 CHALET BUNGALOW | San Jose, California

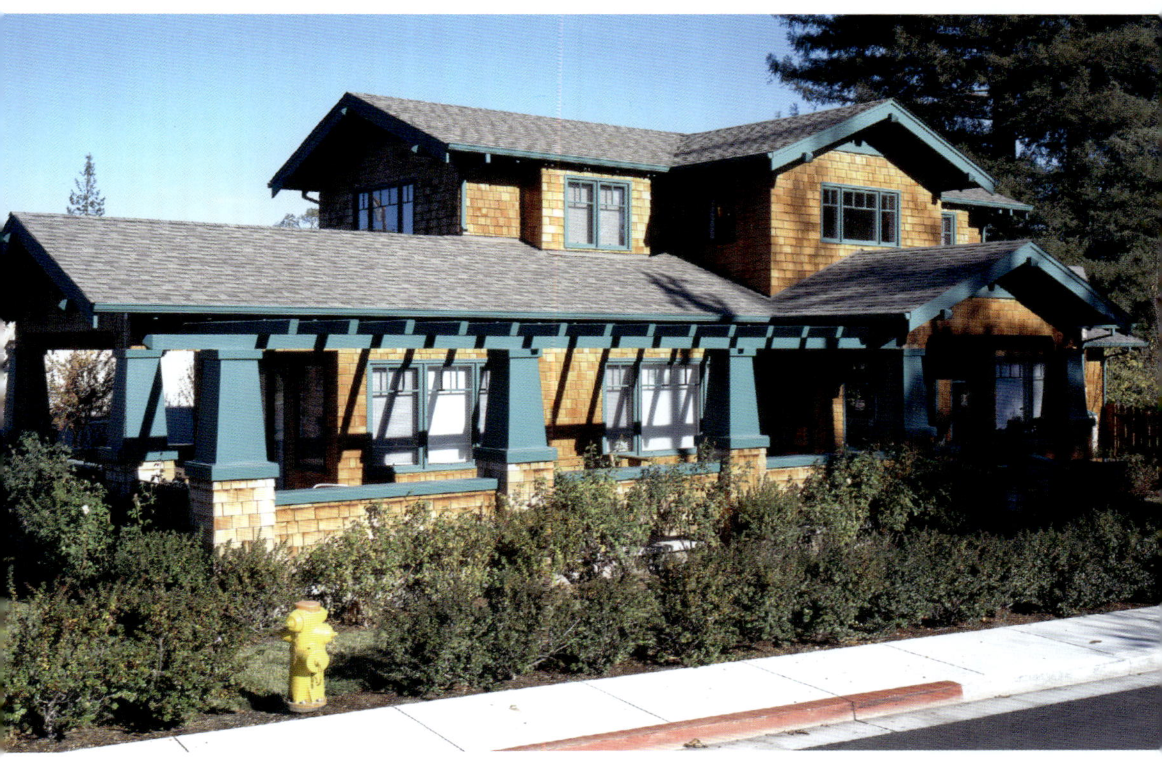

St. Helena, California

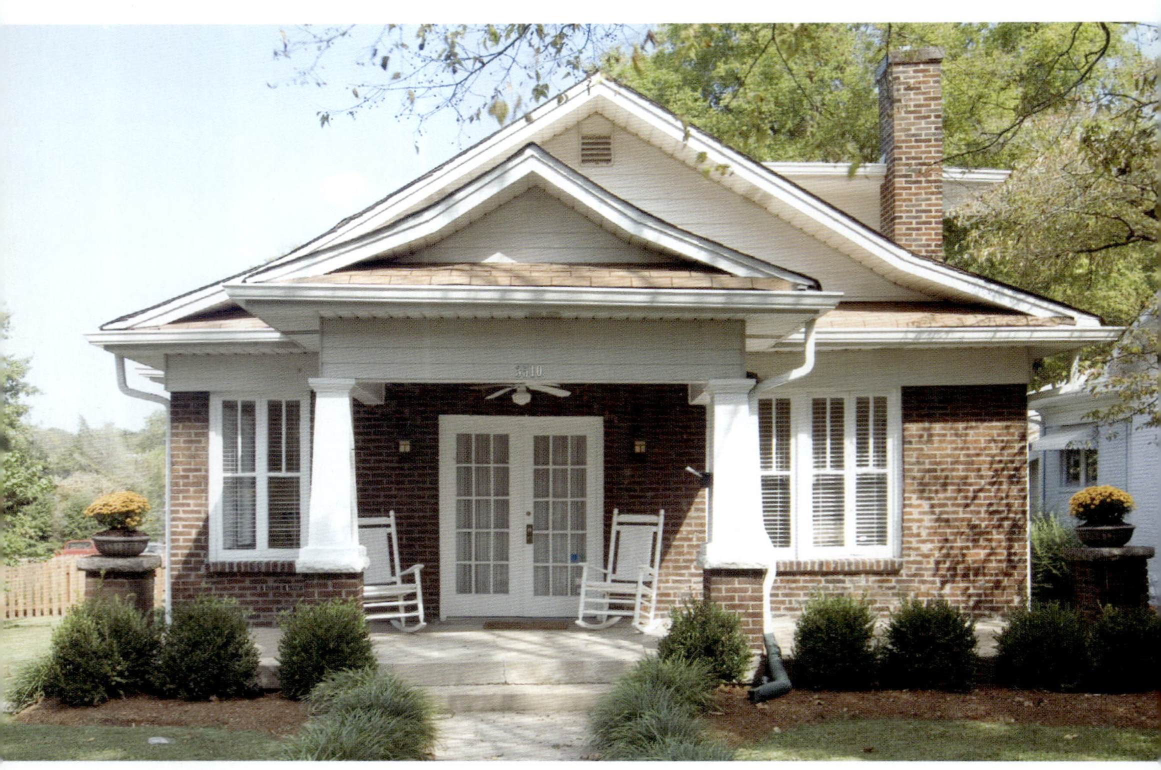

 ORIENTAL BUNGALOW | NASHVILLE, TENNESSEE

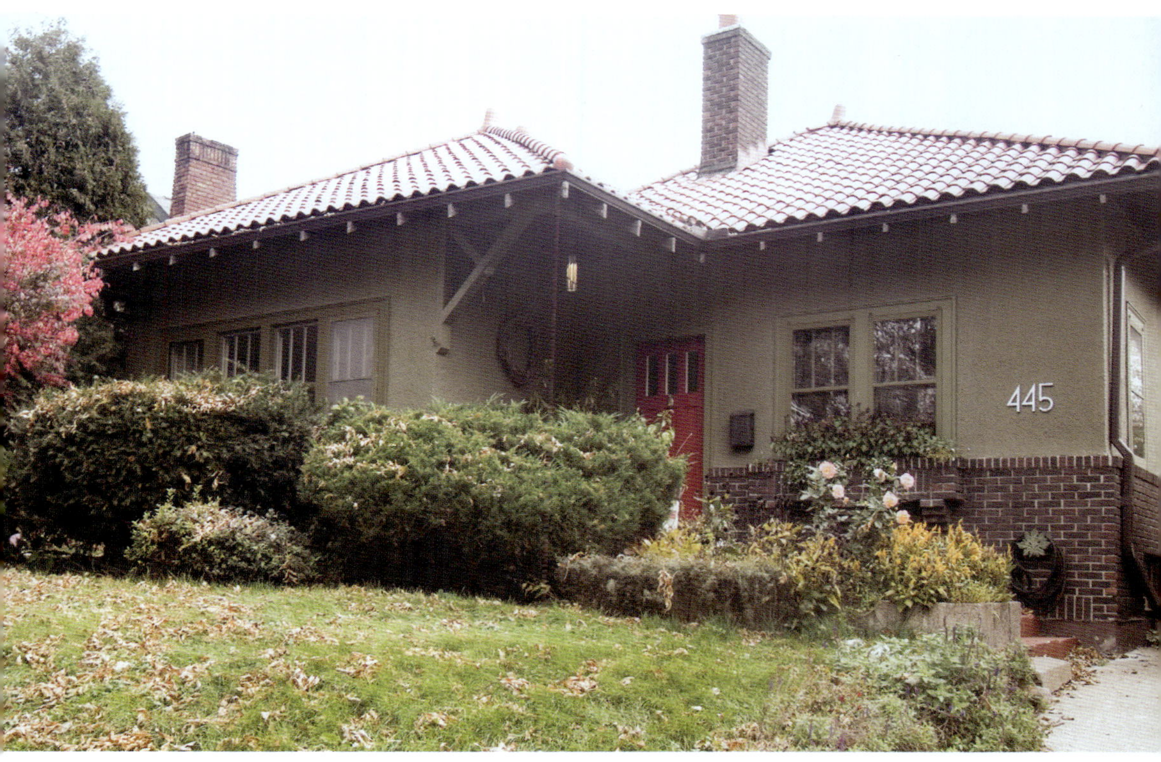
445

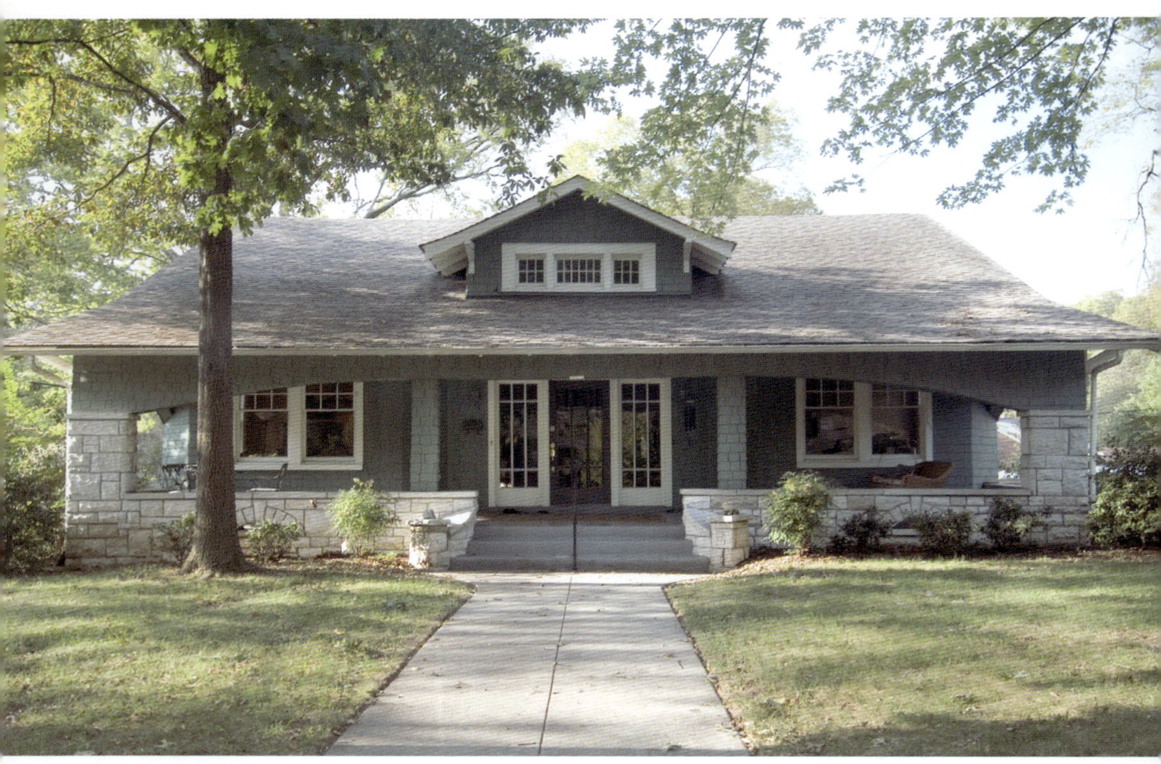

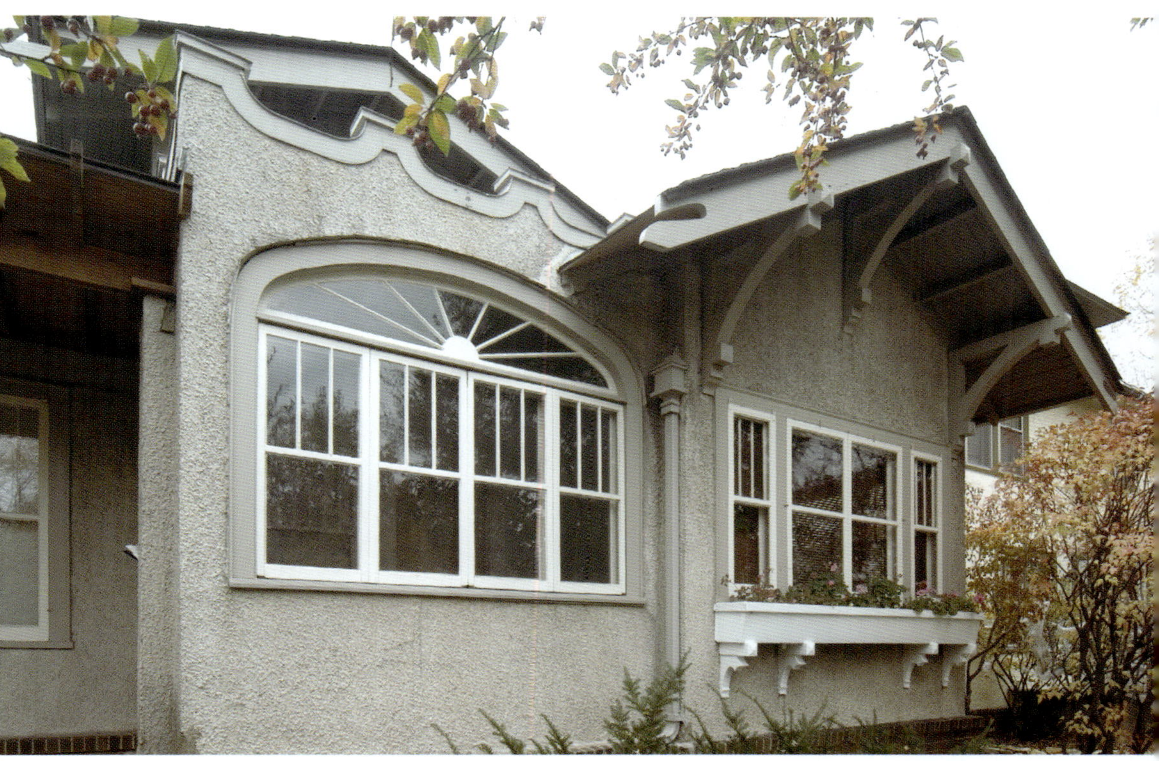

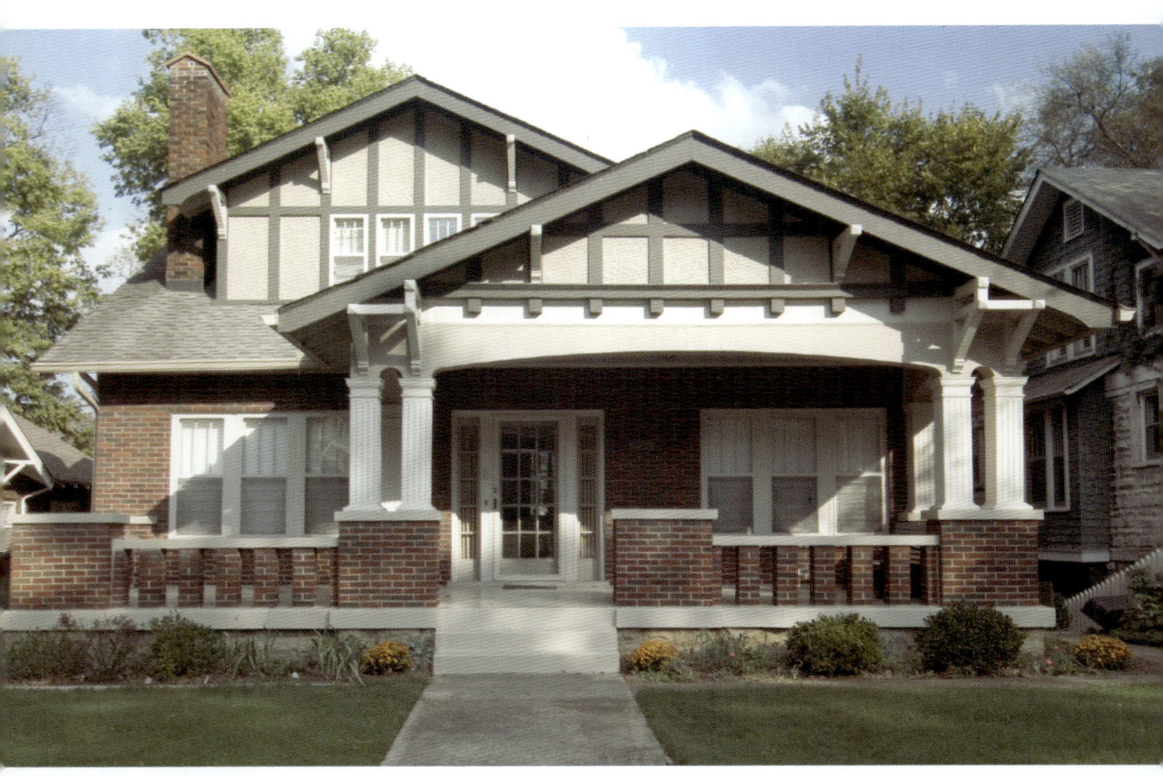

 Nashville, Tennessee

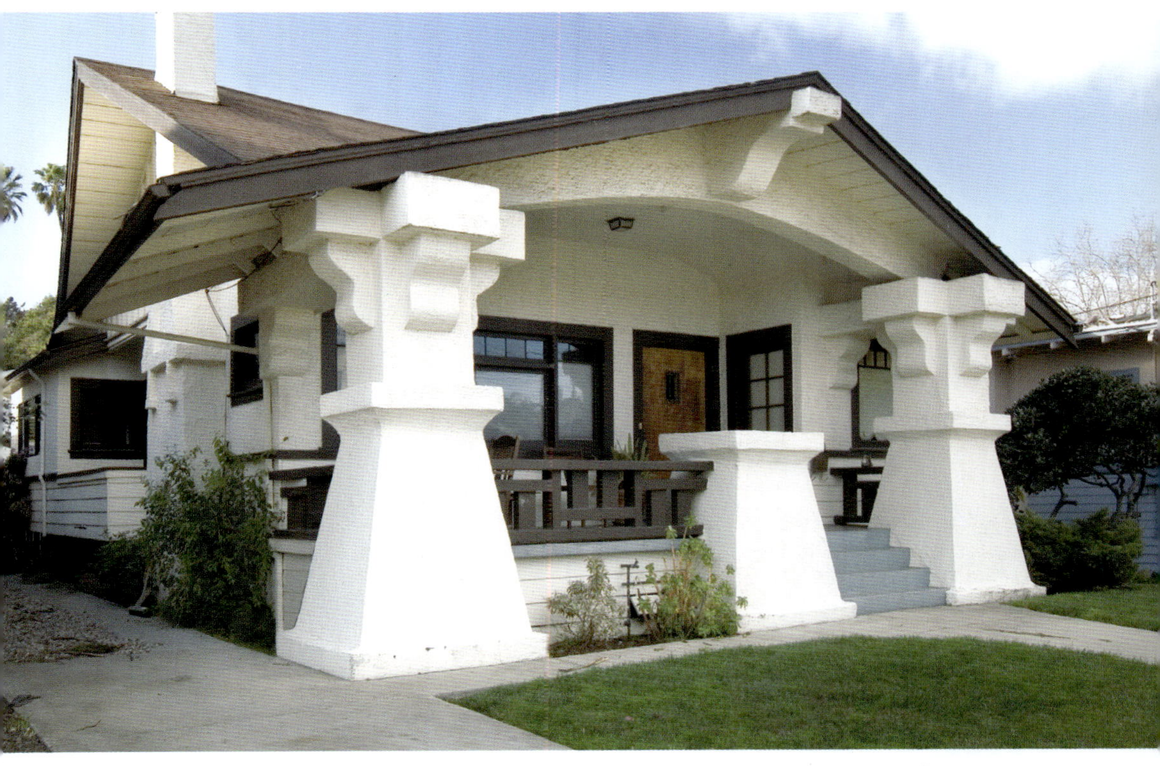

Alameda, California 

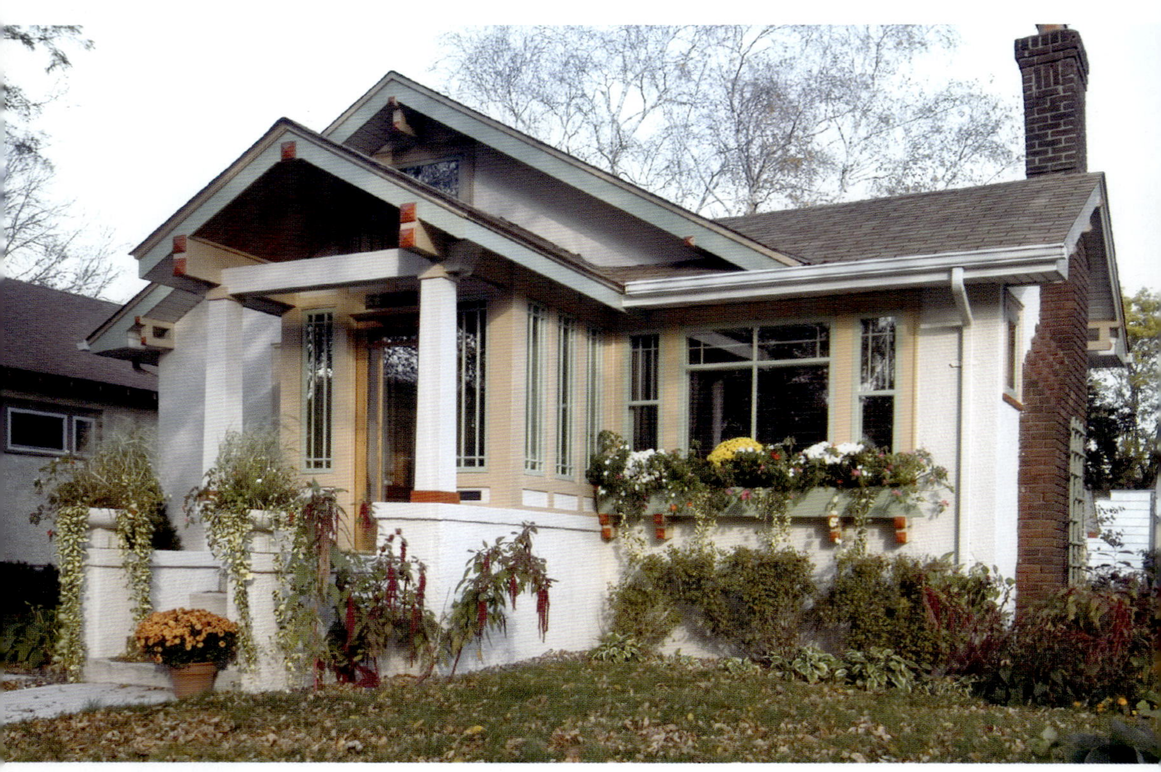

 Minneapolis, Minnesota

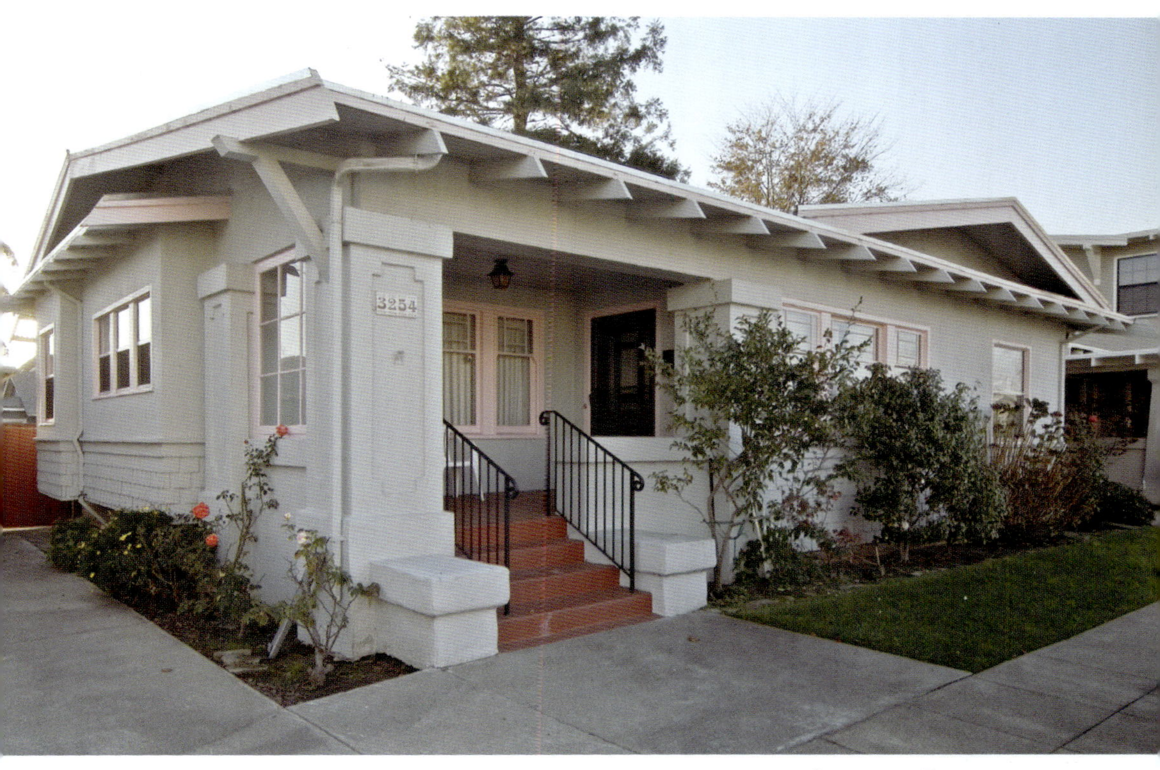


Alameda, California

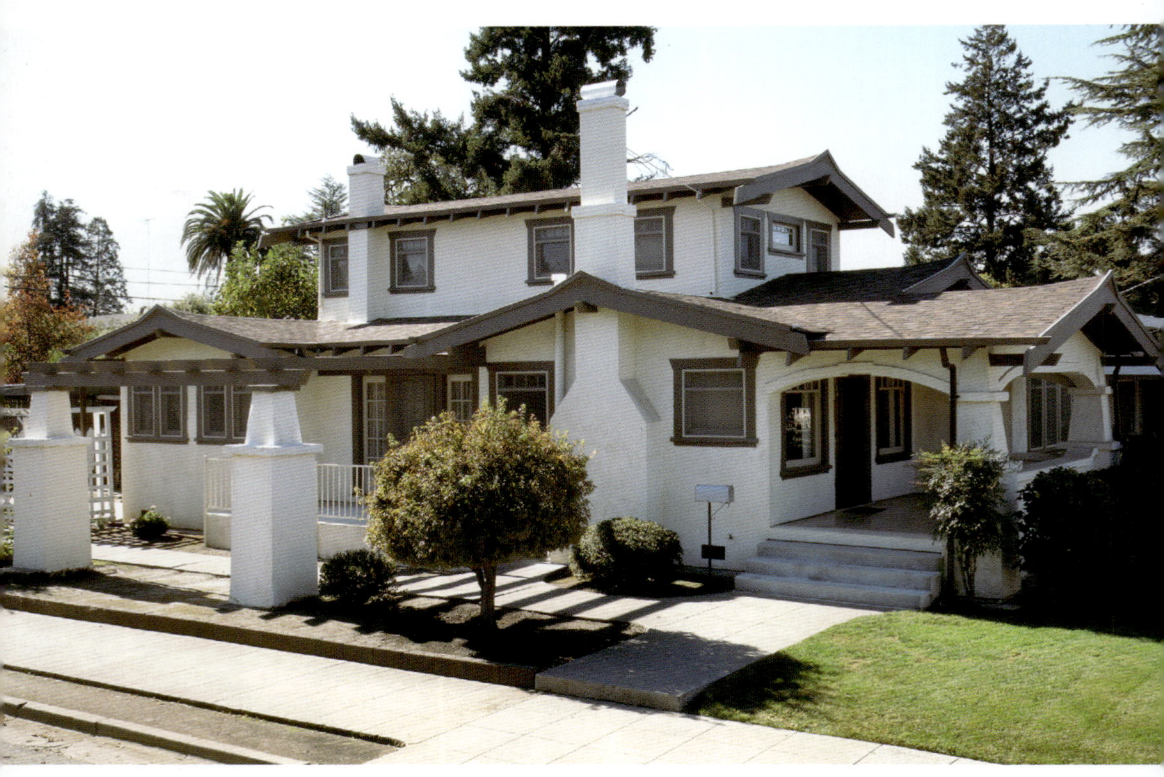

 ORIENTAL BUNGALOW | PETALUMA, CALIFORNIA

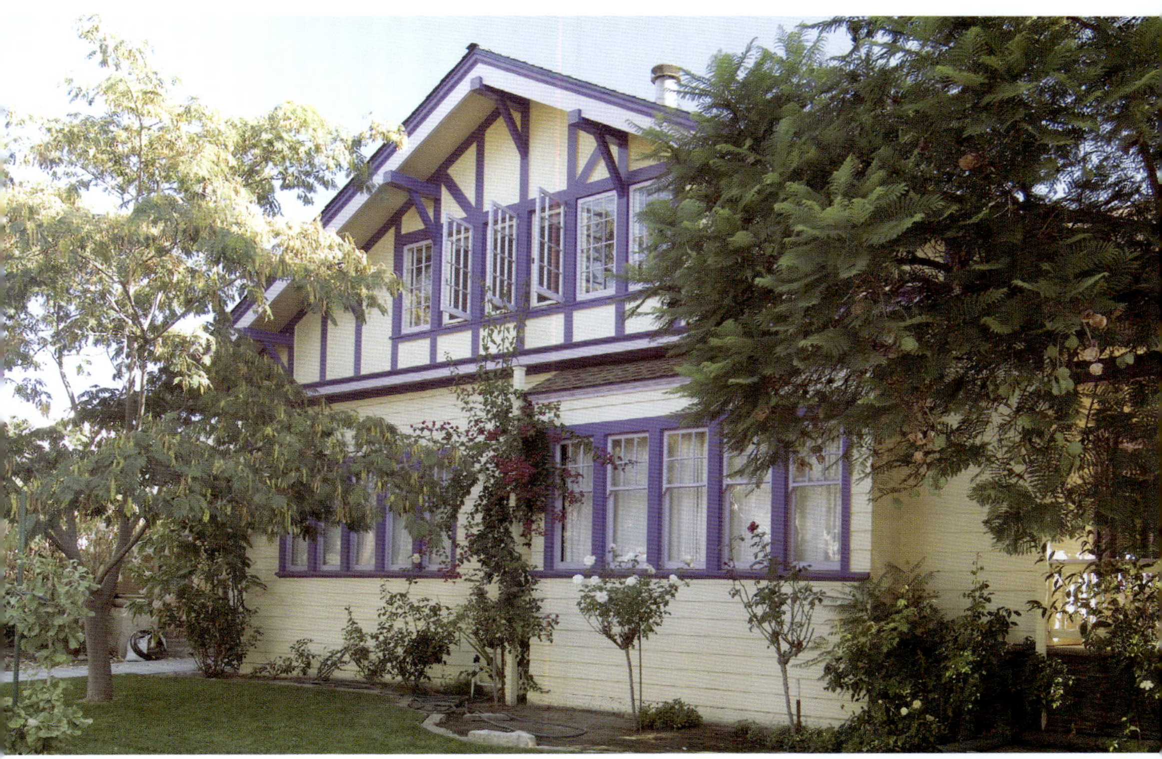

CHALET BUNGALOW | SAN JOSE, CALIFORNIA 

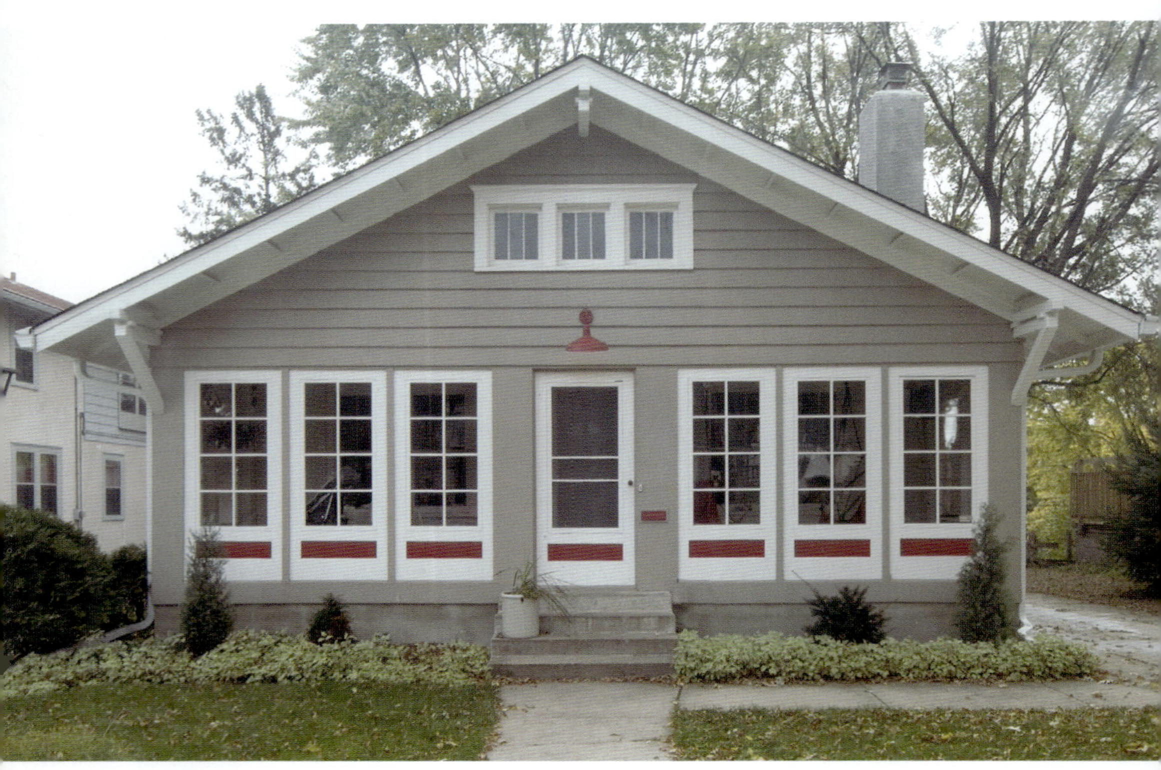

 Minneapolis, Minnesota

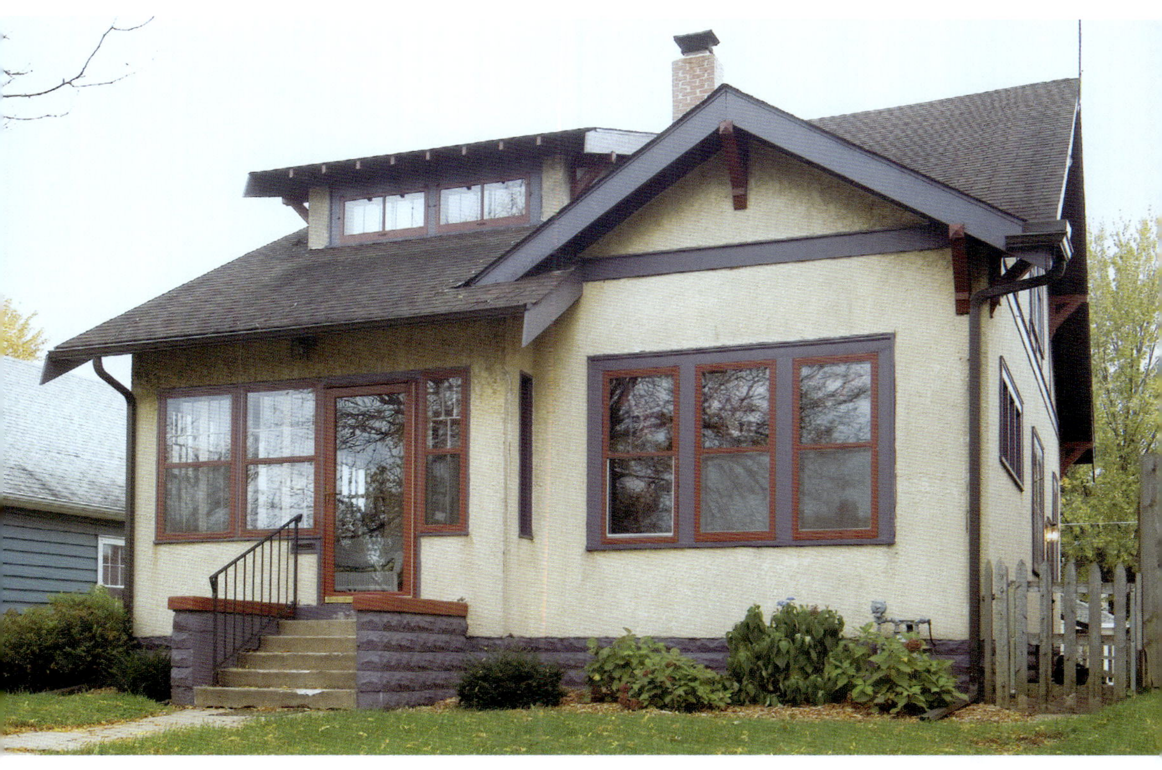

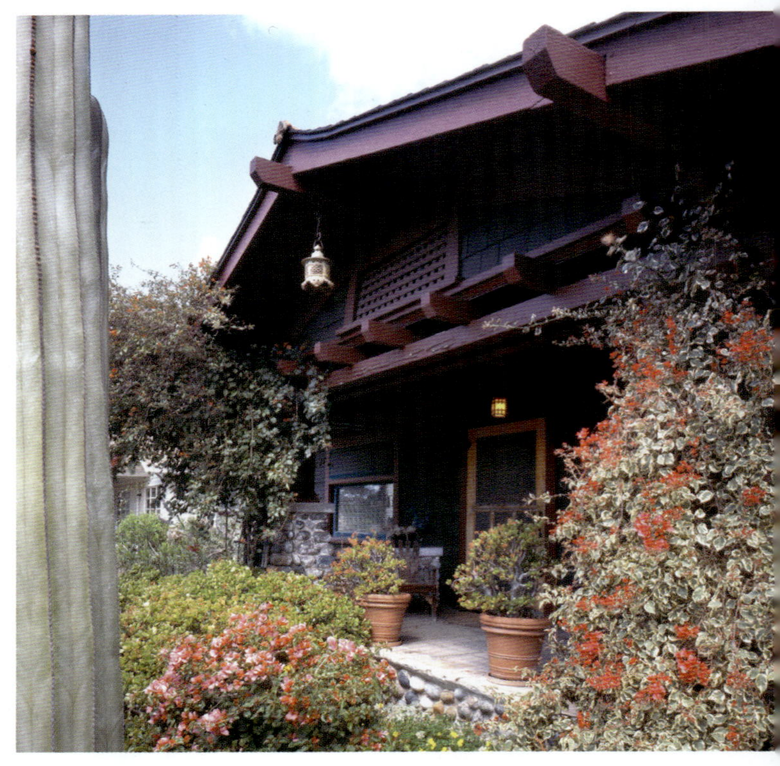

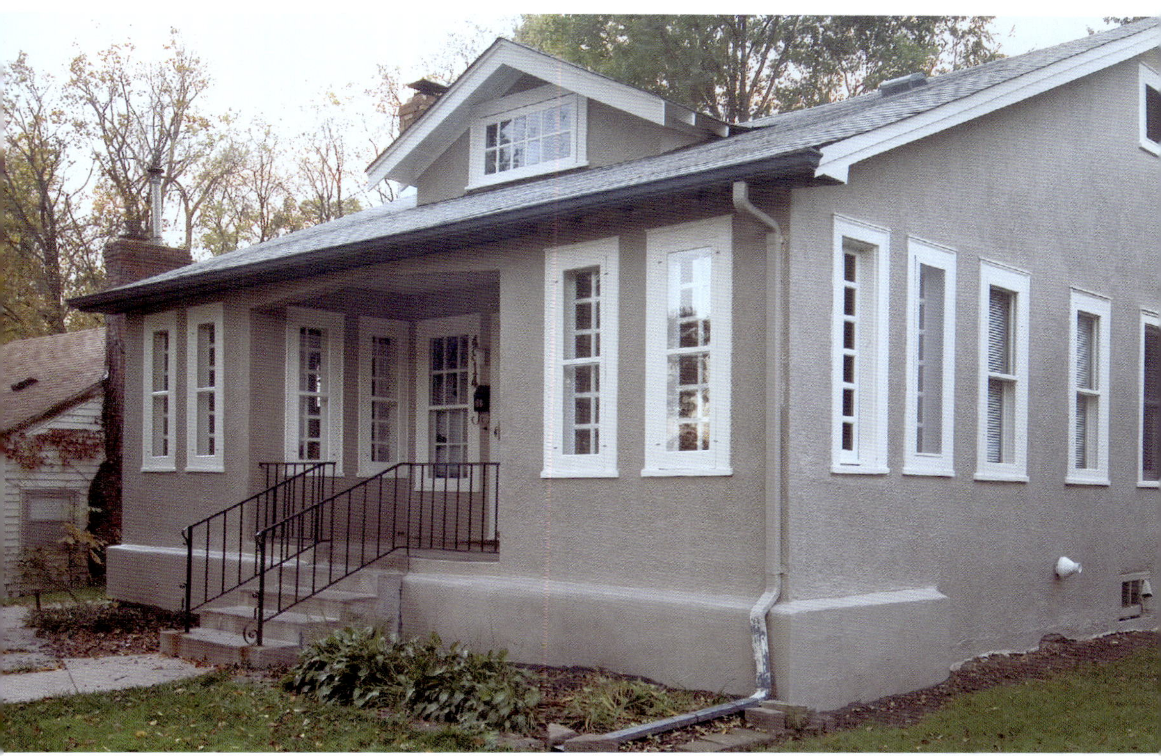

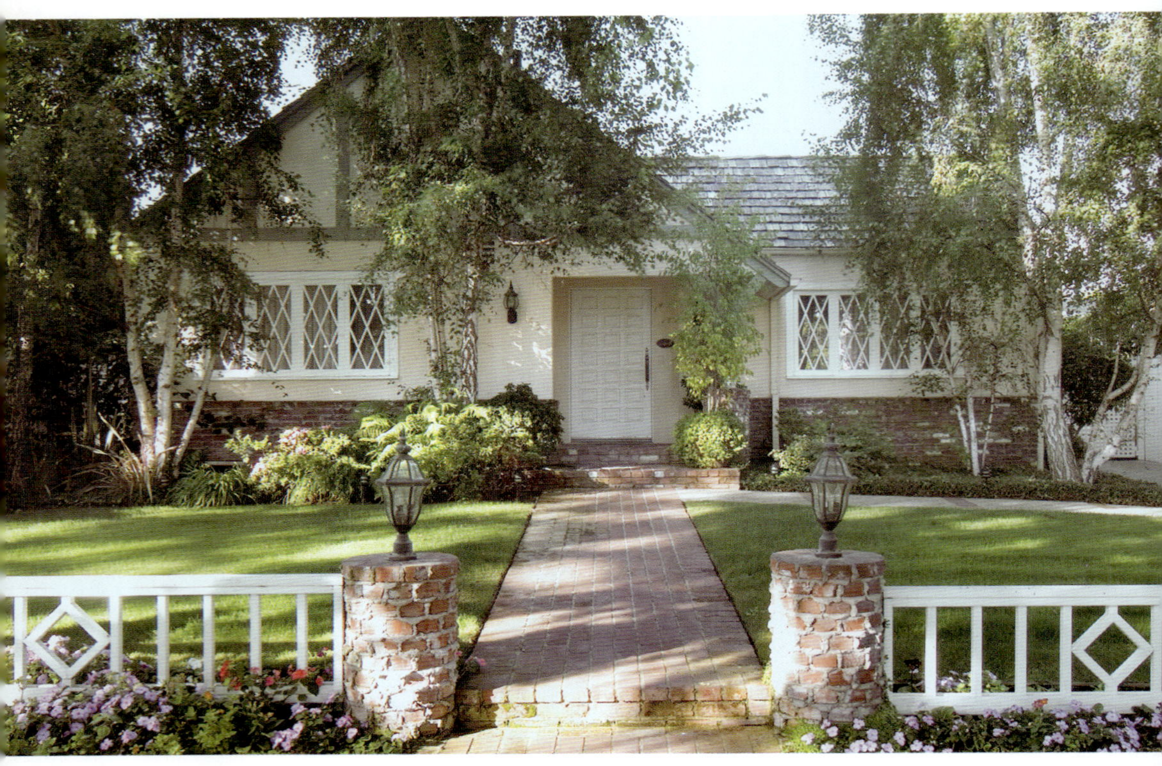

 CHALET BUNGALOW | SANTA MONICA, CALIFORNIA

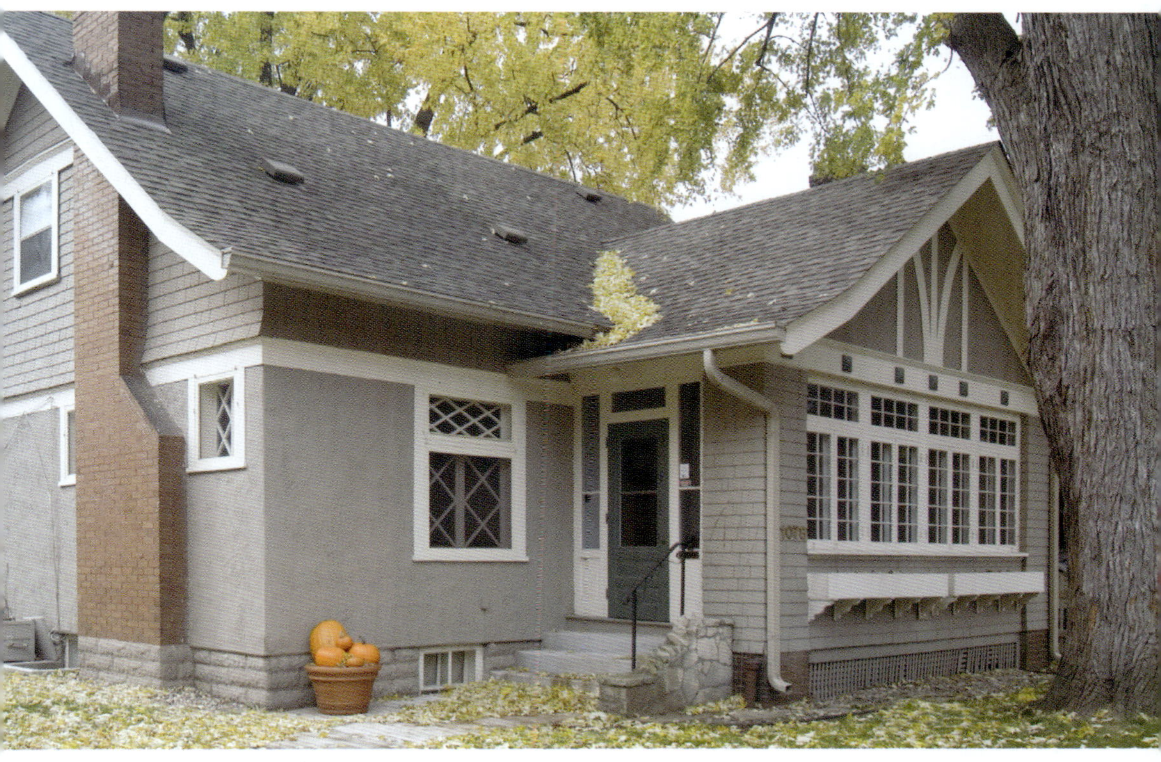

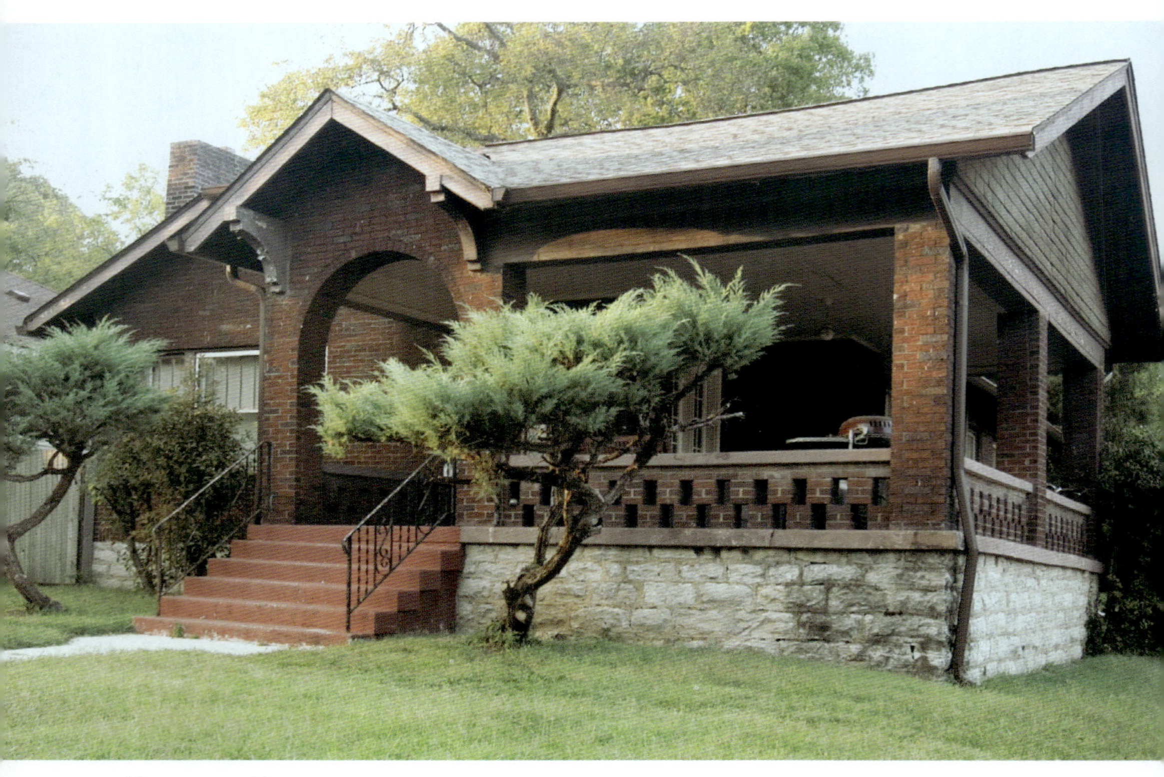

 Nashville, Tennessee

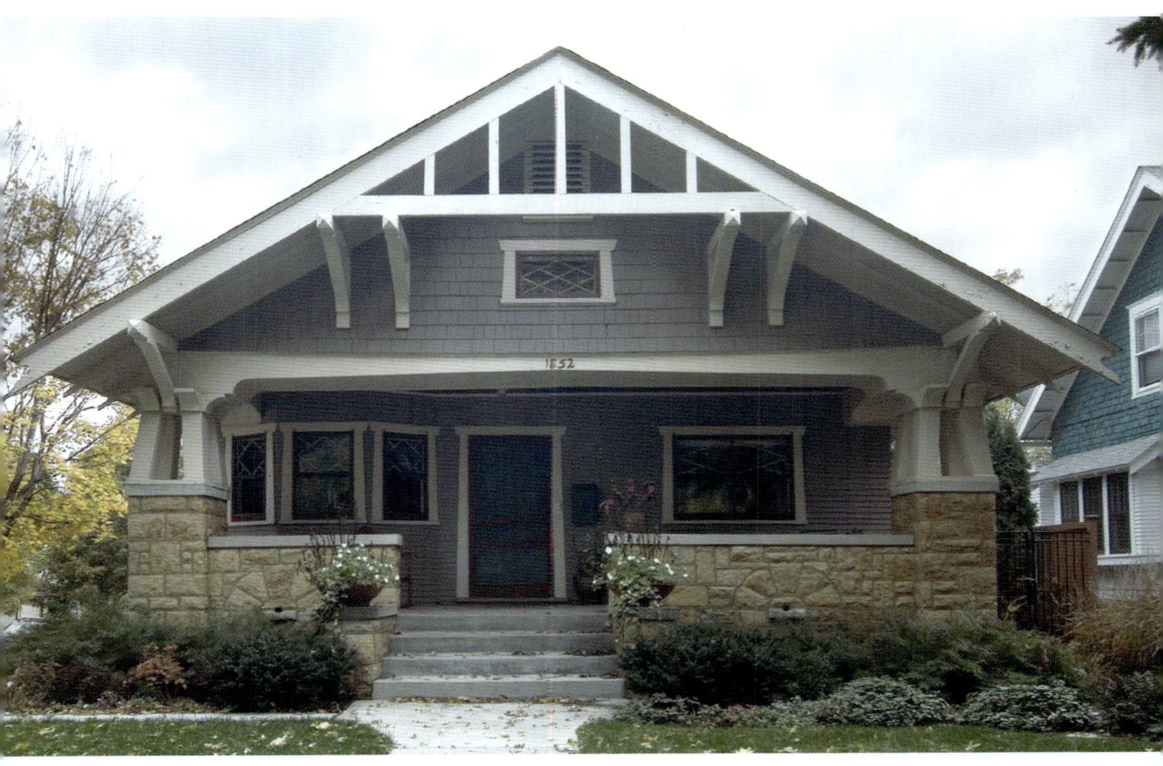
1852

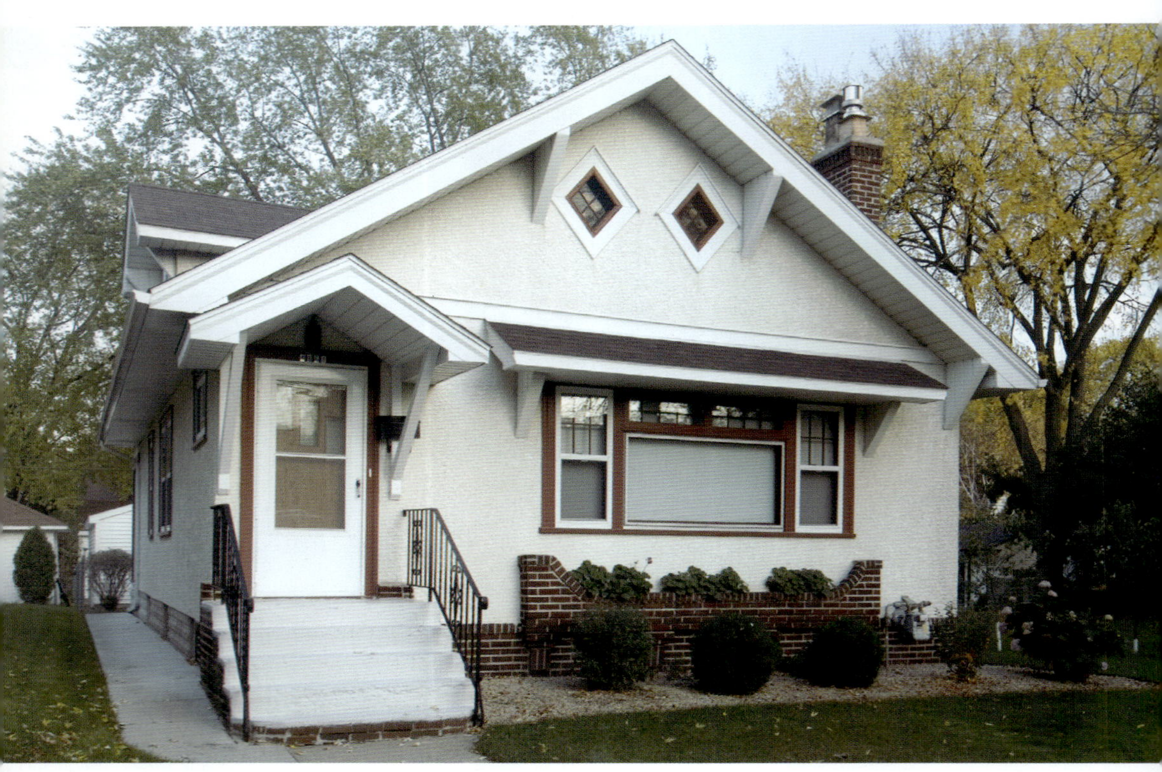

 Minneapolis, Minnesota

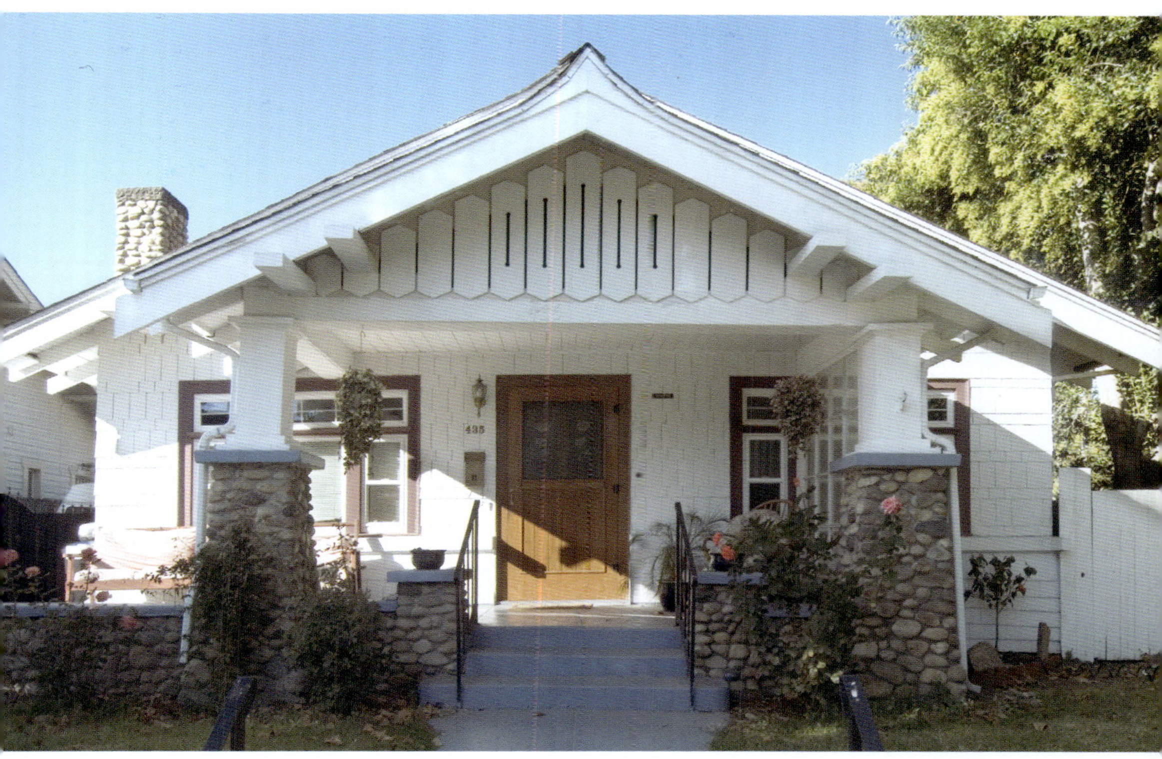


ORIENTAL BUNGALOW | SAN JOSE, CALIFORNIA 

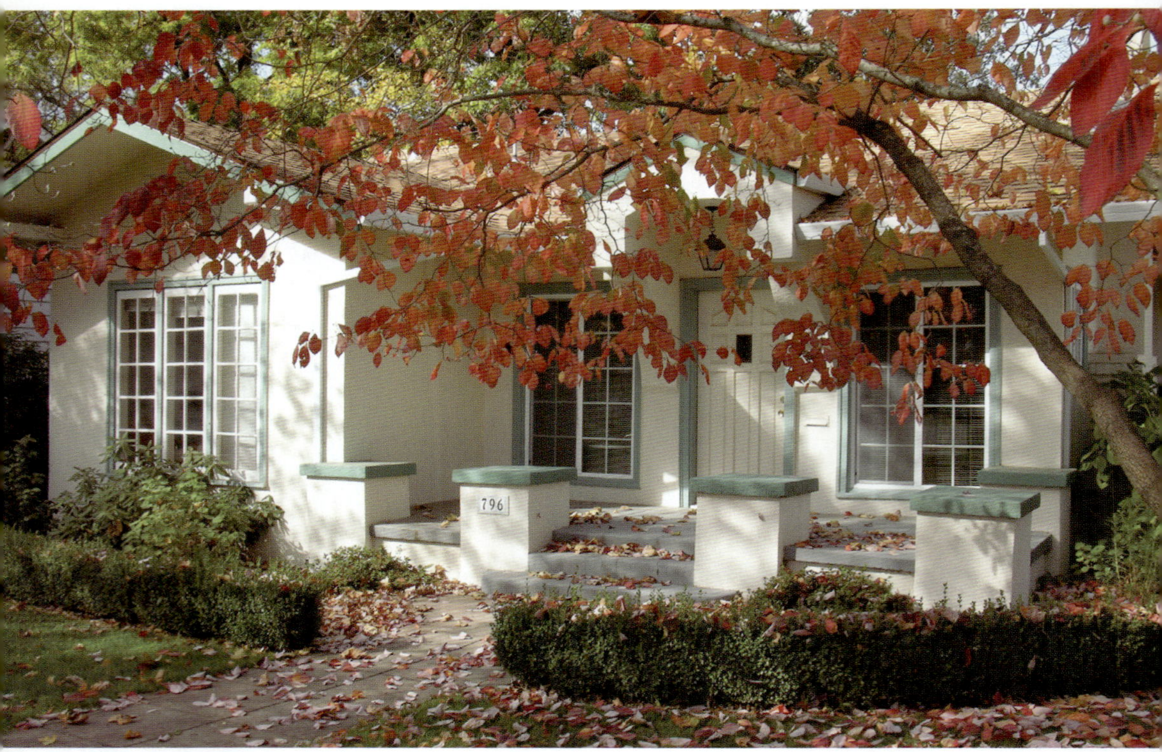

796

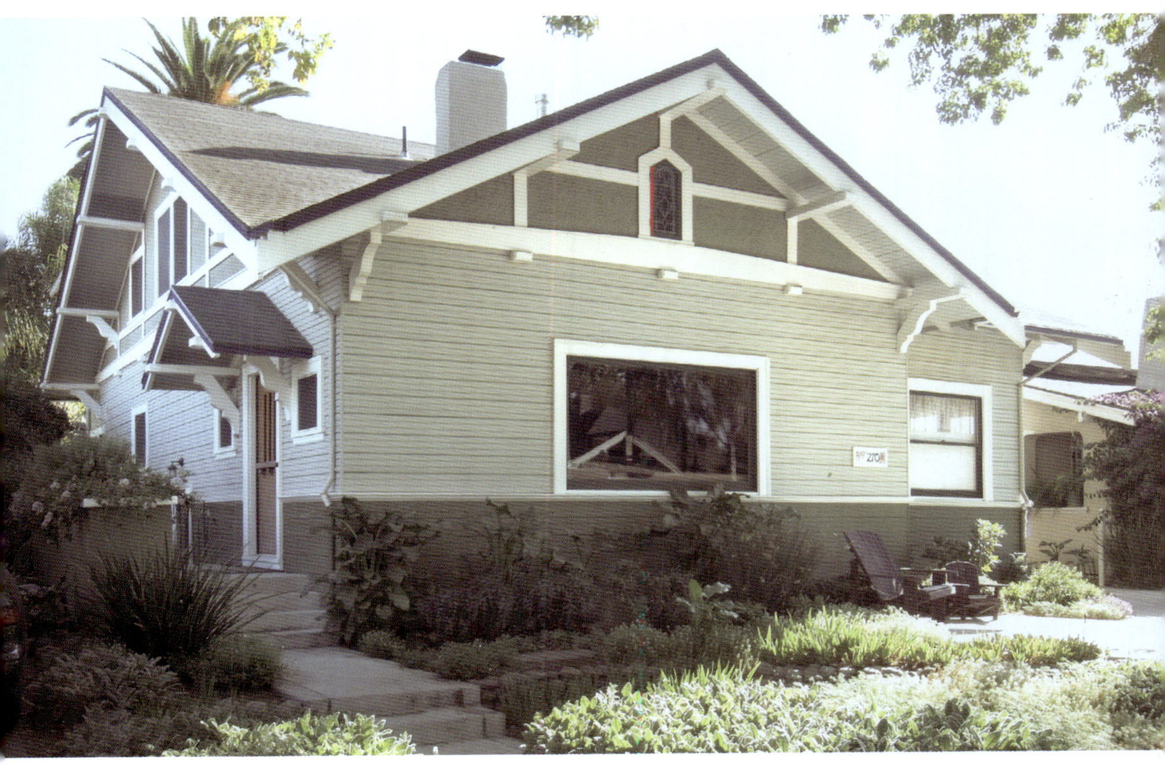


San Jose, California

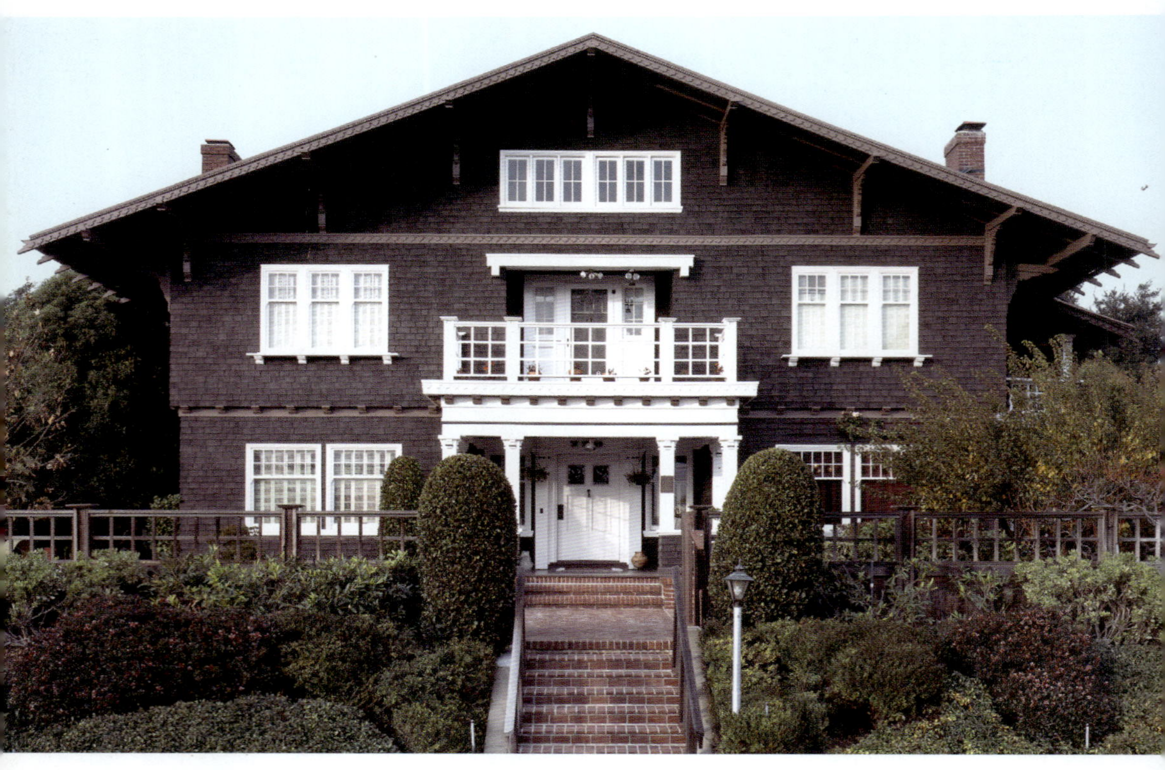

 CHALET BUNGALOW | VALLEJO, CALIFORNIA

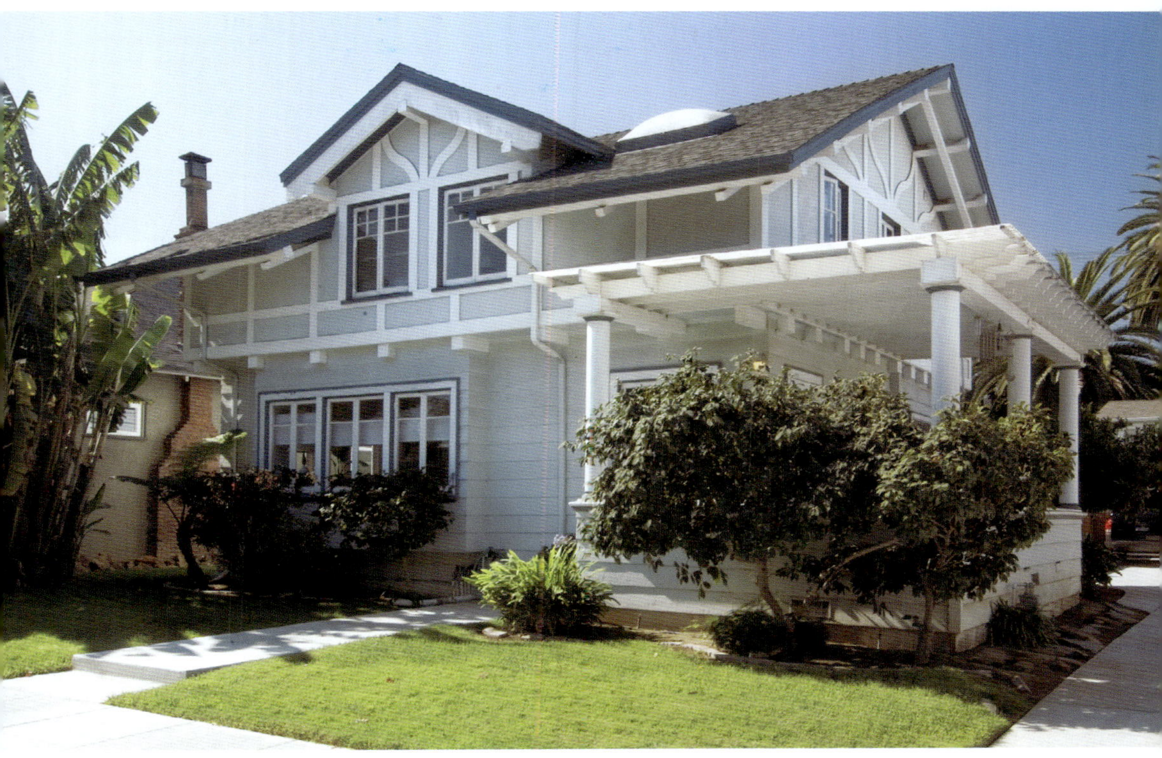

San Jose, California 

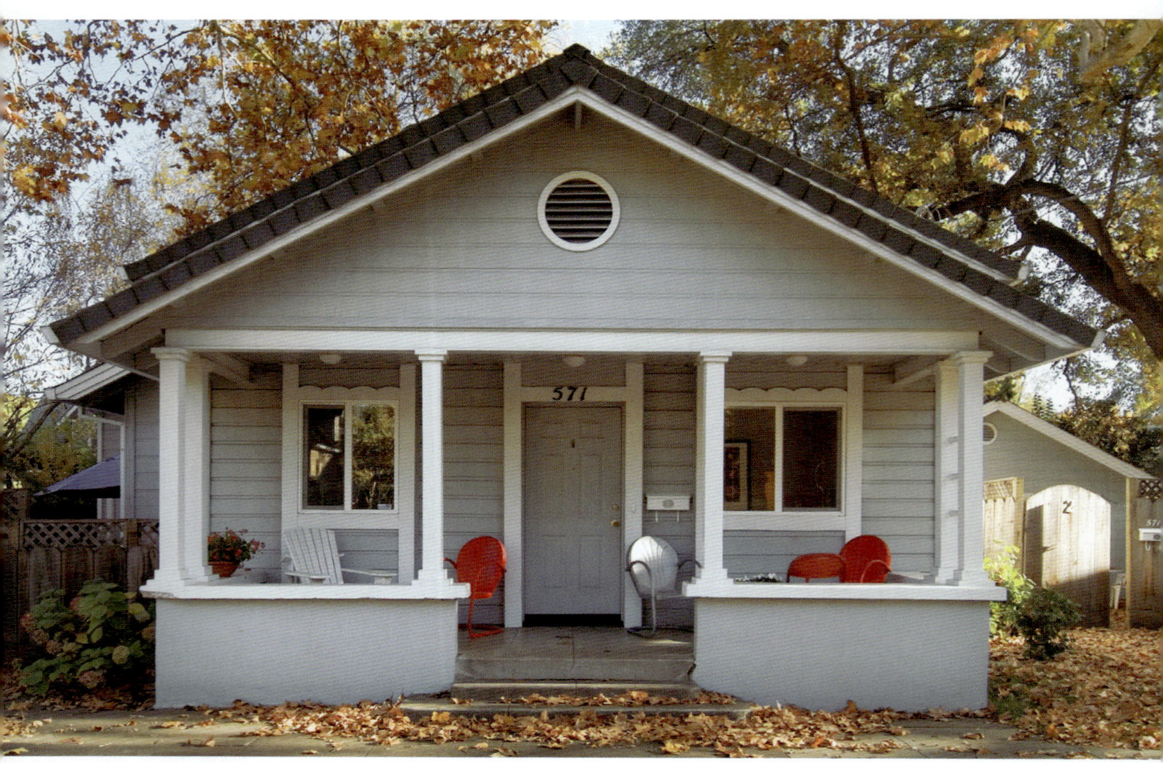


 Chico, California

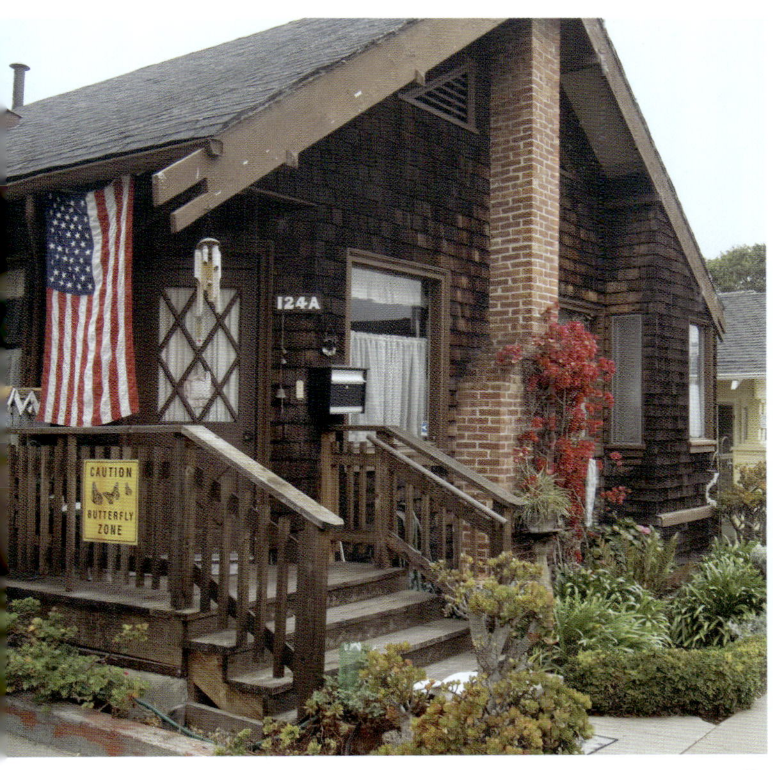


CHALET BUNGALOW | PACIFIC GROVE, CALIFORNIA

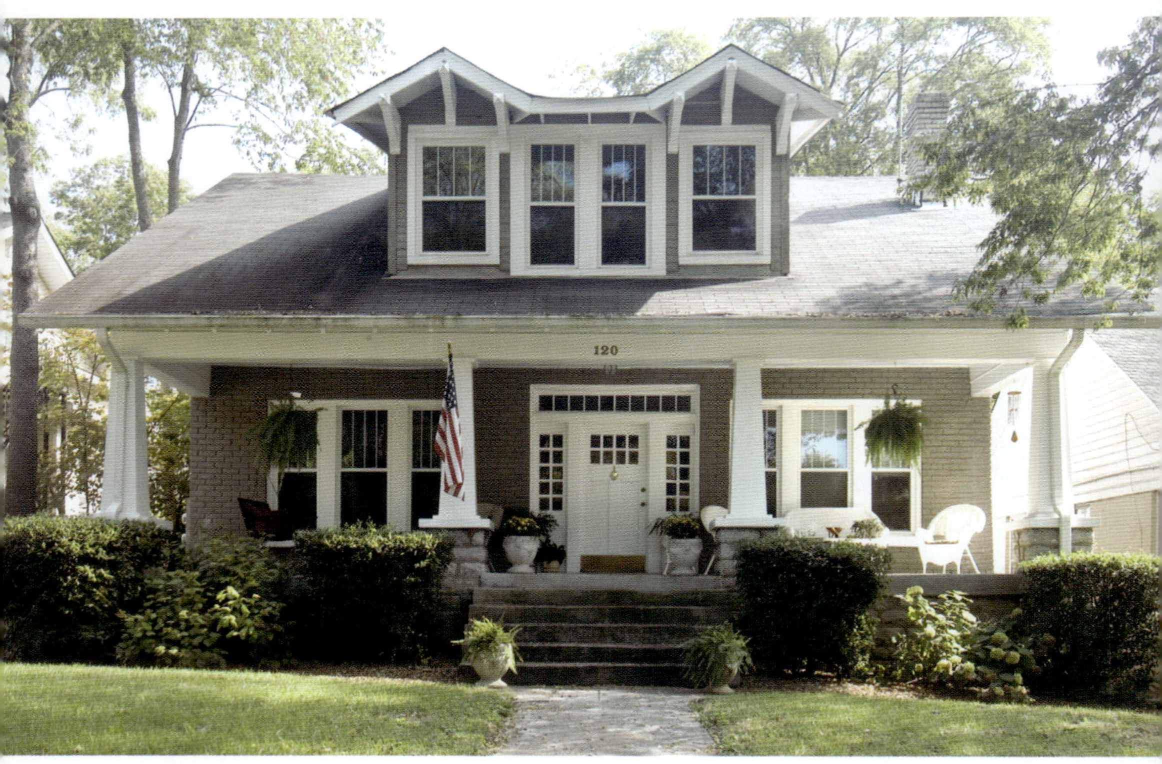


 Nashville, Tennessee

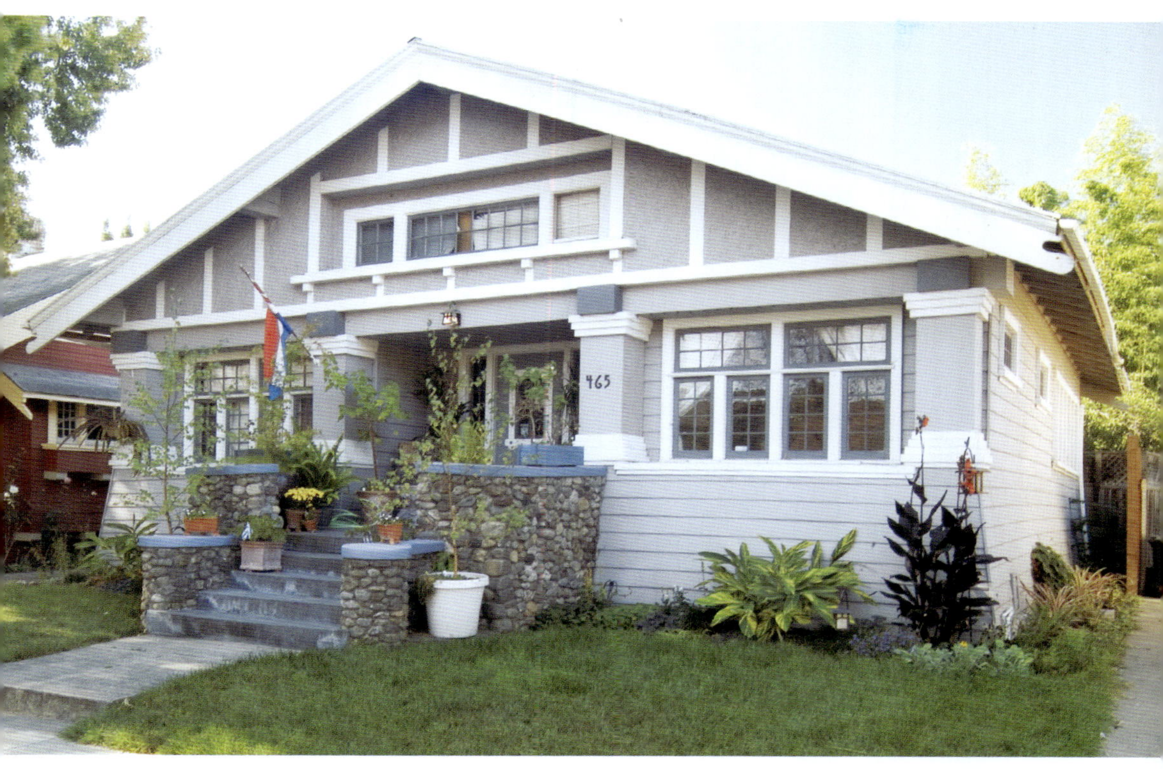


CHALET BUNGALOW | SAN JOSE, CALIFORNIA 

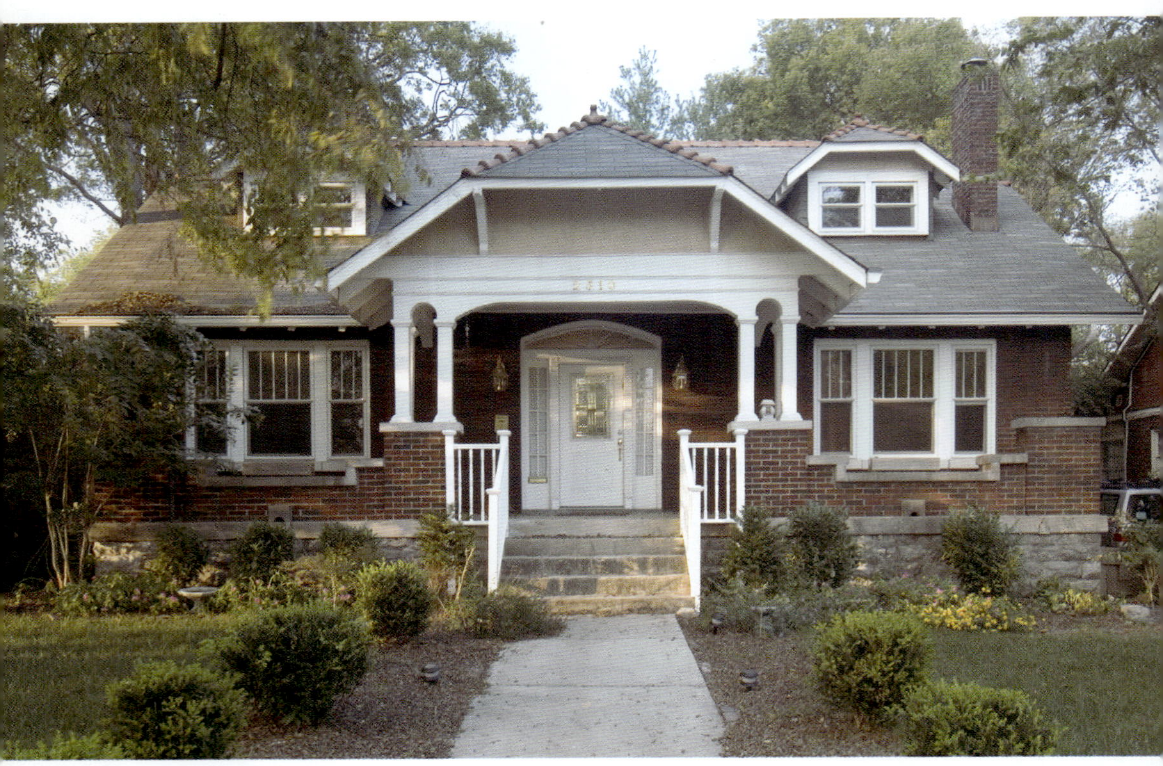

 Nashville, Tennessee

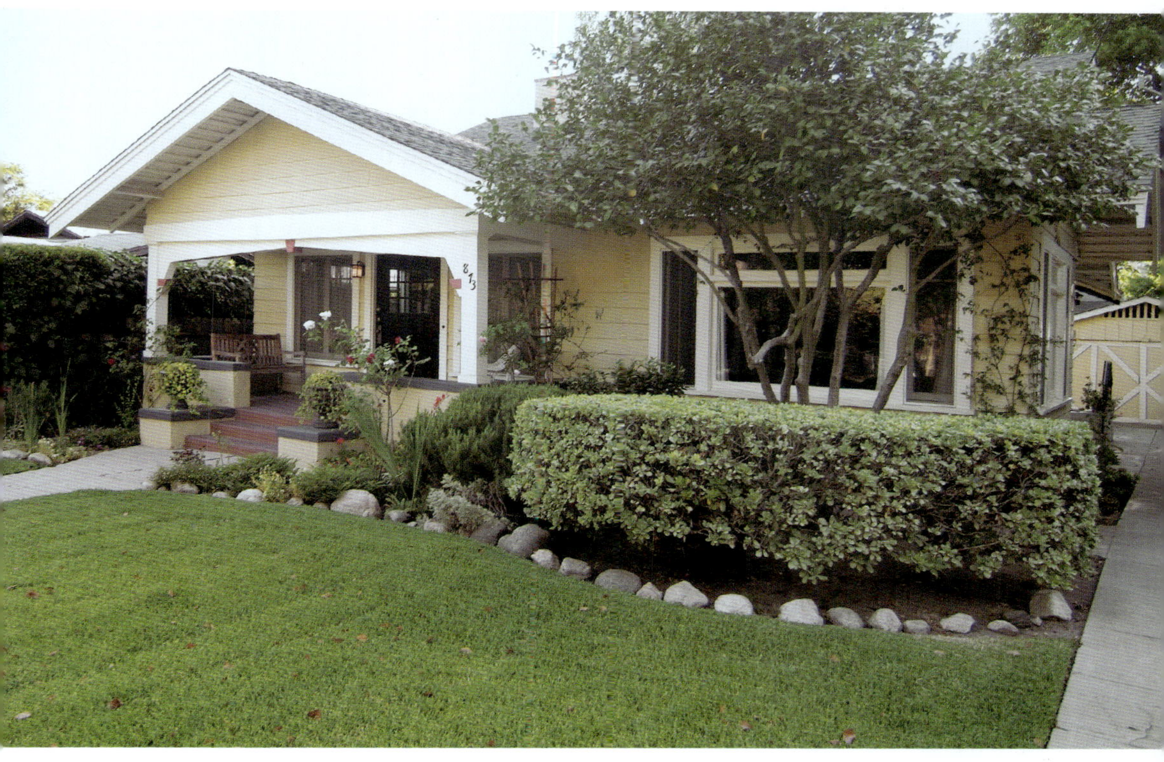

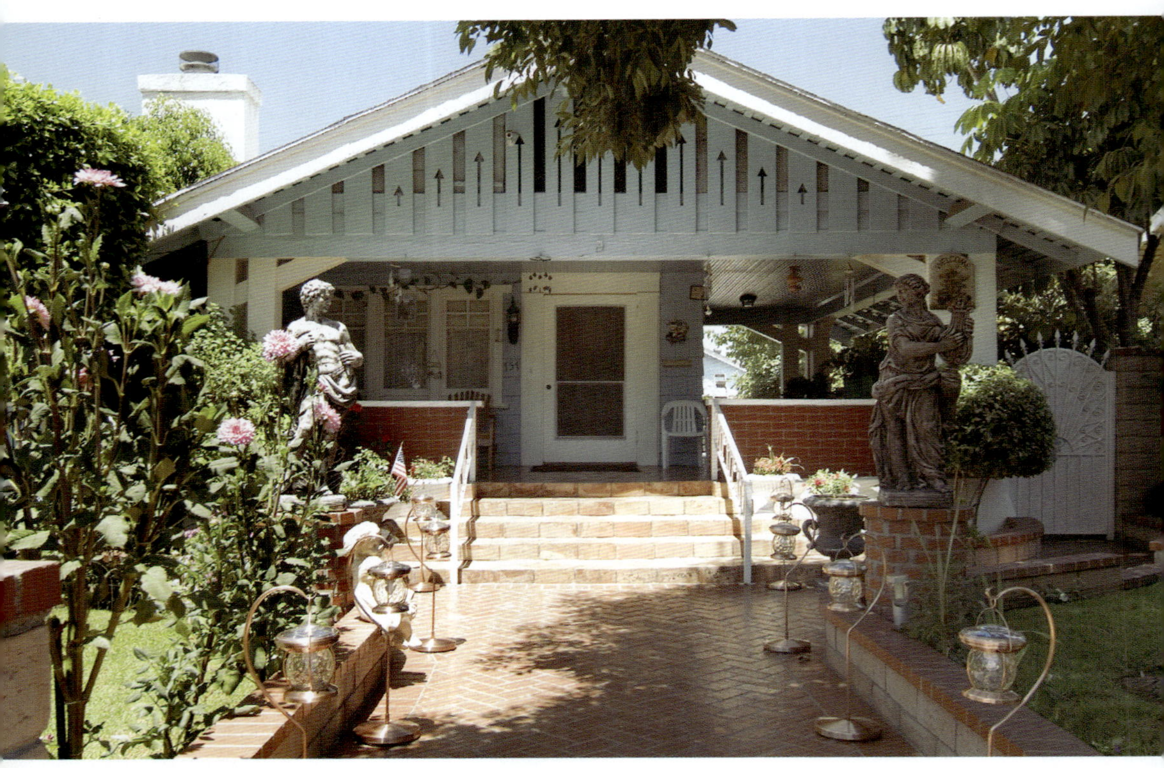

 CHALET BUNGALOW | SAN FERNANDO, CALIFORNIA

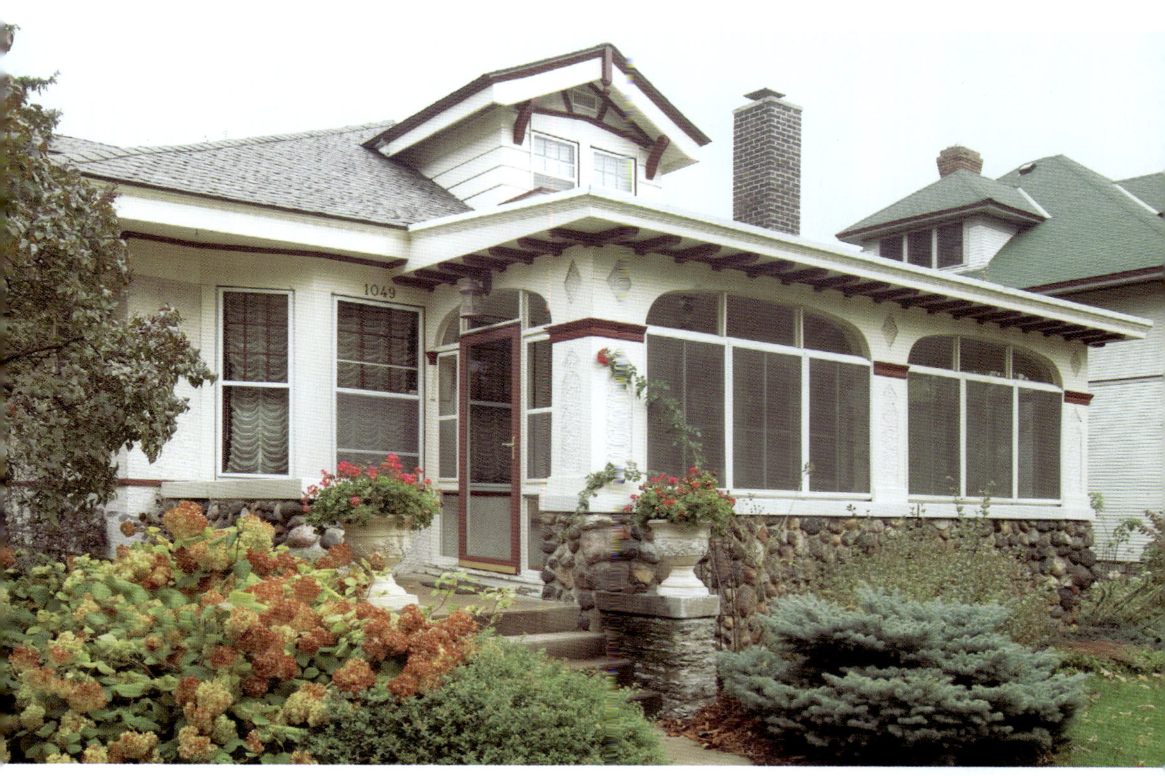
1049

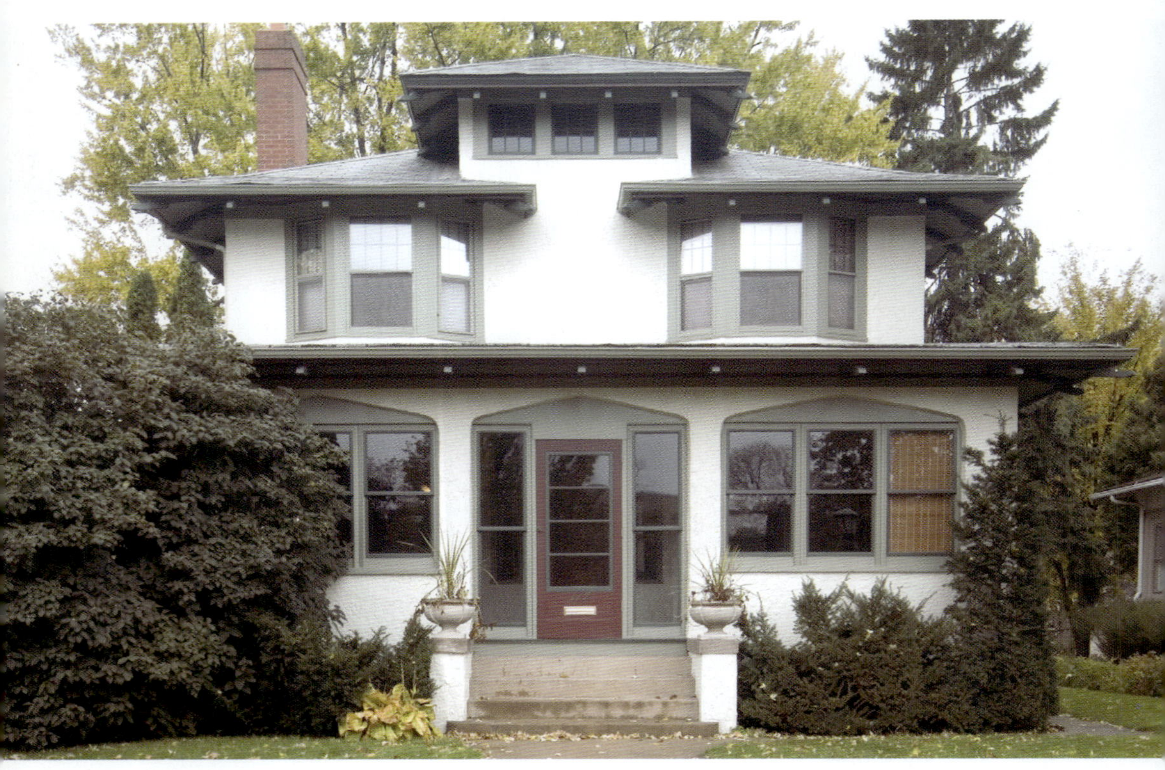

448 St. Paul, Minnesota

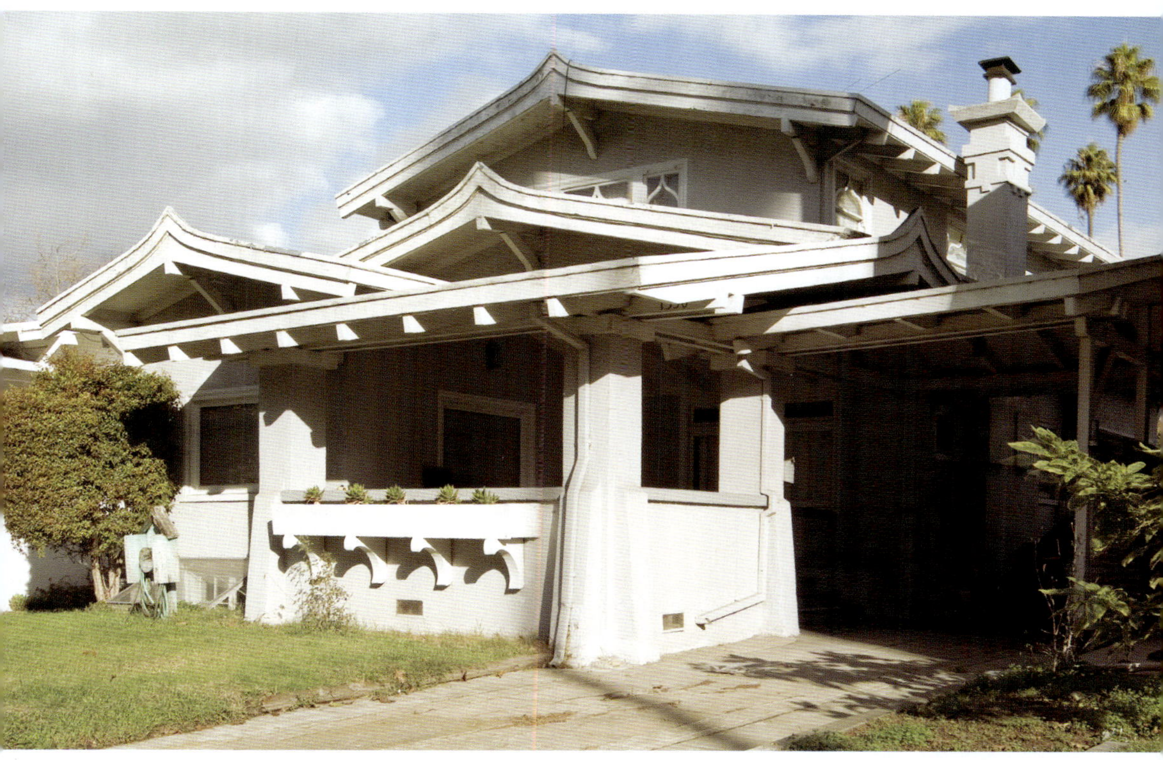

ORIENTAL BUNGALOW | ALAMEDA, CALIFORNIA

BUNGALOW BAZAAR

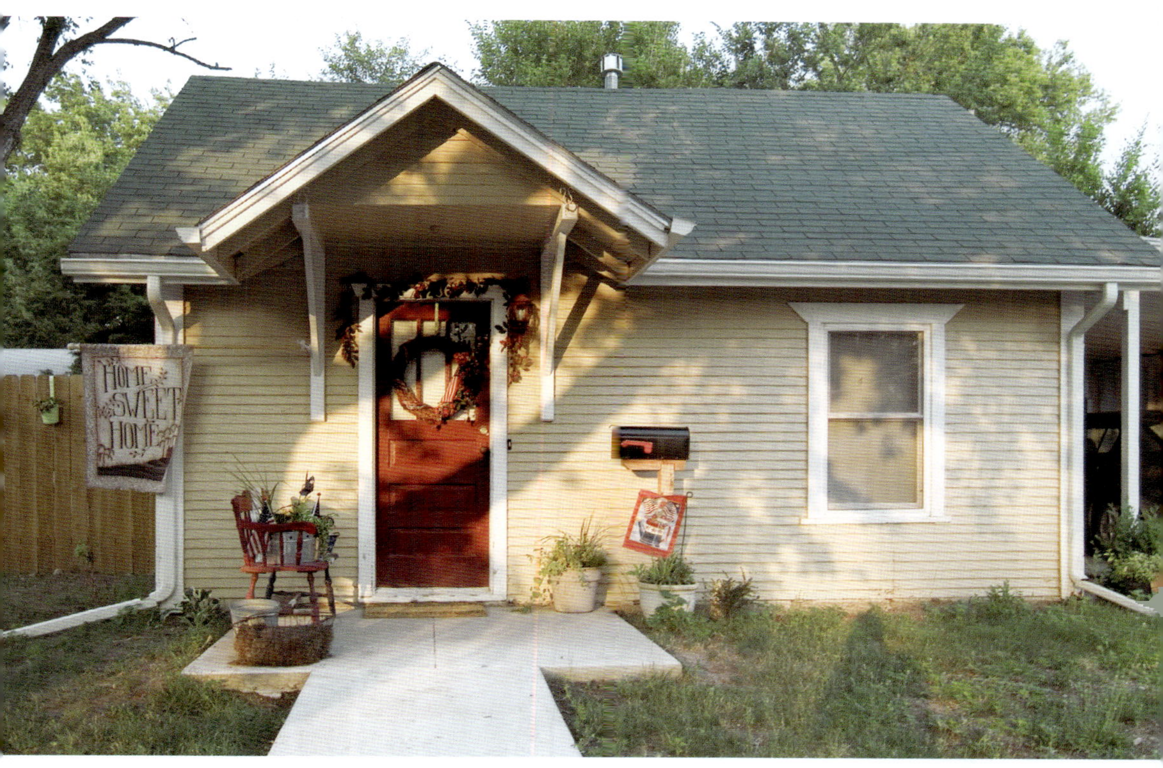
HOME
SWEET
HOME

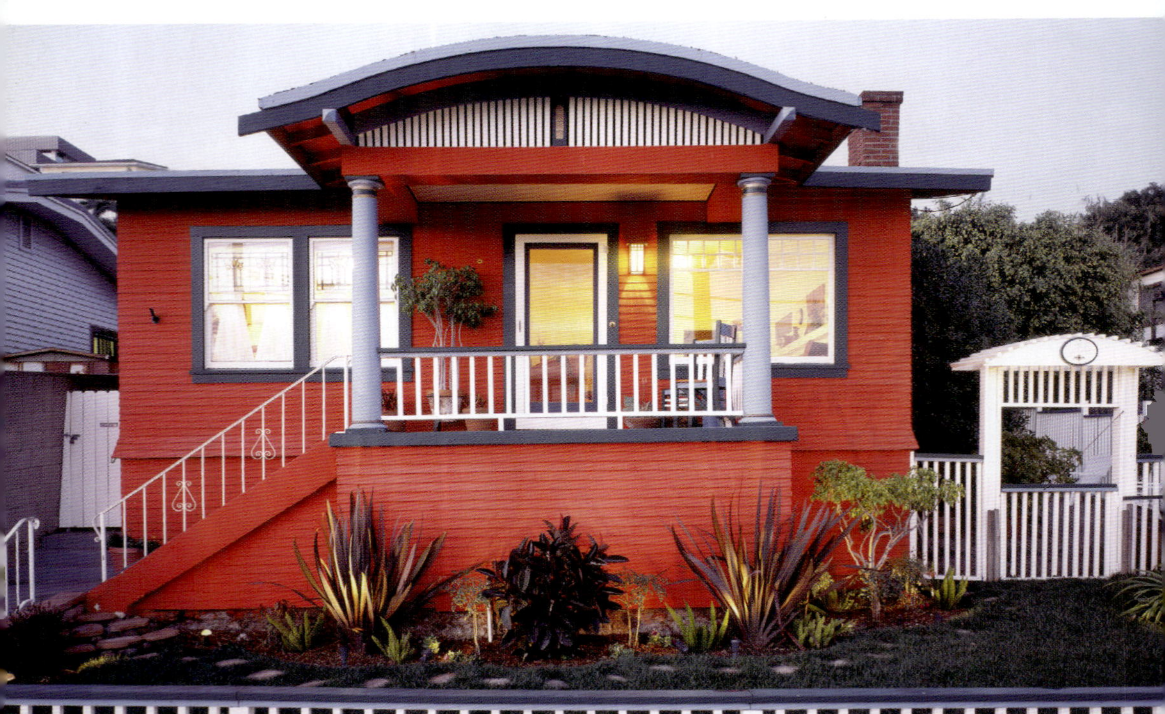

 San Diego, California

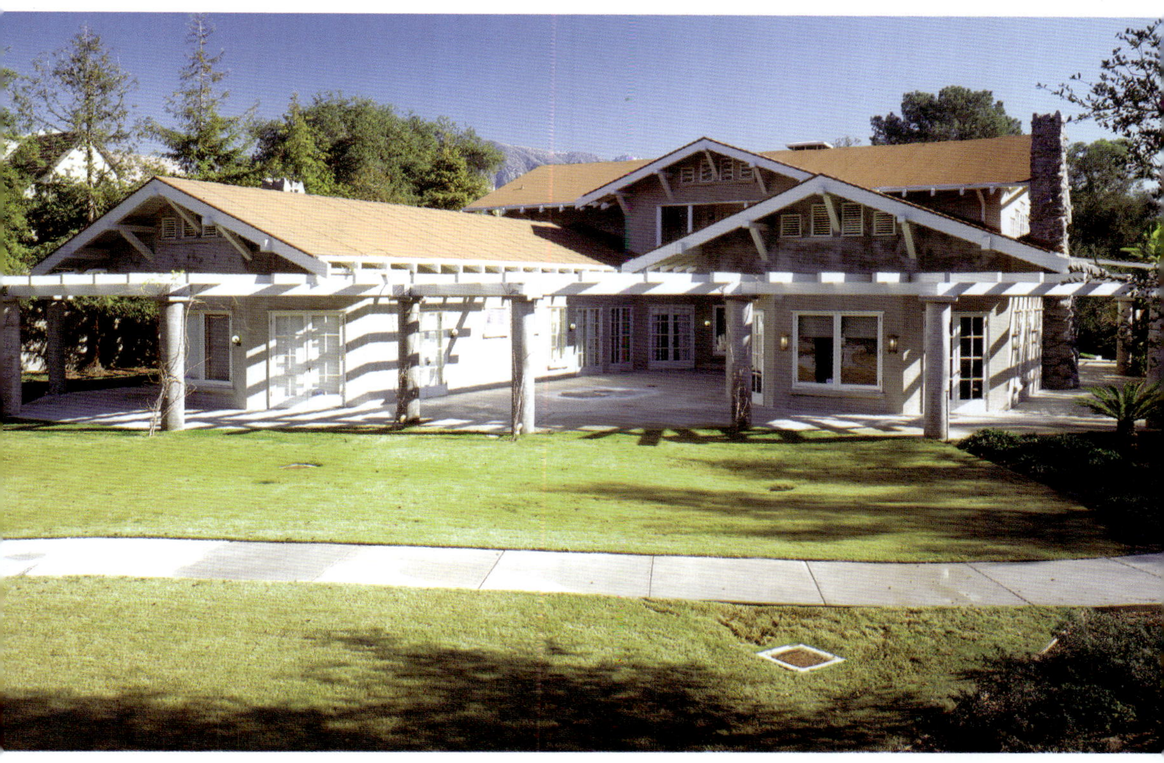

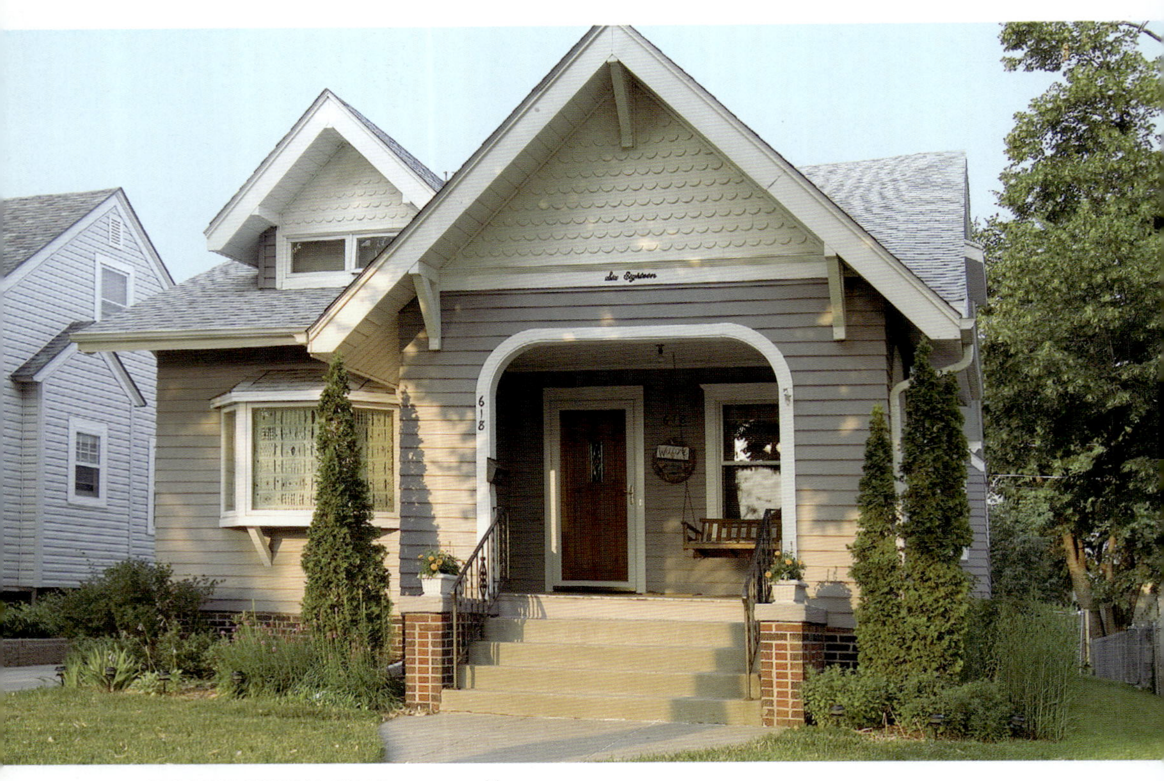


 VICTORIAN BUNGALOW | LINCOLN, NEBRASKA

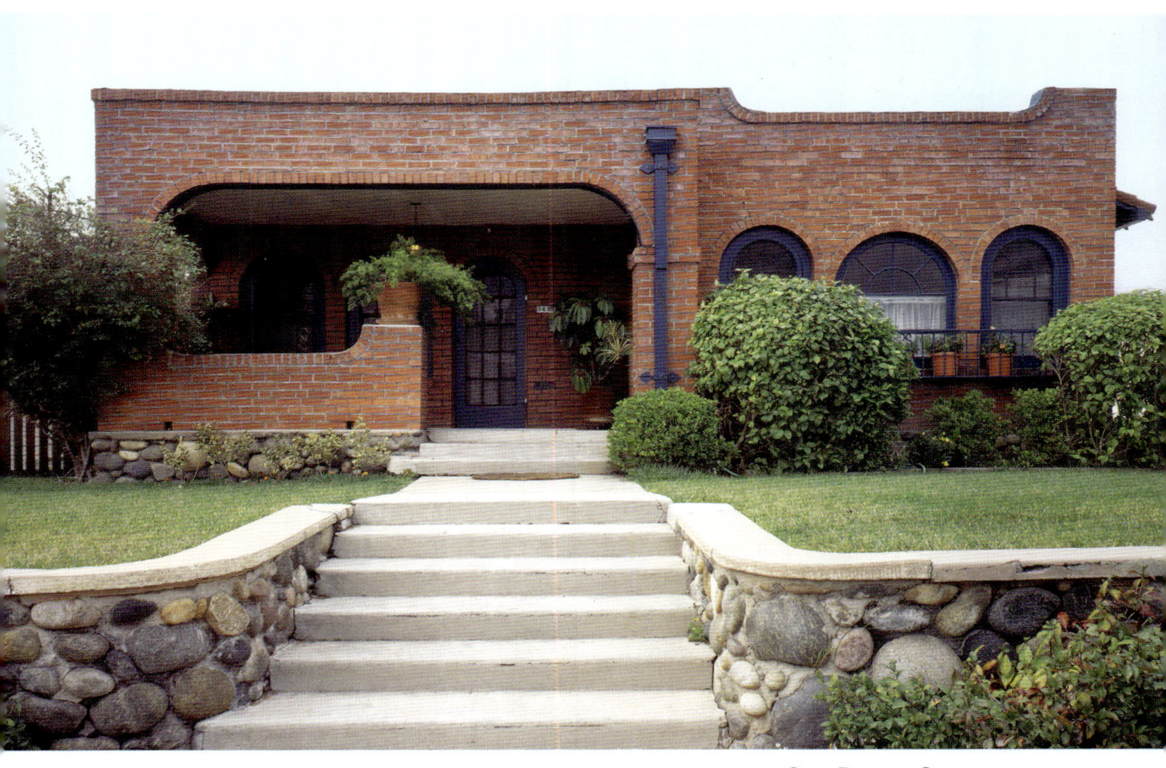

San Diego, California 

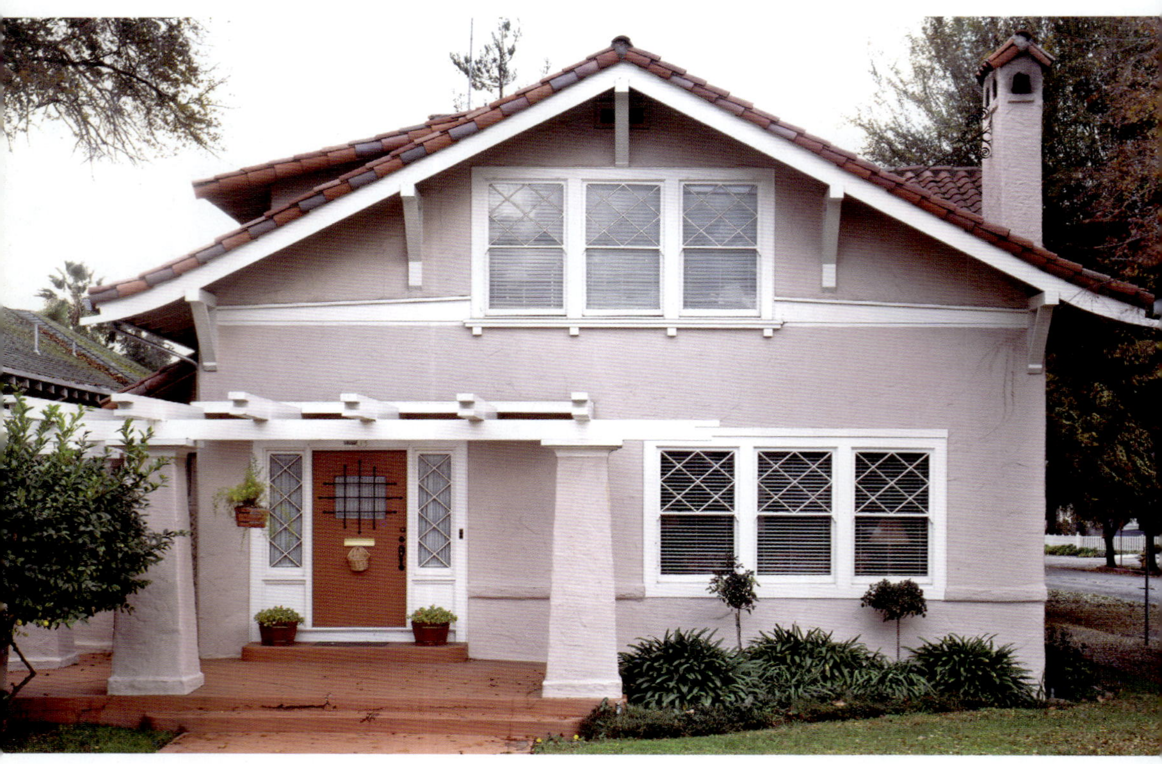

 San Jose, California

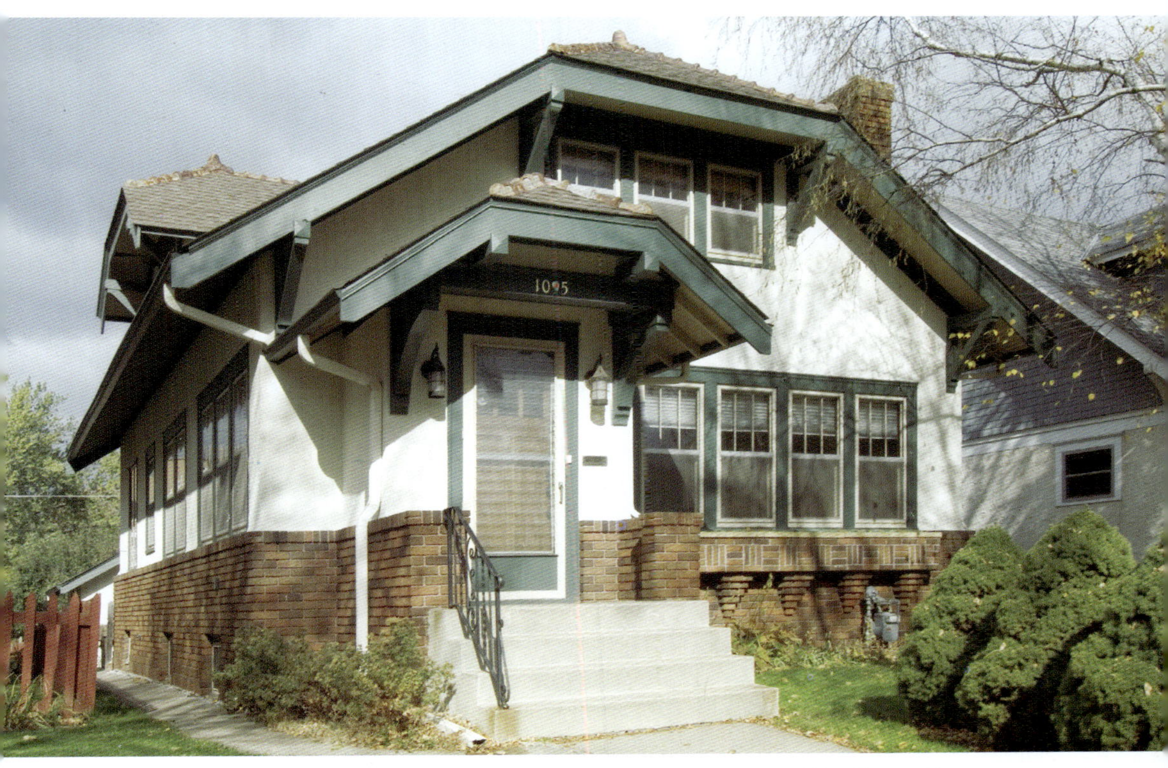


ENGLISH-STYLE BUNGALOW | ST. PAUL, MINNESOTA

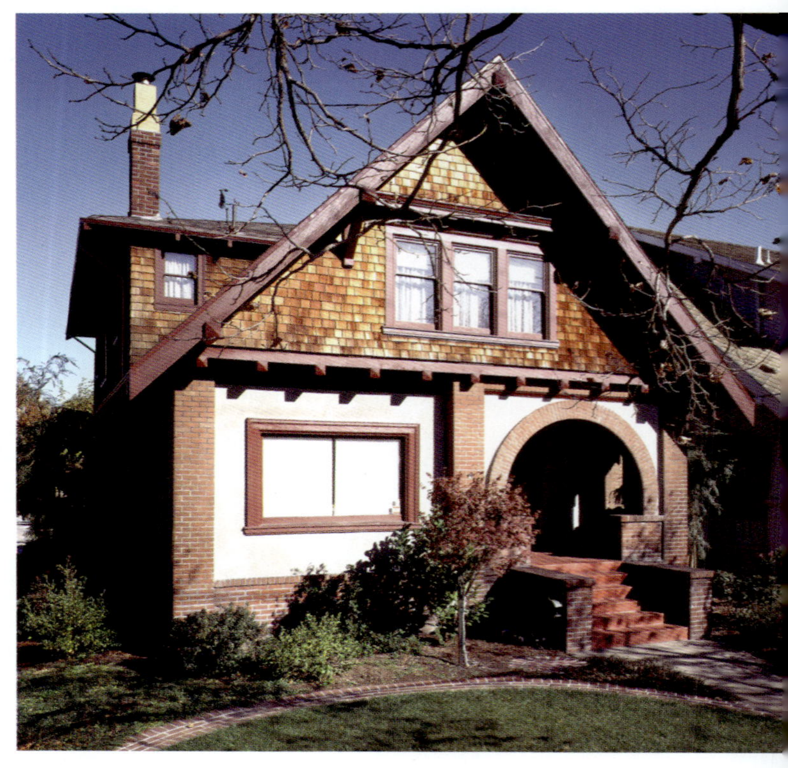

 ARTS AND CRAFTS BUNGALOW | ALAMEDA, CALIFORNIA

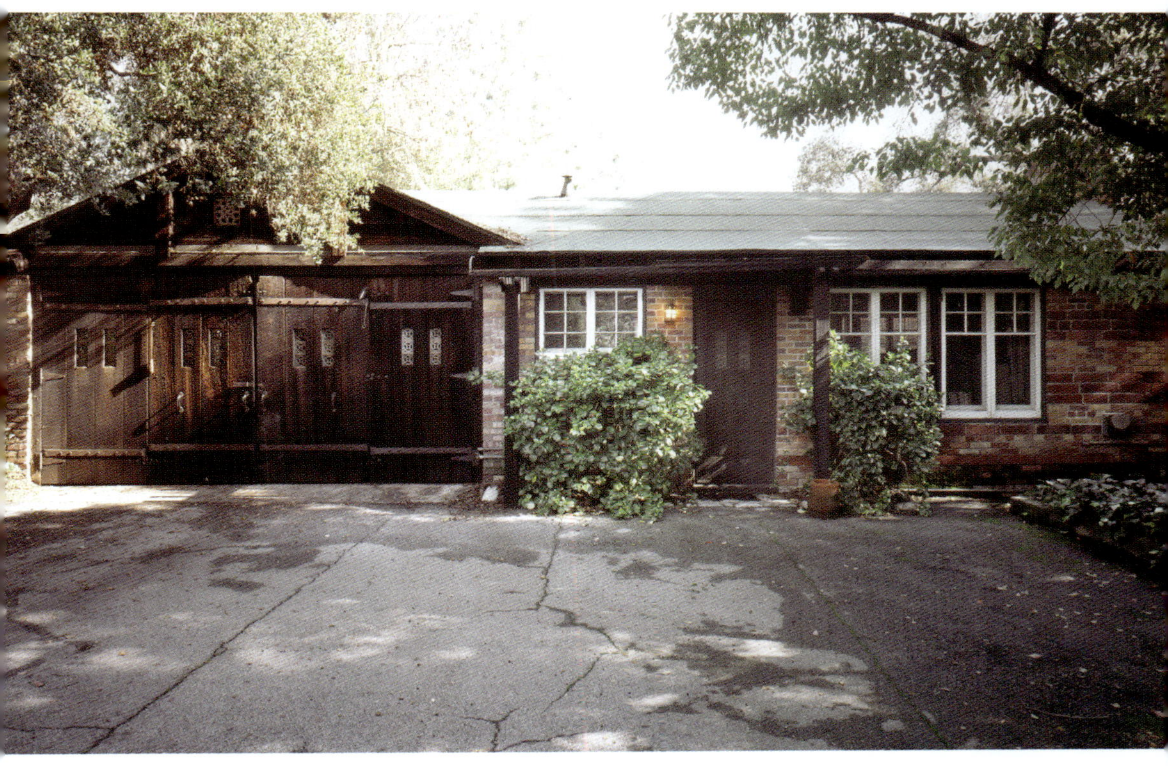

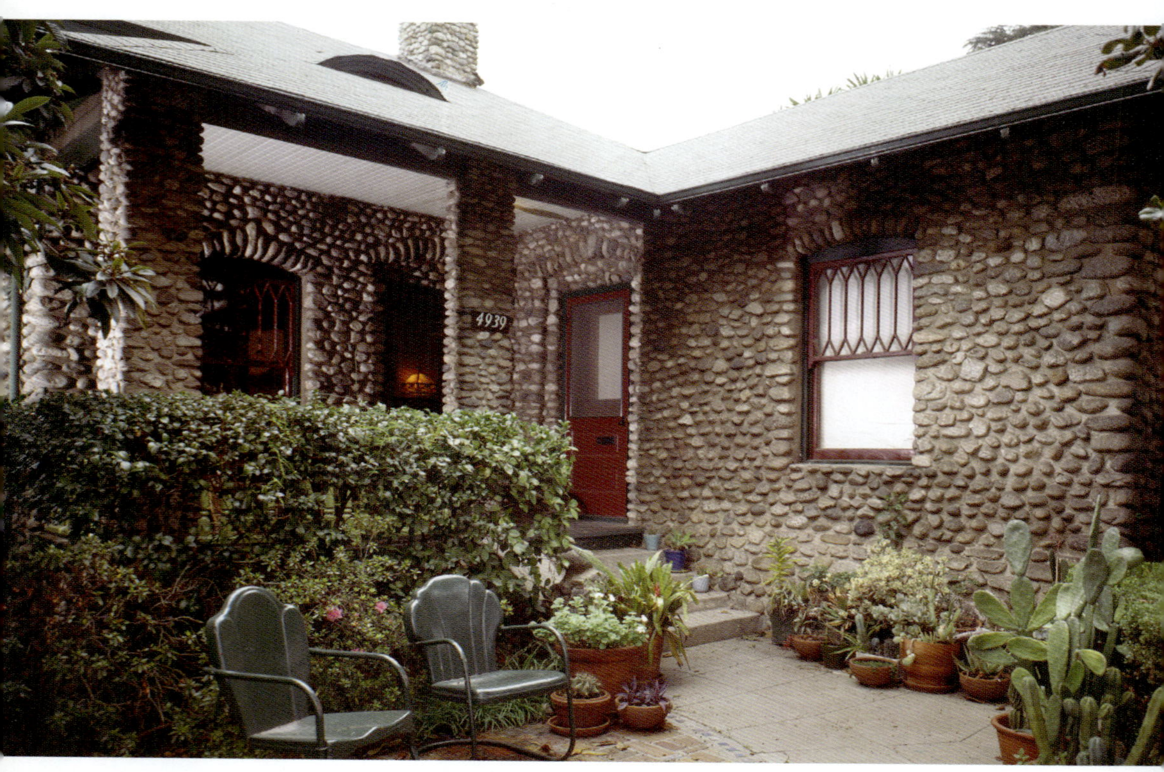


 Los Angeles, California

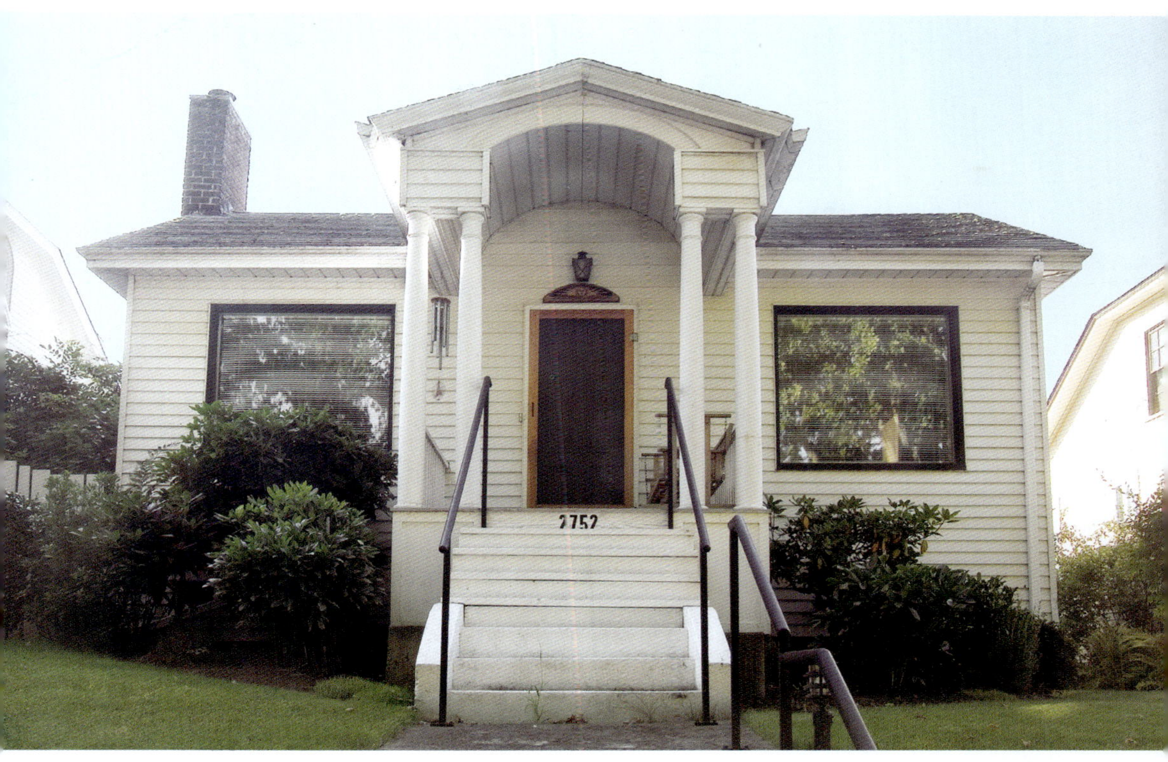


ENGLISH-STYLE BUNGALOW | BELLINGHAM, WASHINGTON

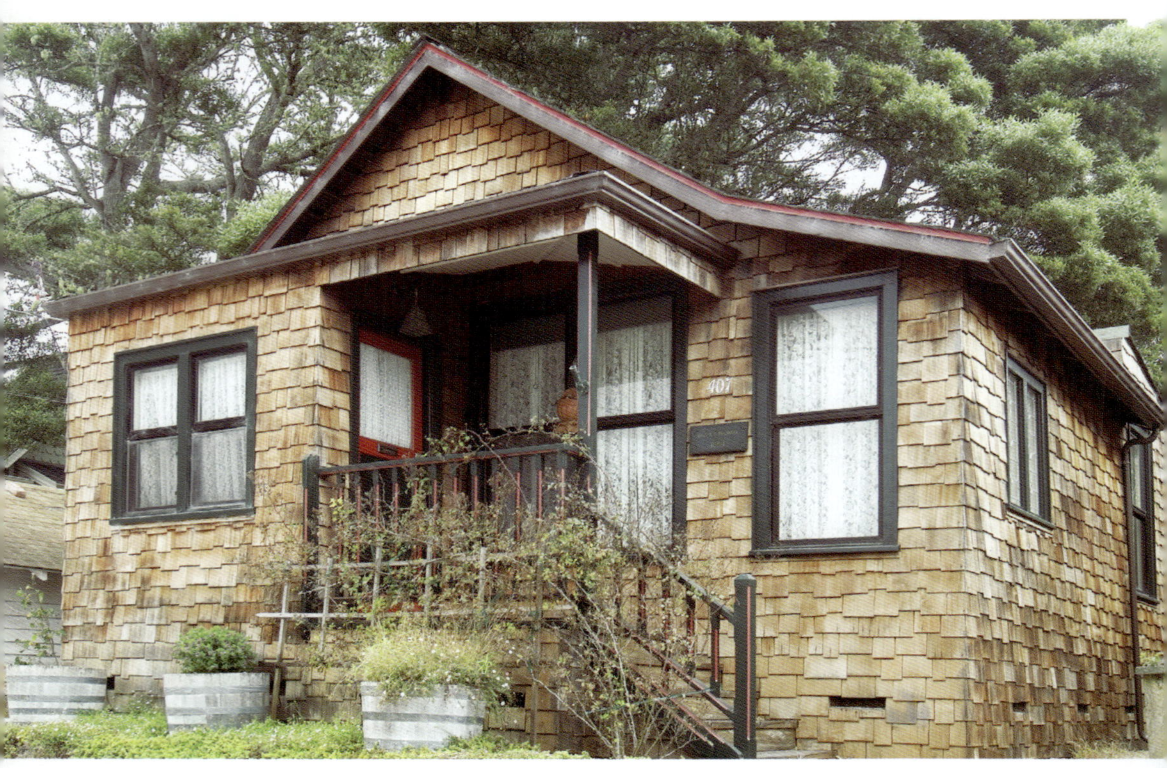


 PACIFIC GROVE, CALIFORNIA

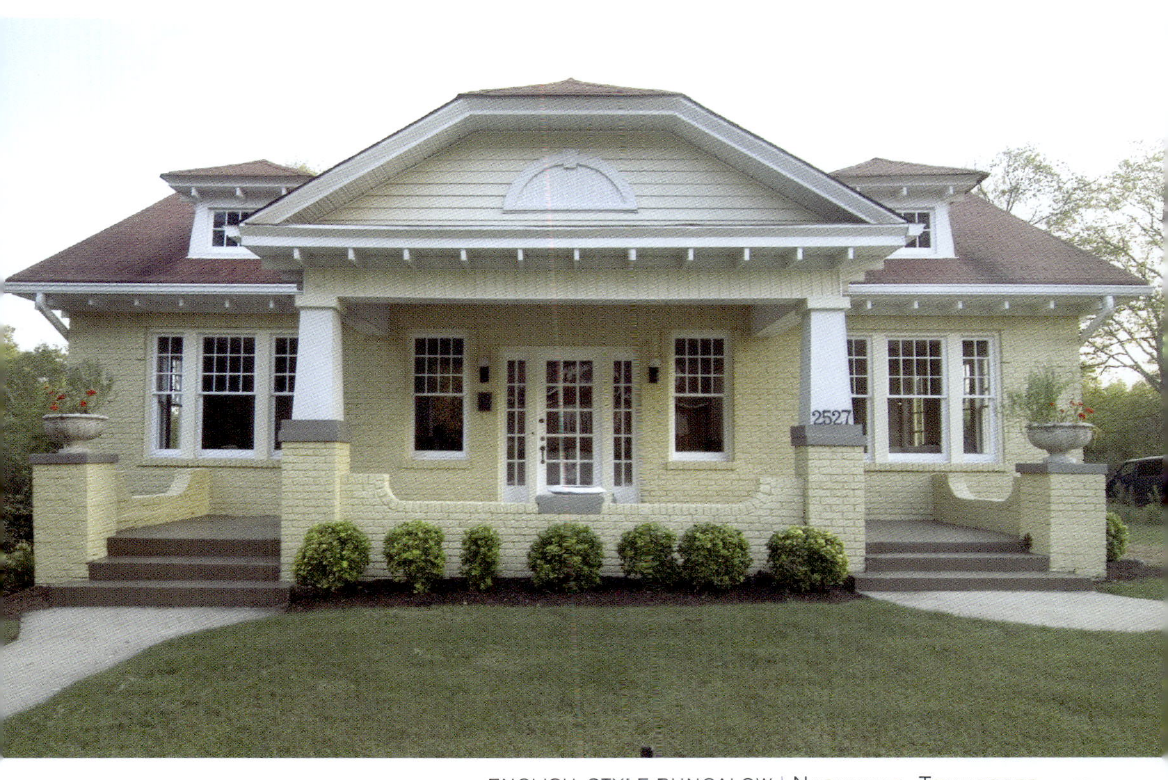
2527

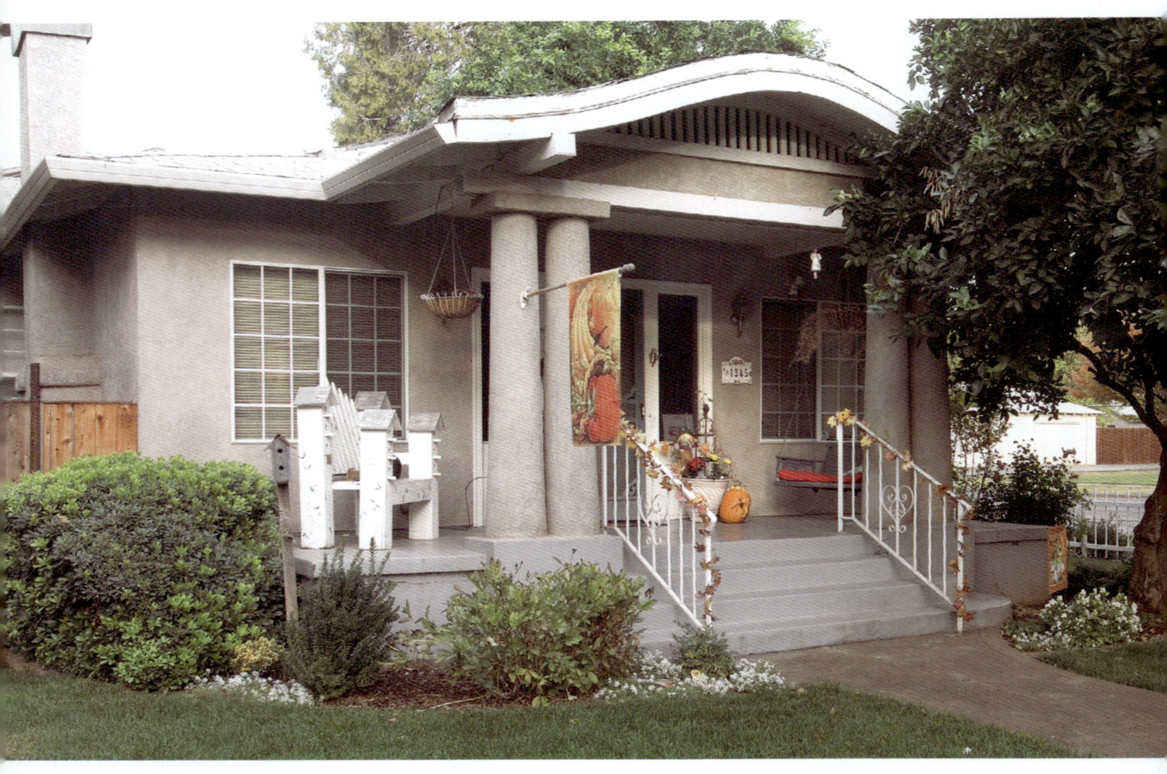

 Chico, California

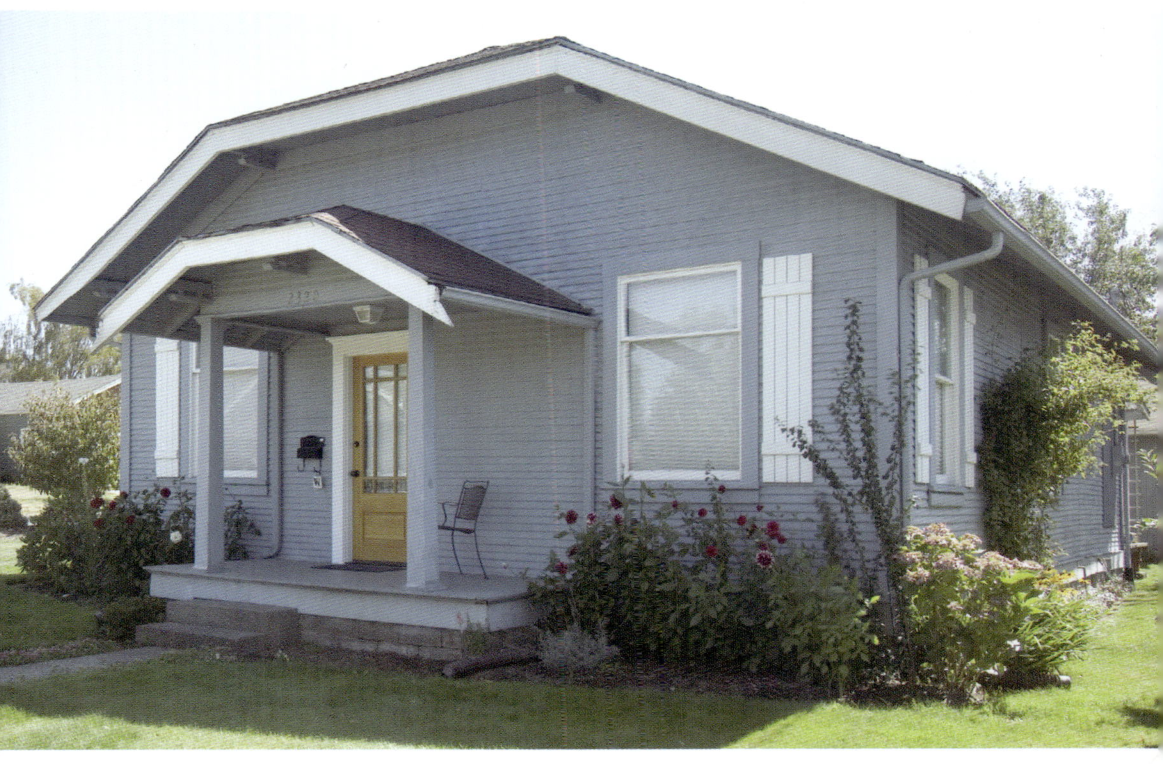

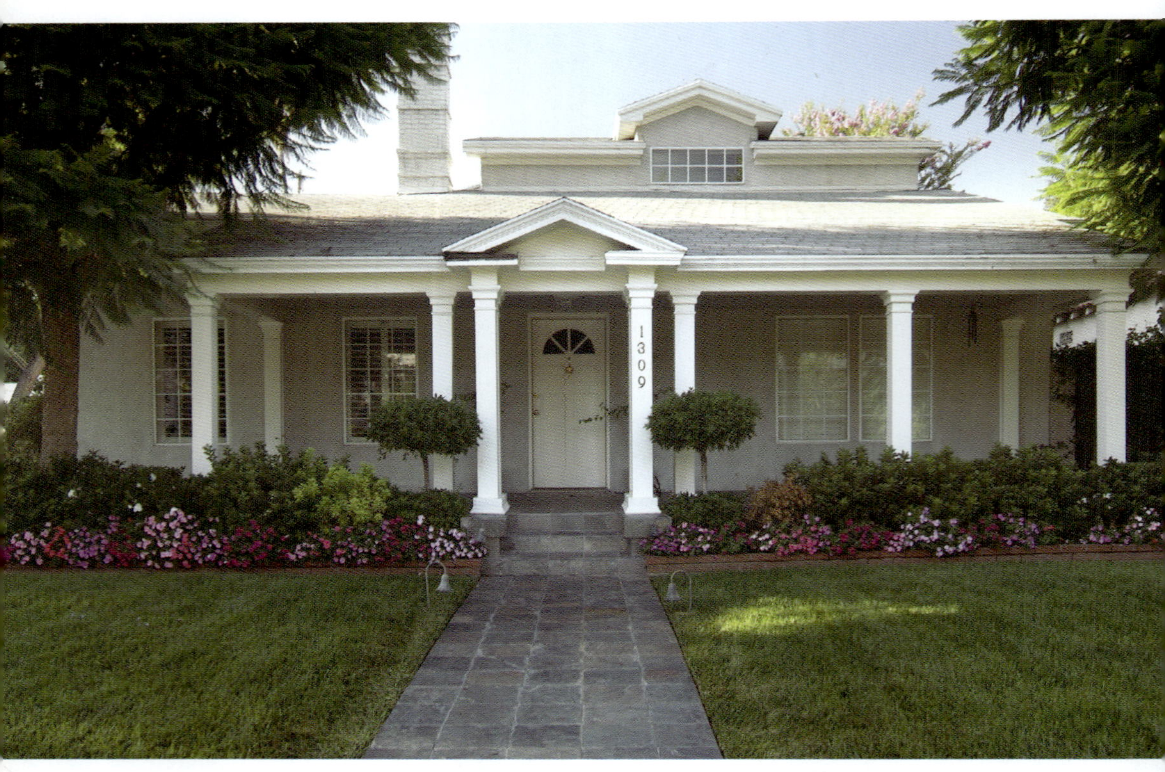


 CLASSICAL REVIVAL BUNGALOW | SANTA MONICA, CALIFORNIA

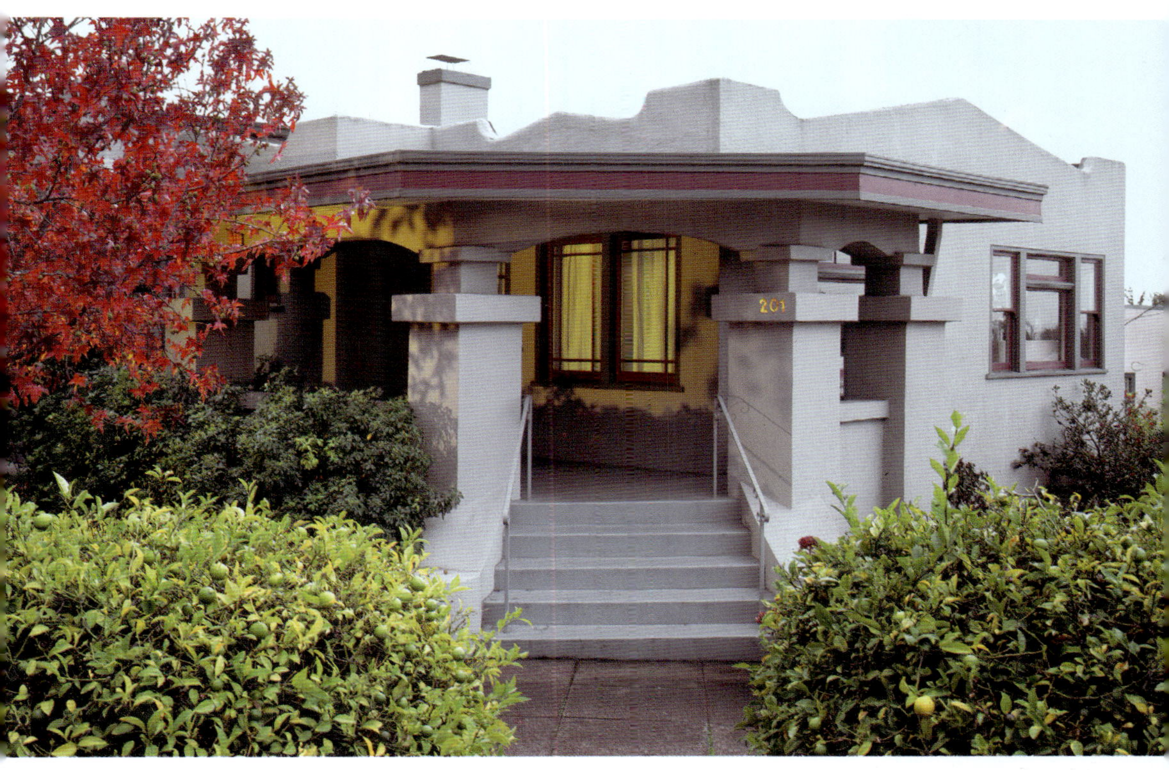


Piedmont, California

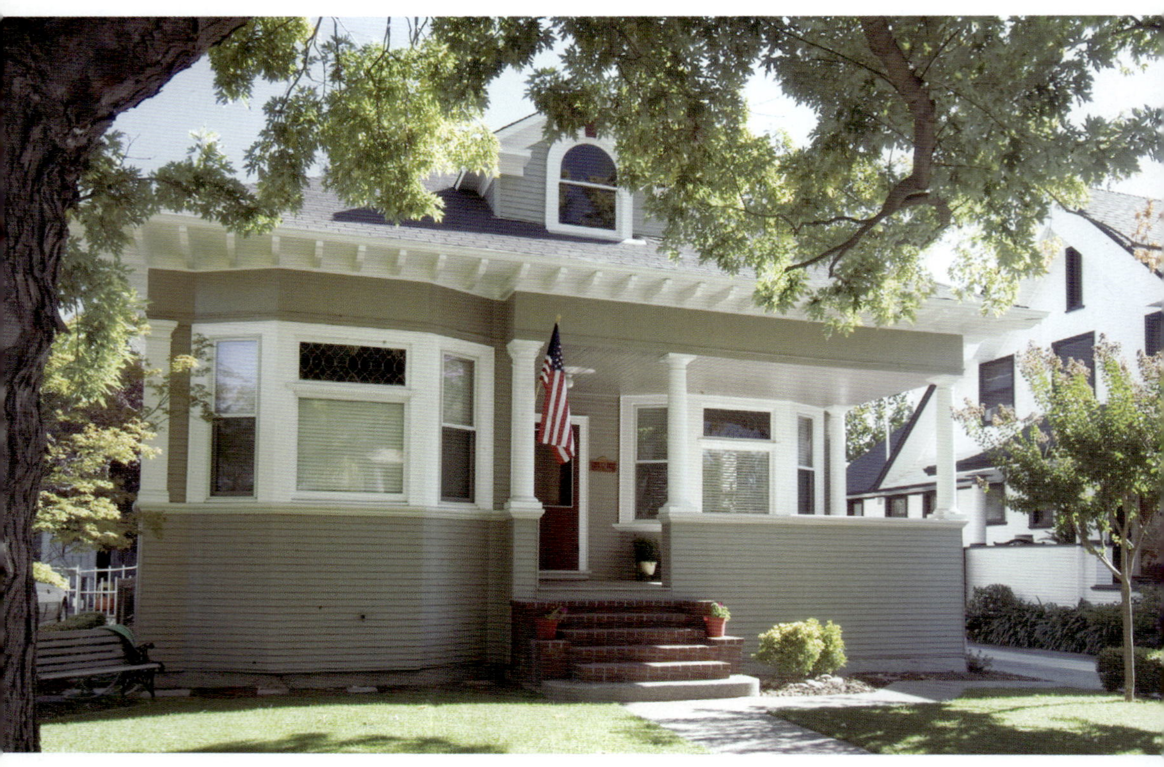

 COLONIAL REVIVAL BUNGALOW | SAN JOSE, CALIFORNIA

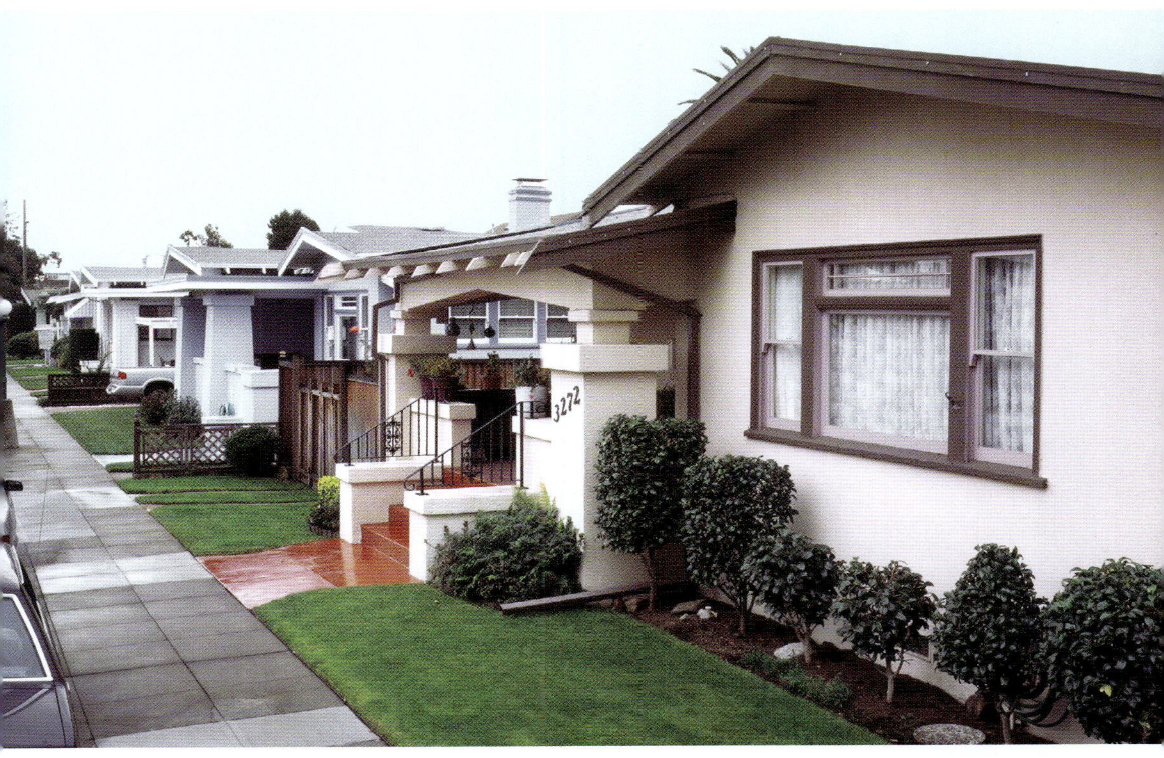


Alameda, California 

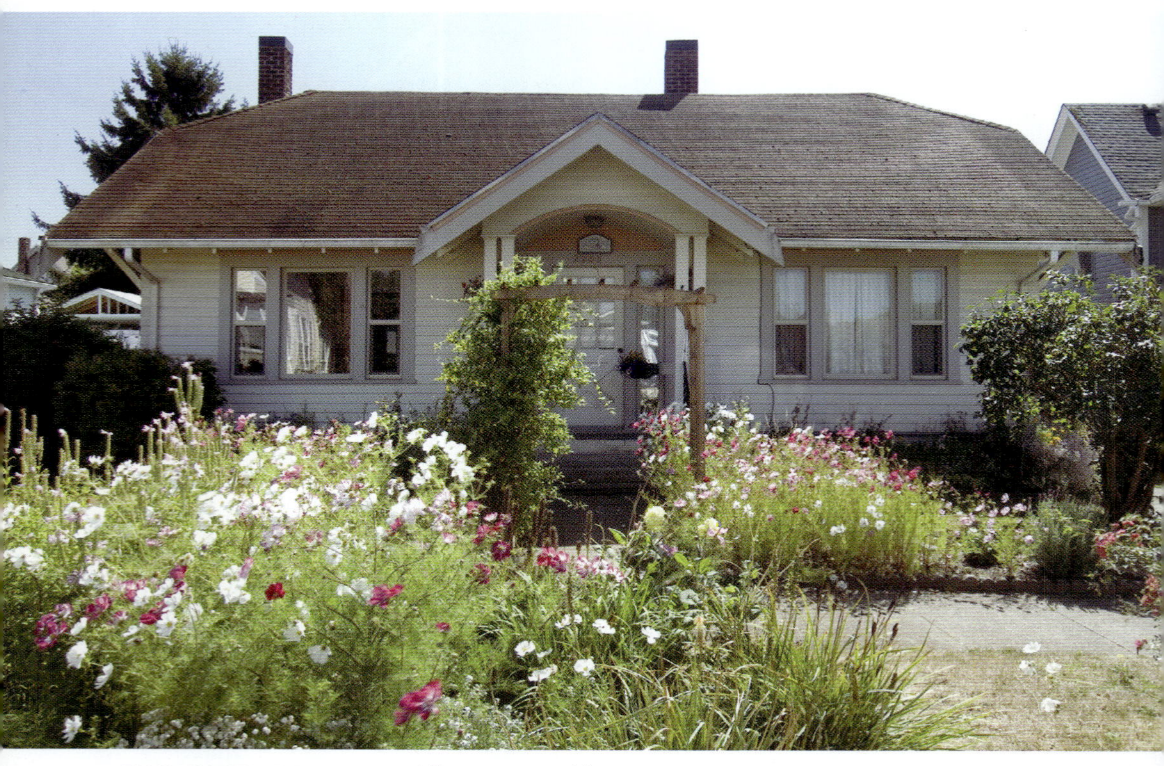

 ENGLISH-STYLE BUNGALOW | BELLINGHAM, WASHINGTON

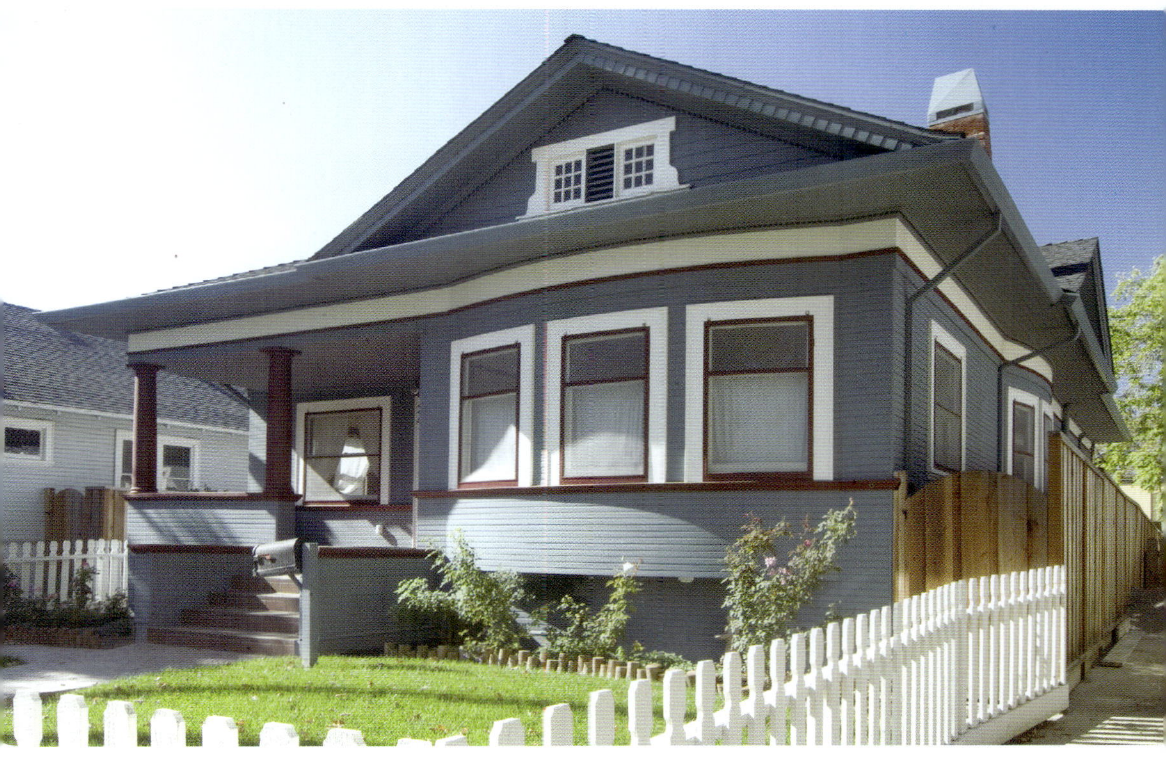

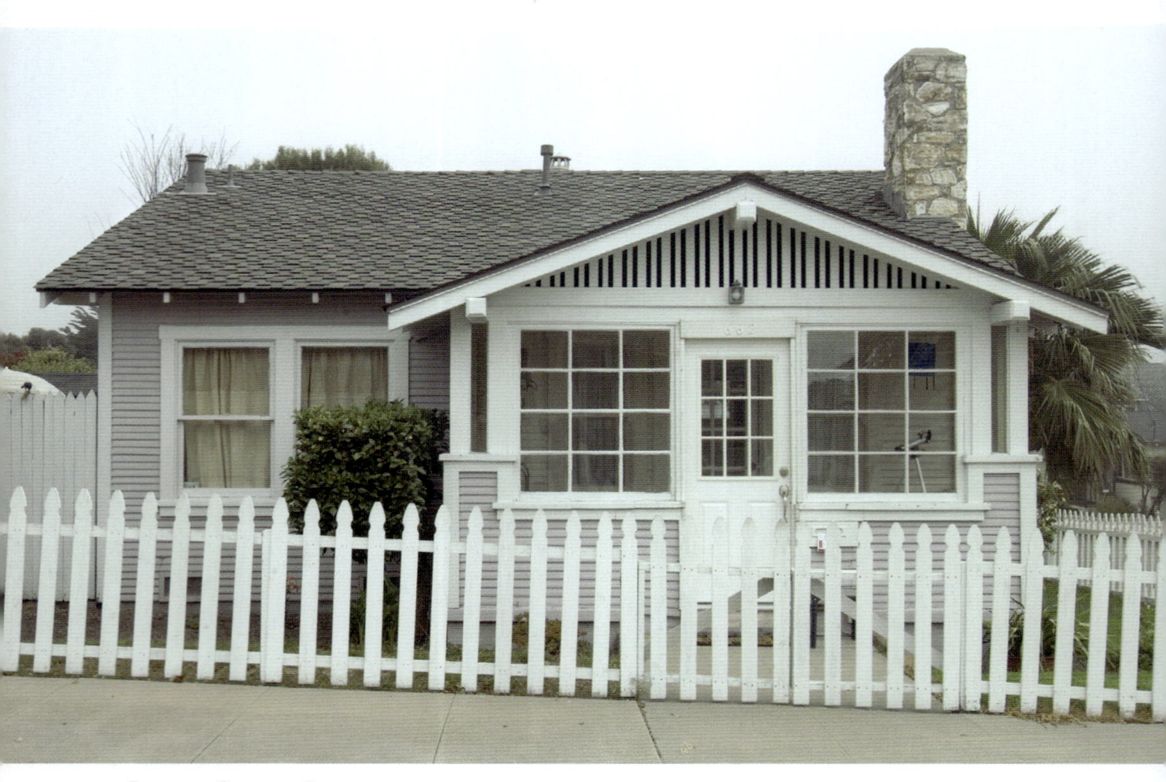

 Pacific Grove, California

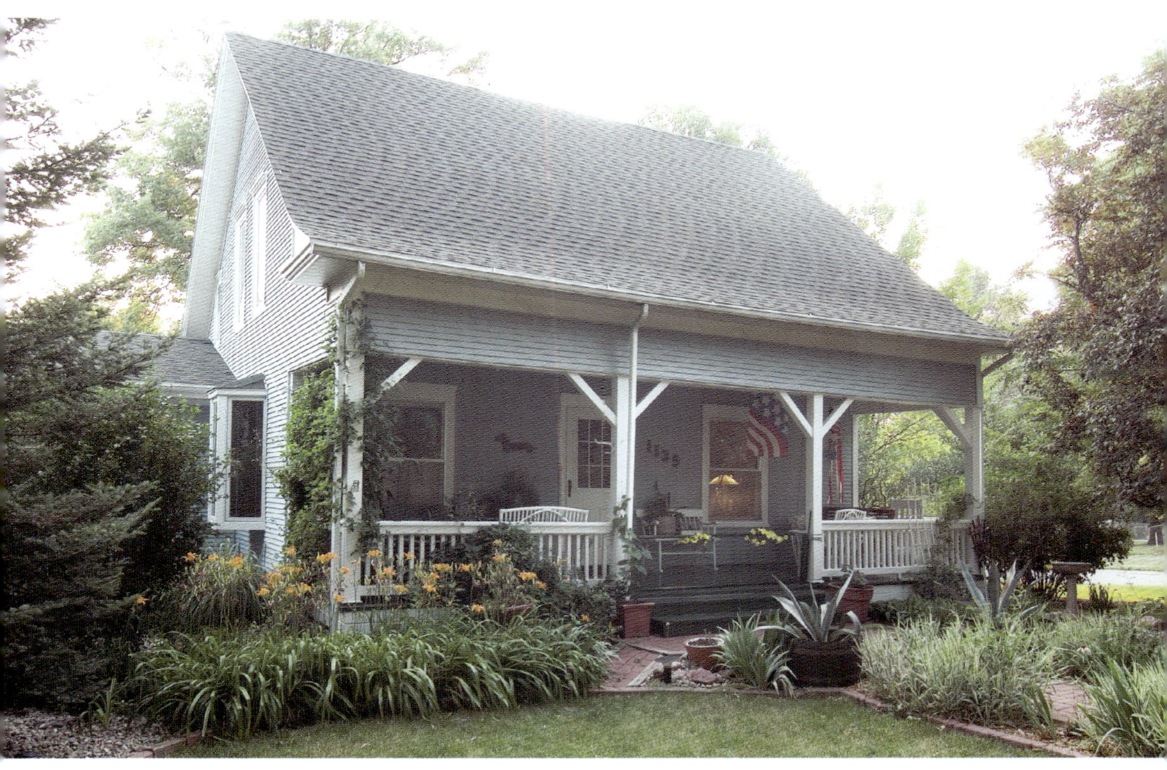

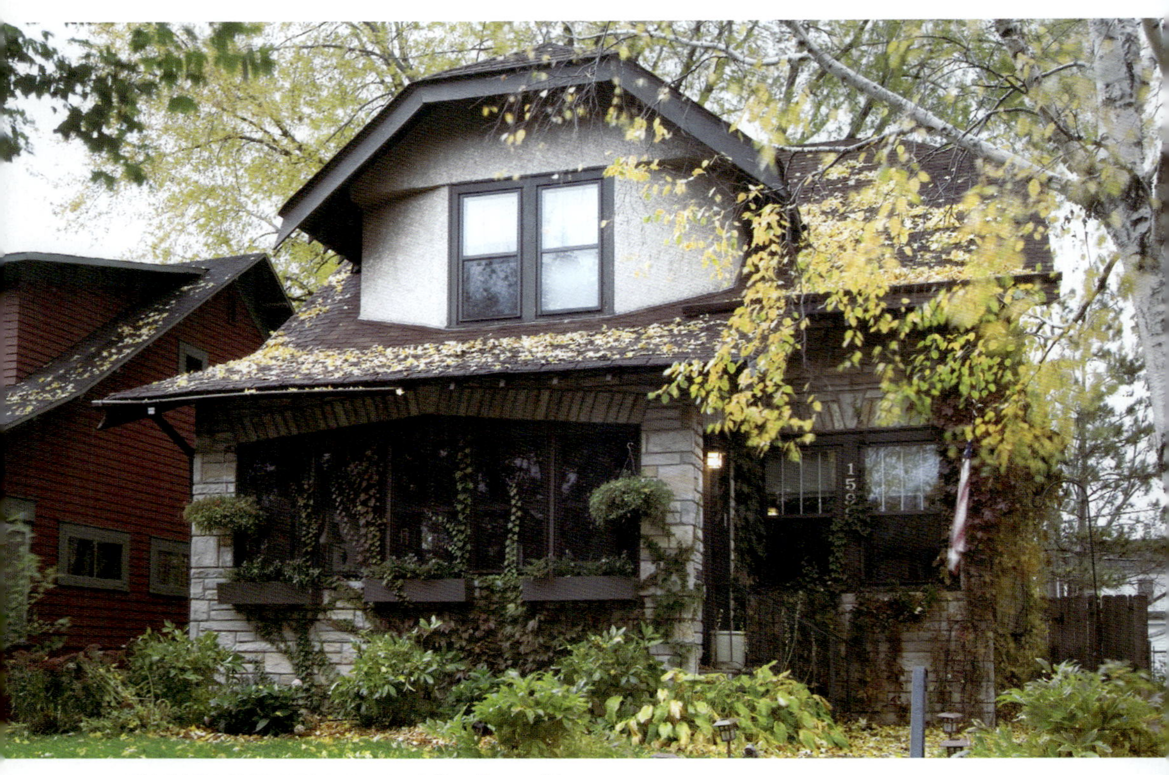

 ENGLISH-STYLE BUNGALOW | St. Paul, Minnesota

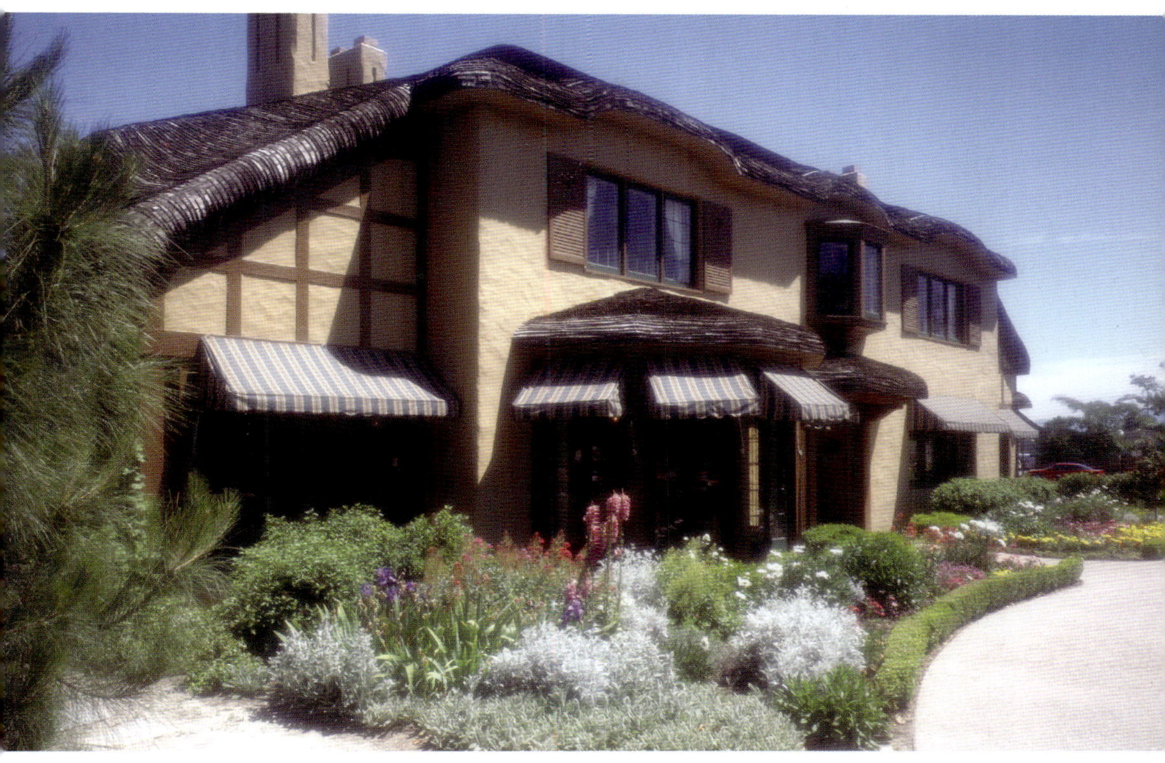

ENGLISH-STYLE BUNGALOW | CAMPBELL, CALIFORNIA

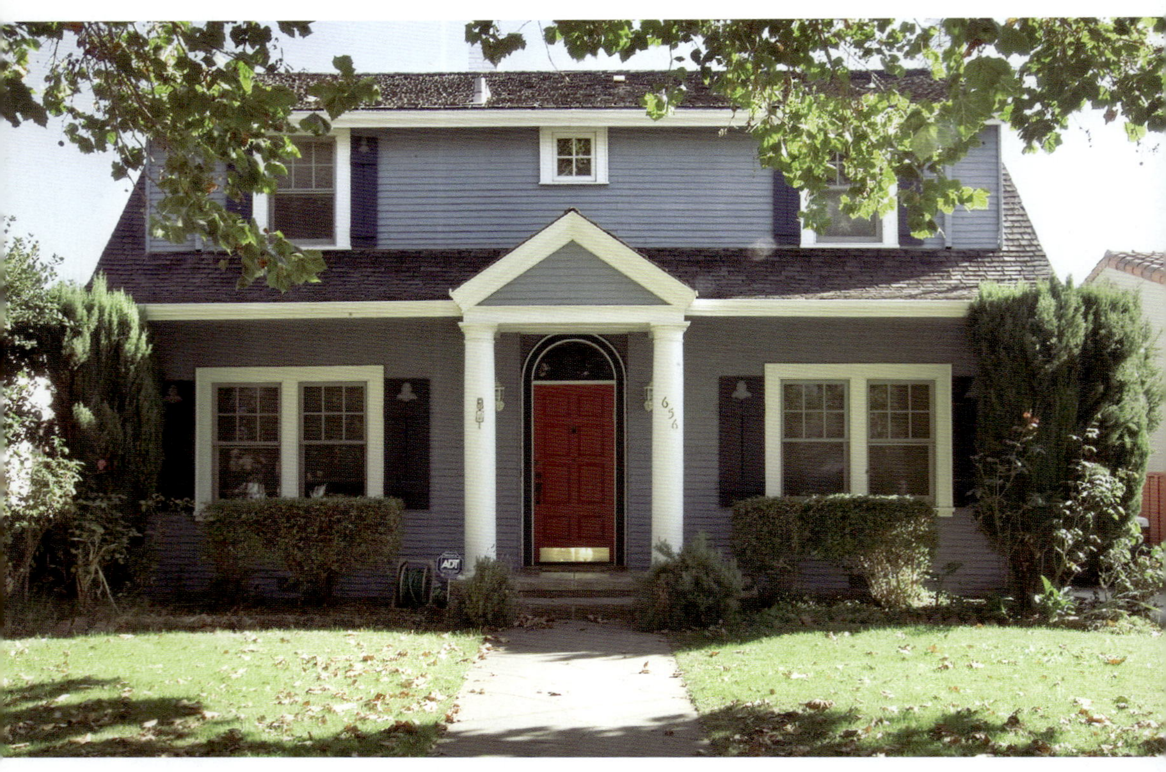


 COLONIAL REVIVAL BUNGALOW | SAN JOSE, CALIFORNIA

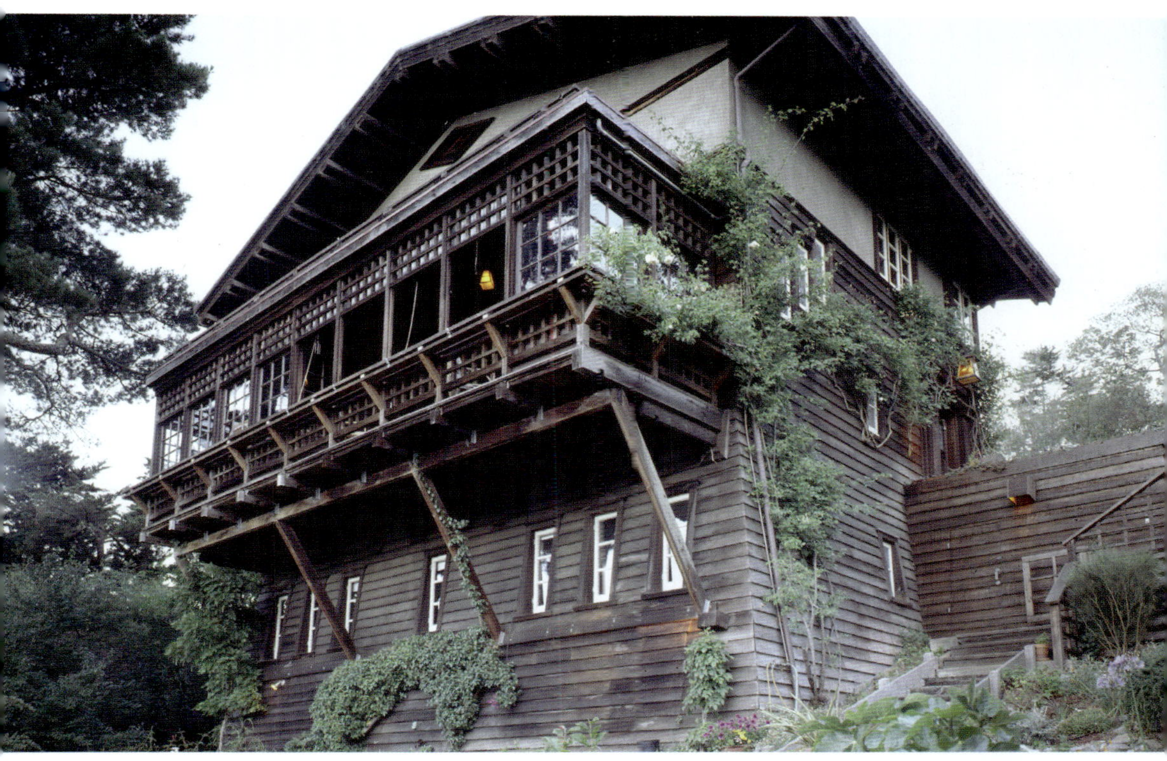

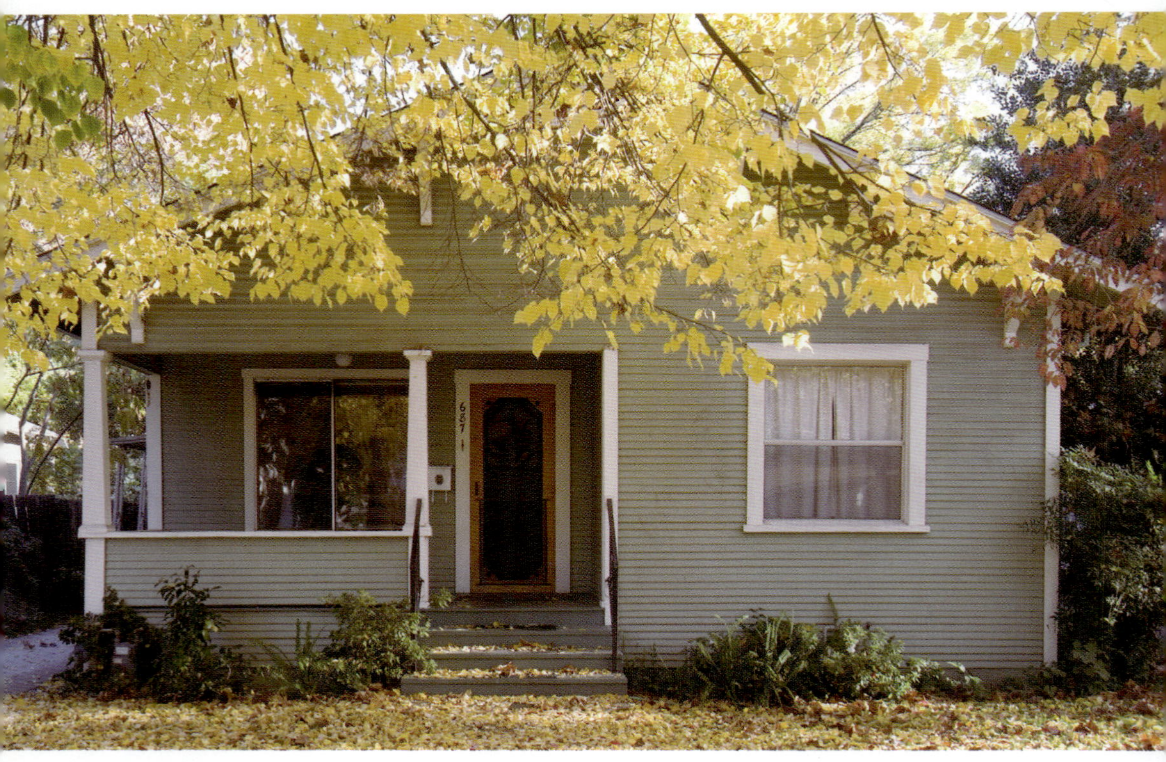


 Chico, California

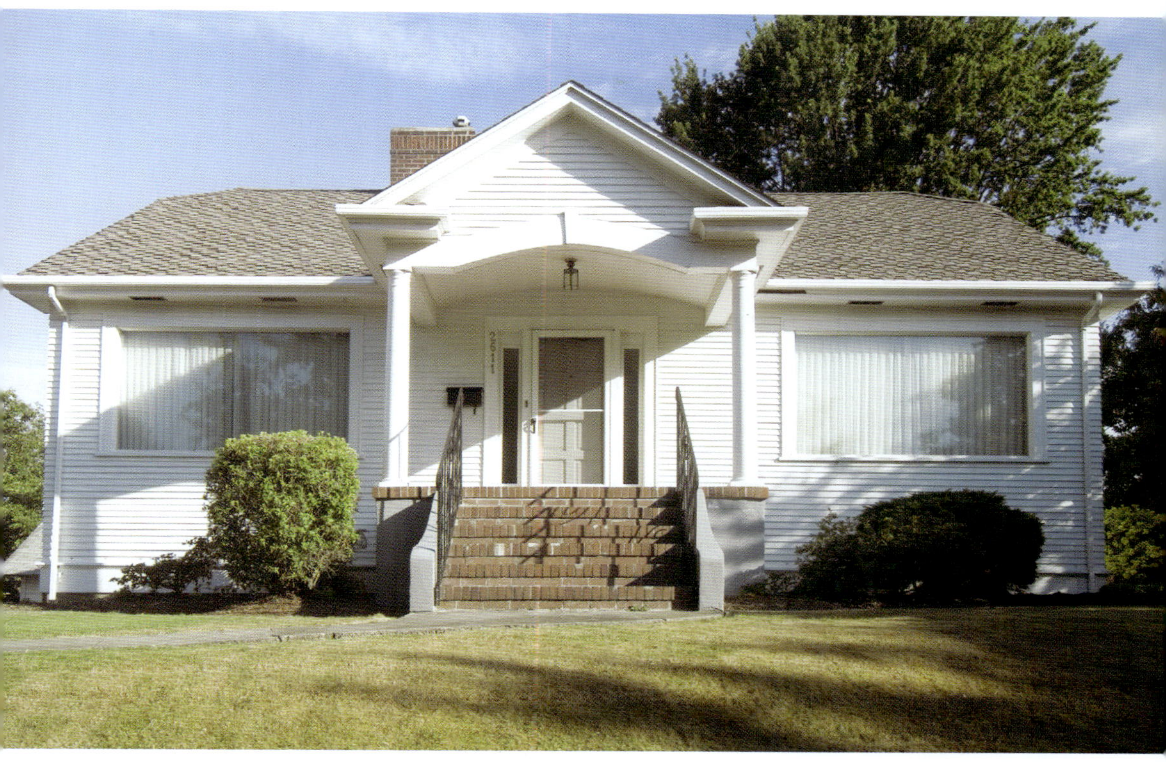


CLASSICAL REVIVAL BUNGALOW | BELLINGHAM, WASHINGTON

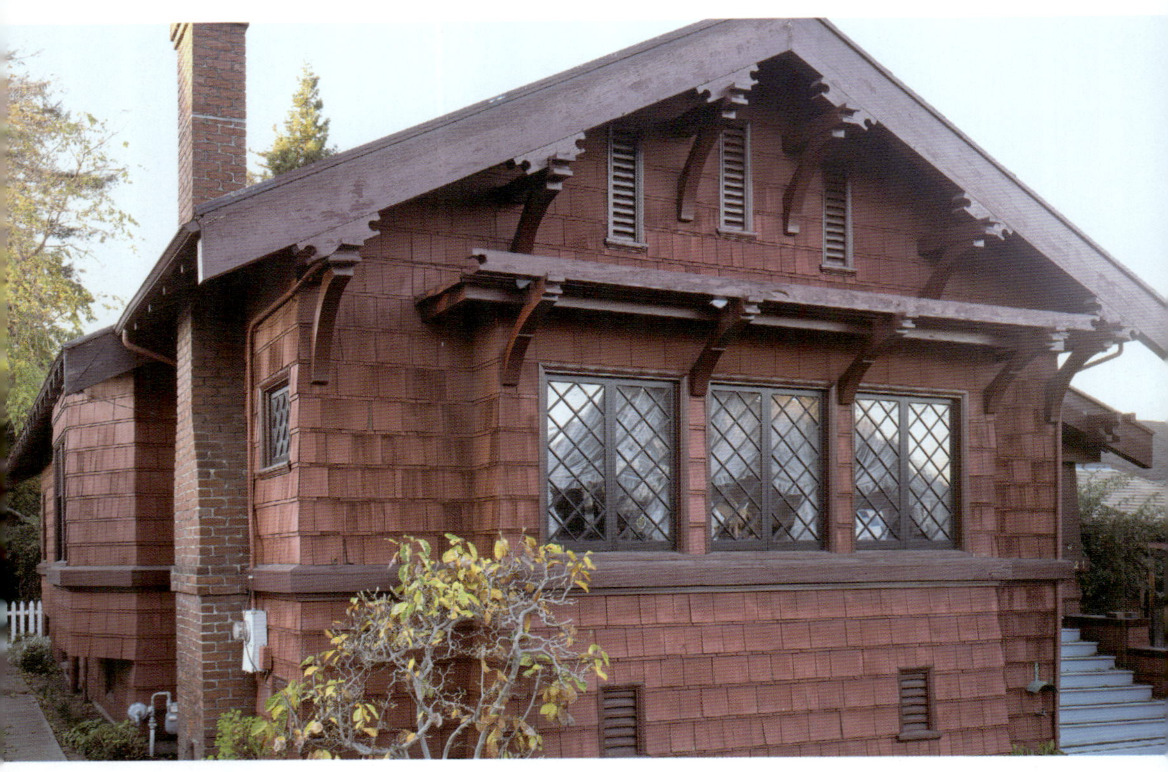

 ENGLISH-STYLE BUNGALOW | ALAMEDA, CALIFORNIA

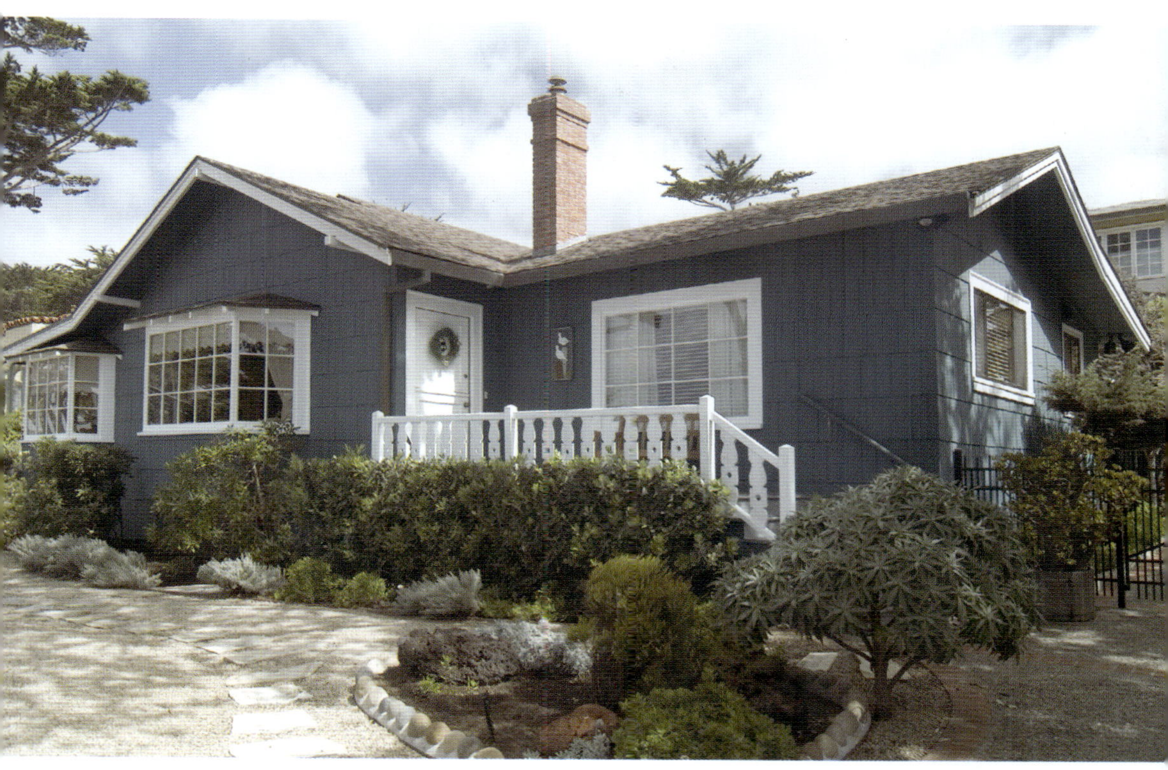

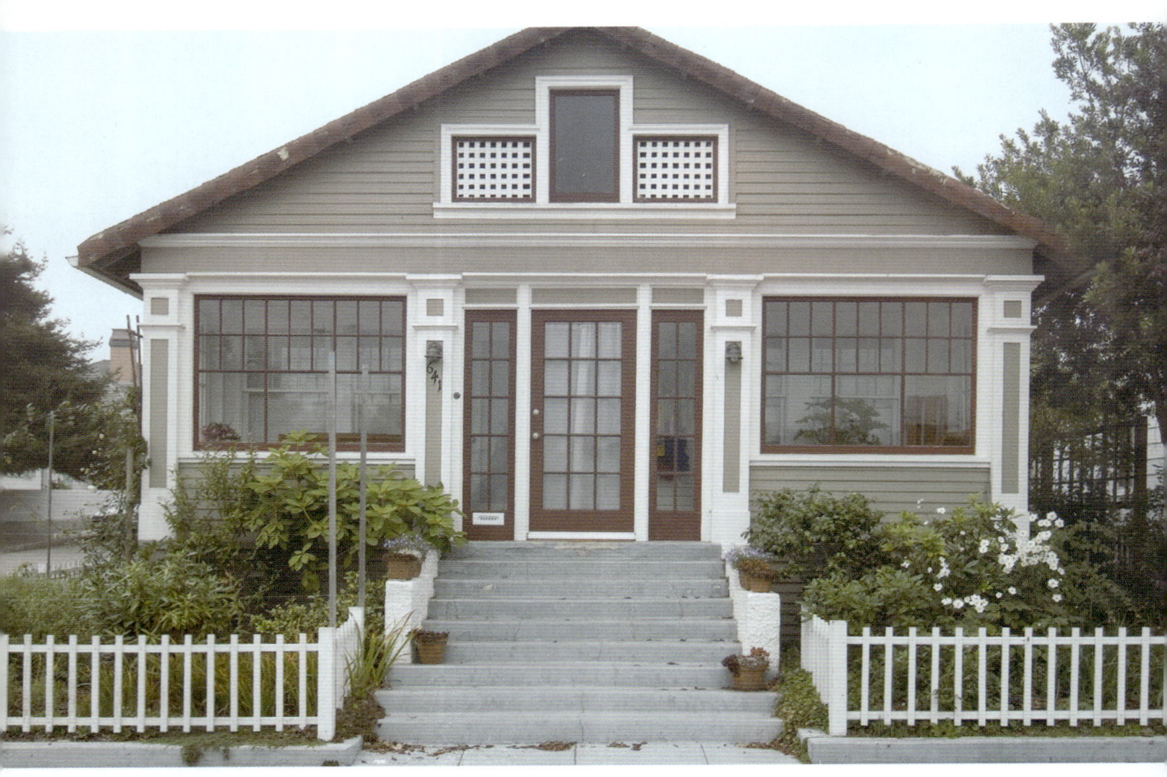


 Pacific Grove, California

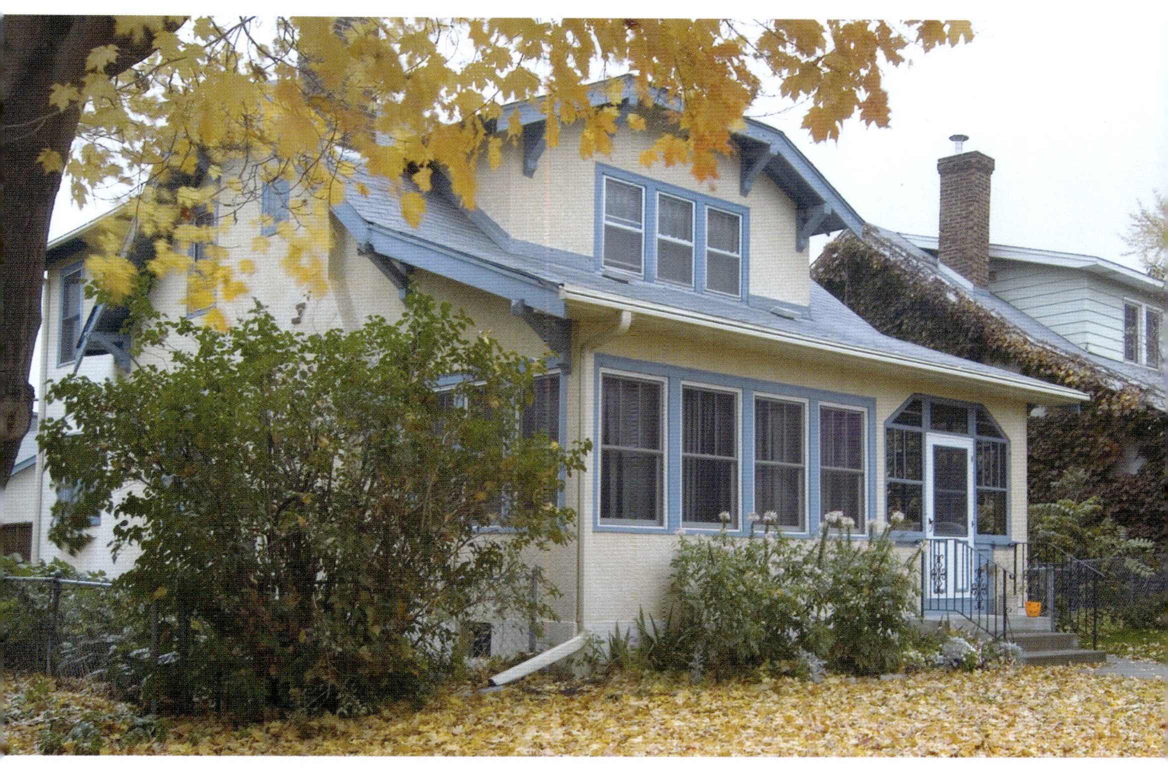

ENGLISH-STYLE BUNGALOW | ST. PAUL, MINNESOTA

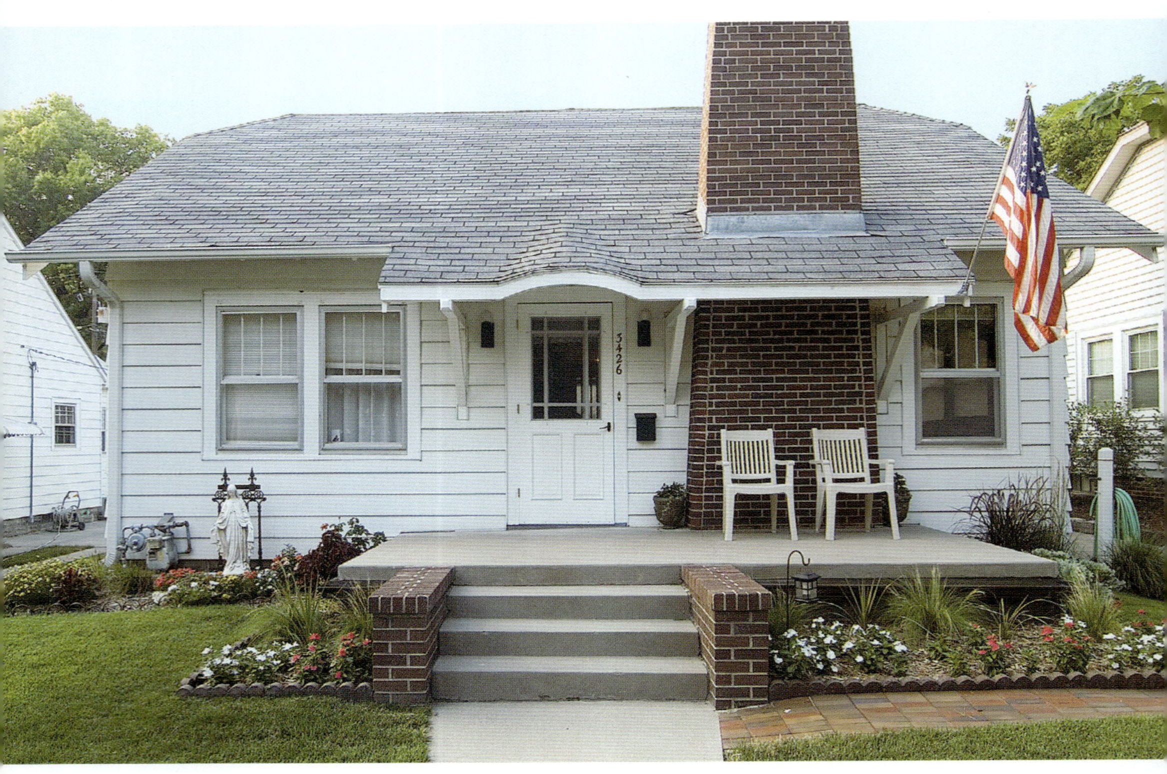


 ENGLISH-STYLE BUNGALOW | LINCOLN, NEBRASKA

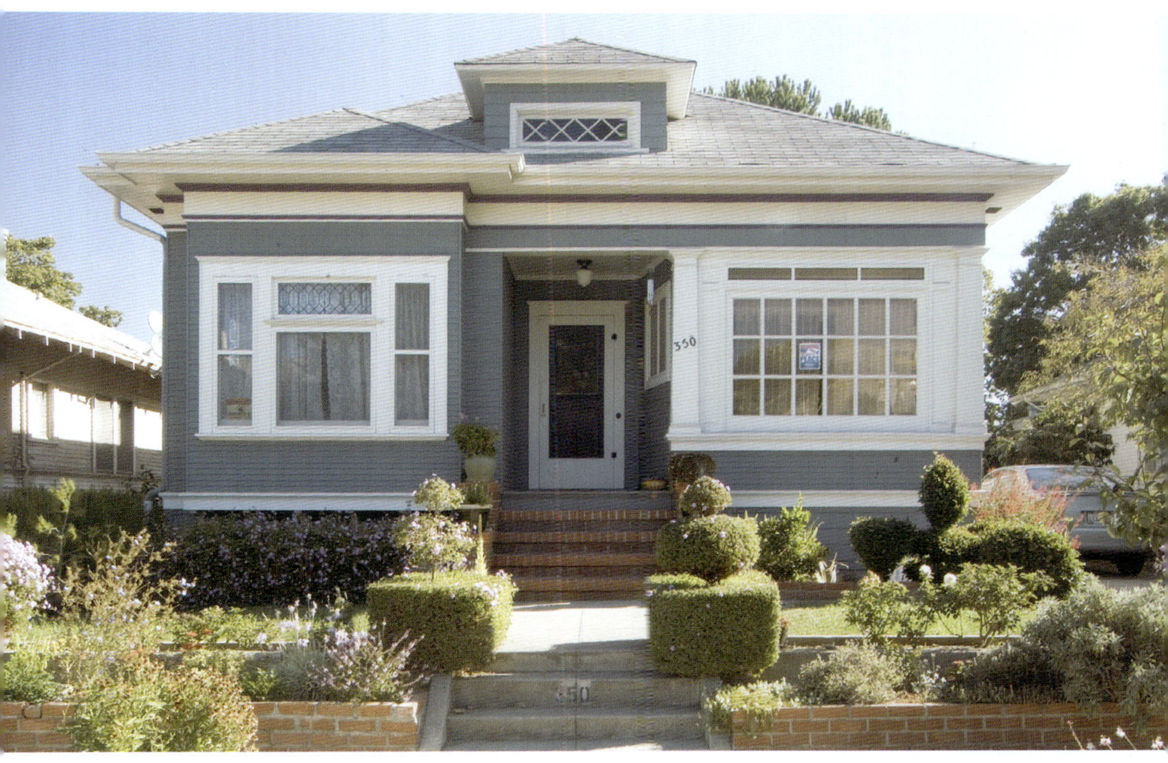


VICTORIAN BUNGALOW | SAN JOSE, CALIFORNIA

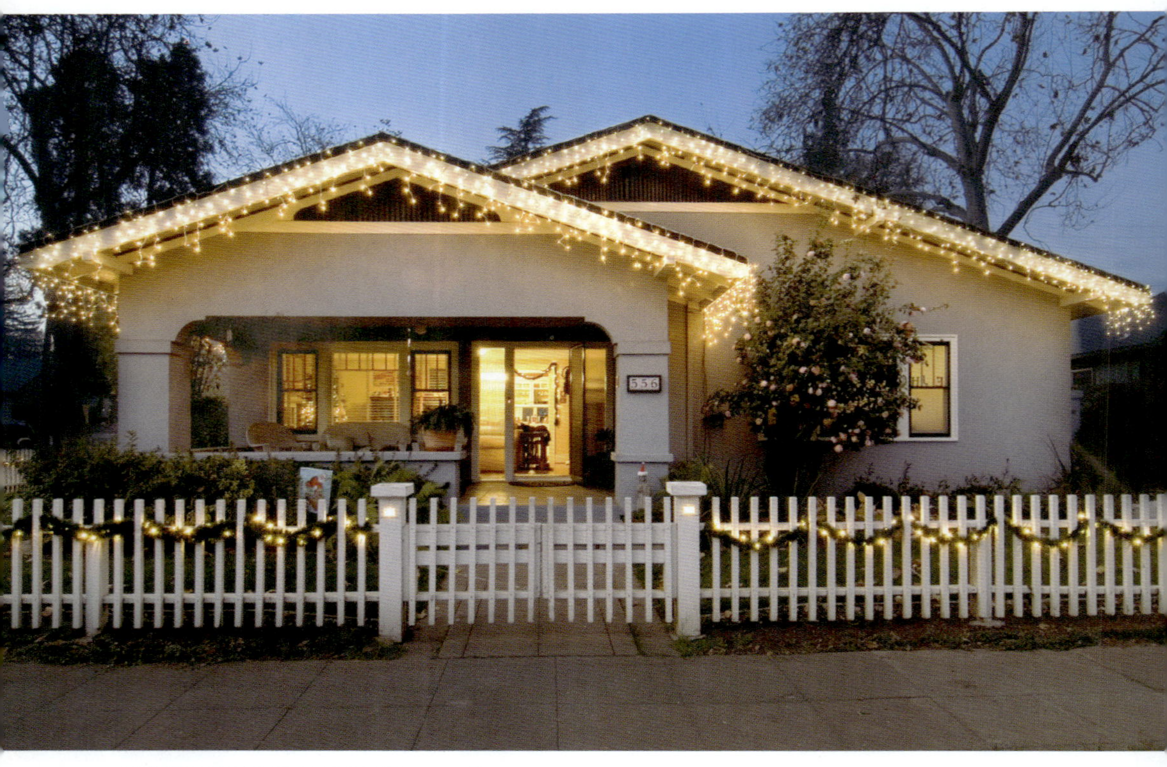


 CHRISTMAS BUNGALOW | CHICO, CALIFORNIA

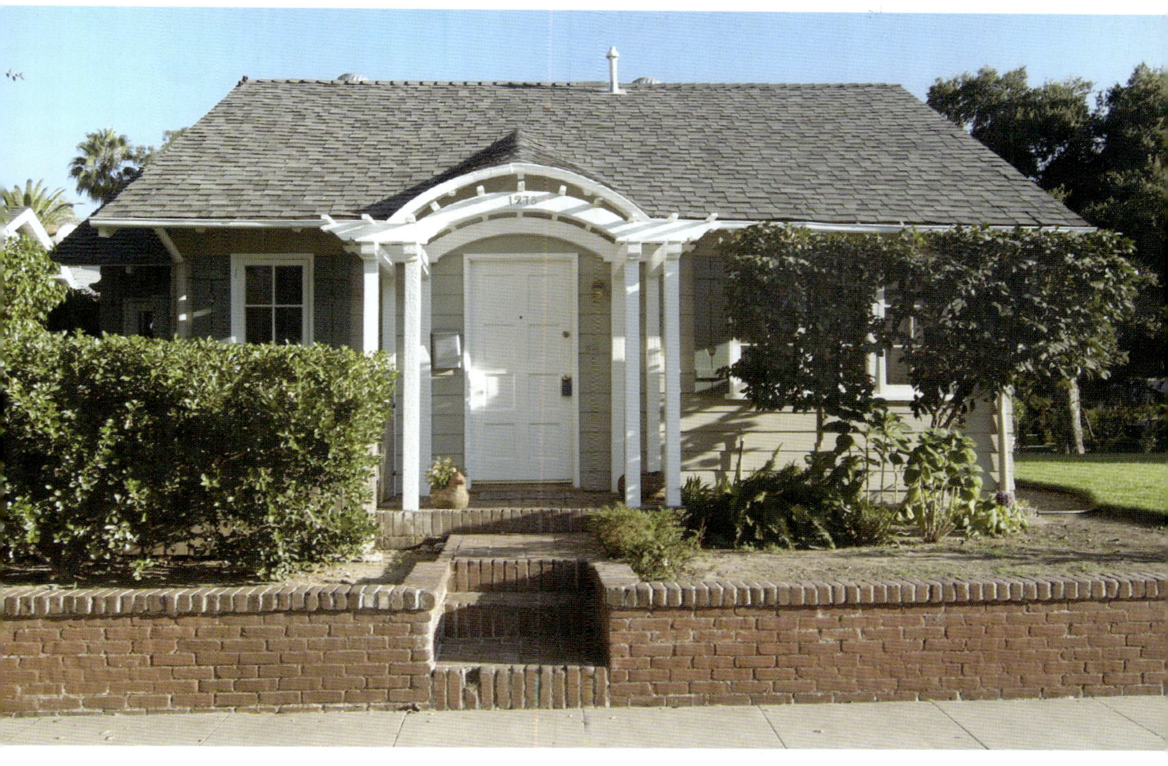

ENGLISH-STYLE BUNGALOW | PASADENA, CALIFORNIA

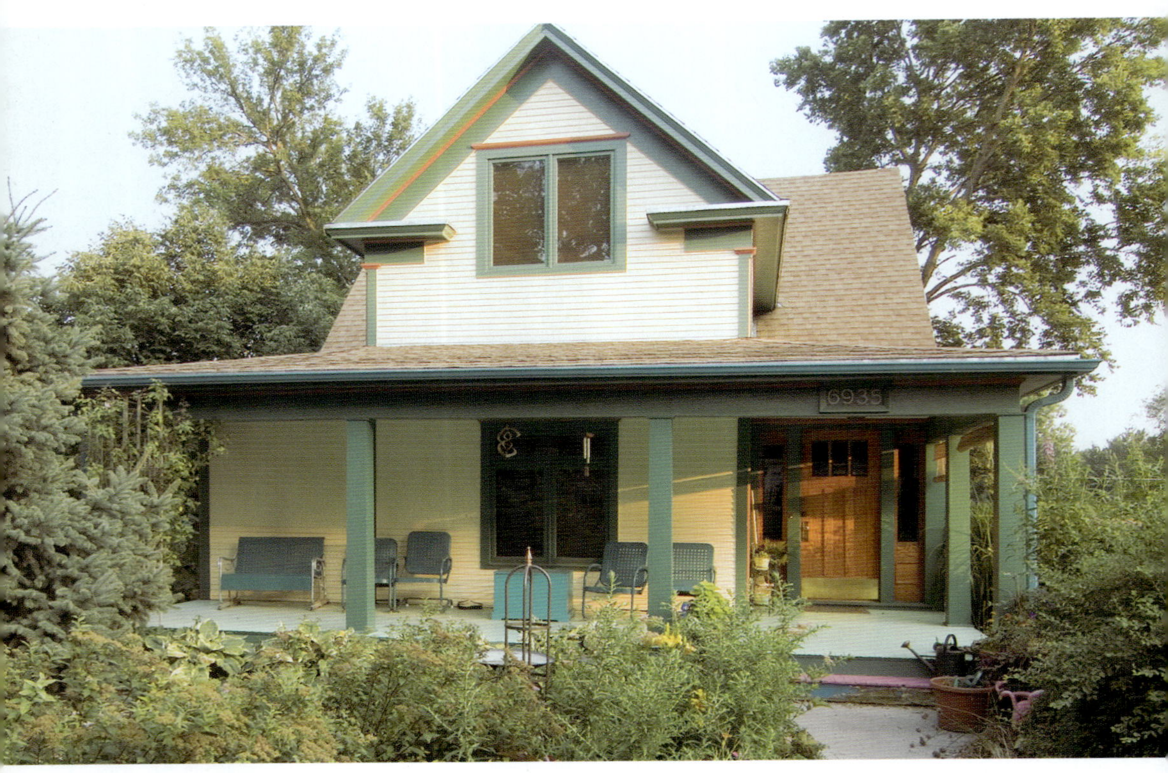


 BUNGALOW FARMHOUSE | LINCOLN, NEBRASKA

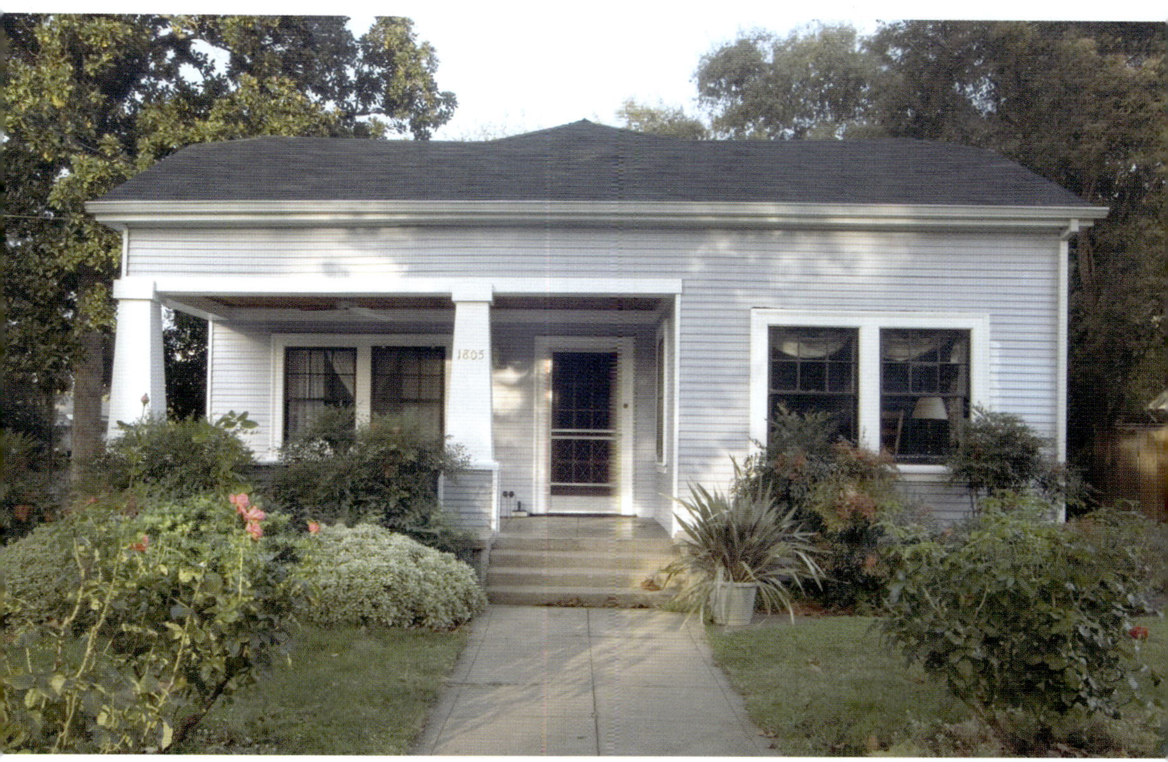


Chico, California 

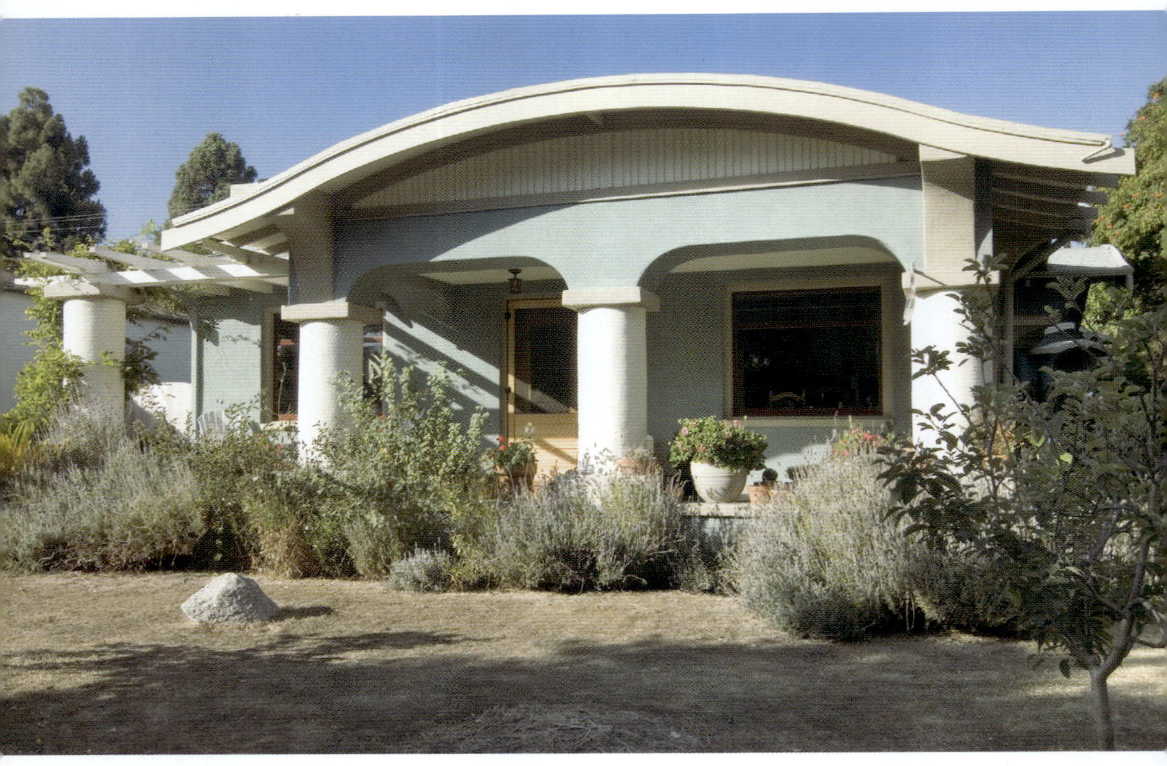

 ENGLISH-STYLE BUNGALOW | SANTA MONICA, CALIFORNIA

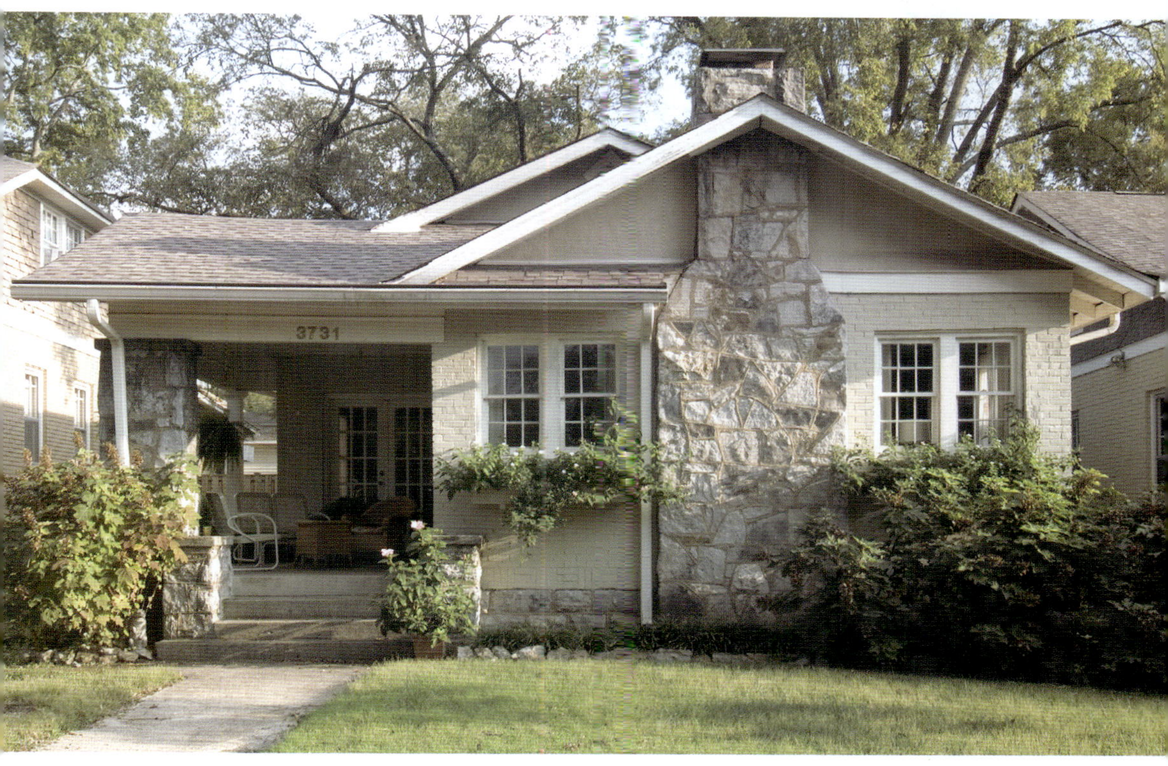
3731

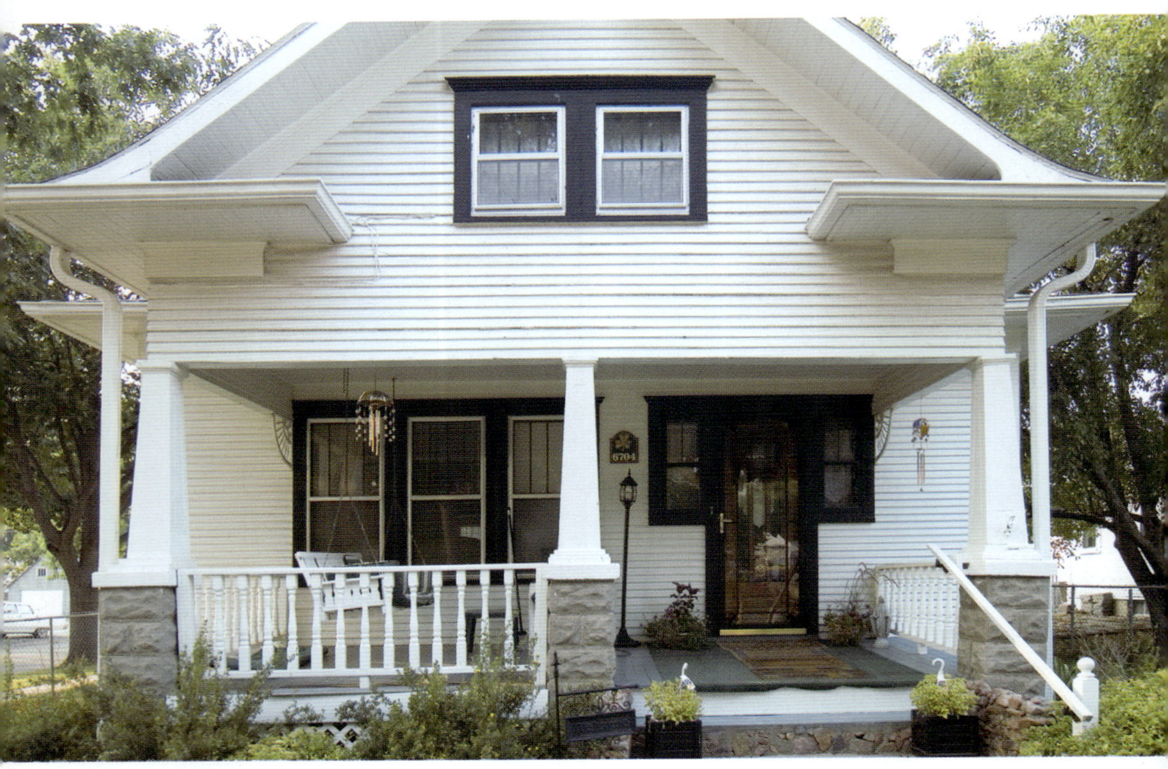


 CLASSICAL REVIVAL BUNGALOW | Lincoln, Nebraska

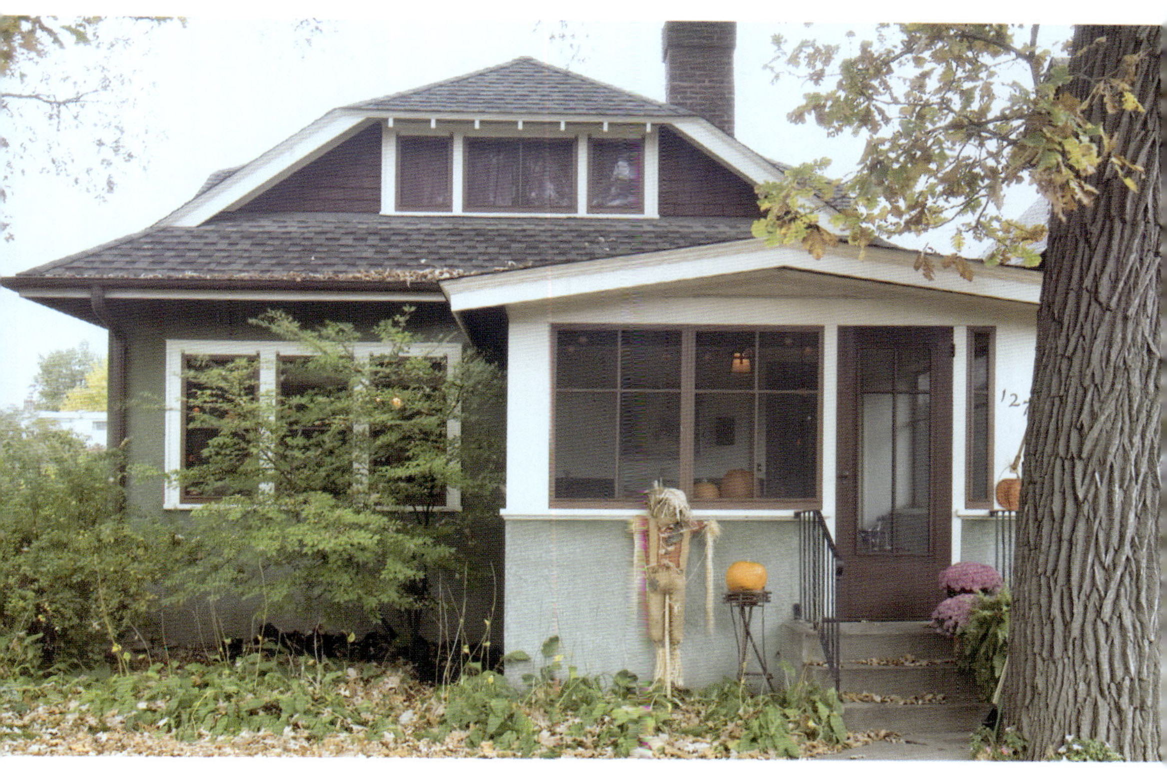

ENGLISH-STYLE BUNGALOW | ST. PAUL, MINNESOTA

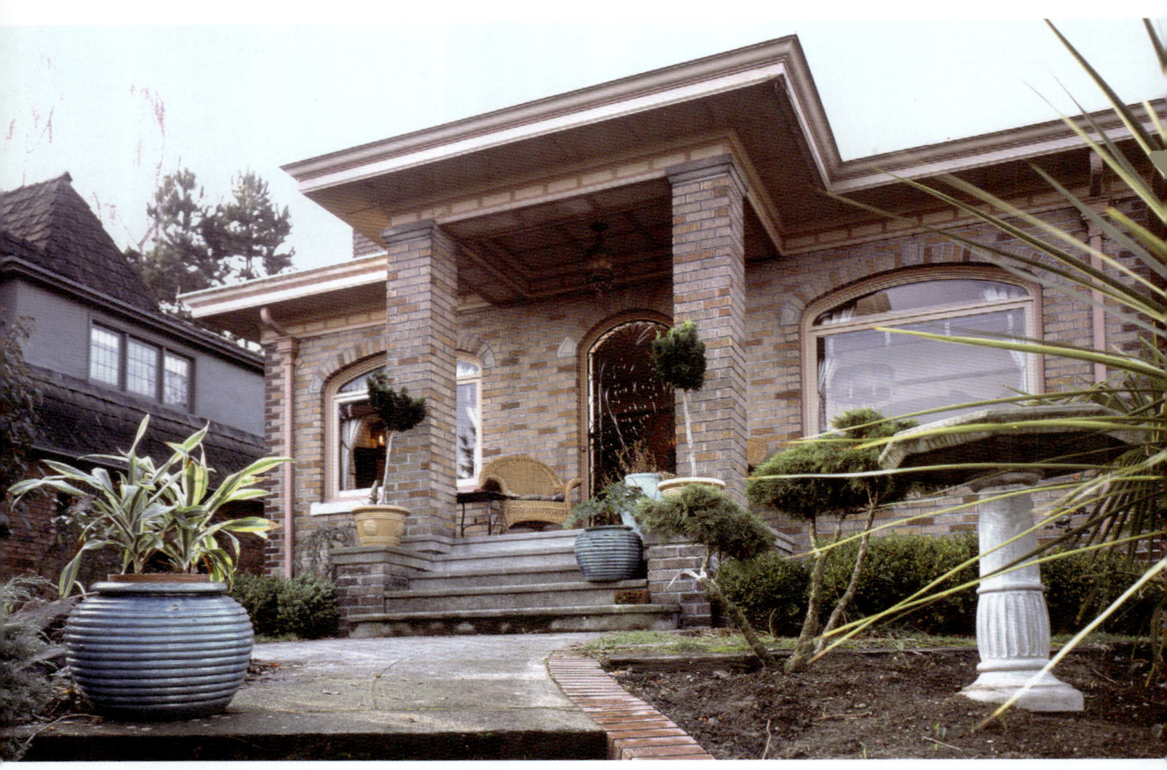

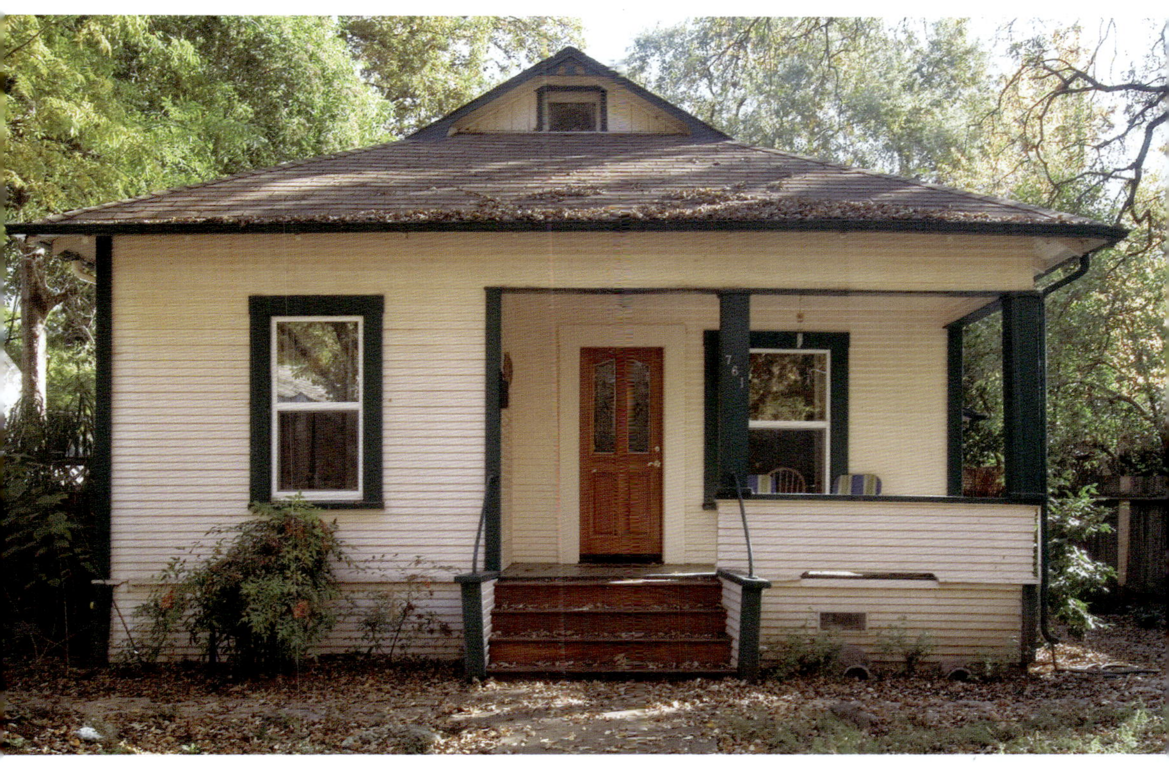


Chico, California

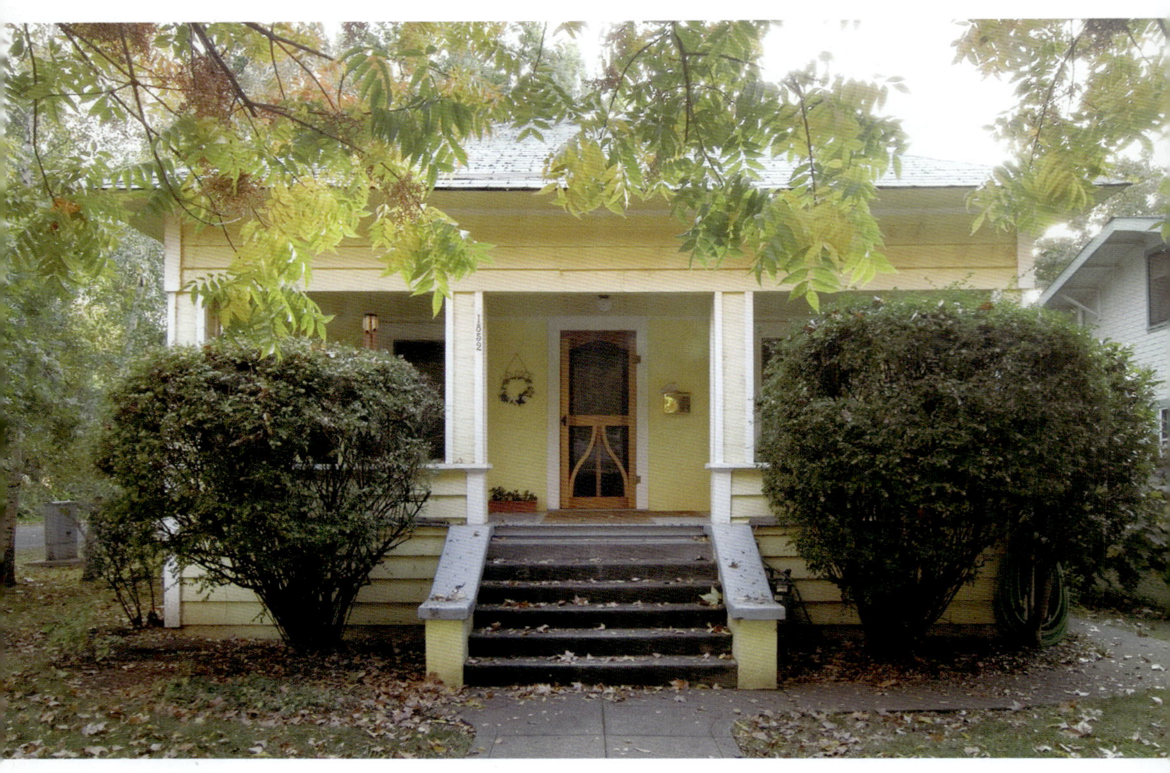


 CHICO, CALIFORNIA

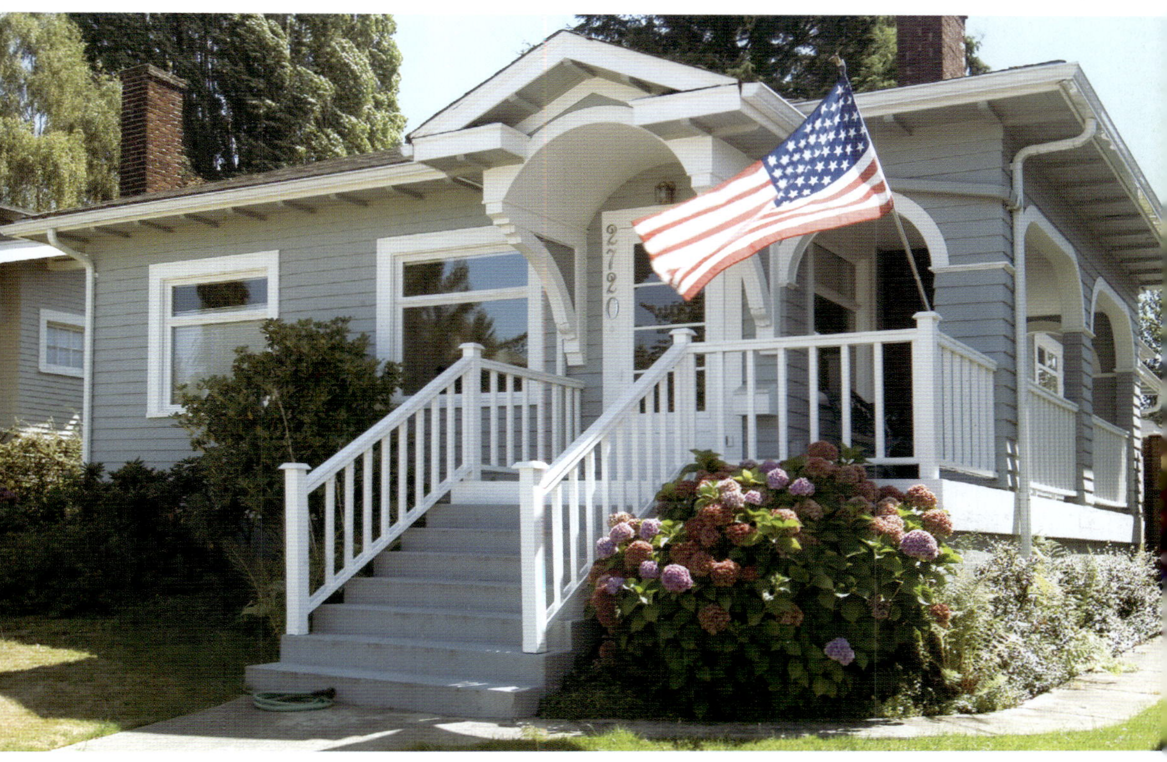


ENGLISH-STYLE BUNGALOW | BELLINGHAM, WASHINGTON

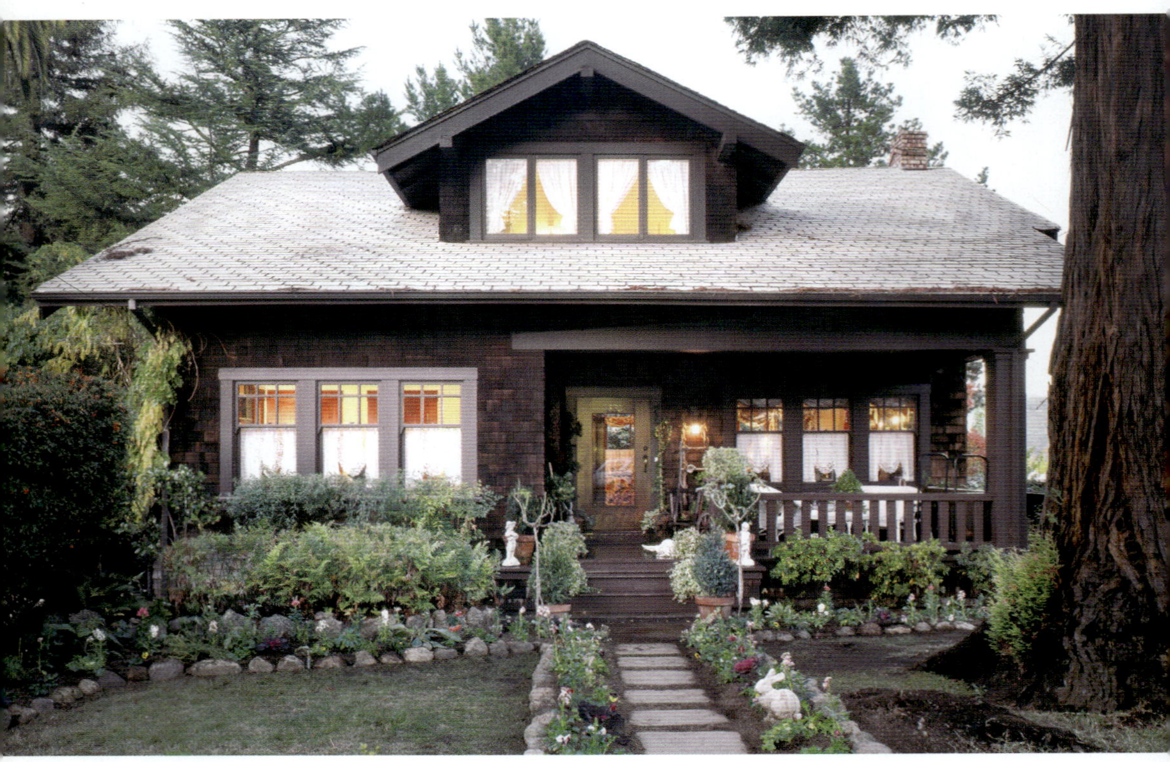

 St. Helena, California

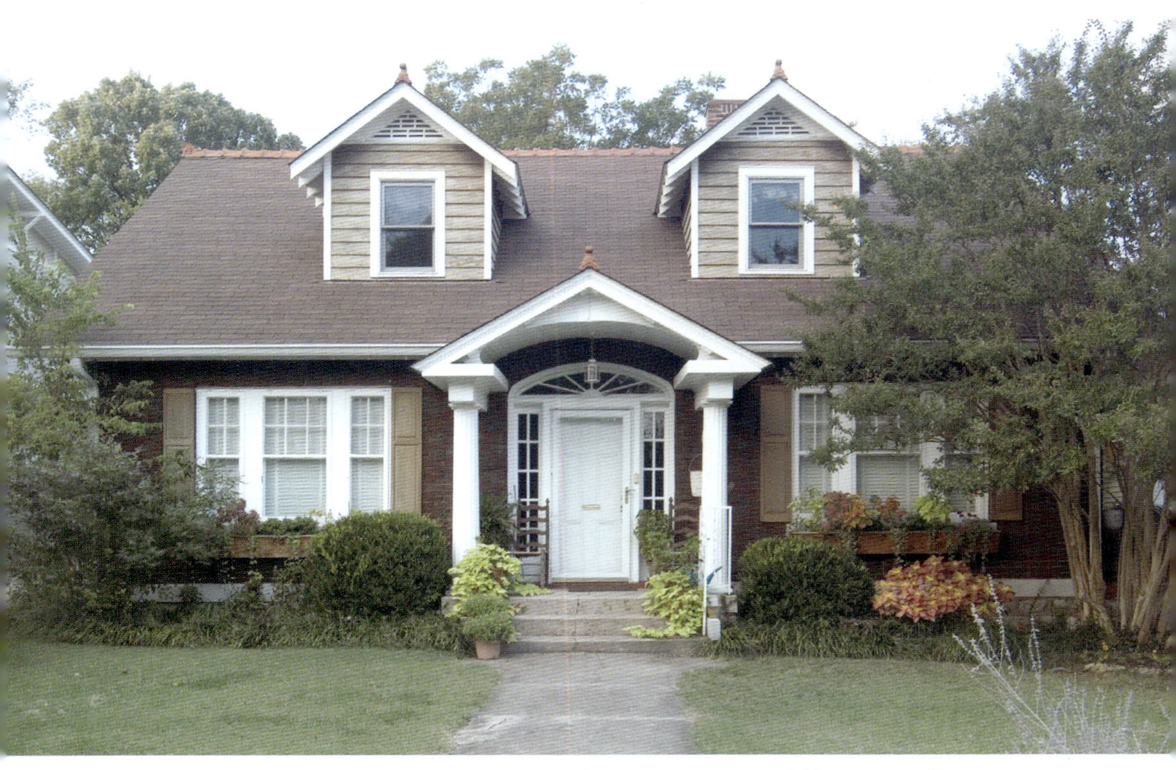

COLONIAL REVIVAL BUNGALOW | NASHVILLE, TENNESSEE

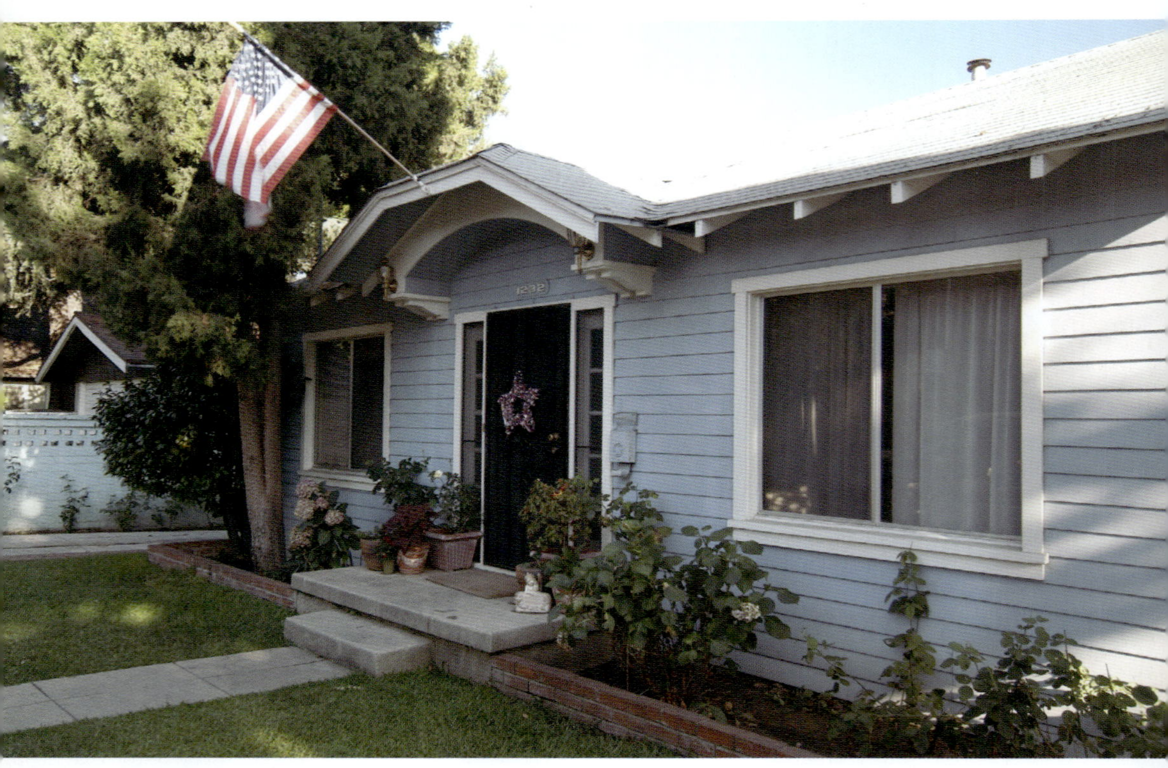

 ENGLISH-STYLE BUNGALOW | Pasadena, California

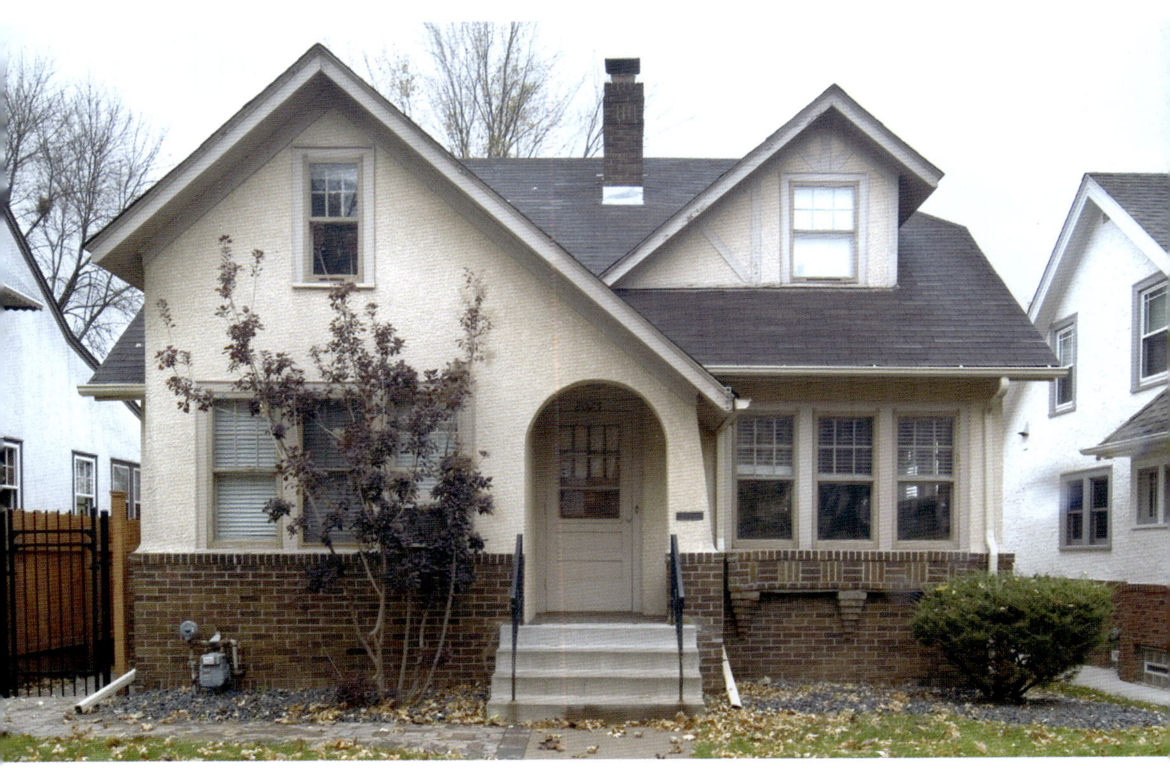

PERIOD REVIVAL BUNGALOW | ST. PAUL, MINNESOTA 

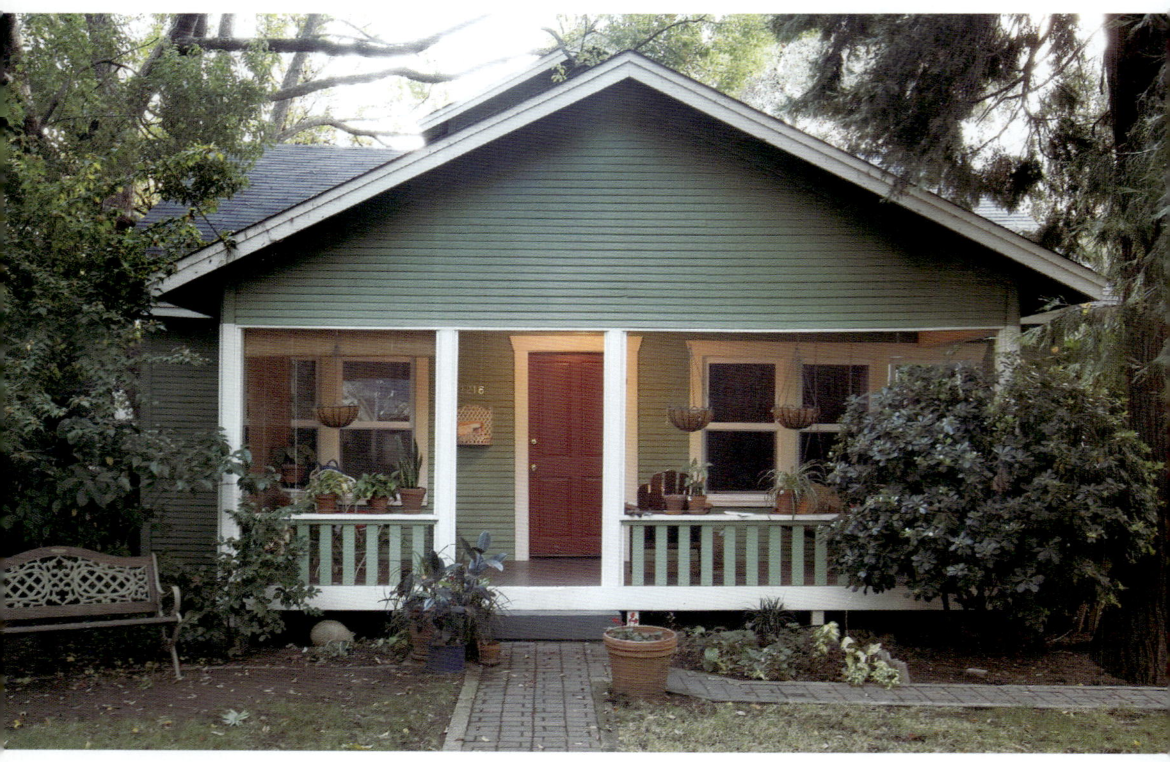

 Chico, California

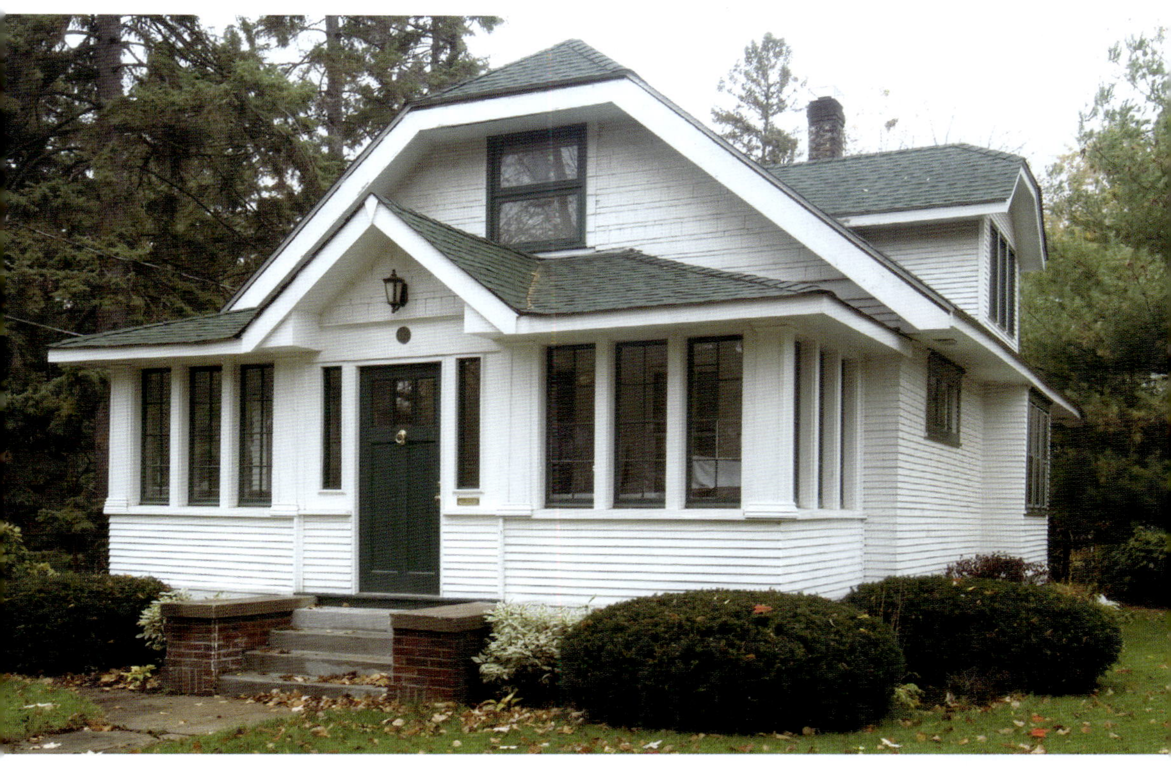

VICTORIAN BUNGALOW | ST. PAUL, MINNESOTA

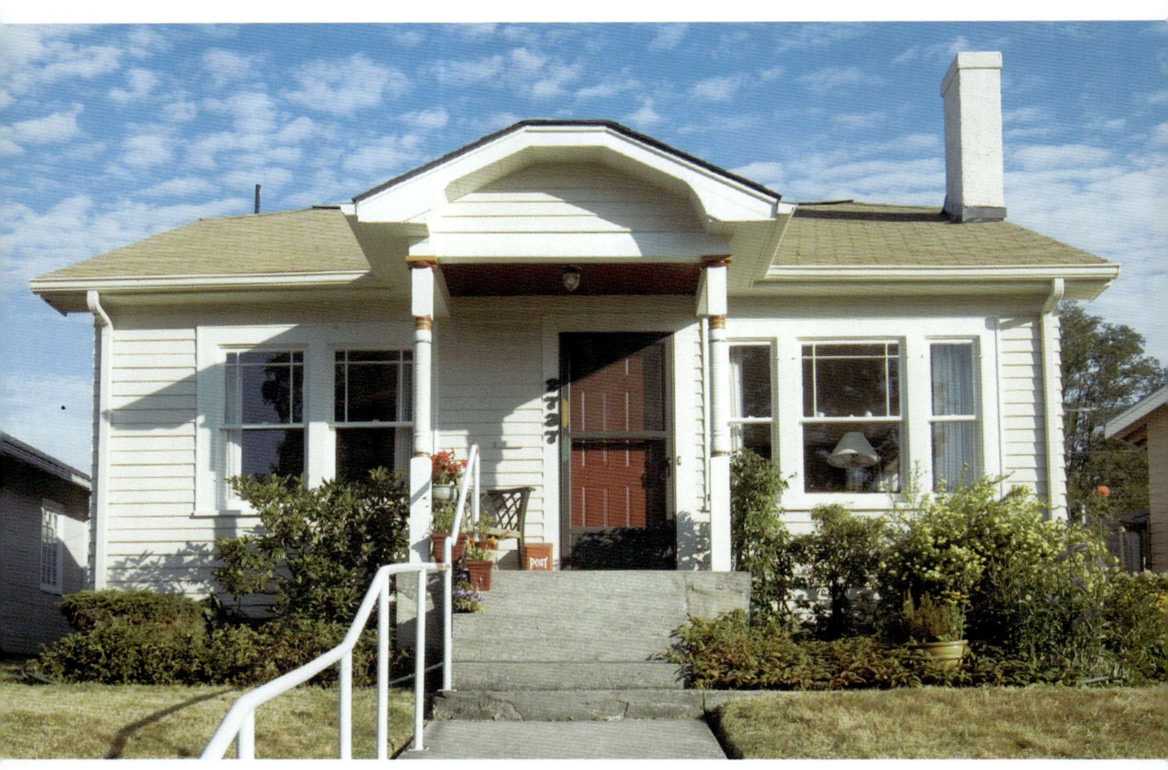


 ENGLISH-STYLE BUNGALOW | BELLINGHAM, WASHINGTON

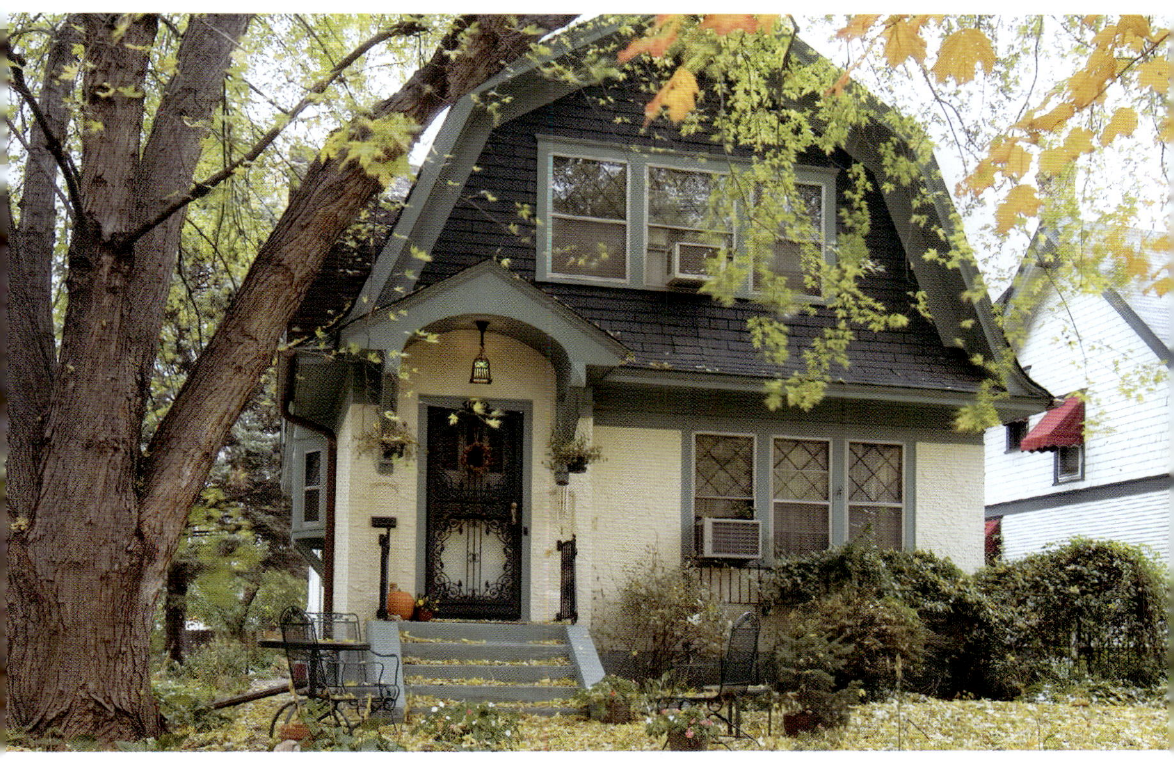

DUTCH COLONIAL BUNGALOW | St. Paul, Minnesota

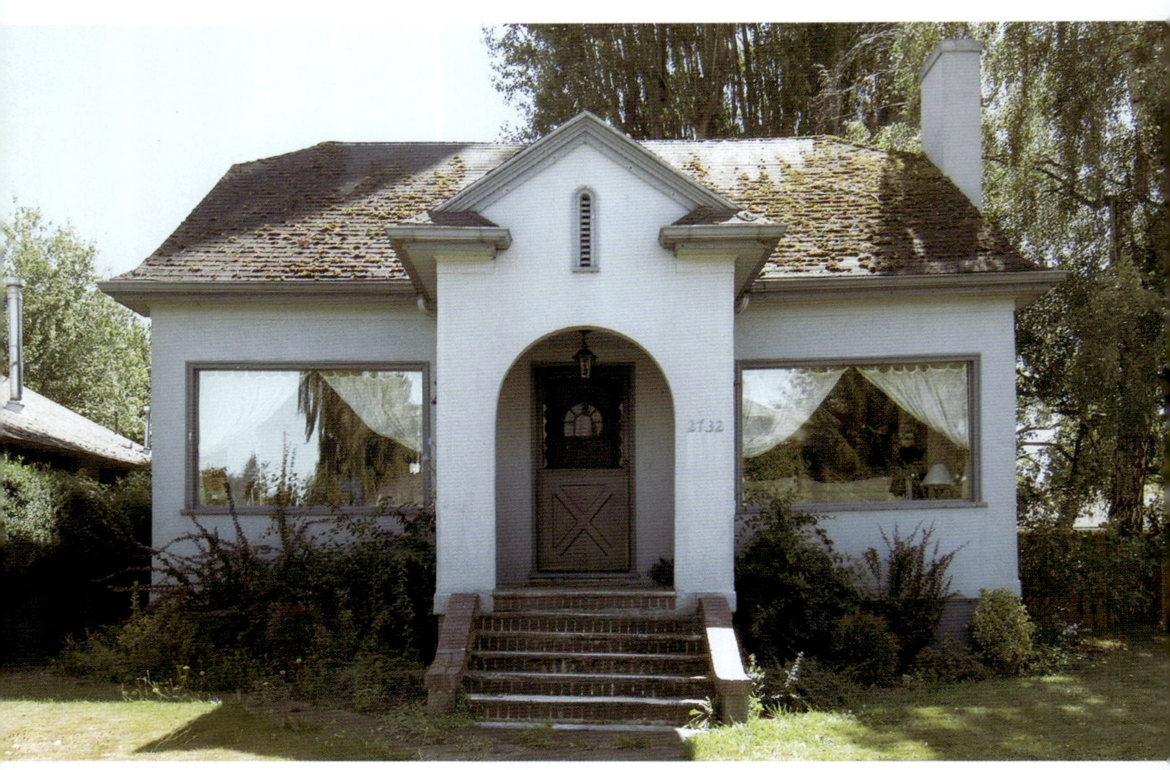


 ENGLISH-STYLE BUNGALOW | Bellingham, Washington

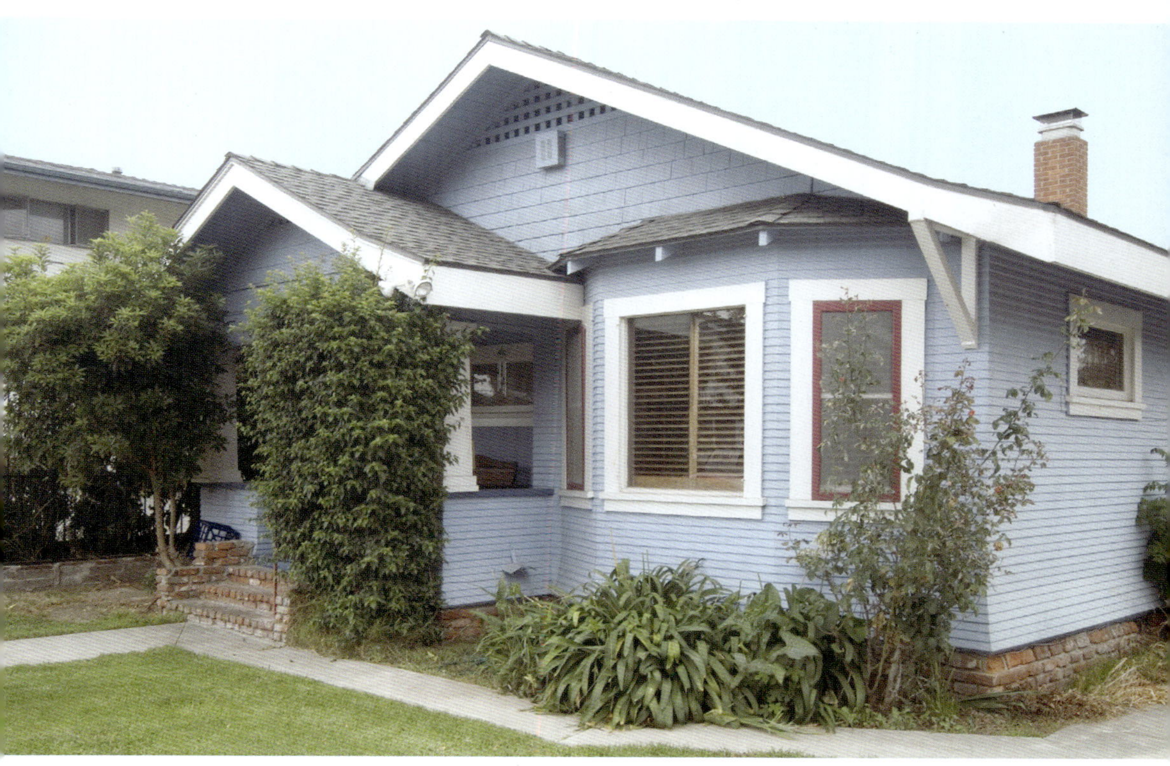

San Diego, California

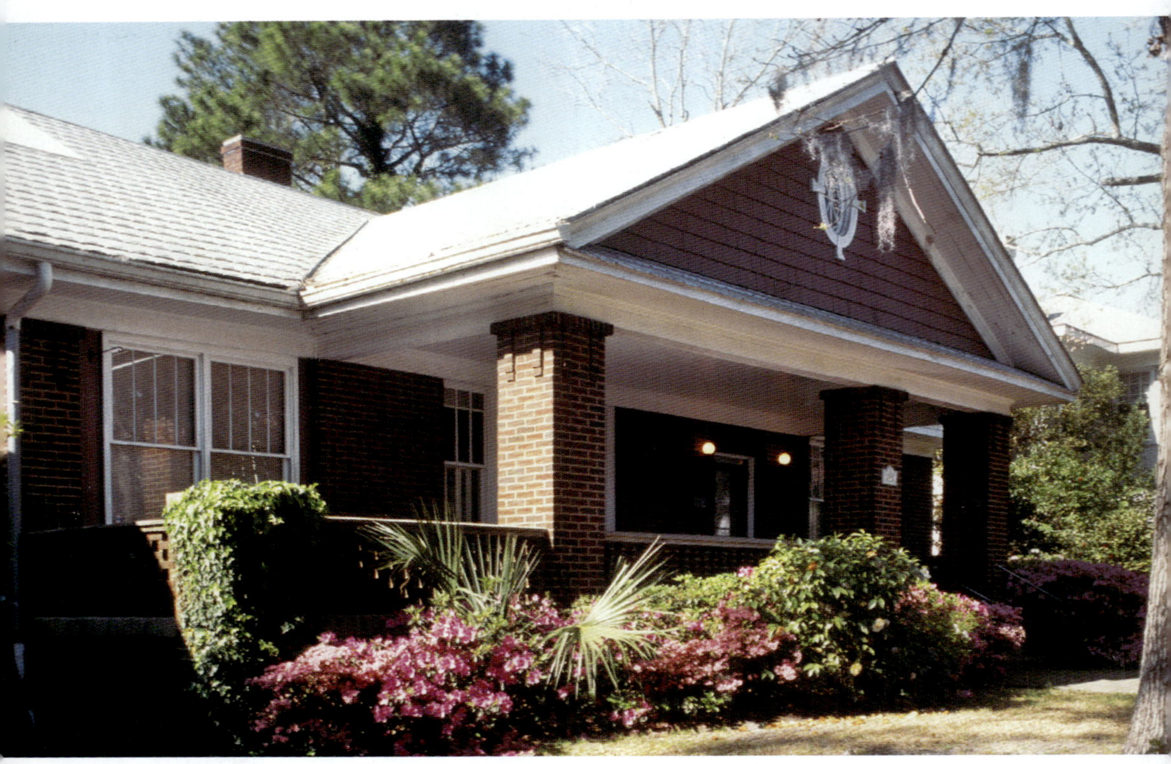

 SAVANNAH, GEORGIA